Other publications from Crowbar Press

Inside Out
by Ole Anderson, with Scott Teal

Wrestlers Are Like Seagulls
by James J. Dillon, with Scott Teal & Philip Varriale

Assassin: The Man Behind the Mask
by Joe Hamilton, with Scott Teal

"Is That Wrestling Fake?"
by Ivan Koloff, with Scott Teal

Bruiser Brody
by Emerson Murray, edited by Scott Teal

Wrestling with the Truth
by Bruno Lauer, edited by Scott Teal

The Solie Chronicles
by Bob Allyn, with Pamela S Allyn & Scott Teal

Wrestling in the Canadian West
by Vance Nevada

Long Days and Short Pays
by Hal West, edited by Scott Teal

Drawing Heat
by Jim Freedman

ATLAS: Too Much, Too Soon
by Tony Atlas, with Scott Teal

The Last Laugh
by Bill De Mott, with Scott Teal

HOOKER
by Lou Thesz, with Kit Bauman

The Last Outlaw
by Stan Hansen, with Scott Teal

NIKITA
by Nikita Koloff, as told to Bill Murdock

The Strap
by Roger Deem

BRISCO
by Jack Brisco, as told to Bill Murdock

The Mighty Milo
by Phillips Rogers

"I Ain't No Pig Farmer!"
by Dean Silverstone, with Scott Teal

The Hard Way
by Don Fargo, with Scott Teal

Whatever Happened to Gorgeous George?
by Joe Jares

"It's Wrestling, Not Rasslin'!"
by Mark Fleming, edited by Scott Teal

**BRUISER
The World's Most Dangerous Wrestler**
by Richard Vicek, edited by Scott Teal

The Mat, the Mob & Music
by Tom Hankins, edited by Scott Teal

**BREAKING KAYFABE
THEY CALL ME BOOKER**
by Jeff Bowdren, edited by Scott Teal

BATTLEGROUND VALHALA
by Michael Majalahti, edited by Scott Teal

Florida Mat Wars: 1977
by Robert D. VanKavelaar, with Scott Teal

When It Was Real
by Nikita Breznikov, with Scott Teal

The Annotated Fall Guys
by Marcus Griffin,
annotated by Steve Yohe & Scott Teal

Pain Torture Agony
by Ron Hutchison, with Scott Teal

Raising Cain: From Jimmy Ault to Kid McCoy
by Frankie Cain & Scott Teal

Master of the Ring
by Tim Hornbaker

--- **Wrestling Archive Project** ---
by Scott Teal
Volume #1 • Volume #2

--- **Through the Lens ... Through the Ropes** ---
Compiled by Scott Teal
— Volume #1 —
Southeastern Championship Wrestling
— Volume #2 —
Championship Wrestling from Florida
— Volume #3 —
All South Wrestling Alliance

--- **The Great Pro Wrestling Venues** ---
Volume #1 — Madison Square Garden
by Scott Teal & J Michael Kenyon
Volume #2 — Nashville, volume 1
by Scott Teal & Don Luce
Volume #3 — Alabama: 1931-1935
by Jason Presley
Volume #4 — Japan
by Haruo Yamaguchi,
with Koji Miyamoto & Scott Teal
Volume #5 — Knoxville: 1905-1960
Volume #6 — Knoxville: 1961-1991
by Tim Dills & Scott Teal
Volume #7 — Amarillo: 1911-1960
Volume #8 — Amarillo: 1961-1997
by Kriss Knights & Scott Teal

--- **Classic Arena Programs** ---
Volumes #1-2 — SLAM-O-GRAM
Volumes #3-4 — Florida
Volumes #5-7 — Knoxville

by Tim Hornbaker

Gallatin, Tennessee

Copyright © 2020 by Tim Hornbaker

All rights reserved. No part of this book may be reproduced or transmitted in any form or by any means, electronic or mechanical, including photocopying, recording, or by any information storage and retrieval system, without permission in writing from the publisher.

Published by Crowbar Press
106 Tattnal Court
Gallatin, Tennessee 37066.

http://www.crowbarpress.com

Book layout and cover design by Scott Teal
Cover photo from the Scott Teal collection

Library of Congress Cataloging-in-Publication Data

Hornbaker, Tim

    Master of the Ring / by Tim Hornbaker

1. Sports—United States—Biography. 2. Wrestling—United States—History. I. Hornbaker, Tim II. Title

Printed in the United States of America
ISBN 978-1-940391-35-9

First Edition / November 2020

TABLE of CONTENTS

Dedication	6
Acknowledgements by Tim Hornbaker	6
Chapter 1: Life Begins on Arlington Street	9
Chapter 2: From Gob to Grappler	23
Chapter 3: The Rohde Brothers	36
Chapter 4: The Atomic Blond	49
Chapter 5: Drawing Blood and Suspensions	62
Chapter 6: Wrestling's Nature Boy	74
Chapter 7: Time for a Change	86
Chapter 8: The Pfefer Curse	99
Chapter 9: A Perennial Champion	112
Chapter 10: Rogers vs. Rogers	125
Chapter 11: Mentoring a Legend	137
Photo Gallery	150
Chapter 12: The Politics of Wrestling	176
Chapter 13: The Path to Capitol	188
Chapter 14: The Ultimate Goal	200
Chapter 15: An Arduous Journey	213
Chapter 16: A Champion on the Ropes	226
Chapter 17: Blind to the Consequences	239
Chapter 18: A King Dethroned	251
Chapter 19: The Next Chapter	266
Chapter 20: Passing the Torch	277
Chapter 21: The Legend Lives Forever	290
Index	307

DEDICATION

This book is dedicated to the legendary "Manager of Champions," Bobby Davis, and his wife Sylvia. Their kindness and friendship will be treasured forever.

Lee Rogers – For her unrelenting assistance, thoughtfulness, and understanding

Debbie Rogers – For her kindness in sharing her memories

Lastly, this book is dedicated to the memories of J Michael Kenyon and Fred Hornby – two of professional wrestling's greatest historians. Their dedication to uncovering the mysteries of the mat business will inspire me forever.

ACKNOWLEDGEMENTS

In the aftermath of finishing *Death of the Territories: Expansion, Betrayal and the War that Changed Pro Wrestling Forever* in 2018, I made the decision to write a book about the famous "Nature Boy" Buddy Rogers, one of the most celebrated and controversial superstars in wrestling history. Going into the project, I knew it was going to be a rollercoaster, and for more than two years, I labored on his complicated story – trying to ensure that all the facts about his time in wrestling were brought to light. Such a project would have been impossible without the love and encouragement of my family and friends.

First and foremost, I'd like to thank my wife, Jodi. Her assistance makes all of these books possible, and I couldn't ask for a better partner and friend. She is everything to our family. I'd also like to thank L.W. Hornbaker, Timothy and Barbara Hornbaker, Melissa Hornbaker, Virginia Hall, Sheila Babaganov, Frances Miller, Debbie and Paul Kelley, and John and Christine Hopkins.

My deepest gratitude goes out to the entire Rogers family. I first corresponded with Buddy's daughter Lee in 2018, shortly after beginning research on this project, and she couldn't have been more friendly and accessible to my never-ending stream of questions. Over the course of the past two years, I've learned so much from her and I want to thank her for her time and incredible insight. During the summer of 2020, I spent more than an hour on the phone with Debbie Rogers, and I want to thank her for her kindness in answering all of my questions. Her knowledge and perspective was very important to my research and gave me the necessary information to complete the book. I also had the privilege of speaking with Buddy's nephew, Mr. Jerry Hauske. Mr. Hauske was also kind enough to share his memories of his famous uncle, and I want to thank him for his assistance. My additional appreciation goes out John and Vera Rohde and David Rogers.

Working on this book gave me the special opportunity of getting to know pioneering manager Bobby Davis and his wife, Sylvia. Bobby and Sylvia are two of the kindest, sweetest, and most engaging people I've ever encountered, and I'm honored to call both of them my friends. I also want to send Bobby and Sylvia my gratitude for sharing their memories with me. Bobby was more than a manager to Buddy Rogers. He was his best friend and confidant. They traveled the highways and byways together and, to this day, Bobby has infinite love and respect for the "Nature Boy." Bobby's assistance throughout the research and writing for this project has been a godsend. As other historians will acknowledge, Bobby Davis is a legend, and for his contributions in professional wrestling, he belongs in every Hall of Fame.

Master of the Ring: The Biography of "Nature Boy" Buddy Rogers has also given me the opportunity to work with Scott Teal, a premier historian and publisher. For years we've discussed the possibility of doing a project together, and our mutual respect for Buddy Rogers made this a natural fit. As I quickly learned, Scott's meticulousness as an editor was just what this book needed, and he helped shape this project into its final form. A big thank you goes to Scott for his work and dedication.

Thank you to wrestling researcher and collector Doug McCullough for his ongoing assistance throughout this project. Doug's immense collection of Buddy Rogers material was critical as I attempted to track down old magazines, programs, and other vital documentation. Doug also contacted Elena McCormack, the wife of the well-known writer, Bill McCormack, who kindly gave him permission to share her late husband's research with me. Mr. McCormack was writing a book about Buddy Rogers prior to his unfortunate death in 2001. Considering his extensive knowledge and impressive writing style, his book would undoubtedly have been a classic tome had he been able to finish it. My gratitude and respect to Bill for his incredible research and to Elena for allowing Doug to share the material with me.

One of the big necessities for a book about Buddy Rogers was a need to dig into the Jack Pfefer Collection at the University of Notre Dame. In late 2018, I ventured to South Bend for the first time in 15 years, and spent nearly a week going through old periodicals, correspondence, and financial records. It was a fascinating journey into wrestling history and I enjoyed every minute of it. Thank you to George Rugg and the entire staff in the University of Notre Dame Rare Books and Special Collections Department in the Hesburgh Library for their hospitality and patience. If you are a wrestling fan, you must visit this collection at some point in your life.

At this point, I'd like to acknowledge a few of the tremendous wrestling historians I've worked with through the years, particularly the late Fred Hornby and J Michael Kenyon. Hornby was a faithful Buddy Rogers researcher for a number of decades, and collected enough results to put out his first Buddy Rogers Record Book, with help from Haruo Yamaguchi, in 1983. In subsequent years, Hornby released five supplements to his original record book, and his work is mandatory reading for people interested in mat history. In conjunction with Steve Yohe, Hornby did his final version of the record book – a massive publication – in 2004. Hornby passed away in 2015. J Michael Kenyon was another historian devoted to accurately reporting the story of Rogers, and his *A Buddy Rogers Tribute*, printed in the 2004 Hornby Record Book, was wonderfully detailed – and told in classic "JMK" fashion. Mr. Kenyon passed away in 2017.

Both Haruo Yamaguchi and Steve Yohe were instrumental in the research and writing for this book on Rogers and I thank them both. An additional acknowledgment and thanks to the following individuals for their assistance: Koji Miyamoto, Karl Lauer, Dave Giegold, Fred Rubenstein, Brad McFarlin, Tommy Fooshee, Dan Westbrook, Brian Last, John Pantozzi, Libnan Ayoub, Michael Omansky, Steve Johnson, Bob Bryla, Bob Oates, Don Luce, Bertrand Hébert, Daniel Chernau, Max Jacobs, Jim Molineaux, Michael Tereshko, Jeff Walton, Bill Apter, David Aquino, Don Robertson, George DiFlavis Jr., Anthony Cottone, Lou Sahadi, Mark Weitz, Jon Boucher, Paul J. MacArthur, Mike Johnson, Will Morrisey, and Steve Ogilvie.

To help understand Buddy's medical history, I want to thank Charles M. Geller, MD, FACS, FACC, FCCP, the Chief of Cardiac Surgery and Associate Chairman of the Department of Surgery for the Crozer Keystone Health System in Delaware County, PA. He serves as a Clinical Associate Professor of Surgery at both the Drexel University College of Medicine and Temple University School of Medicine.

Digging through old magazines, I discovered mention of the "Anti-Buddy Rogers Fan Club," headed by Ray D'Ariano in the early 1960s. Of course, I wanted to learn more about this club, so I contacted him for more information. Ray couldn't have been friendlier. It was a surprise, though, to learn that the "Anti-Buddy Rogers Fan Club" was headed by D'Ariano when he was but 11 years old, and he was actually the group's only member. At the time, he loved to hate Buddy, like most people, but later recognized Rogers's brilliance, calling him the "King of that Era." D'Ariano went on to become well-known in the music industry. My gratitude goes to Ray for sharing his memories. Thank you also to Dick Bourne for his insight into Buddy's tenure in the Mid-Atlantic territory. Check out his awesome website, www.midatlanticgateway.com.

Late in life, between 1988 and 1991, Buddy Rogers did three important radio interviews. The first was Wrestling Hotline with Blackjack Brown in March 1988. This particular interview was historical because Brown brought together Rogers and Bruno Sammartino to discuss their differences for the first time. Rogers also appeared with Tom Burke and Dan Reilly on Wrestle Radio in late 1991. Tom recalled that Buddy initially rescheduled due to a prior engagement, but when he realized he could do the interview after all, he called and apologized. "That is class," Burke said of Buddy's actions. Lastly, Buddy did John Arezzi's Pro Wrestling Spotlight twice in 1991, the first on August 4 and the second on October 20. I'd like to thank Blackjack Brown, Tom Burke, and John Arezzi for sharing the audio of their interviews with Rogers. Getting to hear his comments about history and modern pro wrestling were fascinating.

Bob Greene, the famous columnist and author of many popular books, graciously answered my questions, as did Barbara Condon Marrs, the daughter of sportswriter, David Condon. My appreciation is sent to both for their supportive comments. Researchers Cortney Bangel, Aaron Goodwin, and Dawn King Carson obtained critical information for this project and have my gratitude. Amy Miller and the Interlibrary Loan Department at the Main Library in Fort Lauderdale, Florida always have my appreciation for their incredible work. They've been helping me with my research for the past 20 years. A number of other institutions offered assistance, to include the Atlantic County Historical Society, Greater Cape May Historical Society, Cape May County Library, Newark Public Library, West Virginia and Regional Historical Center (WVU Libraries), Leeds Central Library, Franklin County Probate Court, Los Angeles Superior Court, New Jersey Division of Revenue, and the National Personnel Records Center.

Others who made themselves available to answer questions include: Linda Spiegleman, Erin Henson, Jean Scott, Mike Zim, Kurt Holbrook, Dick Longson, Jerry Vallina, Carol Dodrill, Gary Russo, Holly Gilzenberg, Lydia Tack, Pampero Firpo, Mary Fries, Jim Cornette, Ralph Delligatti, Thomas Bunce, Phil Cohen, Nathan Hatton, Joe Opiela, Jon Langmead, Gary Michael Cappetta, Dave Meltzer, Greg Oliver, Andrew Calvert, Jason Campbell, Pat Laprade, Mike Chapman, Mark Hewitt, Matt Langley, Rock Rims, Jose Fernandez, Rebecca Stump, Kit Bauman, Gary Gabrich, Bob Mulrenin, Manuel A. Torres, Javier Rodriguez, Michael Bauman, Mark James, Ross Schneider, Dave Davis, Evan Ginzburg, Chuck Thornton, Dr. Mike Lano, Diane Devine, Dr. Frank Segreto, Chris Swisher, Bob Barnett, Ray Odyssey, Alex Marvez, Donald O'Keefe, Kathleen C. Wyatt, Harry Bellangy, John Perin, Mike Norrid, Larry Dwyer, Billy Joe Pyle, Sid Parker, Greg Cameron, Ernie Rickert, Toni Laughridge, and Pat Pannella.

Throughout the writing of this project, I relied on additional research from a number of talented researchers and writers to include: Burt Ray, Jim Melby, Georgiann Makropoulos, Jim Zordani, Graham Cawthon, Wade Keller, Bruce Mitchell, David Chappell, Bob Sand, Harry White, Ed Garea, David Skolnick, Karl Stern, Kenneth R. Levitt, Hisaharu Tanabe, Terry Dart, Gary Will, and David Baker.

Chapter 1
Life Begins on Arlington Street

The year was 1961. In the ring was the new heavyweight champion of the world, and he had just spoken a few words into the house microphone, demonstrating his sheer pompousness. It was a glorious display of arrogance as "Nature Boy" Buddy Rogers stepped through the ropes, and walked away from the squared circle as the most hated man in America. More than 38,000 spectators at Comiskey Park in Chicago gave him the works, calling him every name in the proverbial book, and based on his self-centered personality, he deserved every criticism. But no one in the crowd could disparage his performance that night. Rogers had wrestled like a champion. Of course, his tactics weren't always within the realm of sportsmanship, and if he saw an opening to break the rules, he typically went for it. That being said, Rogers proved to be an unparalleled competitor, and his victory over Pat O'Connor for the National Wrestling Alliance championship was one of the greatest moments in wrestling history.

Blond and marvelously tan, Buddy was a heat magnet, which meant he naturally courted the disdain of fans. A wrestling "bad guy" wouldn't be doing his job correctly if he didn't draw a chorus of boos every time he stepped out from behind the curtain, but Rogers took it to another level. Initially compared to Gorgeous George, a master of showmanship, Buddy developed his own style of performance, and drew immense reaction wherever he traveled. His pre-match swagger, including a much-imitated strut, was infuriating to audiences, and Rogers knew exactly what buttons to push. Enjoying a meteoric rise to the pinnacle of professional wrestling, Buddy endured the challenges of promotional rivalries, politics, and resentment. He took it all in stride and overcame one obstacle after another until he reached that crucial occasion in 1961 against O'Connor. A record-breaking crowd turned out to see the pivotal match-up, and Rogers didn't let them down. He gave everyone a performance of a lifetime.

The complex story of Buddy Rogers began on Feb. 20, 1921, when he was born Herman Karl Rohde in Camden, New Jersey.[1] His father, Herman Gustav Max Rohde, a German immigrant from Hamburg, was 48 years of age when his son was born.[2] An adventurous young man in his youth, Herman Gustav yearned to see the world and became a sailor, traveling to a number of countries around the globe.[3] In 1893, he migrated to the United States aboard the transatlantic steamship, the Furst Bismarck, and settled initially in New York before moving to Philadelphia.[4] He married a German woman named Elizabeth, and over an eleven-year period from 1901 to 1912, they had three children; Ida, Anna, and John Charles.[5] John was his youngest, born April 1, 1912. The following January, John was baptized at the Zion German Presbyterian Church in Philadelphia, the family's regular house of worship.[6]

Herman Gustav was a hard worker, ever-determined to provide for his family, and labored as a machinist. During the first half of the 1910s, he uprooted his family from an address northeast of downtown to West Philadelphia, within walking distance of a better-paying job at the Louis Bergdoll and Sons Brewing Company at 29th and Parrish streets.[7] Employed as a chief engineer, Herman put in long hours at the brewery, but maintained his standing in numerous fraternal organizations, including the Loyal Order of Moose and the Independent Order of Odd Fellows. On Feb. 23, 1915, his wife, Elizabeth, passed away of heart disease at the age of 45, leaving a substantial hole in the family.[8] Much of the burden fell to his children, especially Ida, who, incidentally, turned 14 the day after her mother's passing.

The "Temperance Movement," a powerful effort to ban the manufacture and sale of alcoholic beverages, was a major concern to Philadelphia brewers as the 1910s wore on. In fact, by 1918, it was all but certain to become a constitutional amendment. Sure enough, on Jan. 16, 1919, the amendment was ratified by the states and Prohibition officially began the following year. For people employed in the brewing industry, there was a several-year period of uncertainty leading up to the formal ban of alcohol in January 1920. Breweries fought to make a distinction between beer and hard liquor, and beer manufacturers agreed to whittle down the alcoholic content of their product in an effort to strike a compromise. However, they were beaten back by their opposition, and ultimately lost the war.

The little guys in the battle, the actual employees being put out of work by Prohibition, were among the biggest losers. In 1919, the Anti-Saloon League tried to minimize the expected ramifications of the alcohol ban by proposing that breweries could produce cider, grape juice, and malted milk instead.[9] In reality, most breweries boarded up their doors. Depression and despair caught up with many people burdened by the stress of being newly unemployed, and Herman was in line with the rest of them. One of his best friends, Reinhold Baack, a brewery fireman who served as a witness when Rohde applied for naturalization, committed suicide in May 1919 during a bout with temporary derangement, and it is not known what external factors played a part.[10] Sadly, Baack's eight-year-old son died the following year after a fall.[11] He was five days older than Herman's son John.

With things changing at a rapid pace, Herman examined his options, and decided to move his family out of Philadelphia and across the Delaware River to Camden, New Jersey. He found a modest home in South Camden at 976 Woodland Avenue, and utilized his machinist background to obtain employment in the paper industry.[12] Shortly thereafter, he moved the family again, this time to 2033 Arlington Street, firmly imbedded in what is today acknowledged as the Waterfront South section of Camden. Herman rented the property from Annie L. Cannon, but when the home was then sold to John N. Durmann in 1920, the latter became his landlord.[13] At the time, Arlington Street was part of a bustling working-class neighborhood, surrounded by thriving companies and factories. About five dozen wooden row houses littered both sides of the narrow street, and each residence had two stories, usually around six rooms, and all the modern conveniences.

Arlington Street was part of the Eighth Ward, one of 14 specialized districts in Camden.[14] One block east of Arlington was Broadway, Camden's central know about money, bartering, and how to protect himself. It wasn't an easy education, but Herman knew nothing else. This was life, and he was there to help his parents and siblings to the best of his capabilities.

"[Herman] grew up in an area where the merchants were old world Jews and all purchases had to be negotiated," wrestler Billy Darnell later wrote. "He very quickly became fluent in Yiddish, which is basically German, and I believe that this is the reason he became such a good negotiator. Many of his friends were Jewish."[32] At home on Arlington Street, many different languages were spoken. He had neighbors from Yugoslavia, Italy, Poland, Ireland, Scotland, and Hungary. Only a couple families on the block emigrated from Germany by 1930, and a majority were American born. Most households were comprised of adults ranging in age from their 20s to 40s, with a handful of older couples scattered about. For Herman, there were about two dozen kids between seven and 15 in the immediate area around his home, giving him a wide assortment of playmates.[33]

Not unlike many other parts of the country, South Camden dealt with increased levels of crime before Prohibition's repeal in December 1933, and the bootlegging of alcohol was a major source of money for local gangsters. In addition, the rough-and-tumble Eighth Ward, known as the "Bloody Eighth," saw its share of political corruption and violence, and the waters separating government service and organized crime were incredibly shallow. Gambling was a popular vice, and robberies were frequent. Both the family-owned grocery store at one end of Arlington and the saloon at the other were both targeted by criminals at one time or another.[34] One of the more recognizable names of the era was Joseph "Cuzzy" Scarduzio, who the *Camden Courier-Post* called a "colorful Eighth Ward figure in many a political campaign and a well-known character in the nightlife of South Camden."[35] Scarduzio's cousin Samuel lived at 2024 Arlington, just across the street and a few houses down from the Rohde residence.

Providing relief from the constant day-to-day stress, sports were a major source of recreation and entertainment for the people of Camden. Football was a genuine pastime, and it didn't matter if it was playground, scholastic, independent, college, or professional, fans were enthusiastic through and through. Philadelphia's close proximity kept the interest of local supporters, especially when it came to the exploits of the University of Pennsylvania and Temple University. In 1926, the Frankford (Philadelphia) Yellow Jackets won the NFL championship, posting a 14-1-2 record. Seven years later, the Philadelphia Eagles debuted as a franchise. Over in the realm of baseball, Connie Mack's Philadelphia Athletics were five-time World Series champions, having won their last two titles, back-to-back, in 1929 and '30. Boxing was also a beloved sport, and many Camdenites attended the famous 1926 upset that saw Gene Tunney strip the world heavyweight title from the "Manassa Mauler," Jack Dempsey, in Philadelphia.[36]

In December 1930, big-time professional wrestling was established in Camden. Charley Grip, a former trainer at the New York Athletic Club and a talented welterweight wrestler, was the man in charge.[37] Born Karl Aug. Gribul in Riga, Latvia, Grip escaped his homeland in 1914 at the beginning of World War I.[38] He toured as a wrestler, competing in non-heavyweight strongholds, and lived in Columbus, Ohio, for a time.[39] Promoting was a natural progression, and Grip made his bones in Huntington, West Virginia, before settling into a leadership role in Camden. Earlier in 1930, another outfit tried their hand at running the Convention Hall in the city, but bowed out after a few shows.[40] Grip understood the challenges and plowed ahead anyway, determined to remold Camden into a thriving wrestling metropolis.

Importing wrestlers from Boston and Columbus, Grip was moderately successful from day one. On Dec. 10, 1930, an estimated 2,500 patrons attended his inaugural program featuring the likes of "Count" George Zarynoff, Jack Sherry, John Grandovich, and Andy Brown. The latter was the star heel for the evening's presentation, and witnesses were generally pleased when Zarynoff defeated him in two-of-three-falls. Nevertheless, Brown had everyone talking. In fact, fans were so aroused by his villainous tactics that they actually wanted a piece of him after the bout. Police were called in to protect Brown as he left the ring.[41] A few weeks later, the famous "Tigerman" John Pesek made an appearance, and attendance rose to 4,000. An extraordinarily intelligent and aggressive wrestler, Pesek beat Cyclone Ress when his opponent was unable to continue after one fall. On the undercard was a talented 190-pounder named Joe Montana, who originally was from Italy, but was making his home in Camden.[42]

Over the following weeks and months, Grip hit his stride, and crowds skyrocketed to more than 7,500. Joe Banaski, claimant to the world light heavyweight championship, and Henri DeGlane, the recognized AWA world heavyweight champion, made stops in Camden, as did former champion Gus Sonnenberg. On Grip's first anniversary as a local promoter, Tom Ryan, the sports editor for the *Camden Courier-Post*, wrote: "It is a tribute to his matchmaking ability that wrestling has become an institution with South Jersey sports fans."[43] Although it wasn't often publicly discussed, the grappling industry was heavily fractured and separated by rival syndicates. To that point, Grip was playing ball with the Paul Bowser troupe out of Boston, and received a constant flow of popular stars. The business, in 1932, was rattled to its core when the popular Greek sensation, Jim Londos, another claimant to the world heavyweight throne, broke from his New York masters and joined an opposition group.

The move set the wrestling world aflame, and promoters throughout North America struggled to find their footing. Grip was no exception. In August 1932, he declared loyalty to the Londos organization and welcomed a whole host of new performers to Camden. Gino Garibaldi, Rudy Dusek, Milo Steinborn, Floyd Marshall, Pat O'Shocker, and Londos himself, made their debuts, and crowds were reinvigorated. These were regularly featured wrestlers across the river in Philadelphia, and anyone keeping tabs on the business in the newspaper knew who they were. But Paul Bowser wasn't going to lose Camden without a fight. He inked a deal with brothers Frank and Ray Hanly, and began booking his stars to the 114th Infantry Armory. Thus, there was a continuation of his established wrestlers on Camden shows. Every week, there were two live programs in the vicinity, plus those staged in Philadelphia, and fans were never at a loss for professional wrestling action.

It isn't known if young Herman attended any of the pro events offered in Camden during that time, but it is clear that he was influenced by the pro sport and its colorful performers. Frankly, it was difficult not to be. Wrestlers were featured on the front page of the sports section, talked about on playgrounds and in schools, and around proverbial water coolers. In the evenings during the week, lively commentators delivered the play-by-play for the regional festivities on the radio.[44] Jim Londos, Ed (Strangler) Lewis and many of their contemporaries were household names, and whenever they were in Camden or Philadelphia, droves of fans turned out to see them battle. For a child supporter of the sport, being raised during the Depression, there was only so much Herman could do. On the recommendation of his brother John, he turned to the Camden YMCA, and at eight years old, began to learn how to wrestle.[45]

Growing up in a tough neighborhood, Herman already knew how to defend himself from aggressors and bullies. His older brother made sure he knew how to fight.[46] With friends, he wrestled for fun, but there was never any real science or skill behind it.[47] "As long as I can remember, I was wrestling other boys," Herman later recounted. "I always aimed to be a wrestler."[48] Grappling on the playground was one thing, but gaining an education at a formal institution was completely another. That was the difference between an ordinary adolescent combatant and an athlete of genuine ability. The Camden YMCA was the gateway to such an education, and Herman took advantage of the opportunity. Located at 614 Federal Street, the YMCA was a little less than three miles north of Arlington, just off Broadway. It was a bit of a trek, but as a healthy outlet during stressful times, the trip was completely worthwhile.

The greater Camden community felt the same way. The YMCA was a critical sanctuary for athletics, social interaction, and health. Membership cost $15, and gave citizens full access to the gymnasium and swimming pool.[49] With regard to competition, teams from the Camden YMCA were very successful in regional contests. The senior and junior swimming teams were championship grade, and the basketball, volleyball, and handball squads were just as fierce. It wasn't uncommon to see professional boxers and wrestlers sparring on the mat, or muscle-bound bodybuilders lifting weights in the gym. Amongst the amateur wrestlers, 23-year-old Wilson Kerr was considered the best of the best, and he served as coach for the local grapplers.[50] Eccentric in the hair department, Kerr frequently competed on combination boxing-wrestling shows across the region, and in 1933, he won a match on a special amateur show promoted by Charley Grip at the Pennsauken Arena.[51]

Herman learned all about wrestling from Kerr at the Camden YMCA.[52] The lessons were physically arduous, the hours long, and the bruises deep. Kerr wasn't tasked with teaching hopscotch, and he didn't always play nice. Wrestling was a brutal sport, and in learning the offensive and defensive tricks of the trade, one had to experience the pain of being pushed to the limits. That often meant being "stretched," a term used by legitimate wrestlers (shooters) in their efforts to either break in or punish others. Tying up a newcomer in a variety of submissions was an endearing tool for wrestling tutors. If they were trying to weed out weak-minded wannabes, it was the surest way to do so. It was somewhat of an initiation process, and Herman undoubtedly was tested to some extent. The young man embraced the challenge and never gave up. For the next eight years, he trained as a wrestler at the "Y," and his commitment never wavered.[53] There was little fanfare, but a lot of character building, and Herman was on his way to becoming a man.

Schooling was neglected in many families because of the need to contribute financially during the Depression. Herman's mother Frieda was an educated woman and wanted him to continue his studies. In June 1936, at the age of 15, he graduated from the John W. Mickle School and was promoted to junior high school.[54] The following year, he graduated from the Cooper B. Hatch Junior High School with a practical arts certificate. He was an impressive guy, in both looks and confidence, and administrators selected him to present an "address of welcome" speech during the graduation ceremonies.[55] That summer of 1937 was important to the story of Herman Rohde, as he'd later recall achieving his first major athletic honor. It came as a swimmer, and multiple times in press reports, he told the tale of winning a three- or five-mile distance championship, setting a record at Wildwood, New Jersey.[56] The length of the record depended, apparently, on his mood when an interview was recorded. Despite that, no proof of his win has ever surfaced.

That's not to say it didn't happen. Herman was a naturally gifted swimmer and reportedly a standout at the Camden YMCA.[57] Sports and competition came easy to him, and his physical development played a major part. Between the ages of 14 and 17, he experienced a massive growth spurt, blooming to better than 5-foot-10 in height, and swelling from 142 to 180 pounds.[58] He was already towering over his 5-foot-5 father and there seemed to be no end to his growth in sight.[59] Weight training was a contributing factor. He initially expressed worry that lifting weights would increase his bulk and slow him down as a wrestler, but a YMCA trainer convinced him otherwise.[60] It was no secret, however, that a heavier frame was better suited for football. And since most high schools in the area didn't have a wrestling program, Herman was concentrating more on his gridiron skills than his grappling.[61]

In the fall of 1937, he enrolled at Woodrow Wilson High School and was classified as a 10B sophomore.[62] Witty and energetic, he continued to stand out, and was named one of three class leaders, along with Marvin Aronow and Joseph Green.[63] Herman joined the school varsity football team under Coach Grover (Worm) Wearshing, and was impressive in preseason practice.[64] He was good enough to start the right guard position in the opener against Haddon Heights High School on Oct. 2, 1937, but Woodrow Wilson was outplayed as a whole, and shut out, 13-0.[65] Coach Wearshing was unsettled by the inexperience of his line and quickly made a number of changes. Herman was benched, but his removal from the lineup didn't help Wilson improve. They lost three of their next six games and fell to the bottom of the South Jersey Group 4 football standings.

Prior to the beginning of the next school year, Herman transferred from Woodrow Wilson to Camden High School, which was much closer in distance to his Arlington home.[66] Notably, Camden defeated Wilson in a city football championship game on Nov. 25, 1937, before 5,300 enthusiasts at the Farnham Park Athletic Field.[67] The annual contest was always bitterly fought and meant bragging rights for the subsequent year. For Herman, who turned 17-years-old in February 1938, Camden High offered a fresh start and he wanted demonstrate his exuberance on the football field. His new coach, Bill Palese, knew an up-and-comer when he saw one, and thought the 186-pounder had great potential. A local sportswriter for the *Camden Courier-Post* agreed, and believed that if Herman gained better knowledge of the team playbook, he might even achieve a starting position.[68]

Palese, a former Camden High football star in the late 1920s, entered the 1938 season with nine veterans on his roster. If his returning players all remained healthy, that left little room for newcomers in his starting lineup. But football was much different in those days, and players were responsible for going the distance on both offense and defense. That meant Palese needed a deep bench to ensure his team was competitive for an entire 48 minutes. When Camden's season commenced on Sept. 24, 1938, Rohde came off the bench as a substitute in an 18-0 thumping of Philadelphia's Simon Gratz High School.[69] The victory was huge for morale, and Camden tried a similar approach a few days later against Northeast, another Philadelphia school. This time, their rival got the better of them, and Camden was defeated 19-7.[70] On Oct. 8, 1938, Herman was given his first Camden starting shot against Woodbury High, and the "Purple Avalanche," as his team was called, beat their opponents, 25-0.[71]

A week later, Herman started at left tackle again for Camden, but a repeat was not to be. In fact, Camden was shut out, 20-0, by Vineland High, and the local paper reported that Palese's athletes were "outclassed in every department of the game."[72] Their struggles continued, and over the next three games, Camden suffered two defeats and one tie. The November 5 game, a 6-0 loss at Atlantic City, was the last time Herman would start for Camden that season.[73] He played off the bench in a 38-2 victory over Emerson High and then a 7-7 tie versus Merchantville. Finally, on Nov. 24, 1938, in the annual championship game against Woodrow Wilson, Camden retained its honors with a 6-0 win. Rohde again came off the bench and provided a spark when his teammates needed it.[74] Acknowledging his hard work, he was awarded a traditional "C," representing letterman status, during a special assembly on Dec. 22, 1938.[75]

Going into his junior year, Herman was on the cusp of having the biggest year of his athletic life. Football was his prime sport in school, but it wasn't his only passion.[76] He enjoyed swimming, as well, and was exceptionally talented.[77] On June 21, 1939, he passed a series of grueling tests to become a member of the elite Wildwood Beach Patrol. Wildwood was a booming vacation and convention spot, and tens of thousands flocked to the beautiful beaches of Southeastern New Jersey during the summer. Frank Hoffman, director of the outfit, gave a speech to seven new members that afternoon, telling them: "You men are now members of the Wildwood Beach Patrol, which has a record second to none in this country, and it is up to you when you start in on July 1 to help keep that record immaculate. Keep our record of no fatalities clean, be courteous at all times to visitors, and we'll all be one big happy family on this patrol."[78]

A natural beach bum, Herman was addicted to the sun and the water. The constant rays turned his normally brown hair blond, and with his dark skin, gave him a distinctive look. Following a successful season on the beach, he returned to Camden, and began to make preparations for another year on the grid. Also returning was one of his best friends, Dominic (Dom) Doganiero, who was a star in the making at halfback for Camden High. Doganiero, sadly, suffered the sudden loss of his father, Antonio, in March 1939, and was forced to leave school midway through the fall campaign to tend to the family's popular barber shop. [79] Joe Martin, the only player from Camden High to be named to the South Jersey All-Star First Team in 1938, proved to be a versatile backfield specialist.[80] Coach Palese expected him to take a leadership role in 1939 as team captain and part-time quarterback.

Rohde started for Camden's eleven on Sept. 30, 1939, in a rare night game versus New Brunswick, playing right tackle, but the "Purple Avalanche" was outgunned and defeated, 6-0.[81] Rebounding to win the next two, over Perth Amboy and Woodbury, Camden was seemingly headed for the top of the class. On Oct. 21, 1939, they ran into the defending South Jersey Group 4 titleholders, Vineland High, and were promptly dispatched, 19-0, before a crowd of 6,000 at Farnham Park. The beat writer for the *Camden Courier-Post* specifically mentioned Rohde's play as a positive in the loss, but the local aggregation was overwhelmed by a superior team.[82] Now weighing upwards of 200 pounds and nicknamed, "Big" Herman by friends, Rohde was turning a pivotal corner as a football player, and there was no limit to his possible success.

But things were going to take a drastic change. Few people knew that five months earlier, even before his summertime work began in Wildwood as a lifeguard, Herman filled out an application for enlistment in the United States Navy.[83] Such a decision would have halted his education and taken him far from his South Camden roots. There may have been several factors for his interest in naval service. For one, his father had been a sailor in his younger years, and his stories and overall influence might have rubbed off on his son. Herman indicated that he was considering making a career out of the Navy, and the opportunity for stable work with secure paychecks was enticing. Jobs in Camden were hard to come by. It had gotten to the point that Camden High School officials were mailing out letters to local businesses in an attempt to set up future employment for graduates.[84] Companies balked because the education students were receiving was not what they were looking for in terms of commercial employment.

Herman needed specialized training to get a good-paying job and he was motivated to utilize the Navy as a steppingstone. On Sept. 25, 1939, his father signed an authorization form, required by the Navy, giving his blessing for Herman's military service.[85] The rest of his documentation and physical were in order, and on Oct. 30, he was notified to report for duty. In that instant, his high school tenure was over.[86] At some point, Herman was confronted by his principal and told that he'd never amount to anything, apparently because he was dropping out of school.[87] The man's disheartening words were painful and Herman would never forget them. It was true, though, that there were poor prospects for graduates, and even less for dropouts, but the Navy was his career choice and he wasn't afraid to take the next step.

The final documentation for enlistment was signed on Nov. 2, 1939, at the Naval Reserve Station in Philadelphia. Herman agreed to enlist for six years and would receive $21 per month.[88] Putting his athletic experience to use, he qualified in recruit swimming by completing a variation of styles at 175 yards in four minutes and 30 seconds. He also performed a lifesaving component to the qualification, including resuscitation, and was perfectly capable.[89] Herman was soon shipped out to the Newport, Rhode Island, training station and given the rank of Apprentice Seaman. Once there, he took a series of written tests, on which he scored the highest in English with "General Classification" following behind. His lowest marks came in "Mechanical Aptitude," and he did only a little better in arithmetic. Being so far away from family was worrisome, but he knew when he left home that things were "running smooth," and he could focus on his personal mission going forward.[90]

Herman always idolized his father. A hardworking and loyal man, Herman Gustav labored to support his family, and nothing was ever too good for his children. He was smart with his money, and planned ahead to ensure they had a permanent place to live. On Feb. 22, 1930, as the Great Depression was striking the nation, he completed payments on their property on Arlington Street.[91] When his son told him he wanted to join the Navy, he was wholeheartedly supportive, and although seeing young Herman off was painful, he knew it was the right move. What neither knew at the time was that they would never see each other again.

At 8:55 a.m. on Dec. 5, 1939, Herman's brother Johnny sent him a Western Union telegram. It read: "Father Died This Morning See About Leave Come Home Before Buryal (sic)."[92]

Heartbroken, Herman went through the motions, arranged for his leave, and began the painful trip back to Camden. He never could have imagined this happening, and he knew that with his beloved father gone, his life would never be the same.

ENDNOTES - CHAPTER 1

[1] U.S. Social Security Application dated July 28, 1937. Some sources have listed his name as Herman Gustave Rohde Jr. His name and birth date were confirmed by a check with the Office of the Register of Vital Statistics, City Hall, Camden, NJ, performed by the United States Navy prior to Rohde's enlistment. U.S. Navy Enlistment Records, National Personnel Records Center, St. Louis, MO.

[2] Rohde was born on Sept. 7, 1872. Certificate of Naturalization, Jan. 18, 1915, Ancestry.com.

[3] *Gong Magazine*, June 1979.

[4] Rohde arrived in the U.S. on Sept. 15, 1893. Ellis Island Records. According to his naturalization records, Rohde arrived in the U.S. at the Port of New York "on or about" Feb. 11, 1894.

[5] Elizabeth's maiden name is unknown. Ida Rohde, Herman's oldest child, was born on Feb. 24, 1901, reportedly in Philadelphia. U.S. Social Security Applications and Claims Index, 1936-2007, Ancestry.com.

[6] All U.S. Presbyterian Church Records, Ancestry.com.

[7] The Rohde Family moved from 1440 Lawrence Street to 2705 Cambridge Street in West Philadelphia.

[8] Pennsylvania Certificate of Death, File No. 20038.

[9] *Camden Morning Post*, Jan. 21, 1919, p. 9.

[10] Pennsylvania Certificate of Death, File No. 53026.

[11] *Philadelphia Inquirer*, July 26, 1920, p. 1. Pennsylvania Certificate of Death, File No. 75653.

[12] Ida Rohde, 18, also gained employment in the paper field, working at a local paper mill as a box maker. 1920 United States Federal Census. It isn't known what company Herman and Ida worked for, but it is very likely they were employed by the Samuel M. Langston Company at 1930 South Sixth Street, a short distance away from their Arlington Street home. The Samuel M. Langston Company manufactured boxes out of corrugated paper using specialized machinery. Their cardboard and paper boxes were replacing wooden shipping containers, and becoming more and more common in the commercial world. Quaker Oats was one of this company's major clients.

[13] Camden County Property Records, Camden, NJ, p. 137-138.

[14] There were 14 wards as of 1920. *Camden Daily Courier*, Nov. 3, 1920, p. 2.

[15] Employment information was taken from the 1930 United States Federal Census.

[16] *Camden Courier-Post*, Aug. 25, 1920, p. 8.

[17] New Jersey Certificate and Record of Marriage, May 22, 1920. When Herman and Frieda obtained their marriage license at Camden's City Hall, notice was posted in the local newspaper. *Camden Daily Courier*, May 13, 1920, p. 15. According to the recollection of Herman's grandson, Jerry Hauske, Herman and Frieda met in Germany. Interview with Jerry Hauske, June 21, 2018.

[18] Germany, Select Births and Baptisms, Ancestry.com.

[19] Correspondence with Lee Rogers, Aug. 2018.

[20] Frieda traveled aboard the S.S. Nieuw Amsterdam. New York Passenger Lists, Ancestry.com.

[21] New Jersey Certificate and Record of Marriage, May 22, 1920.

[22] *Camden Morning Post*, Dec. 14, 1926, p. 2.

[23] 1930 and 1940 U.S. Federal Census. Ancestry.com.

[24] New York Passenger Lists, Ancestry.com.

[25] Interview with Jerry Hauske, June 21, 2018.

[26] *Camden Evening Courier*, April 23, 1932, p. 1.

[27] 1930 U.S. Federal Census, Ancestry.com.

[28] *Camden Morning Post*, Nov. 26, 1931, p. 1.

[29] *Camden Morning Post*, Nov. 25, 1931, p. 2.

[30] *Buddie Rogers and The Art of "Sequencing"* by Max W. Jacobs, p. 4.

[31] Herman sold copies of the *Philadelphia Daily News*. It was reported that he sold papers around Black Horse Pike (Mt. Ephraim Avenue) and Crescent Blvd., which was southeast of Arlington Street. *Philadelphia Daily News*, June 10, 1969, p. 47.

[32] Billy Darnell letter to Bill McCormack, circa 2000.

[33] 1930 U.S. Federal Census, Ancestry.com.

[34] The grocery store was at 2001 Arlington and the saloon (Rosemont Café) was at 2051 Arlington. The latter was owned by Stanley Wojciechowski until his death in 1936. The business remained in his family until the 1970s. dvrbs.com.

[35] *Camden Courier-Post*, May 17, 1999, p. 13.

[36] Over 120,000 people attended the fight on Sept. 23, 1926. Boxrec.com.

[37] Grip reportedly was an instructor at the New York Athletic Club for six years. *Camden Courier-Post*, Dec. 1, 1930, p. 20.

[38] Grip's last name has been spelled a number of ways, including Greibul, Gribel, and Gribul. In his World War I Draft Registration, dated June 5, 1917, it was spelled, "Gribel." Grip was working as a longshoreman and living in Brooklyn. In his World War II Draft Registration from 1942, his last name was spelled, "Greibul." He was living at 3225 Mt. Ephraim Avenue in Camden with his wife, Violet. Ancestry.com.

[39] Grip was living in Columbus when the 1930 U.S. Federal Census was taken. He was 36-years-of-age. Ancestry.com.

[40] Barry Peshmaylan and Elwood Rigby were the promoters. They began on May 2, 1930.

[41] *Camden Courier-Post*, Dec. 11, 1930, p. 22.

[42] *Camden Courier-Post*, Jan. 27, 1931, p. 16.

[43] *Camden Courier-Post*, Dec. 10, 1931, p. 25.

[44] The Camden Armory shows were broadcast on WTEL.

Life Begins on Arlington Street • 21

45 Herman began wrestling at either 8 or 9 years old, depending on the article. The statement that he started at 8 was made in the *Atlantic City Sunday Press*, March 7, 1982 and *Camden Courier-Post*, Nov. 22, 1984, p. 110. The statement that he started at 9 was made in the *Philadelphia Inquirer*, Aug. 30, 1970, p. 5.

46 His brother Johnny was his first wrestling coach. *Akron Beacon Journal*, June 12, 1950, p. 17.

47 "Almost from the time he first could walk, Rohde was in his wrestling-minded neighborhood." *NWA Official Wrestling*, April 1952, p. 10-11.

48 *Buffalo Evening News*, Nov. 17, 1956, p. 4.

49 *Camden Courier-Post*, Feb. 23, 1935, p. 21.

50 Kerr was acknowledged as the "YMCA titleholder." *Camden Morning Post*, May 4, 1931, p. 13.

51 Kerr would often grow his hair long. *Camden Courier-Post*, Dec. 19, 1931, p. 4. The amateur show was held on July 13, 1933. Kerr defeated Albert DiPatruzio in 7:18. *Camden Courier-Post*, July 14, 1933, p. 18.

52 Rogers was quoted as saying, "I learned all my wrestling under Wilson Kerr." *Camden Courier-Post*, Nov. 22, 1984, p. 110. He reportedly made the YMCA team at age 11. *Akron Beacon Journal*, June 12, 1950, p. 17.

53 Rogers said that he was an amateur for "eight years." Buddy Rogers in the "Apter Chat," with Bill Apter, 1979, part one, Youtube.com.

54 Rohde was part of the 8-A graduating class. *Camden Courier-Post*, June 15, 1936, p. 4. The John W. Mickle School was at South Sixth Street and Van Hook Street. Dvrbs.com.

55 This was ninth grade for Herman. *Camden Courier-Post*, June 15, 1937, p. 10.

56 Herman claimed it was a 5-mile record and said he used the Australian crawl. *Wrestling World*, November 1962. His 3-mile championship was cited in *Sports Pictorial Review*, May 8, 1950, p. 2, Unknown magazine article by Mary McCauley, circa. 1950, *Chicago Sun-Times*, June 12, 1950, p. 53. A Chicago-based article claimed that he won an Atlantic City swimming tournament twice in 1938 and 1939. *Wrestling As You Like It*, Nov. 27, 1947, p. 3.

57 *Wrestling As You Like It*, Oct. 7, 1950, p. 9.

58 He said he weighed 142 pounds at 14 years of age. *Gong Magazine*, June 1979. His height was listed as 5'10" ½" in his United States Enlistment Records.

59 Herman Gustav's height was listed in his Naturalization Record, Jan. 18, 1915. Ancestry.com.

60 *Wrestling As You Like It*, Oct. 7, 1950, p. 9.

61 Many articles in later years claimed that Buddy wrestled in high school, such as the *Evansville Press*, Jan. 29, 1946, p. 10. Some articles stated that he was a four or five-letter man at Camden High School. This would have included wrestling. Examples include the *Santa Cruz Sentinel*, Nov. 30, 1958, p. 12 and the *Akron Beacon Journal*, June 12, 1950, p. 17. "I was the best wrestler at Camden High," Rogers said in one Unknown Magazine Article written by Joe Goldstein, circa. 1956. Rogers corrected these stories in 1982, saying: "They didn't have wrestling in high school in those days." *Atlantic City Sunday Press*, March 7, 1982.

62 Woodrow Wilson High School was at 3101 Federal Street and was approximately five miles from Herman's Arlington home.

63 Herman's last name was spelled, "Rhode." *The Wilsonian*, Nov. 1937, Volume V, No. 1, p. 26. Camden County Historical Society, Camden, NJ.

64 Herman was amongst 25 other players in a team photograph. *The Wilsonian*, Nov. 1937, Volume V, No. 1, p. 22. Camden County Historical Society, Camden, NJ.

65 *Camden Courier-Post*, Oct. 4, 1937, p. 19.

66 Camden High was just over two miles away from Arlington Street, at Park Boulevard and Baird Avenue. On his Navy application, Herman stated that he attended Camden High School for "3 Years" from September 1936 to present. United States Navy Application for Enlistment, May 27, 1939, National Personnel Records Center, St. Louis, MO.

67 *Camden Courier-Post*, Nov. 26, 1937, p. 19.

68 *Camden Courier-Post*, Sept. 23, 1938, p. 23.

69 *Camden Courier-Post*, Sept. 26, 1938, p. 19.

70 *Camden Courier-Post*, Sept. 30, 1938, p. 27.

71 *Camden Courier-Post*, Oct. 10, 1938, p. 15.

72 *Camden Courier-Post*, Oct. 17, 1938, p. 15.

73 Herman started at right tackle. *Camden Morning Post*, Nov. 7, 1938, p. 14.

74 *Camden Courier-Post*, Nov. 25, 1938, p. 32. Camden's final standings were 4-4-2.

75 Players also received "automatic pencils." *Camden Courier-Post*, Dec. 23, 1938, p. 4.

76 Articles written later in his life claimed that he had achieved athletic letters in five sports while in high school, including football, basketball, track, swimming and wrestling. *Chicago Sun-Times*, June 12, 1950, p. 53. In 1962, he was quoted as saying: "I was the top guy in throwing the hammer, putting the shot and throwing the javelin." *Wrestling World*, November 1962. The track and field team at Camden was coached by Bill Palese, but there are no records that he was a member of the team.

77 Rogers quotes: "I was absorbed in playing football and swimming. Above all, I was very good at swimming and swam 23 miles at the age of 14." *Gong Magazine*, June 1979.

78 *Wildwood Leader*, June 22, 1939. A photo of Herman and fellow members of the beach patrol appeared in the *Camden Courier-Post*, June 28, 1939, p. 8. Two members of the patrol, Henry Steingass and Jack Lumsden were champion swimmers in collegiate and AAU meets. They joined at the same time Rohde did.

79 Antonio Doganiero died at the age of 45 on March 19, 1939. He was survived by his wife and eight children. *Camden Courier-Post*, March 21, 1939, p. 4. Also see *Philadelphia Inquirer*, March 2, 1994, p. 72.

80 *Camden Courier-Post*, Nov. 28, 1938, p. 17.

81 *Camden Morning Post*, Sept. 30, 1939, p. 26.

82 *Camden Courier-Post*, Oct. 23, 1939, p. 14.

83 United States Navy Application for Enlistment, May 27, 1939, National Personnel Records Center, St. Louis, MO.

84 *Camden Courier-Post*, June 8, 1938, p. 14.

85 The form was required for the "Enlistment of a Minor Under Twenty-One Years of Age." United States Navy Consent, Declaration, and Oath of Parent or Guardian, Sept. 26, 1939, National Personnel Records Center, St. Louis, MO.

86 Herman listed his education as 10 ½" Grade. United States Navy Application for Enlistment, May 27, 1939, National Personnel Records Center, St. Louis, MO. According to the U.S. Federal Census in 1940, his highest grade completed was third year of high school. 1940 U.S. Federal Census, Ancestry.com. In a 1963 magazine article, he admitted: "I never graduated from high school." *Wrestling World*, December 1963, p. 39-43. He didn't drop out of Camden High School to join the Navy three weeks before his graduation, as indicated in the *Camden Courier-Post*, July 25, 1963, p. 36.

87 Bill Watts told this story in the *Saturday Evening Post*, Feb. 12, 1966, p. 88. The principal at Camden High School was Carleton Roper Hopkins (1892-1976).

88 His discharge date was Nov. 1, 1945. United States Navy Enlistment Records, Nov. 2, 1939, National Personnel Records Center, St. Louis, MO.

89 Ibid.

90 U.S. Navy, U.S.S. Breckinridge Document, March 19, 1940, National Personnel Records Center. St. Louis, MO.

91 Camden County Property Records, Camden, NJ, p. 137-138.

92 Western Union Telegram, Dec. 5, 1939, United States Navy Records, National Personnel Records Center, St. Louis, MO.

Chapter 2
From Gob to Grappler

The recruit depot at Newport, Rhode Island, was one of four specific U.S. Navy bases offering basic training, alongside stations in San Diego, Norfolk, and North Chicago. Hundreds of aspirants turned up at the facility each week and were willing to make the transformation from civilian to sailor.[1] The indoctrination period was extraordinarily challenging, and the first couple weeks of training were jarring both mentally and physically. Recruits were broken down and remolded in the classic military style, programmed by a relentless diet of discipline, teambuilding, and rigorous exercise. Lengthy educational lecture sessions and technical training were also part of the curriculum, and the novice seamen were constantly tested before gaining the qualifications they needed for future naval duty.

Herman Karl Rohde was already 32 days into his training when he was notified of his father's passing.[2] The astonishing reality of joining the military and embracing that life-altering decision, and then so quickly being followed by such a huge personal tragedy, was almost too much to bear. The 13-year-old, full of grief and sadness, was granted emergency leave from his training station and made the journey home.[3] A million thoughts were going through his head, and the well-being of his newly widowed mother was his most pressing concern. He didn't know what was next, nor was he sure that being on a Navy ship potentially stationed thousands of miles away was the best way to show support for his grieving family. First and foremost, he had to personally cope with the heartbreak. Before he could stand as the backbone for his family, he needed to deal with the pain himself, and there were still many questions about the circumstances of his father's death.

The truth was that Herman Gustav suffered from obesity, hypertension and arteriosclerosis. The family physician, Vincent T. McDermott, tended to the Rohde patriarch, but Herman's condition rapidly worsened.[4] On the morning of Dec. 5, 1939, he died at his Arlington home from coronary thrombosis, a blockage of a blood vessel of the heart.[5] He was 67-years-old.[6] Two days later, an obituary and a small biography for Herman ran in the *Camden Courier-Post*. Of note was a list of the six fraternal organizations in which he held membership, including the Brewery Engineers' Union, the German Beneficial Union, and the Kensington Lodge No. 44, Fraternal Order of Beavers. In addition, he was a member of good standing in the Camden Lodge No. 111, Loyal Order of Moose, and the Kane Arctic Lodge No. 115, Independent Order of Odd Fellows.[7] These groups were very important to Herman, who had many friends in the Camden and Philadelphia area.

The funeral was held at Lakeview Memorial Park in nearby Cinnaminson on Dec. 9, 1939. Pastor Otto Dietrich, the same man who married Herman and Frieda 19-years earlier, presided over the services. Before young Herman reported back to Newport the next day, he spent a lot of time discussing the needs of the family with his siblings and how they were going to support Frieda. As a basic recruit, he didn't make much money, but he was willing to send most, if not all of his monthly stipend, back home to help provide for his mother. Herman agreed, with brother John and sisters Ida and Anna, to do what they could for the foreseeable future, and if they needed to reassess things at a later date, they would do so. In the meantime, he was returning to the Navy to continue boot camp, and reported back at 2045 hours on Dec. 10, 1939.[8]

Driven all the more to live up to family expectations and fulfill the goals his father wanted for him, Herman successfully advanced through Naval training and graduated on or around Jan. 12, 1940. Counting his leave time, plus the holidays, he was stationed at Newport for exactly 70 days. With top marks for conduct, he was immediately transferred to his first duty station, the U.S.S. Breckinridge, which was a destroyer assigned to the Atlantic Squadron, and under the leadership of Commander Fred D. Kirtland.[9] The Breckinridge, and its sister ships, were tasked with patrolling the Atlantic and helping escort transport vessels from Europe to the United States. In February 1940, the destroyer was parked at the Brooklyn Navy Yard, and Herman was granted his first "regular" leave, from February 9 to February 13.[10] He took the opportunity to go home and see relatives in Camden.

Upon arrival, he found that conditions hadn't improved for Frieda, and she needed more direct financial assistance. After consultation with family, friends and Pastor Dietrich, Herman agreed to apply for a hardship discharge to help his mother. The decision was a difficult one, but there were no other options. Five days after Herman returned to the U.S.S. Breckinridge following his leave, Commander Kirtland received a letter from Pastor Dietrich. Dietrich indicated that he was writing the letter at the request of Frieda, and explained: "Since her husband's death, Mrs. Rohde has been entirely without support. As Herman is her only son and the only person upon whom she can depend, may I, in her name, respectfully ask you to favorably consider his release from further service in the navy."[11]

While it's true that Herman was Frieda's only biological child, the missive minimized any help received by her stepchildren and extended family. But the overall substance of the letter was powerful and illustrated her need for Herman's discharge. A couple days later, Dr. McDermott, the Rohde's longtime doctor, sent a brief note of his own to Commander Kirtland, and stated: "Mrs. Rhode (sic) depends for support on her only son whom is now in the service."[12] The letters from back home were consequential, but Navy officials refrained from making any formal decision. On the Breckinridge, performing his normal duties as an enlisted man, Herman continued to thrive. On March 2, 1940, he was promoted to Seaman Second Class, and his conduct rating remained high.[13]

On March 11, a third letter from Camden arrived on the desk of Commander Kirtland. This one was from Herman's own cousin, Frank Stech, proprietor of Stech Transportation, a local and long-distance hauling company.[14] Frank was the son of the late George Stech, Frieda's brother, who had passed away six years earlier.[15] He wrote: "I'm writing to let you know I'm willing to give Herman Rohde a position in my firm. His salary will be twenty to twenty four dollars a week. He has worked for me before and his work has always been satisfactory."[16] Herman's wages in the navy were in the neighborhood of $21 a month. After putting in more time, he would see a slight raise to $30. If his cousin was offering him $20 to $24 a week, it was significantly more money, and Herman would've been in a much better position to provide for his destitute mother.

A little more than a week later, Herman submitted a personal request for a "special order discharge." He explained, "Mother and I have tried very hard in keeping our home and living conditions, but have found it impossible due to the fact that I receive such a small salary." Herman mentioned the job opportunity for Stech Transportation and the increased pay. "I know with this income I could support my mother and myself," he concluded.[17] Later that same day, Commander Kirtland forwarded the request and recommended approval.[18] Even though Herman already had the backing of his ship commander, he received a further boost in his efforts from influential U.S. Representative Charles A. Wolverton of New Jersey's 1st District. Wolverton was Camden-born and raised, and had served in the House of Representatives since 1927.

In a letter directly to Rear Admiral Chester W. Nimitz, the Chief of the Bureau of Navigation, Rep. Wolverton wrote: "I am writing in the interest of Herman K. Rohde, now attached to the U.S.S. Breckinridge, who has made application for release from the service. I do hope that it will be possible to act favorably upon this application as I understand the case to be one that merits such action. Whatever you can do consistent with the due performance of your duty will be very much appreciated by all concerned."[19] Rear Admiral Nimitz responded a short time later. On March 28, 1940, he wrote: "I take pleasure in informing you that his request for discharge has been considered favorably. Orders are being issued directing that his release from the service be effected."[20] Commander Kirtland was promptly notified.

The U.S.S. Breckinridge, by this time, was anchored at the Navy Yard in Charleston, South Carolina. Rohde was out-processed from the military and officially released on March 29, 1940.[21] He was authorized five cents per mile travel allowance back to his "place of acceptance [into the Navy]," which was Philadelphia, and provided his final month's pay. From the $51.36 was he given, Herman arranged for transportation, and made the 650-plus-mile trip homeward.[22] Bearing in mind everything that had happened over the previous five months, Herman Rohde was a much different man going home to Camden than he was when he initially left for training the previous November. His eyes were less bright, the bounce in his step diminished, and the idealistic fantasies of globetrotting were gone. Nevertheless, he carried the unmistakable and striking confidence that only a proud military veteran could exhibit.

A new set of responsibilities were ahead of him now, and Herman dutifully accepted the role as primary caregiver for his mother. Only a few days after he returned home to Arlington Street, a government official arrived at his door with a questionnaire needed for the 1940 U.S. Federal Census. Frieda was listed as the head of the household, but confirmed that she was not employed. Herman's stepbrother John was working fulltime as a machinist and admitted to making $1,250 annually. As for Herman, now 19-years-old, he was "seeking work."[23] He was likely expected to start as an employee of his cousin, Frank Stech, but little is known about that experience, or if he actually took that job. By the summer of 1940, Herman accepted an apprentice position at the massive New York Shipbuilding Corporation, working with sheet metal.[24] His salary was only $18.26 a week, but there was room for growth within the company.[25]

In his off-time, he continued to pursue athletics. When Camden's Manufacturers' Committee organized a special Industrial Field Day on Sept. 14, 1940, Rohde agreed to participate as a representative of the New York Shipbuilding firm.[26] Not necessarily known for his speed, Herman might have shied away from the footraces and entered the weightlifting or shot put competitions, but he didn't place. A workmate, Mike DeCastro, won the weightlifting contest in the heavyweight division, and, overall, the New York Shipbuilding Corporation won the team prize with 30 overall points.[27] On the weekends, football was hugely popular in the region, and there were over a dozen independent amateur and semi-professional organizations at any given time.

Indie football was seen as a great way to stay in shape and keep connected with friends. Mike DeCastro, the aforementioned strongman, actually played on a club known as the Shipyard Union during the 1940 campaign.[28] In October of that year, Dominic Doganiero, Mike Leo, Frank Podolski, and John Paul Icart, four of Herman's ex-Camden High teammates, joined the relatively obscure Whitman Park outfit for winter ball.[29] It appeared to be just a matter of time before Herman reunited with his pals in a similar fashion.[30] He resumed workouts at his home away from home, the illustrious Camden YMCA, and reacquainted with a lot of old buddies. One of his newest friends at the gym was Irvin (Zabo) Koszewski, an impressive weightlifter, three years his junior.[31] Zabo was a budding star on the gridiron for Collingswood High School and also an accomplished swimmer.[32]

Herman divided his time between work and athletics, and maintained a fairly active social life. Music was a big hobby of his and would remain so his entire life. He loved the big band sound, and growing up right in the thick of the Swing Era, he appreciated the music of Benny Goodman, Harry James, Billy Eckstine, and Bunny Berigan.[33] Berigan, notably, performed Herman's favorite song from the era, "I Can't Get Started with You," and often played the big clubs up and down the Jersey Shore.[34] Venturing out to dance halls and ballrooms was an especially enjoyable activity for Herman and his friends, and he became a skilled dancer of varied forms.[35] With slicked-back hair, and his Zoot suit style of dress, which included tremendously padded, wide shoulders, he was a fashionable man, and was often in the company of women.[36]

Herman proved to have a bit of a rebellious streak, as well. One particular evening, he crossed the river and enjoyed a night on the town in Philadelphia with friends. There was a big dance at the popular Town Hall at 150 N. Broad Street, and it seemed to be the logical place to go. Things quickly went sideways when Herman and three others tried to get into the establishment without tickets. They were confronted by two of Philadelphia's Finest, and the situation escalated. All four of the young men were nabbed, with Herman and Warren O'Brien headed for jail, and Arthur Anderson and Leonard Polis, both 17, being sent to the Juvenile Court. According to the *Philadelphia Inquirer*, the individuals were charged with resisting arrest, disorderly conduct, and malicious mischief. The newspaper reported that the quartet "attacked two detectives" in an ensuing melee. Rohde and O'Brien were fined $10, and it is unknown if there was any further punishment.[37]

Following the attack on Pearl Harbor in December 1941, and the subsequent declaration of war, the country was united in support of its troops. Military enlistment soared and the people of Camden were committed to the fight in every way imaginable. Patriotism was at an all-time high on Arlington Street, and soon, 31 of its residents were serving in the military. In the center of the block, a large service flag was dedicated in acknowledgement of their sacrifice.[38] Herman's status hadn't changed one bit – he still had a dependant mother. His background in the Navy would have made him a prime candidate for return duty, but for the time being, he remained excluded from service. If there had been a more serious need for manpower, his classification could have changed at any time. From the sidelines, he watched many of his friends go off to war. Among them were high school buddies Joe Martin, Harry Zane, and John Paul Icart, and Zabo Koszewski, Dino Mazzo, and his wrestling coach, Wilson Kerr, from the Camden "Y."

Kerr's instruction, over a period of years, was illuminating and inspiring. Through tireless workouts, Herman's wrestling proficiency improved measurably, and because of his size and strength, he possessed great raw potential. The Camden area had a vibrant amateur circuit where people like Alfred (Pop) Lawrence, Ray Haldeman, Stan Soboleski, Joe Smith, and Les Marshall competed at local recreation halls and athletic centers for the love of the sport. The competition was heavy, and Herman was more of a young lion than a championship-grade wrestler. In his free time, he worked long hours in the gym to increase his base of knowledge.[39] When the opportunity arrived, he accepted a number of small-time amateur exhibitions and continued to build his resume.[40] There was no doubt about it. Herman was talented, but he wasn't naturally gifted as a mat wrestler. He had to strive to be on par with his older contemporaries, and that task didn't come easy.

The notion of making money from wrestling was broached as a genuine possibility by Herman Rohde in 1942, but the initial thought might have occurred to him years earlier. During his childhood, he was fascinated by many of the sport's top stars, and he learned as much as he could about them. "I studied the styles of Joe Stecher, Jim McMillen, and Ed Don George," he later admitted."[41] Jim Londos, the famous Greek powerhouse and the biggest box office attraction to date, set the barometer for "class and science," and Herman was acutely aware of his incredible showmanship.[42] Of all the wrestlers he had seen, though, only one was his true "ideal" in terms of athleticism, and that was Colorado's Everette Marshall, a former claimant to the world title.[43] Marshall feuded with Londos in the mid-1930s and their matches were often catch-as-catch-can mastery with a splash of polished drama. Sporting blond hair and an efficient knowledge of holds, Marshall was a gifted performer and his style was highly influential.

Rohde spent some of his time hanging around the Camden Convention Hall, and demonstrated his enthusiasm by helping carry the luggage of wrestlers to-and-from their automobiles. The great women's wrestler, Mae Young, who was in the very early stages of her career in 1942, later remembered receiving his assistance.[44] The glitz and glamour of professional wrestling was hard to ignore, and for an ex-footballer with an amateur grappling background, it was a vocation to consider. He turned 21 years old in February 1942 and the New York Shipbuilding Corporation remained his only form of income. But that was about to change, and a well-known co-worker at his place of employment would serve as the catalyst.

Wartime brought increased security at the ports along the Delaware River, and the New York Shipbuilding Corporation, with its military contracts, needed a top crew of watchmen at all hours of the day. As part of its extensive troop of civilian guards was a 6-foot-3, 200-pound pro wrestler from Harlan, Iowa, named Fred Grobmier. Grobmier, 46, in his 24th year as a grappler, was perhaps the most inconspicuous-looking athlete ever to grace the squared circle. Exceptionally tall and thin, he was often referred to as wrestling's "bean-pole," and one sportswriter, in 1933, said Grobmier looked like the "skeleton of a big, bad giant." Another remarked that he fooled "fans and foes alike with his slender frame."[45] When it was time to "go" in the ring, he was tricking no one, as Grobmier's legitimate wrestling skill was apparent to observers. Opponents, too, quickly realized he was not someone to push around.

Grobmier came up through the business the hard way, graduating from the farm life in Iowa to makeshift mats in barns and small-time venues across the Midwest. Trained by the legendary Farmer Burns, he wrestled all the greats, including the Zbyszko Brothers, Ed (Strangler) Lewis and Jim Londos. To make extra money, he toured small-town America with a carnival, swindling local tough guys out of their cash by playing the part of an unskilled rube, only to thrash them with unbridled ability. Few were better than him in that respect, and it was all because of the unsuspecting way he looked. "He was the most unique wrestler I'd seen," Herman later recalled. "He was very lean. He had arms like buggy whips and very thin legs. But when he got on you, it's if a cobra had you. And the skin on this man was just like an elephant. You just never got away from him. He just latched on and that was it. And [he was] just the most deceiving individual that a man would ever see."[46]

Rohde and Grobmier didn't meet on the job or through mutual friends. It happened naturally at a benefit exhibition on June 2, 1942. A combined boxing and wrestling show was staged in Westmont, New Jersey, in the auditorium of the Holy Saviour Church.[47] Thirteen matches were booked, but only two of them were wrestling. On one side, Grobmier was slated to compete against Mel Braddock, while Rohde was to face Bob Keys. Braddock didn't show for the affair, so Grobmier was instilled as the referee for the Rohde-Keys exhibition. From his position as the third man in the ring, he had a bird's eye view of Herman's wrestling aptitude, and was impressed.[48] The 400 spectators in attendance probably were, as well.[49] Grobmier pulled Herman aside after the show and it didn't take long for the latter to be completely sold on the idea of turning professional.[50]

It also didn't take long for Grobmier to leave a mark on Rohde in training. "So we went to a gym," Herman later recounted, "and before I knew what had happened, he had my lips bleeding, my eyes swollen, my ears bent back, and I ached all over. He told me, 'If you are going to be a wrestler, you got to learn to take it.'"[51] The punishment continued and Herman never caved. He trusted the grizzled vet, and Grobmier smartened him up to all aspects of the business. Training lasted six weeks, and by the time they were finished, Herman was ready to take the plunge and have his first professional match.[52] Notably, Charley Grip, the man who spiked Camden's attendance for wrestling during the 1930s, was another local influence for Herman Rohde during that time-frame.[53] As a promoter and businessman, Grip was always accessible to the youngsters looking for advice, and was seen as a mentor of sorts. Grip actually had lost his handle on the Camden promotion several years earlier, in 1938, having been a victim of wrestling politics.

The same wrestling politics were going to have a say in Rohde's pro debut, where and when it happened, and if at all. The industry was tightly controlled by various syndicates, and booking agents often exercised much more authority than promoters. In fact, promoters were entirely beholden to syndicate leaders because of the talent they managed. They could make or break promoters by either supplying or withholding headline wrestlers, and in some cases, they could refuse to provide performers at all. If they wanted to push someone out, they could help set up a cross-town promotion and book their box office attractions there instead. In Southern New Jersey, Grip was not the preferred promoter, and booking agent Rudy Dusek helped ensure brothers Frank and Ray Hanly survived the wrestling war and came out on top in Camden. The Hanlys were the local men on the ground running the day-to-day operations, but Dusek was the real power behind the territory.

The expansive Dusek circuit extended from New York City to Washington, D.C. and included Philadelphia and Baltimore. In addition to his leadership duties, Rudy was still an active wrestler and competed up and down the east coast. Like Grobmier, he was originally trained for the mat by Farmer Burns, and had engaged in grappling mayhem for 20 years. He also trained three of his brothers for pro wrestling, Emil, Ernie, and Joe Dusek, and collectively, they were billed as the notorious "Riot Squad." Grobmier had known Rudy for years and was a mainstay in Dusek-controlled towns. In Camden, over the prior months, he worked as a heel, and wrestled the likes of Gino Garibaldi, Tommy O'Toole, and Cowboy Luttrall. For Herman Rohde, Grobmier was his closest contact to Dusek, and it seems altogether likely that Fred would have connected the two, setting up Herman's initial booking.

However, Rohde told the story a different way. During an interview with the *Camden Courier-Post* in 1984, he claimed that he met Dusek while running on the beach in Atlantic City, and that led to his debut match.[54] As for who specifically handled the booking, Herman attributed that to Jess McMahon, a longtime force in both boxing and wrestling in the northeast.[55] McMahon worked for Dusek and assisted with most of the administrative tasks associated with the office. Once Herman was penciled in as a member of the Dusek troupe, McMahon established his first date, and this marked Herman's official introduction to the mat game. But the established history of wrestling has recorded his pro debut in a strange way, mostly because of a string of discrepancies that have perpetuated for decades. Only when tearing back the veneer of his story can the true timeline of events be understood and contrasted against the years of falsehoods.

First of all, a slew of sources, including interviews with the wrestler himself, claimed that he made his debut three years earlier, on July 4, 1939.[56] He would have been a high-schooler at the time, and had joined the Wildwood Beach Patrol two weeks earlier. The assertion was unrealistic from all sides. A widely distributed magazine from 1962 donated an entire segment to Herman's debut, but again, it was more fiction than fact. It was stated that he received his opening bout from the Hanly Brothers and defeated Angelo Savoldi, earning $20.[57] And yet, in nearly every other interview he did, he claimed that his first opponent was Moe Brazin of Brooklyn.[58] He briefly described the match to Bill Apter in 1979, saying: "I guess the match went four or five minutes. I just felt like I was all over him."[59] The only constant across the board was the contention that his first pro match occurred at the Garden Pier in Atlantic City. But could that have been in dispute as well?

Taking all things into consideration, maybe the date was really supposed to be July 4, 1942, with the year being misremembered. As it turns out, Dusek didn't run Atlantic City that day. His local crew was 45-miles south on the Cape May peninsula at Hunt's Auditorium in Wildwood. Could this have been Herman Rohde's real pro debut? Moe Brazin was indeed on the program, connecting one of the dots, but his opponent was not Rohde. It was "Joe Martin," a purported magnesium plant worker.[60] And to top it off, this "Joe Martin" was making his professional debut against Brazin.[61] That was a huge coincidence. The name "Joe Martin" appears in only a few results from the early 1940s and little is known about him.[62] If, for some reason, Rohde used that designation in Wildwood, perhaps to conceal his identity, that information remains unknown. Given that, in regards to the claim that Rohde wrestled Brazin in his pro debut, it may have occurred just like he remembered, but it wasn't reported in either the Atlantic City or Wildwood newspapers.

Herman's first identified professional match occurred on July 18, 1942 at the Garden Pier in Atlantic City.[63] He used the nickname, "Dutch" Rohde for the bout, which was slated to be a one-fall prelim against Angelo Savoldi.[64] Fred Grobmier was also on the card, booked to wrestle Henry Kulkovich. The latter contest went off without a hitch and Kulkovich scored a victory in 19:16. Rohde's match was changed at the last minute, and his original opponent joined Moe Brazin in a team affair against Al Norcus and Maurice LaChappelle. Rohde was instead sent against 30-year-old Eddie King of Philadelphia, a former collegiate football player for Columbia University. King was six-pounds heavier than the 205-pound newcomer, and had seven years experience in the pro ranks.[65] Rohde lived up to expectations and held his own during a 30-minute draw. Afterwards, the *Atlantic City Press-Union* called the bout, "thrilling," and added that both wrestlers "were accorded a big ovation by the fans for their performance."[66]

Preliminary money in wrestling wasn't good, and depending on the town and the promoter in charge, it ranged from $8 to $25.[67] Sometimes it was less. But the higher placement on the card meant more cash in his envelope at the end of the day, and for most grapplers, that was the singular goal. Rohde was riding a personal high, and being on the Dusek circuit had potential, but there was no guarantee wrestling was going pay enough to make it a career. He was willing to take a chance going forward, and he soon left his job at the New York Shipbuilding Corporation.[68] The war was another factor. Wrestling's talent lanes were being depleted by the call to service, leaving opportunities for individuals remaining in the civilian sector. It wasn't under the best circumstances, but jobs were jobs, and Rohde was playing the cards he was dealt.

Nine days after his bout in Atlantic City, he returned to the Garden Pier and achieved his first recorded victory in a match against Jack Vansky, a former amateur from Northern New Jersey.[69] The following day, Rohde made his first serious road trip and traveled 150-miles to Baltimore for a program that night at the Coliseum. He won again, this time over Jim Austeri.[70] In Baltimore, he shared a locker room with Milo Steinborn, the great strongman from Germany, and Rohde immediately gravitated to him.[71] A pro since the early 1920s, Steinborn became a fatherly figure to "Dutch," offering advice and direction, and assisted in his development.[72] When it was opportune, the two shared transportation, navigating the towns on the Dusek circuit, and by September 1942, Rohde had debuted in Washington, D.C., North Bergen, and finally his native Camden.

Appearing as a professional wrestler for the first time before family and friends at the Camden Convention Hall on Sept 21, 1942, was probably an exhilarating moment. Rohde had performed before large hometown crowds before, but nothing compared to being in the middle of the ring and controlling the complete attention of the crowd. An estimated 2,800 spectators watched their local wrestling prodigy battle Angelo Savoldi to a 30-minute draw.[73] There was a common theme for this particular Savoldi bout, as well as other matches against the Jack Vanskys and Michele Leones of the wrestling world. Rohde was always the babyface, and he took a lot of punishment from his madcap rivals. A *Camden Courier-Post* sportswriter explained that "Dutch" spent a lot of his bout with Savoldi "defending himself against [his foe's] off-color tactics, which consisted mainly of strangles, eye gouges and punches to the groin."[74]

Appealing to the crowd by way of his high-quality athleticism and sportsmanship, Rohde was playing his role perfectly, and was learning how to sell against aggressive opponents. Rudy Dusek, himself, set the bar for antagonistic and violent behavior in the ring, and to him, heels were box-office gold. The pure fan favorites in the territory mostly wrestled from an underdog spot, and were compelled to take their lumps, even if they were booked to win. Taking a victory, but keeping the heat on the heel, was one of Rohde's early lessons, and it was very important, solidifying future matches down the line. Altogether, being at the bottom of the totem pole was rough business, but Rohde was in a valuable position to learn from the ground up. He was already building upon his knowledge of wrestling psychology and paying close attention to the reaction of audiences. His ability in the ring was sharpening, as well. Utilizing body slams, a dropkick, and the flying tackle, he displayed a rounded attack. There was some science mixed in, too, including use of the Japanese wristlock, a double leg hold, and the crab hold.

Sportswriters were taking notice of his development, and his ability to survive the onslaught of his crooked foes was noteworthy enough.[75] But there was a higher level of excitement surrounding his meteoric rise. On Oct. 23, 1942, a lengthy article about Rohde was printed in the *Camden Courier-Post*, with the author stating: "Camden finally appears to have the makings of a first-flight wrestler in young Herman 'Dutch' Rohde." Said to be undefeated in 50 matches, Rohde was "believed to be the youngest pro-matman in the country," having turned 21 "recently."[76] In conclusion, his "bright future" was acknowledged, and there was little doubt he had the support of Camden's wrestling faithful.[77] As far as being undefeated, it made for good publicity, but was off the mark. He had suffered his first loss to a wrestler named Tom George on Oct. 2, 1942 at the Philadelphia Arena.[78]

Professional wrestling was changing Rohde's life and he was absorbing the benefits one day at a time. On Oct. 19, 1942, he received his first semi-final berth in Camden, and wrestled Michele Leone to a stimulating half-hour draw.[79] He was still chasing his first main event, but things were going his way. From posing for pictures with the famous orchestra leader Ina Ray Hutton in Wildwood, to having his matches broadcast on WCAM radio by Bill Markward, he was getting a full taste of celebrity.[80] With his sun-bleached blond hair and handsome looks, he was becoming one of the most talked-about young wrestlers in the business, and the sky was the limit.

Things in his personal life changed on Nov. 21, 1942, when he married Kathryn Givnin, the daughter of William and Grace Givnin of Camden County.[81] It was reported that they were wed by Siegfried W. Dietrich, a minister of the Gospel, in Camden, but the latter's name may have been incorrect.[82] The Rohde Family's longtime pastor was Otto Dietrich, and he may have been the one to perform the ceremony. Five days after his wedding, Rohde was called to Trenton for a preliminary match against Joe DeValteau at the Arena.[83] But it was Thanksgiving, and the first holiday for the newlyweds. The wrestling business was proving to be endlessly consuming, and to maintain his positive upward climb, he had to follow through with every booking, regardless of the pay scale or having to forgo a holiday. It was painfully clear that balancing the demands of wrestling with having a family was going to be one of Herman Rohde's biggest challenges.

ENDNOTES - CHAPTER 2

[1] By February 1941, the Newport installation was processing 500 recruits a week. *Paterson Morning Call*, Feb. 7, 1941, p. 21.

[2] Rohde arrived in Newport on Nov. 3, 1939.

[3] Rohde's emergency leave began at 1200 hours on Dec. 5, 1939. U.S. Naval Training Station Leave Certificate, National Personnel Records Center, St. Louis, MO. The trip was approximately 275-miles.

[4] McDermott's office was at 511 State Street in Camden, NJ. He had been the family physician for 10 years. Letter from V.T. McDermott, M.D. to Commander Kirtland, U.S.S. Breckenridge dated Feb. 21, 1940, National Personnel Records Center, St. Louis, MO.

[5] Herman died at 7:30 a.m. Camden Health Department Death Certificate for Herman G. Max Rohde.

[6] His obituary said he was 63. *Camden Courier-Post*, Dec. 7, 1939, p. 4. On his death certificate, Herman's date of birth was listed as "Unknown," and his age was said to be, "about 64." Camden Health Department Death Certificate for Herman G. Max Rohde.

[7] *Camden Morning Post*, Dec. 7, 1939, p. 4.

8 U.S. Naval Training Station, Leave Certificate, National Personnel Records Center, St. Louis, MO.

9 Rohde received a "40" for Conduct while at Newport. Professional Qualifications, Conduct and Marks, National Personnel Records Center, St. Louis, MO. The U.S.S. Breckinridge was classified as DD-148. One article claimed that Rohde was a "second-class fireman" while serving in the Navy. *Camden Courier-Post*, Oct. 23, 1942, p. 36.

10 U.S.S. Breckinridge Leave Form, Feb. 9, 1940 & Authorized Leave Form, National Personnel Records Center, St. Louis, MO.

11 Letter from Otto Dietrich, Pastor of the Nazareth Evangelical Lutheran Church, to Commander F.D. Kirtland, U.S.S. Breckinridge, New York City, NY, dated Feb. 18, 1940, National Personnel Records Center, St. Louis, MO.

12 Letter from Dr. Vincent T. McDermott to Commander F.D. Kirtland, dated Feb. 21, 1940, National Personnel Records Center, St. Louis, MO.

13 Professional Qualifications, Conduct, and Marks, National Personnel Records Center, St. Louis, MO.

14 The address for Stech Transportation was 961 Sylvan Street, Camden, NJ. This was also the home address for the Stech Family for a number of decades.

15 George Jacob Stech died on March 13, 1934. *Camden Morning Post*, March 14, 1934, p. 3. Stech, like Herman Gustav Rohde, worked in the brewing industry, including a lengthy stint at the Camden County Beverage Company. Frank Stech was born around 1914.

16 Letter from Frank Stech to "Sir," dated March 11, 1940. National Personnel Records Center, St. Louis, MO.

17 U.S.S. Breckinridge Request to the Chief of the Bureau of Navigation, dated March 19, 1940, signed by Herman Karl Rohde. National Personnel Records Center, St. Louis, MO.

18 U.S.S. Breckinridge Document to the Chief of the Bureau of Navigation, dated March 19, 1940, signed by F.D. Kirtland. National Personnel Records Center, St. Louis, MO.

19 Letter from U.S. Representative Chas. A. Wolverton to Rear Admiral Chester W. Nimitz, dated March 20, 1940. National Personnel Records Center, St. Louis, MO.

20 Letter from Rear Admiral Chester W. Nimitz to U.S. Representative Chas. A. Wolverton, dated March 28, 1940. It should be noted that Rear Admiral Nimitz initially responded to Rep. Wolverton on March 22, 1940, indicating that Rohde's request for discharge hadn't yet reached the Bureau of Navigation. He indicated that "this case will be considered carefully upon receipt of the enlisted man's official request." Letter from Rear Admiral Nimitz to Rep. Wolverton, dated March 22, 1940. National Personnel Records Center, St. Louis, MO.

21 In his final Navy ratings, Rohde scored a 30 in proficiency and a 40 for conduct. His final average was a 3.75. Professional Qualifications, Conduct and Marks, March 29, 1940, National Personnel Records Center, St. Louis, MO. He served 77 days on the U.S.S. Breckinridge.

22 Rohde got $32.75 for travel allowance. He was recommended for reenlistment. He was discharged on account of "dependency." U.S. Navy Discharge Papers, National Personnel Records Center, St. Louis, MO.

23 The date on the census was listed as April 4, 1940. Their Arlington Street home was valued at $3,000. 1940 United States Federal Census, ancestry.com.

24 *Camden Courier-Post*, Oct. 23, 1942, p. 36, *Boxing and Wrestling*, April 1962.

25 *TV Guide*, Nov. 13, 1953, p. 6.

26 The newspaper mistakenly omitted the "New York Shipbuilding Corporation" name and listed its athletes as being affiliated with the "Public Service" group. *Camden Morning Post*, Sept. 13, 1940, p. 30.

27 *Camden Morning Post*, Sept. 16, 1940, p. 19.

28 *Camden Courier-Post*, Nov. 8, 1940, p. 28.

29 *Camden Courier-Post*, Oct. 4, 1940, p. 26.

30 A "Rohde" appeared in a box score for the Audubon Scholastics in November 1940, as a substitute player in a football game versus the Cramer Hill Wildcats. It isn't known if this was Herman Rohde. *Camden Morning Post*, Nov. 18, 1940, p. 18. In Oct. 1941, a "Herman Lodes" was mentioned as being part of the LaMarr independent football team. The club was managed by Rohde's buddy, Dom Doganiero and included at least two of his former Camden High teammates,

Mike Leo and Ralph Byrd. *Camden Morning Post*, Oct. 10, 1941, p. 34. No other information could be found.

[31] Herman met Zabo at the Camden YMCA. *Muscular Development*, Nov. 1966.

[32] Zabo was captain for the Collingswood football squad in 1942. He played left guard.

[33] He listed Benny Goodman as his "Favorite Orchestra." *Wrestling Chatterbox*, August 1992. Billy Eckstine was named as one of his favorite musicians. *Wrestling and TV Sports*: The Fan Magazine, March 1951.

[34] Denver Wrestling Program, Feb. 13, 1958.

[35] Herman later told Milo Steinborn that he was "a professional" ballroom dancer and Steinborn believed him. *Milo and the Halitosis Kid* by Max Jacobs, p. 230-232.

[36] Milo Steinborn said that he was a "Zoot-suiter." Ibid. Definition of "Zoot suit" from thefreedictionary.com.

[37] *Philadelphia Inquirer*, April 27, 1942, p. 17.

[38] *Camden Courier-Post*, Sept. 13, 1943, p. 5.

[39] *Boxing and Wrestling*, April 1962.

[40] It was claimed in 1942 that he wrestled amateur "for the past seven years." *Camden Courier-Post*, October 23, 1942, p. 36.

[41] *Buffalo Evening News*, Nov. 17, 1956, p. 4.

[42] *NWA Official Wrestling*, April 1952, p. 10-11.

[43] *Chattanooga Times*, Dec. 22, 1946, p. 51.

[44] Bob Oates Letter, *Whatever Happened To...?*, Issue #38, p. 47. Mae Young made appearances at the Camden Convention Hall on February 9 and Feb. 23, 1942, and also on March 9, 1942.

[45] *Harrisburg Evening News*, Oct. 25, 1933, p. 11 and *Wilmington News Journal*, April 26, 1935, p. 26.

[46] Buddy Rogers Interview by Bill Apter, *Apter Chat*, Part One, 1979, youtube.com.

[47] It was about a 15-minute drive from Rohde's home on Arlington Street. The show was a special benefit to purchase athletic equipment for the children of the church. *Camden Courier-Post*, May 27, 1942, p. 23.

[48] *Camden Courier-Post*, Oct. 23, 1942, p. 36.

[49] The finish of the exhibition is unknown. It might have been a draw. *Camden Courier-Post*, June 3, 1942, p. 16.

[50] Like Rohde, Grobmier was also the son of German parentage. Rogers incorrectly called Grobmier his high school wrestling coach. *Chicago Sun-Times*, June 12, 1950, p. 53.

[51] *Evansville Press*, Jan. 29, 1946, p. 10.

[52] *Camden Courier-Post*, October 23, 1942, p. 36. Herman was later quoted as saying, "Fred made a finished product out of me real fast." *Boxing and Wrestling*, April 1962, p. 53. June 2, 1942 to July 18, 1942 was six weeks and four days. In another article, he claimed he was trained for "six months." *Evansville Press*, Jan. 29, 1946, p. 10.

[53] A 1969 newspaper article claimed that Grip met Rohde when he was young and that, "for a brief time," Grip managed him. *Philadelphia Daily News*, June 10, 1969, p. 47.

[54] *Camden Courier-Post*, Nov. 22, 1984, p. 8D.

[55] Buddy Rogers Interview by Dr. Mike Lano and Gary "Gerhardt" Kaiser, *Canvas Cavity*, Circa. 1991-1992, Buddy Rogers Interview by John Arezzi, *Pro Wrestling Spotlight*, Aug. 4, 1991.

[56] Sources include *Gong Magazine*, June 1979, Buddy Rogers Interview by Dr. Mike Lano and Gary "Gerhardt" Kaiser, *Canvas Cavity*, Circa. 1991-1992, Buddy Rogers Interview by Tom Burke and Dan Reilly, *Wrestle Radio*, Nov. 9, 1991, Buddy Rogers Interview, *New Wave Wrestling* magazine, April 1992, *Lancaster Sunday News*, March 2, 1952, p. 28. Several other interviews and sources claimed that he made his debut on July 4, 1940. *Wrestling Revue*, Sept. 1983, Buddy Rogers Interview, *Jim Barniak's Sports Scrapbook*, Dec. 2, 1981, PRISM Network, youtube.com, Buddy Rogers Interview, *Rod Luck Radio Show*, 1983. A 1963 article quoted Rogers as saying that he made his debut on May 5, 1940. *Camden Courier-Post*, July 30, 1963, p. 21.

[57] *Wrestling World*, November 1962.

[58] *Gong Magazine*, June 1979, Buddy Rogers Interview by Bill Apter, *Apter Chat*, Part One, 1979, youtube.com,
Brazin's last name was also commonly spelled, "Brazen." The Brazin Family was involved in the fur industry.

[59] Buddy Rogers Interview by Bill Apter, *Apter Chat*, Part One, 1979, youtube.com.

[60] *Wildwood Leader*, July 2, 1942.

[61] *Camden Evening Courier*, July 4, 1942, p. 16.

[62] A "Joe Martin" appeared in Newark in December 1943 and was said to be a "Madison war worker." It is not known if he is the same man. *Newark Star Ledger*, Dec. 9, 1943.

[63] The show was promoted by Andy Applegate with Matty Engle as the matchmaker. Rudy Dusek was the booking agent.

[64] The local newspaper billed him as "Dutch Rohe, a newcomer from Camden." *Atlantic City Press-Union*, July 18, 1942. Another report called him "a rugged grappler from Camden." *Atlantic City Press-Union*, July 16, 1942.

[65] It was later claimed that when Buddy made his pro debut, he weighed 187 pounds and had a 34 inch waist. *Ottawa Journal*, Feb. 15, 1957.

[66] *Atlantic City Press-Union*, July 19, 1942, p. 7.

[67] He said he had a lot of $8 paydays. *Charlotte Observer*, Aug. 18, 1979, p. 7A.

[68] Rohde left his job at the New York Shipbuilding Corporation sometime after October 1942. He reportedly received his apprenticeship papers, but put the documents away and forgot all about them. Unknown article, Circa. 1950.

[69] Their match took place on July 27, 1942. Rohde would wrestle Vansky five times in his first three months in the business. He'd win four of those bouts and draw the other. Vansky was originally from Kearny, NJ. He'd later be known as "The Neck" because of his extraordinarily large neck measurements.

[70] *Baltimore Sun*, July 29, 1942, p. 15.

[71] Steinborn was quoted as saying: "When I first saw Buddie (sic) Rogers, which is what Rhode (sic) eventually changed his name to, I recognized there was something really unique about him." *Milo and the Halitosis Kid* by Max W. Jacobs, 230-232.

[72] *Jersey Journal*, Jan. 12, 1945, p. 13.

[73] *Camden Courier-Post*, Sept. 22, 1942, p. 16.

[74] Ibid.

[75] A Camden article stated that Rohde was "advancing by leaps and bounds." *Camden Morning Post*, Oct. 15, 1942, p. 39.

[76] Rohde turned 21 eight months before in February 1942.

[77] *Camden Courier-Post*, Oct. 23, 1942, p. 36.

[78] He was billed as "Herman Rhodes." George pinned him in 20:02. *Philadelphia Inquirer*, October 3, 1942, p. 26. He later claimed that he won 66 matches in a row to start his career. *Camden Courier-Post*, July 30, 1963, p. 21.

[79] *Camden Courier-Post*, Oct. 20, 1942, p. 14.

[80] *Camden Courier-Post*, Oct. 23, 1942, p. 36, *Camden Courier-Post*, Sept. 28, 1942, p. 6.

[81] *Rohde v. Rohde*, Superior Court of New Jersey, Case Number 152-491-E/26-653.

[82] Ibid.

[83] Rohde pinned his opponent with a body slam in 18:33. *Trenton Evening Times*, Nov. 27, 1942, p. 26.

Herman (Dutch) Rohde (1942)

Chapter 3
The Rohde Brothers

During the late 1930s, the popularity of professional wrestling diminished in many parts of North America. Bad decisions by industry leaders, a lack of superstar attractions, and a general apathy were all contributing factors, and promoters were desperately looking for new ways to intrigue fans back to arenas. In 1937, "team wrestling" was introduced as the sport's newest innovation, and crowds responded enthusiastically.[1] The rules were simple. There were two wrestlers per team and all four competitors would face off in the ring at the same time in, typically, two-of-three-fall matches. A fall was achieved when both wrestlers on a particular side were defeated and, thus, "eliminated." The same rules applied to the second and third falls, as well.[2] As "team wrestling" gained esteem and debuted in various parts of the United States, the rules also evolved. It was no longer necessary to beat both opponents to win a singular fall, and the elimination aspect was removed.[3]

Team matches were a free-for-all, meaning that anything that could happen usually did. When not throwing their foes from the ring or piling on top of each other to score a three-count, wrestlers would break the rules with impunity, and frequently tricked the referee to achieve an upper hand. "Dutch" Rohde participated in a handful of team bouts during his first couple months in the business. On Nov. 2, 1942, in Camden, he partnered with the 5-foot-3 Abe Coleman, a Jewish grappler from Poland. Having started in 1927, Coleman was a veteran pro who possessed a sound repertoire of moves in the ring, punctuated by a powerful dropkick. That night, they beat Jim Austeri and Angelo Savoldi in two straight falls at the Convention Hall, and demonstrated good teamwork in doing so.[4] The combination of Rohde and Coleman was popular with fans and they received a nice push by booker Rudy Dusek.

Between November 1942 and May 1943, they won every one of the 13 matches they wrestled together. Action was always fast and furious, and each contest was markedly different as the performers added new elements to the fray. In Camden on Nov. 30, 1942, in a rematch against Austeri and Savoldi, the latter pair won the opening fall after Austeri landed groin shots to both Rohde and Coleman. The heroes focused their attack on Austeri in the second, looking for retribution, and achieved a fall to tie the match. In the third, Austeri went out of his way to entangle Rohde's neck in the ring ropes, and then proceeded to pummel him unmercifully. The referee had no other choice other than to disqualify the heels for their behavior.[5] A few weeks later, Rohde and Coleman won from Savoldi and Milo Steinborn in Camden. This time, Savoldi decided to stand idly by while Steinborn was double-teamed in the third fall and pinned. The great Milo then turned on his partner, with Rohde and Coleman comically lending an assist.[6]

As a singles wrestler, Rohde won a good percentage of his matches. He was elevated to his first main event as part of a double-windup at the Camden Convention Hall on Dec. 28, 1942. Saddled with a difficult assignment against the seasoned Gino Garibaldi, a former coal miner from St. Louis, Herman tried to make it a competitive match, but was mostly on the defensive.[7] Garibaldi "roughed and fouled" him on his way to victory in 25:12.[8] Night after night, "Dutch" was in the ring against larger, stronger, and more experienced wrestlers. The Dusek proving-grounds were relentless, probably one of the harshest in the country for a young grappler. Stiff shots, brutal strikes, and drawing blood the hard way was all part of a night's work, and a man had to be physically tough to endure. On April 5, 1943, in Camden, Rudy Dusek, the senior member of the "Riot Squad," smashed Rohde in the nose, causing him to bleed, and "used every foul he knew" before forcing "Dutch" to surrender to a chokehold.[9]

Dusek put Rohde over the following week at the same venue, giving Herman the biggest win of his short career.[10] It was a major vote of confidence from the head of the promotional syndicate, indicative of Dusek's growing confidence in the Camden athlete. The following month, Rohde captured victories over Emil Dusek and Joe Cox, two formidable opponents, and logged a win over Ernie Dusek during the summer. Things were improving, and instead of taking the brunt of the punishment in every bout, he was doling out a fair amount, and sometimes dominating matches with his own style of aggressiveness. For the most part, he was still playing by the rules, but in the midst of a heated battle, fans understood when he needed to fight fire with fire, and supported his efforts even if he punched and kicked in retaliation.

Backtracking a little bit, Feb. 2, 1943, was a personal milestone moment for Rohde. That was the day he debuted in New York City at the St. Nicholas Arena, wrestling to a draw against Rudy Dusek. Dusek had a pretty good stranglehold in New York City, running promotions at St. Nick's Arena on Tuesday nights, plus two key Brooklyn clubs: Ridgewood Grove on Thursdays and the Broadway Arena on Saturday. But the wrestling landscape descended into turmoil in 1943, and a war between syndicates stripped Dusek of two of his primary cities. In March of that year, Rudy lost his control of Washington, D.C. and Baltimore after a smooth-talking rival operator named Joseph (Toots) Mondt stepped in and worked new deals with local promoters.[11] The move was thievery at its best, but in the cold, harsh realm of pro wrestling, it was commonplace.

Toots Mondt was a real character – a man of impressive stature, figuratively and literally. Weighing north of 250 pounds, he was a sizable guy, and had been involved in wrestling to some degree since he was 16 years old.[12] Now 49, he was a legend, respected for his time as a grappler and for his work as a promoter and booking agent. But a recent stint in Southern California didn't end on a positive note, and Toots amassed heavy debt. His reputation as a matchmaker also took a big hit, and there were questions whether he'd ever regain a position of power in wrestling. His resiliency was incredible, and, in 1942, he reestablished himself in New York as a partner of Al Mayer, a former theatrical manager.[13] The Mondt-Mayer outfit locked down a solid crew of wrestling talent and expanded its territory, much to the dismay of Rudy Dusek.

The power play and the politics of the business were new to "Dutch" Rohde. Washington, D.C. and Baltimore were two of his regular stops, but after Toots made his move, they were off limits.[14] During the summer months, as beachgoers returned to the South Jersey Shore in droves, Dusek reopened his Wildwood operation at Hunt's Sports Arena.[15] Rohde was back in familiar surroundings and fans showered him with admiration. While visiting friends and working out in the beach town, he struck up a friendship with a 17-year-old swimming prodigy named Billy Darnell.[16] Rohde and Darnell had a lot in common, starting with the fact that they were both from Camden. Darnell grew up in the northern part of the city, on Grant Street, and was a current student at Camden High.[17] He was going into his senior year when he befriended the wrestler and the two started training together. When he wasn't at the gym, Darnell was a full-time member of Wildwood's Beach Patrol.[18]

Rohde began training Darnell to wrestle professionally.[19] On Saturday, July 3, 1943, the two teamed up in what was Darnell's pro debut at Hunt's Sports Arena. The *Wildwood Leader* noted that their team was comprised of "a former Wildwood lifeguard and a present member of the beach patrol." Their opponents were Tom George and Joe Parelli, but no specifics of the bout, or the result, are known.[20] Darnell resumed his schooling during the fall, but remained an active wrestler. It should be noted that, for financial reasons, a number of athletes jumped from the Dusek circuit to the Toots Mondt group in 1943. Mondt's territorial share was steadily blossoming, and included weekly shows in New York, Newark, Philadelphia, and Wilmington, as well as the aforementioned Baltimore and Washington, D.C. Grapplers in the Northeast could make much more money performing in those cities for Mondt than what Dusek had to offer. Among those to part in the exodus were Michele Leone, Cliff Olsen, Maurice LaChappelle, and Ed (Strangler) White. Billy Darnell also soon went to work for Mondt.[21]

Loyalty was important to young Rohde, and he recognized the consequential role Dusek had played in his budding career. Unquestionably, an amplification of his salary was a great incentive to look elsewhere for work, but for the time being, "Dutch" was content. He reportedly made $8,000 in his first year in wrestling, which was considerably more than what his income would have been in the Navy, working for his cousin, or at the shipyards.[22] He could support his mother quite well, and from his perspective, there was plenty of room to grow. In September 1943, he was given a stronger singles push and headlined his first program in Philadelphia against the Yellow Mask (Barto Hill).[23] The *Camden Morning Post* cited his "brilliant record last season" for his main-event status, and claimed his rise to the top was "probably the most rapid in the history of the grappling game."[24] Rohde battled the Yellow Mask on even terms in Philadelphia, but in the third fall, he lost his cool and was disqualified.[25]

A few months later, in December 1943, Rohde's mentor Milo Steinborn went down the coast and worked the Mid-Atlantic states. The territory was independent from its northern neighbor and run by dynamic promoters Jim Crockett in Charlotte, Henry Marcus in Columbia, and Bill Lewis in Virginia. Steinborn was acutely established in the region, having wrestled throughout the area for a number of years. His reappearance created a nice buzz and carried forward as 1944 approached. Behind-the-scenes, the strongman got into the ears of local promoters and touted Rohde to the high heavens. Word of mouth worked wonders in wrestling, and it didn't take long for Mid-Atlantic impresarios to be sold on the idea of a skilled newcomer with box-office appeal. They wanted him on their cards immediately. This was a chance for "Dutch" to step away from the realm of the Duseks and see what the business looked like under different management. Steinborn made the offer to Rohde and the latter agreed.

Rohde wouldn't be turning up in the Carolinas and Virginia under his real identity. He took the assumed name, "Wally Ward," upon his arrival in Charlotte on Jan. 3, 1944. Such a dramatic alteration was usually spawned by some kind of external factor, and the war might have played a part. It is possible that local promoters didn't want to exhibit a blond-haired German-sounding "Herman 'Dutch' Rohde" on their cards. They might have yearned for the Americanized "Wally Ward," a fresh-faced, sportsmanlike athlete to counter their flock of dastardly heels.[26] A more unlikely possibility was Rohde's efforts to conceal his name from booker Rudy Dusek, especially if he left the northeast without Dusek's blessing. Regardless of the reason for his newfound alias, Rohde, as "Wally Ward," debuted with tremendous publicity and started a successful journey through the Mid-Atlantic region.

Displaying his ring confidence and sharp maneuvers, Rohde was as popular as Steinborn promised he'd be. Audiences quickly embraced him, and he captured exciting wins from Eddie King, George Harben, and Herb Freeman. In the press, stories were vivid, sometimes exaggerated, and writers were awfully confused about "Ward's" background. A Wilmington newspaper called him a "top-flight operator" from St. Louis.[27] The *Columbia Record* went in a different direction, reporting that he was a "University of Southern California glamour boy."[28] In Charlotte, they acknowledged him as a "big, blond 220-pounder out of Philadelphia," which was, to their credit, slightly closer to the truth.[29] And since Steinborn was proudly promoting his protégé, telling everyone who'd listen that "Wally Ward" was "his boy," people started to legitimately think that they were related. A *Charlotte Observer* report actually billed them as "Steinborn and Son," and gave credence to the rumor that Ward was Milo's offspring.[30]

After nearly four weeks on the Mid-Atlantic circuit, Rohde received notice from his military draft board, and was called back home to Camden.[31] He finished up several dates as he worked his way up the coast, and re-emerged in Philadelphia for a team match with Fred Grobmier against Jim Austeri and Herb Freeman on Feb. 4, 1944. Using his real name again, Rohde and his partner were victorious.[32] Just before "Dutch" departed the south, an unusual thing happened to one of his contemporaries. Jim Clinstock, a wrestler Rohde defeated on January 25 in Columbia, died four days later under strange circumstances. The towering, 240-pound Oklahoman was in Charlotte on the evening of January 29, scheduled to have some dental work done. Liquor was consumed and a fight broke out. Clinstock was rendered unconscious and pronounced dead upon arrival at the hospital. Police suspected he was strangled, but there was insufficient evidence, and two suspects were later freed.[33]

On Feb. 11, 1944, Rohde was scheduled to wrestle the 53-year-old legend, Ed (Strangler) Lewis, at the Philadelphia Arena. Lewis was a multiple-time former world heavyweight champion and his matches with Joe Stecher, Gus Sonnenberg, and Jim Londos helped popularize professional wrestling in the modern era. Getting a bout with illustrious "Strangler" was an honor, and a distinction Rohde would remember for the rest of his days. He did just that, too. In 1983, during an interview with *Wrestling Revue* magazine, he talked in detail about his bout with Lewis, stating that the contest lasted around "47 minutes," and that he received $1,500, the "biggest payday" of his career.[34] To put that into perspective, $1,500 in 1944 equates to more than $22,000 in 2020 money, and it was by far the most he'd earned for a single bout.[35] There was only one problem with this story. It's very likely that none of it ever happened.

As far as current records indicate, Rohde never wrestled Lewis; not in Philadelphia, not anywhere.[36] They were advertised to battle on Feb. 11, 1944, but for whatever reason, Rohde wrestled and beat Turkish grappler Ali Adali instead.[37] The probability of "Dutch" making $1,500 for a mid-card bout with the virtually blind Ed Lewis in 1944 was next to zero.[38] If Rohde and Lewis did meet in the ring, and if their match was overlooked by publications at the time, there's but a small chance Rohde would have made more than $100 for such a bout. In late February 1944, Milo Steinborn returned to the Dusek group, and ironically, was only a few months removed from a special tour of Army-Navy bases, entertaining the troops with the man himself, Ed (Strangler) Lewis.[39] Steinborn reconnected with Rohde and influenced the Camden wrestler to make another important decision.

Considering the state of the business in the northeast, Steinborn felt it was time for a change, and between March 17 and March 22, 1944, both Milo and "Dutch" left the Dusek syndicate and joined the Toots Mondt outfit.[40] The defection couldn't have come at a better time. In his debut showing for the Mondt troupe, on March 23, cameras were set up at the Trenton Arena to film the matches for distribution in theaters.[41] It was invaluable exposure for Rohde and a five-minute segment of his match against Tom Mahoney was filmed for the production, *Mat Maulers*.[42] With legendary sportscaster Bill Stern providing narration, Rohde demonstrated wily skill, using forearm smashes, uppercuts, and, ultimately, two dropkicks, to score a pinfall.[43] By an incredible stroke of good fortune, film historian Joe Opiela discovered a nondescript wrestling film reel on eBay in 2005, and it just happened to be the final product of the 1944 Trenton production.[44] He made the material available on YouTube, and to this day, it marks the earliest available footage of Herman "Dutch" Rohde.[45]

On March 28, Rohde made his first appearance in Baltimore since December 1942, and wrestled Michele Leone to a draw. Things in Baltimore were run a little differently and he was billed as "Herman Rhodes," while Leone was known as "Michael Leone."[46] On the whole, the Mondt promotional system was dissimilar from that of Rudy Dusek, and Rohde had to make adjustments. There was a new hierarchy of performers, including a claimant to the world heavyweight title, exclusive to the region. The reigning champion was the 6-foot-4 Babe Sharkey, a former football star at Temple University.[47] Sharkey only had about four years in the profession, but his athleticism was a great equalizer for his relative inexperience. For Rohde, matches with the champion would have signified his placement amongst the top heavyweights in the business, and that was undeniably his goal.

Mondt smartly continued Rohde's push in Philadelphia, where he was already an established figure in grappling circles, and booked him in a number of main event bouts. Conversely, in Baltimore, Rohde was back wrestling preliminary and mid-card matches because, in that city, he was pretty much starting from scratch. Beginning on April 5, "Dutch" started a lengthy feud with Don Evans, a renowned tough guy from New York, and the rivals fought all over the territory. Evans was a major player in the Northeast, and his work as a heel was noteworthy. He gave the world champion Babe Sharkey a run for his money on April 26 in Washington, D.C., earning a 60-minute draw.[48] Since Evans was a top challenger, Rohde needed to beat him in order to get a shot at the title, and the build-up was slow, but valuable. Finally, before a rowdy crowd at Turner's Arena in Washington on July 5, the blond warrior from New Jersey took home a victory and was declared the "leading contender" to Sharkey's crown.[49]

Wrestling Sharkey for the championship at Turner's Arena on July 19, was said to be "the big break of [Rohde's] up-and-coming" career.[50] It was an action-filled bout, and many times throughout the encounter, he wiggled out of tight spots "and reversed the situation" on the titleholder.[51] Rohde "employed speed and strategy" against his heavier foe, and ended up with a draw in 60-minutes.[52] With the fans in his corner and a rematch with the champion being planned for the future, things couldn't have been better. But away from the ring, Rohde was dealing with some significant changes. His marriage to Kathryn Givnin was essentially over before it began, and the two were living apart. His military status was unchanged, but in press reports, the reasoning for his ineligibility for war-time duty was only slightly better defined. A Charlotte newspaper claimed that Rohde was a 4-F classification due to a "punctured ear drum or something."[53] How much of that was true is unknown.

In an effort to further strengthen his ties to the community and remain close to home, Rohde had applied for a civil service job in Camden in 1943. Upon submitting paperwork to become either a police officer or a firefighter, he was declared eligible on Aug. 18 of that year, pending an examination. If he passed, he would be approved to a civil service position within the next three years.[54] Needless to say, Rohde did pass, and when an opening came up for employment on the Camden Police Force, he got the call. On May 11, Camden City Clerk Clay Reesman swore Rohde and four others in, and Public Safety Director Dr. David S. Rhone introduced the quintet as the city's newest police officers. "I am pleased that we have been able to get such a fine group of young men for the department," Rhone declared.[55]

Regarding Rohde's health, it was noted that "some" of the newly assigned officers were 4-F for the military draft, but "had been passed for duty in the police department by doctors for the civil service," according to the *Camden Courier-Post*.[56] The newspaper didn't take it a step further and identify those who were ineligible for Selective Service, but it didn't matter because "Dutch" was performing a crucial wartime function in a time of great need.[57] He would receive a salary of $1,650 a year, and start out wearing plain clothes before receiving an official uniform at a later date.[58] He would be allowed to supplement his income by continuing to wrestle, but it was mandatory that he would curtail his schedule to fit his police obligations.[59] And with that, he cut out the New York end of the circuit almost immediately. In fact, he whittled down his wrestling commitments to just three dates a week: Mondays in Wilmington, Tuesdays in Baltimore, and Wednesdays in Washington.

Additional bookings were made here and there, but generally, that remained his schedule through September 1944. The Camden wrestling season opened on September 18, and Rudy Dusek still held court at the Convention Hall. He was to participate in a team match with Charley Allen against Jim Austeri and Herb Freeman that was sure to incite the crowd. At the last minute, hometown hero "Dutch" Rohde replaced Allen and teamed with Dusek in a three-fall victory.[60] No explanation was offered, but one can surmise that Allen was a no-show, and perhaps Rohde was on hand as a visitor and asked to fill in. In any case, Rohde's showing seemed to lighten whatever animosity there may have been between him and Dusek, and he agreed to wrestle for Rudy's group in Camden and at the Philadelphia Arena during the winter.[61] Rohde's police schedule appeared to have changed, as well, freeing him up for added engagements in New Jersey and New York.

Peculiarly, a report circulated in Pennsylvania newspapers on Oct. 20, 1944, informing readers that "Herman Rhode" (sic) had been "reinstated" by the Pennsylvania State Athletic Commission.[62] A reinstatement by the commission meant he must have been suspended for some reason. The clean-cut babyface, and genuine police officer, was unlikely to have run that far afoul of pro wrestling's rules, but what exactly happened is anybody's guess. A few weeks later, in Philadelphia, Rohde was matched with Tony Martinelli of Clifton, New Jersey, and their bout received national attention. It wasn't because of anything the grapplers themselves did, but for who the special guest referee was. That official was none other than Joe Louis, boxing's current heavyweight champion of the world. Louis was on furlough from the United States Army and agreed to referee the Rohde-Martinelli contest at the Philadelphia Arena for 35 per cent of the gate. After he declared the match a draw, Louis confidently told a journalist: "Ain't much to refereeing wrestling." For his work, the boxing great earned $1,758.75.[63]

Not surprisingly, Rohde's marriage was unsalvageable. A petition for divorce was filed by Kathryn Rohde in the Superior Court of New Jersey on Nov. 2, 1944, and Herman didn't protest it in the least. He submitted an affidavit to the court as required, and when the final hearing occurred, neither he, nor a legal representative, attended on his behalf. Chancellor Luther A. Campbell signed off on the petition, declaring the marriage null and void.[64] Age and immaturity were likely factors in the demise of their marriage.[65] Back home on Arlington Street, life hadn't changed all that much. Working-class families were doing what was necessary to survive, and were caught up in the monotonous daily grind. A few houses down from the Rohde residence, at 2018 Arlington Street, things took a scary turn on the evening of Jan. 9, 1945. A 25-year-old mother of three was murdered in her home by a former boarder. The man who committed the heinous crime then shot himself and later died.[66]

Ever-protective of his mother, "Dutch" Rohde was in Baltimore that night, but always took comfort in the fact that family and close friends were nearby to keep an eye on her when he was on the road. His older brother John still lived at home, as well, but was often away for duty in the United States Maritime Service.[67] John was an athlete during his younger years, mostly at the Camden YMCA, and may have boxed as an amateur in formal competition.[68] Seeing what his brother was accomplishing as a pro wrestler, he considered moonlighting as a grappler on a semi-serious basis. He started training with "Dutch," Joe Cox and Billy Darnell at the Camden "Y," and made significant headway in a short amount of time.[69] Interestingly, in some cities, Darnell had already been acknowledged as Herman's "brother," and the two wrestlers played up the gimmick.[70] It was claimed that Darnell took that last name to avoid any confusion with his famous sibling.[71]

Having a close friend on the circuit with him was appealing to Rohde. He liked the camaraderie, and being able to travel from town-to-town with someone he trusted. But his touring with Darnell was coming to an end. On Dec. 21, 1944, Darnell hung up his wrestling boots and enlisted in the United States Army.[72] Approximately three weeks later, on Jan. 12, John Rohde made his debut as a wrestler at the Garden in Jersey City. The brothers made the journey together and it was decided en route that John would use the name "Buddy Rogers."[73] The *Jersey Journal*, however, called him "Buddy Roger," and reported his victory over Zimba Parker in a preliminary bout.[74] About the same height as "Dutch," John was 15 to 20 pounds lighter, and was fairly strong from his work as a mechanic. He knew the basics of pro wrestling, but needed time to gain experience if he wanted to make it a regular vocation.

Five days later, the *Washington* [DC] *Evening Star* printed an article officially recognizing "Buddy Rogers" as the third Rohde brother.[75] The wrestling career of John Rohde appears to have lasted from Jan. 12, 1945, to April 26, 1945, and he wrestled at least 16 matches.[76] Of those 16, he shared the bill with his brother "Dutch" nine times. In terms of his win-loss record, he won five matches, defeating the likes of Gus Rapp, Joe Ludlum, and John Vansky. Rohde suffered six losses, going down in defeat to George Macricostas, Al Galento, Angelo Savoldi and others. Three of his matches were draws and two results are unknown. Some years later, "Dutch" spoke about John, and said: "My brother used to be a wrestler. He had tough luck – broke his leg in nine places."[77] John was supposedly injured in a match against the famous Joe Savoldi.[78] When asked about it during a 2003 interview, he denied ever wrestling the former Notre Dame Football star.[79]

John admitted that it was his brother who came up with the "Buddy Rogers" name for him to use.[80] In the eyes of the public, the Rohde Brothers consisted of an actual, "Rohde," a "Darnell," and a "Rogers." But where did the name "Buddy Rogers" come from? There are different versions of the story, but a 1952 magazine article told it this way: "As a boy, [Herman Rohde] had been a great admirer of the orchestra leader Buddy Rogers, now a regular television performer and the husband of Mary Pickford."[81] And, thus, he plucked that name out of the air and gave it to John. Buddy Rogers, the musician, had also performed in 37 films by the mid-1940s, and was a regular on the radio. Given Herman's love for music, this wasn't a farfetched theory.

As an in-ring performer, Herman's abilities were diversifying and his matches were becoming more layered. Usually the underdog, he would garner immense support and carry the crowd toward a hot finish, only to miss a flying tackle or land awkwardly on the ropes, causing his defeat. His attitude was visible and changed as the story unfolded. At times, he'd bicker with the referee, and occasionally let the official have it, as he did in Washington, D.C. in May 1944. He had been fully engaged in a contest with his rival Don Evans when referee Babe Craddock interjected himself into the fracas. Upset by Craddock's actions, Rohde punched him, setting up a special "grudge" match for the next week, which "Dutch" won in seven minutes.[82] His reactions, facial movements, and timing were improving exponentially, and regardless of the feud or the angle, he put forth one hundred per cent and maximized the return.

Facing Laverne Baxter in Baltimore in January 1945, his babyface persona was put to the test. In their 36-minute war, "very few of the known illegal tactics were missed" by the two combatants, according to the *Baltimore Sun*. They "fought, grappled, and scratched" throughout, and Baxter's arm was raised in victory after Rohde suffered a shoulder injury. Baxter targeted his weakened limb and forced Rohde to give up.[83] Rohde kept his popularity despite the rough stuff, and at times, he was as violent, if not more so, than his opponents. He continued to chase Babe Sharkey and the latter's heavyweight championship going into 1945, and they had a series of big matches in Washington, D.C. After a 60-minute draw on January 17, and then a Sharkey victory on February 7, the *Washington Evening Star* was still impressed by Rohde's cunning, and called him the "heir apparent" to the throne.[84]

Fans were behind Rohde all the way. They were loud in their support following a win and similarly vocal in their objections to a sour finish. His Washington faithful actually tried to jump into the ring and help him against Don Evans on March 21, 1945.[85] Up against Joe Savoldi in Asbury Park on March 26, he demonstrated his wherewithal in defending himself against the dropkick by falling flat to the mat in a flash whenever Savoldi went for his patented move. Lending to the entertainment value of the bout, Savoldi did the same exact thing when Rohde went for the maneuver. The "bout turned into a roughhouse affair," and punches were flying in all directions. Following a collision in the middle of the ring, Savoldi regained his senses enough to pin "Dutch" and take the win.[86] In another "riotous" battle that went 30-minutes to a draw, Rohde went toe-to-toe with Michele Leone in Camden, and both men were "fouling at will." The *Camden Courier-Post* noted that "Rohde finished strong, dishing out as much punishment as he absorbed."[87]

In March 1945, Rohde was examined by the U.S. Army for induction into the service, and this time around, he passed. He was given three weeks to report to Fort Dix, New Jersey, and it seemed that his wrestling career was going to be interrupted by the war, but he was granted an extension in early April, and fulfilled a handful of dates in familiar haunts.[88] He wrestled Emil Dusek in Camden on April 16, losing after missing a flying tackle and sailing through the ropes into the front row. The referee counted him out and "Dutch" was taken to the locker room area on a stretcher.[89] The next day, it was reported that Rohde was a patient at West Jersey Hospital with a serious injury, stemming from the Dusek bout. He suffered torn muscles in his back and it wasn't known at the time if his classification with the military was going to change as a result.[90]

But it *was* going to change. Everything was altered in the weeks that followed. Rohde avoided being called into the Army for duty, and a combination of his physical condition and his mother's dependency might have been influential factors. As for his wrestling career, he was making progress, but he wasn't experiencing the kind of elevation some of his peers had gotten, even after paying his dues. Rohde was wising up to the game, and he didn't want to continue with the status quo. He wanted to advance to the next level and that didn't mean doing jobs to Dusek's boys for the remainder of time. He was being used in that regard, but he needed to play his own hand to ensure he was getting what he deserved. Breaking away from the Northeast was the logical answer. And that's what he did. "Dutch" Rohde was headed for Texas, and was right on the cusp of becoming the star he was destined to be.

ENDNOTES - CHAPTER 3

[1] Portland promoter Herb Owen was the reported inventor of "team wrestling." *Eugene Guard*, Feb. 21, 1937, p. 10.

[2] Ibid. Also see *Seminole Producer*, Feb. 23, 1941, p. 2.

[3] It was one pin or submission per fall. *Allentown Morning Call*, March 10, 1942, p. 19.

[4] *Camden Morning Post*, Nov. 3, 1942, p. 14.

[5] *Camden Morning Post*, Dec. 1, 1942, p. 19.

[6] *Camden Morning Post*, Dec. 15, 1942, p. 18.

[7] Garibaldi worked as a coal miner in DuQuoin, Illinois, in the southern part of the state.

[8] The other half of the double-windup was "Irish" Jack Kelly vs. Michele Leone. *Camden Courier-Post*, Dec. 29, 1942, p. 20.

[9] *Camden Morning Post*, April 6, 1943, p. 16.

[10] Rohde's win was considered an upset. *Camden Courier-Post*, April 13, 1943, p. 22.

[11] The promoters were Joe Turner of Washington, D.C., and Ed Contos of Baltimore. Toots Mondt seized D.C. beginning on March 25, 1943 and Baltimore a few weeks before, on March 9, 1943. As part of his eastern expansion, Mondt also started in Newark, NJ in February 1943.

[12] Toots Mondt began wrestling in 1910.

[13] Mayer was part of the management for the famous performer, Sarah Bernhardt. *New York Times*, April 1, 1923. He was also involved in managing boxer Luis Angel Firpo.

[14] Rohde didn't appear in Baltimore again until Jan. 24, 1944. His next showing in Washington didn't happen until April 26, 1944.

[15] The promoter in Wildwood was normally Turc Duncan. After he went off to serve in the military during World War II, his wife ran the promotion. She was acknowledged as, "Mrs. Duncan" by the local newspaper. *Wildwood Leader*, July 1, 1943. Hunt's Sports Arena was located at Oak Avenue and the Boardwalk.

[16] Darnell was born on Feb. 25, 1926.

[17] 1930 and 1940 United States Federal Census, ancestry.com. Darnell also played football at Camden High under Coach Bill Palese.

[18] *Wildwood Leader*, July 8, 1943. It was later said that Darnell "rescued as many as thirty persons a day," while a Wildwood lifeguard. *Wrestling As You Like It*, Oct. 7, 1950, p. 15.

[19] Darnell started wrestling as an amateur when he was 12 years old. *Sports Pictorial Review*, April 24, 1950, p. 2.

[20] Rohde was billed as "Herman Rhodes." Ibid.

21 Darnell appeared in Philadelphia, North Bergen, and Newark for the Mondt group. One report stated that he was 23-years-old. *Paterson Morning Call*, Oct. 15, 1943, p. 23.

22 *TV Guide*, Nov. 13, 1953, p. 6. Another report claimed he made only $10,000 in his first two years as a pro wrestler. *Haft Nelson*, Vol. 1, No. 62, Feb. 26, 1953.

23 The match occurred on Sept. 24, 1943 and was promoted by Eddie Gottlieb.

24 *Camden Morning Post*, Sept. 16, 1943, p. 19.

25 *Philadelphia Inquirer*, Sept. 25, 1943, p. 16.

26 There was a stage comedian named "Wally Ward" touring the United States during the 1940s. Ward appeared in Camden at the Towers in November 1942. *Camden Courier-Post*, Nov. 20, 1942, p. 15. He also appeared in Richmond, Virginia in late December 1943, just days before Rohde debut in the region. *Richmond Times-Dispatch*, Dec. 29, 1943, p. 11. There is a possibility that Rohde, or someone close to him, saw Ward perform and recommended the name for him to use.

27 *Wilmington Morning Star*, Jan. 3, 1944, p. 4.

28 *Columbia Record*, Jan. 25, 1944, p. 9.

29 *Charlotte Observer*, Jan. 3, 1944, p. 11.

30 *Charlotte Observer*, Jan. 27, 1944, p. 7. "Ward" denied being related to Steinborn. The local newspaper stated that his build was a "carbon copy" of Steinborn's. *Charlotte Observer*, Jan. 28, 1944, p. 20.

31 A Columbia, South Carolina newspaper stated that Rohde's draft board was in Philadelphia. *Columbia Record*, Feb. 1, 1944, p. 9.

32 *Philadelphia Inquirer*, Feb. 5, 1944, p. 14.

33 *Charlotte Observer*, January 31, February 2, February 3, March 1, 1944.

34 He claimed his loss to Lewis was the first defeat of his career, and said the match happened in 1942. *Wrestling Revue*, September 1983, p. 41. He also talked about wrestling Lewis in *Gong Magazine*. He said: "I think I am one of the few living wrestlers who fought with Ed 'Strangler' Lewis or Jim Londos." *Gong Magazine*, June 1979.

35 CPI Inflation Calculator, data.bls.gov.

36 Wrestling historian J Michael Kenyon mentioned the "supposed match" Rohde had with Lewis in his "Buddy Rogers Tribute" paper. He wrote: "No newspaper account of any kind has been uncovered." *A Buddy Rogers Tribute* by J Michael Kenyon, *Buddy Rogers Record Book*, Circa 2005, p. 6.

37 The advertisement was featured in the *Philadelphia Inquirer*, Feb. 11, 1944, p. 26. The match, billed as a "special attraction," was also mentioned in the *Camden Morning Post*, Feb. 11, 1944, p. 24. Rohde beat "Abe Adali" in 5:30. Lewis's name did not appear in the results. *Philadelphia Inquirer*, Feb. 12, 1944, p. 14.

38 Lewis suffered from trachoma, an eye disease that was causing him to lose his sight.

39 *Wisconsin Rapids Daily Tribune*, April 26, 1944, p. 6. Steinborn reportedly added quotes about the Lewis-Rohde match in *Milo and the Halitosis Kid* by Max Jacobs, p. 230-232.

40 Billy Darnell joined them as well. Darnell had rejoined Rudy Dusek in December 1943. The exact reasons Steinborn, Rohde and Darnell left the Dusek group are unknown, although it could have been about money and/or better opportunities. It appears that Steinborn may not have worked for Dusek all that much after March 1944.

41 In pre-show publicity, Rohde's previous wins over the Dusek Brothers was acknowledged. *Trenton Evening Times*, March 23, 1944, p. 22.

42 *Mat Maulers* was directed by Harry Foster and photographed by Jack Etra for "The World of Sports" program and the Columbia Pictures Corporation. The entire film was ten minutes, with approximately five minutes for the Rohde-Mahoney match and another five minutes for the Babe Sharkey-Don Evans bout. The film was released on June 19, 1944.

43 Rohde's entire match against Mahoney lasted 10:12. The local newspaper stated: "Rhode (sic) displayed a world of speed and a whole bag of mat tricks that are bound to make him one of the most popular grapplers ever to appear at the arena." *Trenton Evening Times*, March 24, 1944, p. 26.

44 Correspondence with Joe Opiela, March 25, 2019.

45 It is available under the title: "Herman 'Dutch' Rohde vs. Ash Mahoney – Early Buddy Rogers Wrestling Match 1940s," youtube.com.

46 The Rohde-Leone bout was said to be "the best battle seen this year." *Baltimore Sun*, March 29, 1944, p. 15. In Wilmington, Delaware, Rohde was often billed as "Dusty Rhodes." For a time, the *Wilmington Morning News* referred to him as "Dutch Rhodes," while the *Wilmington News Journal* called him "Dusty Rhodes." A program from Wilmington dated May 22, 1944 called him "Dutch Rhodes." *Wilmington Official Program*, May 22, 1944.

47 On March 7, 1944, Sharkey won a 16-man tournament in Baltimore, and a week later, triumphed over "Strangler" Lewis for the World Title, recognized by the Maryland State Athletic Commission. *Baltimore Sun*, March 15, 1944, p. 14.

48 *Washington, D.C. Evening Star*, April 27, 1944, p. 19.

49 *Washington, D.C. Evening Star*, July 6, 1944, p. 16. The following week, Rohde defeated Angelo Savoldi, confirming his spot as top challenger to Sharkey.

50 *Washington, D.C. Evening Star*, July 14, 1944, p. 8.

51 *Washington, D.C. Evening Star*, July 23, 1944, p. 19.

52 Ibid., *Washington, D.C. Evening Star*, July 20, 1944, p. 15.

53 *Charlotte Observer*, Jan. 28, 1944, p. 20.

54 Rohde was declared eligible on both the "police list" and the "firemen list." *Camden Courier-Post*, Aug. 19, 1943, p. 3.

55 *Camden Courier-Post*, May 12, 1944, p. 3.

56 Ibid.

57 Officials "decided Buddy could do more good for his country in a prowl car than in an Army or Navy uniform." Denver Wrestling Program, Feb. 13, 1958.

58 Ibid.

59 A Washington, D.C. newspaper wrote that Rohde arranged his police "work schedule so that he [could] come here Wednesday nights" for promoter Joe Turner. *Washington, D.C. Evening Star*, July 10, 1944, p. 9.

60 Rohde was not advertised to be on the show. *Camden Morning Post*, Sept. 18, 1944, p. 12. Results appeared in *Camden Morning Post*, Sept. 19, 1944, p. 16.

61 Rohde returned to the Philadelphia Arena for Dusek beginning on Nov. 3, 1944.

62 Babe Sharkey was also reinstated on that day. *Uniontown Morning Herald*, Oct. 20, 1944, p. 20.

63 *Scranton Times*, Nov. 11, 1944, p. 9. The Martinelli-Rohde bout was not the main event on the card, but the semi-final. The main event was Ernie Dusek vs. George Becker and Louis did not referee that bout. *Philadelphia Inquirer*, Nov. 11, 1944, p. 15.

64 It was effective May 2, 1945. *Rohde v. Rohde*, Superior Court of New Jersey, Case Number 152-491-E/26-653.

65 Herman was 21 and Kathryn was 16 years of age at the time of their marriage in November 1942.

66 *Camden Morning Post*, Jan. 10, 1945, p. 1.

67 U.S. City Directories, 1943, ancestry.com.

68 A "John Rhode" participated in a Moose Amateur Boxing Tournament at the Pennsauken Arena in July 1932. *Camden Courier-Post*, July 7, 1932, p. 22.

69 Interview with John Rohde, Circa September 2003.

70 One newspaper billed Darnell as, "Billy Darnell-Rohde, brother of Dutch Rohde." *Queens Ledger*, Undated, p. 6.

71 *Trenton Evening Times*, Nov. 5, 1944, p. 19.

72 Ancestry.com.

73 Milo Steinborn was also on the Jersey City card, and he wrestled to a draw with Ben Marfuggi. It is unknown if he traveled with the Rohde Brothers to the show. *Jersey Journal*, Jan. 13, 1945, p. 7. John was billed as "Buddy Rhodes" in Baltimore.

74 Ibid. The Rogers-Parker match was not advertised. Parker was originally scheduled to wrestle Angelo Savoldi. *Jersey Journal*, Jan. 12, 1945, p. 13.

75 *Washington, D.C. Evening Star*, Jan. 17, 1945, p. 15. One article claimed Rogers was from California. *Wilmington Morning News*, Jan. 31, 1945, p. 10.

76 John said he wrestled as a professional for "two years." Interview with John Rohde, Circa September 2003. If John wrestled for two years, his matches beyond what is stated here are completely unknown.

77 It was claimed that John Rohde suffered a broken leg in his third pro match. *Columbus Star*, July 19, 1952, p. 2.

78 In a separate piece, it was said: "The older Rhode (sic) Brother, for some time a noted amateur wrestler, turned professional. In his sixth professional bout his leg was broken by 'Jumpin' Joe' Savoldi, effectively ending his career." *Buddie Rogers and The Art of "Sequencing"* by Max W. Jacobs, p. 4.

79 Interview with John Rohde, Circa September 2003.

80 Ibid.

81 *NWA Official Wrestling*, April 1952. The musician-actor, Buddy Rogers was born Charles Rogers. John Rohde's middle name was, "Charles."

82 *Washington, D.C. Evening Star*, June 8, 1944, p. 18.

83 *Baltimore Sun*, Jan. 10, 1945, p. 13.

84 *Washington, D.C. Evening Star*, March 21, 1945, p. 21.

85 *Washington D.C. Evening Star*, March 22, 1945, p. 17.

86 *Long Branch Daily Record*, March 27, 1945.

87 *Camden Courier-Post*, Feb. 27, 1945, p. 18.

88 *Camden Courier-Post*, April 4, 1945, p. 16.

89 *Camden Morning Post*, April 17, 1945, p. 13.

90 *Camden Courier-Post*, April 18, 1945, p. 16.

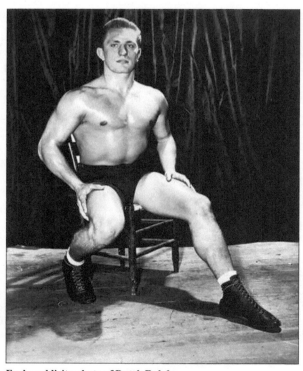

Early publicity photo of Dutch Rohde

Chapter 4
The Atomic Blond

Professional wrestling evolved considerably during the first half of the 20th century, and the sport in 1945 looked nothing like it had 25 to 30 years earlier. The changes were widespread, and impacted every facet of the industry. The implementation of creative storylines to heighten feuds and important matches, the crafted build-up of challengers, and the introduction of colorful gimmicks were box-office gold. Expansive syndicates were born, fostering specific circuits and territories, and wrestling moved out of small venues into the biggest arenas in the world. But of all the modifications to the sport, the establishment and encouragement of the legendary good-versus-evil rivalry was the most consequential. When wrestling was perceived to be on the level, and combatants were sportsmen first and foremost, fans cheered both sides of any given match. Ed (Strangler) Lewis and others began to tease and test emotions during the 1920s, subtly using maneuvers that were borderline illegal. Crowds were appalled and angrily reacted en masse. It was then and there that promoters realized this was the missing ingredient to wrestling's success.

Flash forward to 1945 and there were aspects of professional wrestling that were consistent with all-out mayhem. Rowdy villains like "Dynamite" Joe Cox were responsible for a great deal of it. The 5-foot-11, 235-pound firecracker was a pioneering wrestling heel, a master of crowd manipulation and a proven attraction. Originally from Mercer County, Missouri, Cox was a 20-year veteran of the pro ranks by the 1940s and had wrestled for the world championship many times.[1] He challenged claimants Jim Londos, Danno O'Mahoney, and Lou Thesz, and engaged in long-running feuds with Ernie Dusek and Gino Garibaldi. He defeated Yvon Robert for the Montreal version of the world title in 1940 and held it for nearly three months before dropping the belt to Leo Numa.[2] Based out of Kansas City, Cox wrestled all over the map and was a perennial headliner for Rudy Dusek in the Northeast. In January 1943, he made his return to the Dusek circuit and became acquainted with Herman (Dutch) Rohde for the first time.

In Rohde, Cox saw a talented athlete eager to learn, and he took the young man under his wing. Rohde was appreciative. Having absorbed the lessons of Fred Grobmier and Milo Steinborn, he accepted the guidance of the noted "bad guy," and the education he received was an important part of his development.[3] For months, Rohde had dealt with the intrinsic "power" bestowed to the region's in-ring villains, and heard Dusek espouse the value of keeping their heels strong, but now, he was studying how they worked their magic. Cox, using a wide range of techniques on the performance end of the spectrum, revealed the tricks he used to work crowds into a fury on a regular basis. It was a simple methodology, and most of it was his ruthless aggression toward an opponent, but there were other elements, specifically, the unspoken interaction between the wrestler and the crowd itself. Casual, but menacing, glances out beyond the ring, gestures, and slight mannerisms were tools of the trade, and they drove fans wild.

With reference to Rudy Dusek, the booking agent, Cox understood his shortcomings, and knew Rohde needed to move to another territory for a shot at legitimate, positive advancement. He wanted "Dutch" to succeed, so he reached out to a friendly promoter in Houston named Morris Sigel, paving the way for Rohde's local debut in Texas.[4] But there was another personality involved in this transaction, and that was the 50-year-old Jack Pfefer, a native of Warsaw, Poland.[5] A man of 1,001 idiosyncrasies, Pfefer was a wrestling powerbroker and had been one for more than a decade. His station in pro grappling was undefined to some degree, and he was much more capricious than his peers. Pfefer was moody in tone and whimsical in business, and whereas most promoters had a stable home for operations, he was nearly always on the move.[6] Typically, he could be found touring the countryside with his "mat freaks," the Swedish Angel and Martin Levy, the 640-pound "Human Blimp."

The Angel and Blimp were exclusively gimmick performers and Pfefer thrived on discovering and promoting unusual acts. He was a fatherly figure to them and earned undying loyalty from the wrestlers under his management. Pfefer, by 1945, was interested in building up his roster, and added "Tiger" Jack Moore and Dave Levin, a former claimant to the world heavyweight title during the 1930s, to his catalogue of nomadic stars.[7] The entire troupe was planted in the New York City region in March and April 1945, and Pfefer got to see Herman Rohde up close. On March 13, "Dutch" wrestled and lost to the Swedish Angel at the State Armory in Wilmington after receiving four "head twist" maneuvers.[8] Rohde and Pfefer were introduced and formed a pleasant acquaintance, and it's probable that Pfefer advised the wrestler to leave the Duseks as soon as possible.[9] Notably, Pfefer had a rather extensive list of people he reviled, and Rudy Dusek was at the very top.

Somehow, Pfefer became a middleman in the discussion between Rohde and the Houston office. On March 30, 1945, Morris Sigel's partner in Houston, Frank J. Burke, actually sent Pfefer a telegram requesting that Rohde report on April 8 "prepared for steady bookings" beginning the next evening.[10] And since Pfefer kept impeccable business records, it is known that he sent two telegrams that same day, and then spent $2.60 on a long distance telephone call.[11] It's anyone's guess who he was in contact with, but very likely he replied to Burke with regard to Rohde's status. "Dutch" needed a little more time to work things out, and in the interim, received a call directly from Sigel. "[Herman], you come down, I guarantee you that you'll fare high amongst these guys because you got a lot on the ball," Sigel explained. "This will be something that you can really put your teeth into, and just might be able to come out on top."[12]

"I have a problem," Rohde told Sigel. "Technically, I am a reserve on the police force here in Camden. It is the only way I can keep out of the Army. Is there a way you can help me out?"[13] In response, Sigel said he'd use his connections to get him hired on the "stand-by police force in Houston."[14]

That was music to Rohde's ears, and everything seemed to fit into place. But there was one other big issue, Sigel felt, and he explained the undesired attention the name "Herman (Dutch) Rohde" could bring during wartime, especially if he was going into Texas as a babyface. Sigel wanted him to change his name, and this was something Rohde completely understood. In fact, the name "Wally Ward" might have been born out of a promoter's similar desire to avoid fans mistaking him for a German heel and booing him. Rohde suggested the name "Buddy Rogers," the alias his brother John used earlier in the year, and Sigel loved it.[15] Herman did, too, and the era of Buddy Rogers, the blond wrestling sensation, officially began.

Before he stepped into a Texas ring using his new name, Rogers ventured to South Florida for a brief vacation. Expectedly, he spent most of his time baking in the sun and wound up with a painful sunburn. It was so severe that he had to back out a May 18 wrestling engagement at the Biscayne Arena.[16] His skin was still sore when he arrived in Galveston on May 21, but he was supposed to be just a spectator. Buddy, however, was called into action to replace fan-favorite Bobby Managoff, who was stuck in Houston because of bad weather, and teamed with Otto Kuss to beat Marvin Jones and Hans Schnabel. The match was clinched in the third fall after Rogers pinned Jones, and their victory was said to be for the Texas tag team title.[17] The championship win was significant as it marked the first title Buddy ever captured. But there was little merit to the championship itself, and it doesn't appear that Rogers and Kuss ever teamed again. Their title win was recorded in the proverbial "books," and then promptly forgotten.

On the fast-paced Eastern Texas circuit, Buddy wrestled five to six nights a week in places like Houston, Dallas, San Antonio, and Corpus Christi. Sigel churned out first-class publicity to promote his newest hero, acknowledging his good looks, quickness, and popularity.[18] "Rogers comes here with a great record and is listed as the game's No. 1 gate attraction," a report in the *Houston Post* stated.[19] Buddy being dubbed the sport's top draw was a bit farfetched, but as a sales tactic, it sounded incredible. Following a win over George Lenihan in Houston on May 25, the local paper said that he was "the most sensational grappler to show here since Paul Jones made his debut 22 years ago."[20] In the ring, Buddy's confidence was at an all-time high and he was getting nice cooperation from opponents, many of whom he had never met. His ability to chain wrestle was improving, and he made great use of the ropes, frequently springing off the strands to land his dropkick. As a finisher, he used a "spread eagle hold," which was seemingly a modified body press, and the move was held in high esteem.[21]

Shortly after Buddy's arrival in Texas, Jack Pfefer and his men launched their own campaign in the "Lone Star State." It was almost as if Pfefer wanted to keep tabs on Rogers, and he very well might have been. Jack Moore, a Pfefer stableman, was repackaged as the masked "Golden Angel" and pushed as a heel. Dave Levin, a skilled tactician, was a top opponent for Rogers, and the two matched up well in every department. On June 8, they battled to a 90-minute draw at Houston's City Auditorium, and pundits lauded the fact that the grapplers "went the limit without violating a single rule or even using a short-arm blow."[22] This was demonstrative of Buddy's versatility. In the waning days of his Dusek run, he was combating heels with a fire all his own, and rules were regularly broken. Now, he was back utilizing a clean style and displaying impressive conditioning. The following month, Levin won the Texas title from Bobby Managoff, and Rogers became a leading contender.[23]

Rogers sought his first singles championship and delivered a boastful comment to the press in what amounted to a pre-match promo in those days, declaring: "I know that I am faster than Levin, and I plan to cut out a pace that will kill off the Brooklyn grappler."[24] On July 27, 1945, before 5,000 people at the Houston Coliseum, Rogers toppled Levin in two-straight falls to win the Texas championship.[25] It was a major achievement and was the kind of career progression he longed for, but never saw in the Northeast. Soon thereafter, Pfefer's troupe departed Texas for Southern California, and an interesting thing took place.[26] On Aug. 8 at the Olympic Auditorium in Los Angeles, a new wrestler by the name of "Bummy Rogers" debuted against Brother Jonathan, and claimed to be from New York by way of Texas.[27] This individual was Jack Moore, who was using his second gimmick in as many months.

"Bummy Rogers" was an unabashed Pfefer creation. The promoter would later be known for using derivatives of well-known wrestler's names and hyping them on his cards in an effort to draw fans. The tactic was crude, and once audiences got wind of the imposters, they were fully disgusted. But in 1945, Buddy Rogers was still an up-and-comer. Pfefer's "Bummy Rogers" was undoubtedly purposeful in reference to the Camden athlete, but not likely to mock or injure. However, it is important to note that Pfefer was easily scorned, and if anything on his way out of Texas triggered animosity, that alone would have given him motivation to create the derived gimmick. However, there is no reason to think that was the case here.

In August 1945, Rogers wrestled both the heavyweight and junior heavyweight champions of the world. The former came at Houston on Aug. 3, and he put up a good fight against Bill Longson, the reigning National Wrestling Association champion. Longson carried a far-better claim to the crown than Babe Sharkey and 90 per cent of the other so-called wrestling champions. The 6-foot-2, 235-pound behemoth from Salt Lake City was in the midst of his second reign as the NWA kingpin, and he had held the prized belt since Feb. 19, 1943, when he stripped Bobby Managoff in St. Louis. Nicknamed "Wild Bill," he was a crooked champion, and typically shattered the rulebook with every appearance. But Longson was a talented wrestler when the situation called for it. He could wrestle scientifically, and Buddy needed to be on the top of his game to match holds with someone as experienced as the NWA champion.

Longson viewed Buddy as any great champion would have, and that is completely without ego. An insecure wrestler might have been concerned about the young athlete's potential and the push he was getting from some of the sport's leading promoters. As a smart businessman, though, Longson knew Buddy's marketability opened up a terrific opportunity, and he wanted to maximize that at the box office; not only for the short term, but over a period of years. This was a lesson Buddy himself was learning. For Buddy to have a moneymaking future against Longson, it was critical that they have a competitive match. And that they did. Longson and Rogers went 90-

minutes to a draw in Houston. Longson won the first fall with a piledriver and Buddy tied things up in the second with his spread eagle hold. At the very end, with the clock ticking down, Longson was at the mercy of Buddy's aggressiveness, and the entire scenario was played out perfectly.[28]

The Longson-Rogers feud was just beginning, that much was sure. Four days after his bout with Longson in Houston, Buddy wrestled the 200-pound champion, LeRoy McGuirk, in Dallas. For the match to be considered for the NWA world junior heavyweight title, Buddy had to drop weight, and newspaper reports claimed it was as much as 16-pounds.[29] Such a dramatic weight loss was probably exaggerated for the storyline, but nevertheless played a role in the third fall of the contest. With the match tied at one-fall apiece, Rogers had McGuirk in an airplane spin, hoping to finish his rival off, but succumbed to dizziness and fell to the canvas. McGuirk promptly pinned him to retain his crown.[30] The "dizziness" was attributed to his weight loss, but he was credited for giving the champ a tough bout, and rematches were planned.[31] During the summer of 1945, Rogers saw a number of familiar faces arrive in the territory from back east; among them, Maurice LaChappelle, Don Evans, and Lou Plummer.

Life on the Houston circuit was arduous, but it was paying off. Rogers was making good money, gaining experience and networking, and relishing in his time off. The beaches of Galveston were a particular favorite of his, and the nightlife in and around Houston was plentiful. The Cotton Club and the Old Barn were exciting spots, and the dance scene at the Aragon Club never failed to entertain. Buddy enjoyed socializing, but in his personal life, he was accounted for. The 24-year-old was in a relationship with Ellen Marion Wyman, a talented former night club singer, three years his senior.[32] The daughter of Finnish parents, Ellen grew up in Philadelphia on South Dover Street and attended three years of high school.[33] In the late 1930s, she gained regional fame as a vocalist and dancer, and performed in clubs in Pennsylvania and New Jersey. At some point prior to 1941, she was briefly married and gave birth to a son named Allin.[34]

It is unclear as to when Ellen and Buddy met, but it could have occurred at any time between 1940 and 1945. Ellen, using the name, "Ella Wyman," performed in many South Jersey establishments, including the Penguin Club, Betty's Café, and Club Lido. She was advertised as a dancer at Murray's Inn in Haddonfield as late as April 1945, and soon departed for Texas when Buddy made his big move in May.[35] On Aug. 10, the couple was married in Houston, and received their official documentation from W.D. Miller, the Harris County Clerk.[36] That evening at the Coliseum, Buddy and his longtime foe, Don Evans, put on a wrestling clinic, and fans were on their feet screaming and cheering in response. Evans switched gears mid-match and began fouling, culminating in his disqualification and Buddy's victory.[37] Before the end of the month, Rogers lost his Texas title to Ted (King Kong) Cox in Houston, but regained it the following week on Sept. 7.[38]

Emil and Ernie Dusek, newcomers in Texas during the month of September, were the last people Rogers wanted to see. The duo brought along a message to Morris Sigel from their brother Rudy, who insisted that Rogers owed them two months work for breaking a contract when he left earlier in the year.[39] Buddy disagreed, and was still sore about being manipulated and pushed around by Dusek's cronies. His career had been headed nowhere under the Dusek regime. But Sigel had to bend. Too much business was conducted between New York and Houston, and he needed to keep the peace. As a compromise, he agreed to send Buddy back to the Dusek circuit for a one-month period, and the two promoters were content with the terms. Rogers was anything but satisfied. He was backed into a corner, without any kind of political protection, and risked a widespread blacklisting if he didn't adhere to the agreement. With heavy reservations, he returned to the Northeast, and knew major trouble was ahead.

Starting on Oct. 9, 1945, at the St. Nicholas Arena in Manhattan, Rogers, using his real name again, began a tough whirlwind tour of the Dusek territory. He had a series of hard-hitting matches against Joe Savoldi, Ed (Strangler) White, Laverne Baxter, Don Lee (Masked Atom), and Jimmy Coffield. The local Wilmington paper called his October 11 encounter with Baxter a "wild and savage battle" and the finish had Rogers cracking a chair over the heads of both his rival and the referee.[40] The following night in Newark, he was jobbed out to the 250-pound "Strangler" White in 18-seconds during the third fall.[41] In a separate match against White in Wilmington on October 18, the "Strangler" brutalized Rogers and nearly started a riot.[42] Rogers made his October 19 date at the Jamaica Arena, but walked out on the remainder of his bookings. He was wholeheartedly fed up.

Through hard work, he'd achieved a measure of success and fame in Texas, and was beginning to see the dividends. He had been wrestling the NWA world champion and getting good publicity, but Dusek had him back losing to his crew of roughneck journeymen. It was a huge reversal of fortune. Rogers skipped out on at least five matches between October 22 and October 26, and after missing a bout against Savoldi on October 23, he was suspended by the New York State Athletic Commission "for failure to appear without any excuse".[43] A newspaper promoting a show in White Plains acknowledged his suspension, but claimed it was because Rogers had "aggravated an old shoulder injury."[44] Rogers was fine, and as a matter of self preservation, immediately left the region. Interestingly, Rudy Dusek, an old-school shooter, had wanted one last piece of Rogers in the ring, and was slated to meet Buddy in the closing match of his tour in Queens on October 26. He didn't get his chance and would never have the opportunity to wrestle Rogers again.

As far as Rogers and Morris Sigel were concerned, the debt to Dusek was settled, and Buddy returned to Houston. Upon arrival, Rogers introduced a new finisher known as the "Atomic Drop," and the move received a lot of attention.[45] The innovative maneuver saw Rogers pick up his opponent for a bear hug and then drop him down onto his knee, a slight variation of the inverted atomic drop, which some wrestlers still use to this day. The move was controversial from the start, and Rogers was disqualified for utilizing it against Bill Longson on October 26 in Houston.[46] Rogers was adamant that the finisher was legal, and the Texas Boxing and Wrestling Commission ultimately agreed. He put away a laundry list of foes with the move and went on to recapture the Texas State championship from Jim Casey on November 23, a title he had lost to Ernie Dusek in Fort Worth two months earlier.[47] As Rogers embraced the fanfare that surrounded him, he adopted his first nickname exclusive to the "Buddy Rogers" persona. And since he was the master of the atomic drop, he was billed as wrestling's "Atomic Blond."[48]

A few days before Christmas, Rogers and his wife left Texas for Camden and he enjoyed a two-week reprieve from the grueling mat schedule. Yearning to keep his conditioning, he spent part of his time at a local gym and reconnected with his original teacher, Fred Grobmier, who was more than willing to help polish his skills.[49] Rogers was so much better than he had been a few years earlier, and with his improved abilities, came a sizable raise in income. From 1942 to 1944, he had grossed somewhere between $10,000 and $16,000 in total, a salary that was normal for his age and experience. Wrestling in Texas put him on a different plateau, and it was reported that he made $38,000 in his third year as a pro.[50] "I was sending money home so fast," Rogers later recalled, "my mother [thought that] I was holding up a bank, 'cause we weren't used to all the luxuries I began to receive in '45."[51] As a present for himself, Rogers purchased a brand-new 1946 Chrysler automobile, and initiated a new annual tradition.[52]

Notice of Buddy's success reached the St. Louis office of Tom Packs, one of wrestling's most powerful promoters, and spurred great interest. Packs, a middle-aged man of Greek descent, was in his 22nd year as a grappling impresario, and not only had he survived the tumultuous war years, but he was prospering. In fact, St. Louis was the hottest wrestling city in the United States and far outdoing attendance numbers in New York, Chicago and Los Angeles. Bill Longson was responsible for a great deal of the success, and his drawing power was unmatched. As the NWA champion, a title that Packs controlled, Longson was dominant in St. Louis, and after the success he and Buddy had in Texas, it was little surprise that Rogers entered the territory in January 1946.[53] Buddy's enthusiasm and popularity were great selling points, and Packs quickly pushed him as a challenger to Longson's title. Locals were on board after witnessing his impressive wins over Joe Dusek, Warren Bockwinkel, and Yvon Robert.

In addition to his Texas responsibilities, Rogers joined Packs' circuit and wrestled from Louisville to Atlanta. The fans in Evansville, Indiana, were especially receptive to his youthful exuberance, and female enthusiasts were quite taken by his good looks. "I just swooned all over when Buddy Rogers entered the ring last Wednesday night, and I swooned even more when he got in action," one college-aged supporter said. "Buddy can wear my sorority pin any time." Another girl added: "Buddy is just too wonderful for words. He's the answer to any girl's prayer, for he is a real he-man. Yes, siree, he's a real handsome guy and I could go for him with no trouble at all." A longtime male fan put things into perspective, declaring: "I have never seen anything like Buddy Rogers in the past 20 years. That boy has everything to make a great champion. Color and ability. He showed a brand of wrestling last week that only Jim Londos in his prime showed, but to me he looks even better than Londos and that's a big saying."[54]

To aficionados, Rogers was the logical successor to Longson, and they wanted to see the title change hands. Packs encouraged that sentiment building toward the "Battle of the Decade" at the St. Louis Arena on April 12, 1946.[55] This was the big Rogers-Longson showdown that everyone wanted to see. "Naturally, the biggest ambition of my wrestling career is to become champion," Rogers told a reporter prior to the contest, "and I have every reason and right to believe I can win this match."[56] Much of the crowd believed the same thing, and their hopes and dreams appeared possible when Rogers stormed out of the gate and dominated the early portion of their bout. Dropkicks were his go-to move, and Longson was battered about the ring. Finally, at the apex moment, Longson swiftly dodged a flying kick and Rogers went through the ropes, crashing onto the press table. He was slow to get back into the ring, where the champion easily finished him off to retain.[57]

Rogers sold a severe back injury at the end of the match and his devotees, among the astonishing 17,621 fans in attendance, were gripped by the sensational finish. People rushed toward the ring as officials tended to their fallen hero, and emotions were tugged on as Buddy was helped from the ring and taken to a local hospital for treatment.[58] Later, it was revealed that Rogers had suffered a "transformed process of the fourth lumbar of the fourth vertebrae," and it appeared very serious.[59] Buddy's loss was attributed to tough luck, and his popular underdog status was upheld in St. Louis. And in terms of selling an injury, he was becoming increasingly proficient – a skill that would help him throughout his career. To his supporters in St. Louis, he was bedridden and trying to recover from the brutal match. But, in truth, Rogers was fit as a fiddle, and three nights later, he returned to the ring and beat Leo Numa in Memphis.

It wasn't long after Rogers expanded his schedule to include dates for Tom Packs that he met Lou Thesz for the first time. Thesz, a 29-year-old product of St. Louis, was already a three-time world heavyweight champion, and considered to be the cream of the crop. Classically trained in the legitimate art of pro wrestling, he was a shooter, in addition to being a performer, and his cat-like aggressiveness put him on another level from most of his peers. In March 1946, Thesz was a member of the U.S. Army, and since World War II had ended six months before, he was expecting his discharge later that year.[60] He continued to wrestle when opportune, and traveled between Texas and Missouri, with additional stops elsewhere on the Packs circuit. On March 27 in Evansville, Thesz and Buddy Rogers wrestled for the first time, and the two competitors went 90-minutes to a draw. Thesz won the initial fall, while Rogers took the second in what the newspaper called a "fast and interesting match."[61]

Thesz was about five years older than Buddy, and possessed far greater experience and overall wrestling knowledge, particularly when it came to politics. He had been everywhere on the map since his 1934 debut and knew all the tricks and pitfalls of the game. The ring chemistry between the two men was clear from the very beginning, and looking at their age, a long-running and profitable feud was expected. Importantly, Thesz would have been in a position to teach Rogers many fundamental techniques, improving their ring work, and helping Buddy develop as an individual wrestler. On May 3, 1946, in Houston, they wrestled again. This time, Thesz was on the receiving end of an unintentional low blow in the third fall and Rogers was disqualified. Referee Paul Boesch awarded Thesz the Texas championship as a result.[62] A week later in the same city, Rogers won a rematch and regained his belt. In that contest, Buddy triumphed with one-fall in 90-minutes.[63]

One of the longstanding rules in pro wrestling prohibited "good guys" and "bad guys" from traveling together. Occasionally, it extended to two fan favorites, as well, if they were booked to face each other. Promoters didn't want the opponents being seen getting out of the same car, as it damaged the illusion of competition and ring warfare. In his 2011 autobiography, Hooker, Thesz explained that he shared an automobile with Buddy from St. Louis to Louisville prior to a match they were slated to work against each other sometime in 1946. It was a dangerous move, but they felt it was safe enough to manage. While en route, during a casual conversation, Buddy made a disparaging comment about Thesz's idol, Ed (Strangler) Lewis, who was refereeing their bout.[64] He asked: "Why do we need that fat old bastard?" Thesz was incensed by the question.[65] In fact, he was beyond furious, and that one comment about Lewis was at the root of his lifelong animosity toward Rogers.

Rogers and Thesz were intertwined as wrestling personalities in 1946, but their relationship was hampered by ego, mistrust, and a personal hatred. They were never going to be friends, but their rivalry endured because of the flawless manner in which they matched up in the ring. Their feud was going to draw money and that was the most important thing. In 1946, Rogers encountered another Herculean performer on his way up the wrestling ladder. George Wagner, better known as Gorgeous George, was wrestling's fashion icon, the "Toast of the Coast," direct from Hollywood, California. The 31-year-old was pioneering a colorful style that magnified earlier wrestling gimmicks and would capture the imagination of the mainstream public. With his $10,000 wardrobe, silken robes, and English valet, he was a tremendous character in a world of eccentrics, and his efforts were changing the business, for good or bad.

The "Atomic Blond" wrestled George four times in Texas between May and July 1946, and won two of the matches, lost one, and drew the other. In the midst of that stretch, on June 24 in Fort Worth, Buddy lost the Texas State title to former pro footballer Kay Bell. Things in Texas were winding up and Rogers had lost his winning momentum as a headliner. He needed a break from the territory and dropped matches to the likes of Dave Levin, Ted Cox, and Gino Garibaldi. Throughout this period, Rogers had been doing a lot of thinking, putting things into perspective, and working to set up his next move. It was clear that he was unprotected and had no ability to safeguard his career going forward. Wrestlers in the upper echelon of the business were almost always politically protected by a promoter or manager who shielded them from unscrupulous dealings. As the situation with Rudy Dusek demonstrated, Rogers was vulnerable, and he needed an advocate to look out for his best interests.

The unorthodox Jack Pfefer was roaming the wrestling circuit at a furious pace in 1946. He was doing what he did best; promoting his stable of creations and, generally, keeping the profession just a little off-balance. Buddy knew Jack by this time, understood his management style, and was confident that he could do everything he needed a manager to accomplish. He broached that subject with Pfefer and the two began negotiating. Pfefer saw dollar signs all over Rogers and committed himself to making Rogers a national star. Undoubtedly, the diminutive manager invoked a little salesmanship to close the deal, and when both were satisfied, they shook hands to mark the occasion.[66] From that juncture on, Pfefer was Buddy's official manager. The terms were fairly simple. Pfefer would receive 33-1/3 per cent of every booking, and would pay two-thirds of Rogers' expenses, including travel fare.[67]

Linking up with Pfefer was great in many respects, but depending on who you asked, the benefits were debatable. If you were to ask Dave Levin, he probably would have volunteered his contentment working for such a wayward personality. On the surface, it was easy to judge Pfefer and his quirkiness, but there was much more to it. "I locked up with a guy that's one of the most popular, or unpopular, guys in wrestling, Jack Pfefer," Rogers later told writer Ray Tennenbaum. "Jack Pfefer, when he fought for you, boy, he was all blood and guts. I know he's a son-of-a-bitch, but remember, he's my son-of-a-bitch."[68]

For all intents and purposes, that was the basis of Buddy's move. Pfefer's strong personality and wisdom were going to give him an edge as he traversed the wrestling landscape. If Dusek or someone else came along trying to bring trouble, Rogers knew Pfefer had his back. Beginning on Sept. 23, 1946, Buddy launched a new phase of his career in Denver, Colorado, and won over the massive Blimp. Part of the Pfefer playbook was to have the members of his stable wrestle each other on any given night, and Rogers was in for a string of matches against Jack Moore (Golden Angel), Elmer Estep (Elmer the Great), Dave Levin, and future B-movie star Tor Johnson (Super Swedish Angel). His first week in Pfefer's sphere, Buddy made $451 for four matches, and followed up with $570 the next.[69] He wrestled from Salt Lake City to Rocky Ford in Southeastern Colorado, and was a featured player in cities like Colorado Springs, Ogden, and Pueblo.

Working for Pfefer was an entirely new experience and there were bound to be bumps in the road. The money wasn't perfect, nor was the day-to-day scheduling, but for Buddy Rogers, at this point in his life, he felt it was the best opportunity he had. And there was no question that he planned to make the most of it.

ENDNOTES - CHAPTER 4

[1] Cox was born on Oct. 28, 1900. Ancestry.com. He was reportedly a veteran of both world wars. *Kansas City Times*, Sept. 1, 1945, p. 7.
[2] Cox won the Montreal version of the World Title from Yvon Robert on Feb. 27, 1940 and lost it to Leo Numa on May 20, 1940.
[3] *Buddie Rogers and The Art of "Sequencing"* by Max W. Jacobs, p. 5-6.
[4] It appears that Cox last worked for Sigel in Texas in December 1942 and February 1943 before touring extensively for Dusek in the northeast.
[5] Pfefer had turned 50-years-of-age on Dec. 10, 1944.
[6] Pfefer's old office was at the Times Building in Manhattan. By 1945, he had closed his office and was paying $25 a month for storage of his belongings at an unknown location. He'd stay almost exclusively at the Hotel Piccadilly when in New York.
[7] It is unclear if Dave Levin joined Pfefer in 1944 or 1945. A St. Louis article from June 1944 stated, "Pfefer may become Dave Levin's manager." *St. Louis Star and Times*, June 28, 1944, p. 15. There does seem to be evidence that Levin was touring with Swedish Angel, Pfefer's wrestler, in late 1944. Notably, Levin broke into pro wrestling for Pfefer in the 1930s.
[8] *Wilmington Morning News*, March 14, 1945, p. 14. Swedish Angel's finishing move was also called the "Cobra head twist" and the "neck twist" in various newspaper reports. Angel and Rohde

wrestled one previous time on Oct. 18, 1944 in Washington, D.C., and Angel was victorious there as well.

[9] Researcher Max Jacobs reported that it was Ed Lewis who introduced Rohde to Jack Pfefer. *Buddie Rogers and The Art of "Sequencing"* by Max W. Jacobs, p. 6.

[10] Western Union Telegram from Frank J. Burke to Jack Pfefer at the Piccadilly Hotel in New York City dated March 30, 1945.

[11] Pfefer Business Expense Book, 1945. Jack Pfefer Collection, Joyce Sports Research Collection, Hesburgh Library, University of Notre Dame, Notre Dame, Indiana.

[12] Buddy Rogers Interview by Bill Apter, *Apter Chat*, Part One, 1979, youtube.com.

[13] *Buddie Rogers and The Art of "Sequencing"* by Max W. Jacobs, p. 7. There is no additional data on Rohde's transition from serving as an active police officer to a reserve for the Camden Police Department. A later report stated that he served on the force "for 19 months until his resignation to devote his efforts to wrestling." *Camden Courier-Post*, July 25, 1963, p. 36.

[14] *Buddie Rogers and The Art of "Sequencing"* by Max W. Jacobs, p. 7.

[15] The "Buddie Rogers and The Art of 'Sequencing'" paper by Max Jacobs stated that Sigel came up with the "Buddie Rogers" identify for Rohde. *Buddie Rogers and The Art of "Sequencing"* by Max W. Jacobs, p. 7. Since John Rohde first used the name "Buddy Rogers" in the northeast earlier in 1945, it is implausible that Sigel invented the name. Rogers talked about the name change in several interviews later in life. "Since our country was at war with Germany," he explained in 1992, "I changed my name to an American one, Buddy Rogers." *Puroresu Okoku*, July 1992. In 1983, he said: "It was at the height of World War II and the resentment against anyone of German or Japanese extraction was high. The promoter [in Texas] figured I was too good a wrestler to have that kind of trouble, so he called me Buddy Rogers." *Wrestling's Main Event*, September 1983, p. 21-22.

[16] As "Dutch Rohde, the Flying Dutchman," he was booked to participate in a six-man battle royal. *Miami Herald*, May 18, 1945, p. 16. He was replaced by "Young Gotch." Also in the match were Henry Kulkovich and Tommy O'Toole. *Miami News*, May 18, 1945, p. 15.

[17] *Galveston News*, May 22, 1945, p. 8.

[18] *Houston Post*, May 20, 1945, p. C2.

[19] *Houston Post*, May 25, 1945, p. B6.

[20] *Houston Post*, May 26, 1945, p. 6.

[21] There may have been variations of the "spread-eagle hold" through the years. From an assessment of primary source material, the move Rogers used in Texas didn't appear to have a submission component to it.

[22] *Houston Post*, June 9, 1945, p. 6. The Levin-Rogers bout "was stamped by veteran mat followers as one of the greatest ever staged here." *Houston Post*, July 15, 1945, p. B1.

[23] Levin won the championship on July 13, 1945 in Houston. *Houston Post*, July 14, 1945, p. 10.

[24] *Houston Post*, July 15, 1945, p. B1.

[25] Rogers won the first fall by DQ. *Houston Post*, July 28, 1945, p. 6. In many interviews later in life, Buddy claimed to have won the Texas championship in a tournament. Rogers said: "We held a tournament. There was over three-hundred and fifty wrestlers that went through this thing. About a nine month period. And Morris Sigel was the promoter." Buddy Rogers Interview by Bill Apter, *Apter Chat*, Part One, 1979, youtube.com.

[26] Pfefer was joined by Levin, Golden Angel, the Blimp, and Jules Strongbow. The latter unlikely worked for Pfefer directly, but seemingly made the jump to Los Angeles at the same time.

[27] *Los Angeles Times*, Aug. 8, 1945, p. 11. He was also billed as "Barney Rogers."

[28] *Houston Post*, Aug. 4, 1945, p. 6.

[29] *Dallas Morning News*, Aug. 12, 1945, p. 9.

[30] *Dallas Morning News*, Aug. 8, 1945, p. 8.

[31] McGuirk undoubtedly wanted Rogers to come to Tulsa, his home-base, for a series of matches. Rogers was already being mentioned in the Tulsa press. *Tulsa World*, Sept. 17, 1945, p. 8.

[32] Ellen was born in Philadelphia on April 10, 1918.

[33] She was the daughter of Axel and Helen (Helmi) Wyman. 1940 U.S. Federal Census, ancestry.com.

34 She was listed as "married" in the 1940 Census. 1940 U.S. Federal Census, ancestry.com. Her husband's last name was apparently, "Hanson," but little is known about him. Allin was reportedly born on Jan. 23, 1940.
35 *Camden Morning Post*, April 28, 1945, p. 16.
36 Texas Marriage Records, Certificate #98262, ancestry.com.
37 *Houston Post*, Aug. 11, 1945, p. 6.
38 Rogers lost the championship to Cox using the injury angle on Aug. 31, 1945. He missed a flying tackle and crashed into the turnbuckle. Cox then applied his "cobra clutch" finisher, which was also said to be a variation of the neck twister, and scored a pinfall. He used the same move several additional times after the fall. Rogers was carried to the dressing room and was unable to continue for the third and deciding fall. *Houston Chronicle*, Sept. 1, 1945, p. 5. Rogers won the title back with two-straight falls on Sept. 7, 1945. *Houston Chronicle*, Sept. 8, 1945, p. 3. Years later, Rogers made the claim: ""I held the Texas Title for three years." Buddy Rogers Interview by Bill Apter, *Apter Chat*, Part One, 1979, youtube.com.
39 Information from the research notes of wrestling writer, Bill McCormack.
40 The match was declared a no contest. The referee was Bob Wade. *Wilmington Morning News*, Oct. 12, 1945, p. 32.
41 *Newark Star-Ledger*, Oct. 13, 1945, p. 7.
42 Rogers won by DQ. *Wilmington Morning News*, Oct. 19, 1945, p. 32.
43 New York State Athletic Commission Meeting Minutes, Oct. 26, 1945, p. 4.
44 *Mount Vernon Daily Argus*, Oct. 26, 1945.
45 A newspaper in Houston reported that Rogers had been "vacationing" for the past few weeks. *Houston Chronicle*, Oct. 26, 1945, p. B10. The move was also called the "atomic split." News of the move circulated on the United Press wire and was printed in newspapers from Ohio to Hawaii. The invention of the atomic drop hold was only two months after the atomic bombings of Hiroshima and Nagasaki in Japan, which ended World War II.
46 *Houston Chronicle*, Oct. 27, 1945, p. 4.
47 *Houston Chronicle*, Nov. 24, 1945, p. 4. Rogers lost the championship to Dusek on Sept. 24, 1945 at the North Side Coliseum in Fort Worth.
48 The first references to the "Atomic Blond" nickname appeared in Houston newspapers in October 1945.
49 *Wrestling Program*, Evansville, Indiana, Feb. 6, 1946, p. 2.
50 *Haft Nelson*, Vol. 1, No. 62, Feb. 26, 1953. This number may have been inflated by several thousand dollars.
51 Buddy Rogers Interview by Bill Apter, *Apter Chat*, Part One, 1979, youtube.com.
52 *Wrestling Program*, Evansville, Indiana, March 27, 1946, p. 2.
53 Rogers debut in St. Louis on Jan. 18, 1946.
54 *Wrestling Program*, Evansville, Indiana, Feb. 6, 1946, p. 3.
55 According to one report, Packs wanted Rogers to succeed Longson as NWA champion. Pfefer was against the idea and Rogers agreed with him, primarily based on the notion that the titleholder had to wrestle in "dump" towns. *Buddie Rogers and The Art of "Sequencing"* by Max W. Jacobs, p. 10.
56 *Sports Pointers*, April 12, 1946.
57 *St. Louis Globe-Democrat*, April 13, 1946, p. 13.
58 Rogers was taken to St. Mary's Hospital. Ibid.
59 Ibid.
60 Thesz was stationed at Fort Sam Houston in Texas.
61 *Evansville Press*, March 28, 1946, p. 23.
62 *Houston Chronicle*, May 4, 1946, p. 4.
63 Rogers won the lone fall in 66:40 with a body press. *Houston Chronicle*, May 11, 1946, p. 5.
64 *Hooker* by Lou Thesz with Kit Bauman (2011), p. 127-128. Historians have long been in search for a Rogers-Thesz match refereed by Ed Lewis in 1946, but to this date, it has not been found. A match between the two wrestlers in Louisville has also eluded researchers. In the endnotes of *Hooker*, it is mentioned that the March 27, 1946 match between Thesz and Rogers in Evansville

was probably part of the road trip Thesz talked about. *Hooker* by Lou Thesz with Kit Bauman (2011), p. 136.

[65] *Hooker* by Lou Thesz with Kit Bauman (2011), p. 127-128.

[66] Rogers said there never was a contract with Pfefer. Buddy Rogers Interview by Ray Tennenbaum, February 1985.

[67] *New York World-Telegram and Sun*, March 15, 1950. Jack Pfefer Financial Records, Jack Pfefer Collection, Joyce Sports Research Collection, Hesburgh Library, University of Notre Dame, Notre Dame, Indiana.

[68] Buddy Rogers Interview by Ray Tennenbaum, February 1985. www.ray-field.com.

[69] Jack Pfefer Financial Records, Jack Pfefer Collection, Joyce Sports Research Collection, Hesburgh Library, University of Notre Dame, Notre Dame, Indiana.

Fort Worth TX, Monday, Dec. 10, 1945

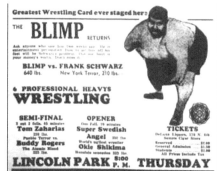

Grand Junction CO, Thursday, Oct. 10, 1946

(left to right) New York, New York : Jan. 30, 1947 — Feb. 20, 1947 — May 6, 1947

Chapter 5
Drawing Blood and Suspensions

A revolutionary shock wave hit the professional wrestling industry in 1946. The newfangled television medium had expanded enough to include weekly episodes of grappling in New York City and Chicago.[1] The growth of TV was going to alter the way the sport was promoted, presented, and enjoyed. Instead of having to visit a local arena to see the unrestrained grappling mayhem, viewers could soak in the action from their living room couch. As a result, an entire generation of new fans would be influenced by wrestling and its colorful performers. From a promotional point of view, leaders wanted to highlight a diverse range of wrestlers, and give a spotlight to those with an innate gift for television, both in terms of overall look and in-ring antics. Personality went a long way, and TV was going to usher in a host of performers with a college degree in showmanship.

The innovative television happenings from the Jamaica Arena in Queens caught the interest of Jack Pfefer and he made arrangements for his crew to return to New York in January 1947. It was a nice homecoming for Buddy Rogers and it was under much better circumstances than his last trip around the territory more than a year earlier. This time, he was exclusively booked by Joe (Toots) Mondt with cooperation from Pfefer, and he would wrestle five-to-six times a week in New York, Washington, D.C., Baltimore, and Trenton, with additional dates in Wilmington and Philadelphia. The name "Buddy Rogers" was cast aside for the tour and he was again using the "Dutch Rohde" designation. Mondt's local publication, *Sports Pictorial Review*, publicized his arrival, and included "Rohde" in its list of the top 40 heavyweight wrestlers in its Jan. 6, 1947 edition. He was placed at number 30 alongside such luminaries as Bobby Managoff, Ruffy Silverstein, and Bronko Nagurski.[2]

The number-one position was occupied by a former farm boy from Ohio named Frank Sexton. Standing more than 6-feet tall, and weighing 230 pounds, Sexton was the reigning world heavyweight champion on the East Coast. He first gained recognition in 1945 when he dethroned Steve (Crusher) Casey for the AWA championship in Boston, and then steamrolled Babe Sharkey for his version of the title on Jan. 29, 1946, in Baltimore.[3] As a wrestler, Sexton easily outclassed most of his peers, and was widely respected for his mat knowledge. He was favored to beat Rogers "with little trouble" in their first ever match-up on Jan. 22, 1947, in Washington, but Buddy surprised the crowd by holding the champion to a draw.[4] Two nights later at Jamaica Arena, Sexton beat Rogers in a hotly contested bout, and the crowd applauded the efforts of both men.[5]

Friday nights at Jamaica Arena were always a high point of Buddy's week because of the television exposure. Professional voice Dennis James, a fellow New Jerseyan, described the matches with a quaint style that endeared him to viewers new to the sport. In a later interview, Rogers claimed to have performed color commentary for James for "the first four [or] five weeks that he was on the air."[6] If the time-frame was correct, this would have given him immeasurable experience, and added to his confidence before TV cameras. Jamaica Arena footage was broadcast live in the local area at 9:00 p.m. on WABD, and at the time, the jury was still out as to whether TV would help at the box office or hinder it.[7] Nevertheless, Toots Mondt was charging forward, and, being the gambling man that he was, he bet on what he thought was a sure winner.

Predictably, Baltimore was one of Buddy's best towns.[8] It had been since his first year in the business, and fans there were heavy supporters of the Camden grappler. When he challenged Frank Sexton for the championship at the Coliseum on March 11, 1947, Rogers carried the final minutes of the match. His demonstrable speed off the ropes, dropkicks, and flying tackles were in full glory, and an upset seemed possible. Near the 16-minute mark, he attempted one final flying tackle, missed, and crashed from the ring, giving Sexton a count-out victory.[9] At the end of the following month, Rogers was booked into a special feature match in Baltimore against ex-heavyweight boxer Tony Galento, who was making his grappling debut. Often a guest referee for wrestling matches, Galento was motivated to become a combatant after learning what Primo Carnera, another former fighter, was making on the pro mat.[10] He wanted a piece of the pie.

Acknowledged as the "roly-poly tavern keeper from New Jersey," Galento weighed in the 270-pound range, and considering his greenness, he needed a skilled ring general to lead him during his initial bout.[11] Rogers was entrusted with the role, and he not only made Galento look like a proficient grappler, but he put him over by pinfall.[12] The match was a huge payday for Buddy as he collected $500, and it would end up being his largest payoff for the entire year.[13] Over the next six nights, Buddy wrestled Primo Carnera, the prize of the Mondt troupe, four straight times. Carnera, a 6-foot-6, 265-pound mastodon, held the world heavyweight boxing crown in 1933-'34, and was undefeated as a wrestler. Like Galento, Carnera was intimidating, but limited in his athleticism, leaving much of the responsibility to his foe during a match. And Rogers handled the workload, as he did in Baltimore versus "Two-Ton" Tony.

In at least three of the four matches with Primo, Rogers used the same dramatic finish, and it was identical to the ending against "Wild" Bill Longson in St. Louis in 1946 and versus Frank Sexton a few months earlier. Buddy would gallantly try for a flying tackle, only to miss, and either sail from the ring in a heap, or smash against the turnbuckle in the corner. Either way, he was knocked silly, and his opponent would win by pin or count-out. This finish was utilized versus Carnera in Philadelphia, Brooklyn, and Trenton, and might have also been used in Queens.[14] Taking into account that Buddy had employed the tactic in title contests with Longson and Sexton, and again versus Carnera, it was easy to deduce that he relied on the maneuver in specific big matches. Each and every time, it drew immense crowd reaction, and Buddy sold the resultant injury as if his life depended on it. From April

30 to May 5, 1947, he was defeated by Primo four times, and adding the Galento bout, gave him five losses in a row.

The Northeastern tour wasn't a failure for Buddy – not at all. He was a steady headliner and gained wins over Dave Levin, Martin Levy, Ben Morgan, Bobby Stewart, and Sandor Kovacs, plus had good showings against Sexton, Carnera, and Galento.[15] Behind the scenes, he scored points with guys like Toots Mondt and Willie Gilzenberg, Galento's manager, for his slick abilities in crucial matches. All in all, Jack Pfefer was happy, and ready to take his gang back on the road. On May 9, Rogers and Levin departed for the Colorado territory, where they planned to stay about two months.[16] Wrestling again as "Buddy Rogers," the blond fan-favorite won the Rocky Mountain championship shortly after his arrival in the region, capturing the title from Everette Marshall in Colorado Springs on May 14. He lost the crown back to Marshall the following week in the same city.

Rogers received the opportunity of a lifetime in Denver on June 23. He was booked to wrestle the legendary Jim Londos, and unlike the weird situation with Ed (Strangler) Lewis early in his career, this was a match that was definitely going to happen. At 53-years-of-age, Londos was still in great physical condition, and his ability to draw had remained strong. An estimated 3,000 spectators turned out for their Mammoth Garden match, and after 33-minutes of "furious action," Londos was declared the victor.[17] Years later, Buddy recalled the memorable moment, and told researcher Max Jacobs: "Jim was really marvelous. He did some old stuff, like take advantage of me when I was down. He hit me with his forearm when I broke clean, a technique not much in use then. He charged me when my back was turned and ran away when I turned to face him, that sort of stuff. His only problem was that his timing was a little off and he kneed me in the mouth and knocked out my two front teeth."[18]

The Rocky Mountain area was scenic, but it wasn't necessarily a moneymaker for wrestlers in 1947. On June 17 in Pueblo, Buddy made $17 for his bout with Charley (Red) McCarthy, and only $15 in Greeley on June 20.[19] For the Londos match, and a show that 3,000 fans turned out for, Buddy collected but $125. His largest payday in the territory was only $10 more, on May 26, for a draw against Dave Levin in Denver.[20] By the middle of July, Jack Pfefer had moved his workers into the Tulsa region for promoter Sam Avey and the transition was going to prove historically valuable to Rogers in more ways than one. At the time, Pfefer was advertising Levin as the world heavyweight champion, of course, exclusive to his group. Before leaving New York, he hired a local company to create a new wrestling belt, which Levin used to represent his title.[21] Once the group was in Tulsa, Levin's championship was front and center, and Buddy was recognized as the number-one contender.[22]

The Tulsa press loved Buddy right off the bat. The *Tulsa Daily World* stated that he looked "like a combination of Atlas and Hercules," and promoter Sam Avey "said Rogers was as fine looking an athlete as he ever saw."[23] Carrying a good bit of momentum, he challenged Levin at the Tulsa Coliseum on July 21, 1947, and prevailed in three falls, winning his first world heavyweight championship. Three-falls were staged in around 30-minutes of a clean bout, and Buddy won the second and third to capture the title. The moment was personally significant, and in his post-match exuberance, Rogers danced around the ring, hugged and kissed the referee, Jack League, as well as "playfully" shaking a radio announcer and police officer. Tulsa athletic commissioner C.C. McCrary also got a hug after presenting Buddy with the gold belt.[24] At 26-years-of-age, with five years of pro experience, Rogers was finally a claimant to the "world heavyweight title."

Wrestling in Tulsa was covered in a unique fashion, and there was a greater emphasis placed on the personalities of the athletes and the pre-match build-up than in most other cities. It gave Buddy a chance to work on his promos, and although the written words in the newspaper were "delivered" much differently than what a TV interview would later accomplish, the task of hyping a specific match or talking about an opponent, was an important lesson. Prior to an August 1947 bout against the Blimp, Rogers assertively said: "Every day, I read in the papers that the Blimp weighs 640 pounds and that he's likely to step on your toe or sit on you and mash the daylights out of you. So what? No one made me take the match with the Blimp, and I don't care how much he weighs, how much he eats, whether he can do the rhumba, or how many wrestlers have worn themselves out trying to get him down. Don't worry about me. I can take care of myself."[25] On Aug. 4, Rogers beat the Blimp in two-of-three-falls before 4,500 fans.[26]

Overall, the "Atomic Blond" continued to wrestle clean, but occasionally resorted to fisticuffs and other unsportsmanlike tactics. There were instances when he was not the clear-cut hero and even booed for one of his in-ring actions. In terms of fan support, Tulsa already had an established local wrestling celebrity on a permanent basis, and that was Leroy McGuirk. He was a hometown product, a former NCAA champion, and the reigning NWA world junior king. Every wrestler who ventured into Tulsa had to contend with his overarching superiority, and it was obvious Sam Avey was angling for a feud between McGuirk and Rogers. The two wrestlers knew each other well from their matches in Texas, and big things were anticipated. However, Buddy started to take some heat, first from McGuirk, and then from Sterling (Dizzy) Davis, an eccentric roughneck from Houston.

McGuirk criticized Buddy's championship, saying that it might have been "a little on the synthetic side."[27] Davis made things personal and went right for the jugular. He called him a "pretender," said he couldn't wrestle, and declared: "When I get through with that egotistical bum, well, the fans won't want any more of him; not with McGuirk or anybody else."[28] In response, Rogers calmly replied: "I haven't been wrestling as long as Davis has, but in the few years I've been in the business, I've learned that matches are settled in the ring – not in the newspapers. If you want a quotation from me regarding the match Monday night, you can just say that I'll show up as usual."[29] Despite the platform to rail against his adversaries and engage in some competitive trash talking, he was resistant. In fact, Buddy was not known as a "talkative athlete," and one publication cited his belief in "letting his actions in the ring speak for themselves."[30]

Rogers triumphed over McGuirk to exact some revenge on Aug. 25 in Tulsa, and also beat Davis on September 1.[31] The victory over McGuirk was particularly satisfying, but their war was far from over. On Sept. 8, 1947, McGuirk used brutal knee lifts to take the third fall from Rogers and win his claim to the world heavyweight title.[32] Two weeks later, on September 22, Buddy used his missed flying tackle gimmick at the finish of their contest in Tulsa, and he was carried to the locker room unconscious.[33] Rogers and McGuirk battled two additional times, and the latter won both matches, much to the delight of his Tulsa loyalists.[34] Local enthusiasts were privy to another engaging feud involving Rogers beginning November 24. That night, he faced Hollywood's Danny McShain for the first time, and beat the rugged warrior "in one of the goriest struggles ever seen on the Coliseum mat."[35]

McShain, a nine-time NWA world light heavyweight champion, was, according to a rival, "the roughest guy in the game," and violence was always heightened during his matches.[36] They fought again a week later and it was more of the same. There was intense brawling, fighting amongst the crowd, and bloodshed. McShain, in the midst of the fray, got his neck caught in-between the top and second ropes, allowing Rogers to freely pummel him as he was choked by the pressure. The two foes traded hectic falls until McShain scored the final to win the bout.[37] Aside from his notably vicious style, McShain was a tremendous showman, and worked as a fast-and-furious heel, as well as a crowd pleaser. He wore flashy robes prior to matches and his assorted mannerisms were both exciting and exasperating to fans. McShain's approach to wrestling was multifaceted and intelligent, and Rogers was highly influenced by his ring artistry.

Plotting his next big move, Jack Pfefer orchestrated a deal with Chicago wrestling majordomo Fred Kohler, and arranged to give Buddy more television exposure. But before the first show in the "Windy City," Pfefer went out of his way to bolster the gimmick surrounding his up-and-coming star, and demonstrated his own creativity at the same time.[38] An elaborate story was concocted giving Buddy an artificial background, focusing on a so-called world tour he participated in several years earlier. The trip was said to have taken him from London to the Orient, and included a stay in South Africa, where he went lion hunting with members of the Zulu Nation.[39] While traversing the globe, Rogers acquired a priceless artifact, simply branded "The Robe," an item that once belonged to Catherine the Great of Russia.[40] Pfefer hyped the robe as being worth a million dollars, complete with beautiful rhinestones, emeralds, and rubies.[41] In reality, the garment had little real value, and the story was all fabricated.

"The Robe" was actually first given to the Golden Angel (Jack Moore) by Pfefer a year earlier in the Rocky Mountain territory.[42] It was now Buddy's turn, so Pfefer sent advance publicity on Rogers and his invaluable robe to Fred Kohler in Chicago for his local program, *Wrestling As You Like It*.[43] Between Pfefer and Kohler's public relations agent, Dick Axman, the ballyhoo preceding Buddy was incredible. He was called "Gorgeous" Buddy Rogers, dubbed "the magnificent," and referred to as the "idol of the bobby soxers." The Chicago publication, in its October 23 issue, stated: "Ever since [wrestler] Gene Stanlee left for the West Coast, many of our lady fans have been looking for a new idol. Buddy Rogers will fill this bill. The Atomic Blond has the personality that made Frank Sinatra, Buddy Rogers of the old movie days, and Clark Gable, a hero with the ladies."[44]

With all of the hoopla in place, Buddy had a lot to live up to entering Chicago for his debut on Wednesday, Oct. 29, 1947, at the Rainbo Arena. Facing a familiar opponent, Dave Levin, he was victorious, and following the bout, Buddy was lauded by Chicago's wrestling press. "[Rogers] proved to be one of the most colorful wrestlers to have ever appeared here," a pundit for *Wrestling As You Like It* noted. "His gorgeous robes coupled with his body beautiful and his great ability in the ring gave everyone a thrill. Buddy Rogers has given the heavyweight division the color and dazzle that is needed at this time."[45] Attracting fans with his honorable wrestling methods, he didn't need a lot of time to become popular, and was a natural TV star.[46] Buddy wrestled Levin again a week later at the Rainbo, and the two competitors went 60 minutes to a draw.

The heavyweight championship picture changed in 1947 after four years with Bill Longson atop the National Wrestling Association ranks. Wild Bill was dethroned by the popular Whipper Billy Watson, who, in turn, was defeated for the belt by Lou Thesz. Rogers challenged Thesz at least eight times for the championship that year, losing seven of the contests and drawing once.[47] On November 7, Buddy was back at the Kiel Auditorium in St. Louis to face Longson, but their match didn't go as planned. An errant knee to the lower part of Buddy's face caused a deep wound, and because of the heavy blood, they closed out the match quicker than most normal main events – in 10-minutes and 35-seconds. Buddy was taken to Firmin Desloge Hospital and received 15 stitches in his chin.[48] A Chicago report described the injury a little differently, stating that 10 of the stitches were placed inside his mouth, and five were outside.[49]

Rogers was advised by physicians to take a rest from wrestling to allow his wound to heal.[50] He returned home to Camden and recuperated for 13 days, missing matches in Chicago, Louisville, and Cleveland.[51] On November 21, he reemerged from his hiatus in Buffalo and battled Dave Levin to a draw at the 11:00 curfew.[52] Over the next week, he put in nearly 2,600 miles on the road, first from Buffalo to Tulsa, then to Minneapolis and Cleveland. It was another 950 miles from Cleveland back to Tulsa, which capped, perhaps, his harshest travel schedule to date. Promoter Tom Packs booked the highly charged rematch between Buddy and new NWA world champion Bill Longson on December 5 at the Kiel Auditorium. Longson had dethroned Lou Thesz for the title on November 21 in Houston and was beginning his third reign. With the fans behind him, and a scar on his chin from their last encounter, Buddy was racing for the gold, and led most of the way.[53] A missed flying tackle did him in, and Longson retained with a pin.[54]

In January 1948, Buddy reconnected with his old friend, Billy Darnell. Since getting out of the Army in late 1946 and joining the Toots Mondt circuit in 1947, Darnell was a much-improved grappler. He'd more recently worked in Ohio and Missouri, and turned his sights to the Northeastern region after the first of the year. It wasn't long before Darnell also took Jack Pfefer as his manager. In fact, by the middle of January, Pfefer was already making inquiries about the possibility of Darnell, Rogers and Dave Levin touring Australia.[55] His contact in that area was Ted Thye, a former wrestling champion from the Pacific Northwest.[56] Thye expressed an interest in Rogers and Levin, but was open to other athletic grapplers, as well.[57] Pfefer was predictably protective of his wrestlers and wanted to know what other performers were going to be on the tour. "I hate to see my boys in the dressing room with some Bolsheviks or drunks," he told Thye by letter. "[It's a] bad atmosphere and is bad for the business."[58]

The trip to Australia never materialized and there could have been a dozen or so reasons why it failed to happen, all of them having to do with Pfefer's peculiar micromanagement style. However, his decision to bring Darnell into the troupe was brilliant and started to pay off almost immediately. Dedicated fans knew Darnell well. They remembered him from even before the war, and those enthusiasts with a good memory recalled that he was nearly always acknowledged as Buddy's younger brother.[59] But now, in 1948, Rogers (wrestling again as Dutch Rohde) and Darnell were the perfect ring rivals, and Pfefer wanted to eradicate any claims that they were siblings. The *Long Branch Daily Record* proclaimed: "Billy and Dutch are no strangers, since the mistaken conclusions have been voiced in print that they are brothers, but actually they are only old teammates who have separated to come together in opposite corners."[60]

It was revisionist pro wrestling at its very best, and who was going to challenge the word of promoters? Well, there was one man with the gall and motivation to call out the shenanigans of wrestling when he saw something crooked. That was Dan Parker, an influential sportswriter from New York City. Parker had been detailing wrestling's tomfoolery since the early 1930s, and at one point, was responsible for releasing insider secrets that nearly destroyed the business in New York. And throughout it all, his most important source for such knowledge was Jack Pfefer. In Parker's Jan. 12, 1948, column, he asserted that Buddy and Darnell were indeed brothers, and mentioned they were wrestling that night in the Bronx.[61] That declaration went directly against Pfefer's ploy, and it's unclear why Parker was doing it.

Five days later, the sportswriter struck again, writing: "Will Dutch Rhode (sic) continue to hit the road, wrestling his brother, Billy Darnell, every second Tuesday, rather than return to Camden and face the challenge of his fellow townsman, Joe Montana, who would like to meet him in the first shooting match of Dutch's career."[62] Parker bringing the 40-year-old Montana into the picture was an interesting development, and may have been prompted by Rudy Dusek in an effort to discredit Rogers on his home turf. Montana had wrestled out of Camden for years, but rarely weighed over 200 pounds, and because of his size, was limited in terms of success. In a shoot versus Rogers, he undoubtedly would have had the upper hand based on his superior skill, but that kind of match would never have happened on Pfefer's watch.

Officially, the Rogers-Darnell feud kicked off on Jan. 12, 1948, at the Winter Garden in the Bronx, and over the next five months, they wrestled 21-times in the northeast territory.[63] Considering the fact that Buddy trained Darnell and the latter patterned much of his in-ring style after his Camden pal, their matches were remarkably competitive because of just how well they knew each other. They added an additional layer of substance to their bouts by working out diverse finishes, trying to tell each "story" a little differently from the last. In truth, their matches were like public training sessions, as they could experiment with different moves and scenarios against a trusted ally without any kind of hesitation. They benefited from each contest, and as history would later confirm, their marathon feud was just beginning.

Rogers also went to war with one of Pfefer's largest monstrosities, the Super Swedish Angel. Standing 6-foot-3 and weighing more than 350 pounds, this version of the Angel gimmick was portrayed by Tor Johnson, a hulking bald behemoth.[64] For Buddy, matches against a large opponent were booked differently than his bouts with Darnell or Dave Levin, and required a harsher sense of violence rather than an emphasis on athleticism. Of the 18 matches Buddy had with the Angel between February and April 1948, at least six of them ended in near riots.[65] Their matches were extreme brawls with bloodshed, the use of chairs, and a variety of knockout-collision finishes. On March 26 in Reading, Buddy picked up his massive foe and threw him onto the referee, sending both men to the mat. As the referee tried to regain his composure, Rogers had the Angel pinned four separate times, but there was no official to make the count. Finally, the ref returned to his feet, and DQ'd the popular Rogers, giving the Angel the victory.[66]

In a rematch on April 9, fans were turned onto their heads when Rogers became entangled in the top two ropes, and was being choked by the neck in a hanging-type situation.[67] It was the same technique Danny McShain had used so effectively in Tulsa several months before, and Buddy extracted similar results. The neck-caught-in-the-ropes routine was immensely dangerous, but when successfully pulled off, it generated an intense level of heat amongst the crowd, which approached all-out pandemonium. Rogers decided to apply the gimmick again at the Jamaica Arena on April 23 versus Darnell, and his efforts were incredibly real. Observers felt he was turning purple while being strangled by the ropes, and officials were enraged by the stunning turn of events.[68]

Rogers was blamed for attempting to incite a riot. New York State athletic commissioner John M. Christensen issued a report of the wild affair during a meeting of the commission on April 30. Based on his recommendation, Rogers was indefinitely suspended "for acts considered detrimental to the best interests of wrestling."[69] In 1981, Buddy spoke with Jim Barniak for an episode of *Sports Scrapbook* on the Philadelphia-based cable network, PRISM. He recalled being suspended by the New York commission, but explained that it was due to his actions following a bout with Primo Carnera at St. Nicholas Arena. "Right after they raised my hand," he said, "I was going out of the ring, and [Primo] was up on one knee, and I just went over and shoved him off his knee back down onto the mat."[70] Maybe Buddy wasn't told that his suspension wasn't for the Carnera bout on April 27, but instead for his previous contest with Darnell. Nonetheless, the Primo match was his last in New York for the foreseeable future.

The Pfefer road show departed the East Coast toward the end of May 1948 and "Dutch" was back to using his full "Atomic Blond" Buddy Rogers moniker. On May 26, he made his debut in Columbus, Ohio, for veteran promoter Al Haft, and beat Darnell. Haft was a longtime ally of Pfefer's and an important figure in wrestling politics. He was also a good judge of talent. Getting support from Haft went a long way in the industry, and from initial good impressions, there seemed to be a place for Rogers in Columbus down the road. In the meantime, Rogers and Darnell continued to awe fans in cities like Memphis, Cincinnati, and Tulsa. On May 31, at the Tulsa Coliseum, Buddy pulled out one of his best known tricks, a sly move he would use throughout his career. He began the match by charging Darnell right at the bell, landing several dropkicks, and then tossing Billy out of the ring. Darnell didn't waste any time. He jumped right back onto the mat, snagged Rogers in an airplane spin, and pinned him in about a minute's time.

Darnell was the aggressor in the early part of the second fall as Rogers still appeared to be dizzy from the airplane spin. Landing a perfectly executed shoulder block off the ropes, Darnell went for a pin, and at the count of two, Buddy reached around and tapped his back. Darnell, thinking he was notified by the referee that he had won the match, released his hold and stood up. Rogers bounded upwards, locked in a giant swing, and put Darnell down for the count. This pat on the back trick created unfaltering excitement, either pro or anti-Rogers, depending on the mood of the crowd, and usually led to a Buddy triumph. The earliest recorded instance of Buddy utilizing the ruse was in 1944; actually the filmed bout against Tom Mahoney in Trenton, which is available on YouTube.[71] Additionally, he used it a few times in Camden against Tony Martinelli, Gino Garibaldi, and Emil Dusek in late 1944 and into 1945.[72]

On May 21, 1948, in St. Louis, Buddy challenged Bill Longson for the NWA world heavyweight championship, and pulled out all stops. He missed a flying tackle, got his neck tangled in the ropes, and "almost hung himself to death," as noted by sportswriter Harry Mitauer of the *St. Louis Globe-Democrat*. He was counted out by referee Charles Schwartz and the champion retained his NWA belt.[73] At the Louisville Armory on June 1, the maneuver was applied again, and Buddy, "limp from lack of air," was carried to the locker room and unable to continue versus Lou Thesz.[74] In both instances, the audiences reacted vociferously as they had been hoping to see Buddy emerge victorious. Promoters wisely booked rematches in both towns and played the drama for all that it was worth.

Rogers returned to the Houston territory on June 18 and didn't miss an opportunity to spend time on the beach in Galveston. As Buddy's skin darkened from the sun, Jack Pfefer told him about their next big gambit. They were headed for Hollywood, California, where Buddy was going to alter his persona from top to bottom. He was going to inhabit a fresh new gimmick and his world was going to change forever.

ENDNOTES - CHAPTER 5

[1] Wrestling on TV debuted on Wednesday nights on WBKB in July 1946 from the Rainbo Arena in Chicago, and was hosted by Russ Davis. The New York show was presented from the Jamaica Arena in Queens on Friday nights, broadcast on WABD. That show was hosted by Dennis James and launched around October 1946.

[2] *Sports Pictorial Review*, Jan. 6, 1947, p. 2.

[3] Sexton dethroned Casey in Boston on June 27, 1945.

[4] *Washington Evening Star*, Jan. 23, 1947, p. C2.

[5] For his work, Rogers earned $149, which was his largest payoff of the year so far. Jack Pfefer Financial Records, Jack Pfefer Collection, Joyce Sports Research Collection, Hesburgh Library, University of Notre Dame, Notre Dame, Indiana.

[6] Buddy Rogers Interview by Bill Apter, *Apter Chat*, Part One, 1979, youtube.com.

[7] Rogers told writer Ray Tennenbaum in 1985 that when wrestling on TV first started, "all" of the wrestlers were against it because of their fear it would hurt their income. "We all thought that people would not come to the arena to watch the matches when they could get it for free at home," Rogers explained. Buddy Rogers Interview by Ray Tennenbaum, February 1985.

[8] Rogers was consistently billed as Herman (Dusty) Rhodes in Baltimore.

[9] *Baltimore Sun*, March 12, 1947, p. 16. Rogers made $200 for this match. Jack Pfefer Financial Records, Jack Pfefer Collection, Joyce Sports Research Collection, Hesburgh Library, University of Notre Dame, Notre Dame, Indiana.

[10] *Fort Lauderdale News*, April 29, 1947, p. 10.

[11] *Baltimore Sun*, April 29, 1947, p. 21.

[12] The match lasted 10-minutes. *Baltimore Sun*, April 30, 1947, p. 16. It would not be surprising to learn that Rogers helped train Galento to some degree prior to his debut match.

[13] Jack Pfefer Financial Records, Jack Pfefer Collection, Joyce Sports Research Collection, Hesburgh Library, University of Notre Dame, Notre Dame, Indiana. Financial records for Buddy Rogers are not available prior to September 1946. There is a good possibility that this match with Galento earned him the largest payoff of his career.

[14] *Philadelphia Daily News*, May 1, 1947, *Long Island Daily Press*, May 2, 1947, *Trenton Evening Times*, May 6, 1947, p. 15.

[15] Bobby Stewart wrestled as "Robert Ashby."

[16] Pfefer didn't head for Denver until May 24, 1947. Jack Pfefer Financial Records, Jack Pfefer Collection, Joyce Sports Research Collection, Hesburgh Library, University of Notre Dame, Notre Dame, Indiana. Ben Morgan soon joined the Pfefer troupe and worked as the "Volga Boatman."

[17] According to the newspaper report, Buddy knocked himself out after going through the ropes "attempting a 'body slam.'" *Denver Post*, June 24, 1947, p. 32. However, this might have been another missed flying tackle finish.

[18] *Buddie Rogers and The Art of "Sequencing"* by Max W. Jacobs, p. 9-10.

[19] The Greeley bout was also against Charley "Red" McCarthy.

[20] Jack Pfefer Financial Records, Jack Pfefer Collection, Joyce Sports Research Collection, Hesburgh Library, University of Notre Dame, Notre Dame, Indiana.

[21] Pfefer paid $100 for the new belt. Jack Pfefer 1947 Expense Book, Jack Pfefer Collection, Joyce Sports Research Collection, Hesburgh Library, University of Notre Dame, Notre Dame, Indiana.

[22] Levin was acknowledged as the World champion during his tour of the Rocky Mountain region, and even lost his claim to Volga Boatman. In Tulsa, it was said that Levin "acquired his handsome belt and title claim in the spring of 1944 with a conquest of big Orville Brown." *Tulsa Daily World*, July 20, 1947, p. 22. Rogers was billed as the Texas Junior Heavyweight champion when he arrived in Tulsa. *Tulsa Sunday World*, July 13, 1947, p. 22. A New York publication also reported that Buddy had been a light heavyweight champion in Texas "several years ago," but said that he had outgrown the division. *Sports Pictorial Review*, March 15, 1948, p. 1. No records of Buddy holding a non-heavyweight title in Texas have been found.

[23] *Tulsa Daily World*, July 15, 1947, p. 12.

[24] *Tulsa Daily World*, July 22, 1947, p. 12.

[25] *Tulsa Daily World*, Aug. 4, 1947, p. 7.

[26] Rogers used "football tactics" to win the third fall. *Tulsa Daily World*, Aug. 5, 1947, p. 12.

[27] *Tulsa Daily World*, Aug. 24, 1947, p. 22.

[28] *Tulsa Daily World*, Aug. 31, 1947, p. 20.

[29] *Tulsa Daily World*, Sept. 1, 1947, p. 11.

[30] *Wrestling As You Like It*, Dec. 4, 1947, p. 1.

[31] *Tulsa Daily World*, Aug. 26, 1947, p. 12 and Sept. 2, 1947, p. 14.

[32] Rogers weighed 20-pounds more than McGuirk, 215 to 195. The World Title belt was not given to McGuirk in the ring. *Tulsa Daily World*, Sept. 9, 1947, p. 14. It appears that McGuirk was later given the "MWA" Title belt. *Tulsa Daily World*, Oct. 7, 1947, p. 12. His September 8 loss was in the midst of a six-match losing streak that extended from September 2 in Little Rock to September 10 in St. Louis.

33 *Tulsa Daily World*, Sept. 23, 1947, p. 14.

34 It should be noted that after this tour, Rogers never had another match against McGuirk or Dizzy Davis again.

35 *Tulsa Daily World*, Nov. 25, 1947, p. 12.

36 *Los Angeles Times*, Feb. 17, 1947, p. 11.

37 *Tulsa Daily World*, Dec. 2, 1947, p. 18.

38 A sports reporter called Pfefer, ""an elfin dude, with a gravel voice and an unshackled imagination." *New York World-Telegram and Sun*, March 15, 1950.

39 Rogers was quoted about his purported time lion hunting in South Africa. *Buffalo Evening News*, Nov. 26, 1947, p. 22.

40 Ibid.

41 "The Robe" was predominantly red in color. *Wrestling As You Like It*, Oct. 16, 1947, p. 3. Around the same time, Buddy wore another robe that was "gleaming carnelian (orange colored) … trimmed in gold braid." *Buffalo Evening News*, Nov. 22, 1947, p. 5.

42 *Salt Lake Tribune*, Oct. 6, 1946, p. 22.

43 *Wrestling As You Like It*, Oct. 16, 1947, p. 3. A similar story was printed in *Buffalo Sports Magazine*, Nov. 21, 1947, p. 4.

44 Buddy was also called the "Fashion Plate of the Wrestling Ring." *Wrestling As You Like It*, Oct. 23, 1947, p. 1, 3.

45 *Wrestling As You Like It*, Oct. 30, 1947, p. 2. Buddy was billed as being from Houston, Texas. *Wrestling As You Like It*, Nov. 27, 1947, p. 2. Between October 29 and Nov. 4, 1947, Buddy made his debut in Chicago, Cleveland, Buffalo, and Minneapolis.

46 The host for the Rainbo telecast was Wayne Griffin, a well-established Chicago sportsman on WBKB. Griffin and Rogers became good friends, and Buddy later told *TV Guide* that the commentator gave him much needed advice at a personally depressive juncture in his career. "I was ready to quit [the sport] when Wayne showed me what an asset television was for wrestling and for me," Buddy explained. "Wayne Griffin is the greatest announcer and the nicest person that you would want to meet." *TV Guide*, Nov. 13, 1953. The timing of this incident is not known. In later interviews, Buddy would often mention that he received the "first 13 week segment" at the Rainbo Arena in Chicago. Buddy Rogers Interview by Bill Apter, *Apter Chat*, Part One, 1979, youtube.com. He would also make the claim that he was the "first performer in the history of TV." Ibid, Buddy Rogers Interview by Ray Tennenbaum, February 1985. In a separate interview, Rogers said he was involved in the first telecast out of Rainbo Arena in Chicago. *Philadelphia Daily News*, June 20, 1967.

47 The draw occurred on Sept. 29, 1947 in Memphis and set up a rematch on October 20, which Thesz won.

48 *Sports Pointers*, Dec. 5, 1947, p. 1. The *St. Louis Star and Times* initially called it a "lower lip" injury. *St. Louis Star and Times*, Nov. 8, 1947, p. 13. Publications during the 1950s, mentioned Buddy's injury, and said he needed anywhere from 14 to 39 stitches.

49 *Wrestling As You Like It*, Nov. 13, 1947, p. 3.

50 In his personal financial book, Jack Pfefer wrote that Buddy was "Hurt" in his match against Longson. Buddy made $430 on the night, his largest payday since July 1947, and his third largest payoff of the year. Jack Pfefer Financial Records, Jack Pfefer Collection, Joyce Sports Research Collection, Hesburgh Library, University of Notre Dame, Notre Dame, Indiana.

51 The Louisville match was against Lou Thesz, originally set for Nov. 11, 1947. *Louisville Courier-Journal*, Nov. 10, 1947, p. 11.

52 Rogers was called a "four-star show-stopper." His match with Levin lasted 23:03. *Buffalo Evening News*, Nov. 22, 1947, p. 5.

53 Buddy's scar was mentioned in *Sports Pointers*, Dec. 5, 1947 and the *St. Louis Star and Times*, Dec. 20, 1947, p. 12.

[54] The show drew 8,581 spectators. *St. Louis Globe-Democrat*, Dec. 6, 1947, p. 18. Rogers made $464.50 for the match. Jack Pfefer Financial Records, Jack Pfefer Collection, Joyce Sports Research Collection, Hesburgh Library, University of Notre Dame, Notre Dame, Indiana. Typically, Buddy's biggest paydays from this time-frame were in St. Louis.

[55] Talk of Buddy making a tour of Australia and New Zealand in 1948 appeared in *Sports Pictorial Review*, March 15, 1948, p. 1 and *The Ring*, November 1947, p. 28-29.

[56] Letter from Jack Pfefer to Ted Thye, dated Jan. 14, 1948, Jack Pfefer Collection, Joyce Sports Research Collection, Hesburgh Library, University of Notre Dame, Notre Dame, Indiana.

[57] Letters from Ted Thye to Jack Pfefer, dated Jan. 9, 1948 and Jan. 26, 1948. Jack Pfefer Collection, Joyce Sports Research Collection, Hesburgh Library, University of Notre Dame, Notre Dame, Indiana.

[58] Letter from Jack Pfefer to Ted Thye, dated Jan. 14, 1948, Jack Pfefer Collection, Joyce Sports Research Collection, Hesburgh Library, University of Notre Dame, Notre Dame, Indiana.

[59] In a couple territories during 1947, Darnell worked as "Billy Rogers," and was again billed as Buddy's brother.

[60] *Long Branch Daily Record*, Feb. 14, 1948, p. 7. In Toots Mondt's home program, *Sports Pictorial Review*, it said: "Billy Darnell and 'Dutch' Rohde are definitely not half-brothers, nor are they related to each other. Billy Darnell hails from Camden, NJ, the same town as Rohde, which probably explains some of the rumors you heard." *Sports Pictorial Review*, April 5, 1948, p. 4.

[61] Parker's column was called, "The Broadway Bugle." *Montreal Gazette*, Jan. 12, 1948, p. 17. Parker was syndicated from New York into Montreal and also Camden, NJ.

[62] *Montreal Gazette*, Jan. 17, 1948, p. 7.

[63] The first public face-off between Rogers and Darnell actually occurred during a benefit show in Camden on Dec. 14, 1944 at the Convention Hall. The two athletes wrestled a 15-minute exhibition. *Camden Morning Post*, Dec. 15, 1944, p. 40. Of the 21-matches they had the northeast, Buddy won 16 of them, drew four times, and lost once (4/23/48 at the Jamaica Arena).

[64] Pfefer said that Johnson was "sure much better and bigger than all the other Angels combined." Letter from Jack Pfefer to Ted Thye, dated Jan. 14, 1948, Jack Pfefer Collection, Joyce Sports Research Collection, Hesburgh Library, University of Notre Dame, Notre Dame, Indiana.

[65] In Pfefer's records, he listed the February 25, March 26, April 7, April 9, April 14, and April 21 matches as having started riots. Jack Pfefer Collection, Joyce Sports Research Collection, Hesburgh Library, University of Notre Dame, Notre Dame, Indiana.

[66] *Pottsville Republican*, April 7, 1948, p. 17.

[67] *Pottsville Republican*, May 5, 1948, p. 17.

[68] *New York World-Telegram and Sun*, March 15, 1950.

[69] His suspension was effective April 28, 1948. New York State Athletic Commission Meeting Minutes, April 30, 1948, p. 2. On his entry for April 23, 1948, Pfefer wrote the word, "Suspended" next to Buddy's match with Darnell. Jack Pfefer Collection, Joyce Sports Research Collection, Hesburgh Library, University of Notre Dame, Notre Dame, Indiana. Buddy had been booked for a rematch against Darnell at Jamaica Arena for April 30, but that match was cancelled due to his suspension.

[70] Buddy Rogers Interview, *Jim Barniak's Sports Scrapbook*, Dec. 2, 1981, PRISM Network, youtube.com. Buddy wrestled Primo at St. Nicholas Arena on April 27, 1948 and they went to a draw.

[71] The match occurred on March 23, 1944.

[72] The dates were Oct. 2, 1944, Jan. 1, 1945, and April 2, 1945, respectively.

[73] *St. Louis Globe-Democrat*, May 22, 1948, p. 18.

[74] Thesz was billed as "Don Luis Thesz" in Louisville. *Louisville Courier-Journal*, June 2, 1948, p. 20.

Chapter 6
Wrestling's Nature Boy

With the exception of a few cities in North America, there was an industry-wide collapse during the late 1930s. The popularity of pro wrestling dropped significantly and financial numbers were abysmal. New York, Chicago, and Los Angeles, the three most populated areas in the United States, were equally decimated by the downturn, and promoters struggled to survive in spite of weak attendance. Cal Eaton of Los Angeles was one of those promoters. He was the man in charge of the Olympic Auditorium, which for years had been the top wrestling venue on the West Coast. Eaton was known for his business smarts, but he wasn't an influential powerbroker behind-the-scenes. He relied on a central booking agent to control talent and arrange matches. In previous years, matchmakers Joe (Toots) Mondt and then Nick Lutze endeavored to rebuild the territory, but bad decisions and public apathy hindered their success. By 1946, though, there was a new man in charge, and in many respects, John James Doyle was the visionary Los Angeles needed.

The 37-year-old Doyle spent his younger years as an assistant promoter in several eastern cities before landing in Los Angeles and ultimately assuming control of the local office.[1] He was faced with repairing years of inconsistent booking and went to work implementing a fresh strategy that improved the box office in a matter of months. Without question, his biggest move was the hasty push of Enrique Torres, an agile, former amateur grappler who immediately captured the hearts and minds of regional fans. Torres, billed as being from Sonora, Mexico, was still a rookie when he ascended to headliner status, and what he lacked in experience, he made up for in athleticism. On Dec. 11, 1946, he beat George Becker for the California-based world heavyweight championship, and his supporters couldn't have been happier. Doyle was equally happy with the positive response, but he knew that to properly balance his promotion, he also needed a noteworthy and capable villain.

From stage-left marched George Wagner, better known in many parts of the country as "Gorgeous George." Sporting curly locks, an exaggerated pre-match routine, and a highfalutin' valet, George was much different when he arrived in Los Angeles in November 1947 compared to just a few years earlier. Knowledgeable enthusiasts likely recognized George from his stint in the area in 1944-'45, but he was no longer the straight-laced battler they once enjoyed.[2] He was now the living embodiment of the character, Gorgeous George, the profession's greatest gimmick to date, and an original wrestling novelty act. For casual fans, he was a treasure, and his dramatized performance began the moment he stepped out from behind the curtain.

The pomp and circumstance and the fanciful performance were provoking and heralded at the same time, and George's striking customs only added to the amazing success Los Angeles was achieving.[3]

The arrival of television and a weekly telecast from the Olympic on KTLA in May 1947 served to magnify the interest in George, turning him into a must-see attraction across all socioeconomic levels.[4] And to the concern that TV would hurt the box office, people wanted to see George's incredible showmanship in person and live gates boomed. The coffers of Cal Eaton and Johnny Doyle were well stocked, and the Los Angeles territory as a whole, from Bakersfield in the north to San Diego in the south, was primed for huge business. The growth had a sizable impact on Hollywood promoter Hugh Nichols, who ran a non-heavyweight circuit from his office at the Legion Stadium. Nichols was an adversary to the Eaton-Doyle combine, and somewhat of an underdog in the promotional game. With smaller, and sometimes more entertaining grapplers, he never failed to put on a good show, but his operations were dwarfed by the productions and bankroll of his cross-town rivals.

Nichols, a hardened ring warrior originally trained by the celebrated Farmer Burns, had been putting bodies in seats at the Legion Stadium since 1939.[5] He wasn't one to back down from a fight, and he wasn't going to cave to the increasing pressure stacking up against him. Throughout this period of time, Jack Pfefer kept in close contact with Nichols, his longtime friend, and wanted to know the happenings in Southern California. He had always been at odds with the larger syndicates, and if there was an ongoing wrestling war, he typically wanted to be involved. Not surprisingly, Pfefer was unimpressed by Gorgeous George. In fact, he wanted to help Nichols and supplant the "Gorgeous One" with none other than Buddy Rogers. Pfefer told Nichols by letter on June 9, 1948, "To make the Gorgeous Guy look like a lemon, and you can be sure after the first showing of the 'Nature Boy' Buddy Rogers, they will think nothing more but of Rogers,"[6]

Putting the nickname, "Nature Boy" aside for a moment, the date of this letter illustrated Pfefer's forethought in not only entering the Los Angeles territory, but of completely rebranding Rogers. "For the first appearance of Rogers," Pfefer continued, "get an accordion player who shall play the song 'Nature Boy' when Rogers [comes] out from the dressing room."[7] In addition, he requested that Nichols line up two "beautiful models" to accompany Buddy to the ring, and to dress them up in Amazonian costumes, recommending that the promoter rent the outfits from a store in Hollywood. He touted Buddy's "exquisite and expensive" capes, and stated: "Please listen to my suggestions, and I am sure you will have many sell-outs in the near future."[8] Pfefer had it all figured out and was going to market Rogers in direct competition with Gorgeous George. For Buddy's debut in Hollywood on June 28, Pfefer wanted the spectacle played out exactly like he envisioned it in his head.

"Nature Boy" was the title of Nat King Cole's newest jazz hit, which was reigning at number one on *Billboard's* popularity charts. Written by Eden Ahbez and released on March 29, 1948, the song was "haunting, rich and compelling," as one pundit described it, and the album sold more than a million copies.[9] Pfefer felt the general ambiance surrounding the tune, combined with Buddy's handsome features, well-built frame, and exceedingly dark tan, was a perfect fit. Rogers had faith in Pfefer's creative powers and agreed with him, thus, the "Nature Boy" moniker was born. On June 25, 1948, Buddy closed out his final date in Houston, losing to Primo Carnera, and ventured to California to make preparations for his Hollywood debut. And, in accordance with Pfefer's vision, Rogers was repackaged from head to toe.

Three nights later, on June 28, the new and improved "Nature Boy" Buddy Rogers debuted at the Hollywood Legion Stadium to much fanfare. The match was over in a flash, and spectators were awed with the wrestling skill of the victor. In just 90 seconds, Rogers steamrolled over Frank Gonzales, finishing off his opponent with a bodyslam.[10] But they were even more struck by his grandeur. For his walk down the aisle to the ring, Buddy wore an extravagant cape, "stunningly designed with all sorts of stones and colors."[11] Lifting his head toward the rafters with an air of conceit, his eyes closed and he expanded the large cape across his back in impressive fashion, displaying its full beauty. Underneath the cape, Buddy wore a form-fitting one-strap bodysuit-type top, also remarkably decorated with colorful sleeves on both arms.[12]

Prior to the bell, he unfastened his cape, and the Amazonian-clad model Pfefer hired carefully removed it from his person, and folded it neatly.[13] Buddy then unzipped his bodysuit top on one side, removed the strap from his shoulder, and slowly peeled it down his legs. When the bejeweled gear was off, he was back in his customary wrestling trunks and ready to fight. From time-to-time, he still wore "The Robe," and publicists continued to hype its so-called grand heritage.[14] The elaborate pre-match entrance was especially tailored to contrast the efforts of Gorgeous George, and Buddy worked the crowd with every step he took. In some cities, Pfefer was able to add to the pageantry by having a venue's lights turned completely off and a single spotlight focused on Rogers as he strolled to the ring.[15] In total, his ring entrance could last up to 10 minutes, and Buddy used every second of it to whip onlookers into a fury.

There was another aspect to Buddy's gimmick. As he reveled in his flamboyance and self confidence, looking down his nose at the crowd, his female companion would tend to his every need. She was there to apply cold cream to his face between falls, and give him deodorant for his armpits.[16] When the moment called for it, she used a "cologne-filled atomizer" to purify the ring area, similar to what Gorgeous George's valet did.[17] Wearing tattered clothing, the model acted just like Buddy's slave, and would become known as, simply, the "Slave Girl."[18] Interestingly, the original Slave Girl was a tallish, dark-haired woman, who appeared for a series of promotional photos alongside Rogers. In one of the shots, she was holding his luxurious cape, and in another, she was applying cream to his face as Buddy stared into a mirror. These pictures were professionally done and paid for by Pfefer for promotional advertisements in newspapers and programs.[19] Unfortunately, the name of the original Slave Girl has been lost to history.

The introduction of a slave girl, as opposed to a male valet, was a stark difference between Rogers and Gorgeous George. However, as soon as Buddy started visiting a hair salon as part of his shtick, it was clear that he was stealing George's material. He was photographed getting his hair done and nails filed, and in July 1948, a California sportswriter referred to him as the "Perfumed, well-decked-out, walking beauty shop."[20] It was unmistakable, and an intense personal feud was started because of it. Depending on the publication, and which side of the war had better press contacts, Buddy was either a full-blown copycat or doing the "Gorgeous George act" better than George was. The *San Diego Union*, a newspaper in a Hugh Nichols-run town, stated: "Buddy Rogers popped up with a routine that probably left Gorgeous George spluttering with envy."[21] Bleaching his hair blond, and even growing it a tad longer, he pulled out all the stops, and Pfefer loved every minute of it.

The "Nature Boy" nickname caught on just as Pfefer had hoped. A couple years later, in 1950, Buddy was asked how the handle was developed, and he told New York reporter Lester Bromberg it was essentially by accident. He claimed that after the Hollywood Legion Stadium crowd saw him take off his robe, they naturally started calling him "Nature Boy."[22] It made for a good story, and Buddy reiterated this version in interviews long after his retirement.[23] But, as Pfefer's June 9, 1948, letter to Nichols illustrated, he had the "Nature Boy" nickname figured out weeks before Buddy's Hollywood debut. Rogers was also acknowledged as the "Nature Boy" in the newspaper prior to the show, making any spontaneous reaction to his distinct appearance impossible.[24] Pfefer was the mastermind behind the idea, and no amount of revisionism can change that fact.

Taking on the new gimmick forced Rogers to change his appearance, the manner in which he dealt with fans, and his style in the ring.[25] For years, he'd cultivated the favor of enthusiasts with his clean-cut methods and sportsmanlike approach. But the "Nature Boy" was anything but honorable. He was a bone-bending, arrogant heel, and it was finally time to utilize the repertoire of tricks he'd seen others use with great success. Wrestlers like Jim Austeri, Michele Leone, Angelo Savoldi, Don Evans, and even the Duseks were masterful proponents of the villainous arts. More recently, Bill Longson and Danny McShain gave him insightful knowledge on how to maximize the heat from rowdy audiences. Rogers was subscribing to both the over-the-top and the subtleties of being a wrestling desperado, which means he would overtly break the rules and work the crowd with small gestures, grimaces and sneers. He applied aggressiveness and underhanded tactics, all while actively telling a story with each match.

He still had a lot to learn and the challenge of being a full-blown heel was a test of his own abilities. He took careful note of which particular techniques worked better than others and strengthened his ring psychology. In terms of actual tactics, the customs of a wrestling evildoer were fairly standard — eye-gouging, punches, kicks, and hair-pulling. After being in the ropes and the referee calling for a clean break, Buddy was a relentless cheat, often delivering a swift knee to the stomach. At times, a simple slap to the face was enough to incite immense reaction amongst spectators. At other times, he'd force the reaction by engaging ringside fans. He wasn't above sticking out his tongue or motioning toward a member of the audience. Occasionally, when pushed to his limits, he'd spit at a ringside tormentor, but that was rare.[26]

Buddy's deliberate high-brow antics were enough to drive people through the roof. "The crowd went wild when Rogers, during the rest period between falls, stopped to put on face cream, deodorant, and sprayed himself with perfume," a reporter in Bakersfield noted on July 1, 1948.[27] One of his personal favorites was an exaggerated, staggered walk that seemed to grind fans right in their gut each and every time he performed the move. It was a strut, but unlike anything wrestling had seen before. In fact, it was the strut of all struts, and Buddy trademarked the maneuver right then and there. His simple, pretentious saunter was infuriating, and fans let him know just how hated he was. When asked why he was such a rough character, he answered: "I always want to win, and I'll do anything to accomplish that end."[28]

In selling the "Nature Boy" gimmick in Southern California, Jack Pfefer bestowed Rogers the "International Heavyweight championship," a fictional title the promoter invented. Buddy wore a belt, which was more than likely the same Pfefer-branded strap they had used in Tulsa the year before.[29] It soon morphed into a straight "world" title claim, and it was exclusive to Pfefer's crew.[30] The Southern California Pfefer circuit was usually a five-day work week, beginning with Hollywood on Mondays, followed by San Diego, Bakersfield, Santa Barbara, and Huntington Park. Pfefer added Saturday bookings in Visalia and Pomona, and mixed things up a bit with weekday shots in El Monte and Pismo Beach. Buddy resumed his feuds with Super Swedish Angel and Billy Darnell, and in September 1948 at Hollywood, he wrestled his first tag team match in more than a year when he partnered with Pierre LaSartes to beat Darnell and Frank Gonzales.[31]

By that time, Rogers was working with a new Slave Girl, and this one was more in tune with the happenings inside the squared circle. She was a blond professional wrestler named Helen Hild.[32] The 19-year-old was originally from Grand Island, Nebraska, and had attended high school in Omaha.[33] She was briefly married to wrestler Al Galento and faced off with the likes of June Byers and Nell Stewart. Christy Gregg, the sports editor of the *San Diego Union*, featured an interview with the "Slave Girl" on Sept. 5, 1948. Hild admitted her wrestling past, but refused to give her real name. She said she met Buddy in Columbus, Ohio, and he offered her a flat $200 a week to be his Slave Girl. When Gregg asked her if she was in love with Rogers, she replied: "No, he just sort of fascinates me."[34] With her background and level of physicality in the ring, Hild was more than a passive second. She was an active participant, and if a match called for her involvement, she was right there willing to slug it out.

Following a card in Pismo Beach on Sept. 21, 1948, Buddy became sick with a throat infection and missed six shows.[35] He returned the following week for two matches in Redondo Beach and Santa Barbara, but went out of action again on October 1. Trying his best to fight through it, he made five matches from October 5 and October 9, but his condition worsened. Two days later, he went into the hospital to have his tonsils removed.[36] The specifics of Buddy's health condition are unknown other than what was printed in the newspaper and a brief note in Jack Pfefer's personal date book. But there was obviously more to the story because, when Rogers filled out his physical questionnaire to join the Navy in 1938 and he was asked if his tonsils were out, he replied in the affirmative.[37] Nevertheless, a week after his operation, Buddy rejoined his mates on the circuit and beat Red Koko (Red Ryan) in Hollywood.

In various articles, it was mentioned that Buddy was a prime candidate to become a motion picture actor and was being scouted by directors.[38] While he was in Southern California, Cecil B. DeMille was filming his newest epic, *Samson and Delilah*, starring Hedy Lamarr and Victor Mature. The movie also featured two pro wrestlers, Mike Mazurki and Wee Willie Davis, and another, Kay Bell, was Mature's stand-in. Two years earlier, Buddy had dropped the Texas title to Bell, and at the very least, they were passing acquaintances in the locker room. It was rumored that Rogers appeared in *Samson and Delilah*, and, if true, he was more or less an uncredited extra.[39] Little more was ever spoken about it. Back in the San Diego ring on Oct. 26, 1948, Rogers was stripped of his world title by Billy Darnell in what was considered an upset.[40]

The politics of wrestling experienced a number of highs and lows in 1948, and one of the major news stories involved the organization of a new promoter's union based in the Midwest. The National Wrestling Alliance was founded during the summer by a handful of enterprising leaders hoping to shore up talent trading deals and the recognition of a single heavyweight champion. At about the same time, Tom Packs, a primary antagonist to the NWA, decided to retire and sell off his interests to a consortium led by Lou Thesz. For several years, Sam Muchnick had promoted in St. Louis as an independent, and he was consistently at a disadvantage against Packs. With Thesz now in charge of his opposition, nothing was expected to change, and the ongoing war continued.

Muchnick was a member of the new National Wrestling Alliance, and his outfit was actively searching for ways to expand. His partner in the organization, Orville Brown, a mainstay in the Kansas City territory for well over a decade, was the NWA's first and reigning world heavyweight champion and was committed to giving the Alliance credibility on a national scale. On Nov. 1, 1948, he accepted the challenge of Buddy Rogers in Hollywood and beat the "Nature Boy" with one fall in 60-minutes.[41] Brown's venture to the West Coast was somewhat abnormal, but it served a dual purpose. On one hand, he wanted to enlist the membership of Hugh Nichols, and on the other, he sought to recruit Rogers. Buddy had previously worked for the Packs syndicate and it was expected that he would wrestle for the Thesz group, as well.[42] But Jack Pfefer, who respected Brown and Muchnick, was prepared to shake things up, and he authorized Buddy's jump to the outlaw organization.[43]

It was a landmark move and Muchnick was exceptionally appreciative. Rogers finished up his West Coast commitments and spent $112 to fly to St. Louis for his match there on Nov. 26, 1948.[44] In advance of his showing, he splurged for a new outfit, a sprayer, cold cream, powder, and perfume, and then was ready to break ground locally as the "Nature Boy."[45] But St. Louis fans weren't expecting a revamped Buddy Rogers, and cheered him like normal at the Kiel Auditorium as he beat Jim Wright with a crab hold in 11:27. The *St. Louis Star and Times* affirmed that Buddy was the "favorite of the bobby soxers."[46] The attendance was 10,176 and it was the biggest crowd Muchnick had ever achieved. Personally, Buddy made his largest single paycheck in more than a year, earning $450 for the appearance, an amount that dwarfed most of his recent payoffs in California.[47]

During the next two shows in St. Louis, Rogers made it clear that he was the bad guy, shattering the image fans had of him. On Dec. 22, he took pleasure smashing the face of Bobby Bruns into the ring post, opening up a bloody cut, and pinned his foe soon thereafter.[48] Elsewhere in the territory, which extended through Missouri and into Kansas, Rogers was completely unhinged, eliciting the ire of spectators with his increasing violence and the entire "body beautiful" act. And in place of the Slave Girl, he was accompanied by a masked male valet, performed by Jack Pfefer's guy, Izzy Becker.[49] Regional sportswriters were impressed by his routine. He was called a "good entertainer" by a journalist in Kansas City and the *St. Joseph Gazette* flatly declared: "He is the most colorful wrestler ever to appear here."[50] The writer in St. Joseph added that Rogers was a "highly adept wrestler and, though unpopular, drew grudging admiration from the fans."[51]

That was an important fact that would follow him throughout his career. In spite of his aggression and cruel ring methods, Buddy was still able to build a base of true, die-hard supporters. Whether it was his appearance, his magnetism, or a combination of both, Rogers possessed an innate ability to connect with enthusiasts, and a love-hate relationship between the athlete and wrestling fans was already being formed in 1948. However, there were a lot of people who hated him with a passion, and in the Midwest, they made their voices heard during Buddy's feud with the ever-popular Orville Brown. On Dec. 17, in St. Joseph, the two battlers drew the largest house in the history of the City Auditorium with more than 6,500 in attendance, and rocked the building to its foundations. But toward the end, Rogers had Brown busted open, and he was eventually disqualified for hitting the title claimant with a cold-cream jar.[52]

The reaction of the crowd was ideal, and Rogers was overjoyed. He whipped up a letter to Pfefer telling him all about the exciting affair. "Jack, last nite in St. Joe, Orville made me the biggest killer in the town," Buddy exclaimed. "I villained over him all the way [and] he was bleeding all over the ring. I knocked him out and they carried him to the dressing room. They let me go crazy like [Everette] Marshall did with [Jim] Londos. I got disqualified after knocking out Orville – Izzy – the referees, newspaperman and the ring was full of people. We sure had a thriller."[53] The Rogers-Brown feud did good business in Wichita, as well, luring a record 5,500 to the Forum on Jan. 3, 1949. That night, they went 90-minutes to a draw in a match full of action. Right in the midst of things, when it appeared that Brown had the "Nature Boy" pinned for the count, Buddy worked his magic once again. He reached around and gave the NWA champion a nice tap on the back. Brown nonchalantly got up and the rest was history.[54]

People continued to compare Rogers with Gorgeous George, and there wasn't much being said publically in response from George's camp.[55] In October 1948, he made a rare, brief comment to a Tulare, California, newspaper, confirming that he thought Buddy was "stealing" his "stuff."[56] After hearing the news that Rogers was headed to St. Louis to wrestle for Sam Muchnick, George cancelled future bookings with the latter in reprisal. He considered Muchnick a good promoter and had promised not to work for the Thesz group in opposition, but he was now wavering. The bad blood toward Rogers was just too much. Muchnick understood and released George from his promise.[57] On Dec. 17, 1948, George headlined for Thesz at the Kiel Auditorium and drew 10,042 fans. He beat Larry Moquin in 8:50 and made a huge splash with spectators, especially when he was handing out his famous "Georgie pins."[58]

Rogers spent the holidays with his family in Camden and went right back to work after the first of the year.[59] Notably, he was going into his fourth year of matrimony to Ellen Rohde. His extensive travel made things difficult and it was impossible for the couple to enjoy a customary marriage. By this time, though, Ellen had made up her mind to become a professional wrestler herself. She later told a newspaper writer that she took up the sport because she was tired of seeing Buddy "come home covered with wrestling honors."[60] Taking on the stage name of "Ellen Olsen," she worked out with many of the top women grapplers in preparation for her debut. The 5-foot-5 former singer was embraced by booking agent Billy Wolfe, the man in charge of the female troupe, and the husband of world champion Mildred Burke. As a matter of ritual, Wolfe gave her a fabricated history, and claimed she was originally from Minneapolis.[61]

While Buddy was shuttling back-and-forth between dates in the Midwest and working the Southern California loop for Jack Pfefer in early 1949, Ellen joined the women's circuit wrestling alongside June Byers, Nell Stewart, Juanita Coffman, and other well-known stars. So, even with the couple in the same profession, they still were light-years away from each other. Incidentally, it was in 1949 that newspapers started referring to Ellen as the "former" wife of Rogers, and if that was any indicator, their marriage was surely on the rocks.[62] Buddy returned to the Kiel Auditorium in St. Louis on Feb. 4 and delivered Sam Muchnick his first ever sellout. Attendance was 10,651 with an estimated 3,000 turned away to see Rogers beat Don Eagle in 21:55. Eagle dominated much of the bout, but missed a dropkick at the finish, and Buddy achieved a pinfall.[63]

Back in Hollywood, Rogers defeated Sheik Lawrence on Feb. 28 to capture the Pfefer world heavyweight title.[64] A couple weeks later, he participated in two contests in Southern California before flying to St. Louis for a big rematch with Don Eagle on March 18. Billy Darnell was on the show, and he came out to the ring to challenge the winner of the Rogers-Eagle bout. Eagle responded kindly, shaking Billy's hand. In contrast, Rogers ignored him, prompting Darnell to attack. Buddy sailed from the ring, and when Darnell finished his assault, Rogers was bleeding from a forehead cut. It was then that his match with Eagle began. Their fight lasted just over 28 minutes and ended with a disqualification victory for the "Nature Boy" after Eagle tossed him over the top rope. This show at the Kiel was only a few hundred shy of a sellout, and Rogers earned $528.[65]

Speaking of Billy Darnell, Buddy and his chum were constant opponents and wrestled more than 30 times through the first six months of 1949. Considering their friendship and history, their matches were undoubtedly a walk in the park. After his St. Louis bout with Eagle, Rogers took a break from wrestling and went home to Camden.[66] The reasoning, other than just a need for time off, is not known. Being back in the East was always important to Rogers, particularly when it came to seeing his family. In early 1949, a report surfaced that he was being looked at for a future spot on a card at Madison Square Garden.[67] The reporters must not have been aware of the fact that Buddy was still under suspension in New York. Meanwhile, there was a new face on wrestling cards in New York City, a young high-flyer under the sponsorship of Toots Mondt. "Argentina" Antonino Rocca debuted at Ridgewood Grove on March 31, 1949, and his arrival on the scene was a game-changer.[68]

As Buddy was getting back in gear from his time off, Jack Pfefer was relocating his office from Hollywood to Toledo, Ohio. Setting up his new headquarters at the Secor Hotel, he aligned himself with local promoter Cliff Maupin, a trusted ally.[69] For Rogers, it was a pretty good situation, and eliminated the regular cross-country trips between the Midwest and California. Toledo was a good-drawing town, and with that, his pay was above average. Pfefer's bookings concentrated on the area in and around Ohio, including arenas in Indiana and Illinois, plus dates in St. Louis and Kansas City. Rogers had one of his best weeks during a six-day span beginning April 18, 1949, in Wichita. The following night at Kansas City, he pulled out his head-in-the-ropes stunt and started a near-riot against Orville Brown.[70] On April 20, Rogers made his first appearance in Chicago in more than a year, defeating Pierre Lasartes.[71] Rounding out his week in Toledo, Lorain, and Akron, he banked $1,257 – a hefty amount in 1949.[72]

Rogers' return to Chicago was a significant moment, and once again, the local publicity machine went into overdrive. This time around, though, they had plenty of new material to work with. "The loads of clippings that have come into Fred Kohler's office singing the praises of 'Nature Boy' Rogers are terrific in their enthusiasm," an article in *Wrestling As You Like It* claimed. "They are reminiscent of the first days of Frank Sinatra's success when the bobbysoxers swooned in droves over the personality of the crooner."[73] Another column addressed his new gimmick, stating: "He may appear effeminate to some, but his wrestling in the ring contradicts this argument."[74] Buddy was an affirmed heel in Chicago, and was greatly improved as a promo-man.[75] Prior to a bout with "Farmer" Don Marlin, he told a reporter: "The man is positively repulsive, but he needs to be given a lesson, that is why I am wrestling him. I believe he is a detriment to wrestling and I will send him back to the backwoods of Michigan where he belongs."[76] It was classic heel work and a sign of things to come.

The war in St. Louis was at the core of professional wrestling in the late 1940s, and by the summer of 1949, it was much more than a localized conflict. It involved promoters from coast to coast, meant millions of dollars in revenue, and held the future of both the National Wrestling Association and the National Wrestling Alliance in the balance. Sam Muchnick's recent success leveled the playing field against Lou Thesz, and tightened the competition in a major way. In addition, Muchnick managed the political side of things far better than Thesz, and was a considerable factor in the NWA's stunning growth. Running on empty, Thesz agreed to a compromise with Muchnick to end the war, and they would split financial returns going forward.[77] There were many details that needed to be worked out, but for the sake of the business, the deal was signed and peace reigned supreme.

The tides in the conflict rippled on Nov. 26, 1948, and completely turned on Feb. 4, 1949, when Muchnick scored his first sellout. Newspaper writers and historians didn't have to study long and hard to figure out the common thread. They knew that Buddy Rogers, and Buddy Rogers alone, was responsible. Everyone in the profession was paying attention, and following the miraculous settlement in St. Louis, the 28-year-old "Nature Boy" was arguably wrestling's greatest star.

ENDNOTES - CHAPTER 6

[1] Doyle settled in Los Angeles around 1939 as the promoter at the Eastside Arena. In 1944-'45, he took control of the Southern California booking office (heavyweights).

[2] Wagner wrestled at the Olympic Auditorium under his real name as late as Feb. 14, 1945.

[3] By far, Los Angeles was outdrawing both New York City and Chicago in the 1946-'49 time-frame.

[4] The KTLA broadcast debut on Wednesday, May 7, 1947 with Dick Lane as commentator.

[5] Nichols' wrestling career lasted from at least 1919 to 1938 and he was a multi-time world champion.

[6] Letter from Jack Pfefer to Hugh Nichols dated June 9, 1948. Jack Pfefer Collection, Joyce Sports Research Collection, Hesburgh Library, University of Notre Dame, Notre Dame, Indiana.

[7] Ibid.

[8] Pfefer explained that all the models had to do was walk Rogers to the ring and take his cape. Ibid.

[9] *The Billboard*, April 3, 1948, p. 28. Americanradiohistory.com. Eden Ahbez wanted his name spelled in lower case letters.

[10] *Los Angeles Times*, June 29, 1948, p. 34 and *North Hollywood Valley Times*, June 29, 1948, p. 6.

[11] ACME Photo Wire Citation Sheet, Aug. 13, 1948. At times, his cape was said to be worth a million dollars. Over a five month period, from July 1948 to November 1948, Pfefer spent $344.45 to rent various capes for Rogers, an amount greater than $3,600 in 2019 dollars.[12] It was an expensive investment, but critical to Pfefer's plan. Jack Pfefer Collection, Joyce Sports Research Collection, Hesburgh Library, University of Notre Dame, Notre Dame, Indiana. Inflation calculator, Data.bls.gov.

[13] The sleeves on his arms were also called gauntlets and/or "gloved arms and hands." His top was referred to as a leotard.

[14] It is unclear whether Rogers had one or two models with him when he debut in Hollywood.

[15] A previously written publicity piece on "The Robe" appeared in the Los Angeles program, *The Knockout*, Feb. 26, 1949.

[16] Toledo, Ohio was one of the cities Pfefer made this arrangement. *Toledo Blade*, April 15, 1949, p. 39.

[17] *San Diego Union*, June 30, 1948, p. 21. After being handed his cape and top, the Slave Girl went to the back area, quickly returning to Buddy's side with a tray of cosmetics. On the tray were the cold cream, deodorant, a comb, mirror, powder, perfume, and a face towel. Buddy used Chanel No. 5. *San Diego Union*, Sept. 5, 1948, p. 3B.

[18] *Windsor Star*, Aug. 30, 1949, p. 21.

[19] An early Slave Girl report stated that she was wearing "abbreviated deerskins." *San Diego Union*, June 30, 1948, p. 21. The Slave Girl would occasionally have chains around her ankles. *New York World-Telegram and Sun*, March 15, 1950 and *Lancaster Sunday News*, Dec. 17, 1950, p. 47.

[20] In Pfefer's expense book for 1948, he listed an entry for "Photos" on July 12, 1948 for $45.00. The next day, the earliest promotional photo of Buddy with his original Slave Girl appeared in the newspaper. *Santa Maria Times*, July 13, 1948, p. 2. There is a common misconception that these pictures were taken at the Legion Stadium the night Rogers debut in Hollywood. That is false. There were several variations of the promo photos and they can be identified by the dark gauntlets Buddy was wearing at the time.

[21] *San Luis Obispo Telegram-Tribune*, July 10, 1948, p. 5.

[22] *San Diego Union*, Sept. 5, 1948, p. 3B.

[23] *New York World-Telegram and Sun*, March 15, 1950.

24 Buddy told this story many times, including: Buddy Rogers Interview by Bill Apter, *Apter Chat*, Part One, 1979, youtube.com and Buddy Rogers Interview by Dr. Mike Lano and Gary "Gerhardt" Kaiser, *Canvas Cavity*, Circa. 1991-1992.

25 *North Hollywood Valley Times*, June 28, 1948, p. 8.

26 Buddy later admitted that he took on the gimmick to make better money. *Minneapolis Star*, Nov. 5, 1957, p. 10B.

27 It happened in Lancaster in 1951. *Lancaster Intelligencer-Journal*, April 12, 1951, p. 17.

28 *Bakersfield Californian*, July 1, 1948, p. 22.

29 *Wrestling As You Like It*, Oct. 7, 1950, p. 9.

30 The belt was not exceptionally well made and needed to be repaired twice between July and November 1948. Jack Pfefer Collection, Joyce Sports Research Collection, Hesburgh Library, University of Notre Dame, Notre Dame, Indiana.

31 It was billed as a world heavyweight title as early as September 1948. *The Knockout*, Sept. 18, 1948.

32 The Rogers-Angel feud was billed as "Beauty vs. The Beast." *The Knockout*, Aug. 7, 1948. He last appeared in a tag bout in Oklahoma City on Sept. 5, 1947.

33 Rogers spoke about Hild during a 1991 interview. Buddy Rogers Interview by John Arezzi, *Pro Wrestling Spotlight*, Aug. 4, 1991.

34 Hild gave her age as 22. *San Diego Union*, Sept. 5, 1948, p. 3B. Also *Omaha World-Herald Magazine*, Oct. 22, 1950, p. C5.

35 *San Diego Union*, Sept. 5, 1948, p. 3B.

36 His throat infection was mentioned in the *Bakersfield Californian*, Sept. 23, 1948, p. 28. Another report stated he was "sidelined with a strep throat." *Los Angeles Times*, Sept. 28, 1948, p. 46.

37 Jack Pfefer Collection, Joyce Sports Research Collection, Hesburgh Library, University of Notre Dame, Notre Dame, Indiana. The removal of his tonsils was mentioned in the *Los Angeles Times*, Oct. 18, 1948, p. 53.

38 U.S. Navy Applicant's Physical Questionnaire dated May 27, 1938. National Personnel Records Center, St. Louis, MO.

39 *Wrestling As You Like It*, Oct. 16, 1947, p. 3 and *North Hollywood Valley Times*, June 28, 1948, p. 8.

40 Chicago Wrigley Field Program, June 21, 1950, p. 2. Part of the filming locations for the movie occurred at the Paramount Studios in Hollywood. Imdb.com.

41 *San Diego Union*, Oct. 27, 1948, p. 21.

42 *Los Angeles Times*, Nov. 2, 1948, p. 42.

43 Rogers last worked St. Louis for the Packs group on June 4, 1948 versus Bill Longson.

44 Pfefer and Muchnick corresponded a lot about Rogers in October and November 1948. Muchnick wondered if the Thesz group had an "exclusive contract" on Buddy in St. Louis. He told Pfefer he heard that they did. Letter from Sam Muchnick to Jack Pfefer dated Nov. 3, 1948. Jack Pfefer Collection, Joyce Sports Research Collection, Hesburgh Library, University of Notre Dame, Notre Dame, Indiana. Rogers later explained that Muchnick called him and said, "Buddy, if I had you on the card, I could sell out the Auditorium. Do me a big favor, because man, I'm going down the drain." Muchnick told Rogers that he wanted to book him against Don Eagle. Buddy Rogers Interview by Bill Apter, *Apter Chat*, Part One, 1979, youtube.com.

45 Rogers flew on Thanksgiving, Nov. 25, 1948. Jack Pfefer Collection, Joyce Sports Research Collection, Hesburgh Library, University of Notre Dame, Notre Dame, Indiana.

46 Rogers spent $24 for the various items, which were part of his "beauty kit." Ibid.

47 *St. Louis Star and Times*, Nov. 27, 1948, p. 6. Muchnick informed fans that Buddy was a heel in the *St. Louis Post-Dispatch*, Nov. 17, 1948, p. 3D.

48 It was his largest payoff since November 1947, which was $464.50 for a bout in St. Louis against Bill Longson. Jack Pfefer Collection, Joyce Sports Research Collection, Hesburgh Library, University of Notre Dame, Notre Dame, Indiana.

49 *St. Louis Star and Times*, Dec. 23, 1948, p. 17.

50 Becker's real name was Thomas "Tommy" Phelps. The masked valet was called "George." *St. Joseph Gazette*, Dec. 10, 1948, p. 10. He was called "George or Jeeves" in a separate paper. *St. Joseph: The Journal for Progressive Stockmen, Farming and Businessmen*, Dec. 9, 1948, p. 2.

[51] *Kansas City Times*, Dec. 1, 1948, p. 21 and *St. Joseph Gazette*, Dec. 4, 1948.
[52] *St. Joseph Gazette*, Dec. 4, 1948.
[53] *St. Joseph Gazette*, Dec. 18, 1948.
[54] Rogers letter to Jack Pfefer dated Dec. 18, 1948. Jack Pfefer Collection, Joyce Sports Research Collection, Hesburgh Library, University of Notre Dame, Notre Dame, Indiana.
[55] *Wichita Beacon*, Jan. 4, 1949, p. 25.
[56] In St. Joseph, Buddy was advertised as "the Midwest version of Gorgeous Georges (sic)." *St. Joseph Gazette*, Dec. 3, 1948.
[57] *Tulare Advance Register*, Oct. 9, 1948, p. 2.
[58] Muchnick letter to Jack Pfefer dated Nov. 3, 1948. Jack Pfefer Collection, Joyce Sports Research Collection, Hesburgh Library, University of Notre Dame, Notre Dame, Indiana.
[59] *St. Louis Star and Times*, Dec. 18, 1948, p. 12. The matchmaker for Thesz's group was Bill Nelson, and shows were sponsored by the Mississippi Valley Sports Club.
[60] In a letter to Pfefer in California, Rogers said that he spent Christmas afternoon with the Darnell Family. Rogers letter to Jack Pfefer dated Dec. 27, 1948. Jack Pfefer Collection, Joyce Sports Research Collection, Hesburgh Library, University of Notre Dame, Notre Dame, Indiana.
[61] The writer was Betty Harries. *Palm Beach Post-Times*, Aug. 28, 1949, p. 5.
[62] As the story went, she fought off an inebriated customer at a Minneapolis nightclub, and then was offered a contract by promoter Tony Stecher. *Tampa Tribune*, Aug. 5, 1949, p. 17.
[63] *Lexington Herald*, March 17, 1949, p. 6 and *Paterson Evening News*, Oct. 12, 1949, p. 30.
[64] *St. Louis Globe-Democrat*, Feb. 5, 1949, p. 4C. A panoramic photograph of this huge crowd is in Pfefer Collection. Jack Pfefer Collection, Joyce Sports Research Collection, Hesburgh Library, University of Notre Dame, Notre Dame, Indiana.
[65] The title change was on the undercard of a Jim Londos main event. *Los Angeles Times*, March 1, 1949, p. 50.
[66] *St. Louis Globe-Democrat*, March 19, 1949, p. 14 and *St. Louis Star and Times*, March 19, 1949, p. 6. Also, Jack Pfefer Collection, Joyce Sports Research Collection, Hesburgh Library, University of Notre Dame, Notre Dame, Indiana.
[67] In Pfefer's date book, Rogers was listed as being "Home" between March 19 and March 27, 1949. Jack Pfefer Collection, Joyce Sports Research Collection, Hesburgh Library, University of Notre Dame, Notre Dame, Indiana.
[68] *Ottawa Citizen*, Jan. 26, 1949, p. 21.
[69] Rocca had previously worked in Texas and St. Louis. He was born in Italy, but raised in Argentina, where he was discovered by Kola Kwariani.
[70] Buddy's local residence was also at the Secor Hotel.
[71] Rogers lost to Brown by DQ. The attendance was 8,223 and Rogers was billed as the "Gorgeous Nature Boy." *Kansas City Times*, April 20, 1949, p. 18. In his date book, Pfefer wrote that it was a "Riot." Jack Pfefer Collection, Joyce Sports Research Collection, Hesburgh Library, University of Notre Dame, Notre Dame, Indiana.
[72] His last appearance in the "Windy City" was on Jan. 28, 1948.
[73] Jack Pfefer Collection, Joyce Sports Research Collection, Hesburgh Library, University of Notre Dame, Notre Dame, Indiana.
[74] *Wrestling As You Like It*, April 14, 1949.
[75] *Wrestling As You Like It*, June 2, 1949, p. 4.
[76] Izzy Becker was working with Buddy in Chicago as his valet.
[77] *Wrestling As You Like It*, Aug. 4, 1949, p. 3.
[78] The deal occurred around August 1949.

Chapter 7
Time for a Change

Bordering on the edge of Lake Erie, the city of Toledo was a haven for professional wrestling in 1949. Under the promotional management of Clifford Cleo (Cliff) Maupin, the son of a Kansas farmer, the sport flourished with a steady line-up of talented grapplers.[1] For years, Maupin had gotten more out of compelling feuds with hard-working journeymen than by relying on superstar-caliber names from other areas. Matches at the Sports Arena were full of life, mixing catch-as-catch-can science with unreserved violence, and Maupin's formula was a big hit with fans. The influx of Jack Pfefer's assorted characters in April 1949 was enthusiastically welcomed by the wrestling populace and aficionados were increasingly supportive at the box office. Besides Buddy Rogers, the newcomers included Billy Darnell, the Demon of Death Valley, Tony Sinatra, Ivan the Terrible, and the Polish Angel.[2] One of Pfefer's most gifted athletes was Ohio State alumni George Bollas, who appeared as the masked Zebra Kid.

Entering Toledo, Rogers quickly learned two things. For one, the rules and regulations were extremely liberal. In Ohio, there was no central state athletic commission governing pro wrestling like in Missouri or New York. Instead, Toledo and other major cities had local boxing and wrestling commissions, which established a paltry set of guidelines, usually with feedback from the leading promoter.[3] Without nosy state bureaucrats getting mixed into every situation, things were much easier to manage from a wrestling standpoint. Maupin named his own referees and there was an anything-goes vibe each Thursday night at the Arena.[4] The second thing Buddy quickly discovered was that he was making better money in Toledo than in Hollywood, Cincinnati, Detroit, and a number of other large cities. The pay was astronomical, ranging from $200 on the low side all the way up to more than $500. And that was every week. With the right opponents and build up, they were primed to do huge business.

Buddy's first significant conflict in Toledo was against the Demon, and the "Nature Boy" Nature Boy went over in three-falls on May 26, 1949.[5] Two weeks later, they fought again, and a sizable audience witnessed a rougher-than-normal encounter. The Demon, using the ring post to maim his foe, was disqualified for his relentless onslaught, and Rogers was awarded the win. Battered and bloody, Buddy staggered to the middle of the ring to have his arm raised by the referee, but then fell to the mat unconscious.[6] He was rushed to Robinwood Hospital by ambulance, where he was medically evaluated by physicians and released the next day. It was Buddy at his very best; selling the "brutal" beating for the live crowd, the ambulance driver, and the attendants at the hospital. Hours after the show was over, with only with a handful of onlookers, he was still working the injury angle, and Jack Pfefer was footing the entire bill. The ambulance, a brief stay at St. Vincent's Hospital, and the full emergency treatment at Robinwood amounted to $45.[7]

On June 16, Rogers gave the Demon exactly what the fans hoped he would – a thorough mauling – and gained revenge when his rival was unable to continue.[8] That same month, Buddy entered into a feud with the 300-plus-pound Zebra Kid, the aforementioned George Bollas. An NCAA heavyweight wrestling champion in 1946, Bollas was an incredible shooter and a legitimate force of nature. With that being said, he was also an extraordinary performer, and took Rogers to his limits in terms of riotous conduct. The Zebra Kid captured the world title from Rogers on July 7 in a Toledo match that saw Buddy miss the flying tackle and knock himself out on the concrete floor.[9] It was his patented big-match finish. Emotions were riding high for their return engagement and Pfefer billed their July 21 bout as the "Battle of the Century" and the "biggest championship match ever presented in Toledo for the world's title and championship belt."[10]

Buddy put up a good fight against Zebra, but a ref bump cost him the match, sending the crowd home dissatisfied.[11] Toledo fans had to wait until September 1 to see him beat the masked giant, and by that time, the Zebra Kid was no longer in possession of Pfefer's belt. Dave Levin had dethroned him a few weeks earlier. The pandemonium continued north of the border as the hard-hitting Rogers-Zebra feud carried over into Windsor, Ontario, in September and October 1949. They turned things up a notch on September 12 by utilizing chairs and fighting with the referee, resulting in a wild no-contest.[12] On September 26, the Zebra Kid won the opening fall, and lost the second in nine seconds after being hit by three successive dropkicks. Rogers proceeded to dish out the "worst shellacking ever administered in a Windsor Arena mat battle," and reporter Vic May added that the bout "was packed with thrills, spills, and attempted mayhem."[13] The match was eventually stopped due to its violence and to prevent injury.[14]

Windsor was also the scene of a highly charged series of bouts between Buddy and Billy Darnell, and a specific match on Aug. 15 left a permanent mark. The two wrestlers did a head-on-collision finish and the audience was up in arms. Fans swarmed him and a hazardous situation quickly escalated. "Overpowered by weight of numbers," Vic May wrote in the *Windsor Daily Star*, "Buddy only reached the dressing room after battling his way through an infuriated mob, which clawed, struck and kicked him as he sped past."[15] While the "Nature Boy" was en route, a determined female "fan" used a nail file to gouge a lengthy scratch across his shoulders. In the dressing room, Rogers reacted to the assault, telling May: "They're entitled to their fun, but this is going a little too far, and somebody might get hurt some time."[16] May stated that the "price of the ticket [didn't] entitle [fans] to claw, strike or gouge the performers just because their tactics do not appeal to them."[17]

Drawing the kind of heat Buddy did on a consistent basis was extremely dangerous, especially at arenas without the proper security measures in place. He had to protect himself from potential attackers and remain on high alert at all times. Fans wielding knives, broken bottles, and even hatpins were worrisome, and Rogers benefitted from having a second in his corner to watch his back. Izzy Becker was competent in that role, and resumed his work as a valet for Rogers in September 1949.[18] Many times in both Toledo and Windsor, he got involved in the action, and was usually carried from the ring area discombobulated. Off and on, Rogers had been accompanied by a Slave Girl, and it isn't known how many individuals performed in that role after Helen Hild in 1948. During the summer of 1949, a "Slave Girl Toni" was in the position, and a rare photo of her spraying Rogers with cologne was printed in the *Windsor Daily Star* on Aug. 30.[19]

There has been considerable curiosity as to whether Buddy's wife Ellen ever portrayed the Slave Girl at any time. An exhaustive search turned up no verifiable information. In Jack Pfefer's archive at the University of Notre Dame, payoff records for shows throughout 1949 were available, however, the Slave Girl was listed only as "Girl."[20] No proper name was used. Lillian Ellison, who later achieved fame as the Fabulous Moolah, described working as the Slave Girl for Rogers in her 2002 autobiography, *The Fabulous Moolah: First Goddess of the Squared Circle*.[21] In terms of a proper time-frame, it's likely that Ellison performed in that spot sometime in 1949 or 1950 on Pfefer's Ohio-Indiana circuit. To date, very little supporting information about her time with Rogers has been found and that includes no surviving photographs. More has been located about Ellison's role as a slave girl for the Elephant Boy in 1951 than about any previous time with Rogers.[22]

With the various Slave Girls in their leopard-skin clothing, a high-brow valet, and all the regular chaos both in the ring and backstage, Rogers was enjoying the best his manager Jack Pfefer had to offer. Rarely was there a dull moment in the Pfefer camp, and Jack's own attitude waivered as easily as the turn of the winds. He was an exceptionally cunning, but complicated man. He was generous, kindly, and thoughtful, going beyond what was needed to ensure his friends were taken care of. And yet, he was also remarkably suspicious and probably miserable as a result. When he was wrapped up in the politics of professional wrestling, he was at his absolute worst. The peace accord in St. Louis between Sam Muchnick and Lou Thesz particularly bothered him, and he didn't hesitate to lash out at Muchnick. Pfefer told the latter he was a "sucker" for entering into a deal and warned of double-crossers.[23] He then spitefully vetoed Muchnick's plan to use Buddy Rogers for his Sept. 23, 1949, show.[24]

Muchnick shrugged it off. "While Rogers is a valuable man, the United States carried on without Franklin D. Roosevelt and survived, so until he contacts us, we'll just have to get along without him," he told promoter Tony Stecher by letter.[25] Pfefer pulling the plug on dates in St. Louis undoubtedly put a crimp in Buddy's monthly take, but Rogers was a dutiful player and had to accept things for what they were.[26] Matters in Chicago were upended by politics as well, and Pfefer made another drastic decision. In 1949, Fred Kohler became one of the most powerful promoters in wrestling with two semi-national television programs. His longtime Wednesday offering from the Rainbo Arena was featured on a dozen or so stations belonging to ABC, whereas his Saturday program at the Marigold was presented to viewers on the DuMont network. It was tremendous exposure, and Rogers made appearances on both shows, including Kohler's Sept. 17, 1949, debut on DuMont.[27]

Later that year, Kohler pulled back from the Rainbo and ended his run on ABC. Difficulties with Rainbo owner Leonard Schwartz were at the root of his issues, and with money and egos involved, it became deeply personal. Typically, this wouldn't have really mattered much, and maybe Kohler thought cutting Schwartz off from top wrestling talent would have destroyed his business. But the ABC-TV contract was worth a fortune, so Jack Pfefer swooped in and made a deal with Schwartz, breaking from Kohler in the process.

Notably, Kohler had booked Rogers into a high-profile bout at the International Amphitheatre in Chicago on Oct. 28, 1949, and like Muchnick, he had to swiftly rearrange his card without the services of the "Nature Boy."[28] Once again, Buddy was on the losing end, financially, as nearly 11,000 fans paid $23,645 to attend the Amphitheatre event. Instead of making an exorbitant amount of cash that night, he was in South Bend, Indiana, where he earned $85 for a match with Zebra Kid.[29]

Pfefer's lack of faith in the St. Louis agreement matched his dubious feelings toward the budding National Wrestling Alliance. He was against the NWA and its possible monopolistic power, just as he hated the unforgiving "Trust" in the 1930s. A consequential November 1949 meeting of the Alliance took place in St. Louis, and Pfefer was considered to be an outsider – completely alienated from the group. However, it was all his own choosing and that's the way he liked it. In an effort to strengthen his own position politically, he reconnected with Joe (Toots) Mondt of New York. The year before, Mondt had founded the Manhattan Booking Agency with Milo Steinborn and Rudy Miller, and he was running a successful operation with Primo Carnera and Antonino Rocca as his top stars. Similar to Pfefer, but likely for different reasons, Toots was less inclined to believe in the positive benefits of a national organization, and refused to join the NWA.

From Buddy's perspective, he was watching the manipulations of a master in Jack Pfefer, and despite losing moneymaking opportunities in St. Louis and Chicago, he was being promised great things. And it didn't take long for Pfefer's scheming to start paying off. In late 1949, the unkempt promoter scored the booking rights to the Cleveland Arena after dissolving his previous partnership with promoter Jack Ganson.[30] Within days, the Cleveland promotion also added live television coverage sponsored by the Duquesne Brewing Company.[31] Rogers was the central attraction and he started to build a win streak with victories over Billy Darnell, Zebra Kid, and Lord Spears.[32] On Dec. 19, 1949, he resumed his long-running feud with Primo Carnera and drew a couple thousand to the Cleveland Arena. Rogers was the aggressor during the third fall and tied Primo up in the ropes. Referee Vic Tanski attempted to step in and free the former fighter, but Rogers punched him, earning a disqualification.[33]

Ex-boxer Tony Galento turned up in Cleveland, as well, and wrestled the "Nature Boy" twice. Rogers hadn't met Galento since the latter made his pro debut in 1947, and by this time, "Two-Ton" Tony was much more experienced. They put on a pair of wild brawls at the Arena and Rogers was victorious in both matches.[34] The Carnera and Galento bouts drew moderately well, but by early 1950, fans only wanted to see one wrestler in Cleveland, and that was "Argentina" Antonino Rocca. Unquestionably, Rocca was the hottest property in the business, and devotees everywhere were clamoring for live appearances. Toots Mondt was handling his newest sensation perfectly and TV was being used to increase interest from coast-to-coast. Cleveland was the beneficiary of a CBS telecast out of New York City on Tuesday nights, and Rocca was prominently featured.[35] A few weeks later, the barefooted South American athlete drew more than 8,000 to the Arena for his local debut.[36]

With Rogers established as the primary heel in the territory and Rocca the incredibly popular babyface, wrestling's next "Battle of the Century" was a foregone conclusion.[37] On March 27, 1950, they wrestled for the very first time, and a massive crowd of 13,210 people were in attendance for the thrilling affair. Buddy, acknowledged as the "long-haired, perfumed villain" by the *Cleveland Plain Dealer*, split the opening two falls with Rocca before throwing all the rules out the window. He battered his rival unmercifully and was disqualified.[38]

The show was an all-around success, drawing a gate of $26,224 with Buddy making the largest single-day payoff of his career. He earned $1,620, while Rocca did a little better, making $1,944.60.[39] Obviously, a rematch was scheduled and held at the Cleveland Arena on April 10, 1950. This time, they went to a draw finish, and Rogers picked up another $1,065.[40]

Backtracking a couple months, "Toots," Pfefer, and Rogers had shared a common goal, and that was to get Buddy back into the New York City market. During his lengthy suspension, the Northeastern territory was transformed by a stunning revival, and there were two wrestlers at the forefront of the resurgence. One, of course, was Antonino Rocca. The other was Eugene Stanley Zygowicz of Chicago, better known as Gene Stanlee. Billed as "Mr. America," Stanlee was well-built, blond and bronzed, and exceedingly popular with female fans. In addition, he wore colorful outfits and capes, making him a close carbon copy of Buddy Rogers. Rogers made no bones about it; he felt Stanlee was an imitator, plain and simple. "Gene came to California to watch me wrestle," he explained in 1950. "He studied my style closely, copied every move I made, then returned east and started using my originations."[41] Without the presence of the "Nature Boy" in New York, Mondt pushed Stanlee as the local glamour boy, and he became a heartthrob, credited with converting 25,000 women into diehard mat enthusiasts on the East Coast.[42]

Rogers was in a strange position. In Los Angeles, he was compared to Gorgeous George and called a copycat. Over in New York, he was likened to "Mr. America," and his particular ring act was already a well-known thing, although performed by someone else. Since Stanlee was a draw and protected by "Toots," there was little Buddy could do about it. Their similarities in appearance and style had fans confusing them for brothers, and wrestling publications played it up. *Wrestling As You Like It*, published out of Chicago, stated that Rogers and Stanlee "not alone [sic] resemble one another, but wrestle like twins."[43] That was an important fact to understand because in the regular realm of pro wrestling, babyface Stanlee booked against heel Rogers was a dream match. The problem was they were too much alike, and the constant comparison actually hurt each individual man, especially Stanlee, who wasn't as polished as Rogers.

In wrestling, bookers usually wanted opposites to wrestle. The pretty boy against the behemoth, for instance, and the variances of the performers made for an interesting match. Two wrestlers with an identical gimmick and techniques was not an appealing concept. But that didn't mean a Rogers-Stanlee match wasn't in the cards. However, first things first. Buddy was still suspended in New York and that had to be resolved before making his long-awaited return to the Northeast. In early February 1950, the New York State Athletic Commission was petitioned and the regulatory body decided to reinstate "Herman Rohde, wrestler."[44] It was great news and a major step for Rogers. Since his last appearance in 1948, he had adopted the "Nature Boy" persona and had made wrestling's "Buddy Rogers" a household name in many parts of the country.

Television viewers in the New York City area had seen Rogers competing on the WJZ-7 ABC footage from the Rainbo in Chicago.[45] They knew he was no longer "Dutch" Rohde, the clean-cut sportsman, but a vile villain with an entirely new image. Toots Mondt's promotional publication, *Sports Pictorial Review*, did a huge cover story on Buddy's return, and mentioned his transition from Rohde to Rogers. "The handsome blond atomic star was nothing short of sensational in his last matches," an anonymous writer noted. The article stated that Rogers was looking for matches with Rocca, Stanlee, and the reigning world champion Frank Sexton.[46] Shortly after he arrived back in New York, Buddy spoke with Lester Bromberg of the *New York World-Telegram and Sun*, and was revealing with his comments. He praised Jack Pfefer for "the routine" and "costumes," and said that "Dutch" Rohde was "popular, but poor." Rogers also asserted that he was making $30,000 a year.[47]

Substantially pushed in the Northeast, Buddy went undefeated between February and April 1950 and took wins from the Golden Superman, Super Swedish Angel, Mike Mazurki, and Sandor Kovacs. On Feb. 17, he faced off with Gene Stanlee for the first time at the Armory in Paterson, New Jersey. Their match was advertised by promoter Turc Duncan as the "Battle of the Blonds," and 3,500 spectators were in attendance.[48] A report in the *Paterson Evening News* stated that their bout was "thoroughly enjoyable," and that the bobbysoxers were "left limp by the excitement." The contest ended in a draw in 37 minutes at the 11:00 curfew.[49] The next day, longtime New Jersey referee "Doc" Gehman sent a letter to Jack Pfefer advising him of the situation in Paterson. He said the gate was $2,000 less than anticipated and felt that Rogers hadn't been on TV enough to "build up his old following." It was a mistake, the referee wrote, not to bill him as "Dutch Rohde, now known as 'Nature Boy' Buddy Rogers."[50]

Apparently, Gehman believed more of an emphasis needed to be placed on his original ring name, rather than focusing on "Buddy Rogers," which was not as established. Nevertheless, *Sports Pictorial Review* tossed out Buddy's name as a potential foe for Antonino Rocca in the upcoming March 6, 1950, main event at Madison Square Garden.[51] When it came right down to finding the right match-up, Toots went with the guaranteed draw, Stanlee, rather than risk a Paterson-like disappointment.[52] There might have been a financial motivation for Mondt to push his two stars into the main event, as well, seeing that he got a personal cut from both wrestlers as their booker. Despite his overall good showing in the territory, Rogers still had some work to do in Northeastern rings. But the stringent members of the New York athletic commission, who didn't want gimmicks in their state, continued to be annoyed by Rogers, and in a surprising decision, the body ordered him to stop using the "Nature Boy" moniker locally. It effectively stripped him of the nickname he had made famous.[53]

The full revitalization of pro wrestling in New York was also being experienced in Chicago, where 13,877 paid $53,744 for a big spectacular at the Stadium on Feb. 3, 1950. Promoted by Ray Fabiani in conjunction with Mondt, the card featured Rocca, Stanlee, and Don Eagle. The following month, a second Stadium effort was organized with Rogers wrestling Stanlee in the third match from the top. The March 24 program had Rocca in the main event, with Jim Londos in the semifinal, and another large crowd was expected. But the loaded card failed to interest fans and the show drew a measly 3,101.[54] In May 1950, Rogers was back at the Rainbo Arena in Chicago and scored two controversial wins over Billy Darnell. In those matches, he was a stone-cold heel, proving to be the opposite of the fan-favorite he had been months earlier. After one of his rough victories, there was a mass letter-writing campaign in protest, and Fabiani claimed to have received nearly 5,000 complaints.[55]

The Illinois State Athletic Commission wasn't happy with Rogers and issued a warning about his in-ring behavior.[56] It proceeded to suspend Jack Zeravich, the assigned referee for the Rogers-Darnell bout, for 30 days, citing his failure to uphold the rules, and authorized a third and final match-up to settle matters.[57] On May 31, Buddy beat Darnell for a third-straight time at the Rainbo, and with all the added attention, the "Nature Boy" was in position for yet another huge stadium affair. This time, though, he was going to main event a world championship match. But in the preceding days leading up to that announcement, a few startling things occurred, including a legitimate, and rare double-cross. The dominos began to fall on May 23 when Chief Don Eagle ended the lengthy reign of Frank Sexton as world champion. Three days later, at the International Amphitheatre in Chicago, Gorgeous George pinned Eagle for his championship, and it was a completely unscheduled title switch. George, with political backing from Fred Kohler and help from a referee, executed a double-cross on Eagle.[58]

Kohler was motivated to pull the stunt because of Don Eagle's ties to his rivals, Ray Fabiani and Leonard Schwartz. Prior to the unexpected finish, Eagle was the reported choice to face National Wrestling Alliance world heavyweight champion Lou Thesz on June 21 at Wrigley Field.[59] Thesz, it can be remembered, was a several-time National Wrestling Association champion, and after peace was brokered in St. Louis, he ascended to the top of the Alliance, as well. In fact, he became the Alliance kingpin following the car accident that ended champion Orville Brown's career in late 1949.[60] Once Eagle was knocked out of the picture, Kohler needed a worthy opponent for Thesz, and got in touch with Jack Pfefer, who had no problem playing all sides. At one minute, he was with the Mondt-Fabiani group, and the next he was doing business with Kohler and the NWA. Sometimes, loyalties went where the money was, and the Wrigley Field show certainly meant big money.

At least, that's what they figured. During a meeting of the Illinois Athletic Commission on June 5, 1950, Rogers was announced as Thesz' opponent, and a percentage of the take was going to the Chicago Heart Association.[61] The charitable component of the event was going to help bring in mainstream publicity, and Kohler arranged for the supremely popular Jack Dempsey, ex-heavyweight boxing champion, to be the special guest referee. These factors, in addition to the excitement surrounding the main event itself, appeared to be a winning promotional strategy. In a little of the pre-match hullabaloo, Rogers talked up his abilities and suggested that he could "take Thesz using scientific wrestling." Kohler was against the idea, and said: "Don't change your style. The fans want to see if you can use those piledrivers, dropkicks, airplane spins, and other roughneck holds on a man as good as Thesz."[62]

The piledriver was a finishing move Rogers had been using since at least the summer of 1948.[63] Thesz insisted that Buddy "stole" the maneuver from Bill Longson, and it's hard to doubt the latter's influence.[64] With the important June 21 contest approaching, the Illinois Commission approved the match as officially being for the world championship, an uncommon distinction in a state that recognized wrestling bouts as exhibitions. And for Rogers, it was probably the biggest match of his career. He'd wrestled Thesz many times in the past, but not in more than two years, and during that time, a good dose of political and personal animosity had built up. However, there was enough respect between them, and in-ring chemistry, to give the people of Chicago a good show. The night of the event, 7,638 paid their way into Wrigley Field, below Kohler's 10,000-person estimate, and the gate amounted to $30,265.01.[65]

Rogers and Thesz had a great match. They mixed science with brawling, used terrific psychology, and thrilled viewers. The action was fast-paced, and Rogers kept up with Thesz, countering holds and applying "back alley tactics."[66] He used his piledriver to win the first fall, and, looking out at the spectators, proudly pointed to his head with his right index finger as an illustration of his superior mental faculties. Thesz rebounded for the second fall, pinning Rogers following an airplane spin. At that moment, Buddy's male valet, who was formally dressed in a tuxedo jacket, wiped the sweat off his face with a towel and combed his hair back. Such a demonstration was a magnet for crowd heat, and Rogers played it to the gills. As the match went past the half-hour mark, Rogers started landing shoulder blocks off the ropes. In quick succession, he hit two in a row, but on his third attempt, Thesz avoided contact, and Buddy went head first into the ropes.[67]

Strangled between the top and middle strands, Rogers was counted out – a dramatic finish he had done many times before. Gene Kessler of the *Chicago Sun-Times* wrote that "the weird ending [was] met with applause despite Buddy's agony."[68] This match displayed the continued love-hate relationship fans had with Rogers. His aggravating style could blow the lid off even the most passive of enthusiasts. But in Chicago, and especially places like Toledo and Akron, he was cheered and booed, and it often depended on who his opponent was, and how criminal he was acting. With that being said, his crooked manipulations were just galling enough to be a pleasurable aspect of the pro wrestling experience. Earlier in 1950, Akron promoter Walter Moore picked Rogers as the top favorite of local fans, explaining: "The women love him and the men look at him kind of doubtful when he struts around the ring in his robe, but when he takes off that robe and starts dishing it out, they like him."[69]

In trying to clean up the sport, the Illinois State Athletic Commission put more pressure on Rogers to perform in a more honest fashion, and in September and October 1950, he did just that. The publication, *Wrestling As You Like It*, noted: "Buddy Rogers has curbed his temper and stayed within the sportsmanlike rules of wrestling. The consensus of opinion is that Buddy is again enjoying the good will of fans by adapting clean and sportsmanlike methods."[70] Rogers expressed a desire to wrestle Thesz again, and announced: "I should be the world's champion. I can beat Thesz and all others without violating the rules."[71] His metamorphosis in Chicago was part of a slow, but significantly larger shift in style and gimmick. It was clearly time for a change, and Buddy wanted to move far away from the glamour boy image. Financially, being a villain had worked out for him, and that was a sound part of his in-ring repertoire.[72] But the valets, the Slave Girls, and the Gorgeous George-esqe performance was on its way out.

"I hate the so-called glamour lads," Rogers told a reporter in 1950.[73] There was definitely a place in wrestling for the prissy, effeminate performers, and at Jack Pfefer's urging, he had gone as far as he could go utilizing those techniques to get heat. But the comparisons to Gorgeous George and Gene Stanlee were personally upsetting, and Buddy wanted to define his own image. In an interview with Harold V. Ratliff of the AP, he denied ever copying George, and said there were several differences between them. "George goes in for histrionics and is fastidious to an extreme," the article stated. "I am the arrogant he-man type," Rogers added. He also denied bleaching his hair like George did, although that was untrue.[74] Giving up the capes, the elaborate entrance, and valet were three other elements Rogers wanted to eliminate, finalizing his transformation.

When it came to his in-ring performance, he was the opposite of the prancing fan-favorite, who shook hands with ringsiders, blew kisses to the crowd, and doled out bobby-pins. He was actually a relentless fighter, ready and willing to engage in bloody brawls. One wrestling publication stated: "His handsome appearance belies the fact that he can get tough in the ring, but once the gong sounds to start the bout, Buddy is one of the hardest boiled wrestlers in the game, if the occasion warrants."[75] In a 1949 issue of *Wrestling As You Like It*, a pundit wrote: "'Nature Boy,' who loves to strut around the ring in expensive capes and gala attire, is a Dr. Jekyll and Mr. Hyde in his wrestling maneuvers. He can be quite peaceful before the gong rings to start him his way in a wrestling match. Once the match gets going full force, the cruelty and haughtiness comes to the fore in Buddy's disposition and character and he is a tough hombre."[76]

"Fans say I am a dirty wrestler," Rogers explained to a kayfabe magazine. "They try and tell me I am too tough, that I punish my opponents too much. They forget that when a man is in the ring, it's either pin or be pinned. If you don't try with all you've got to beat your man, you are not only going to lose the match, but any prospects of future employment. I am in the ring for two reasons – to wrestle and to win. A tough wrestler I might well be – but a dirty one, never."[77]

Around November 1950, Buddy began wearing a jacket to the ring instead of a fancy cape.[78] In fact, an astute reporter for the *Toledo Blade* commented that Rogers was wearing a completely "new outfit" that same month, confirming his wrestling makeover.[79] Soon, publicity photos of Rogers in a custom-made jacket were distributed for use in promotions, and they replaced the older shots. Within a short time, Buddy would amass a collection of 27 jackets, some of them costing as much as $300 apiece.[80] A Lancaster, Pennsylvania, reporter described one of Buddy's jackets in the following way in January 1951: "He was stunningly attired in a lavender jacket trimmed with gold sequins and having as its crowning glory a stiff white collar, reminiscent of the days of knighthood in merry England."[81]

Stanley Weston of *The Ring* magazine had advised fans about Buddy Rogers three years earlier, saying that he showed "a lot of promise," and thought the youngster "should go a long way in wrestling."[82] In early 1950, Weston offered a more comprehensive statement: "When asked to tell who is my favorite grappler of the present era, I could think of only one man who in my opinion possesses the qualifications, not only to make things interesting, but to give the spectators that something that keeps them in a spirit of expectation at all times. His name? Buddy Rogers." Weston admitted that Buddy was "not a great wrestler" in the technical sense, but "as a master showman and workman, he rates tops in my book."[83]

Being a New Yorker, Weston saw Rogers during his previous tour through the Northeast and was taken by his new attitude. "His style has changed quite a bit since he last showed here," Weston noted. "Now he goes in for the rough villain role and fans around New York boo him to the rafters. But how they turn out to see him!" It didn't seem to matter that Buddy was a straight heel, strutting across the ring and roughing up his opponents, as fans, journalists and insiders were transfixed by his level of performance. In many ways, he held the emotions of the audience in the palm of his hands, yet little did everyone know that the best was still to come.

ENDNOTES - CHAPTER 7

[1] The Maupin Family was from Osborne County, Kansas.
[2] The Demon of Death Valley was also called the "Death Valley Demon." His real name was Jack O'Brien. Tony Sinatra wrestled as Frank Gonzales in other areas for Pfefer. He was Cherry Vallina (Jerry Vallino). Ivan the Terrible was Don Lee and the Polish Angel was Wladislaw Talun.
[3] Incidentally, Toledo had both a "Toldeo Wrestling Commission" and a "Toledo Boxing Commission." *Columbus Dispatch*, Feb. 17, 1953, p. 11.
[4] In most states, the athletic commission appointed wrestling referees.
[5] *Toledo Blade*, May 27, 1949, p. 43.
[6] It was reported that Rogers "fainted." *Toledo Blade*, June 10, 1949, p. 43 and June 12, 1949, p. 52.
[7] Rogers was initially taken to St. Vincent's Hospital at 2213 Cherry Street and visited the emergency room. His stay there cost Pfefer $2. From there, he was driven by ambulance to Robinwood Hospital, at the corner of Robinwood and Delaware Avenues. His examination and stay at that hospital cost $33. Harold's Ambulance Service was hired to drive Rogers, and cost $10. Receipts from the ambulance company and the two hospitals were found in the Jack Pfefer Collection, Joyce Sports Research Collection, Hesburgh Library, University of Notre Dame, Notre Dame, Indiana. $45 in 1949 equals over $480 in 2019 dollars. Data.bls.gov.
[8] *Toledo Blade*, June 17, 1949, p. 39.

96 • Master of the Ring

[9] *Toledo Blade*, July 8, 1949, p. 35. Following this match, Rogers went home to Camden for a 13-day vacation. Jack Pfefer Collection, Joyce Sports Research Collection, Hesburgh Library, University of Notre Dame, Notre Dame, Indiana.

[10] *Toledo Blade*, July 17, 1949, p. 54.

[11] *Toledo Blade*, July 22, 1949, p. 33. Pfefer wrote "Riot" for this match in his personal date book. Jack Pfefer Collection, Joyce Sports Research Collection, Hesburgh Library, University of Notre Dame, Notre Dame, Indiana.

[12] *Windsor Daily Star*, Sept. 13, 1949, p. B2.

[13] *Windsor Daily Star*, Sept. 27, 1949, p. B2.

[14] Their Windsor warfare ceased on Oct. 3, 1949 with a Rogers victory by countout before 2,200 spectators at the Arena. Reporter Jack Dulmage wrote that Rogers was "jubilant" with the victory. *Windsor Daily Star*, Oct. 4, 1949, p. B2.

[15] *Windsor Daily Star*, Aug. 16, 1949, p. B2.

[16] Ibid.

[17] Ibid.

[18] Becker resumed his work as a valet on Sept. 5, 1949 in Windsor. Jack Pfefer Collection, Joyce Sports Research Collection, Hesburgh Library, University of Notre Dame, Notre Dame, Indiana.

[19] *Windsor Daily Star*, Aug. 30, 1949, p. 21. Toni made between $15 and $30 for an appearance. Jack Pfefer Collection, Joyce Sports Research Collection, Hesburgh Library, University of Notre Dame, Notre Dame, Indiana.

[20] Ibid.

[21] *The Fabulous Moolah: First Goddess of the Squared Circle* by Lillian Ellison with Larry Platt (2002) p. 61-65.

[22] Ellison adopted the name, "Slave Girl Moolah" before changing it to the "Fabulous Moolah."

[23] Pfefer sent Muchnick a "nasty letter," according to Muchnick. Sam Muchnick letter to Tony Stecher dated Aug. 19, 1949. Department of Justice Investigation into the National Wrestling Alliance, National Archives, College Park, MD.

[24] Muchnick wanted to book Rogers against Yvon Robert in St. Louis on Sept. 23, 1949. Ibid. After that plan fell through, he arranged Don Eagle to battle Robert. *St. Louis Star and Times*, Sept. 24, 1949, p. 7.

[25] Department of Justice Investigation into the National Wrestling Alliance, National Archives, College Park, MD.

[26] Rogers' last St. Louis date had been May 13, 1949.

[27] Rogers wrestled and beat Billy Darnell that night.

[28] Rogers was booked to face Hans Schnabel with Jack Dempsey serving as the referee. Similar to the situation in St. Louis, Rogers was replaced by Don Eagle. Kohler's local arena program stated: "Rumor is to the effect that Buddy was wary of wresting Schnabel. It is further thought that Kohler paid heed to the many protests lodged against Rogers for his unruly conduct in the ring." *Wrestling As You Like It*, Oct. 20, 1949, p. 4. Fred Kohler later claimed that he pulled Rogers from this card as a favor to Al Haft and "underwent tremendous expense in reprinting circulars and window cards." Fred Kohler Letter to Sam Muchnick dated Dec. 9, 1950, Department of Justice Investigation into the National Wrestling Alliance, National Archives, College Park, MD.

[29] Jack Pfefer Collection, Joyce Sports Research Collection, Hesburgh Library, University of Notre Dame, Notre Dame, Indiana.

[30] Pfefer worked out a deal with James C. "Jim" Hendy, the general manager of the Cleveland Arena for shows every Monday night. Jack Ganson continued to promote at the Central Armory on Tuesdays with talent from Al Haft of Columbus.

[31] Bob Shelley was the announcer. The show was featured on WNBK. *Cleveland Plain Dealer*, Oct. 29, 1949, p. 11.

[32] For his matches, Lord Spears (Abe Stein) was accompanied by a Slave Girl, as arranged by Pfefer.

[33] The local newspaper cited two different attendance figures: 2,263 and 3,263. *Cleveland Plain Dealer*, Dec. 20, 1949, p. 26. Rogers and Carnera had four matches on the circuit in Dec. 1949. Carnera won three of the matches, two by DQ, and the fourth was a draw.

34 The contests occurred on Jan. 2 and Jan. 9, 1950.

35 The CBS show debut in Cleveland on WEWS on Jan. 10, 1950. Bill Johnston Jr. was the announcer. *Cleveland Plain Dealer*, Jan. 10, 1950, p. 24.

36 Rocca beat Tom Marshall. *Cleveland Plain Dealer*, Feb. 14, 1950, p. 18.

37 The "Battle of the Century" slogan for Rogers-Rocca was listed on the local Cleveland program. It was also stated that: "This historic match is the dream of every promoter in the country – but the Arena offered the biggest purse. $10,000 cold cash." *Wrestling Program*, March 20, 1950, p. 4.

38 An estimated 1,000 fans were turned away. *Cleveland Plain Dealer*, March 28, 1950, p. 24.

39 Jack Pfefer Collection, Joyce Sports Research Collection, Hesburgh Library, University of Notre Dame, Notre Dame, Indiana.

40 Ibid.

41 *Television Guide*, Feb. 25, 1950, p. 22. A 1950s magazine confirmed that Stanlee "studied" Buddy's "bouncing, spectacular style of mat maneuvering." Stanlee also studied the styles of Gorgeous George and Lou Thesz. Unsourced magazine, circa 1950s. Stanlee reportedly copied Rogers style after watching him in California in 1948.

42 Stanlee was receiving 1,500-2,000 fan letters a week. *Wrestling As You Like It*, Jan. 5, 1950, p. 8.

43 *Wrestling As You Like It*, Jan. 26, 1950, p. 8.

44 He was reinstated effective Feb. 2, 1950. New York State Athletic Commission Meeting Minutes, Feb. 3, 1950, p. 4.

45 The *Trenton Evening Times* acknowledged the name change, stating: "Trenton fans watching Chicago wrestling matches on television saw a familiar figure operating under an unfamiliar name the other night. The Chicago announcer called him Buddy 'Nature Boy' Rogers, but it was none other than Herman 'Dutch' Rohde, a popular favorite at the Trenton Arena a few years back." *Trenton Evening Times*, Jan. 6, 1950, p. 24.

46 *Sports Pictorial Review*, Feb. 6, 1950, p. 1.

47 *New York World-Telegram and Sun*, March 15, 1950.

48 Duncan promoted Rogers, as "Dutch" Rohde, in Wildwood, NJ in 1943.

49 *Paterson Evening News*, Feb. 18, 1950, p. 19.

50 Letter from Dr. Jesse Mercer "Doc" Gehman to Jack Pfefer dated Feb. 18, 1950. Jack Pfefer Collection, Joyce Sports Research Collection, Hesburgh Library, University of Notre Dame, Notre Dame, Indiana. Stanlee and Rogers wrestled two additional times in 1950, on February 23 in Brooklyn and March 24 in Chicago. Both matches were draws.

51 *Sports Pictorial Review*, Feb. 20, 1950, p. 1.

52 Rocca and Stanlee drew 16,979 and a gate of $51,962.81 at the Garden on March 6, 1950. *Wrestling in the Garden: The Battle for New York* by Scott Teal and J Michael Kenyon (2017), p. 121.

53 "Sports Chatter" columnist Harry Singer mentioned this decision. *New York Post*, April 3, 1950.

54 Rogers and Stanlee wrestled to a 30-minute draw. The gate was $7,178. *Chicago Daily News*, March 25, 1950, p. 13.

55 *Chicago Sun-Times*, May 31, 1950, p. 45. Another report stated that "more than 4,000 letters" were received by the TV station in complaint. *Chicago Tribune*, May 31, 1950, p. 38.

56 Rogers might have actually been on probation with the Illinois State Athletic Commission at this juncture.

57 *Chicago Daily News*, May 31, 1950, p. 39.

58 Eagle was quoted as saying: "I don't know what kind of a double-cross this is." 5,200 fans were in attendance and a "riot" occurred after the bout. *Chicago Sun-Times*, May 27, 1950, p. 4.

59 It was also reported that Ray Fabiani had planned for a big Don Eagle-Jim Londos match during the summer of 1950, and that was also going to be impacted by the double-cross. *Chicago Sun-Times*, June 5, 1950, p. 41.

60 Thesz was declared National Wrestling Alliance champion on Nov. 27, 1949.

61 *Chicago Sun-Times*, June 6, 1950, p. 40.

62 *Chicago Sun-Times*, June 12, 1950, p. 53.

63 *Los Angeles Times*, Aug. 24, 1948, p. 43.

[64] *Chicago Sun-Times*, June 18, 1950, p. 66.
[65] *Chicago Sun-Times*, June 22, 1950, p. 57. Kohler also predicted a $50,000+ gate. *Chicago Sun-Times*, June 19, 1950, p. 55.
[66] Buddy's "back alley tactics" were mentioned by commentator Russ Davis. Buddy Rogers vs. Lou Thesz, Chicago Film Archives, F. 2008-04-0082, youtube.com.
[67] Ibid.
[68] *Chicago Sun-Times*, June 22, 1950, p. 57.
[69] *Akron Beacon Journal*, Feb. 19, 1950, p. 25.
[70] *Wrestling As You Like It*, Nov. 4, 1950, p. 3.
[71] *Wrestling As You Like It*, Sept. 30, 1950, p. 4.
[72] Rogers was quoted as saying: "The first year I emerged as the villain of the mat, I made $33,000 more than the year before." *Lancaster Sunday News*, Dec. 17, 1950, p. 47.
[73] *Sports Pictorial Review*, May 8, 1950, p. 2.
[74] *Lancaster Sunday News*, Dec. 17, 1950, p. 47. Rogers again denied stealing George's act and compared the two in the *Lancaster Sunday News*, March 2, 1952, p. 28.
[75] *Wrestling As You Like It*, Nov. 27, 1947, p. 2.
[76] *Wrestling As You Like It*, Oct. 6, 1949, p. 4.
[77] *Wrestling*, July 1951.
[78] The earliest reference to Rogers wearing a jacket was found in a Windsor newspaper in November 1950.
[79] *Toledo Blade*, Nov. 26, 1950.
[80] *Columbus Star*, July 19, 1952, p. 2.
[81] *Lancaster Intelligencer Journal*, Jan. 4, 1951, p. 11.
[82] *The Ring*, November 1947, p. 28-29.
[83] *The Ring*, May 1950, p. 28.

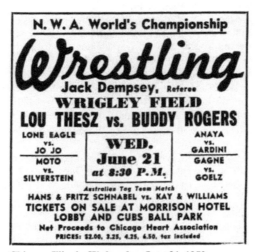

Chicago, Illinois: Wednesday, June 21, 1950

Chapter 8
The Pfefer Curse

The establishment of the National Wrestling Alliance in 1948 was a historic milestone for the industry fostered by six forward-thinking entrepreneurs.[1] The creation of a structured coalition entirely for booking agents was a powerful decision, but at the time, few people considered the NWA consequential. Coastal wrestling leaders were unimpressed by the new organization and were essentially ready to ignore the happenings in the Midwest. But the real benefits of the Alliance were being realized, and membership grew from a half dozen to 24 by 1950. Among the perks of affiliation with the NWA was recognition of exclusive territories, protection against rivals, and the acknowledgment of a single world heavyweight champion. The latter was an imaginative concept as most parts of North America already had at least one wrestler claiming the title. Whittling that number down to a single champion was a grand initiative, and the NWA put its faith behind Lou Thesz to get the job done.

The inventive strategies of the Alliance only complicated the political environment of pro wrestling. That included controversies surrounding the delineation of territories and the specific "ownership" of those regions. Chicago was a central battleground in that regard with long-time promoter Fred Kohler in a dominant position. His Saturday evening television show from the Marigold Arena was broadcast semi-nationally on the DuMont Network, and he was earning enormous sums of money. Leonard Schwartz was less experienced as a wrestling promoter than Kohler, but was in just as valuable a position with his Wednesday telecast from the Rainbo Arena on the ABC Network. Kohler, an NWA member, felt he was entitled to exclusivity in Chicago and wanted the Alliance to help him push back against Schwartz, a non-member. What took place, instead, was the opposite of the kind of cooperation and protection that the National Wrestling Alliance promised, and Kohler was furious.

Schwartz initially received assistance from Jack Pfefer in early 1950, but he soon sought help from Ray Fabiani, who was in cahoots with Toots Mondt and the Manhattan Booking Agency. Since none of those individuals were involved in the NWA, Kohler had little recourse other than fighting them tooth-and-nail for the territory. But things took on a different shape by August 1950 when NWA member Al Haft began sending troops from Columbus, Ohio, to work for Schwartz at the Rainbo. Then, two months later, Toots Mondt was approved for membership in the Alliance. Finally, to justify the help Haft and Mondt were giving Schwartz, the NWA hierarchy declared Chicago an "Open City," which gave any member permission to book in opposition to Kohler. It was a knife to the back, and Kohler resigned from the Alliance in protest.² He quickly realigned with Pfefer, a move he knew would get under Haft's skin, and pushed Buddy Rogers back to the top of his promotion.³

On Dec. 8, 1950, the "Nature Boy" headlined at the International Amphitheatre against NWA champion Lou Thesz and had another critically acclaimed match. The competitors wrestled 60 minutes with Thesz taking the only fall and retaining his title.⁴ Attendance was underwhelming at 5,432, and bad weather was blamed for the mediocre crowd.⁵ Despite Buddy's loss, press reporters maintained his credibility as a challenger, pointing out that Thesz' recent victory, and his win at Wrigley Field, were both indecisive. They also played up Thesz' reported hesitancy to face Rogers again, as if he was fearful of losing his championship to a better man. A column in *Wrestling As You Like It* claimed that Thesz had been guaranteed a percentage of the gate to get him to sign for a rematch.⁶ Such a statement was textbook storyline fodder, but it worked well and sold a lot of tickets.

The third Chicago bout between Rogers and Thesz occurred on Jan. 26, 1951, at the Amphitheatre and drew 7,536 spectators. The gate was around $17,000.⁷ Much like their previous matches, the action went back-and-forth, and neither was overly commanding. Near the end, however, Rogers had the champion weakened and a journalist noted that "Thesz was never closer to defeat than in this match."⁸ The fact that Thesz continued to sell so well for Buddy was telling, and based on their history, it was likely more about future business than personal respect. At the end of an hour, the match was declared a draw, and Thesz retained his belt. Dick Axman, the veteran scribe, wrote: "Buddy proved himself to be definitely of championship caliber, and if the blonde Eastern heavyweight continues his campaign for a rematch, he may still wind up as the titleholder."⁹

During that same time-frame, Jack Pfefer was busily doing what he did best — ruffling the feathers of his promotional contemporaries. After New York impresarios Toots Mondt and Rudy Dusek both signed on with the National Wrestling Alliance, a nauseated Pfefer went east and joined up with fellow indie booker Al Mayer. Mayer, having established a weekly Saturday television program broadcast on WPIX from the Naval Base at Bayonne, New Jersey, needed an upgrade in talent, and Pfefer was more than willing to lend a hand. In doing so, Pfefer featured his stars in opposition to Mondt and Dusek, while also garnering nice TV exposure in the New York City area.¹⁰ A few weeks later, Pfefer and Mayer convinced the promoter in Camden, New Jersey, to leave the Mondt syndicate and sign on with them.¹¹ As a result, Rogers made his homecoming on Jan. 15, 1951.

The largest crowd of the Camden wrestling season turned out to see Buddy's first local match in nearly six years, and the 2,800 people in attendance weren't disappointed. Fans that remembered his previous battles at the Convention Hall back in 1945 could clearly see that he was a much better wrestler and performer. He lived up to the advanced hype, and although he was in front of a friendly audience, perhaps including family and neighbors, Rogers didn't go the typical babyface route. He was "vicious," as the *Camden Courier-Post* affirmed, and earned boos from the crowd for repeated punches and kicks.¹² Rogers was committed to his role and worked over his opponent,

Tony Sinatra, inside the ring and out. They were equally bloody by the match's end, which came at the 60-minute mark, and the bout was declared a draw.[13]

There was still the question of the red flag that had been raised by the New York State Athletic Commission about Buddy's use of the "Nature Boy" moniker. Pfefer heard complaints about him utilizing the "Buddy Rogers" name when he was originally known in the territory as "Dutch Rohde." Taking everything into consideration, Pfefer decided to bill him as "Dutch 'Nature Boy' Rohde," and figured it was the best of both worlds. New York area newspapers were careful in their advertisements, calling him by his legitimate name, and then stating that he was also known as "'Nature Boy' Buddy Rogers."[14] Between January and March 1951, Rogers worked many dates in the Northeast, as well as in the Midwest, and his endurance was put to the test. Being constantly on the road gave him plenty of time for quiet reflection, and Buddy had a lot on his mind. Deep contemplation about his status in wrestling and future opportunities were front and center, and everything cycled back to his relationship with Jack Pfefer.

For more than four years, Rogers had put his entire livelihood in the hands of Pfefer and had faith in his manager's expertise as a manipulator. In many ways, Pfefer had been much more than just the administrator of his business affairs, and served as a valuable mentor and guide. Adhering to his manager's wishes, Buddy kept precise weekly financial records of his bookings, and that in itself was an important lesson in discipline. The notion of having a fierce watchdog protecting his best interests at all times was appealing to a certain degree, and Rogers benefitted from that kind of supervision. There were personal aspects of their relationship, too. Buddy knew that Pfefer cared about his well-being and he felt the same way about Jack. At times, Rogers was heartened by Pfefer's thoughtfulness, especially when it came to the latter sending gifts to Buddy's mother at Christmastime.[15] If he needed money, Pfefer graciously helped out, and over the previous two years, Buddy was rewarded with a couple of week's vacation away from the grind of wrestling.

Rogers relished in the positives of his association with Pfefer and realized he owed much of his success to his dwarfish boss. But Buddy, who was turning 30 years old in 1951, was not the same naïve upstart that he had been in 1947, and he had grown weary of having an authoritarian in charge of his career. He was tired of turning over a good-sized chunk of his earnings to someone else and envisioned a time in which he was more in control of his own destiny. On top of that, Rogers was increasingly annoyed by Pfefer's maddening eccentricities, and was mentally exhausted by his overbearing attitude, vile language, and erratic behavior.[16] As a political entity in wrestling, Pfefer was a disrupter, and not a team player. He stood outside the syndicates and sewed discord amongst fellow promoters at every turn. Playing by his own rules was one thing, but Pfefer's troublemaking spirit was costly to Rogers, both in standing and financially.

Buddy had to accede that being an outsider like Pfefer, and at constant war with various promoters, was a destructive enterprise, and one that wasn't going to aid his ascension up the proverbial wrestling ladder. In truth, Pfefer was now standing in his way, and Rogers was ready to cut all ties. The exact chronological series of events surrounding the Rogers-Pfefer break-up are unclear, but one particular date in the midst of things stands out, and that is March 22, 1951.[17] On that evening at the Toledo Sports Arena, Lone Eagle, the "Indian Nature Boy," beat Rogers in two straight falls.[18] The surprising finish came on the heels of an intense argument between Rogers and Pfefer, and Pfefer's insistence that Buddy put the Indian wrestler over.[19] He did what his manager wanted for a final time and then dissolved their arrangement. "I couldn't take it no more," Buddy later explained. "He was always right, you were always wrong. And in due time, I don't care who you are, you're going to walk away from that."[20]

Although the decision was made, Rogers was still on the hook for payments to Pfefer through April 13, 1951, according to Pfefer's business records.[21] In the meantime, though, Buddy had washed his hands of the Pfefer circuit and immediately left Toledo. He worked a couple dates in Michigan, New Jersey and Indiana before spending five days in Missouri and Kansas. On April 13, Rogers was in St. Louis for an important bout with Lou Thesz at the Arena, a card that drew 12,183 fans.[22] Thesz went over in 28:25 to retain his NWA world title and Rogers collected a handsome sum of $979.95 for the appearance.[23] That tidy amount, plus earnings for three previous matches over the preceding four days, gave Buddy $1,424.95 on the week, of which $500 went to Pfefer in what would be the latter's final compensation from their severed partnership.[24] Not altogether shockingly, Billy Darnell joined in the exodus, and abandoned the Pfefer camp right around the same time.[25]

Having achieved his independence, Rogers was in a position to better direct his career, and he had many plans for the near future. But he also had a major concern. In addition to his service as a manager, Pfefer had been Buddy's booking agent, and had coordinated a robust schedule that kept him on the move. Being busy meant a healthy income, and Rogers didn't want his bottom line hurt by his newfound sovereignty. He still needed help in that respect, and while he wasn't willing to sign a managerial deal with anyone else, he was in the hunt for a new booking agent – one he knew he could trust. During his last stay in St. Louis, Rogers spoke with Sam Muchnick and inquired about the possibility of the local office booking him. Muchnick weighed the positives and negatives, and ultimately told Buddy he wasn't interested because of his strong sense of loyalty to Pfefer. He advised Rogers to take a "summer vacation" and allow cooler heads to prevail. The St. Louis promoter wanted to meet with Pfefer and work everything out.[26]

There was extreme danger in jumping into business with Rogers right away, and Muchnick recognized that fact. He'd be crossing the perpetually vindictive Pfefer and start a war he didn't want to fight. Other promoters were in the same boat. Pfefer had a lot of acquaintances in wrestling, and many people didn't want the stress of open hostilities with the rogue operator.[27] Rogers understood the reasoning, but that didn't lessen his personal need for allies. He was fending for himself now and had to play his own hand of political hardball. In late April 1951, Buddy sent a wire message to Muchnick with a straightforward declaration: "I am now a free agent. I am no longer managed by Pfefer." Rogers went on to blame "numerous dissatisfactory bookings and constant aggravations" as the reason for the break, and affirmed that it was "not instigated by any Alliance member nor the champion [Lou Thesz]."[28]

Rogers was a verifiable box-office moneymaker and he was going to land on his feet, without question, but it was a matter of timing. He wanted back in the saddle and a substantial push to boot. He soon found out that not all promoters were weak in the knees when it came to Jack Pfefer. In fact, some prominent wrestling figures sought ways to antagonize him. One such man was Edmund Regan (Eddie) Quinn, a product of the western suburbs of Boston, and a longtime associate of "Beantown" promoter Paul Bowser. Quinn was a gregarious fellow with an unyielding appetite for success, and after taking over the Montreal promotion in 1939, had solidified himself as one of the best enterprisers in the field. With firm capital reserves and a thriving territory, he was undaunted by the threat of Pfefer and welcomed the opportunity to work with Rogers.[29]

Negotiations were swift, and within days, a deal was reached between Rogers and Quinn that was satisfactory to both parties. On May 2, 1951, Buddy made his Montreal debut at the Forum and triumphed over Manuel Cortez in auspicious fashion.[30] A local newspaper mentioned his "bewildering aerial attack" and "spectacular grips," and observed his flair for showmanship as he entered the ring under a bright spotlight.[31] His pre-match shenanigans were compared to Gorgeous George, but he was considered to be "a far better wrestler than the Gorgeous One."[32] In the closing seconds of his bout with Cortez, Buddy knocked his foe out with a piledriver and scored a pinfall.[33] The new Rogers-Quinn partnership was off and running and journalists were quick to offer a few words of commentary. Gerald Fitzgerald, a columnist for the *Montreal Gazette*, revealed that Rogers was "under contract" to Quinn, and wondered if the promoter might have "hit another jackpot" in landing him.[34]

Dan Parker, the dogged reporter for the *New York Daily Mirror*, who had made several unfavorable statements about Rogers three years earlier, also referenced his contract with Quinn. He sardonically remarked that the document "was written under water with invisible ink on cellophane."[35] The specific contractual terms are unknown, but it is possible that Quinn was receiving as much as 20 per cent as Buddy's agent.[36] For that reason, Quinn had every intention of pushing Rogers right to the top of his promotion. And he wasn't going to waste any time doing so. Buddy only had one Montreal match under his belt before being booked into a bout with regional world title claimant Bobby Managoff on May 9.[37] His impressiveness and the well-earned hype gave Rogers credibility, and the *Montreal Daily Star* acknowledged him as a favorite "in many quarters" to win the championship.[38] Quinn gave the nod, and Rogers displaced Managoff as champion in a grueling and bloody one-hour contest at the Forum.[39]

Six days later, Buddy went another hour on the mat, this time a thrilling no-falls draw in Cleveland with former rival Don Eagle.[40] Quinn was on hand for that show, as well, having made the trip to attend a special promoters' meeting. Considering he booked most of the talent for the Cleveland program, Al Haft of Columbus was likely one of the other dignitaries present at that conference.[41] Haft was a valuable ally for both Quinn and Rogers, and it made sense to solidify a future working agreement. But since Rogers had spent a lot of time in Ohio under Pfefer's umbrella, a hasty return wasn't a winning long-term formula. He needed a break, and then a smartly-booked fresh start in the territory.[42]

Meanwhile, Rogers was expanding his horizons. Signing with Quinn allowed him to debut in Boston on May 3, 1951, where he beat Les Ryan in a semifinal contest in front of 7,000 at the Arena.[43] That same week, Buddy appeared on the front cover of *New England TV Guide* and was called "Wrestling's New Wonder Man." His success at the box office was highlighted inside the issue, and Rogers was said to have drawn "the biggest houses of the current season."[44] The publicity was ideal, and Buddy was already achieving the kind of prosperity he wanted for his post-Pfefer career. He was a claimant to the world heavyweight title, was wrestling in new markets like Boston and Toronto, and was getting incredible press.[45] In Montreal, he was given the royal treatment and was invited to partake in celebrity events at high end downtown establishments. On one occasion, he mingled with burlesque dancer Lili St. Cyr and comedian Hal Fisher at the Penthouse atop the famous Windsor Steak House overlooking Dominion Square.[46]

Being in Montreal and working with Quinn had many perks. The financial and social benefits were personally gratifying, but in terms of wrestling promotions, Buddy's voice was finally being heard behind the scenes. He was involved in a plot to utilize Quinn's talent on cards staged by Al Mayer in Pennsylvania and New Jersey, and because Mayer was an indie booker, the maneuver drew heavy criticism. NWA member Toots Mondt blamed Rogers for the hostile act and believed Quinn was "following suggestions" made by the blond wrestler.[47] A rumor also circulated that Rogers had officially taken over as matchmaker at the Montreal Forum and that Quinn was moving away from wrestling to greener pastures.[48] The report fed gossipmongers, but had little basis in reality. Quinn wasn't going anywhere. Later in 1951, an article claimed Rogers was a "part-time promoter" in his hometown of Camden.[49]

The success of Rogers made Jack Pfefer furious. He wanted nothing more than for Buddy to be destitute and longing for a reunion. At the core of his emotions, he felt betrayed, and with that came an unhealthy desire for vengeance. In his usual way, he condemned anyone who promoted Rogers and cast aspersions on others if he thought they were even closely aligned with him.[50] As for Rogers, Pfefer maligned him in every way he knew how. His favorite custom was to give inferior performers names that closely resembled Rogers, but differed only slightly. The ritual mocked Buddy, but at the same time, capitalized on his fame. "Bummy" Rogers was a classic example. When Pfefer's creativity ran out, he casually promoted "Young Buddy Rogers" and the "Nature Boy."[51] Eddie Faieta, an up-and-coming wrestler, ran into the real Buddy Rogers on the road in Quebec during the summer of 1951, and told him about Pfefer's new "Nature Boy." Needless to say, Buddy wasn't thrilled.[52]

An old-school promoter from the Old World, Pfefer carried his hatred for Rogers like an albatross around his neck. It was also a badge of honor, which motivated his daily actions. On the cruel underbelly of pro wrestling, there was a way of exacting revenge, and that was to hire a shooter to legitimately injure a rival on the mat. The tactic was malicious and nearly out of practice by the 1950s, but remained a staple in the arsenal of some battle-scarred promoters. Rogers knew all about the possibilities of a double-cross, as did Quinn, and they maintained a strict calendar of dates and a short list of trusted opponents, all regulated from Montreal. Unconcerned, Buddy's former manager set into motion the full effects of the bizarre "Pfefer Curse," as he affixed magazine cut-outs of black cats onto photos and articles about Rogers in his personal collection.[53] His actions were done in superstitious fashion, and he eagerly waited to celebrate any kind of bad news involving his former star.

For Sam Muchnick in St. Louis, siding with Pfefer was all about self preservation. But losing Rogers was significant, and Muchnick suffered a major financial loss. In need of a wrestler with a similar ability to draw, Muchnick corresponded with Toots Mondt about the possibility of using Gene Stanlee. Toots was more than happy to oblige, telling Muchnick: "I am sure [Stanlee] will supplant Rogers for you quick."[54] "Mr. America" did venture to St. Louis for appearances in November and December 1951, building toward a title match with Lou Thesz on Dec. 28, 1951. The NWA champion retained his crown that night with a pinfall victory over Stanlee in 15:21.[55] And to the question: Did Stanlee successfully replace Rogers as a box office attraction in St. Louis, a scientific comparison can't be made. However, if you compared Stanlee versus Thesz, and then Rogers against Thesz, the audience differential was 5,576 in Rogers' favor.[56] Stanlee was a draw, but he certainly didn't displace the "Nature Boy" as hoped.

Rogers remained a valuable force in Montreal throughout 1951. As expected, he entered into a feud with local hero Yvon Robert, and a big championship match was held in an outdoor baseball stadium on July 13.[57] Before more than 10,000 spectators, Rogers vaulted through the air and was caught between the second and top ropes — a repeat performance of his hanging routine. Once freed by referees, Rogers fell to the mat unconscious and was rushed to an area hospital for treatment. Robert was declared winner by default and captured the world title.[58] Over the next couple months, Buddy worked a relatively light schedule, and watched as Quinn laid the foundation for his return to Ohio. The effort reinforced his relationship with Al Haft and the NWA, and peace was brokered with New York promoters.[59] On October 18, Rogers made his first appearance in Columbus in well over two years, defeating Maurice Roberre in 8:44.[60]

The Haft circuit included Cincinnati, Cleveland, and Akron, plus additional bookings into outlying towns and parts of Pennsylvania. Haft, who turned 65 in November 1951, was the type of promoter to shy away from overbearing showmanship.[61] A former wrestler himself, he long appreciated the finer art of the profession, but that didn't mean he didn't recognize extraordinary talent when he saw it, regardless of the style. Haft was a businessman and he knew Rogers meant big bucks. Whatever apprehension he might have had disappeared in light of Buddy's marketability, and he was ready to give him a featured spot. The arrangement was rewarding to Rogers, too, and increased his workload measurably. He maintained his obligations to Quinn and expanded his range of travel, bouncing quite steadily between Quebec and the Upper Midwest. On Wednesday nights, he was frequently called to Chicago for matches at the familiar Rainbo Arena, and was prominently showcased on the ABC telecast.

Almost immediately after joining Haft, Rogers was assigned a "policeman" to help safeguard the interests of the "Nature Boy" and his handlers. The choice was a 5-foot-8 Chicagoan named Ralph (Ruffy) Silverstein, a veteran of 14 years on the pro mat. Silverstein was a heralded shooter, having won Big Ten and NCAA honors in college, and was more recently an AWA world heavyweight champion and TV sensation in Chicago. He agreed to take the position, earning a modest slice of Buddy's gates, and in exchange would ward off dangerous opponents from ever getting their chance at a double-cross.[62] If a potentially untrustworthy rival stepped forward with a public challenge, Rogers could respond by telling the foe to wrestle and beat Ruffy first. And if the individual was bold enough to face Silverstein, there was little chance he could beat him, leaving Rogers safe from outward pressure to take any match he didn't want. Simply put, Silverstein was a deterrent. Nobody wanted to shoot with Ruffy.

"We hit it off right away," Rogers later said of his association with Silverstein. "He was the best wrestler I ever worked with. He was the ideal policeman."[63] Backstage, the two were friendly stablemates, but in the ring, they were fierce opponents. Their rivalry kicked off at a high school gym in Aliquippa, Pennsylvania, on Oct. 20, 1951, and they were in no mood to trade holds in an exposition of wrestling science. They went completely in the other direction, brawling in the ring and out, and were both disqualified. In Johnstown, Pennsylvania, on November 23, Buddy and Silverstein did it again, and their unrestrained, extreme violence nearly started a riot. The former took delight in bashing Ruffy's head into the ring post, opening up a wound, and after a few minutes, blood was everywhere. They were covered in plasma, and one ringside spectator fainted from the gruesome sight. The referee stopped the match in the midst of the chaos, disqualifying the competitors, and police held back irate spectators from entering the ring.[64]

On November 30, in a non-televised affair at the Rainbo, Rogers won his first match over his "policeman" when Silverstein was disqualified for failing to break an illegal hold in the third fall.[65] In Ohio, Haft had already initiated a special tournament, and was running weekly eliminations from a television studio in Dayton.[66] It was the second annual WLW tourney, sponsored by the Crosley Broadcasting Corporation, and it was enormously popular across the state. Silverstein had captured the prized WLW Television championship belt the year before. This time around, Ruffy was going to meet the tournament finalist in defense of his crown, and it seemed natural that Rogers would be his eventual opponent. Buddy advanced through the eliminations and, on the afternoon of Feb. 2, 1952, he beat Pierre LaSalle for the right to wrestle Silverstein.[67]

The championship finals occurred on February 9 at the Coliseum in Columbus, and nearly 9,000 enthusiastic spectators were in attendance. Jack Dempsey was imported to be the guest referee, and considering the mayhem in recent Rogers-Silverstein matches, having a former boxing champion officiate was probably a good idea. The wrestlers split the opening falls, and in the third, Rogers caught Ruffy in a corner of the ring. When he unloaded with his usual rough tactics, Dempsey disqualified him, ending the bout.[68] Buddy's heel antics had been expected, and Ohio crowds were quick to vocalize their collective disdain for his "wild and woolly" behavior. His actions only intensified the fan support for his opponents, and made for a good show. When Al Haft booked Rogers against a fellow heel, which he often did, fans were left to choose between the lesser evil.[69] If Rogers was up against a wrestler fans hated more, they'd cheer him. And that actually happened in matches against the likes of Mr. Moto and Killer Kowalski.

Sometimes, though, the hatred for Rogers turned well-established "bad" guys into heroes. George Drake, a Californian in his early twenties, was working as a heel in part of Indiana, prior to a contest with the "Nature Boy." A writer for the *Muncie Star Press* noted that Drake, when "pitted against that rascal Rogers," was "taken to the bosoms of the very customers who denounced him one week before." The journalist added: "This was not surprising, since Rogers, the scoundrel, could make a hero out of Hitler."[70] Yet still, in a March 1952 issue of Haft's Columbus arena program, appropriately dubbed *Haft Nelson*, said that Buddy was the "pride and joy of the bobby soxers – and some of the grown-ups."[71] It was that group of people, the fans who enjoyed Rogers regardless of his nightly duties, that Haft wanted to reach, and he advocated for Buddy to play into his "softer" side. The middle ground between a favorite and a heel was awfully gray, and was a moneymaking spot if handled the correct way.

Haft felt Rogers could handle it. As 1952 wore on, there was more of an emphasis on Buddy's charm and personality. On April 12, 1952, the "Nature Boy" made a special live appearance at Luckoff's Department Store in Columbus, and it was a perfect opportunity to socialize with fans.[72] Generally, Buddy remained an anti-hero in most cities, but the crossover affect was potent, and certainly helped his box office appeal. The *Lancaster New Era* newspaper summed it up: "While he's a villain, he has maintained his popularity with the fans, which is a neat trick few toughies have mastered."[73] In a kayfabe defense of his villainy, Rogers said: "I do not realize, many times, that I am getting too rough. After all, I'm out to win each and every match and I put my heart and soul in every bout. Some of the fans do not like me, for which I am sorry, but just the same, I'll always try to win as quick as I can, and I may get a little rough accomplishing my end."[74]

Everything surrounding Buddy Rogers was going to be black or white – or gray, for that matter. His in-ring wrestling was going to be part hero and part heel, his interviews were going to be masterful storytelling, and out-of-the-ring, he was going to glad-hand and smile his way into the hearts of fans. On one night, he'd be slamming his rival's head into the metal post and bathing in his blood, and on another, he would be playing it clean from bell-to-bell, and signing autographs after the bout. You never really knew what you were going to get with Buddy Rogers, but for his growing horde of supporters, they didn't care. They wanted to be entertained, and Rogers was a born performer. Stoic professional wrestlers were a dime a dozen, and their welcome was worn. It was a new era, and fans were embracing the calculated mixed bag of the "Nature Boy." He represented unpredictably, arrogance, and unscrupulous wrestling at its very best. But with a crooked grin, it was all washed away. He was their hero.

ENDNOTES - CHAPTER 8

[1] The National Wrestling Alliance was founded on July 18, 1948 in Waterloo, Iowa.

[2] Kohler described his grievances in a letter to Sam Muchnick dated Dec. 9, 1950, Department of Justice Investigation into the National Wrestling Alliance, National Archives, College Park, MD.

[3] Notably, Pfefer had already forgiven Sam Muchnick for his perceived indiscretions in St. Louis. Rogers had returned to St. Louis on July 21, 1950 after a more than a year absence. Muchnick was elected to the presidency of the NWA in September 1950 at its annual convention in Dallas.

[4] *Chicago Sun-Times*, Dec. 9, 1950, p. 29.

[5] *Wrestling As You Like It*, Dec. 23, 1950, p. 3. Rogers earned $795 for the match. Jack Pfefer Collection, Joyce Sports Research Collection, Hesburgh Library, University of Notre Dame, Notre Dame, Indiana.

[6] *Wrestling As You Like It*, Jan. 20, 1951, p. 3.

[7] *Chicago Daily News*, Jan. 27, 1951, p. 12.

[8] *Wrestling As You Like It*, Feb. 10, 1951, p. 2.

[9] Ibid, p. 3.

[10] Rogers debut on the telecast on Dec. 23, 1950 and also appeared the following week. He beat Jack Steele in his first appearance and then Hal Kanner in his second.

[11] The promoter was Joe Valentine.

[12] *Camden Courier-Post*, Jan. 16, 1951, p. 22.

[13] Ibid.

[14] *Long Island Star Journal*, April 11, 1950, p. 17.

[15] Rogers letter to Jack Pfefer dated Dec. 27, 1948. Jack Pfefer Collection, Joyce Sports Research Collection, Hesburgh Library, University of Notre Dame, Notre Dame, Indiana.

[16] Rogers spoke about Pfefer and his "very vicious way" during a 1991 interview. Buddy Rogers Interview by Tom Burke and Dan Reilly, *Wrestle Radio*, Nov. 9, 1991.

[17] Wrestling historian Bill McCormack theorized that Rogers "exercised his 90 day notice on his contract" with Pfefer sometime after a Jan. 12, 1951 date in St. Louis. Research notes of Bill McCormack. On Jan. 12, 1951 in St. Louis, Rogers defeated Lord Pinkerton and made $299.13 on the evening. No additional info about Buddy's "contract" with Pfefer was located. No such document was in existence at the Jack Pfefer Collection, Joyce Sports Research Collection, Hesburgh Library, University of Notre Dame, Notre Dame, Indiana.

[18] *Toledo Blade*, March 23, 1951, p. 38.

[19] George Grant Interview, *Wrestling Archive Project, Vol. 1* by Scott Teal, p. 265.

[20] Buddy Rogers Interview by Tom Burke and Dan Reilly, *Wrestle Radio*, Nov. 9, 1991.

[21] Jack Pfefer Collection, Joyce Sports Research Collection, Hesburgh Library, University of Notre Dame, Notre Dame, Indiana.

[22] The show was an unabashed success, yet the attendance was 5,600 less than what Rogers and Thesz achieved at the same venue a month earlier. On March 16, 1951 at the St. Louis Arena, Thesz pinned Rogers before 17,796 fans. Several thousand were turned away. *St. Louis Globe-Democrat*, March 17, 1951, p. 4C. This attendance topped the record setting crowd that Rogers and Bill Longson drew in April 1946 by 175 people and is believed to be the largest of Buddy's career, to date.

[23] *St. Louis Globe-Democrat*, April 14, 1951, p. 19. Two of Pfefers' workers, Lone Eagle and Elephant Boy, were also on this card. Jack Pfefer Collection, Joyce Sports Research Collection, Hesburgh Library, University of Notre Dame, Notre Dame, Indiana.

[24] That week, Rogers earned $107 in Camden, $235 in Lancaster, and $103 in Lebanon. Jack Pfefer Collection, Joyce Sports Research Collection, Hesburgh Library, University of Notre Dame, Notre Dame, Indiana.

25 Darnell's reasons for leaving Pfefer were probably similar to Rogers' complaints. It has been said that Rogers directly influenced Darnell's move, and it is likely true. Darnell had been advertised for the March 29, 1951 show in Toledo, but no showed the event. *Toledo Blade*, March 30, 1951, p. 42. Notably, Rogers' friend Tony Sinatra (Jerry Vallina) had broken from Pfefer around February 1951 and went to work for Al Haft in Ohio.

26 Rogers also spoke with Lou Thesz and Bill Longson. Sam Muchnick letter to Toots Mondt, dated July 7, 1951.

27 In addition to Muchnick, Rogers approached Orville Brown and Fred Kohler about a possible deal to be his booking agent. Ibid.

28 Sam Muchnick letter to Jack Pfefer, dated April 29, 1951. Jack Pfefer Collection, Joyce Sports Research Collection, Hesburgh Library, University of Notre Dame, Notre Dame, Indiana. It is not known if Rogers sent this same message to other NWA members.

29 Yukon Eric was the middleman between Rogers and Eddie Quinn. Research notes of Bill McCormack. It was rumored that Lou Thesz facilitated the Rogers-Quinn deal, and specifically put Rogers in touch with Quinn, who was his longtime friend. Muchnick later denied that story. Sam Muchnick letter to Toots Mondt, dated July 7, 1951.

30 Billy Darnell also made his Montreal debut at that event. Some people didn't believe Rogers had left Jack Pfefer. One rumor stated that Pfefer had sent Rogers to Montreal to take over the territory. Letter from Eddie Faieta to Jack Pfefer, June 24, 1951. Cortez used the name "Frank Scarpa" in Boston. Years later, Rogers told a story of a match against Scarpa, saying: "I'll carry a long scar down my back as long as I live – a present from Scarpa. We were wrestling in Boston back in 1952. He hit me with a flying block and knocked me out of the ring. Clear over the top rope I sailed, landing back first on a row of chairs. One of the chairs splintered and a razor-sharp piece of wood ripped across my back." He reportedly needed more than 20 stitches. *Big Book of Wrestling*, September 1970. In 1952, Rogers had two big matches with Scarpa in Boston, one on February 28 and the other on April 24. If the year was correct, it's believed that the incident happened during one of these two bouts.

31 *Montreal Daily Star*, May 7, 1951, p. 36.

32 Ibid.

33 *Montreal Daily Star*, May 8, 1951, p. 30.

34 Fitzgerald wrote the column, "On and Off the Record." He explained that Rogers was "under contract," and was the "only one of Quinn's stable so committed." He added that Yvon Robert, Larry Moquin "and his other stars" were "on verbal pacts only." *Montreal Gazette*, May 7, 1951, p. 4.

35 *Camden Courier-Post*, May 14, 1951, p. 21.

36 A report in the *Columbus Dispatch* in 1953 claimed that Quinn made $7,000 during a six-month span in which Rogers earned $32,777. This would have been in the neighborhood of 21 per cent. However, the numbers in the article were not altogether precise and leaves room for further speculation. *Columbus Dispatch*, Feb. 22, 1953, p. 56. Although 20 per cent was still a large amount of money to turn over to an agent, Rogers was being booked into better towns and larger venues, significantly increasing his pay. The trade off was worth it.

37 Rogers knew Managoff from his time in Texas during the summer of 1945. He had both wrestled and partnered with the second generation grappler from Chicago.

38 *Montreal Daily Star*, May 8, 1951, p. 30.

39 The match lasted 1:02:15. Managoff sold a back injury late in the bout. Rogers used a flying scissors to score the final pinfall. *Montreal Daily Star*, May 10, 1951, p. 52.

40 *Cleveland Plain Dealer*, May 16, 1951, p. 24. This was the first Rogers-Eagle match in two years. They last faced on April 26, 1949 in Des Moines.

41 The Cleveland show featured Bill Miller, Jack Vansky, Frankie Talaber, Jackie Nichols, and Roy Shire. Ibid.

42 Sam Muchnick stated that Al Haft was bitter against Rogers. Letter from Sam Muchnick to Toots Mondt dated July 7, 1951.

43 *Boston Herald*, May 4, 1951, p. 52. Rogers' original foe was said to be Miguel Torres. *Boston Traveler*, May 3, 1951, p. 27.

44 The writer of the magazine article was speculative about Buddy's potential to supplant Gene Stanlee "in the hearts of the fans." He added that "authorities" inside the business felt it would "never happen." *New England TV Guide*, Week of May 5-11, 1951, p. 16-17. The author was Bill Johnston. It is unclear, but very likely, that this was Bill Johnston "Jr.," the son of the late boxing promoter, Jimmy Johnston, and the nephew of Charley and Bill Johnston. The latter, notably, passed away in May of 1950.

45 Rogers debut in Toronto on June 14, 1951 with a victory over Sonny Kurgis.

46 The Windsor Steak House was a well-known eatery for celebrities in Montreal. Dominion Square is now known as Dorchester Square. Harry Labe owned the Elbow Room bar as part of the establishment. Rogers attended a special "Meet the Stars" event at the Penthouse with Lili St. Cyr, Billy Vane, and Jackie Miles. *Montreal Gazette*, June 18, 1951, p. 13. He was photographed with St. Cyr, Laura, a former Miss Miami, and Hal Fisher. *Montreal Gazette*, June 21, 1951, p. 3.

47 Letter from Toots Mondt to Sam Muchnick dated July 11, 1951.

48 Letter from Eddie Faieta to Jack Pfefer dated June 24, 1951, Jack Pfefer Collection, Joyce Sports Research Collection, Hesburgh Library, University of Notre Dame, Notre Dame, Indiana.

49 *Lancaster New Era*, Dec. 13, 1951, p. 46. Between September and December 1951, Rogers wrestled in Camden seven times.

50 In a letter to Toots Mondt, Muchnick discussed the places Rogers appeared, and stated that the promoters must have had no scruples about using him. Letter from Sam Muchnick to Toots Mondt, July 7, 1951.

51 Tommy Phelps, who worked as Buddy's valet (Izzy Becker), used the "Nature Boy" gimmick for Pfefer in 1951.

52 Letter from Eddie Faieta to Jack Pfefer, July 10, 1951, Jack Pfefer Collection, Joyce Sports Research Collection, Hesburgh Library, University of Notre Dame, Notre Dame, Indiana. Faieta was working the indie circuit for promoters Bob and Paul Lortie.

53 After reviewing materials in the Pfefer Collection, it appears that the black cat image that he frequently liked to use was taken from "My Sin" fragrance advertisements by Lanvin. Jack Pfefer Collection, Joyce Sports Research Collection, Hesburgh Library, University of Notre Dame, Notre Dame, Indiana.

54 Mondt also explained that Stanlee received "ten percent of the net after legal taxes." Letter from Toots Mondt to Sam Muchnick, Aug. 25, 1951.

55 *St. Louis Post-Dispatch*, Dec. 29, 1951, p. 7.

56 Rogers and Thesz drew 12,183 at the St. Louis Arena on April 13, 1951. *St. Louis Globe-Democrat*, April 14, 1951, p. 5C. Stanlee and Thesz drew 6,607 at the Kiel Auditorium on Dec. 28, 1951. *St. Louis Globe-Democrat*, Dec. 29, 1951, p. 4C.

57 The show was held in the stadium of the Montreal Royals, a minor league team.

58 *Montreal Daily Star*, July 14, 1951, p. 25.

59 Toots Mondt still believed Rogers was at fault for their previous difficulties and bragged that he was working with Quinn to get him "straightened out." Letter from Toots Mondt to Sam Muchnick, Sept. 27, 1951. In a return letter, Muchnick said that he appreciated Mondt's efforts. Letter from Sam Muchnick to Toots Mondt, Oct. 1, 1951.

60 His match was a semifinal, underneath a bout between MWA Junior champion Marvin Mercer and Jackie Nichols. The show was staged at the Memorial Hall and 3,100 fans were present. *Columbus Dispatch*, Oct. 19, 1951, p. 33. Prior to the show, Rogers was billed as a "glamour boy," and said to be "one of the top 'villains' of the mat." *Columbus Dispatch*, Oct. 18, 1951, p. 21. Buddy's last Columbus appearance was Feb. 17, 1949.

61 Haft was born on Nov. 13, 1886.

62 In a later interview, Rogers said that Fred Kohler introduced him to Ruffy Silverstein. *Buddie Rogers and The Art of "Sequencing"* by Max W. Jacobs, p. 9.

63 Ibid.

64 *Altoona Tribune*, Dec. 1, 1951, p. 10.

65 *Chicago Daily Tribune*, Dec. 1, 1951, p. C4.

⁶⁶ The tournament launched on November 24 and there were 16 wrestlers involved. *Columbus Dispatch*, Nov. 18, 1951, p. F16.
⁶⁷ The Rogers-LaSalle bout was advertised for broadcast on WLW-T, channel 4, at 10:30 p.m., *Cincinnati Enquirer*, Feb. 2, 1952, p. 28. One newspaper called this particular contest "the final preliminary match of the WLW-TV championship tournament." *Marion Star*, Feb. 8, 1952, p. 18.
⁶⁸ *Columbus Dispatch*, Feb. 11, 1952, p. 13.
⁶⁹ Rogers feuded with many "rulebreakers" to include Nanjo Singh, Roy Shire, and Ed Francis. The latter two wrestlers were managed by Jack Hunter and Bobby Wallace, respectively.
⁷⁰ *Muncie Star Press*, Nov. 14, 1952, p. 36.
⁷¹ *Haft Nelson*, Vol. 1, No. 12, March 6, 1952.
⁷² A contest was held during this appearance for fans. If someone could guess Rogers' "specifications," they'd win a prize. Rogers was there between noon and 1:00 p.m. *Haft Nelson*, Vol. 1, No. 16, April 3, 1952.
⁷³ *Lancaster New Era*, March 5, 1952, p. 22.
⁷⁴ *Haft Nelson*, Vol. 1, No. 7, January 1952.

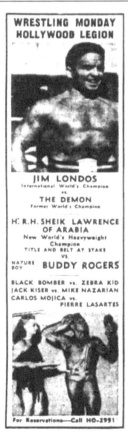

Los Angeles, California: Monday, Feb. 28, 1949
The night Rogers won the Pfefer version of the world heavyweight title for the second time.

Chapter 9
A Perennial Champion

Television was the source for a renewed popularity and mass exposure of professional wrestling in the late 1940s. In many parts of the United States, box office revenue increased significantly, and promoters worked overtime to strengthen their arrangements with influential TV stations, both locally and nationally. The mainstream prominence of wrestling, and its valuable prime-time placement on television, was a powerful new recruitment tool for promoters to use in discussions with athletes considering a future in the sport. Between 1947 and '51, a fresh crop of rookies entered the grappling business, and many of them were highly-touted prospects right out of college. Verne Gagne was an NCAA, Big Ten, and AAU champion from Minnesota, while Mike DiBiase captured three Big Seven titles at the University of Nebraska. Bob Geigel and Bill Miller were two other former amateur stars to make the transition to the pro ranks, and their success was all but guaranteed.

One newcomer with just as much potential as his university-educated colleagues was John Theodore Wisniski, better known as Johnny Valentine. Originally from Hobart, Washington, Valentine faced hardship from a young age, and prioritized work over schooling to survive. The 6-foot-2 youngster was discovered as a teenager by the Zbyszko brothers, Stanislaus and Wladek, two former world champions.[1] With little money, but the motivation to make a career in wrestling, he ventured to the Missouri farm of the Zbyszkos, and was provided with a first-rate mentorship of his own. The lessons were grueling, but life-altering, and by 1947, he made his pro debut in South America. Over the next few years, he toured extensively from Florida to California and furthered his ring education. Ohio's Al Haft reveled in Valentine's ability and exuberance, and recognized him as a throwback-type wrestler from his generation.[2]

Billed as Johnny "Baby Face" Valentine, for his youthful looks, he gained notoriety in Columbus by challenging the more experienced Buddy Rogers to a bout on Nov. 1, 1951, at the Memorial Hall.[3] This, their first ever match-up, kicked off an intense rivalry that continued for the next 11 years. And to illustrate how fiery their combat was, following their initial contest in Columbus, both men were suspended by the Columbus Boxing and Wrestling Commission for innumerous infractions. The epic scene was rasslin' violence at its best as they pummeled each other mercilessly, drawing blood, and sending the crowd into a riotous frenzy.[4] After the bout was declared a no-contest, an estimated 500 fans "trailed" Rogers as he left the ring, and the *Columbus Dispatch* affirmed that the wrestler "had to use his fists several times to keep from being struck."[5]

Rogers and Valentine each put up a $250 forfeit prior to their return match on November 21, and the "Nature Boy" used a piledriver and a submission hold to achieve victory.[6] A few weeks later, on December 13, a third contest between the foes was scheduled, and this time, it was a special 10-round boxing match with both athletes wearing regulation gloves. The Columbus Boxing and Wrestling Commission officially sanctioned the fight because the two had so often resorted to fisticuffs. For Rogers, he was right at home in a boxing environment. He trained as a pugilist while a member of the Camden YMCA during his early years and closely followed the sport.[7] In response to a hypothetical about the road not taken, Rogers was typically boastful, stating: "I could have been the sensation of the [boxing] heavyweights. A real killer."[8] He proved capable in his worked fight with Valentine and won in six rounds. Rogers put over Valentine's strength and was knocked to the mat "no less than five times."[9]

As noted after Buddy's first match with Valentine, there were times in which Rogers was in legitimate physical danger. He was almost always outnumbered and police protection was mandatory. On such occasions when his heel antics pushed crowds to the boiling point, Rogers had to take precautionary steps, and he was hyper-alert to incoming aggressors. He wasn't afraid to fight back if he felt he was in jeopardy, but sometimes, the circumstances were just beyond his control. In a 1950 interview, Rogers recalled a harrowing episode in Mexico City, saying: "Every time I would get the Mexican hero flat on his back ready for the count, the fans would pile into the ring and pull me off. Finally, on the 12th try, I pinned. Then the fun started. Someone knifed me in the leg. After fighting for 20 minutes, I went down from loss of blood. Then they began feeding me show leather. I finally lost consciousness. To top it off, the police threw me into jail for three days for inciting a riot."[10]

In 1952, Rogers was caught in several risky situations. The first may have occurred at a spot show in April, and little is known about it. A brief write-up that appeared in a Pennsylvania newspaper only mentioned that he had been stabbed by a "West Virginia hillbilly."[11] A month later, in Springfield, Ohio, he was stabbed again, and his assailant got him right in the back as he was leaving the ring.[12] Rogers swiftly reacted to the attack and reportedly grabbed a woman by the arm to prevent further violence. The woman claimed she was bruised and the two each filed assault charges on the other.[13] The case was ultimately dropped.[14] Another incident happened in Columbus during the summer when Rogers was poked by a sharp hatpin.[15] Instinctively, he "flailed his arms" and seemingly "struck" Mrs. Jessie Lamp in the process.[16] She also filed charges against Rogers, but dropped the case within a couple days.[17] In each of these events, Rogers, and the fan involved, were both lucky to have escaped serious injury.

The feud between Rogers and Ruffy Silverstein continued to sell a startling amount of tickets. On June 12, 1952, the "policeman" took a rare pinfall win from the "Nature Boy" before 5,000 onlookers at Haft's Acre in Columbus.[18] Rogers used his piledriver to even the score on July 10 and drew 5,781 to the same venue.[19] Silverstein was leading things on Aug. 28, but made a costly error late in the match and was pinned. That contest was held in Columbus, as well, and was witnessed by 5,811 spectators.[20] By this time, Al Haft was advertising Rogers as the "kingpin of Eastern Heavyweights," and the championship added to his prestige.[21] But the territory itself was overloaded with title claims and it was nearly impossible to chart any lineage with any sort of accuracy. The "AWA" world championship had been Haft's central heavyweight crown, and the belt carried a great deal of respect following the lengthy reign of Frank Sexton from 1945 to '50. Sexton was succeeded by Don Eagle in May 1950.

The following year, without a clear explanation, Ruffy Silverstein was suddenly acknowledged as the "AWA" champion in Chicago, which was a sharp divergence from AWA recognition in Ohio and Boston. On May 1, 1952, Bill Miller won Haft's Ohio version of the title with a victory over Eagle, but since the latter was still champ in New England, there were now three different AWA claimants.[22] As strange as all this sounds, it got even weirder. Don Arnold, a talented upstart from San Diego, beat Miller in Dayton on September 2 and was proclaimed champion.[23] Eleven days later, Miller was a finalist in a TV tournament in Pittsburgh, but was defeated by Buddy Rogers.[24] Rogers, as a result, was pronounced the initial Tri-State titleholder, recognized in Pennsylvania, Ohio and West Virginia. On face value, the tournament went to a logical conclusion and the new championship added to Buddy's list of honors.

But sportswriter Win Fanning of the *Pittsburgh Post-Gazette* denoted that something else had happened when Rogers beat Miller. He stated that their tournament final was actually for a claim to the world heavyweight title, and after Rogers won, he was to receive the diamond-studded belt worth $5,000.[25] Fanning didn't see the belt handed over to Rogers on the television broadcast, nor did commentator Wayne Griffin clarify the "status" of the championship in clear terms.[26] With questions remaining, Al Haft used his Columbus arena program, *Haft Nelson*, to subtly confirm that Buddy was the "new heavyweight champion" of the AWA and held the prized belt.[27] The addition of Rogers to the growing list of AWA claimants was mindboggling, but par for the course in pro wrestling. There were now four simultaneous AWA champions: Silverstein, Eagle, Arnold, and Rogers.

From an outside perspective, this kind of booking was jumbled and chaotic. What earthly purpose did having two AWA champs in Ohio, one in Chicago, and another in Boston serve?[28] If it was going to draw money, Haft was in for it, but otherwise, the situation needed to be cleaned up quickly. On Oct. 14, 1952, at Sucher Park in Dayton, Rogers defeated Arnold for his claim to the AWA championship. Referee Archie Turner called for the bell after Arnold was thrown from the ring and deemed unable to continue.[29] Three nights later in Chicago, Buddy beat Silverstein to end his run as AWA champion. The three-fall victory occurred at the Rainbo before 1,500 fans.[30] And as quick as that, the "Nature Boy" had eliminated two of the three other claimants. Don Eagle was the last remaining rival, but injuries had caught up with him, and the title was declared vacant in Boston.[31] Local promoter Paul Bowser yearned to fill the void on December 2 at a special charity show at the Boston Arena.[32]

Feeling the pressure from the National Wrestling Alliance, of which he was a member, Bowser began to distance himself from independent recognition of a world champion. Instead of calling it the AWA "world" heavyweight crown, he was now content labeling it the AWA "Eastern" or "East Coast" heavyweight belt. Al Haft joined him, although publicity reports frequently misidentified the title.[33] The December 2 bout in Boston drew a crowd of 5,000, with Rogers winning two straight falls over Wladek (Tarzan) Kowalski to capture the championship.[34] The process of uniting the various versions of the AWA lineage further cemented Rogers' fame, and the positive press kept pouring in. A Columbus piece put out by Haft praised his drawing ability, and lauded his recent appearances in Montreal, Pittsburgh, Chicago, and Boston. "Shows before [Rogers arrived in these locations] did not draw big crowds," the article asserted.[35] In a Georgia promotional item, Rogers was said to have been "rated as almost the best thing to come along since toothpaste" by his peers.[36]

Financially for Rogers, things were in tip-top shape. As he'd say to his friends and reporters, he was "in the velvet," literally meaning that he was in the money, and it was a much better economic class than he was used to. A child of the Depression, Rogers had seen poverty first-hand, and he could recall the struggle of his parents as they labored to put food on the table. His memories were haunting, and Buddy never wanted to experience that kind of lifestyle again. From a young age, he had been committed to preserving his cash intake, and he was already sitting on a nice-sized nest egg.[37] There was another memory deeply ingrained in his mind, which also motivated him to preserve his financial wellbeing. Many years earlier, he was witness to the resultant effect of "living beyond your means" when he saw a famous retired professional athlete in the poorhouse and "dependent on charity."[38]

NWA Official Wrestling magazine, in 1952, revealed that tidbit of information, but didn't specify anyone in particular. Rogers subsequently did an interview and brought up the name, Ed (Strangler) Lewis, stating that he "grossed $15 million in the wresting game and didn't have fifteen bucks to his name" later in life. "It made me think and I've been nursing every nickel ever since," Rogers added.[39] The "Strangler" was indeed one of the most recognizable superstars in the sport's history, and it was very true that he was insolvent. He was hired by friends in the National Wrestling Alliance as Lou Thesz' manager and given a modest salary to keep his head above water. But other than that, he was broke. Rogers didn't want that to happen to him, and vowed to maintain and build upon his fortune.

Rogers was much more frugal than frivolous, but he did have his weaknesses. "I love clothes, flashy cars and diamonds," he told the *Columbus Star*.[40] His wardrobe included more than three dozen tailor-made suits and he owned $26,000 worth of diamonds.[41] On his left pinky finger, he wore an opulent 14-karat diamond ring that cost more than most people made in a year.[42] Buddy's car preference was Cadillac, and he liked to purchase a new automobile on an annual basis.[43] His model in 1952 was a Cadillac convertible, red in color, with a blue hard top.[44] Driving was an important part of a wrestler's life, and Rogers wanted to be extremely comfortable (and stylish) while cruising the byways and highways of America. He couldn't be caught in any old jalopy. He was a champion wrestler, after all, and, of course, the "Nature Boy." It was all about image. As a driver, Rogers was known for his heavy foot. He loved to speed from town-to-town, and there was never a dull moment when he was behind the wheel.[45]

Camden was Buddy's hometown, but it wasn't a lucrative wrestling city. Sure, it had a long history of pro grappling, but it was far from being the cornerstone of the Northeastern territory. Through the years, Rogers lived in a lot of places, sometimes for months at a time, but Camden was always his home of record. However, he was spending much of his time in Columbus, Ohio, and fell in love with the city. "You can't meet any nicer people anywhere," he later said.[46] Rogers lived in downtown Columbus at 224 S. High Street, a short distance from Al Haft's office and gymnasium.[47] The surrounding area was bustling with first-class eateries, nightlife, and entertainment. The popular Coney Island Restaurant was a few doors away and drinks were available at the High Beck Tavern down the block.[48] A 24-hour establishment, the Hi-Fulton Grill, was advertised as "the favorite eating place of the wrestlers," and served steaks and seafood.

Live music and dancing was abundant, and that too was a major plus for Rogers. When wrestling didn't occupy the Memorial Hall, world-class performers took center stage. Crooners Tony Bennett, Louis Jordan, Frankie Laine, and Billy Eckstine were among the big names to captivate audiences. Ella Fitzgerald and Dinah Washington, two of Buddy's favorites, also toured through Columbus with engagements at the Hall. Great music emanated from the Ionian Room at the Deshler-Wallick Hotel and the Columbus Room at the Seneca Hotel. Free-time during the summer was spent swimming at the famed Bath Club at 570 Nelson Road.[49] It was the perfect environment to work out, improve his tan, and socialize. The *Columbus Star* newspaper caught Buddy hanging out with Miss Columbus 1951, Nancy Eversole, on the outdoor deck of the club in July 1952. The two were photographed performing an impressive acrobatic feat, with Rogers doing a handstand while balancing atop a prone Eversole.[50]

Working for Al Haft proved worthwhile. Columbus was a significant hub for pro wrestling and Haft booked wrestlers in six different states.[51] An older man with a bald head and distinctive cauliflower ears, Haft was meticulous in his business, and earned international respect. His High Street office was a hotspot for talent, promoters, and fans hoping to get a look at their favorite stars. Additionally, on the third floor of the building, a wrestling ring was set-up to train aspiring wrestlers. Rogers frequently worked out in Haft's gym, as did Ruffy Silverstein, Bill Miller, Joe Scarpello, and scores of others. The territory saw the very best in the industry, and match-ups were physically skillful and creative. Loyalists expected nothing less. Rogers was given plenty of leeway to work his magic, and he was still learning on the job.

Haft was a wise mentor and offered advice, constructive criticism, and encouragement. His experience was valuable, and at the time, Rogers had nothing but good things to say about him. "I've had some great teachers in the game," he explained in 1952. "Columbus' own Al Haft is one of them. When you take a place like Red Lion, Pennsylvania, with a population of 1,200 people, and see 3,000 turn out for a match, you wonder where they come from. Then you realize that good promoting has brought them in from miles around." Shrewd to the bone, Haft refused to play ball with other members of the National Wrestling Alliance at times if an issue contradicted his personal dealings. For example, Chicago promoter Fred Kohler expressed a desire to receive bookings for Rogers and feature him on his Saturday TV program on the Dumont Network. An appearance of that magnitude was beneficial, and everyone involved knew it. But Haft didn't care. He blocked the booking, and likely cited Kohler's past transgressions for his reasoning.[52]

On Feb. 3, 1953, Buddy returned to Boston to wrestle his long-time adversary, Yvon Robert, in defense of his "East Coast" championship.[53] Rogers, in the third fall, pulled off his hanging in the ropes stunt, and dropped the title.[54] It was the same way he had lost his Montreal belt to Robert in 1951. The "Nature Boy" remained champion in Ohio. In fact, he was acknowledged as both the Eastern and Tri-States titleholder.[55] Rogers put both championships on the line against "Professor" Roy Shire on January 22, 1953, in Columbus, and their match drew considerable attention. Shire, who was 10 months younger than Buddy, was also a notorious blond-haired heel, and their pairing drew 3,800 to Memorial Hall. A strange thing happened during their bout, and the roles were reversed at the finish. Shire ended up hanging by the ring ropes, and upon falling to the arena floor, was rushed to a hospital in an unconscious state – a la Buddy Rogers.[56]

The Rogers-Shire feud was moderately successful at the box office, although their rematch in Columbus on February 12 drew 100 less spectators than their first contest.[57] In all, Rogers went undefeated against Shire, winning at least nine bouts, and their May 8 match in Cincinnati was the last time they would ever wrestle. Another blond ruffian named the Great Scott, a grappler purportedly from St. Andrews, Scotland, joined the Haft circuit in early 1953. Scott, born John Schweigart and nicknamed "Dutch," was really from Haddonfield in Camden County, New Jersey, and was practically a neighbor of Rogers. The tall athlete was a standout football player in high school and became a champion wrestler in the Navy during World War II.[58] Following his discharge, he was a wrestling coach at the Camden YMCA before turning pro in 1946. Schweigart and Rogers were old pals, and his arrival gave Haft an exciting new headline match-up to exploit.[59]

The Great Scott was a formidable battler, and, like Rogers, could garner immense heat from his off-the-wall ring behavior. Combined, their shenanigans were noteworthy, and crowds were in a constant near-riot mode. In Dayton on February 24, 1953, the kilt-wearing Scot pitched Rogers from the ring during the second fall and the latter was injured. The match was stopped and Scott immediately claimed the Eastern championship.[60] Shortly thereafter, officials, citing the controversy of the bout, declared both the Eastern and Tri-State Titles vacant.[61] During a rematch in Columbus on March 12, Scott appeared to have the victory well in hand, but he "went berserk," pummeling Rogers, and the referee, Frank Baker, who reversed his decision and disqualified Scott.[62] Finally, on April 2, Rogers triumphed over the Great Scott and regained possession of his two championships.[63] Indicative of a warming trend toward Rogers, the Columbus audience enthusiastically applauded his win.[64]

While Al Haft had re-designated his American Wrestling Association championship the "Eastern" title, Cleveland matchmaker Jack Ganson stuck with its original name. On March 5, 1953, Rogers defended his AWA belt against Antonino Rocca, and it was nearly three years to the day after their historic match at the Cleveland Arena.[65] This time around, the attendance was less than half of what they formerly drew; 13,210 down to 6,292, and

Buddy again came out the loser. Rocca scored the second and third falls and captured the AWA title.[66] The following month, Rogers regained the championship, taking two-of-three from the high-flying Rocca.[67] Notably, the Cleveland Boxing and Wrestling Commission stripped the "Nature Boy" of his belt in May, with a local storyline accusing Rogers of dodging a defense against Ruffy Silverstein.[68] Rogers willingly relinquished one of his other championships, the Tri-States title, because it was said that he wanted to focus on his Eastern crown.[69]

However, he added to his laurels in Cincinnati on May 16, 1953, when he prevailed over Frankie Talaber in the finals of the WLW-TV tournament. His victory culminated weeks of rousing action and the build-up lured a stunning 16,000 fans to the Cincinnati Gardens.[70] Four nights later, Buddy put forth a memorable performance in Richmond, Indiana, once again going the extra mile to prove his master thespian abilities. He won the opening fall from Bill Miller at Municipal Stadium, but accidentally bumped the referee from the ring in the second. Miller gained the advantage and silenced Buddy's run with a devastating backbreaker in the middle of the ring. Without an official to break the hold, Miller maintained his pressure for a good number of minutes, well after Rogers expressed his desire to submit. Buddy crumpled to the mat in agony and was taken by ambulance to Reid Memorial Hospital, where he simulated the dramatic effects of Miller's hold for several hours. As for the match, he was pronounced the winner.[71]

Outside of Ohio, Lancaster, Pennsylvania, was one of Buddy's best-drawing towns. On April 2, 1952, he wrestled Ruffy Silverstein at the Maple Grove Field House and established a post-war local attendance record with an audience of 4,673.[72] The following month, he was heralded by the public as the hero versus the Great Moto, master of the sleeper hold and a noted mat terror. 3,877 spectators attended their charged bout on May 21, and after Rogers was victorious, Moto's manager, Fuji, who had previously rubbed rice in Buddy's eyes, was chased from the ring by several dozen rabid fans.[73] Most of the time, it was Rogers who carried the disdain of the majority, and he often needed police protection himself from Lancaster rowdies. During a particularly vicious match against Johnny Valentine in October 1952, Rogers went over and above his normal savageness, and repeatedly fouled his opponent en route to a three-fall victory. Afterwards, a disgusted fan said: "That wasn't wrestling, it was murder."[74]

A female member of that Lancaster crowd displayed her displeasure with Rogers' conduct by throwing her shoe at the blond grappler. Buddy responded by destroying it; tearing off the heel and tossing it back into the audience with a chuckle.[75] Unquestionably, Rogers saw the best and worst of fans in Lancaster, but their unabashed enthusiasm meant he was doing something right.[76] Over in Philadelphia on June 5, 1953, a raucous throng witnessed an animated contest between Rogers and Antonino Rocca. The rulebook was declared null and void by the athletes in the ring and the official ultimately disqualified both men.[77] According to a report in *TV Guide*, a distraught observer went after Rogers with a knife, furious at the "Nature Boy" for his relentless brutality toward his idol. Experienced in such situations, Buddy maneuvered his body out of the way and "pushed" Rocca toward his attacker as a measure of defense. Rocca, in turn, received a superficial cut, but the quick move might have saved Buddy's life.[78]

In the midst of his travels in 1953, Rogers made a one-night jaunt to New York City on March 24 for his first-ever booking at Madison Square Garden.[79] Al Haft gave his blessing for Rogers and Johnny Valentine to make the trip, and their ready-made match-up was the semifinal under Rocca and NWA champion Lou Thesz. Despite the significance of the moment, there was minimal local TV hype going into the appearance, and nothing specific to build tension for Rogers and Valentine going into their bout.[80] That being said, the two wrestlers knew each other well, and could be trusted to deliver a fast-paced and emotionally charged contest. And they did. The Rogers-Valentine match went 8:31, and the "Nature Boy" used a "neat head butt with an aerial scissors" for the victory.[81] The show drew 9,300 and the only photo from the event to appear in the newspaper was of Rogers hammering Valentine with a forearm to the noggin.[82]

In summer 1953, Rogers welcomed a high school pal from Camden to the Ohio wrestling circuit. Dominic (Doc) Doganiero had been a football teammate at Camden High and had briefly wrestled two years earlier when Rogers and Jack Pfefer were working with Al Mayer in Camden. Doganiero was a natural athlete, and with coaching from Rogers, became a capable journeyman. He was Buddy's third close friend from home to take to wrestling, following Billy Darnell and the Great Scott. On July 30 in Marion, Ohio, Doganiero demonstrated some of the more off-color lessons received from Rogers. He ignored the referee, failed to break a hold, and was disqualified. His opponent was 17-year-old Ray Stevens, a baby-faced youngster from West Virginia, who was also a protégé of Rogers.[83] Stevens had made his professional debut in late 1952 and was already surpassing expectations. With Al Haft and Rogers giving him the support he needed to prosper, Stevens was on track to have a great career.

Even with 11 years in the business, Rogers was still developing himself. Beginning around April 1953, he introduced a new finishing hold dubbed the "figure-four grapevine."[84] Going back to his earliest days in the profession, Buddy exhibited a basic knowledge of leg holds, which were taught to him by Fred Grobmier. The various moves, ranging from the double leg hold to the figure-four scissors, were effective over the years, but Buddy placed more stock in finishers like the atomic drop and piledriver. His figure-four was a variation of a maneuver he learned from Grobmier, and it replaced all others as his go-to signature hold.[85] Rogers took full credit for its invention, telling a reporter: "It was in Camden, New Jersey. I was working out with a young friend and I had been thinking of this hold. I applied the figure-four leglock on him and he couldn't break it no matter how hard he tried. He finally gave up. I knew I had a hold no other wrestler had. I had the perfect hold."[86]

The figure-four was a game changer and Buddy embraced all of its possibilities. Before a massive live audience and an expansive viewership at home, he used the novel finisher to put away Frankie Talaber for the TV championship on May 16, 1953, in Cincinnati. Two months later in Baltimore, he "puzzled" spectators and officials as he applied the hold and extracted a win from Clyde Steeves at the Coliseum.[87] Down in Nashville, he made a "human pretzel" of Tarzan White and tore the latter's leg ligaments.[88] By crossing his opponent's right leg over his left and administering pressure, the figure-four was a viable submission hold and was thoroughly convincing to fans. Rogers and the figure-four would soon become synonymous, and it was an exceptional addition to, not only his repertoire, but his image. He confidently offered $1,000 to the first person who could break the hold, and appeared invincible at times as he strutted around the ring after forcing his rival to concede.

The creation of the figure-four was a historic moment, and Rogers was frequently asked about it later in life. His story was usually the same, but occasionally, little details differed from interview-to-interview. For instance, in a 1979 discussion with a journalist from *Gong* magazine, Rogers said he first applied the figure-four to his "sparring partner" Wilson Kerr, his old-time coach from the Camden YMCA.[89] Kerr was approximately 14 years older than Buddy, and wasn't exactly the "young friend" he mentioned in his aforementioned statement.[90] Putting aside any inconsistencies told decades after the fact, there is little doubt Rogers made a huge imprint on the business with the arrival of the figure-four leglock. It wasn't known at the time, though, that the move would become one of the most recognizable and popular finishers in wrestling history and still be commonplace nearly 70 years later.

ENDNOTES - CHAPTER 9

[1] The Zbyszkos were originally from Poland and established themselves as wrestling legends between the 1900s and '20s, holding several claims to the World Heavyweight championship.

[2] It is believed that Haft's active career lasted from the 1900s to the late 1910s. He often performed under the name, "Young Gotch."

[3] Valentine reportedly issued the challenge to Rogers on Oct. 25, 1951 after the "Nature Boy" had beaten Tommy O'Toole in Columbus.

[4] The match was said to be "the roughest mat event staged in Columbus in many years." *Columbus Dispatch*, Nov. 2, 1951, p. 34.

[5] Ibid.

[6] Rogers used a "Japanese torture hold" to win the match. 4,000 fans were in attendance, the largest crowd of the Columbus indoor season. *Columbus Dispatch*, Nov. 23, 1951, p. 33. Illustrating the talent-trading relationship between Al Haft and Eddie Quinn, Yukon Eric made his local debut on this card. Eric was one of Quinn's stars.

[7] A 1946 article claimed that Rogers, before he turned to wrestling, had won a New Jersey amateur boxing heavyweight title and that some of his friends wanted him to turn pro. Rogers was quoted as saying: "I just didn't go for it. I thought I was pretty good, but the game didn't appeal to me." *Evansville Press*, Jan. 29, 1946, p. 10. In a separate article, Rogers talked more about his boxing interests, saying: "I spent a lot of time with boxers in the gyms around Philadelphia." *Buffalo Evening News*, Nov. 17, 1956, p. 4.

[8] *Columbus Dispatch*, Jan. 6, 1952, p. D1.

[9] *Columbus Dispatch*, Dec. 14, 1951, p. 50. Rogers also had boxing matches against Joe Christie and Frankie Talaber.

[10] Rogers reportedly suffered a three-inch wound above his knee in this attack. These quotes were featured in a column by Phil Dietrich. *Akron Beacon Journal*, June 12, 1950, p. 17. There are several other versions of this story. A 1953 article in Columbus stated that he needed '17 stitches" for a wound he received in Mexico in his left knee. *Haft Nelson*, Vol. 1, No. 62, Feb. 26, 1953. In a 1962 magazine article, Rogers was quoted as saying that he received a right forearm wound during a 1946 appearance in Mexico. *Boxing and Wrestling*, April 1962, p. 50. No independent information about Rogers' tour of Mexico has ever been found.

[11] *Lancaster Intelligencer Journal*, May 8, 1952, p. 23. This likely happened in late April. Rogers appeared in Huntington, WV on April 28, and a search of that newspaper turned up no references to him being injured at the hands of a knife-wielding fan.

[12] The show occurred on May 26, 1952 and Rogers defeated Mike Roberts prior to the incident.

[13] It was also claimed that Rogers tore her dress. She filed charges first and he pleaded innocent. *Massillon Evening Independent*, June 4, 1952, p. 13. The woman's name was Ida Rafferty.

[14] Rogers and Rafferty decided to drop all charges against each other. *Coshocton Tribune*, June 29, 1952, p. 13.

Also see *Columbus Dispatch*, Aug. 26, 1952, p. 2.

[15] The incident occurred on Aug. 14, 1952 after Rogers' win over Frankie Talaber.

[16] *Columbus Dispatch*, Aug. 26, 1952, p. 2.

[17] *Columbus Dispatch*, Aug. 29, 1952, p. 34.

[18] *Columbus Dispatch*, June 13, 1952, p. 42.

[19] *Columbus Dispatch*, July 11, 1952, p. 29.

[20] *Columbus Dispatch*, Aug. 29, 1952, p. 6B.

[21] *Columbus Star*, June 14, 1952, p. 25. Rogers, at times, was also billed as the Ohio Heavyweight champion. *Columbus Dispatch*, Aug. 25, 1952, p. 12.

[22] Miller dethroned Eagle in Pittsburgh, winning by disqualification. *Pittsburgh Post-Gazette*, May 2, 1952, p. 23.

[23] Arnold was billed as the AWA titleholder in Dayton and Lexington, two of Haft's cities, but might not have been recognized in Columbus.

[24] The event was held at the Islam Grotto and sponsored by the Fort Pitt Brewing Company. It was broadcast on WDTV. The final match-up of the tournament was held on Sept. 13, 1952 and Rogers won in 19:06, capturing the title and special Michael Berardino trophy. *Pittsburgh Sun-Telegraph*, Sept. 14, 1952, p. D3. Rogers took two famous publicity photos with the AWA belt and the Michael Berardino trophy – one sitting and one standing.

[25] Fanning wrote that the "event announced as [being for] a regional championship suddenly developed into a 'contest' of world-wide significance. And all in the course of about 35 minutes." *Pittsburgh Post-Gazette*, Sept. 18, 1952, p. 31.

[26] Fanning wrote that Griffin was "secretive" on the broadcast. Ibid.

[27] *Haft Nelson*, Vol. 1, No. 42, Oct. 2, 1952. An article featured in an issue of *TV Digest*, affirmed that Buddy won his "world" "heavyweight crown" in the Pittsburgh tournament. *TV Digest*, Dec. 6, 1952, p. 21.

[28] Multiple champions gave Haft better drawing power in various parts of his territory all at the same time. Ironically, the NWA wanted him to eliminate heavyweight claimants that rivaled Lou Thesz, but instead of doing so, Haft was temporarily adding more.

[29] *Dayton Daily News*, Oct. 15, 1952, p. 14. Arnold was billed as the defending champion. Rogers was said to be holding the Tri-State and "Canadian" heavyweight titles. *Dayton Daily News*, Oct. 14, 1952, p. 11.

[30] *Chicago Daily Tribune*, Oct. 18, 1952, p. 32.

[31] Bill McCormack noted that this match was made necessary by a legit injury to Don Eagle. Research notes of Bill McCormack.

[32] To earn his place in this match, Rogers beat Ruffy Silverstein and Billy Darnell in the same evening, on Nov. 25, 1952 at the Boston Arena. *Boston Daily Record*, Nov. 26, 1952, p. 17.

[33] At different times, it was called the "East Coast," "Eastern," "AWA," and "Midwest" championship.

[34] Jack Dempsey was guest referee. The first fall was with a "cross leg-lock" and the second was by DQ for "unnecessary roughness." *Boston American*, Dec. 3, 1952, p. 22. The benefit was for the Christmas Festival Committee Fund, headed by Boston Mayor Hines, to help send Christmas presents to soldiers in Korea. A photo appeared in at least one magazine of Paul Bowser presenting his famous AWA belt to Rogers.

[35] *Haft Nelson*, Vol. 1, No. 7, January 1952.

[36] *Aug.a Chronicle*, Aug. 10, 1953, p. 7.

[37] A Columbus article mentioned that he was saving his money. *Columbus Star*, July 19, 1952.

38 *NWA Official Wrestling*, April 1952, p. 10-11.
39 This was part of the column, "Inside Stuff" by Joe McCarron. *Allentown Morning Call*, July 11, 1960, p. 14.
40 *Columbus Star*, July 19, 1952, p. 2.
41 Ibid, *Haft Nelson*, Vol. 1, No. 62, Feb. 26, 1953.
42 A report claimed that the 14-karat diamond ring was worth $20,000. He was said to have had a different ring, which he wore on the pinky finger of his right hand. That ring was valued at $10,800. *TV Guide*, Nov. 13, 1953, p. 6. In a 1952 article, his ring was described as having a "five-karat diamond surrounded by 54 15-point stones." *Columbus Star*, July 19, 1952, p. 2. Rogers' diamond pinky ring was purchased from a Columbus, Ohio jeweler. Correspondence with Lee Rogers, September 2019.
43 *NWA Official Magazine*, April 1952, p. 10-11 and *Lancaster New Era*, Oct. 28, 1952, p. 16.
44 *Columbus Star*, July 19, 1952, p. 2. In 1953, he had both a Cadillac and a Lincoln. *Haft Nelson*, Vol. 1, No. 62, Feb. 26, 1953. He was driving a Cadillac Coupe de Ville, according to an article in *TV Guide*. *TV Guide*, Nov. 13, 1953, p. 6.
45 *The Hard Way* by Don Fargo with Scott Teal (2014).
46 *Columbus Star*, Aug. 17, 1957, p. 6.
47 Rogers lived in apartment 5. Haft's office was at 261 S. High Street.
48 The Coney Island Restaurant was at 243 S. High Street and the High Beck Tavern was located at 564 S. High. The High Beck Tavern, which opened in the 1920s, is still open to this day.
49 The Bath Club was the largest private swimming club in Columbus. Jim Haydu, husband of the late Lola LaRay, recalled that Buddy also used to work out at the YMCA in downtown Columbus on Long Street. Jim Haydu post on Facebook, February 2019.
50 *Columbus Star*, July 19, 1952, p. 2.
51 Haft booked wrestlers in Ohio and parts of Indiana, Illinois, Pennsylvania, West Virginia, and Kentucky.
52 Letter from Sam Muchnick to Jack Pfefer dated Aug. 3, 1953, Jack Pfefer Collection, Joyce Sports Research Collection, Hesburgh Library, University of Notre Dame, Notre Dame, Indiana. The specific reasoning for Haft's decision to block Rogers from appearing for Kohler is unknown.
53 Robert said he'd retire from wrestling if he didn't beat Rogers. *Boston American*, Feb. 2, 1953, p. 16.
54 The show was at the Boston Arena before 3,500 fans. Rogers was carried from the ring on a stretcher. *Boston Daily Record*, Feb. 4, 1953, p. 18.
55 Haft, in late 1952 and early '53, phased out any references to the "American Wrestling Association" in his primary towns with the exception of Cleveland. According to some press reports, the Eastern championship was recognized in "17" states.
56 *Columbus Dispatch*, Jan. 23, 1953, p. 16. One report claimed that Shire was unconscious for a "three hour period" at White Cross Hospital. *Columbus Star*, Feb. 14, 1953, p. 26.
57 The finish of this bout, again, saw Shire use a very familiar Buddy Rogers tactic. He missed a flying tackle and the "Nature Boy" got the pin in 10:10. The attendance was 3,700. *Columbus Dispatch*, Feb. 13, 1953, p. 28.
58 Schweigart attended Haddonfield High School. He was the heavyweight wrestling champion of the South Pacific Fleet. *Camden Courier-Post*, April 1, 1946, p. 18.
59 Prior to joining the Navy, Schweigart worked at the New York Shipbuilding Corporation. U.S. World War II Draft Cards Young Men, 1940-1947, Ancestry.com. Rogers recommended that he get in contact with Jack Pfefer for a possible spot on the latter's roster. Letter from John Schweigart to Jack Pfefer dated July 12, 1949.
60 Rogers won the first fall and was thrown out of the ring during the second fall. He was given an 11-minute rest period, but still was unable to continue. The match was given to Scott. *Dayton Daily News*, Feb. 25, 1953, p. 13. Instead of being governed by the "American Wrestling Association," which had been the case in previous years, officials were said to be representing the "Midwest (or Midwestern) Wrestling Association." The MWA was Al Haft's longtime local organization with roots in the early 1930s. When he joined forces with Paul Bowser, however, the AWA took precedence in the Ohio territory.

⁶¹ Once again, publications misidentified the championships involved. *Haft Nelson*, surprisingly, was one of them. It stated that the "Tri-State and Midwest Heavyweight championship belts" were declared vacant by Ross Leader, acting president of the MWA. *Haft Nelson*, Vol. 1, No. 64, March 12, 1953. According to the same publication, the Midwest Wrestling Association, helped "to direct wrestling in this section." Ibid. Also see the *Columbus Dispatch*, March 10, 1953, p. 16. Rogers held no claim the Midwest Title at this time.

⁶² *Columbus Star*, April 4, 1953, p. 26, *Columbus Dispatch*, March 13, 1953, p. 45.

⁶³ Scott was counted out. *Columbus Dispatch*, April 3, 1953, p. 9B.

⁶⁴ *Haft Nelson*, Vol. 1, No. 68, April 9, 1953.

⁶⁵ There are reports that Rogers beat Don Arnold for the AWA belt in Cleveland on Jan. 29, 1953. However, there was no build up for a championship match, nor did the *Cleveland Plain Dealer* mention a title change the next day. *Cleveland Plain Dealer*, Jan. 30, 1953, p. 18. It was reported that Rogers' Cleveland claim stemmed from a victory over Don Eagle in Pittsburgh in June 1952. Cleveland Wrestling Program, Dec. 16, 1952, p. 2. No record for that match has been found.

⁶⁶ *Cleveland Plain Dealer*, March 6, 1953, p. 16.

⁶⁷ The match occurred on April 9, 1953 at the Cleveland Arena. *Cleveland Plain Dealer*, April 10, 1953, p. 23.

⁶⁸ *Cleveland Plain Dealer*, May 17, 1953, p. S6. Cleveland promoter Jack Ganson initially wanted to hold a tournament to determine a new AWA World champion. He scrapped that idea, probably because of National Wrestling Alliance pressure. When wrestling returned in October 1953, Ganson's first main event was NWA World champion Lou Thesz against Bobby Managoff.

⁶⁹ *Dayton Journal Herald*, April 27, 1953, p. 7. The Tri-State championship represented Ohio, Pennsylvania and West Virginia. After Rogers vacated the title, it was said that tournaments were going to be held in each individual state to fill the local heavyweight crowns. On May 12, 1953, Bill Miller beat Gino Martinelli in a tournament final in Dayton to win the vacant Ohio State championship. *Dayton Journal Herald*, May 13, 1953, p. 10.

⁷⁰ *Wrestling World*, July 1954. Other sources claim that attendance was 14,164. It was reported that Rogers won the $3,000 prize in the WLW-TV tournament. *Aug.a Chronicle*, Aug. 10, 1953, p. 7.

⁷¹ Rogers was declared winner based on his first fall victory. There was no second fall finish. *Richmond Palladium-Item*, May 21, 1953, p. 23. Also see *Cincinnati Enquirer*, May 21, 1953, p. 30.

⁷² Rogers performed the neck in the ropes trick and lost to Silverstein. He was carried from the ring on a stretcher. *Lancaster New Era*, April 3, 1952, p. 41 and *Lancaster Intelligencer Journal*, April 3, 1952, p. 21.

⁷³ *Lancaster Intelligencer Journal*, May 22, 1952, p. 23.

⁷⁴ *Lancaster New Era*, Oct. 30, 1952, p. 40.

⁷⁵ A second shoe was thrown and Rogers did the same thing. Ibid.

⁷⁶ Rogers appreciated the spirit of fans in Lancaster. *Lancaster New Era*, April 10, 1951, p. 20. Later, "Gentleman" Ed Sharpe was quoted as saying that Lancaster was the "worst town for riots." He added that "Buddy Rogers could start up a riot quicker than anyone." *Whatever Happened To...?*, No. 47, February 2001, p. 45.

⁷⁷ *Philadelphia Inquirer*, June 6, 1953, p. 16.

⁷⁸ *TV Guide*, Nov. 13, 1953, p. 7.

⁷⁹ In addition to it being Buddy's first Garden appearance, it was also quite possibly his first showing in New York City since April 1950. The current version of the *Buddy Rogers Record Book* has a possible date for Rogers in New York on Jan. 1, 1953, but no confirmation for that bout has been found. *Buddy Rogers Record Book* by Haruo Yamaguchi, February 2020.

⁸⁰ This is assuming the local TV show booked by Toots Mondt acknowledged the upcoming matches at the Garden. No specific information is known.

⁸¹ Article by Chris Kieran. *New York Daily News*, March 25, 1953, p. 80.

⁸² Photograph was taken by Walter Kelleher. Ibid.

⁸³ *Marion Star*, July 31, 1953, p. 18.

[84] The earliest recorded match of Rogers using the figure-four grapevine occurred in Indianapolis on April 14, 1953 during a tag team bout. Rogers was teamed with Bob Clay to defeat Dr. Frank Gallagher and Bull Montana. In the second fall, Rogers "pinned" Gallagher with "a figure-four and grapevine hold." *Indianapolis Star*, April 15, 1953, p. 28. An earlier possibility shows up in a Boston newspaper in December 1952. It stated that Rogers used a "cross leg-lock." It's not known if this was the figure-four grapevine. *Boston American*, Dec. 3, 1952, p. 22.

[85] Interview by Evelyn Lesh, *Nature Boy's News*, August 1962, p. 5. Rogers said that he got a "hint" for the figure-four grapevine "from the figure-four body scissors Fred Grobmier was using." *Gong Magazine*, June 1979.

[86] *Wrestling's Main Event*, September 1983, p. 23.

[87] *Baltimore Sun*, July 22, 1953, p. 15.

[88] *Nashville Tennessean*, July 15, 1953, p. 20.

[89] In the article, his coach's name was spelled, "Wilson Carr." *Gong Magazine*, June 1979.

[90] Additionally, Rogers remembered that he introduced the hold in the early 1950s, but offered at least two different years in terms of time-frame. In a 1992 interview, Rogers stated that it happened at the YMCA in 1950. *Puroresu Okoku*, July 1992. He gave another interview and said he believed he invented the hold in 1954. *Wrestling's Main Event*, September 1983, p. 23.

Uniontown, Pennsylvania: Friday, March 6, 1953

Chapter 10
Rogers vs. Rogers

During the final year of World War II, a prominent figure in the equestrian world became a noted sports columnist for the *Chattanooga Times* newspaper. Her name was Edna Wells, and she wrote a regular feature entitled, "As a Woman Sees Sports." In December 1946, she turned her attention to pro wrestling and placed a rather large spotlight on the popular hero, Buddy Rogers. The evening of the interview, Rogers was challenging Bill Longson for the NWA world heavyweight championship, and Wells was curious about his background.[1] She asked the "great big hunk" about his parents, athletic history, and then his relationship status. "He's married, girls," Wells announced. "His wife, Ellen, is that 'gawgus' blonde with the leopard coat you saw sitting over near the press box that night."[2] To complete the assignment, Wells was an astute observer of the compelling Rogers-Longson match, which went 60 minutes to a draw. She wrote that Buddy "wrestled his heart out and the fans went with him all the way."[3]

The publicity surrounding Rogers in Chattanooga was all positive, and the insightful column offered a rare glimpse into his personal life. Buddy and Ellen were about 16 months into their marriage, and her support for his budding career was ever apparent. By 1949, Ellen had taken the plunge and donned wrestling boots to blaze her own path in the business. But because of the arduous travel schedule, there was little time for a conventional home life, especially when Ellen was headed off in one direction and Rogers the other. Buddy, always on the move, was traversing Eastern and Midwestern states at a fast clip in the early 1950s. It was pivotal to meet the box office demand for appearances and his income was improving each year. Conversely, Ellen's commitment to wrestling waned in 1951, and she was residing back in the Camden-Philadelphia area.[4] Their seven-year marriage had run its course and they decided to call it quits.

In Franklin County, Ohio, on Dec. 18, 1952, Rogers appeared before Common Pleas Judge Joseph M. Harter and expressed his desire for a divorce. "I asked her to keep me a normal home," he told the court, "but she wouldn't do it."[5] According to the official Decree of Divorce, the judge, citing a "gross neglect of duty," approved the dissolution of their marriage.[6] That same document revealed something else almost as important. Three months before, Rogers made another significant, life-altering decision through the courts in Columbus. On September 9, Franklin County Probate Judge C.P. McClelland approved his application for a formal name change. Legally, he would no longer answer to his birth name, "Herman Karl Rohde," and from that point forth, he would be known as "Buddy 'Nature Boy' Rogers."[7] This news wasn't widely reported, although Jerry Nason of the *Boston Globe* did briefly mention it in his October 4 column.[8]

Even before his divorce was finalized, Rogers was talking about his future plans. In July 1952, he meticulously described his dream home to a writer for the *Columbus Star*, and said that "it would have a couple of kids running around; a boy first, a girl next." When he disclosed that he hadn't "found the wife yet," journalist Mary Joos asked him what he looked for in a potential mate. Rogers was candid and detailed in his response, and provided a list of six characteristics he found important in a woman. "She must have brains, be a good hostess, and a good mixer," he stated. "I don't ask that she is beautiful. She doesn't have to be a Lana Turner, but I do want a woman that keeps her body in good physical condition." Among his other preferences were being a good cook and possessing style in clothing and hair. The *Columbus Star* reporter declared: "They hate him in the ring, but off-stage, he's the golden god on a pedestal in the female admiration society's book."[9]

Rogers was seldom without companionship from the opposite sex. He was a natural in the social environment and eternally self-confident. Meeting women was never a problem for him, and Buddy enjoyed life to the fullest. Considering his profession, he was careful to protect his conditioning and physical health, telling a newspaper, "I know when enough's enough."[10] To the question of getting remarried, the twice-divorced wrestler took a more pragmatic approach to the possibility in a 1953 statement to *Haft Nelson*. Acknowledging the fact that he was never home, and the difficulties he'd experienced, he said he'd think about doing it again once he was retired from the mat.[11] But that wasn't going to be the case. While visiting a friend in an apartment building in Columbus, Buddy passed an intriguing young woman in the lobby area. After expressing a desire to meet her, his friend brought the two together, and Buddy was formally introduced to the beautiful 21-year-old Iva Audrey "Terry" Jackson.[12]

Originally from Gallipolis, Ohio, Terry was the second of four children born to Malcolm and Iva Jackson, and was a graduate from Gallia Academy High School.[13] She had been a member of the school's talented Dett Choir, and was in Columbus to continue her education at Ohio State University.[14] Prior to their initial meeting, Terry was unaware of the famed "Nature Boy," as she wasn't a wrestling fan, nor was she interested in a possible relationship.[15] But they connected, and a romance soon developed. On January 3, 1954, Buddy and Terry were married in Florida, and, as part of his tour of the territory, spent some time in Cuba on their honeymoon.[16] The newlyweds planned to make their home in Columbus, in an apartment building that Rogers had purchased the summer before. The two-story brick residence was just east of the university at 53 West Tulane Road, set back off the road on a small hill.[17]

Rogers and his bride occupied the entire first floor and rented "efficiency apartments" tailored for single people, businessmen, and couples. Rent, which included utilities, typically ranged from $90 to $95 for an apartment and $50 for a room.[18] He also provided lodging for friends in the wrestling industry.[19] On one particular afternoon, Buddy answered a knock on his door. It was a young wrestling fan, and as an example of his easygoing personality, Rogers welcomed him inside. The boy, perhaps 12 years old, was meeting his idol for the first time and the "Nature Boy" was beyond welcoming. They shared a brief conversation and the youngster left with a memory that would last a lifetime. Buddy didn't know it at the time, but it wasn't going to be the last time he would interact with that baby-faced wrestling enthusiast. They would meet again in a few years. The young man's name was Bobby Davis.[20]

A few months before tying the knot, Rogers received a booking to appear in St. Louis, one of his best drawing towns. But in the aftermath of his break from Jack Pfefer, he was aced out of the city due to Sam Muchnick's loyalty to the caustic manager. More than two years had passed, and both Rogers and Muchnick were losing financially by the unofficial ban. Muchnick realized the pointlessness of the situation and decided to bring Buddy back to town. He knew he'd have to deal with Pfefer, though, and sent the latter a letter on Aug. 3, 1953, stating: "I hope that you and I won't have to be engaged in any controversies or battles if I bring Rogers in."[21] With Pfefer, anything was possible, but Muchnick was no longer concerned.[22] Twelve days later, Rogers reemerged at the St. Louis House for a TV match against Frankie Talaber, and won with his figure-four in 13:14.[23] As for his return to the Kiel Auditorium, which occurred on November 20, a crowd of 6,024 watched him defeat Don Eagle by count-out.[24]

For a special tag team tournament held in Al Haft's territory, Buddy partnered with his real world Camden buddy, the Great Scott, who, up to that point, had been a major ring rival. The eliminations, which began on Oct. 8, 1953, in Columbus, saw Rogers and Scott prevail over Bill Miller and Frankie Talaber by disqualification. That result was unsatisfactory for local commission officials, who overturned the decision, declaring the bout a no-contest.[25] The tournament continued in Huntington, West Virginia, at the Radio Center Arena, with Rogers and Scott winning over Nick Roberts and Marco Polo in three falls on October 12.[26] The following week, at the same venue, the blond brawlers slugged their way to a tournament victory over the Dark Secret and Great Durango.[27] With the achievement, they were crowned the American tag team champions and presented a special trophy and belt.[28] Red Kirkpatrick, Scott's sly assistant, assumed managerial duties for the team, but his tenure was brief.[29]

Several days after winning the tag championship, Buddy met defeat in Columbus and was stripped of his Eastern Heavyweight crown. It happened on October 22 at Memorial Hall and his conqueror was Bill Miller. But at the end of the bout, Miller looked nothing like a triumphant new champion. In fact, Rogers was the aggressor, stomping and kicking at Miller's injured leg. Rogers' undoing, however, came about when he locked Miller in the dreaded figure-four and was disqualified for refusing to release the hold. Miller, nevertheless, had his arm raised and was handed the title belt.[30] That kind of defeat only served to strengthen the credibility of Rogers and his finisher, and gave logical reasoning for a rematch. In Indianapolis a few months later, Buddy went the identical route with NWA world champion Lou Thesz in their first contest in nearly three years.[31] On Feb. 20, 1954, Rogers had Thesz in the figure-four, and once again, was disqualified. Fans, surprisingly, were on Buddy's side in the matter.[32]

On March 13, Rogers returned to Southern California for a consequential TV match-up at Hollywood Legion Stadium. The last time he had appeared in the region was 1949 when his "Nature Boy" gimmick was still in its infancy. Now he was back to wrestle Sandor Szabo in front of a nationwide audience on the CBS network. Their Saturday afternoon battle was witnessed live by fans from coast to coast, and Rogers was in rare form. During the third fall, Buddy secured his figure-four and gained a submission victory.[33] The exposure was immeasurable and further elevated his thrilling finishing hold. Back in the East, Al Haft swung a major deal by acquiring the booking rights to Baltimore, and his troops marched into that city in May.[34] For Rogers, Baltimore was a familiar old haunt, and he was immediately put over as the top heavyweight. On May 18, he was presented with a gold belt "in honor of his wrestling achievements" by J. Marshall Boone, chairman of the Maryland State Athletic Commission.[35]

By this juncture, the prestigious Eastern heavyweight title was back in Buddy's grasp, having defeated Bill Miller in Charleston in February.[36] The Eastern crown became the primary sectional championship in Baltimore, and Rogers engaged in intense warfare with Ruffy Silverstein and Oyama Kato, the Japanese Judo expert.[37] Bloody, unconventional matches were the norm, and at times, more action took place on the concrete floor than on the canvas. Rogers and Kato packed the Coliseum on Aug. 24, 1954, and the fire department had to turn away an estimated 2,000 people because of maximum capacity limits. The other 5,000 lucky patrons were given an old-school lesson in punishment as Rogers utilized every under-handed trick known to man in an attempt to maim his opponent. The referee, Gil Schneider, was first sent to the mat, then flung from the ring during the carnage, and Rogers disobeyed all warnings. Schneider, with no other option, disqualified Buddy and awarded the Eastern title to Kato.[38]

In Ohio, the championship picture was intermittingly confusing. The addition of "Midwest" title recognition, and the occasional transposition between the latter and the Eastern belt in publicity reports, was perplexing. Rogers was billed as the defending Midwest kingpin versus Bill Miller on Sept. 18, 1954, in Akron, but he was again penalized for foul tactics and lost his championship.[39] A couple nights later, in Baltimore, Rogers used a piledriver to incapacitate Oyama Kato and score a pinfall in 40 seconds, thus launching his third reign as Eastern champion. Interestingly enough, Rogers was a fan-favorite in Baltimore, and his victory over Kato was roundly cheered.[40] Buddy was due back in Akron on October 2, and to spice up his rematch with Miller, officials held-up the Midwest title.[41] That evening at the Akron Armory, Rogers won two of three falls from Miller and regained the Midwest belt.[42]

Over on the tag team side of things, Rogers and the Great Scott were champions for a good portion of 1954. Lexington, Kentucky promoter Red Fassas called them, "the greatest and most colorful tag team in business today," and they lived up to that praise each time they stepped through the ropes.[43] Reportedly, there were talks by the NWA to give the duo sanction as "world" tag team champions, a highly unique honor that never materialized.[44] Between March and November, they lost and regained the American tag championship three times, and feuded with the likes of Bill Miller and Len Montana, and Oyama Kato and Danny McShain. During the summer, Rogers went to Montreal and had his first match against the popular Pat O'Connor, a 30-year-old former amateur champion from New Zealand. O'Connor was the reigning Montreal world champion, and their Delorimier Stadium contest drew 16,000 fans on Aug. 25. Jack Sharkey, the guest referee, disqualified Rogers for "unnecessary roughness" in the third fall.[45]

Buddy met another ex-amateur on October 16 in Canton, and suffered defeat again. But this time, it was a two-straight-fall loss to a man with three NCAA championships under his belt, Dick Hutton, who was in his second year as a pro. Hutton was in the Ohio territory gaining experience from the tutelage of Al Haft's master grapplers, and Rogers had no trouble putting the promising athlete over in a big way. Earlier that night, Buddy defeated Ruffy Silverstein, only to be challenged by Hutton afterwards. Hutton agreed to donate $1,000 to charity if he was defeated, and Rogers agreed. Spectators were wowed by Hutton's ability, and his triumph instantly boosted his reputation amongst local heavies.[46] They battled two additional times in Canton before the year was out and fan interest was immense. Rogers won their second bout by disqualification and captured a more decisive victory on December 11 in front of 3,471 at the Auditorium.[47] Rogers smartly dodged a flying tackle and Hutton knocked himself out.[48]

Being the sun worshipper that he was, Buddy returned to Florida for a three-week tour in January 1955, and was surrounded by familiar faces. Jack Vansky, Angelo Savoldi, and Gino Garibaldi were in the territory, guys he had known since his first year in the business. The Great Scott soon joined him, but instead of teaming up as they had in Ohio, they clashed in Tampa and Miami Beach. In Fort Lauderdale on January 13, Rogers and Danny McShain rekindled their longtime rivalry at the War Memorial Auditorium, and fought to a furious no-decision. They generated enormous heat by their violent hostilities and police were called in to prevent a full-blown riot.[49] The following week, the "Nature Boy" and "Dangerous Danny" went to a no-decision again in a special "Texas Duel Match" before nearly 2,000 onlookers. The match was supposed to end when one of the combatants was unable to continue, but fearing McShain was in serious trouble, referee Herb Freeman halted the brawl when McShain suffered a cut above his eye.[50]

In actuality, they were setting up the finale to the exciting feud. Joe Kolb, the sports editor of the *Fort Lauderdale News*, helped sell the advance hype by describing a post-match run-in with Rogers in the dressing room. Promoter Buck Weaver mentioned Jack Dempsey as a possible referee for their next bout, and confidently said the wrestlers wouldn't "clown around" with the boxing legend officiating. "Whaddya mean?" Buddy asked. "No sixty-year-old man is going to push me around. I'll tie him in a pretzel. You can get Dempsey and [Rocky] Marciano, too, in the ring and I'll tie them both in knots. Every time I come to Florida, I'm involved in a disputed decision. I'm getting sick of it. I wrestle the way I want to wrestle and I'll wrestle anybody, anytime."[51] Dempsey was hired to keep the peace for their January 27 contest, and compared to their two prior bouts, Rogers and McShain were relatively composed. They went two of three falls without the need of police protection, and Rogers was declared the winner.[52]

Back in Ohio, Rogers put over former footballer Wilbur Snyder in their first-ever match-up at the Cleveland Arena on Feb. 15, 1955. He missed a flying tackle and was unable to continue, giving Snyder a claim to the Eastern heavyweight championship. However, Buddy said he was fouled and disputed the decision.[53] On March 1, they wrestled to a 60-minute draw in Cleveland, and as promoter Jack Ganson was handing the belt to Snyder, Buddy grabbed it and fled for the back area.[54] On March 15, frustrations overtook Snyder in their third Cleveland bout and he was disqualified for punching referee Charlie Kivi. The loss wiped out his claim to the Eastern belt and reestablished Buddy as the champ.[55] In Columbus on April 20, Rogers retained his title over Snyder at Memorial Hall, earning a referee's decision after an hour of wrestling.[56]

Among the members of the NWA, it was quite common for one promoter to contact another and place a request for talent. In late 1954, Hugh Nichols of the Hollywood office sent a telegram to Al Haft expressing interest in Rogers.[57] He wanted Buddy as soon as possible, but the Eastern champion was booked several months in advance. Finally, on May 2, 1955, Rogers arrived in Hollywood and beat Sandor Szabo at the Legion Stadium.[58] He received a huge push, and by the end of the month, he had won 19 matches in Southern California. To heighten his local persona, Buddy reverted back to his "Nature Boy" gimmick, and brought back the Slave Girl to complete the act.[59] Of course, it quickly touched a nerve with the public. W.H. Cronkhite, a fan from Wilmington, sent a letter to the editor of the *Long Beach Independent Press-Telegram*, stating: "Being against the law for years to have slaves, why put up with this open defiance of having a slave? I believe [the Nature Boy] should be put in his place by law enforcement."[60]

Buddy's "egotistical, arrogant, conceited and sadistic" behavior incited the wrestling populace to no end.[61] Jerry Powers, a Long Beach enthusiast, complained to the Department of Justice about the "brutal wrestling" in Los Angeles and specifically named "big bully Rogers" as one of the culprits. He said there were no rules in California and the likes of Rogers took "all the sport out of wrestling."[62] The California Athletic Commission was fed up with the protests and commentary, and during a meeting on June 15, 1955, decided to bar Rogers from using the Slave Girl in any future matches.[63] The commission cracking down on his gimmick was a testament to the success he was having, but it was also a major thorn in his side. He didn't appreciate the fact that a group of out-of-touch board members were telling him how he should present his craft.

In recent weeks, Rogers had been reinvigorating the box office through his gripping feuds with Danny McShain, Sandor Szabo, and "Cowboy" Rocky (Johnny) Valentine. But, at the same time, he was dealing with a significant out-of-the-ring legal action that had very serious implications. On May 13, 1955, a complaint was filed against Rogers in Los Angeles County Superior Court on behalf of Charles (Buddy) Rogers, the famed musician and actor. The latter charged the "Nature Boy" with having "adopted and appropriated the name Buddy Rogers" with the "intent" of defrauding the actor of his excellent reputation and to deceive the public. He claimed that his standing as a "cultured, well-mannered gentleman of great personal character and integrity" was "severely damaged" by "an individual of offensive and vulgar traits." The actor wanted the court to restrain Rogers from using that name and pressed for damages in the amount of $200,000.[64]

The plaintiff in the suit, as noted in chapter three, was more than likely an influence in the original decision to adopt the name "Buddy Rogers" for wrestling purposes in 1945.[65] But since that time, the wrestler had established his own clear-cut identity, which would, in no way, be confused for the musician and actor. Buddy was a blond-haired athlete, 17 years younger, and never once sold himself as being even related to the orchestra leader. The wrestler was represented by the law firm of Covey & Covey, and in attorney Manley C. Davidson's response, he asked how Buddy "did any act, thing or matter, to deceive the public generally or anyone into the belief that defendant [was] the same person as the plaintiff."[66] That was the big question. The one thing the plaintiff's attorney noticeably admitted was that they didn't know Buddy's "true name," and the dark-haired Hollywood thespian was unaware that the mat star had legally changed his name to "Buddy 'Nature Boy' Rogers" in 1952.

Comically, and in typical pro wrestling fashion, a promoter in Pittsburgh wanted Charles (Buddy) Rogers to wrestle the Camden-born grappler "to determine who had the right to use the name." It would be a "great publicity stunt," the promoter felt.[67] The actor-musician was not amused, needless to say. The court case received national attention, but was nothing more than a nuisance that needed to be rapidly resolved. In mid-July, an out-of-court settlement was announced and the case was formally dismissed by the court on July 21, 1955.[68] According to the *Los Angeles Times*, a compromise was reached, and the wrestling "Buddy Rogers" agreed to be known as "Nature Boy Rogers" from that point forth. In fact, the article asserted that he promised "never to use the names Buddy and Rogers together again in his professional life." No money was exchanged in terms of damages, and with that, the court drama was a thing of the past.[69]

Rogers lost his Eastern heavyweight championship to "Big" Bill Miller on July 26 in Dayton, and the perpetual rivals feuded across four cities between July and October 1955.[70] Their contests in Columbus, Toledo, Dayton, and Baltimore were must-see for aficionados, and the more they wrestled, the better the matches got. That same summer, a political firestorm erupted when Baltimore promoter Ed Contos abruptly severed ties with NWA bookers Bill Lewis and Toots Mondt, and reconnected with Al Haft.[71] The move was part of a larger reconfiguration of the Northeastern territory, and during the transition, Haft's regional influence grew considerably. At the center of things was the inauguration of a brand-new studio wrestling TV show from New York City. The DuMont Network launched a two-hour Thursday evening program from its Telecenter in Manhattan beginning on Aug. 4, 1955.[72] Haft and Eddie Quinn were the primary bookers for the show, and that gave them unparalleled power in the territory.

Baltimore was a strategically important wrestling city. On Tuesday nights, its live grappling TV program from the Coliseum was shown in the local area; Philadelphia, Wilmington, and Washington, D.C.[73] Usually, the Baltimore television exposure resulted in an uptick at the box office if the same talent pool worked each city. After Contos signed with Haft, Philadelphia promoter Ray Fabiani saw the writing on the wall and followed suit. To help bolster ticket sales for his season opener at the Adelphia Athletic Club on Oct. 17, 1955, Fabiani got Buddy Rogers to make a rare public appearance at Gimbels Department Store in downtown Philly. He was joined by Pat O'Connor and Jim Leaming, the sports director for radio station, WIP.[74] That night, Buddy beat Chief Big Heart in two of three falls to win the headline contest, while O'Connor drew with Bill Miller.[75]

Rogers returned to New York City for a show at Madison Square Garden the next evening. Unlike his last appearance, when he was in the semifinal, Buddy was in the fourth match from the top, and faced off with Paul Baillargeon. He achieved victory, using a knee smash to attain a pinfall in just under 14-minutes.[76] The Garden program was a financial failure. It drew only 6,792 spectators, despite the DuMont TV push, and was 700 less than the previous program in May.[77] Talent wasn't an issue, nor was there a lack of exposure, but something was amiss in New York. Whether it was a management problem or a series of external factors, promoters were having real trouble selling out the Garden. The outfit in charge wanted to stage eight big events at the venue that season, but they were forced to cancel the next card on November 14 due to lackluster advance sales.[78] They ran the Garden in December and drew 8,000, but the numbers were well below satisfactory, and the rest of the planned shows were cancelled.[79]

Things elsewhere on the Northeastern circuit were progressively improved. Technically, Rogers was Haft's agent on the ground and was the central booker for their operations.[80] In addition to Baltimore, Philadelphia, Wilmington, and several smaller cities in New Jersey and Pennsylvania, the group expanded into Washington, D.C. on January 6, 1956.[81] The new D.C. promotion was run by Ray Fabiani and was in direct opposition to entrepreneur Vincent James McMahon, who was already established as the local NWA affiliate. But Fabiani was no longer playing by the rules of the Alliance. He was tired of being strong-armed by incompetent bookers with inferior performers. Rogers had a much better overall ensemble, led by the "Nature Boy" himself, and it included Bill Miller, the 6-foot-7 Karl Von Albers, Oyama Kato, Lenny Montana, Chief Big Heart, and Don Arnold.

Rogers brought along his buddies, Billy Darnell, the Great Scott, and Doc Doganiero, plus protégés Don and Ray Stevens and Buddy Rosen. The gigantic Don Lee was also part of the tribe. Weighing better than 275 pounds, Lee and Rogers became friends while under Jack Pfefer's management in the late 1940s. At that time, Lee went by the name "Ivan the Terrible," and in the ring, he was as intimidating and outlandish as his name implied. With his trusted unit of workers and a moneymaking circuit, Rogers had created an environment very similar to the old Pfefer blueprint. It was as if Buddy saw the benefits of surrounding himself with people he could depend on as he pulled the strings behind-the-scenes. Since he controlled the talent, he dictated the terms to promoters, and his booking scheme was the only scheme. If he wanted to use one of his friends in a top spot, he'd make the final call regardless of the original plan.[82]

The situation dramatically increased Rogers' personal political power. He was also making money hand over fist. In Baltimore, he remained a hero, and his feud with the German powerhouse Karl Von Albers was impressively exploited. Buddy was wearing the Eastern championship belt again following his win over Bill Miller in Columbus on Oct. 13, 1955, and the title was the main focus of their storyline.[83] On November 8 at the Baltimore Coliseum,

Von Albers won the strap by disqualification after the Great Scott interfered on Buddy's behalf.[84] Rogers tried to regain the championship on Jan. 10, 1956, and the rivals fought "one of the wildest exhibitions" ever at the Coliseum. At the finish, he was bleeding from his forehead, nose and eyes, and the referee determined that he could no longer continue.[85] Two weeks later, with boxing great Joe Louis as guest referee, Rogers beat Von Albers to recapture the Eastern crown before a joyous capacity crowd.[86]

The title change had an asterisk, though. The *Baltimore Sun* reported that Von Albers actually lost a title match to Don Lee (now wrestling as Cowboy Rocky Lee) in Washington on Friday, January 20.[87] As a result of that decision, Lee was recognized as titleholder in D.C. and Pennsylvania, but Von Albers retained his claim in Maryland until losing to Rogers. A second asterisk acknowledged the fact that there had not been a grappling program in Washington, D.C. on January 20. The switch really occurred the night prior to the Baltimore bout on January 23.[88] Although Rogers was popular in his towns, he was routinely booed in other cities. On February 9, he went to Rochester and wrestled 26-year-old Johnny Barend for the first time. Buddy's persistent "gouging, kneeing and butting tactics" quickly turned the audience against him. Several angry patrons crossed the line and became physically involved, working to tie his legs in the ropes. But Rogers prevailed, winning two-of-three-falls – the third with his figure-four.[89]

The Eastern championship chaos continued. Rogers agreed to beat Billy Darnell and Rocky Lee in separate matches within an hour's time-limit on February 21 in Baltimore. Unlike most bouts with similar rules, Buddy's title was on the line, and would transfer to the man who beat him.[90] Rogers managed to subdue Darnell, but was in poor condition after their heads collided. Lee took advantage of the circumstances and was declared the winner when Buddy couldn't go on, thus taking a controversial claim to the title.[91] All of this turmoil culminated in a special three-way, one-night elimination series in Baltimore on March 13, 1956. Von Albers beat Lee in the opening bout, but was busted open in the process. The blood loss left him in a weakened state, and Rogers didn't help matters by focusing on the wound. Referee Joe Louis stopped the match and, once again, Rogers was the undisputed Eastern heavyweight champion.[92]

Louis' presence added another element to the wrestling scene in early 1956, and promoters made the most of it. Having the former boxing champion onboard as a guest official was a boon to ticket sales, and Rogers wanted to reap the rewards as much as possible. He had first seen the positive benefits of Louis' ability to draw back in 1944, and things hadn't changed much nearly 12 years later. People loved him. They enjoyed seeing him back in the squared circle, flashing his deadly fists, and making the villains of wrestling pay for their in-ring crimes. But there was a legitimate reason why Louis was more involved in the mat business, and word of income tax problems circulated on sports pages across the globe. Promoter Ray Fabiani saw an opportunity at hand and hoped to capitalize on a mutually beneficial arrangement. The prospective deal also involved Rogers, and if everything fell into place, it meant lucrative money. At least, that's what they figured. A whole new chapter was about to begin.

ENDNOTES - CHAPTER 10

[1] Rogers wrestled Longson to a 60-minute draw. *Chattanooga Times*, Dec. 13, 1946, p. 21.

[2] *Chattanooga Times*, Dec. 22, 1946, p. 51.

[3] *Chattanooga Times*, Dec. 13, 1946, p. 21.

[4] By 1952, Ellen's address was listed as the Kesmon Hotel in Philadelphia. *Herman Karl Rohde vs. Ellen Marion Rohde*, Decree of Divorce, No. 69262, Dec. 18, 1952, Franklin County Clerk of Courts, Columbus, Ohio.

[5] *Akron Beacon Journal*, Dec. 18, 1952, p. 76.

[6] *Herman Karl Rohde vs. Ellen Marion Rohde*, Decree of Divorce, No. 69262, Dec. 18, 1952, Franklin County Clerk of Courts, Columbus, Ohio.

[7] Matter of Changing the Name of Herman Karl Rohde to Buddy 'Nature Boy' Rogers, Order 150289, Sept. 9, 1952, Franklin County Probate Court, Columbus, Ohio.

[8] Nason misspelled his last name, "Rodgers" and said that it happened on "Sept. 9, 1951," which was a year too early. *Boston Globe*, Oct. 4, 1952, p. 7. His name change was also mentioned in the *Dayton Journal Herald*, Dec. 24, 1952, p. 6.

[9] *Columbus Star*, July 19, 1952, p. 2,7.

[10] Ibid.

[11] *Haft Nelson*, Vol. 1, No. 62, Feb. 26, 1953.

[12] Correspondence with Lee Rogers, Aug. 2018.

[13] 1940 U.S. Federal Census, ancestry.com. *Athens Sunday Messenger*, Feb. 14, 1954, p. 2.

[14] Gallia Academy High School Yearbook, 1949, ancestry.com.

[15] Correspondence with Lee Rogers, Aug. 2018.

[16] Ibid. Notice of their marriage appeared in a number of different newspapers to include the *Dayton Daily News*, Feb. 14, 1954, p. 55, *Athens Sunday Messenger*, Feb. 14, 1954, p. 2, *Canton Repository*, Feb. 21, 1954, p. 69, and the *Long Beach Independent Press-Telegram*, March 14, 1954, p. 59. Depending on the source, their marriage occurred in either Bradenton or Lakeland, Florida. In attempt to locate a copy of their marriage certificate, a request was sent to the Florida Bureau of Vital Statistics. No record was found.

[17] Rogers purchased the property from Rutherford A. Hawley. The transfer of ownership occurred on Aug. 17, 1953. Warranty Deed supplied by Robert Oates, who received it from the Franklin County Recorder's Office, Columbus, Ohio, September 2018. Also see *Columbus Dispatch*, Aug. 23, 1953, p. 59.

[18] Various issues of the *Columbus Dispatch*, including March 25, 1955, p. 42 and Dec. 8, 1958, p. 29.

[19] Johnny Valentine was one of the wrestlers who stayed in Buddy's building.

[20] Interview of Bobby Davis, Buddy Rogers Tribute Tape.

[21] Letter from Sam Muchnick to Jack Pfefer dated Aug. 3, 1953, Department of Justice Investigation into the National Wrestling Alliance, National Archives, College Park, MD.

[22] Notably, Pfefer was in Dallas in 1953 and was engaged in a promotional war against the local NWA affiliate. He was also booking Tommy "Nature Boy" Phelps.

[23] *St. Louis Globe-Democrat*, Aug. 16, 1953, p. 14.

[24] *St. Louis Globe-Democrat*, Nov. 21, 1953, p. 14.

[25] *Columbus Dispatch*, Oct. 9, 1953, p. 38.

[26] *Huntington Herald Dispatch*, Oct. 13, 1953, p. 11.

[27] Durango pinned Scott for the first fall and Rogers beat Durango with his figure-four, which was called the "octopus grapevine," in the second. Durango was injured and unable to continue. Scott pinned Dark Secret for the final fall. *Huntington Herald Dispatch*, Oct. 20, 1953, p. 15. Durango was also billed as the "Mysterious Durango."

[28] Rogers and Scott won the tournament on October 19. However, six days earlier, a newspaper in Akron said they were the "recent winners of the American tag wrestling championship trophy and belt." *Akron Beacon Journal*, Oct. 13, 1953, p. 45. This championship, like other instances in the Ohio territory, was referred by several different names, including the "Midwestern Tag Team Title."

[29] Rogers, Scott and Kirkpatrick took a well-circulated publicity photo with the trophy and belt. Rogers and Scott were wearing white varsity-type jackets.

[30] *Columbus Dispatch*, Oct. 23, 1953, p. 21B.
[31] Rogers and Thesz last wrestled on April 13, 1951 in St. Louis. It is believed that Sam Muchnick's loyalty to Jack Pfefer played a part in this nearly three-year hiatus. Muchnick was the booker of Thesz as NWA champ.
[32] This show drew 7,000 fans. Rogers was DQ'd for failing to break his hold when instructed by the official. The newspaper called Thesz's victory a "highly unpopular decision." *Indianapolis Star*, Feb. 21, 1954, p. D1. Rogers and Thesz did another variation of this same finish in St. Louis on April 23, 1954. *St. Louis Globe-Democrat*, April 24, 1954, p. 19.
[33] *Los Angeles Times*, March 14, 1954, p. 69.
[34] This deal was brokered after local promoter Ed Contos broke with Joe Toots Mondt.
[35] *Baltimore Sun*, May 19, 1954, p. 22.
[36] Rogers regained the Eastern Heavyweight Title on Feb. 1, 1954 in Charleston, West Virginia.
[37] Kato also wrestled as "The Great Kato."
[38] *Baltimore Sun*, Aug. 25, 1954, p. 16.
[39] The local newspaper misidentified Bill Miler as "Dick Miller." *Akron Beacon Journal*, Sept. 19, 1954, p. 46. It was claimed that Rogers won the Midwest crown from Miller on July 6, 1954 in Dayton. The *Dayton Journal Herald*, on July 6, 1954, indicated that Rogers was defending his "Eastern" championship against Miller. There was no indication that Rogers won a title on that show. *Dayton Journal Herald*, July 6, 1954, p. 8.
[40] There were nearly 5,000 people in attendance. *Baltimore Sun*, Sept. 22, 1954, p. 16.
[41] Reportedly, the NWA made the decision. *Akron Beacon Journal*, Sept. 25, 1954, p. 13.
[42] *Akron Beacon Journal*, Oct. 3, 1954, p. 44.
[43] *Lexington Herald*, Dec. 4, 1953.
[44] *Wrestling World*, July 1954.
[45] *Montreal Gazette*, Aug. 27, 1954, p. 20. The Aug. 27 issue of the *Montreal Gazette* stated that the card was held "last night." Other notices in the same paper stated that the card was to be held on Aug. 25. Unless there was a postponement, which was not reported in the *Gazette*, the show was held on the 25th as scheduled. See *Montreal Gazette*, Aug. 24, 1954, p. 20.
[46] Hutton had also wrestled earlier in the evening, having defeated Whitey Whittler. 2,402 fans were in attendance. *Canton Repository*, Oct. 17, 1954, p. 67.
[47] Their second match occurred on November 27 and Hutton promised to pin Rogers in two-straight falls in an hour or donate $500 to charity. Rogers posted a $1,000 check as a guarantee that Hutton wouldn't succeed. *Canton Repository*, Nov. 28, 1954, p. 6.
[48] *Canton Repository*, Dec. 12, 1954, p. 73.
[49] Rogers worked as the babyface. *Fort Lauderdale News*, Jan. 14, 1955, p. 21.
[50] *Fort Lauderdale News*, Jan. 21, 1955, p. 21.
[51] *Fort Lauderdale News*, Jan. 21, 1955, p. 22.
[52] *Fort Lauderdale News*, Jan. 28, 1955, p. 20.
[53] *Cleveland Plain Dealer*, Feb. 16, 1955, p. 29.
[54] Angry spectators threw chairs at Rogers as he made his way toward the dressing room with the belt. *Cleveland Plain Dealer*, March 2, 1955, p. 29.
[55] *Cleveland Plain Dealer*, March 16, 1955, p. 34.
[56] *Columbus Dispatch*, April 21, 1955, p. 41.
[57] Hugh Nichols telegram to Al Haft, Dec. 28, 1954, Department of Justice Investigation into the National Wrestling Alliance, National Archives, College Park, MD.
[58] *Los Angeles Times*, May 3, 1955, p. 74.
[59] The Slave Girl's name was Tanya. *San Bernardino County Sun*, May 4, 1955, p. 26.
[60] *Long Beach Independent Press-Telegram*, May 22, 1955, p. B6.
[61] *San Bernardino County Sun*, May 11, 1955, p. 28.
[62] Jerry Powers letter to James M. McGrath, Acting Chief, Los Angeles Office, Antitrust Division, Department of Justice, June 20, 1955, Department of Justice Investigation into the National Wrestling Alliance, National Archives, College Park, MD.
[63] *Los Angeles Times*, June 16, 1955, p. 37.

64 It was alleged in court documents that a cease and desist demand had been sent to the wrestler previously, but ignored. In response, Buddy's lawyer asked "When and in what manner, whether orally or by writing" the plaintiff sent a "cease and desist from using said name of 'Buddy Rogers.'" *Charles Rogers, a.k.a. "Buddy Rogers" v. Buddy Rogers*, Los Angeles County Superior Court, Case No. 644124. Also see *Los Angeles Times*, May 14, 1955, p. 17.

65 In a 1955 affidavit signed by Charles Rogers, it was said that he contacted "the defendant's manager in Pittsburgh, Pennsylvania within the past several months. The defendant's manager stated, 'The defendant is a fan of yours – that he likes you and therefore adopted your name.'" *Charles Rogers, a.k.a. "Buddy Rogers" v. Buddy Rogers*, Los Angeles County Superior Court, Case No. 644124.

Rogers later specifically denied that he took his name after the musician-actor: He said: "You know, some magazines said that I took the name 'Buddy Rogers' from an actor, Charles 'Buddy' Rogers, but that wasn't so. I don't know where they came up with that notion." *Wrestling's Main Event*, September 1983, p. 21-22.

66 Covey and Covey was the law firm of brothers Jules and Sylvan Covey. Jules was a former chairman of the California State Athletic Commission and represented promoter Cal Eaton. He was also a pallbearer at Hugh Nichols' funeral in 1956. *Pomona Progress Bulletin*, Dec. 19, 1956, p. 18.

67 *Charles Rogers, a.k.a. "Buddy Rogers" v. Buddy Rogers*, Los Angeles County Superior Court, Case No. 644124.

68 Ibid.

69 *Los Angeles Times*, July 15, 1955, p. B3.

70 *Dayton Daily News*, July 27, 1955, p. 16.

71 Haft wrestlers appeared in Baltimore beginning on Sept. 13, 1955.

72 *Bridgeport Post*, July 28, 1955, p. 27.

73 The telecast was presented locally in Baltimore on WMAR, channel 2, at 10:30 p.m. The show was also featured in Wilmington on WPFH-12, which extended into Philadelphia.

74 *Philadelphia Inquirer*, Oct. 17, 1955, p. 19.

75 *Philadelphia Inquirer*, Oct. 18, 1955, p. 38.

76 *New York Daily News*, Oct. 19, 1955, p. 82. A photo of Rogers applying a head scissors on Baillargeon appeared on the back cover of the *New York Post*. *New York Post*, Oct. 19, 1955, p. 94.

77 This program drew an estimated 7,500.

78 *New York Daily News*, Oct. 19, 1955, p. 82. On the November 14 show, Rogers was again booked to appear, but was slated for a preliminary against Chief Big Heart.

79 Rogers did not appear on the December 1955 Garden program.

80 Don Fargo talked about this in his book. *The Hard Way* by Don Fargo with Scott Teal (2014).

81 Other cities included Union City, Scranton, Lancaster, Altoona, and Hagerstown.

82 Bill Watts was later quoted as saying: "It's like Buddy Rogers used to do. He would bring in his own crew and tell the promoter what to do." *Pro Wrestling Torch Weekly*, Aug. 1, 1991.

83 Rogers beat Miller by countout in the third fall to capture the Eastern Title for a fifth time. *Columbus Dispatch*, Oct. 14, 1955, p. 34.

84 The newspaper initially indicated that Rogers would retain the title by DQ. *Baltimore Sun*, Nov. 9, 1955, p. 18. However, the same paper clarified the status of the championship a few days later, stating that Von Albers won the title. *Baltimore Sun*, Nov. 13, 1955, p. 7D.

85 *Baltimore Sun*, Jan. 11, 1956, p. 18.

86 *Baltimore Sun*, Jan. 25, 1956, p. 20.

87 Ibid.

88 *Philadelphia Inquirer*, Jan. 24, 1956, p. 24. The proper date of the title change was acknowledged in the *Baltimore Evening Sun*, March 8, 1956, p. 56.

89 *Rochester Democrat and Chronicle*, Feb. 10, 1956, p. 22.

90 *Baltimore Sun*, Feb. 21, 1956, p. 18.

91 *Baltimore Sun*, Feb. 22, 1956, p. 24. Lee also beat Rogers on February 20 in Philadelphia, but he wouldn't have lost his Maryland claim in that city. *Philadelphia Inquirer*, Feb. 21, 1956, p. 31.

92 *Baltimore Sun*, March 14, 1956, p. 19.

Chapter 11
Mentoring a Legend

Standing just under six feet, the rail-thin Aurelio Ray Fabiani was a dignified man of culture in an unscrupulous environment. He was born in Naples, Italy, in 1890 and dedicated his early life to playing the violin, first in Europe and then in the United States.[1] He joined the Chicago Civic Opera Company and achieved first chair, an honor given to the very best, and his music aptitude garnered him widespread recognition.[2] As fate would have it, he befriended talented wrestler Jim Londos, and the Greek superstar convinced him to become a promoter. In 1923, he launched his inaugural wrestling promotion in Baltimore and debuted in his hometown of Philadelphia soon thereafter. Fabiani lost a fortune during the Great Depression, but he rebuilt his bankroll and enjoyed good business in Los Angeles and Chicago before returning to Philadelphia in the 1950s. Despite the combustible nature of pro wrestling, he displayed solid instincts, and proved to be a hardnosed scrapper in adversarial situations.

When Fabiani dumped Toots Mondt and the NWA eastern combine to align with the prosperous Buddy Rogers troupe, he drew a line in the sand. He proclaimed his independence from bookers who didn't have his best interests at heart. Philadelphia, he felt, deserved a top-notch roster of performers on a regular basis, and gradually, that standard had diminished. But with Rogers and his crew providing an intriguing blend of histrionics and athleticism, Fabiani expected the box office to rebound in a big way. Prior to a February 1956 show in Wilmington, a city that Fabiani also controlled, the former musician visited a local newspaper in the hopes of gaining a little extra publicity. He brought along Rogers and Karl Von Albers to assist, and the presence of the two wrestlers did the trick. As a result of the sojourn, Al Cartwright, a sportswriter for the *Wilmington News Journal*, devoted an entire column to their appearance and described the entertaining scene in full.

"Just call me, Nature Boy," Rogers confidently told the reporter. "I have been the country's number two wrestler for the last seven years. I have held every sectional title in the United States, Canada, Cuba, Mexico, and Chester, PA." Cartwright noted Buddy's size and commented that he "even had muscles in his smile." When the journalist inquired as to what his favorite move was, Rogers replied: "I'm glad you asked. I feature the figure-four grapevine, a leglock, which I defy anyone to conquer. I have a standing offer of one grand that no wrestler can break this hold. Care to try?" Cartwright politely declined.[3] Fabiani worked the room like a pro, shook all available hands, and masterfully hyped the upcoming program. The employees of the newspaper were sold on the excitement, but the sports-going public was seemingly busy the night of the card. Only 900 turned out at Fournier Hall to see Rogers beat the masked Golden Terror in two straight falls.[4]

Fabiani was an unfaltering optimist when it came to promoting wrestling, and when there was potential money to be made, he was aggressively enthusiastic. In early 1956, a prospective windfall dropped into his lap, and he was quick to seize the moment. Joe Louis, nicknamed the "Brown Bomber" during his legendary boxing career, was the world champion from 1937 to 1949. He was a sports icon, revered for his abilities and accomplishments, and admired by pundits and the public alike. His name could be found daily on the sports pages of newspapers across North America, often in celebration of his heroic fistic feats. But his name was also frequently being mentioned for another reason, one much less favorable. Stories about his income tax problems had been circulating for months, and the Internal Revenue Service imposed a handful of liens against him. In the Jan. 7, 1956, issue of the *Saturday Evening Post*, Louis revealed that he owed the Government more than $1 million in back taxes and interest.[5]

Facing an immensely difficult financial challenge, the 41-year-old Louis was hoping for a settlement to resolve the crisis. In the meantime, he was contending with the possibility that the government was going to raid the trust fund his ex-wife Marva had established for their children.[6] Rightfully concerned, Louis was more open-minded about his employment opportunities, specifically the one offered by Ray Fabiani to become a full-time, traveling professional wrestler. For more than 10 years, Louis had associated with figures within the grappling field and participated in matches as a guest referee. He understood the culture of wrestling and knew the physicality of it. In February 1956, he was asked by a Dayton reporter if he enjoyed officiating mat contests. "It's not bad," Louis explained. "It's a lot tougher than refereeing boxing. In boxing, you move around and don't get hit. But this wrestling, you've got to get right in there with them, and sometimes they're not too gentle."[7]

To elevate the impact of Louis as a referee, promoters worked him into match finishes in various parts of the country. Typically, in the main event contests he officiated, he wrangled with the devious heel in one way or another, setting in motion the final sequence. For example, in Albuquerque on March 28, 1955, Louis got between Jack Claybourne and the Golden Terror in an attempt to break them up, and the latter hit him. The former fight champ retaliated swiftly by punching the Terror in the stomach, and Claybourne then landed a dropkick for the final pinfall.[8] In Baltimore for the Buddy Rogers-Karl Von Albers bout on Jan. 24, 1956, the German followed the same playbook, knocking Louis to the canvas. This time, though, Louis didn't exact revenge. But Von Albers was so focused on his assault of Louis, he left himself open to a blindside attack by Rogers. A dropkick later and Von Albers was counted out.[9]

Between January and March 1956, Louis served as the third man in the ring for eight matches involving Rogers. They varied the finish slightly, but the principle remained pretty standard. Having Louis on the Rogers circuit was illuminating and worthwhile, and upon hearing the dramatic news about Joe's debt, Ray Fabiani made his proposition. He offered Louis an annual $100,000 guarantee for his wrestling contract, an astronomical sum, and persuaded him to give it a shot.[10] Louis soon went into secret training to learn the essentials of the profession with Rogers as his primary coach.[11] Buddy had faced off against a number of boxers, including Primo Carnera, Tony Galento, and Natie Brown, and understood the distinctive limitations that fighters characteristically brought to the wrestling ring. Interestingly, back in 1948, Rogers told a New York publication that he wanted to face then-champion Louis in a boxer versus wrestler contest. "I believe I could win that one," Rogers declared.[12]

Rogers and Louis traveled and trained together during the weeks leading up to Joe's mat debut, slated for March 16, 1956, in Washington, D.C.[13] In addition to learning how to properly bump and safely maneuver around the ring, Louis attempted to lose weight and strengthen his conditioning. Joe admitted to being 240 pounds, but a sportswriter for the *Arizona Daily Star* noticed the "roll of fat" that protruded "over the top of his trunks" during an appearance the year prior.[14] Nevertheless, Rogers successfully taught Louis "about six holds," and on March 16, Joe knocked out Rocky Lee with two of his famous right crosses to officially begin his wrestling career.[15] His match lasted about 11 minutes and the crowd of 4,179 at the Uline Arena was overjoyed by Louis's performance.[16] After the card, a journalist asked Louis if transitioning to a pro wrestler was undignified for a former boxing world heavyweight champion. "Who says so?" Louis asked, irritated by the question. "It's an honest living. It's not stealing."[17]

In late March 1956, Rogers escaped the chilly north for a brief solo tour of Florida before being joined by Louis on April 2 in Tampa. Together, they began a grueling six-straight-night run of matches, which tested Joe's aptitude and commitment to wrestling. He confessed that he was unsure of his future in the mat business, and the trip around the Florida circuit was going to help him make up his mind.[18] It didn't take long for Louis to realize that he disliked the traveling.[19] Rushing out of an arena after a bout to catch a plane to the next city was a nerve-wracking task, and left little time for needed rest. Rogers was a busy man. He was in charge of booking Louis, working as his agent and ring mentor, and arranging for their transportation.[20] He also wrestled each night, battling the likes of Gino Garibaldi and Bob Langevin. But handling Louis was his principal job, and when something irregular surfaced, it was Buddy's responsibility to smooth things over.

On the third night of their journey, controversy sparked up in St. Petersburg. Louis was so irked by the circumstances that he almost refused to perform. Rogers was on the spot as expected, but the matter was far beyond his control. The local promoter, Pat O'Hara, would only allow a white audience to attend his April 4 show at the Armory, claiming the facility was too small for a desegregated crowd. The main reason, it was stated, was because there wasn't a separate rest room for whites and blacks.[21] Louis was surprised and upset by the news and told Rogers, "I ain't going on." Rogers and *New York Post* sportswriter Milton Gross watched the former champ leave the dressing room. Buddy explained that it was the second time that day that they had encountered racial discrimination. At the Tampa airport after their arrival, they went inside for a bite to eat. Instead of putting Louis and Rogers amongst the public, they sat them in a secluded back room. Louis was disgusted and told Buddy, "[I] lost my appetite."[22]

After returning to the dressing room, Louis stated, "I shouldn't go on. I ain't going on." Rogers, trying to reassure him, made a guarantee that it wouldn't happen again. "Before I ask what the percentage will be, I'll ask if colored people will be allowed," Buddy responded. Louis asked what Gross thought, and he replied: "It's your problem. You've got to make up your mind." Rogers made a comment, to which Gross retorted: "You and I can't fully appreciate this as Joe can." Rogers immediately said, "Can't I? I've got a colored wife."[23] His spouse, Terry, was of mixed heritage, and the couple was often the target of discrimination.[24] After their marriage, Buddy received hate mail by "fans" who disliked his choice in partner and was called a "n——- lover."[25] Despite the overt racism, Rogers was generally "unfazed by outsider opinions," but as shown by the situation with Louis, he did take things personally.[26] Louis struggled with his decision, but after considerable thought, he agreed to go on with the show.[27] In the main event, he landed a powerful right to the chin of Shag Thomas, an ex-football star for Ohio State, and achieved victory.[28] In all six of his Florida contests, Louis relied on his famous fists, and his opponents put him over each time. And despite the constant complaints of critics, fans loved it.[29]

Rogers was completely supportive of Louis and talked him up at every opportunity. "He's the strongest man I've ever taught," Buddy told a reporter for the *Fort Lauderdale News*.[30] While his initial bouts were a little shaky, Louis improved steadily, and by his sixth match in Daytona Beach, he was commended for his effort.[31] Money-wise, they made about what they anticipated for the six-day tour. Commanding a percentage ranging from 25 to 35 per cent of the gross, Louis and Rogers earned in the neighborhood of $2,500.[32] Louis received the lion's share, of course, taking home about two grand. Rogers earned close to $500, plus additional money for his wrestling appearances. Louis admitted that he enjoyed wrestling, but he made it clear that his other business responsibilities would prevent him from being a regular fixture on the mat circuit.[33] "I just can't be away from them too much," he said. "If they'll let me take a week off now and then to wrestle, okay, I'll do it. But I can't make a full-time tour."[34]

Louis continued to grapple, but did so on his own terms. He ventured with Rogers to Havana, Cuba, for an event at the Sports Palace on April 19, 1956, and both were triumphant. Louis won over Eduardo Perez and Rogers beat Bob Langevin.[35] The following month in Ohio, the teacher and student were matched up for the first time on May 3, and drew 3,500 patrons to the Toledo Sports Arena. Rogers and Louis split falls and went to a no-contest.[36] They did the same finish in Dayton a few weeks later, as well.[37] The wrestler versus boxer concept was a hot ticket, and Al Haft decided to exploit another feud involving Rogers, this time with former world heavyweight champion "Jersey" Joe Walcott. Walcott and Rogers were longtime friends going back to their shared hometown of Camden, and had worked out together in the past.[38] Their simulated hostilities began in Akron on March 3 when Walcott punched out Rogers during a boxing contest between Buddy and Billy Darnell.[39]

Haft quickly booked them for a mixed match at the Memorial Auditorium in Columbus on March 15. Walcott, who was a few months older than Louis, was physically prepared for the bout, and knocked Rogers to the canvas in the second round. In the third, he was leading by a good margin, but the "Nature Boy" cunningly avoided defeat. He caught Walcott off-guard, grabbed one of his legs, and applied what the newspaper called a "step-over toehold and head twist" to win the match.[40] By that point, the Northeastern circuit Rogers previously managed had deteriorated, and his absence was a big factor. Towns were reabsorbed into the Eastern NWA syndicate, and many of the wrestlers Buddy used fanned out elsewhere. For instance, the talented Stevens brothers (Don and Ray), remerged in Ohio and were acknowledged as the American tag team champions. In Northern California, Karl Von Albers dropped the German gimmick and became "Ed Miller," a purported brother of Bill Miller.

For Rogers, it was an important transitional time. He was no longer a booker or the agent for an international sports celebrity. He was headed back on the road, ready to make his first start in Texas in nearly six years.[41] Wrestling in the "Lone Star State" for promoter Morris Sigel was always personally meaningful, and he never forgot the break Sigel had given him 11 years earlier. Buddy was pushed to the top of the heavyweight ranks in his first match in the territory, June 1, 1956 in Houston, and went over Pepper Gomez for the Texas State crown. Gomez reigned as champion for nearly ten months and was extraordinarily popular.[42] The victory of Rogers and the way he injured Gomez with a "vicious octopus clamp," instantly made him public enemy number one.[43] Spanish-speaking enthusiasts were particularly angered, and fan-favorite Ramon Torres took on the role of Buddy's chief rival.

Torres beat Rogers by disqualification on June 8 in Houston and won again, under handicap rules, on June 27 in San Antonio.[44] They also drew, tied at one-fall apiece, in San Antonio on July 4.[45] Aside from Torres, Rogers wrestled familiar opponents like Duke Keomuka and Ed Francis, and soon resumed his enduring feuds with Johnny Valentine and Danny McShain, both of whom arrived in Texas in July. Rogers was positioned as a leading heel and headliner, but often had to share the spotlight and work semifinals due to the abundance of talent in the region. He was overshadowed at times by the rule-breaking antics of "Iron" Mike DiBiase and "Bulldog" Danny Plechas, and when pitted against one of the two Nebraskans, people begrudgingly supported him because of their hatred for his opponent. The Dallas arena program actually told patrons that Rogers "should really be the choice of the fans" versus DiBiase on July 3 at the Sportatorium.[46] That night, Buddy prevailed in a hotly contested bout.[47]

Alternating use of his "octopus clamp" and a "paralytic headlock" as his finishers, Rogers originally intended to spend six months in Texas.[48] But after only two and a half months, he cut the tour short. On the way out, he dropped the Texas title back to Pepper Gomez on Aug. 3, and put over Ramon Torres on Aug. 8 in San Antonio and Gene Kelly the following night in Galveston. Kelly, a brawny former football star, would later be known as "Gene Kiniski." On Aug. 14 in Dallas, Buddy challenged NWA world champion "Whipper" Billy Watson. He won the initial fall, but was counted out in the second after a mid-ring collision. Rogers was unable to continue, lost the bout, and left the territory.[49] Gomez, in a 1996 interview, stated that Buddy campaigned to Morris Sigel to keep the Texas belt on him despite an earlier agreement to lose the title to Pepper when he returned.[50] Sigel refused to modify his plans, and that decision may have contributed to Buddy's hastened departure.

During the summer of 1956, the studio program based in New York City was cancelled and replaced by a telecast from Washington, D.C., produced by Vincent J. McMahon.[51] Since McMahon was not a booking agent, he relied on help from Alliance members Jim Crockett and Bill Lewis of the Mid-Atlantic region, and also New York's Toots Mondt. Fred Kohler of Chicago pitched in, as well, by sending Verne Gagne and Hans Schmidt to the Capitol Arena for its weekly broadcast. The influential, new TV series with an expansive reach grabbed Buddy's attention, and two nights after his Dallas loss to champion Watson, Rogers defeated Dick Steinborn in front of cameras in Washington. On Aug. 21, he wrestled a competitive 60-minute draw with Antonino Rocca at the Baltimore Coliseum, and although his loyalists were glad to see him back in town, Rogers was clearly a changed man.[52]

Buddy displayed "explosive and unusual tactics" in his bout with Rocca, and rather than embracing his previous popularity, he went full-blown heel.[53] The next week in Baltimore, he went after Timmy Geohagen with a fury, and constantly tossed him from the ring to the Coliseum floor. Around the 20-minute mark, Rogers applied "a new hold he acquired on his trip south" and gained a win.[54] His latest finisher was the same "paralytic headlock" he used in Texas, and the move was quickly established as one to be feared.[55] The maneuver incapacitated two opponents, Dick Steinborn and Jack Allen, in Baltimore on September 11, with the former having to be carried to the back area.[56] Again acknowledged as the Eastern States champ, Rogers teamed with newly crowned U.S. titleholder Hans Schmidt on September 18 in Baltimore and September 24 in the Bronx, but their partnership was brief.[57] Surprisingly, Rogers no-showed the next three dates, made an event in Canton, Ohio, and then returned to Florida.[58]

Newspapers in Baltimore and Rochester, two of the cities in which Buddy failed to appear, excused Rogers because of injury.[59] However, he managed to perform in Canton on September 29 without incident. His withdrawal from the Northeast was probably more for personal and political reasons, and his central objection rested with booker Toots Mondt. A year earlier, Rogers wrestled for Mondt at Madison Square Garden on a night in which attendance was far below expectations. It was indeed a setback for the local promotional syndicate, but Rogers fulfilled his obligation, and anticipated his full and complete pay in return. Instead, he was "short-changed", and when it came to money issues, Buddy took matters very seriously. He knew the value of a dollar, and in that respect, was the polar opposite of the irresponsible Mondt. Toots had a well-known gambling vice and was a regular at New York metropolitan horse tracks. Over the course of his life in wrestling, he had amassed and lost several sizable fortunes.

Rogers and Mondt mixed like oil and water. Despite their shared interest in greenbacks, they had little use for each other. Notably, Mondt had been the driving force behind Gene Stanlee's ascension in the late 1940s, and Stanlee was, in many opinions, the East Coast version of Rogers at the time. With Rogers suspended in New York, Stanlee became a superstar, and Mondt coined a mint.[60] From Buddy's point of view, he didn't need anything from

Mondt, Fred Kohler, or his more recent ally Ray Fabiani.[61] The choice of working for promoters he had problems with or leaving for friendlier regions was not much of a choice at all. Rogers left the Northeast with no intention of returning anytime soon.[62] And with regard to the money he was owed for his Garden appearance, Buddy informed the New York State Athletic Commission about the situation, and an investigation was opened.[63] Chairman Julius Helfand, the man who was trying to straighten out boxing, added the mat business to his purview, much to Mondt's dismay.

In Canton, on Sept. 29, 1956, Rogers beat Chest Bernard in two-of-three-falls.[64] The local periodical, the *Canton Repository*, indicated that Buddy was in a hurry to make a benefit event in Miami, and his main event bout was pushed up from its usual spot.[65] Miami Beach promoter Chris Dundee was planning a special benefit boxing program for the late Babe Didrikson Zaharias, the legendary golfing champion, on October 3.[66] Zaharias, however, died of cancer the week before at the age of 45. Married to ex-wrestler and promoter George Zaharias, Babe was enormously popular and respected in athletic circles, and Rogers was very fond of both. "They're real people," he told a reporter in 1952. "[They were] an ideal couple."[67] Apparently, Rogers was unable to attend the Miami benefit because of a conflicting booking in St. Petersburg. On October 1 in Tampa, Buddy shared a locker room with George Zaharias' brother Chris, and surely expressed his deepest sympathies.

Having endured a rocky patch, Rogers rejoined his primary advocates, Al Haft and Eddie Quinn, and turned his focus to a moneymaking circuit that included Boston, Toronto and St. Louis. In Boston, where he hadn't wrestled since 1953, Buddy drew 3,500 for a match with Killer Kowalski on October 15. Promoter Paul Bowser, enthused by the attendance, told the *Boston American* that he "wouldn't be surprised to see a wrestling renaissance this year." Rogers took a loss to Kowalski and was to have a rematch the next week, but missed the show due to bad weather.[68] On October 29 at the Arena, Buddy drew with Lou Thesz before another good crowd.[69] Over in St. Louis, Rogers received two shots at the NWA world title against Billy Watson. In their first contest, which took place on September 14, he put on a wild demonstration, throwing the champ from the ring and fighting on the floor of the Kiel Auditorium. He was disqualified, and in protest, he knocked down referee John Turner and tore his shirt.[70]

Missouri State Athletic Commissioner Charles W. Pian fined Rogers $25 for the disorderly scene, and it was evidence of a job well done. But the real validation of Buddy's hard work rested in the attendance figures of their rematch on October 5. A swarm of 7,649 witnessed the second program, topping the previous affair by more than 1,600, and fans weren't disappointed. The Rogers-Watson match-up was relatively brief, only 11:21, but it was full of action from bell-to-bell. At the end, the two wrestlers used a variation of the finish they worked in Dallas in Aug. – a collision leading to a count-out. To add to the drama, Rogers was given a ten count because he was in the ring, whereas Watson was outside the ropes and provided 20 seconds to return. Rogers awoke first and noticed that the champion was unable to continue. When referee Jack Sharkey signaled for the bell, Buddy thought he was the victor and new titleholder. But, in reality, he had already been counted out, and the match was a no-decision.[71]

A scary real-world incident occurred on November 30 in Buffalo. Rogers, in town to face the ever-popular Ilio DiPaolo, resorted to unsportsmanlike tactics to win by count-out. As the two fought outside the ring, DiPaolo pushed Rogers with all of his might, sending Buddy off balance. To brace himself, Buddy extended his arm, and it went through a plate glass window, severely cutting his wrist. The shattered glass cut DiPaolo, as well, and both were rushed to Buffalo Emergency Hospital for immediate treatment. Rogers lost a lot of blood and needed 15 stitches to close the wound.[72] The cynical and sarcastic columnist Dan Parker, in noting Buddy's condition, wrote: "Won't it be a black Christmas in Montreal when the news reaches there that Nature Boy Rogers, the Elvis Presley of the mat, is listed as ill and unavailable on the New York State Athletic Commission's weekly bulletin?"[73] Rogers missed at least two weeks of in-ring action.[74]

1956 was a difficult year for the wrestling industry. Public reports of a widespread Department of Justice investigation into the National Wrestling Alliance for monopolistic practices were revealed, and the NWA's future was in jeopardy. There was a great deal of evidence of wrongdoing across the board, and the Government was set for prosecution with the intent of disbanding the organization. Without the judicious maneuverings of several key figures, that would have happened. But a settlement was reached in advance and a specialized Consent Decree was drawn up, essentially giving the Alliance a second chance at life.[75] The wrestlers under the NWA umbrella weren't really affected by the decision. It was status quo for the most part, but with the added media scrutiny, they needed to protect the business at all costs. Rogers never had a problem with that, and with a sincere need to boost attendance figures, the "Nature Boy" was a central player on the national circuit.

A winter working-vacation in Florida was nearly mandatory for Rogers, and he enjoyed a three-week tour in January and February 1957. In Tampa on February 4, an audience of 4,000 saw him challenge Lou Thesz for the NWA world title. Thesz had dethroned Billy Watson in November, and promoter Cowboy Luttrall pushed the Thesz-Rogers contest as the headline attraction for his annual Gasparilla card. It was a worthy choice. Thesz and Rogers gave a spirited performance with the champ winning the second and third falls after Rogers took the opener.[76] A few days later in Fort Lauderdale, Buddy met 6-foot-6 Don Leo Jonathan, a second-generation grappler from Utah. They had wrestled before, but this time, Rogers went out of his way to put Jonathan over as a bruising behemoth. He was pummeled unmercifully throughout their match, and took a chair to the head at the conclusion, earning a DQ win. Laughably, Rogers tried to fight back, only to see Jonathan shrug off his punches in superhuman fashion.[77]

The manner in which Rogers sold for the 25-year-old "Mormon Giant" turned Jonathan into the city's top heel. Buddy was leaving the territory, and he boosted an up-and-comer on the way out. As a result, Jonathan, on February 14, drew "one of the biggest houses in the last three years" in Fort Lauderdale against Thesz.[78] Rogers remembered the kindness Don Leo's father, Brother Jonathan, showed him in Texas when he was a greenhorn in 1945, and was more than willing to help elevate the towering athlete. Buddy also recalled an extraordinary talent Brother Jonathan had. "The normal chest expansion, even for a big wrestler or weight-man, is about four inches," Rogers told a reporter. "Brother Jonathan's expansion was more than eight inches. It was the most amazing thing I ever saw."[79] From Florida, Buddy went to Montreal, and again got into it with Jersey Joe Walcott, the referee for his bout with rising star Edouard Carpentier of France. Rogers, punched by Walcott, sailed from the ring and was counted out.[80]

On Feb. 18, 1957, he made his first appearance in Memphis in more than six years and defeated Billy Blassie. That particular show was important to Memphis wrestling because it marked a changeover in booking office from Tulsa to St. Louis. NWA President Sam Muchnick and his booker, Bill Longson, did not operate a territory in the usual sense. They promoted St. Louis and a few smaller towns in Missouri, but they had valuable booking rights to cities outside their normal jurisdiction. Those locations included Indianapolis, Evansville, and Louisville, and the addition of Memphis was a consequential financial acquisition.[81] Rogers' arrival was perfectly timed to help Muchnick boost attendance. Already on the circuit were several of his old running buddies, and the aforementioned Billy Blassie was one of them. Blassie had wrestled alongside Rogers in 1949-'50 as part of the Pfefer troupe, using the guise, "Tom Marshall." In recent years, he often wrestled under his real name, Bill McDaniel.

Billy Darnell, George Bollas (Zebra Kid), and Bob McCune were also wrestling on that loop, having graduated from Pfefer's School of Hard Knocks. For Rogers, he was comfortably surrounded by friends and trusted rivals, making for an easier environment and better-quality matches for fans. His contests with Darnell and the Zebra Kid were legendary, and a well-designed angle could set up three to four weeks of exciting action. Rogers was known for taking younger wrestlers under his wing, and there were at least two upstarts on the St. Louis-based tour to have been influenced by him in one way or another.[82] Frank Townsend was a tall, 24-year-old athlete from Camden County, New Jersey, and was directly trained and mentored by Rogers.[83] Ian Campbell of Scotland was similarly skilled, and had learned from Rogers previously in Ohio and Texas, and now on the St. Louis circuit. Although Townsend and Campbell were still preliminary guys, they were definitely headed for bigger and better things.

Demonstrating his versatility, Rogers was a fan-favorite in Indianapolis and Memphis, a heel in Evansville, and a tweener in St. Louis, all during the same stretch. He squared off with heroes Billy Darnell and Bobby Managoff in Evansville, and then teamed with them in Memphis and Indianapolis, respectively. In Indianapolis, he feuded with Fritz Von Erich, and turned around and tagged up with him in Evansville. Without the Internet or national wire reports, fans were none the wiser. Some publicity reports, in pushing Buddy as a babyface, resurrected his old nickname, the "Atomic Blond," instead of the "Nature Boy."[84] The Zebra Kid and Golden Terror combined to pulverize Rogers at the Armory in Indianapolis in March 1957, and the sides were evened up when Buddy was joined by former bodybuilder Bob McCune. On April 4, Rogers and McCune sent the crowd home happy when they beat their foes in two straight falls.[85] At the same venue on May 2, he refused a fall over Red Lyons because he felt he accidentally fouled his opponent. The match continued and Rogers won, legally, with his figure-four.[86]

In Evansville on March 27, as a crooked desperado, he tried to pin Bill Longson using the ropes for leverage, and initially got away with it. The referee quickly learned what had occurred and reversed the decision.[87] The next week, Rogers and Fritz Von Erich cheated to beat Lyons and Longson, but the official again found out and gave the heroes the win.[88] A good-sized Evansville audience witnessed a chaotic brawl between Rogers and Billy Darnell on April 24. Buddy had made the claim that he could defeat both Darnell and Lou Plummer within an hour. He went to the mat with Darnell first, and after 25-minutes, they shifted from a straight wrestling match to an out-of-control war. With fists flying in every direction, they battled up the aisle and into the crowd. They next moved into the lobby of the Coliseum, giving spectators an up-close look at the mayhem. It took many minutes before officials were able to calm things down, and as a result of the carnage, the bout was declared a no-contest and purses were held-up.[89]

Buddy's drawing power remained consistent. When he challenged Lou Thesz for the world title in Evansville on March 20, 1957, they lured the "largest wrestling audience" in city history. A record 6,000 fans packed the Municipal Stadium for the championship affair, and the two professionals put on great show. Rogers was riding a wave at the finish, bowling Thesz over with flying tackle after flying tackle. The champ dodged the last one, which resulted in a disqualification for Rogers when he plowed into the referee.[90] A few weeks before that, he defeated Mike Paidousis at the Indianapolis Armory in front of 3,200 spectators, and the *Indianapolis Star* noted that it was the "largest attendance in two years."[91] Sure enough, the wrestling business was experiencing a downturn in public support, but superstar names and blazing hot feuds could still put butts in seats. As his tour of the St. Louis circuit proved, Rogers attracted crowds for both reasons. And it didn't matter if he was a good guy or bad, the "Nature Boy" just had "it."

ENDNOTES - CHAPTER 11

[1] Various genealogical resources at ancestry.com.
[2] *Lancaster New Era*, May 5, 1932, p. 14.
[3] *Wilmington News Journal*, Feb. 15, 1956, p. 32.
[4] *Wilmington News Journal*, Feb. 17, 1956, p. 23.
[5] Louis said that he didn't know for sure the final amount he owed. The article was "As told to Edward Linn." *Saturday Evening Post*, Jan. 7, 1956, p. 22-23.
[6] Ibid. Also see *Elmira Advertiser*, Feb. 3, 1956, p. 13.
[7] *Dayton Journal Herald*, Feb. 29, 1956, p. 7.
[8] *Albuquerque Journal*, March 29, 1955, p. 14.
[9] *Baltimore Sun*, Jan. 25, 1956, p. 20.
[10] *Chicago Tribune*, March 9, 1956, p. 46. Some reports claimed Louis was promised as high as $150,000 a year.
[11] The public announcement of the deal was made on March 8, 1956 and circulated in newspapers the next day. Louis was training in secret beginning in February, and had a month of tutelage under his belt prior to his first match. United Press Wire Photo Caption Sheet, March 14, 1956.
[12] *Sports Pictorial Review*, April 12, 1948, p. 2.
[13] The pair was spotted at the Hickory Barbecue in Cincinnati while passing through town. *Cincinnati Enquirer*, March 7, 1956, p. 6.
[14] Louis fought wrestler Danny Plechas in a boxing bout at the Tucson Sports Center. Louis won a third round TKO before 4,000 spectators. *Arizona Daily Star*, April 1, 1955, p. 35.

15 *Elmira Advertiser*, July 3, 1956, p. 15.
16 *Washington, D.C., Evening Star*, March 17, 1956, p. 12.
17 Ibid.
18 *Miami Herald*, April 5, 1956, p. 5D. Louis said that Florida was "sort of a proving grounds for me." *Fort Lauderdale News*, April 4, 1956, p. 25.
19 *Orlando Evening Star*, April 9, 1956, p. 12.
20 Tampa Times, April 3, 1956, p. 9. Rogers coordinated the entire tour through Herb Freeman, who worked in the office of "Cowboy" Luttrall, head of the Florida circuit. Freeman may have traveled with Rogers and Louis.
21 O'Hara said he wanted to allow everyone to attend, but had to restrict the audience to whites only. *St. Petersburg Times*, April 1, 1956, p. 3.
22 *New York Post*, April 5, 1956, p. 53.
23 Ibid.
24 Terry personally identified as Spanish. Correspondence with Lee Rogers, July 13, 2020.
25 Ibid.
26 Ibid.
27 Louis had previously refused boxing engagements because of segregation. It is not known if this was the first time he actually appeared before an all-white audience, which had resulted from a ban on black fans.
28 Notably, the "Black Panther" Jim Mitchell was advertised as Louis' opponent. It was claimed that Mitchell did not make the show because of a protest against the ban on African American fans. *St. Petersburg Times*, April 5, 1956, p. 29. However, Louis denied that was the truth. "They used Mitchell's name because he's a wrestler that is known," he explained. "Nobody pulled out." *New York Post*, April 5, 1956, p. 53. Mitchell, in fact, wrestled on a show in Toledo, Ohio that same evening, and defeated the Blimp by disqualification. *Toledo Blade*, April 5, 1956, p. 43. It is quite possible that Thomas was hand-picked by Rogers to make the trip to Florida, where he wrestled Louis three times. Thomas was a product of Al Haft's gym in Columbus and Rogers may have had an influence on his training. Thomas also went by the name, "King Tobey (Toby)." In the days prior to the Florida match, Thomas had been wrestling in Ohio.
29 Many sportswriters were hard on Louis for taking this chance at wrestling. Jimmy Burns of the *Miami Herald* wrote that, "Many boxing fans, preferring to remember Louis as a great fight champion, did not care to see him rassle." *Miami Herald*, April 7, 1956, p. 12. Baltimore writer Paul Menton stated that the "glamour surrounding his fine career as heavyweight boxing champion [was] rapidly fading as he tries to become a wrestler." *Baltimore Evening Sun*, April 16, 1956, p. 29.
30 *Fort Lauderdale News*, April 2, 1956, p. 25.
31 *Daytona Beach News-Journal*, April 8, 1956, p. 15. Rogers believed Louis was improving with every match. *Fort Lauderdale News*, April 6, 1956, p. 22.
32 In Fort Lauderdale, their percentage was 25, while it was 30 in Miami, and 35 in St. Petersburg. See *Miami Herald*, April 7, 1956, p. 12 and *St. Petersburg Times*, April 5, 1956, p. 29.
33 *Miami Herald*, April 6, 1956, p. 61.
34 *Daytona Beach News-Journal*, April 8, 1956, p. 15.
35 *Diario de la Marina*, April 20, 1956, p. B3. The newspaper indicated that Rogers was making his debut in Cuba. *Diario de la Marina*, April 19, 1956, p. B3.
36 *Toledo Blade*, May 4, 1956, p. 39.
37 *Dayton Daily News*, May 30, 1956, p. 16.
38 *Sports Pictorial Review*, April 12, 1948, p. 2, *Columbus Dispatch*, Jan. 6, 1952, p. 51.
39 Rogers hit Walcott first and then "Jersey Joe" struck back, ending the bout. *Akron Beacon Journal*, March 4, 1956, p. 46.

40 *Columbus Dispatch*, March 16, 1956, p. 54. There were 4,000 people in attendance. Keeping up with kayfabe, Walcott told a reporter that he accepted the match because Rogers' challenge "made it impossible for me to live in Camden with him as a neighbor if I turned it down." *Indianapolis Star*, March 26, 1956, p. 18. In a separate article, Walcott said about Rogers: "We never got along at home. Rogers challenged Louis, Rocky Marciano or me to a match, so I accepted." *Mansfield News-Journal*, March 15, 1956, p. 15.

41 Rogers last wrestled in Houston on Aug. 25, 1950.

42 Gomez dethroned Mr. Moto for the championship on Aug. 5, 1955 in Houston.

43 Houston Program, June 15, 1956, p. 1. Gomez left Texas for a tour of the Pacific Northwest.

44 Rogers was disqualified for throwing Torres over the top rope in Houston. In San Antonio, Rogers agreed to beat Torres in two-straight falls or forfeit the match. He won the first fall, but lost the second and forfeited. *San Antonio Express*, June 28, 1956, p. 19.

45 *San Antonio Express*, July 5, 1956, p. 27.

46 *Rasslin'*, Dallas Wrestling Program, July 3, 1956, p. 1.

47 *Dallas Morning News*, July 4, 1956, p. 9.

48 *Gallipolis Daily Tribune*, July 2, 1956, p. 2.

49 *Dallas Morning News*, Aug. 15, 1956, p. 12.

50 *The Wrestling Archive Project*, Volume 1, by Scott Teal, p. 391.

51 McMahon's television show made its debut in New York City on June 21, 1956.

52 *Baltimore Sun*, Aug. 22, 1956, p. 20. Rogers-Rocca was billed as a "promoter's dream match." *Baltimore Sun*, Aug. 19, 1956, p. 43.

53 *Baltimore Sun*, Aug. 26, 1956, p. 44.

54 *Baltimore Sun*, Aug. 29, 1956, p. 22 and *Baltimore Sun*, Sept. 2, 1956, p. 19.

55 Rogers was said to have specialized in the headlock. *Washington, D.C. Evening Star*, Aug. 30, 1956, p. C2. This may have been a variation of the sleeperhold.

56 *Baltimore Sun*, Sept. 12, 1956, p. 20.

57 Schmidt won the United States Title from Wilbur Snyder on Sept. 15, 1956.

58 The no shows were in Baltimore on September 25, New York City on September 26, and Rochester on Sept. 27, 1956.

59 *Baltimore Sun*, Sept. 26, 1956, p. 26, *Rochester Democrat and Chronicle*, Sept. 28, 1956, p. 33.

60 Rogers claimed Stanlee studied and copied his style. *Television Guide*, Feb. 25, 1950, p. 22.

61 Rogers hadn't wrestled for Fred Kohler in over five years. Rogers skipped out on a Philadelphia booking on Sept. 21, 1956. He was scheduled to team with Hans Schmidt versus Gino Garibaldi and Tony Martinelli. He was replaced by Fritz Wallick. *Philadelphia Inquirer*, Sept. 22, 1956, p. 20. It is unclear if Rogers and Fabiani had a falling out in the aftermath of the Joe Louis deal.

62 After Rogers left the northeast, Lancaster promoter Danny Templeton Jr. spoke about his departure to a local newspaper. He said: "Rogers has taken off for Florida, and he's dividing his time between shows there and in Cuba. He's cleaning up in Cuba, too, for its wide open down there and wrestling is drawing tremendously. Buddy flies over for shows every week and then flies back to Florida." *Lancaster New Era*, Nov. 26, 1956, p. 37.

63 *New York Post*, Jan. 10, 1956, p. 52.

64 *Canton Repository*, Sept. 30, 1956, p. 80.

65 *Canton Repository*, Sept. 29, 1956, p. 12.

66 The show was featured on national television and was headlined by Jimmy Beecham and Hector Constance. Half of the gross was going to the Babe Zaharias Cancer Foundation. *Miami Herald*, Oct. 3, 1956, p. 49.

67 *Columbus Star*, July 19, 1952, p. 2,7.

68 *Boston American*, Oct. 16, 1956, p. 28, *Boston Daily Record*, Oct. 23, 1956, p. 15.

69 Attendance was 3,500. *Boston Daily Record*, Oct. 30, 1956, p. 16.

70 *St. Louis Globe-Democrat*, Sept. 15, 1956, p. 10.

71 *St. Louis Globe-Democrat*, Oct. 6, 1956, p. 13.

72 *Buffalo Courier-Express*, Dec. 1, 1956, p. 20.

[73] *Camden Courier-Post*, Dec. 12, 1956, p. 32.
[74] An unverified report claimed that Rogers appeared in Houston on December 14. However, his next bout may have been December 20 in Toronto.
[75] The Government's case was officially closed on Oct. 15, 1956.
[76] *Tampa Times*, Feb. 5, 1957, p. 9.
[77] The match occurred on Feb. 7, 1957. *Fort Lauderdale News*, Feb. 8, 1957, p. 22.
[78] Thesz was victorious. *Fort Lauderdale News*, Feb. 15, 1957, p. 22.
[79] *Fort Lauderdale News*, March 7, 1957, p. 29.
[80] Show occurred on Feb. 13, 1957. *Montreal Gazette*, Feb. 14, 1957, p. 35.
[81] Muchnick shared booking profits, at different times, with the Nick Gulas-Roy Welch group in Tennessee and with Jim Barnett, and others, in Indiana.
[82] There were three if you counted Billy Darnell.
[83] Rogers convinced Townsend to become a wrestler. *Boxing Illustrated, Wrestling News*, June 1959, p. 52-53.
[84] *Indianapolis Star*, March 31, 1957, p. 59.
[85] Rogers won the second fall with a sleeperhold. *Indianapolis Star*, April 5, 1957, p. 29.
[86] *Indianapolis Star*, May 3, 1957, p. 31.
[87] *Evansville Courier and Press*, March 28, 1957, p. 22.
[88] *Evansville Press*, April 4, 1957, p. 54.
[89] *Evansville Press*, April 25, 1957, p. 48.
[90] *Evansville Press*, March 21, 1957, p. 48.
[91] *Indianapolis Star*, Feb. 22, 1957, p. 28.

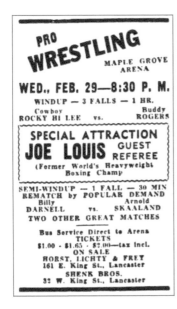

(above) Dayton, Ohio: Tuesday, Feb. 28, 1956
(left) Lancaster, Pennsylvania: Wednesday, Feb. 29, 1956

150 • Master of the Ring

PHOTO GALLERY

Buddy's social security application

Documents from the
Tim Hornbaker collection

Buddy & Ellen Hanson marriage certificate

Photo Gallery • 151

Navy identification record

Buddy's Navy application

Documents from the
Tim Hornbaker collection

Houston, Texas: Friday, May 10, 1946   Courtesy of Dr. Bob Bryla

Early publicity photo   From the Scott Teal collection

Photo Gallery • 153

Buddy with slave girls

Photos on this page from the Chuck Thornton collection

Page from a 1948 arena program sold at Hollywood Legion Stadium

History of Nature Boy's Fabulous Robe

The robe which adorns Buddy Rogers is one of his prize possessions. Much is known about "The Robe," much is still untold regarding its history and worth. Its actual value probably is a question which cannot be answered. Of course, it would be possible to evaluate the worth of each of the precious stones which go to make up the glamour and glitter of the garment, but its background and history would probably increase its value to such a figure that it could not now be purchased from Buddy. The garment itself is made up of rubies, emeralds, and rhinestones. It was fashioned originally for Catherine The Great of Russia, and was her favorite opera attire for many years. Since it has become a wrestler's ring attire it has been press-agented as being worth $1,000,000.00. While this figure is too much for us to comprehend, we do know that The Robe now carries its own insurance policy in the amount of $5,000.00, which, while being a far cry from $1,000,000.00, is still in the large potato class. It will be noticed that whenever The Robe is worn into the ring it is promptly carried back to the dressing room. One of the clauses of the policy, couched in very legal sounding language, means in just plain English: "No, no . . . mustn't touch."

At first The Robe was a problem to The Atomic Blond. Souvenir hunters became the principal worry of the master. As he came down the aisle clothed in The Robe, hands would reach from all sides in an attempt to snatch "just one stone," Rogers said. "While I would like to see all of the fans have such a token, I wouldn't have a robe for very long if all who reached get what they are after." He is now attempting to have color photos made of the creation to give to interested fans, and will soon be offering them in lieu of a piece of The Robe itself.

Many owners of famous diamonds have paste copies made for the sake of protection from theft or loss. These copies are so authentic that only an expert can detect them from the original. Buddy has followed this example to a degree. While it would be impossible to duplicate, the Robe, using the same sort of precious stones with which it is made, it was possible for a famous New York costume jeweler and a famous stylist to combine their efforts and make for The Atomic Blond a second robe, which to the eye has just as much appeal as the Russian original. For the sake of variety the first New York creation employed a different color scheme than the Russian model, and all viewers (excepting gem experts) proclaimed it to be just as beautiful as its more valuable forerunner. In fact, the first substitute was

Nature Boy—Buddy Rogers

such a success that Buddy had still a second one made, employing still a different color scheme. In view of all of this, when you see him enter the ring wrapped in a beautiful opera cape, you may suppose it to be the "famous," most valuable of the three, providing that you have no means of knowing whether you are looking at the famous Russian model or one of the two handsome New York substitutes.

If you are interested in robes, here is a tip: Rogers usually wears the very valuable creation into the ring for the first fall of his match. A second tip: The Russian creation is predominently red in its coloring.

In addition to this fabulous robe which Buddy uses, he has eight robes which make Hollywood producers envy him.

Colors and shades of colors with sequence and stones that shine in dazzling brilliance when exposed to the ring lights are dramatic and beautiful beyond description when he makes his dramatic entrance into the ring to the "ahs" of the crowd.

Page from a 1948 arena program sold at Hollywood Legion Stadium

156 • Master of the Ring

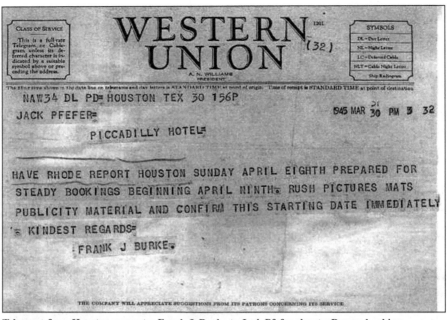

Telegram from Houston promoter Frank J. Burke to Jack Pfefer about a Rogers booking.

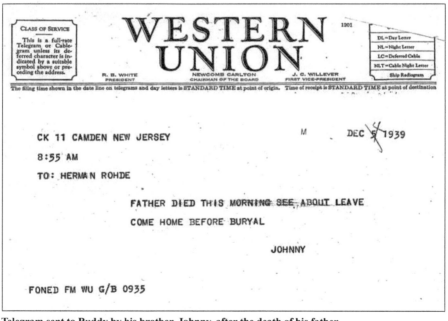

Telegram sent to Buddy by his brother, Johnny, after the death of his father.

Documents from the Tim Hornbaker collection

Photo Gallery • 157

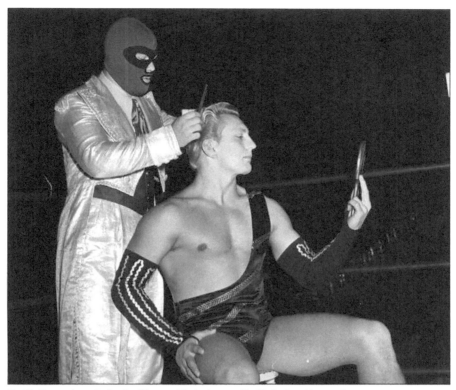

Buddy Rogers' masked valet (Tommy Phelps) preps Buddy before his match.

August 1961

Photos from the Scott Teal collection

(top left)
Rogers photo taken by famous photographer Tony Lanza
from the Scott Teal collection

(top right)
Rogers in Columbus, Ohio
from the Scott Teal collection

(left)
Rogers admiring the Michael Berardino trophy that he won on the Sept. 13, 1952, tournament in Pittsburgh.
from the Scott Teal collection

Photo Gallery • 159

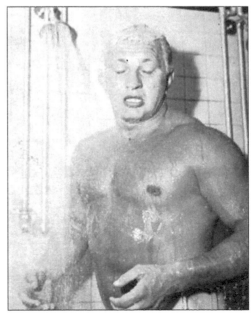

(top left)
Rogers with Ken Linn, who handled TV commentary for studio wrestling at WFBM in Indianapolis and WCPO in Cincinnati.

(above)
Panoramic photo of the crowd at Comiskey Park for the June 30, 1960, card at which Rogers won the NWA world heavyweight title from Pat O'Connor.

(top right) Rogers during his June 30, 1960, match against Pat O'Connor.

(right)
Rogers caught in the shower on Sept. 1, 1961, after defeating Pat O'Connor in their first Chicago return match.

All photos on this page are
from the Scott Teal collection.

(right) Bobby Davis publicity photo
from the Scott Teal collection

Buddy, Ray Morgan, Bobby Davis & Bob Orton Sr.
from the Scott Teal collection

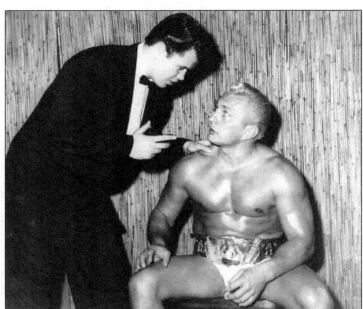

Buddy listens intently as Bobby gives him advice before his match.

(top left) Bobby enjoys a cigar in the dressing room after a match.

(top right) At ringside, Bobby shouts instructions to his champion.

(above) Bobby congratulates Buddy Rogers for winning a return match against Pat O'Connor on September 1, 1961, in Chicago's Comiskey Park.

(right) Bill Cardille interviews Bobby at ringside at the Pittsburgh WIIC-TV tapings.

Buddy Rogers promotional pamphlet produced and distributed by Sam Muchnick. 8-1/2 x 11, fold-out

from the Scott Teal collection

Photo Gallery • 163

NWA secretary Sam Muchnick presents the NWA belt to Rogers.

From the Sam Muchnick collection

CEntral 7486

Sam Muchnick...

Sports Attractions

Suite 230-32   HOTEL   CLARIDGE
CEntral 7900

1800 Locust Sts.   St. Louis 3, Mo.
                                        April 29, 1951

Dear Jack:-

I received the following wire from Buddy
Rogers this morning.

Sam Muchnick, Claridge Hotel, St. Louis, Mo.

To Sam Muchnick, Pres. Alliance members and non-members.
and Jack Pfefer.

I am now a free agent I am no longer managed by Pfefer.
My break with Pfefer was due to numerous dissatisfactory
bookings and constant aggravations. This was not instigaged
by any Alliance member nor the champion this is strictly
my personal doings and ideas I remain your friend

Buddy Rogers

Jack:--Thought you would want to know above. Regards.

Sam

Flyer distributed by Jack Pfefer after Rogers left him in 1951.

(left) Brattleboro, Vermont: Friday, Oct. 14, 1955
Classic Jack Pfefer — Bummy Rogers vs. Lou Kesz

And then there's the real deal ...
(top to bottom) Louisville, Sept. 23, 1947; St. Louis, Dec. 30, 1955
Indianapolis Feb. 20, 1954

> November 15, 1962
>
> Miss Joyce E. Freeland, C. P. A.,
> Leopold & Linowes,
> Certified Public Accountants,
> Woodward Building,
> Washington, D. C.   Re: <u>Capital Wrestling Corporation</u>
>
> Dear Miss Freeland:
>
>   Received your letter of November 13, 1962, and contents noted.
>
>   The Capitol Wrestling Corporation has on deposit with the National Wrestling Alliance a Performance Bond for Champion Buddy Rogers, of $10,000.00. The accumulated interest to date is $442.27, or a total of $10,442.27.
>
>   As the Bond was deposited on July 5, 1961, we have informed Mr. Vince McMahon, from time to time, the amount of interest as it accrued.
>
>   If there is any further information you would like, please do not hesitate to call upon me.
>
>   Sincerely,
>
>   Sam Muchnick, Executive Secretary, Treasurer,
>   National Wrestling Alliance.

> Dec. 17, 1962
>
> Mr. Vince McMahon,
> Franklin Park Hotel,
> Washington, D. C.
>
> Dear Vince:-
>
>   Again I am lettering my heart rule my head. But I believe that friends should help each other out. Toots told me that you fellows are about to make a loan and that this check would save you from making it, so I told him that if this was the case I would like to send back part of the performance bond. I told him that you would lose some interest and he told me that you had to pay interest if you would make the loan so it didn't make any difference. I can see where losing a man like Rogers at critical times especially as he was a "key" man in your operations, would hurt. Let's hope it doesn't happen again when he returns.
>
>   Now in regards to Buddy's dates. If he makes the Montreal date with Kowalski on Jan. 16, the date in Toronto could be Jan. 31st. (I would first have to check with Tunney). However, if it is after that I want him definitely for Houston on Feb. 1 or the entire week of Jan. 28th. There are others who are asking me for the champion's services but I am holding them off.
>
>   There are still people who don't believe he broke his ankle. They claim it could have been an old x-ray. What non-believers!
>
>   ---
>
>   I was typing this letter and sent my secretary over to get the check. They just called me and told me that by taking it out now instead of Dec. 28 you would lose approximately $50.00. Therefore I told them to let it go and I would be in touch with you. IF YOU STILL HAVE TO HAVE IT BEFORE THEN, LET ME KNOW.
>
>   Let's get together on Rogers dates as quickly as possible etc.
>
>   Sincerely,

December 28, 1962

Mr. Vince McMahon
Franklin Park Hotel
Washington, D. C.

Dear Vince:

Enclosing, herewith, check for $5,559.75. I have written you previously regarding the $442.27 accumulated interest. The latest interest accumulated was $117.48, which would have been lost had I drawn the money out last week. This leaves a balance for the Performance Bond of $5,000.00.

Now, I know I am using very poor business judgment in releasing this money, because I am responsible to the National Wrestling Alliance for it. However, sometimes you use bad business judgment to do friends a favor and Toots told me by getting this money it will prevent you fellows from making a loan. That's what friends are for - to help each other out, and despite a lot of things that have happened I still consider you fellows my friends.

Please acknowledge receipt of this check.

Best Wishes for the Holiday Season, I am,

Sincerely,

Sam Muchnick, Executive Secretary,
Treasurer,
National Wrestling Alliance.

Jan. 28, 1963

Mr. Vince McMahon,
Franklin Park Hotel,
Washington, D. C.

Dear Vince:=

Enclosed is a check for $5,000.00 the balance of the Buddy Rogers performance bond.

Have not received one cent as yet on the NWA booking money on Rogers from the time he returned to action.

I have kept my end of the bargain. You have not kept yours to date. So let's close our business relationship so far as the booking of Rogers is concerned with a nice note by having your office send in the booking money as agreed upon.

I may not have a lot of money but at least people in our business and in other businesses can always say:--"Sam Muchnick is a man of his word."

At any rate when you send the checks in this deal does not necessarily mean that it is the end of our business relationship. We can continue to do business, if you desire, for many years to come--

At any rate..I told you I would send you your final check money. It's enclosed, as I promised.

Best wishes.

Sincerely,

Sam Muchnick

Check #15523,
postal Pleaza
enclosed...

May 24, 1963

Mr. Vince McMahon
Franklin Park Hotel
Washington, D. C.

Dear Vince:

Thanks for sending me the memorandum on the Contos case. I had our attorney look it over and he was very much impressed with the Judge's decision, and said the Judge was well up on Anti-Trust laws. As soon as I am finished studying it I will return to you.

It was nice talking to you on the 'phone while I was in Tulsa. I agree with you on everything but the title situation. I believe our business would be better off if we only recognized one World Champion, as we did five or six years ago. In other words, I believe if we only got to use the Champion once or twice a year, the prestige of our business would be better off than it is today. However, I may be wrong, as I have been wrong on many other occasions.

Hope Buddy recovers from his set-back and is well again real soon.

I am still hoping to be able to visit Washington the early part of June.

With kindest personal regards, I am,

Sincerely,

Sam Muchnick

SM:mn

The letters on this and the previous two pages are from the Sam Muchnick collection

Family photos of Buddy and wife Terry with their daughter Lee.
Photos courtesy of Brian Last /
The Arcadian Vanguard Wrestling News Archive

CERTIFICATE OF INCORPORATION

OF

BUDDY ROGERS ENTERPRISES

THIS IS TO CERTIFY THAT WE, BUDDY ROGERS, JOHN C. ROHDE AND FRIEDA ROHDE, DO HEREBY ASSOCIATE OURSELVES INTO A CORPORATION, UNDER AND BY VIRTUE OF THE REVISED STATUTES OF THE STATE OF NEW JERSEY 1937, TITLE 14:1-1 ET SEQ., AND THE AMENDMENTS AND SUPPLEMENTS THERETO, AND DO SEVERALLY AGREE TO TAKE THE NUMBER OF SHARES OF CAPITAL STOCK SET FORTH HEREIN, OPPOSITE OUR RESPECTIVE NAMES.

FIRST: THE NAME OF THE CORPORATION IS BUDDY ROGERS ENTERPRISES.

SECOND: THE LOCATION OF THE PRINCIPAL OFFICE IN THIS STATE IS 716 MARKET STREET, CAMDEN, NEW JERSEY.

THE NAME OF THE AGENT THEREIN AND IN CHARGE THEREOF, AND UPON WHOM PROCESS AGAINST THE CORPORATION MAY BE SERVED, IS ALBERT J. SCARDUZIO.

THIRD: THE OBJECTS FOR WHICH THIS CORPORATION IS FORMED ARE: TO BUY, SELL, EXCHANGE, LEASE, MORTGAGE AND OTHERWISE ACQUIRE, DEAL IN AND DISPOSE OF REAL ESTATE OF EVERY KIND, OR ANY INTEREST THEREIN, WHEREVER SITUATE AND TO HOLD, OWN, CONTROL, DEVELOP, IMPROVE, LEASE, MANAGE, AND OPERATE SAME FOR ANY PURPOSE WHATSOEVER.

TO PURCHASE OR OTHERWISE ACQUIRE, LEASE, ASSIGN, MORTGAGE, SELL AND DEAL IN PERSONAL PROPERTY OF ALL TYPES, SORTS AND DESCRIPTIONS INCLUDING TRADE NAMES, TRADE MARKS, INVENTIONS, PATENTS AND COPYRIGHTS.

TO ACQUIRE IN ANY LAWFUL MANNER, MAINTAIN,

(top left, clockwise)
Oct. 14, 1969, Oct. 21, 1966, Nov. 1, 1967,
Sept. 30, 1968, Oct. 14, 1969

```
SUPREME COURT OF THE STATE OF NEW YORK
COUNTY OF NEW YORK
------------------------------------ X
BUDDY NATURE BOY ROGERS and              Index No.
RUTH AGNES ROGERS,

                    Plaintiffs,

          -against-

MADISON SQUARE GARDEN CORPORATION,
MADISON SQUARE GARDEN BOXING INC.,
TITAN SPORTS INC., also known as
and/or doing business as "WORLD          VERIFIED COMPLAINT
WRESTLING FEDERATION", and CAPITOL
WRESTLING CORPORATION, also known as
and/or doing business as WORLD
WRESTLING FEDERATION,

                    Defendants.
------------------------------------ X
```

    Plaintiffs, by and through their attorneys, Slater, Vanderpool & Breakstone, complaining of defendants, allege as follows:

AS AND FOR A FIRST CAUSE OF ACTION ON BEHALF OF THE PLAINTIFF BUDDY NATURE BOY ROGERS

    FIRST: That at all times herein relevant, the plaintiff BUDDY NATURE BOY ROGERS was and still is a resident of the State of New Jersey.

    SECOND: That at all times herein relevant, upon information and belief, the defendant MADISON SQUARE GARDEN CORPORATION (hereinafter referred to as MSG) was and still is

1

From the Tim Hornbaker collection

```
 1  BULL LAWRENCE
    10748 Washington Blvd.
 2  Culver City, California
 3  VErmont 9 1221
 4  Attorney for Plaintiff.
 5
 6
 7
 8          IN THE SUPERIOR COURT OF THE STATE OF CALIFORNIA
 9              IN AND FOR THE COUNTY OF LOS ANGELES
10
11  CHARLES ROGERS, a.k.a.    )
12  "BUDDY ROGERS",           )   NO.  644124
                              )
13              Plaintiff,    )
                              )   C O M P L A I N T
14       vs.                  )        for
15  BUDDY ROGERS,             )   INJUNCTION, UNFAIR COMPETITION,
16  DOE I, DOE II, DOE III,   )   INFRINGEMENT OF TRADE NAME,
17  DOE IV, AND DOE V,        )   INVASION OF RIGHT OF PRIVACY.
                              )
18              Defendants.   )
19  ─────────────────────────
20       The plaintiff complains and alleges:
21                          I.
22       That the true names and identities of the defendants,
23  DOE I, DOE II, DOE III, DOE IV, AND DOE V, are presently unknown to
24  the plaintiff. That the plaintiff will request leave of Court to
25  amend his complaint accordingly when same becomes known to him.
26                         II.
27       That the plaintiff for a period in excess of twenty years
28  has been engaged in the entertainment industry as a producer, actor
29  and musician in motion pictures, television, radio, the legitimate
30  theater and other facets of the entertainment industry. That through-
31  out said period, the plaintiff has been known throughout the world
32  generally, professionally and socially, as "Buddy Rogers".
```

FILED
MAY 13 1955
HAROLD J. OSTLY, County Clerk
by L. M. Shoreson
L. M. SHORESON   DEPUTY

From the Tim Hornbaker collection

Nature Girl & Nature Boy, Debbie & Buddy Rogers   From the Dan Westbrook collection

Photo Gallery • 175

(above left) First publicity photo taken of Rogers wearing the NWA world heavyweight title belt.
(above right) Dick Steinborn took this shot of Buddy at his house just one month before he passed away.
from the Scott Teal collection
(below) Buddy Rogers, courtesy of Dr. Bob Bryla

Chapter 12
The Politics of Wrestling

For some active wrestlers in the post-war era, working within the industry was just a means to an end. The profession offered a steady paycheck and, in many cases, provided a better-than-average way of life. Traveling was a burden, especially if it meant venturing from territory to territory every three or four months. Wrestlers with families were constantly forced to uproot and the routines rarely got easier. Certain grapplers found a reliable base territory and worked out of the local office with limited outside exposure. It wasn't a lucrative spot, but it guaranteed the athlete much more time at home. But being on the road meant more money, and for guys in the upper-echelon of the vocation like Buddy Rogers, traveling was a necessity. Rogers knew that better than anyone else. He was always out on the circuit, in-between towns, and putting in the work. After 15 years in the professional ranks, he was a battle-tested veteran, and he had the scars to prove it.

The mat business wasn't just a job to Rogers. "Wrestling to me is an art," he told a reporter early in his career.[1] He praised catch-as-catch-can grappling for being "so abundantly rich in many fine holds," and decried roughness as being the "last refuge for those who lack the fundamentals."[2] His comments predated his transition to the "Nature Boy" and the change in style that came with it. As a fan-favorite in the 1940s, he generally abided by the rules unless goaded, and was all about sportsmanship and honesty. His knowledge of holds and maneuvers grew by the year, and Rogers was never afraid to test out new techniques. Members of the press acknowledged him as a high-flyer for his dropkicks, flying tackles, and his effective flying head scissors. The conniving "Nature Boy" went about things a little differently, and if there was a rule to break, he was gung-ho about it. That was the essence of his character, and Rogers was not one to give less than 100 per cent.

Rogers talked about the art of wrestling in its athletic form, and he subscribed to that basic principle during his time as a novice. But by 1957, the art of wrestling meant something different to Buddy Rogers. Instead of spending years training in gym sessions to expand his catch-as-catch-can repertoire, he focused that same amount of time and energy developing his wrestling intellect. He was now a master of psychology and crowd manipulation, and few wrestlers in history were comparable. He also knew how to book matches and feuds to maximize returns, both on a short and long-term scale. Finishes were crafted on a match-by-match basis, and a number of factors were taken into consideration, including if he was a favorite or heel, for how long a specific feud was going to run, and if a larger-scale contest was being groomed for down the road. A simple match was not so simple as Buddy carefully read the mood of the audience, and precisely coordinated efforts with his opponent to play to their whims.

In contrast to most of his contemporaries, Rogers actually thought like a promoter in the way he prepped towns. With stunning forethought, he utilized his in-ring abilities to spur on greater attendance and build anticipation for future matches. It was a natural part of his work in any new territory, and local leaders who understood the way he operated usually allowed him the liberty to push forward without much supervision, as long as he followed the longer-term scheme of the promotion. For instance, his 1956 run in Texas was a perfect example of what Rogers was able to accomplish in a territory, the freedom he achieved, and the limits of his power. He immediately won the state title, wrestled in a compelling manner, and gave back to the leading fan-favorites to keep them strong over a period of two months. And in doing so, he showed his aptitude to maintain his own credibility. Politically, Rogers tried to maneuver behind-the-scenes, but the local booker kept to the original plan, and Buddy acquiesced.

The benefit of having a well-informed wrestler with vast showmanship and skill, who also had a talent to help arrange the booking schedule to increase profits, was a terrific bonus for promoters. However, it was problematic at times, too, especially when Rogers dabbled in politics and tried to assume more control. The booker in Houston wasn't having any of it. In Akron, Ohio, in 1956, promoter Walter Moore severed his ties to Rogers and his crew because he thought Buddy was trying "to run my shows."[3] Al Haft was the opposite. He conceded a lot of power to Rogers to bring wrestlers into the territory and dictate the arrangement of matches. If Buddy didn't like what Haft had scheduled, he had the authority change the plans and do what he wanted.[4] But that kind influence didn't carry over to very many places. It was firmly established that NWA members were the ruling class and wrestlers were their subordinates. With that being said, Rogers fell into line with everyone else.

There was a deeper level to Buddy's wrestling intellect, and it centered on the way he framed matches and controlled the action. Rogers was what was commonly known as a ring general, which meant he was ordinarily responsible for calling the shots and setting the tempo for a match. His opponents relied on him to guide them through the motions, and, in turn, obtain the best of their abilities. And Buddy was exceptionally good at it. In bouts against some of his more regular rivals, Rogers developed and perfected a technique called "sequencing,"[5] a method of establishing a precise artistic arrangement to a full-length contest. The sequences were tailored to keep fans on the edge of their seats, and Rogers was an expert at creating a furious pace that held the attention of spectators. Moves were strung together in chain fashion, but then built into a larger narrative, all the while carrying the emotions of fans toward a breathtaking conclusion.

It was Wrestling Storytelling 101 and was years beyond the normal workrate of his peers. Rogers turned this type of performance into his standard fare, and it was an engrossing spectacle. The entire process was a science within itself, one that Buddy practiced and labored to improve. He required a versatile and trusted opponent to really bring the sequencing to life, and of course, Billy Darnell was his ideal foe in that regard.[6] They were the Ric

Flair-Ricky Steamboat of the 1950s; a perfect combination of chemistry and compatibility. Having trained and wrestled together so often, their matches were creative, briskly paced, and set a standard for the era. Rogers was known for his improvisation. He could adjust to the size and skill-level of his opponent, with the instinctive ability to do whatever was necessary to make his rival appear better than he actually was. He did it by playing up their strengths and selling heavily for each move his foe performed. And, typically, only the finish was known when he entered the ring. Buddy filled in the rest with his imaginative mind.

Against opponents of greater athletic ability, such as Lou Thesz or Ruffy Silverstein, Rogers still managed to tell the story *he* wanted to tell, mostly because he carried the gift for showmanship. His 1950 Wrigley Field bout with Thesz ended with his dramatic hanging gimmick, a finish he'd perfected – and one the crowd ate up. Deferring to Rogers in those situations was a good decision since the high-tension finish was his specialty. As a heel, he garnered an immense reaction to his cunning behavior, and his aggressive attack was demonstrated in many unique ways. For example, from a standing chin-lock position, he slyly slipped into a chokehold, and calmly strangled his adversary. The referee ultimately caught on and the hold was broken. The third man in the ring was a fundamental component of the ongoing action, and Rogers utilized the official to inspire further volatility from the audience. On occasion, he would apply a headlock, and purposely turn his body so the referee was behind him and his foe. Buddy would then sock his rival squarely in the face several times with a closed fist. From the crowd's perspective, he was getting away with illegal punches, and fans roared in disapproval.

Upon being tangled in the corner, Rogers and his foe were slowly peeled apart by the official, only to see Rogers bring a sharp knee up into to the stomach of his unsuspecting rival. Rogers followed up with a series of uppercuts and straight jabs, gouges to the eyes, and a sudden strut across the ring to display his arrogance. He was an agitator of the highest degree. At other times, Buddy would complete a chain sequence and step out into the middle of the ring with both arms raised, as if he had solidified his standing as the best wrestler in the world. People hated his haughtiness with a passion, and the more they protested, the more he instigated them. Matches involving Rogers were usually fast-paced, driven by a sense of urgency and a visible desire to achieve victory. A Baltimore reporter dubbed him "Mr. Perpetual Motion" for his sustained movement during the course of a bout, and he lived up to that moniker.[7] Watching him skillfully bounce off the ropes in the midst of a heated exchange was a true sight to behold.

Rogers, as a popular hero, was surprisingly accessible to arena patrons. He would smile, charm spectators en route to the ring, and pose for photos with youngsters. Between falls, he would frequently sign autographs for eager supporters, giving them a thrill of a lifetime. Over the previous decade, his popularity had skyrocketed in certain geographical areas, but it was also safe to say he had a national following, as well. In 1949, he was receiving 300 pieces of mail a week from enthusiasts.[8] The next year, it was 500 letters, and he did his best to respond to each missive with a personal note of his own.[9] Fan clubs in his honor sprung up like wildfire, with the main organizations based in Toledo, Columbus, and Verdun, Quebec.[10] The Columbus club was formed in 1955 and run by President Ruby Burns. Rogers was supportive of Burns and offered his personal thanks to her and the members of "Rogers Internationale" in April 1956 on the first anniversary of the club's creation.

"I'd like to express a personal word of appreciation to all who have contributed in any way to the success we have so far achieved," Rogers wrote. "I am deeply grateful for the interest, the time, and the effort expended on my behalf. I have enjoyed our friendship and association in the past year and hope we may look forward to many more happy years."[11] Buddy exhibited his gratitude by spending time with Burns and other members at a fan club convention at the Southern Hotel in Columbus in August 1955.[12] Burns, in response to Buddy's efforts, stated: "We want to thank Buddy for everything. The interest and time he has given means so much to his many friends. This past year has been a great pleasure and one that will forever be cherished in our volume of memories. And to Buddy, we will say again, it has been a marvelous year working for the Club, and to see it expand into the biggest and best ever. And to you and yours, [we wish] the best of everything in life for your happiness."[13]

Buddy's Columbus supporters were undoubtedly thrilled when he returned to the city after nearly five months on July 11, 1957.[14] That night, he battled the 6-foot-6, 265-pound Bearcat Wright to a no-contest.[15] A former Golden Gloves and professional boxer, Wright was demonstrably tough, and was a dynamic opponent for Rogers. Between July and September, they met at least a dozen times in the Ohio territory and laid the foundation for a rivalry that would last for years.[16] In Mansfield, Ohio, Buddy faced off against the masked Mighty Zorro, a muscular athlete from the Netherlands. Zorro was a known figure without the hood, having gained a measure of fame using the name "Dutch Howlett." In fact, Howlett adopted the moniker "Nature Boy" in 1949 and used it off and on for about two years. In a sense, he was Al Haft's version of the "Nature Boy," at a time in which Rogers was working for Jack Pfefer.

On October 9, Rogers and his counterpart clashed in Mansfield and put on a real show. Fiercely assaulting each other with reckless abandon, Rogers and Zorro quickly roused the patrons at the Ashland Road Armory. They split the initial two falls with Rogers the worse for wear, suffering a bloody cut to his face. He was incensed by the wound and motivated to repay the favor, chasing his masked enemy through the crowd. The wrestlers pushed their way out the front door of the venue and continued to fight in the street, completely halting traffic. Fans filed out after them, unwilling to miss a moment of the action, and the scene became even more chaotic. But officials had seen enough and put an end to the brawl.[17] Their rematch the following week was an essential event for grappling aficionados, and as expected, Rogers and Zorro engaged in another barbaric tussle. Rogers was busted open above his eye and defeated by his opponent, but two members of the Mansfield Boxing and Wrestling Commission reversed that decision. And for his illicit deeds, Zorro was suspended for 30 days.[18]

Once again billed as the Eastern heavyweight champion, Rogers encountered the 6-foot-3 Fritz Von Goering on September 30 in Springfield,

Ohio, and it is believed he lost his claim to the title on that program.[19] Von Goering, a 27-year-old from Northern California, had previously used the name, "Fritz Von Ulm" during tours of the Upper Midwest and Texas. A prototypical German villain in the vein of Karl Von Albers and Hans Schmidt, he not only beat Rogers in Springfield, but in several subsequent rematches.[20] Being in his home territory gave Buddy the opportunity to spend time with family and friends, but by November 1957, he was headed back on the road.[21] On November 5, he appeared in Minneapolis for the first time in almost nine years and teamed with Al Kashey to beat Hard Boiled Haggerty and Kinji Shibuya by disqualification.[22] Rogers was a fan-favorite, and in a Minneapolis press report, he talked up "straight wrestling" as opposed to using a "gimmick."[23]

Lou Thesz, who epitomized conventional mat practices, still reigned as the NWA world heavyweight champion. He had just returned from an extended tour overseas in Australia and Japan and ventured to Minneapolis for an important bout against Rogers. The result of his contest against the "Nature Boy" wasn't in any doubt because it was guaranteed that he would retain his belt. Thesz had already agreed to lose his championship to Dick Hutton two nights later in Toronto. His match against Rogers was basically a warm-up to break the jet lag.[24] For 60 minutes, "the champion and the challenger wrestled with speed of middleweights and [as result], the contest was packed with action," according to the *Minneapolis Star Tribune*. Thesz won the opening fall, but Rogers evened things up with a pinfall in the second, exciting the crowd. Buddy was heavy on the offense during the final minutes and the bout was declared a draw.[25] Two days later, as anticipated, Thesz passed the mantle to Hutton.

The decree authorizing the transfer of the world championship from Thesz to Hutton was not made in a smoke-filled boardroom, which was normally the standard operating procedure for the National Wrestling Alliance. This time around, Thesz himself made an executive decision, superseding the original plans established by NWA leadership. In Thesz's autobiography, *Hooker*, he revealed that the choice of the Alliance's championship committee to succeed him as champion was none other than Buddy Rogers.[26] Buddy's elevation to such a position was an affirmation of his hard work, backstage maneuvering, and box-office success. He had protected his image and value, implemented his own booking strategies at times, and improved the overall conditions of professional wrestling. But to that point, he had been on the periphery of the NWA's big decision-making, and had been overlooked for one reason or another.

Politics were at the center of things and continued to be strikingly destructive. The business was divided into cliques and syndicates, and many big-money match-ups people wanted to see were off-limits. It also hindered the inclusion of certain wrestlers for NWA title consideration. After Rogers broke with Jack Pfefer in 1951, he was repelled by a certain segment of the Alliance. He didn't receive a single shot at the NWA championship between April 1951 and February 1954. In March 1953, NWA President Sam Muchnick polled the membership to determine which wrestler they would back as titleholder "in the event of an accident, or serious injury to the champion." Eight wrestlers received at least one first-place ballot. They included Verne Gagne, Killer

Kowalski, Bill Longson, Yvon Robert, Ruffy Silverstein, Antonino Rocca, Don Beitelman, and Ray Gunkel.[27] Rogers didn't receive a single vote and was not a part of those deliberations.

By January 1955, though, Muchnick was publicly ranking Rogers alongside the top heavyweights. "Thesz is a great champion, probably the greatest since [Frank] Gotch," Muchnick proclaimed. "Right behind him I'd rate, although not necessarily in the order named, [Leo] Nomellini, Wilbur Snyder, Verne Gagne, Buddy Rogers, Wladek Kowalski, Mike Sharpe, Dick Hutton, and Pat O'Connor, a New Zealander. Any one of them might be able to take Thesz once Lou begins to slip."[28] With that, Rogers had finally been acknowledged as a prospective candidate. While his bad boy image and the "Nature Boy" gimmick were typically disqualifying factors, Buddy had worked enough as a fan-favorite and tweener to gain support inside the NWA hierarchy.[29] Muchnick, in particular, wanted the world champion to be relatively upstanding in terms of sportsmanship, but able to ride the line depending on his opponent. Even if the NWA board of directors thoroughly endorsed Rogers, there was still one major hurdle left to go.

That lone obstacle was Lou Thesz. The legendary St. Louis grappler possessed an iron-trap memory and the ability to hold a longstanding grudge. Eleven years earlier, Rogers made an off-the-cuff, albeit completely insensitive comment about Ed "Strangler" Lewis, and Thesz never forgot. Thesz, who honored Lewis for being a fatherly-type figure to him, took the remark personally, and wanted to sustain his punishment to Rogers. Part of that ongoing retribution was a burning desire to veto any proposal put forward by the NWA authorizing the shift of the championship to Rogers. The fact that Buddy was deemed a "performer" rather than a legitimate wrestler added to Thesz' reasoning.[30] He didn't want his successor to be a showman. "If you want the belt back," Thesz told Muchnick, "get me a wrestler."[31] The NWA bigwigs were backed into a corner and had no choice but to adhere to Thesz' directive. Members agreed to push Dick Hutton to the championship and Thesz, who admired Hutton's raw abilities, gave his blessing.

As a rule, fans didn't follow professional wrestling for the shooters and genuine mat stars with amateur credentials. It was a plus to have former collegiate athletes on the bill, but most upper-echelon draws combined authentic physicality, charisma, and a heighted level of performance. Hutton was a monster of a wrestler, standing 6-foot-1 and weighing more than 270-pounds. He was agile as a cat, brilliantly skilled, and the only living grappler comparable might be Brock Lesnar. But, in terms of his ring personality, Hutton was lacking, and only time would tell if the NWA's call to boost him to the championship would work out at the box office. To cement the transition, Hutton officially dethroned Thesz on Nov. 14, 1957, at Maple Leaf Gardens in Toronto.[32] Buddy Rogers didn't have a say in the matter, and it's not known if he was even told about the conversations that were held. He continued to plod away like normal, but his tour of the Minneapolis territory ended on a sour note when he suffered a back injury.[33]

During his brief time in the aforementioned region, Rogers received a strange bit of press in Winnipeg. Local promoter Alex Turk touted Buddy's arrival and explained that he got the blond wrestler to agree to make Winnipeg his new wrestling headquarters. "I had to give him more [money] than I expected,"

Turk said, "but he's a terrific wrestler and a great performer and I don't think I or Winnipeg wrestling fans will be sorry."[34] A separate report indicated that Rogers was "now making his home in Winnipeg," but the whole tale seemed to be nothing more than a publicity stunt.[35] Convalescing, Buddy was on the shelf for 12 days, wrestled two matches in Ohio, and then went to Florida, where he spent the next two weeks. He was back to his old self, waging war against Swedish powerhouse Karl Karlsson in historic St. Aug.ine.[36] On December 4, Rogers and his 6-foot-5 opponent fought to a bloody no-contest at the Armory. The match was halted after the referee was knocked out by an errant flying tackle from Rogers.[37]

The wild Rogers-Karlsson brawl "spilled over into the seats," and afterwards, the big Swede told the *St. Aug.ine Record*: "I didn't mean to cut [Rogers]. I just got carried away."[38] Buddy won a decision over Karlsson in St. Aug.ine on December 11, but the purses of both men were held up by appalled officials following another brutal match.[39] The violence of their contest was overstated by a Tampa newspaper, which claimed Rogers lost two of his teeth and was hospitalized with a fractured jaw.[40] It's true that he missed a subsequent booking in Tampa on December 16, but it wasn't because he was hurt, despite the statement.[41] Buddy wrestled the next three nights in Eau Gallie, St. Aug.ine, and Fort Lauderdale, and finished his Florida commitments. In St. Aug.ine, he capped his feud with Karlsson by winning a special Texas death match with chicken wire fencing around the ring, and the largest crowd of the local wrestling season was on hand to witness the battle.[42]

A 28-year-old native of Atlanta, Georgia, named Buddy Austin was also in the Florida area in December 1957. He was actually the referee kayoed by the flying tackle during the first Rogers-Karlsson bout in St. Aug.ine. Austin was in his rookie year as a grappler, still with a lot to learn, and a friendship with Rogers soon formed. Within a few months, Austin relocated from Florida to Ohio and began a crash course mat education provided by Al Haft's experienced roster of grapplers.[43] As for Rogers, he was prepared to trek into an unfamiliar region, and he closed out 1957 and began his new year in West Texas. The territory was quite expansive, from Odessa in the south to Lubbock and Pampa, with Amarillo as the central hub. In nearby New Mexico and Colorado, he made appearances in Albuquerque and Colorado Springs, and made his first date in Denver since 1947.[44] Amarillo promoter Dr. Karl Sarpolis, who ran the West Texas circuit, planned to give Rogers a huge push.

Unlike his recent work in Ohio and Minnesota, Buddy entered the area an unambiguous heel, and the "Nature Boy" was in fine form. In the ring, he utilized all of his known tricks, and made new ones up on the fly. His figure-four put a number of foes out of commission, but he didn't rely on that hold exclusively.[45] He pulled out the "paralytic headlock" at times, and started using a "knuckle submission," a move that saw him jab his fist into his rival's temple until they quit. He choked, punched, and gouged the eyes of his opponents, ignoring all the warnings of the referee, and drove fans nuts. But perhaps the biggest alteration to his overall gimmick was the accompaniment of an aggressive manager named Bobby Wallace. The long-haired, tuxedo-wearing Wallace had managed Roy Shire and Edmund Francis in years prior, and since he was a former wrestler himself, he wasn't afraid to get physically involved in his charge's bouts.⁴⁶ And he often did, much to the disdain of spectators.

This was an important shift in the career of Buddy Rogers. Years earlier, his slave girls were not much more than eye candy, although they garnered plenty of attention. Sometimes, they purposefully distracted Buddy's rival or played a minimal role in a contest, but their job rarely went further than that. Wallace was in a different league. He was actively involved in matches, antagonizing wrestlers and officials, and used his cane to impact the results. For example, on Jan. 16, 1958 at the Sports Arena in Amarillo, Dory Funk Sr. was headed toward victory in the third fall over Rogers, and was going for his famed spinning toe-hold. Wallace interjected, reaching out under the bottom rope with his cane, and tripped Funk, effectively saving his man from defeat. Funk was enraged. He was so caught up in the argument with Wallace outside the ring that he ignored the referee, and was counted out.⁴⁷ The perception that Rogers now needed his manager or outside interference to win matches was a big departure for him.

But with that said, it was a fresh way to attract crowd heat and strengthen his heel image. The addition of Wallace was a new dynamic for Rogers to build upon, and the routine achieved short-term success in West Texas. Karl Sarpolis helped bolster Buddy's reputation by calling him "the greatest attraction in wrestling today" in the Amarillo press.⁴⁸ He also hyped him as possibly "the only wrestler who holds an edge over Amarillo-born Dick Hutton, new heavyweight champion of the world."⁴⁹ On January 23, Rogers prevailed over Dory Funk to win the North American heavyweight championship in most unconventional fashion. He lost the first fall, but Funk refused to let up on his spinning toe-hold, even after the bell rang. Wallace jumped into the ring and smashed Funk with his cane, forcing the latter to break. In the ensuing chaos, Rogers got Funk in a figure-four and maintained the pressure for "ten minutes." Funk was carried to the dressing room, clearly unable to continue, and lost the belt.⁵⁰

Funk, the region's principal hero and a silent partner in the ownership of the territory, was knocked out of commission with purported torn ligaments in his knee.⁵¹ Putting him out of action was a big deal, and served to amplify the public outcry against the "Nature Boy." A week later, Buddy won a 14-man tournament in Amarillo, going over Johnny Barend in the finals.⁵² His prize was twofold. He received $1,000 and a shot at NWA champion Dick Hutton, which took place on February 6. In that match, Rogers lost a single fall in the 60-minute time limit and was defeated.⁵³ During his tour of West Texas, Buddy engaged in several other hard-hitting feuds, one of them against the popular Rip Rogers. Rogers formerly wrestled under his real name, "Eddie Gossett," and appeared on shows with Buddy in Ohio and Florida.⁵⁴ Having adopted the bleached-blond look and Buddy's old trademark finisher, the atomic drop, Rip was cut from the same cloth as the "Nature Boy" and was comparably skilled on the mat.

Interestingly, the Rogers-Wallace managerial deal ended without explanation by the first week of March 1958.⁵⁵ Buddy kept a presence in West Texas, but shifted his booking schedule further and further west. Phoenix became an important locale for him beginning on March 24, and on that evening, he drew with Lou Thesz before more than 2,000 fans. The *Arizona Republic* stated that their bout was "unlike most modern wrestling matches [as it was] a scientific duel a good share of the way." Both wrestlers achieved a fall with Rogers taking the second with his figure-four, but the match was declared a draw when the time-limit expired.[56] He challenged Dick Hutton again on March 31 at Phoenix's Madison Square Garden, but instead of battling through a full three falls in a competitive affair, Buddy was attacked by Fritz Von Goering mid-match. He suffered a "deep gash" over his eye and the referee stopped the bout.[57] The Rogers-Von Goering feud was revived and they met three straight times in Phoenix, with Buddy winning twice.[58]

It should be noted that Rogers returned to Amarillo and dropped the North American championship back to Dory Funk on April 3, 1958.[59] But, strangely enough, four days later in Phoenix, Buddy was still acknowledged as the North American champion. While it was sometimes the error of the promoter to publicize a wrestler as champion, even though they had lost their claim, this was certainly not the case. Phoenix impresario Rod Fenton tied Buddy's title to an entirely new and fictitious lineage, stating that he "recently" dethroned Art Nelson in Oakland, California.[60] The story was made up to provide a basis for Fenton's localized title. On April 9, Rogers reemerged in Los Angeles for the first time in nearly three years, and beat Sky-Hi Lee at the Olympic Auditorium. In Southern California, Rogers was surrounded by familiar faces and friends, beginning with Billy Darnell, his old Jack Pfefer troupe-mate, Dave Levin, and the 600-pound Country Boy Calhoun, who he had teamed up with in Memphis in mid-1957.

Irvin (Zabo) Koszewski, a champion bodybuilder from Camden, was another good friend in Los Angeles. "Zabo," a mainstay on Muscle Beach in Santa Monica, was nicknamed "Mr. Abs" for his chiseled abdominals and was remarkably popular. He expressed an interest in wrestling following the success of a growing number of Muscle Beach alumni to join the grappling business. Eric Pedersen and Bob McCune were among the first to do so, and each did a stint under the management of Jack Pfefer as "Superman Apollo" and "Lord Pinkerton," respectively.[61] Soon thereafter, Henry Lenz, Malcolm Brenner, and Seymour Koenig turned pro wrestler, and Buddy's longstanding relationship with Zabo connected him to the larger community of bodybuilders in Southern California.[62] He had wrestled and toured with Pedersen, McCune and Brenner previously, and on April 16, he put Lenz over at the Olympic Auditorium.[63]

During Rogers' stay in Los Angeles in 1958, Pedersen and Koenig were also in the territory, and a good amount of socializing occurred. George Eiferman, a bodybuilding legend originally from Philadelphia, was a mutual acquaintance, as well, and they all enjoyed getting together.[64] Rogers began training Zabo and made arrangements for a summer tour of Ohio.[65] Buddy's wife Terry accompanied him to California in April 1958 when she was approaching her ninth month of pregnancy. Since their marriage four years earlier, Terry had been exceptionally supportive of her husband's career, and traveled with him when the opportunity arose. In 1956, she spent time with Buddy in Florida and the couple ventured over to Havana, Cuba, where Rogers had a scheduled match.[66] A few months later, Terry packed up their automobile and, with their two dogs, Booboo and Baby, drove alone from Ohio to Texas to meet Buddy in Houston.[67]

But the constant traveling was a major negative for Terry. "No woman likes to live out of a suitcase, and I quickly tired of the road," she later explained.[68] However, there was equal distress staying home and being lonely, and thus, the entire lifestyle was a constant challenge.[69] Terry essentially remained out of the public eye, but every now and then, a photo of her appeared in a publication. When the *Columbus Star* persuaded Rogers to open up about his significant other in 1957, he said: "The wife is the boss at home. Whatever she says I do. That's the way it should be." The newspaper included a candid photo of the two with the caption: "This picture illustrates the fairy tale 'Beauty and the Beast,' doesn't it?"[70] Upon landing in California, Buddy and Terry established a temporary residence in a posh section of Beverly Hills, off Wilshire Boulevard, near the Beverly Comstock Hotel.[71] It was a beautiful area, and depending on traffic and the route taken, it was about a 20-minute drive to the Olympic Auditorium in Downtown LA.

On the night of May 28, 1958, Rogers headlined the Olympic for promoter Cal Eaton. A crowd of 5,300 fans saw him defeat Sandor Szabo in two of three falls, taking the first and third to capture the winner's purse.[72] After the show, he raced over to UCLA Medical Center to meet his expectant wife, as the day they had been waiting for had finally arrived. At 1:56 a.m., Terry gave birth to a daughter, whom they named Frieda Alberta Rogers.[73] Both her first and middle names were given in tribute to influential people in Buddy's life. Frieda was the name of his mother, while Alberta was chosen in homage to Al Haft.[74] A traditional announcement of her birth was printed in Terry's hometown newspaper, the *Gallipolis Daily Tribune*, a few days later.[75] Buddy's family had grown, and his responsibilities as a father and husband were balanced against the constant demands of professional wrestling. And for a man sought by promoters all over North America, he was busier than ever.

ENDNOTES - CHAPTER 12

[1] *Sports Pictorial Review*, Jan. 26, 1948, p. 1.
[2] Ibid.
[3] *Akron Beacon Journal*, May 2, 1956, p. 29.
[4] Don Fargo gave an example of this in his book, *The Hard Way* by Don Fargo with Scott Teal (2014).
[5] *Buddie Rogers and The Art of Sequencing* by Max W. Jacobs. Interview of Max W. Jacobs, March 5, 2007.
[6] Ibid.
[7] *Baltimore Evening Sun*, Jan. 10, 1956, p. 23.
[8] *Wrestling As You Like It*, May 26, 1949, p. 8.
[9] Rogers said most of the letters were from women. He said they ranged from, "Drop dead," to "Do you want money or friends?" He replied to the latter note with: "If I have money, I'll have friends." *Lancaster Sunday News*, Dec. 17, 1950, p. 47.
[10] It was said that his "greatest" fan club was in Toledo. *Sports Pictorial Review*, May 8, 1950, p. 2. The Quebec-based club was headed by Dennis Canty of Verdun and Robert Weeks of Montreal. There was a smaller club in Stollings, West Virginia, led by Genny Workman. *Wrestling World*, July 1954.
[11] *Rogers Internationale Bulletin*, April 1, 1956, Issue #6, p. 2.
[12] The convention was held on Aug. 6-7, 1955. *Pat Schnee's International Set*, Fall 1955, p. 13.
[13] *Rogers Internationale Bulletin*, April 1, 1956, Issue #6, p. 3.
[14] Rogers was supposed to wrestle Chris Averoff in Columbus on July 4, 1957, but the show was rained out.
[15] *Columbus Dispatch*, July 12, 1957, p. 23A.

16 Rogers was usually a fan favorite in Ohio. He displayed his babyface qualities on Aug. 10, 1957 in Akron when he refused a victory over Wright after the latter suffered a groin injury. The match was declared a draw. *Akron Beacon Journal*, Aug. 11, 1957, p. 68.

17 *Mansfield News-Journal*, Oct. 10, 1957, p. 37.

18 *Mansfield News-Journal*, Oct. 17, 1957, p. 33.

19 *Cincinnati Enquirer*, Oct. 12, 1957, p. 15.

20 Von Goering beat Rogers in a rematch in Springfield on October 20 and also in Cincinnati on November 29. He also won by countout in Columbus on Oct. 26, 1957.

21 While in the Ohio territory, Rogers had been surrounded by many of his friends and allies, including Billy Darnell, Buddy Rosen, Jack Vansky, Ray Stevens, Johnny Barend, George Bollas, and Rocky Columbo. He participated in a Summer Wrestling Fan Club Party in Columbus during the summer of 1957 and was joined by Darnell, Rosen and Bollas. *Pat Schnee's International Set*, Winter '57/'58.

22 Rogers and Kashey won the third fall by DQ. Minneapolis Star, Nov. 6, 1957, p. 2F. The last time Buddy had worked Minneapolis was December 1948 for promoter Tony Stecher. This time around, he was wrestling for Stecher's son Dennis and matchmaker Wally Karbo.

23 *Minneapolis Star*, Nov. 5, 1957, p. 10B.

24 The Minneapolis match was Thesz's first stateside bout since Aug. 23, 1957.

25 Attendance was 3,289. *Minneapolis Star Tribune*, Nov. 13, 1957, p. 35.

26 *Hooker* by Lou Thesz with Kit Bauman (2011), p. 204.

27 Letter from Sam Muchnick to Fred Kohler dated March 12, 1953, Department of Justice Investigation into the National Wrestling Alliance, National Archives, College Park, MD.

28 *San Francisco Examiner*, Jan. 25, 1955, p. 29.

29 It is unknown if Rogers' increased work as a fan favorite and "straight wrestler" in 1957 was building his case toward a run with the NWA championship. By this time, he had dropped his fancy capes and jackets and toned back his showmanship. A few years later, a fan sent a letter to *Wrestling Revue* magazine and expressed disappointment that he had given up wearing his famous jackets. *Wrestling Revue*, December 1961, p. 6. As to why he had stopped wearing them, Rogers was quoted as saying: "I discovered that a thousand dollar jacket isn't worth a plug nickel once you take it off. I never had one win a single match for me. So one day I asked myself why in hell am I throwing away all this money? I got rid of the whole trunkful the next day. I figured that it was me the people came to see, not my jackets." *Wrestling Revue*, December 1961, p. 20. After he retired his jackets, Buddy went to the ring only carrying a white towel.

30 *Hooker* by Lou Thesz with Kit Bauman (2011), p. 204.

31 Ibid.

32 *Toronto Globe and Mail*, Nov. 15, 1957, p. 18.

33 Rogers was injured in St. Paul on Nov. 16. *Eau Claire Leader*, Nov. 20, 1957, p. 11. His opponent was Joe Christie, who was wrestling as the "Masked Mauler." Rogers would miss matches in Minneapolis on November 19 and Winnipeg on November 22. A report out of Dayton claimed that Rogers had suffered a leg injury. *Dayton Journal Herald*, Nov. 26, 1957, p. 16.

34 *Rasslin' Roundup*, Nov. 15, 1957, p. 2.

35 *Winnipeg Free Press*, Nov. 16, 1957, p. 40.

36 Karlsson was also known as "Tiny Carlson" and "Krusher Karlson."

37 Rogers used a Boston Crab to win the second fall. The match was stopped by matchmaker Saul Weingeroff. *St. Aug.ine Record*, Dec. 5, 1957, p. 5.

38 *St. Aug.ine Record*, Dec. 5, 1957, p. 5 and Dec. 9, 1957, p. 7.

39 *St. Aug.ine Record*, Dec. 13, 1957, p. 9.

40 *Tampa Tribune*, Dec. 15, 1957, p. 2B.

41 Tampa promoter Cowboy Luttrall had wanted to feature Rogers and Karlsson on December 16 and/or Dec. 23, 1957, but neither match took place.

42 *St. Aug.ine Record*, Dec. 19, 1957, p. 9.

43 Austin ventured to the Ohio territory in May 1958.

44 Albuquerque was independently booked by Mike London. It shared some talent with West Texas. On Feb. 13, 1958, Rogers made his first Denver appearance since July 7, 1947.

45 The figure-four was called the "Texas Grapevine" in West Texas. He offered $1,000 to anyone who could break the hold. *Amarillo Globe-Times*, Jan. 3, 1958, p. 8.

46 Wallace managed Francis in 1952-'53 and then became the manager of Shire later in 1953. He also used the name, "Yvon 'Frenchy' Ouimett," and was billed as being from Montreal.

47 *Amarillo Globe-Times*, Jan. 17, 1958, p. 8.

48 *Amarillo Globe-Times*, Jan. 1, 1958, p. 11.

49 *Amarillo Globe-Times*, Jan. 2, 1958, p. 16.

50 Wrestlers and referees were called in to break Rogers' hold. *Amarillo Globe-Times*, Jan. 24, 1958, p. 9.

51 *Amarillo Globe-Times*, Jan. 28, 1958, p. 9.

52 Rogers beat Bob Geigel earlier in the evening. *Amarillo Globe-Times*, Jan. 31, 1958, p. 10.

53 Hutton won the lone fall with his abdominal stretch. *Amarillo Globe-Times*, Feb. 7, 1958, p. 10.

54 Gossett took the name "Rip Rogers" in West Texas around September 1955.

55 Wallace was said to be Buddy's "erstwhile manager." *Odessa American*, March 4, 1958, p. 17. Several weeks later, Wallace would briefly manage Joe Christie in West Texas. In a later interview, Rogers spoke about his tuxedoed manager, saying: "Wallace was too aggressive for me. He tried to change me and I wouldn't put up with that." *Wrestling's Main Event*, September 1983, p. 21-22.

56 *Arizona Republic*, March 25, 1958, p. 25.

57 *Arizona Republic*, April 1, 1958, p. 26.

58 Their first bout, on April 7, 1958, was a no contest. *Arizona Republic*, April 8, 1958, p. 19. Rogers won the second bout under "Texas Rules" on April 14. *Arizona Republic*, April 15, 1958, p. 20. He also won the third, which was staged under "German Rules" on April 21. *Arizona Republic*, April 22, 1958, p. 20.

59 Rogers' loss was a lopsided two-straight fall affair. He was counted out in the first and unable to continue for the second after suffering the effects of Funk's spinning toe-hold. *Amarillo Globe-Times*, April 4, 1958, p. 9.

60 *Arizona Republic*, April 7, 1958, p. 33. Rogers did wrestle and beat Art Nelson on March 11, 1957 in Fort Worth, but didn't win any kind of championship. According to current records, his Oakland debut was a few months away, in September 1958.

61 McCune won "Mr. Muscle Beach" honors in 1947.

62 Lenz was a former "Mr. Muscle Beach" (1952).

63 *Los Angeles Times*, April 17, 1958, p. D2. Brenner used the names "Samson" Brenner and "Farmer" Brenner, and toured with Rogers in Ohio in 1957.

64 Rogers would hang out with Eiferman in Westwood, California. Correspondence with George DiFlavis, Feb. 4, 2019. Around 1949 or 1950, Eiferman considered a career in pro wrestling. He went to New York to train with the Steinborn Family. He didn't venture any further into the mat business. Dick Steinborn, Wrestling Classics Message Board, Nov. 20, 2001. Armand Tanny, a bodybuilder and occasional wrestler, likely also socialized with this group.

65 *Muscular Development*, November 1966, p. 33. "Zabo" would use the wrestling name, "Jungle Boy."

66 Buddy and Terry Rogers flew on a National Airlines plane from Miami International Airport to Rancho-Boyeros Airport in April 1956. Florida Passenger Lists, Ancestry.com.

67 *Gallipolis Daily Tribune*, July 2, 1956, p. 2.

68 *Wrestling Confidential*, July 1964, p. 22-27.

69 Ibid.

70 *Columbus Star*, Aug. 17, 1957, p. 6.

71 They lived at 10330 Wilshire Boulevard. According to newspaper reports from 1958, apartment rentals at that address ranged from $65 to $325 a month

72 *Los Angeles Times*, May 29, 1958, p. D3.

73 Certificate of Live Birth, Registrar-Recorder/County Clerk, County of Los Angeles, State of California. Frieda Alberta Rogers was Buddy's first and only biological child.

74 Correspondence with Lee Rogers, Aug. 18, 2018 and Sept. 14, 2019.

75 *Gallipolis Daily Tribune*, June 2, 1958, p. 3.

Chapter 13
The Path to Capitol

The Southern California wrestling landscape in 1958 was much different than it had been 10 years earlier when the "Nature Boy" gimmick was born. Promotional wars and television squabbles had reshaped the region, and Cal Eaton at the Olympic Auditorium was the sole survivor. Gone were Johnny Doyle, the mastermind behind the rise of Gorgeous George and "Baron" Michele Leone, and Hugh Nichols, the longtime impresario at the Hollywood Legion Stadium. Doyle had abandoned the territory for greener pastures in the East, while Nichols struggled with depression and committed suicide in 1956.[1] Buddy Rogers could never forget the importance of Nichols and the area always brought back fond recollections. But at the same time, new memories were forged. Rogers spent time with his wife and newborn baby, close friends, and enjoyed the picturesque Los Angeles scene. The weather couldn't have been better and Buddy was at the beach as much as possible.

Under the leadership of Eaton, and more importantly, his matchmaker Jules Strongbow, the popularity of wrestling was rebounding after a few turbulent years. The gross gate at the Olympic improved from a low of $36,201 in 1953 to $104,218 in 1957.[2] They were on pace to surpass that figure in 1958, and the presence of Rogers gave them a significant boost. Buddy was at his villainous best against babyfaces Sandor Szabo, Billy Darnell, and Country Boy Calhoun. The 23-year-old Calhoun was billed as the "Eighth Wonder of the World" and his mammoth size made him a big attraction.[3] Wearing overalls and wrestling barefoot, Calhoun was the opposite of Rogers in just about every way. In the ring, their styles clashed, but Rogers had experience working with oversized opponents dating back to his bouts with the 600-pound Martin (Blimp) Levy in the 1940s. He knew how to frame contests in just the right way to keep his heat, propel his rival, and entertain the audience.[4]

Szabo, on the other hand, was approaching his 30th year in the field and was a multi-time former world heavyweight champion. He held the coveted National Wrestling Association belt in 1941-'42, and was in the midst of his seventh reign as the "Beat the Champ" champion in 1958. Following his May 28 loss to Rogers at the Olympic, Szabo was the recipient of some expert trash-talking by his conqueror. Smugly, Buddy asserted that Szabo was hiding behind the standard 15-minute time limit for "Beat the Champ" bouts. To prove him wrong, Sandor accepted a two-of-three-fall rematch on June 4 with the crown on the line. He did insist that Rogers put up a check for $2,450, an amount equaling the "Beat the Champ" prize, and Buddy agreed. "I don't aim to lose my money to that old man," Rogers said with insatiable swagger.⁵ But that's exactly what happened. Szabo, the venerable battler, achieved a third fall DQ victory and retained his title.⁶

Another former NWA champion, Lou Thesz, was also in the territory, defending his uniquely branded International heavyweight championship. On June 11, 1958, he clashed with Rogers at the Olympic Auditorium in the televised main event, and it was a classic "donnybrook." The finish was a bit different than their usual fare as Rogers dove from the "upper elastic in the corner" onto Thesz' back, injuring him.⁷ The match was declared a draw and Thesz was taken to a local hospital for treatment.⁸ In subsequent press, Cal Eaton's publicist played up Thesz' need for revenge and claimed that Buddy had been avoiding a rematch. When the bout was locked in for July 23 at the Olympic, Thesz promised that "Rogers [was] in for the beating of his life."⁹ That night, the eternal foes wrestled at breakneck speed, and extended each other to their limits during a 60-minute draw.¹⁰ "The ferocity of the match was almost unbelievable," one report stated.¹¹

Rogers feuded with Fritz Von Goering and Lord James Blears in Southern California, as well, and although he often fought known heels, he was rarely the one chosen by fans as the favorite.¹² For his fiercest grudge matches at the Olympic and Hollywood Legion Stadium, officials removed the first two rows of ringside seats to protect spectators from the chaotic violence.¹³ "Every time that troublemaker [Rogers] wrestles, I have to put on extra police, and keep wrestlers standing by in case he goes after the fans," promoter Eaton complained. "I'm getting darn tired of the risk I'm taking."¹⁴ Rogers continued to terrorize the region well into September, and completed his tour with a couple explosive bouts against Czaya Nandor and Billy Varga. A few days later, Buddy made his debut in Northern California on the circuit operated by NWA member Joe Malcewicz, and was fully ready to make another big impact.

A promoter with 45 years in the business, Malcewicz knew all the tricks of the trade. He had already concocted a shrewd strategy for Rogers and believed it was a surefire moneymaker. His idea was to book Rogers as the world heavyweight champion, and like Buddy's recent stint as North American champion in Phoenix, it was completely fictitious. The claim was reportedly based on a 1952 tournament, which included 411 participants, and saw Rogers gain recognition in "28 Eastern states."¹⁵ While it was true that Rogers did win a Pittsburgh TV tournament that year, his legitimate title claims stemming from that victory were long gone.¹⁶ Nevertheless, Malcewicz went forward with his plan and advertised the "Nature Boy" as champion. In turn, NWA President Sam Muchnick contacted the San Francisco promoter, and reminded him that it was against Alliance rules to acknowledge a titleholder other than the official NWA-sponsored champ.

"Don't get excited," Malcewicz wrote Muchnick in response. "[Dick] Hutton is our world's champion. Rogers is only the claimant."¹⁷ He minimized the controversy in the sphere of NWA politics and pressed on with business as usual. Rogers got off to a fantastic start in the San Francisco territory, a region encompassing a dozen towns from Marysville in the north to Fresno in the south. He received stellar publicity and quickly established himself as a dominant force to be reckoned with.¹⁸ Still everlastingly confident, Rogers was back to being a fan favorite, and it didn't take long for a bitter feud to develop between Buddy and ex-weightlifter-turned-wrestler Gene Dubuque.

Billed as being from Hollywood and nicknamed the "Strutter," Dubuque was of the "Nature Boy" variety, and portrayed a nefarious instigator perfectly.[19] Rogers took a commanding early lead in their rivalry, teaming with Ronnie Etchison to strip the world tag team championship from Dubuque and Mike Valentino in Oakland on October 3.[20]

In Santa Rosa on October 10, Rogers won the "fastest match ever seen at the Pavilion" over Valentino. He won the first fall in 12 seconds and then the second by submission with his figure-four in 2:04. Enraged by the turn of events, Dubuque attacked Rogers from behind, pounding him with an array of punches and kicks. Those actions changed the mood of the crowd from a contented mass into a rabid mob, and fans genuinely wanted to hurt Dubuque for what he did. He was chased and menaced by people wielding chairs and police were called in to break things up. With blood covering his face and intermixed with his blond hair, Rogers spoke to the audience from the ring moments later. He said: "If you think I'm entitled to get even with Dubuque, why don't we get the promoter out here and make the match right now?" Onlookers roared in approval.[21]

Rogers got his hands on Dubuque in Santa Rosa on October 25 and a very similar story unfolded before the 1,400 patrons in attendance. Rogers won in two straight falls, was bloodied in the fracas, and was again brutalized after the bell by an outsider. Dressed in street clothes, Fritz Von Goering entered the ring to stomp Rogers into submission. The fans went wild. They screamed and shouted, threw everything they could their hands on, and surrounded the ring with the hopes of settling the score on behalf of the fallen Rogers. This "near riot" atmosphere went on for about 15-minutes until police were able to restore calm.[22] Dubuque's aggressiveness continued on October 28 in Santa Cruz when he smashed Rogers with a chair, ripping open his forehead at the conclusion of a tag match that he wasn't a participant in. Buddy and Ronnie Etchison beat Karl Von Schober and The Mask prior to the unexpected assault.[23]

Back in Santa Rosa on November 7, Rogers undertook the daunting challenge of both Dubuque and Von Goering in a special rules contest. Yet again, it was a frenzied battle, and police were called upon to prevent a full-scale riot. Instead of it being a regular handicap match, in which Dubuque and Von Goering would wrestle one at a time, the official allowed them to act as a tag team. Rogers was required to beat both men to win, and if he was defeated for a fall, he would forfeit his purse. Buddy was game and had his opponents on their heels throughout the bout. He won the first fall, but his foes conspired to have him counted out in the second, arousing the crowd. Fans physically assailed Von Goering and Dubuque in post-match mayhem, and in the midst of the reckless brawling, the referee altered his decision, giving Rogers the win.[24] The involvement of spectators was risky business, and considering the heat they were generating, it was just a matter of time before a customer took things too far. Such a situation arose in San Jose on November 12 when Von Goering was confronted by a knife-wielding fan during his clash with Rogers at the Auditorium. In the resulting chaos, wrestler Clyde Steeves was slashed on the arm and required medical attention.[25]

Rogers wasn't booked as an invincible grappler. In fact, it was quite the opposite. He displayed his vulnerabilities while propping up the strengths of his rivals, setting up payoff matches in the various cities on the circuit. In the end, though, he was unquestionably the top star. He overwhelmingly won his feud with Gene Dubuque, winning nine of their 10 matches in the territory; two by disqualification and another was declared a no-contest. He was a claimant to the world heavyweight title and co-holder of the world tag team championship at the same time, and was constantly lauded in newspaper articles. One publication went as far as to call him, "Wrestling's greatest individual attraction of the modern era."[26] When Rogers was in front of a reporter and on top of his game, he was exceedingly boastful. "I'm afraid of nobody and the guy doesn't live that I wouldn't take on," he told a journalist. "I'm not conceited. I'm merely the greatest."[27]

Prior to a December 11 show in Napa, in which he was going to team with George Drake against the Red Mask and Hans Schnabel, Rogers cut a promo for a local newspaper and let it all hang out. "Who are the Red Mask and Hans Schnabel?" he asked. "I deserve only the biggest, roughest, toughest men in the wrestling business, not palookas like them. It's hard to get opponents worthy of my ability. The only thing that bothers me is not getting tough enough competition." The reporter mentioned rival title claimants Dick Hutton, Killer Kowalski, and Lou Thesz, and Rogers replied: "They're cheese champions. I could lick all three of them at one time and they know it. That's why they keep avoiding a title elimination match with me."[28] Promoter Ad Santel wanted to arrange a Rogers-Hutton championship bout in Oakland, but the contest failed to materialize.[29] In fact, Rogers never received another NWA title shot during Hutton's reign.[30]

Notably, throughout Buddy's tenure in California, he was constantly and specifically referred to as "Nature Boy Rogers." The reasoning was simple: He wanted to avoid any additional possible legal entanglements with the actor Buddy Rogers, who had a significant presence in the "Golden State." According to their 1955 settlement, Buddy-the-wrestler agreed never to use the name "Buddy Rogers" in association with wrestling. Outside California, it was less of a concern, but since he was within striking distance of the famed actor and musician, he wanted to adhere to the established decree. Rogers was finished with his West Coast tour by the middle of December, but only lost one of his championship titles on his way out. On November 21, he and Ronnie Etchison dropped the world tag belts to Dubuque and Von Goering in Oakland.[31] His claim to the world heavyweight championship remained intact until the end of his run, and then seemingly disappeared.[32]

In 1958, Rogers made around a half dozen trips back to Ohio to wrestle for Al Haft. Following the birth of his daughter, his family trekked cross-country to introduce his baby to her grandmother and namesake, Frieda Rohde, in Camden in July 1958.[33] After leaving the Los Angeles region in December, the Rogers clan returned to their home in Columbus and spent the holidays in Ohio. Buddy had a little free time on his hands and visited the office of Al Haft to reconnect with old acquaintances. Among the familiar faces was a tall, good-looking young man named Bobby Davis. A handful of years earlier when Davis was but a teenager, he made an unannounced trip to Buddy's home, and the "Nature Boy" couldn't have been more hospitable.[34] They formed an instant friendship and Rogers was delighted to hear of Bobby's recent success in the wrestling business.[35] Beginning in 1956, Davis had begun a whirlwind campaign as a second for the likes of Don Stevens, Dr. Jerry Graham, Ricki Starr, and Edmund Francis.

While Rogers was on the West Coast, Davis was in the New York area, solidifying himself as one of the best managers in professional wrestling. At only 19-years-of-age, he was causing unprecedented trouble for fan-favorites and went to great lengths to support his charge, Jerry Graham. His disorderly actions earned him a suspension by the Maryland State Athletic Commission in May 1957.[36] Davis went the extra mile to help his wrestler achieve victory, and it wasn't uncommon for him to be "caught" by the hero and taught a lesson after a bout in which he interfered. Fans might have been depressed by the decision, but they loved to see Davis get what was coming to him. Despite those instances, Bobby's smugness never diminished, and spectators were always turned on their collective heads by his innate ability to draw heat. In mid-1958, he unified the talents of Dr. Jerry and Tennessean Eddie Gossett, fashioning the iconic Graham Brothers tag team. The colorful Grahams were a game changer in the northeast.

Davis managed the Grahams for the last six months of 1958 and was back home in Columbus for a short Christmas vacation. His reunion with his hero, Rogers, in Al Haft's office was personally satisfying and professionally constructive.[37] They talked about aligning their interests in 1959, both inside the ring and out, and turning the Ohio territory into their own pet project. Rogers and Davis would work in conjunction with Haft, but would control most of the booking and advance the promotional end of their operations across the state. A coordinated push with Rogers on the scene full-time had the potential to rejuvenate the entire region. And that was music to Haft's ears. He had lost his influential studio TV show in October 1955, and business hadn't been the same since. As the deal to bring Rogers back was being arranged, Haft was negotiating a high-profile return to television, cementing Ohio's complete wrestling renaissance.

Joseph Alexander (Lex) Mayers was the owner of a successful Columbus automobile dealership. He was known for his enthusiastic TV commercials, hyping his newest Chevrolets on Sunday nights.[38] Interested in taking his television sponsorship to a new level, he came up with a new innovation involving wrestling, and Haft was immediately onboard. Mayers wanted to host a two-hour Saturday afternoon grappling program at the old Memorial Hall, and feature his cars at the same time. It was a crafty plan, only made possible because of Mayers' financial investment, and the show, dubbed "Lex's Live Wrestling," debuted on Jan. 17, 1959, on WLW-C.[39] In great shape, mentally and physically, Rogers was ready to get things started, and his first major feud was against Buddy Austin, who had become somewhat of a protégé. They wrestled in Dayton and Mansfield the first week of January, then teamed up in Cincinnati and Canton a few days later.[40] The latter two matches ended with Rogers and Austin fighting each other.[41]

The Rogers-Austin rivalry captured headlines, and in terms of bloody warfare, they went all out. One newspaper called their ongoing quarrel "a feud reminiscent of the Hatfields and McCoys."[42] Austin portrayed the heel and received incredible backlash for being repeatedly disqualified in matches throughout the territory.[43] Rogers and Austin had chemistry in the ring, making the work easy, and with Rogers leading the way, played to each other's strengths. In keeping with past traditions, the title situation in Ohio was as vibrant as ever. Before turning their attention to each other, Rogers and Austin apparently won the Ohio tag team belts from Leon Graham and Frankie Talaber in Cincinnati on Jan. 2, 1959.[44] The following week at the Emery Auditorium, their personal brawl cost them the title in a rematch with Graham and Talaber.[45] The following month, Rogers and the Great Scott revived their ancient American tag team title and defended their claim for the first time in several years.[46]

In early 1959, Buddy formed a short-lived tag team with the popular Leon Graham. On two occasions in Mansfield, they challenged the Fargo Brothers (Don and Jackie Fargo) for the world championship. It was notable because the Fargos were handled by Buddy's old manager, Jack Pfefer.[47] Rogers wasn't eager to engage a Pfefer product looking to possibly hurt him for revenge points, and had been cautiously aware of such situations since their split in 1951, but he trusted Don Fargo. They had traveled together and were friends.[48] Buddy didn't expect anything out of the ordinary and went ahead with the bouts. On January 14, the Fargos won in three falls, and two-weeks later, Rogers and Graham took a DQ victory.[49] A Mansfield report in February claimed that Rogers broke Don Fargo's leg in Cincinnati, and that Jackie wanted vengeance.[50] A match was scheduled for February 25, but Jackie mysteriously backed out of the affair a few days before it was to take place.[51]

The Eastern heavyweight championship was pulled out of mothballs essentially as soon as Buddy returned to Ohio, and Rogers resumed defending the belt. On February 14 in Canton, he ran into Sweet Daddy Siki, a talented upstart from Texas with four years as a pro.[52] A relative newcomer to the region, Siki was already a big hit and was garnering rave reviews for his "sensational" style.[53] Rogers put Siki over in two straight falls and lost the Eastern title in what was their first singles encounter.[54] Buddy Austin, a constant thorn in Rogers' side, was in Siki's corner that night, and things escalated quickly. Rogers received timely help from the Great Scott and Bobby Davis, who was now their manager, but it didn't save his championship.[55] Once again riding the line between babyface and heel, Buddy was extracting both cheers and boos, and many times, the hostilities were elevated based on the popularity of his rival. Siki, for instance, was a top- tier fan-favorite, and in that feud, Rogers usually resorted to his old tricks.

Austin got some residual praise when partnered with Siki against Rogers and Scott, but otherwise, he was the traditional "bad guy" in matches against Rogers. And Rogers was beloved. The exciting action, slick matchmaking, and premier talent transformed Ohio just as Al Haft had hoped, but it was no longer just about increasing the box office for short-term financial gain – it was about the survival of his entire territory. Over in Cincinnati, a new promotional outfit moved in and secured a live studio television show on WCPO. The syndicate was run by Jim Barnett and Johnny Doyle, two non-NWA operators with deep pockets and lofty plans. Their first big show at the Cincinnati Gardens on Jan. 23, 1959, drew more than 8,000 spectators and a gate of $16,700, dwarfing Haft's enterprises not only in Cincinnati, but anywhere in the state.⁵⁶ With a deep talent pool, Barnett and Doyle were primed to expand further, and Haft suspected that Columbus might be next.

The Haft-Rogers combine had reason to be concerned, but instead of conceding cities to the opposition, they went on the offensive. In Steubenville, Ohio, near the borders of West Virginia and Pennsylvania, their organization set up a new studio television show with reach to all three states.⁵⁷ Canton promoter Vince Risko was in charge of the operation, and he made it clear that he intended to stage shows in the vicinity of Pittsburgh, the largest city in the area. Barnett and Doyle were far too busy elsewhere to pay much attention, but news of Haft's expansion reached the Northeastern office of the Capitol Wrestling Corporation, and jaws hit the floor. Capitol Wrestling had been established in 1957 by Toots Mondt and Vincent J. McMahon as a way to consolidate the booking operations across their unified territory from Washington, D.C. to New York City.⁵⁸ The company was managed primarily by McMahon and he astutely kept Mondt and his destructive tendencies from hindering their success.

McMahon and Mondt knew what Rogers was capable of. A few years earlier, Buddy had been in the Northeast with TV and a line-up of skilled performers, and did well for himself as a booker. Now, with the right momentum, he could edge his way back in and put up a grand fight for Philadelphia, Baltimore, and possibly New York. The owners of Capitol Wrestling didn't want a full-fledged invasion on their hands and decided to put money and support into shoring up the Pittsburgh promotion, which was, in many respects, a gateway hub to the Eastern territory.⁵⁹ The tireless Ray Fabiani of Philadelphia, who gravitated to Mondt and McMahon following the collapse of the Rogers circuit in 1956, took on the task of rejuvenating Pittsburgh, and initiated a weekly studio TV show on Saturday nights.⁶⁰ Johnny Valentine, billed as the television champion, was his headline attraction, and the latter's confrontational interactions with host Mal Alberts sparked great interest.⁶¹

But Pittsburgh needed more time to once again fully embrace wrestling, and the best Fabiani could muster were bi-monthly shows at the Palisades in suburban McKeesport. Rogers managed to operate only a handful of times in Pennsylvania in 1959, and a further push east was not viable.⁶² Between Rogers and Bobby Davis, most of the promotional and booking aspects of Haft's business were covered, while Haft tended to the normal administrative duties.⁶³ At 72 years of age, Haft was less involved in the day-to-day, and allowed Rogers to do most of the decision-making.⁶⁴ Davis was literally a half century younger than Haft, and even though he was comparatively inexperienced, he was a natural in every phase of the sport. In Marion, Ohio, he was the promoter of record, and he assertively handled all responsibilities with the expertise of a much older man.⁶⁵ For Rogers, it was another opportunity to run the show, and since he had Haft's trust, he arranged things just how he liked them.⁶⁶

Over the course of 1959, Buddy utilized many of his old crew, including Great Scott, Buddy Rosen, Billy Darnell, and Fritz Von Goering, plus the aforementioned Buddy Austin and a more recent addition to his tribe, Johnny Barend.⁶⁷ Rogers welcomed talented wrestlers of all shapes and sizes, color and creed, and among them were several athletes he personally had classic rivalries with: Ruffy Silverstein, Bearcat Wright, Oyama Kato, and Karl

Karlsson. His feud with Austin spanned much of the year, and there were few gimmicks they neglected to attempt. In Zanesville on April 27, they took their violence to the extreme, battling with ringside chairs before fighting their way from the Auditorium onto North Fourth Street. Needless to say, their bout was declared a no-contest.[68] Houses popped for Rogers and his troupe, from 4,000 fans at Memorial Hall to more than 8,000 at the Fairgrounds Coliseum.[69] On Aug. 8, Haft claimed "over 10,000" people were on hand for a Coliseum show headlined by Rogers and Von Goering.[70]

Truth be told, Buddy Austin was a bit of a troublemaker outside the ring. On the evening of Sept. 9, 1959, he was hanging out at the Musical Bar in Columbus with wrestlers Juan Sebastian and Jay York, enjoying a vast supply of alcoholic beverages. As the night wore on, the wrestlers got into a scrap with the bartenders and patrons, and all hell broke loose. Tables and chairs were broken, blood was shed, and at least one man was knocked out. A newspaper photographer who arrived on the scene to take pictures–was attacked by the grapplers, as well. Police arrested the three men and booked them on charges of intoxication, destruction of property, and assault and battery. When Austin was asked his name by law enforcement officials, he said he was "Austin W. 'Buddy' Rogers," and subsequent reports affirmed that "Buddy Rogers" had been involved in the late night ruckus.[71] However, the real Buddy Rogers was not in Columbus on September 9, but was wrestling in Montreal.[72]

Upon returning to Columbus, Rogers informed the press of its error and the *Columbus Dispatch* printed an article on September 11 clarifying that it was indeed Buddy Austin, and not Rogers.[73] But by that time, news had spread far and wide, and Rogers was furious. He spoke privately with Bobby Davis and the two decided to turn the incident and all the bad publicity into an angle. The next day, Rogers appeared on *Lex's Live Wrestling* and spoke from the heart, telling the viewing audience that he was a family man, and that he was crushed by the accusation that he had been involved in a drunken bar fight. On the verge of tears, his emotional speech was as real as a worked pro wrestling scenario could get, and Rogers punctuated the moment by challenging Austin to a bout at the Fairgrounds Coliseum that night.[74] He wanted revenge. All advertising for the show had hyped Rogers against Donn Lewin on September 12, but considering the circumstances, the main event was changed at the last minute, and Rogers got his match.[75]

Austin, who was managed by Davis, was about to get the beating of his life. With blood in his eyes, Rogers tore after his enemy right from the bell, quickly opened a cut above his eye, and put him down for the count. The time was two minutes and three seconds. Austin never got in even a fraction of offense, and was so badly injured that he was unable to continue. Fans celebrated around Rogers as his vanquished foe was carried from the ring and rushed to University Hospital for urgent care.[76]

The Eastern heavyweight championship was the major prop on the Ohio circuit, and Rogers lost the championship at least three different times in 1959.[77] Rarely did reports in various towns coincide with each other, and he was often acknowledged as a champion in one town, but not in another. Perennial babyface Johnny Barend turned heel, took Davis as his second, and stripped Rogers of the belt on Sept. 26, 1959, in Cincinnati.[78]

Buddy's feud with Barend lasted several months and their bouts were high energy from beginning to end. Their "Death Match" on October 31 in Cincinnati sold out the Music Hall Arena (4,200 tickets), and Rogers gained an important win in their saga.[79] On Jan. 2, 1960, Rogers regained his Eastern championship from "Handsome" Johnny in Columbus, winning in two-of-three-falls.[80] During the last four months of 1959, Rogers made regular trips to Montreal and was just as successful there as he was in Ohio. He used his figure-four grapevine to beat Killer Kowalski and capture the Montreal version of the world heavyweight title on September 16.[81] Two weeks later, he dismantled fan-favorite Edouard Carpentier with the same move, but scrapped with his old rival "Jersey" Joe Walcott, the night's special referee, after the contest. Actually, it wasn't much of a scrap, but a lopsided pummeling with the ex-boxing champion doling out the punishment.[82]

The stage was set. Promoter Eddie Quinn immediately scheduled a 10-round boxer versus wrestler match for the Montreal Forum on October 7. The local sports populace was enthusiastic about the concept and an estimated 10,000 fans were in attendance for the epic Rogers-Walcott battle. Buddy put over Walcott's punching power early in the fracas and appeared to be headed for a loss, but he recovered and triumphed in 1:07 of the third round.[83] Rogers dropped the Montreal belt back to Killer Kowalski on December 2, only to regain it on January 13, 1960.[84] On the political side of the business, Quinn had created a lot of controversy after instigating a war in Chicago against the weakened operations of Fred Kohler. He was also planning to soon invade Boston. Rogers, notably, wrestled in a mid-card spot on Quinn's inaugural "Windy City" program on Aug. 1, 1959, defeating Buddy Rosen by DQ.[85]

Back up in Montreal, Quinn scored a home run when he kick-started the first feud between Rogers and Antonino Rocca in more than three years.[86] On Feb. 24, 1960, the two superstars drew 11,300 spectators to the Forum and fought to a hectic double-disqualification.[87] For their rematch on March 9, an incredible crowd of 15,206 were witness to another intense bout. Buddy won the first fall using his famed piledriver, but was taken to the mat by a flying head scissors and a pin in the second. Felonious actions on the part of Rogers earned him a DQ, and Rocca's supporters were dismayed to learn that the world title could not change hands on a disqualification.[88] The next day, Rogers made a unique showing in West Hempstead, Long Island, New York, as part of a massive card at the Island Garden Arena. He teamed up with Eddie Graham, formerly Rip Rogers, to beat Don Curtis and Mark Lewin. Billy Darnell, Sweet Daddy Siki, Primo Carnera, and Johnny Valentine were on the bill, as well.

The expansion efforts of Quinn opened up new talent-sharing opportunities, and a loose promotional clique was formed between the Montreal promoter, Al Haft, Toots Mondt, and Vince McMahon. The latter were partners in Capitol Wrestling, the outfit in charge of the West Hempstead event. Bearing in mind his rocky history with "Toots," Rogers was one of the least-likely athletes to participate on a Capitol program. But something was different in early 1960. Egos were in check and the attention of promoters was focused on moneymaking over and above personal grudges. The timing was right, and "Nature Boy" Buddy Rogers was headed back to the Northeastern territory with a smart manager, astute bookers, and a possible chance to attain the most coveted prize in professional wrestling: the National Wrestling Alliance world heavyweight title.

ENDNOTES - CHAPTER 13

[1] Nichols passed away on Dec. 15, 1956 in Hollywood, California. He was 58 years of age.

[2] *Los Angeles Times*, Jan. 16, 1954, p. 9, Jan. 7, 1958, p. 61.

[3] *Olympic Auditorium News*, July 23, 1958, p. 3.

[4] During this time-period, Rogers and Calhoun wrestled six times in Southern California, four times in Ohio, and once in Arizona.

[5] *Olympic Auditorium News*, June 4, 1958, p. 3.

[6] Rogers refused to break a hold and was disqualified. *Los Angeles Times*, June 5, 1958, p. 79.

[7] It was said that Thesz "suffered damaged vertebrae." Rogers also used this maneuver against Fritz Von Goering. *Olympic Auditorium News*, July 23, 1958, p. 2. His injury was said to be "minor" in a separate report. *Los Angeles Times*, June 13, 1958, p. 82. Thesz was back in the ring by June 14, 1958 in San Bernardino.

[8] *Los Angeles Times*, June 12, 1958, p. 71.

[9] *Olympic Auditorium News*, July 23, 1958, p. 1.

[10] Attendance for their second bout was 4,200, up from 2,500 in their last Olympic encounter. *Los Angeles Times*, July 24, 1958, p. 65.

[11] *Official Hollywood Wrestling Program*, Aug. 4, 1958, p. 4.

[12] A description of a Rogers-Blears bout in San Diego was described in *Wrestling Life*, June 1958, p. 10-11.

[13] This happened at the Olympic on July 30, 1958 for a Texas Death match against Von Goering and at the Legion Stadium on Aug. 11 for a bout with Tosh Togo.

[14] *Olympic Auditorium News*, Aug. 6, 1958, p. 2.

[15] *Santa Cruz Sentinel*, Nov. 30, 1958, p. 12. Malcewicz initially said Rogers was "recognized in 18 states." He also billed him as being from Germany. *San Francisco Examiner*, Sept. 30, 1958, p. 32. A more specific report stated that he was from Heidelberg, Germany. *San Francisco Chronicle*, Sept. 25, 1958, p. 4H.

[16] A photo of Rogers standing with the Michael Berardino Trophy, which he won in the 1952 Pittsburgh tournament, was printed in the same Santa Cruz article. Ibid.

[17] Letter from Joe Malcewicz to Sam Muchnick dated Nov. 6, 1958.

[18] Rogers was the recipient of topnotch press in the *Oakland Tribune*. He was called the "body beautiful of the wrestling mat," and said to claim "the most perfectly framed physique" in the sport. *Oakland Tribune*, Sept. 26, 1958, p. 48.

[19] Dubuque used the name "Gene Darval" in Florida earlier in 1958, and was billed as the "Strutter." *Orlando Evening Star*, April 12, 1958, p. 7. He was also advertised as "Strutter Dubuque" before a Fresno card on Oct. 18, 1958.

[20] *Oakland Tribune*, Oct. 4, 1958, p. 15.

[21] *Santa Rosa Press Democrat*, Oct. 12, 1958, p. 5C.

[22] *Santa Rosa Press Democrat*, Oct. 27, 1958, p. 9.

[23] *Santa Cruz Sentinel*, Oct. 29, 1958, p. 7 and Nov. 4, 1958, p. 5.

[24] *Santa Rosa Press Democrat*, Nov. 9, 1958, p. 25.

[25] After the fan displayed the knife, both Rogers and Von Goering ran for cover. Their match was declared a no contest. Reports of this match went out over the Associated Press wire. *Sacramento Bee*, Nov. 13, 1958, p. E1.

[26] *Santa Cruz Sentinel*, Oct. 19, 1958, p. 15.

[27] *Salinas Californian*, Oct. 7, 1958, p. 13.

[28] *Napa Register*, Dec. 11, 1958, p. 16.

[29] *Oakland Tribune*, Oct. 31, 1958, p. 53.

[30] According to current records, Rogers never wrestled Hutton again. Their last match was on March 31, 1958 in Phoenix, and Hutton was victorious.

[31] Dubuque and Von Goering won the third fall by countout when Rogers was incapable of returning to the ring. *Oakland Tribune*, Nov. 22, 1958, p. 15. Rogers and Etchison also lost a controversial title match to Dubuque and Clyde Steeves by disqualification on Nov. 18, 1958 in Santa Cruz. *Santa Cruz Sentinel*, Nov. 19, 1958, p. 8.

[32] Rogers was billed as the world heavyweight champion through his final California appearance on Dec. 16, 1958 in San Diego. That night, he beat "Crusher" Bill Savage in two-of-three-falls. *San Diego Union*, Dec. 17, 1958, p. 24.

[33] Hollywood Wrestling Program, July 21, 1958, p. 4. Terry Rogers introduced Frieda to her parents in Gallipolis, Ohio in September 1958. *Gallia Times*, Sept. 13, 1958, p. 4.

[34] Davis also used to hang around the arena in Columbus and carry Buddy's luggage.

[35] Rogers saw Davis's work firsthand in November 1957 when Bobby was managing Edmund Francis in Ohio. During the third fall of Buddy's bout against Francis in Mansfield on November 6, Davis smashed Rogers from behind, and a near-riot broke out. *Mansfield News-Journal*, Nov. 7, 1957, p. 34.

[36] *Hanover Evening Sun*, May 15, 1957, p. 21.

[37] Davis said that he and Rogers hung out during Christmastime "for a couple weeks." Interview of Bobby Davis, Buddy Rogers Tribute Tape.

[38] He sponsored "Lex Mayers Theater."

[39] An article, entitled "World's Wackiest Mat Show," about the new TV program was featured in *Wrestling Revue*, Fall 1959, p. 55-58, 70." Some biographical information about Mayers appeared in *The Ohio Alumnus*, November 1959.

[40] Rogers beat Austin in Dayton on January 6 and in Mansfield on Jan. 7, 1959. They teamed in Cincinnati on January 2 and January 9, and also in Canton on January 10.

[41] In Canton, following the split between Rogers and Austin, Buddy was fined $50 for using profanity and fighting outside of the ring. Rogers and Austin were defeated by Leon Graham and Frankie Talaber. *Canton Repository*, Jan. 11, 1959, p. 66 and Jan. 15, 1959, p. 36.

[42] *Dover Daily Reporter*, Jan. 19, 1959, p. 11.

[43] In Dayton, the newspaper stated that Austin had "been disqualified in every bout in which he [had] participated since the indoor season opened." *Dayton Daily News*, Dec. 26, 1958, p. 10.

[44] Rogers and Austin won by DQ in the third fall. *Cincinnati Enquirer*, Jan. 3, 1959, p. 15.

[45] *Cincinnati Enquirer*, Jan. 10, 1959, p. 20.

[46] Rogers and Great Scott hadn't participated in a regular tag team match together since January 1956.

[47] Rogers had wrestled the Fargos in Memphis and Nashville in 1957, but that was prior to taking Pfefer as their manager.

[48] *The Hard Way* by Don Fargo with Scott Teal (2014).

[49] During the January 14 bout, Rogers put over Don Fargo for the first fall. He beat Don for the second and Jackie Fargo went over Graham for the third fall. *Mansfield News-Journal*, Jan. 15, 1959, p. 30. On January 28, Don pinned Graham for the first fall and Graham beat Jackie for the second before the Fargos were disqualified. *Mansfield News-Journal*, Jan. 29, 1959, p. 49.

[50] *Mansfield News-Journal*, Feb. 19, 1959, p. 20.

[51] *Mansfield News-Journal*, Feb. 21, 1959, p. 9. Fargo was replaced by Juan Sebastian, who also had to pull out due to injury. On February 25, Rogers wrestled and beat Little Boy Blue. *Mansfield News-Journal*, Feb. 26, 1959, p. 34.

[52] Siki was billed as being from Jamaica.

[53] *Canton Repository*, Feb. 8, 1959, p. 62.

[54] *Canton Repository*, Feb. 15, 1959, p. 60. The second fall was decided by disqualification. After this match, Siki claimed the championship, but Rogers complained that he couldn't lose his title by DQ. A rematch to settle the dispute was scheduled for April 11 in Canton. A special contract signing to hype the event was staged on Steubenville TV on Sunday, March 29. *Canton Repository*, March 29, 1959, p. 56. On April 11, Rogers beat Siki when the latter was unable to continue. *Canton Repository*, April 12, 1959, p. 66.

[55] *Canton Repository*, Feb. 17, 1959, p. 14. It was later said that Davis bought Rogers' contract from Jules Strongbow for $78,000. *Boxing and Wrestling*, April 1962, p. 50. Davis briefly talked about this on the Buddy Rogers Tribute Tape.

⁵⁶ The Cincinnati Boxing and Wrestling Commission earned more from this one show than they did for the entire year of 1958. Attendance was 8,663. *Cincinnati Enquirer*, Jan. 28, 1959, p. 35.

⁵⁷ The program was shown on WSTV, channel 9, on Sunday afternoons. Ernie Roth was the commentator. *Canton Repository*, Feb. 27, 1959, p. 34.

⁵⁸ Ironically, Johnny Doyle was also an original incorporator for the Capitol Wrestling Corporation. He held 16 percent ownership in the company in 1957-'58.

⁵⁹ Dr. Jerry Graham explained that Capitol Wrestling "sent" Phil Zacko to operate in Pittsburgh. The reasoning was "to keep Buddy Rogers out. They figured that if they extended that far out, then they could stop this other talent from coming in." Department of Justice Investigation into the National Wrestling Alliance, National Archives, College Park, MD.

⁶⁰ The show made its debut on Nov. 15, 1958 on WIIC from the Channel 11 Studios. *Pittsburgh Sun-Telegraph*, Nov. 15, 1958, p. 4.

⁶¹ Valentine reportedly won the TV Title in a tournament in Chicago, defeating Verne Gagne in the finals. *Pittsburgh Post-Gazette*, Dec. 19, 1958, p. 34. The tournament reportedly occurred "two months ago." *Pittsburgh Sun-Telegraph*, Dec. 24, 1958, p. 11.

⁶² Rogers ran shows at Delvitto's Auditorium in Jeannette and at the Fairgrounds in Nazareth. See *Latrobe Bulletin*, March 12, 1959, p. 19 and *Stroudsburg Daily Record*, July 14, 1959, p. 8.

⁶³ It is very likely that Haft's longtime associate Frankie Talaber helped with the booking.

⁶⁴ Don Fargo also talked about this in his book. *The Hard Way* by Don Fargo with Scott Teal (2014).

⁶⁵ *Marion Star*, Feb. 14, 1959, p. 13.

⁶⁶ One report stated that Buddy himself was promoting in the "Troy and Middletown arenas." *Dayton Daily News*, Jan. 19, 1960, p. 10.

⁶⁷ Notably, Scott and Rosen were coming off a run for the Mondt-McMahon group.

⁶⁸ *Zanesville Times Recorder*, April 28, 1959, p. 10.

⁶⁹ Rogers and Austin wrestled before 4,000 at Memorial Hall on March 19, 1959. *Columbus Dispatch*, March 20, 1959, p. 23B. On December 12, Rogers and Lou Thesz drew "some 8,000 fans" to the Fairgrounds Coliseum. *Columbus Dispatch*, Dec. 13, 1959, p. 36B.

⁷⁰ The local newspaper stated that the Coliseum seating capacity was "only around 8,000." *Columbus Dispatch*, Aug. 9, 1959, p. 34B.

⁷¹ The photographer worked for the *Columbus Star* newspaper. *Columbus Dispatch*, Sept. 10, 1959, p. 5A.

⁷² On Sept. 9, 1959, Rogers defeated Joe Christie and Frank Valois in a handicap bout. He beat Christie in 22-seconds and Valois in 6:11. *Montreal Gazette*, Sept. 10, 1959, p. 32.

⁷³ *Columbus Dispatch*, Sept. 11, 1959, p. 3A.

⁷⁴ Interview with Bobby Davis, May 27, 2019.

⁷⁵ *Columbus Dispatch*, Sept. 11, 1959, p. 6B.

⁷⁶ *Columbus Dispatch*, Sept. 13, 1959, p. 34B. Also see New Philadelphia Daily Times, Sept. 14, 1959 and Ohio Sentinel, Sept. 19, 1959.

⁷⁷ Rogers lost the title to Sweet Daddy Siki, Fritz Von Goering, and Johnny Barend.

⁷⁸ *Cincinnati Enquirer*, Sept. 29, 1959, p. 34.

⁷⁹ *Cincinnati Enquirer*, Nov. 2, 1959, p. 42.

⁸⁰ *Columbus Dispatch*, Jan. 3, 1960, p. 34B.

⁸¹ Kowalski won the first fall and Rogers took the second by submission. Kowalski was unable to continue and Buddy captured the championship. *Montreal Gazette*, Sept. 17, 1959, p. 36.

⁸² Rogers kept up his attack on Carpentier after the bout and Walcott stepped in to stop his onslaught. *Montreal Gazette*, Oct. 1, 1959, p. 34.

⁸³ *Montreal Gazette*, Oct. 8, 1959, p. 25.

⁸⁴ *Montreal Gazette*, Dec. 3, 1959, p. 25. Rogers again used his figure-four to beat Kowalski when he regained the title on January 13. *Montreal Gazette*, Jan. 14, 1960, p. 23.

⁸⁵ The show occurred at Chicago Stadium. *Chicago Tribune*, Aug. 2, 1959, p. 37.

⁸⁶ Their last singles bout took place on Aug. 21, 1956 in Baltimore.

⁸⁷ *Montreal Gazette*, Feb. 26, 1960, p. 25.

⁸⁸ *Montreal Gazette*, March 10, 1960, p. 26.

Chapter 14
The Ultimate Goal

Affable Vincent James McMahon, a 45-year-old product of New York, was credited with being the stabilizing force in the Northeastern region after years of mismanagement. His action-packed television show from Washington, D.C. revitalized the box office and thrilled long suffering fans. Off camera, he stylishly maneuvered between the larger-than-life personalities involved in the New York promotional scheme, and was usually a few steps ahead of his opposition. In truth, the entire territory was balanced by grudges and grievances, and since there was a ripe history of double-crosses, nearly everyone was paranoid. McMahon avoided the pitfalls of his predecessors and let those around him get caught up in the maddening shenanigans. He followed his vision, and by 1960, he had three functional TV outlets serving 14 states from Ohio to Maine. In addition to his television programs in Washington and Pittsburgh, he launched a flavorful live weekly show from the City Arena in Bridgeport, Connecticut.[1]

Despite McMahon's success, the New York market remained extremely fragile, and the influence of Jack Pfefer and Pedro Martinez in 1959-'60 only complicated matters. But things were about to take a negative turn for the head of Capitol Wrestling, starting with the announcement of a $300,000 lawsuit brought on by the family of a recently deceased promoter.[2] The widow and son of the late Edward Contos, the longtime operator in Baltimore, filed the suit in Washington, D.C. District Court on Feb. 26, 1960, charging McMahon and Toots Mondt with antitrust violations.[3] The complaint was one thing, but it had broader implications relating to the 1956 Consent Decree signed by the members of the National Wrestling Alliance, who collectively vowed not to restrain trade in the field of pro wrestling. McMahon didn't sign the Decree, but Toots did, and he was on the hook for prosecution if Federal investigators determined he acted with malicious intent.

Capitol Wrestling was rocked by the news. It soon became apparent that officials from the Department of Justice were looking into the situation and assessing the credibility of the claims. As that issue was hanging over McMahon's head, he executed one of his shrewdest moves to date, and brought "Nature Boy" Buddy Rogers back to the territory. But to backtrack a little bit, the first conversation about a possible return to "New York" actually occurred months earlier in Ohio between Rogers and his close pal, Bobby Davis. Davis had spent a good chunk of 1957 and '58 in the Northeast, and not only solidified himself as a heat magnet, but had effectively networked with industry leaders in the area. They loved his work. He was a quick-thinking, fast-talking operator, and fit right in with the New York crowd. Toots was especially taken by Bobby's abilities and they formed a solid friendship.

When Davis left in December 1958, the door was open for his reemergence sometime down the line.

Rogers and Davis got into a discussion and Buddy expressed his desire to wrestle in the East again.[4] He wanted to be closer to his mother in Camden, and felt he could do good business if the occasion presented itself. Rogers explained his problems with Mondt and was convinced that it was impossible. Brimming with confidence, Davis called Toots and spoke about Buddy's recent success in Ohio. When he mentioned the possibility of future appearances in the New York region, and Mondt instinctively recoiled. After digesting the information and considering the potential, Toots asked Davis an important question. He wanted to know if Bobby could "handle" Rogers.[5] That meant, in the event they did tour the Northeast, could Davis temper Buddy's natural appetite for power behind-the-scenes. Naturally, Rogers wouldn't have the same leeway that he had with Al Haft, and he would have to conform to an entirely new system. Toots recognized the economic opportunities and told Davis: "If you can control him, bring him in."[6]

Money was the keyword for both Rogers and Mondt. Trust between the two men was already fractured, but if anything could mend fences, it was a steady diet of hard cash. With Davis in Buddy's ear and McMahon keeping the overall peace, there was little room for selfish manipulations. Personally, Rogers had extra incentive to make the jump to Capitol. For the first time in his career, he was being properly sponsored as a serious prospective candidate for the National Wrestling Alliance world heavyweight title. Beginning with Davis and continuing with McMahon and Mondt, Buddy had consensus support behind him from day one, and it was gratifying. In a way, it was an acknowledgment of his importance in pro wrestling and recognition of his astonishing success. But campaigning for the NWA title was an arduous political task and not something that happened overnight. Rogers had to be patient. In the meantime, Capitol had come up with an ingenuous plan to push Buddy straight to the top.

First, he had to make his local debut as a full-time employee. That came on April 14, 1960, at the Capitol Arena in Washington, D.C.[7] Buddy wanted to make his initial appearance special, so he brought his handpicked opponent, Buddy Rosen, with him from Ohio. Rosen, a high-school track star from Philadelphia, was one of his protégés, and they were acutely familiar with each other's style in the ring.[8] With precision, Rogers called the match, and gave Rosen most of the offense. In fact, Rosen looked to be the better grappler and was on his way to getting a pin. At the last second, Rogers turned the tables and achieved victory. On the road that night, Davis asked the "Nature Boy" why he went to such great lengths to prop up Rosen's mat ability, and Buddy wisely replied: "You're only as tough as the guy you beat."[9] Interestingly, Buddy's match was placed mid-card underneath a tag bout featuring the Bastien Brothers and a handicap prominently starring 24-year-old Italian strongman Bruno Sammartino.[10]

Six-days later, Rogers "outclassed" Arnold Skaaland during a broadcast from Bridgeport, further establishing him on Capitol TV. This match was different than his bout with Rosen, and all of his strengths were on display. He was obviously a heel, utilizing debilitating kicks and punches, and proceeded to injure Skaaland's leg in a short time. From there, he wrapped up the match with his patented figure-four grapevine and celebrated on the way out with manager Davis by his side.[11] Like Rosen, Sweet Daddy Siki had migrated to the Northeast for bookings and appeared on the same Bridgeport show. Two other names on the program were significant, not so much to the active storylines or the draw, but for the personal history of Buddy Rogers. Jack Vansky partnered with Tony Altomare in a loss to the Bastiens, and Jim Austeri, working under a hood as the "Zebra Kid," was polished off by Siki. Incredibly, 18-years earlier, in 1942, Vansky and Austeri were Buddy's opponents in his second and third known pro matches.[12]

The imaginative idea McMahon came up with to bolster Rogers' standing was to give him a noteworthy new championship honor. Prior to his Bridgeport debut, Buddy was billed as the "reigning United States heavyweight wrestling champion," a creative distinction with a fantastical lineage. It was later alleged that his title claim was spawned by a 1950 tournament victory over Ruffy Silverstein.[13] No such event ever took place, but in the fog of wrestling, who was going to complain? Capitol touted Buddy as the best wrestler in the country, and by watching Rogers on television, he often looked it. But he was equally controversial, and there seemed to be no limit to his villainous ways. On May 4, 1960, in Bridgeport, he forced Jack Davis to submit, and then surprise-attacked the popular Chief Big Heart in the aisle leading to the ring. Fans were outraged as he smashed Big Heart in the head with a chair, opening up a forehead wound. Buddy was satisfied with his actions and left him in a pool of blood.[14]

The attack was unprovoked and senseless in the eyes of spectators, and it was just another reason why Rogers was already the most-hated wrestler in the region. The basic blueprint of his matches usually went one of two ways. He either dominated from start to finish or he portrayed the vulnerable champion on the verge of losing. For the latter, it didn't matter who his opponent was because he sold heavily for both newcomers and journeymen. Buddy cowered in the face of defeat, and the people loved it. They wanted to see him pinned. However, Rogers was far too crafty and did whatever it took to win. Many times, when he was on the verge of losing, he'd casually drape his leg across the bottom rope to save himself, causing the audience to moan in unison. His timing was perfect. Rogers would cheat, trick, and swindle his way to victory in those situations, and stagger from the ring with his title belt in his hand. But fans knew Rogers was as skilled as he was cowardly, and he won as many matches by brawling or scientific means leading to his figure-four submission finisher.

The "Buddy Rogers" wrestling persona had evolved numerous times since 1945, and in each territory he visited, he found ways to improve. He was always learning how to work smarter instead of harder, while maintaining the same results. He never gave up his heat, and his early showings in Capitol demonstrated that he was actually better than ever. And it was clear that Rogers was positioned to possibly have the most profitable year of his career by doing far less of the physical work he did previously. Matches in the Northeast were framed differently than they had been in California or Texas. The violence was tempered to a certain degree, and it was more about psychology than insane bumps. His hangman stunt, the reckless flying tackle, and other old favorites were either retired or rarely used, and Buddy adopted a saner approach to his bouts. Manipulating the emotions of the crowd was his greatest asset.

Rogers was different physically, as well. The 39-year-old still looked fit and conditioned, but he was heavier. Some of the changes he made were out of necessity and part of the natural lifespan of a pro wrestler. He just couldn't do certain moves anymore. But to preserve his top spot, he sharpened his repertoire and added more depth to the personality of his on-camera character. Based on that element alone, his brief tenure in Capitol Wrestling was already a triumph. But if an alert fan, who remembered seeing Buddy in all his glory 10 years earlier, caught the Bridgeport show and witnessed the modern "Nature Boy" in action, that person would have likely been very surprised. Rogers was playing the game in a whole new way, and considering the results to this point, he was doing everything correctly. Bobby Davis was an invaluable asset, and his ringside behavior was making crowds insane. Wise beyond his years, he knew the right buttons to push at the right time, and regularly triggered a frenzied response.

The combination of Rogers and Davis was magical at times. They turned things up a notch for TV, knowing it would impact shows down the line. For instance, during the June 15, 1960, Bridgeport telecast, Rogers put Arnold Skaaland out with his submission hold, and Davis joined him in the ring. They gloated over their fallen adversary, and Davis added a sharp kick to Skaaland's torso for good measure. The audience was appalled. Before things went any further, Bearcat Wright ran out to make the save and battered Davis mercilessly. Rogers also was socked in the melee, giving fans exactly what they wanted.[15] The Bridgeport show was broadcast in Chicago and Vince McMahon managed to cut a deal with local promoter Fred Kohler to run cooperative events in the "Windy City." The Rogers-Wright angle went over like gangbusters, and 30,275 Chicago enthusiasts paid just under $90,000 to attend a July 29 program co-headlined by the pair at Comiskey Park. Rogers won that bout in 12:40.[16]

Television from Bridgeport aired later in Washington, and McMahon was able to benefit from two creative outlets promoting his high-profile matches in the District of Columbia.[17] The Rogers versus Wright feud received the same attention and their success was undeniable. On July 18, 1960, they drew the largest audience "ever" for wrestling in Washington, a massive throng of 16,521 to Griffith Stadium, and the gate totaled $41,363.[18] It amazingly topped a landmark 1931 stadium extravaganza featuring Jim Londos and Rudy Dusek, which attracted 15,000 persons.[19] Buddy's box-office power was evident, but there was a notable aspect of his early run in Capitol. Contrary to reports of his oversized ego, Rogers displayed a willingness to be a team player, and didn't arrogantly command the spotlight. He routinely worked under the main event and accepted his role as established by McMahon. His casual attitude came as a shock, especially to those who questioned his motivations.

McMahon's close associate in New Jersey, Willie Gilzenberg, had been leery about Rogers for years. When Buddy was booking his troupe in the Northeast in 1955-'56, he approached Gilzenberg about adding Newark to his circuit, and the latter emphatically rejected the offer.[20] There was no love lost as a result. The decision to bring Rogers in was risky, and Gilzenberg expressed his misgivings in correspondence with Jack Pfefer. Particularly, he felt the "Nature Boy" had been gone "too long" to make an impact, and cast shade on billing him as the United States champion.[21] Pfefer's hatred for Buddy was beyond words, and he enjoyed negative reports about his old protégé. But after Gilzenberg started to recognize Rogers' positive effects in the territory, and realized McMahon's absolute confidence in the wrestler, he began to clash with Pfefer.[22] This was also concurrent to a larger-scale series of hostilities between Capitol and the New York office run by Kola Kwariani.

In mid-June 1960, the conflict escalated and ties were severed completely, ending Capitol's involvement at Madison Square Garden.[23] Pfefer was aligned with Kwariani against McMahon and Gilzenberg in the promotional war, and was pushing his men, Ricki Starr and the Fargo Brothers, into big money matches. He was glad to see Rogers ousted from the Garden, and would have happily taken credit for the move. While Gilzenberg sought to find harmony, pleading with Pfefer to make up with McMahon, lowdown tricks were being used to ensnare talent.[24] Bruno Sammartino, a promising up-and-comer in his second year in the business, was lured away from Capitol and Kwariani was directly to blame. McMahon was known for taking care of his employees. He spent thousands of dollars to help his aged former ring announcer Jimmy Lake, and would treat many of his grapplers to dinner at Goldie Ahearn's restaurant after shows.[25] He inspired loyalty, and in most cases, he received it back in spades.

Rogers continued to earn praise. Emmett Spillane of the *Bridgeport Telegram* acknowledged his star performance on July 27 at the City Arena, and Buddy's extracurricular actions commenced a profitable feud with Sweet Daddy Siki. He brazenly attacked his old rival from behind and bloodied him, only to get served a dose of his own medicine. Bobby Davis was beaten even worse and was assisted to the dressing room. It was an emotional rollercoaster for fans, as Siki was jumped, regained his composure to dish out punishment, and was once again thrashed by the "Nature Boy". Rogers had the last laugh. He beat up Siki and proceeded to defeat Pete Sanchez by submission.[26] Rogers and Siki wrestled across the territory through the end of the year, battling at least 14 times. At Comiskey Park in Chicago on August 19, Buddy and Eddie Graham fought Siki and Bearcat Wright to an exciting double-disqualification. More than 17,000 people paid $52,350 to witness the program.[27]

A week later, on Aug. 26-27, 1960, dignitaries of the National Wrestling Alliance gathered in Acapulco, Mexico, for the organization's annual convention. Sam Muchnick relinquished the NWA presidency after 10 consecutive terms, and Frank Tunney of Toronto was elected in his place. Muchnick remained the group's executive secretary and treasurer, and continued to book the world heavyweight champion. The sanctioned titleholder, by this juncture, was Pat O'Connor, who beat Dick Hutton for NWA recognition on January 9, 1959, in St. Louis. In addition to Muchnick, Tunney, and O'Connor, others to attend the festivities in Mexico were Fred Kohler, Leroy McGuirk, Sid Balkin, Toots Mondt and Vince McMahon. McMahon's appearance was noteworthy as he wasn't a member of the Alliance. He was willing to submit his name for membership, and those on hand took unprecedented steps to approve him.[28] For the sake of fellowship and prosperity, McMahon was admitted to the coalition.

Cunningly, McMahon was ready with an immediate suggestion. He asked his brethren to recognize Buddy Rogers as the official "NWA" United States heavyweight champion, an extraordinary request. Since its founding in 1948, the Alliance had only bestowed formal NWA sanction to three championships: the heavyweight, junior heavyweight and light heavyweight titles. Muchnick purposefully steered away from endorsing a U.S. champion seven years earlier, but the political environment was different in 1960.[29] The NWA was a shell of its former existence, broken by government interference in the mid-to-late 1950s, and McMahon's new involvement was uplifting to the organization. The best way to express gratitude was to give the Washington, D.C. promoter exactly what he wanted, and that's what the NWA did.[30] But on the back side of the decision, there was a hefty benefit for a small segment of the Alliance, including for several of the members present. It was financial in nature, of course, and Rogers was going to play a major part.

McMahon and Toots Mondt were not finished there. They also floated the idea of Rogers possibly replacing O'Connor as world heavyweight champion. It was a bold tactic in the midst of a fluid strategy, but seeing that NWA members were already eating out of their hands, they decided to advocate a push of Rogers to the very top. Why settle for the United States championship when there was an even greater honor above it? In terms of having support, Rogers was in the best position of his career, and the leaders in Acapulco were an example of that. Fred Kohler was onboard with McMahon and Mondt, while Sid Balkin of Houston was an old friend going back to the 1940s.[31] Muchnick and Tunney were well aware of his achievements at the box office, as was Leroy McGuirk, who feuded with Rogers in Oklahoma and Texas before he became wrestling's "Nature Boy." The discussions were preliminary, and a successful run as U.S. champion would go a long way to help his cause.

To commemorate receiving official sanction as U.S. champion, Rogers went to Chicago for a photo-op in Kohler's office at the Marigold Arena. He took individual promotional pictures with both Kohler and Muchnick, being presented the championship belt emblematic of the U.S. title.[32] The latter, though, was not a newly fashioned strap direct from an eminent jeweler, but a "prop" Rogers had used in Al Haft's territory dating back to at least 1953.[33] But since it was shaped like the United States, the belt was decidedly perfect for the job. That same month, an unfortunate happening occurred in Bridgeport. Rogers gained his customary victory, beating his opponent, Marvin Mercer, in rapid time. As he was busy strutting around the ring, Bobby Davis entered to add insult to injury. He walloped Mercer and probably was going to do more damage when the 600-pound Haystack Calhoun made his presence known. He threw Rogers and Davis around like "they were bags of cement," and set Davis up for his big splash.[34]

Haystack went about business as normal, but the bump proved too much for Davis. He suffered three broken vertebrae in his back and was taken to a local hospital, where he stayed for more than two weeks.[35] A feud with Calhoun was only natural for Rogers at that point, and fans in Chicago eagerly awaited their finish encounter on Sept. 16, 1960.[36] It was another humongous turnout at Comiskey Park as 26,731 paid $81,549.40 to see the live show from beginning to end. In the semifinal, Rogers defeated Calhoun in 12:02, knocking off his rotund foe with superior speed and skill.[37] By early November, Buddy became embroiled in yet another intense quarrel, this time with Johnny Valentine.[38] At the Paterson Armory on November 5, they engaged in a barnburner before a capacity house, and Rogers put his old friend over as a dangerous threat to his U.S. championship. At the conclusion, Buddy was bleeding from cuts to his face and head, and barely managed to survive with a disqualification victory.[39]

The match set a new Paterson gate record with $11,080 paid into the till, and the heat was off the charts. But shockingly, Rogers and Valentine opted to team together in Teaneck, New Jersey, and challenge the Fabulous Kangaroos for the U.S. tag team title on Nov. 19. Prior to the contest, Rogers told a reporter: "The promoters and other wrestlers convinced us to merge. They pointed out there's no reason for us to keep belting each other, pointing out it would be more successful instead for us to be the greatest combination in the world."[40] Despite their reputations as cruel customers, the two blonds earned the favor of the Teaneck crowd, and by the end of the bout, the audience was cheering hysterically for them to win. Finally, Rogers locked in his figure-four on Al Costello and forced him to submit for the third fall, and Buddy and Johnny were the new United States champions.[41]

The feelings of jubilance didn't last long.[42] In Newark on November 26, they overcame the challenge of Bearcat Wright and Sweet Daddy Siki in two of three falls, but argued after the match. Their harsh words quickly turned to fisticuffs, and it took a gaggle of special police and officials to pry them apart in the locker room. In tune with the kayfabe storyline, Valentine said: "Rogers will never stop being a showoff. He wants all the glory."[43] Peace was out the window, and so was any chance of defending their championship as a cohesive unit. In fact, Buddy walked away from the tag team title, leaving Valentine to choose Chief Big Heart as his replacement partner.[44] Valentine became a fan favorite during the angle and his popularity soared. On December 9 at the International Amphitheatre in Chicago, Buddy and Valentine battled to a 21-minute "blood splattered draw" in front of 12,011 spectators. The $35,132 gate set a new local indoor record.[45]

When the NWA gave Rogers sanction as U.S. champion, it was understood that he would represent all members across the board. Like the world champion, he would be obligated to accept bookings everywhere on the Alliance map, and fulfill dates to help support the whole organization. But after he became an official NWA champion, the "Nature Boy's" busy schedule had been skewed toward a select grouping of territories, and the preponderance of dates were in his "home" region, the Northeast. He was also satisfying bookings for Fred Kohler in Chicago and Sam Muchnick in St. Louis, with a few additional appearances elsewhere. Muchnick was aware of the problem. He sent a bulletin to the membership in December 1960, stating: "[Rogers] has met all requirements discussed in Mexico, insofar as the St. Louis, Chicago and Washington promotions are concerned, but whether we should 'tag' him as U.S. heavyweight champion, recognized by the NWA, still remains a question because of his unavailability to all members."[46]

Although Muchnick was gaining financially from the arrangement, he demonstrated an impartial tact in an effort to keep morale high. He asked the NWA membership its advice on Rogers, and what steps needed to be taken, if any at all.[47] But nothing seems to have come from it. Buddy continued with his Alliance backing and resumed his tour of preferred NWA cities. Before the end of the year, Vince McMahon emerged on top in the New York wrestling war, clearing the way for a return of his workers to Madison Square Garden. On December 23, McMahon successfully drew 11,612 to the famed arena and a gate of $31,029.[48] It was a star-studded affair headlined by Antonino Rocca and Johnny Valentine wrestling to a no-contest against the Fabulous Kangaroos. Rogers beat Haystack Calhoun and Bearcat Wright won from Eddie Graham by DQ. The upgrade in talent was welcomed by fans and McMahon's interest in future Garden shows guaranteed the kind of match-ups people really wanted to see.

Speaking of Eddie Graham, he was another fierce competitor with whom Rogers had a love-hate relationship inside the squared circle. Between July 1960 and January 1961, Graham was Buddy's main tag team partner, and they combined to have 17 contests together.[49] But in Tampa, where Graham was the lead babyface, they were avowed enemies, and fought several grueling bouts. As illustrated in their October 11 battle, Rogers and Graham were all for creative storytelling and they went the whole nine yards to give enthusiasts an emotional workout. Buddy went ahead in the first fall, using his figure-four to gain a victory. The move injured Graham's knee, and suddenly, the handicapped hero was fighting from behind with the fans cheering his every twist and turn. He won the second fall, but during the third, both men smashed into a turnbuckle at the same time. As they fell backwards, Buddy landed on top, and the referee counted to three.[50]

Graham awoke to find out that he'd lost, but rather than leave the ring, he got on top of the still-unconscious Rogers and self-administered a three-count to the satisfaction of the crowd.[51] Two things happened. Rogers retained his title belt and his aura of being unbeatable, and Graham was not only established a verifiable future champion, but was the biggest fan favorite in Tampa wrestling history. The next time they met in Tampa, on November 15, Buddy sold even more for Graham, and had the clock not run out, fans were sure their idol would have won.[52] Rogers' ring methodology was never about short-term, ego-driven victories, and that's why he gave as much to Gene Dubuque in California as he did to Graham in Florida. He was building the heat of the feud to capitalize on its box office value, and with visions of a grand payoff, he worked consistently hard to make it a reality.

Interestingly, when Rogers was on the road, he was always on the lookout for a potential fresh face to oppose, and it didn't matter if his new rival was the greenest of the greenhorns. Rogers knew he could deliver a good match. It was more about the appeal and "look" of his opponent, and the science behind their feud's development. For example, Rogers scouted an incredibly built 6-foot-4 former weightlifter named Art Thomas while in the Chicago territory in late 1960. Some weeks later, based on Buddy's glowing recommendation, Vince McMahon called Thomas and invited him to Washington, D.C. to start a run on his circuit.[53] They trained him, put him on TV in Bridgeport and Washington, and by the third week of February 1961, he was in the ring with Rogers, making money. "Sailor" Art and the "Nature Boy" had big matches in Chicago, Newark and Philadelphia, and Buddy propped Thomas up to be his apparent successor as U.S. champion.[54] But like everyone else, Thomas took the loss, and Buddy remained supreme.

At the heart of professional wrestling was violence, and Rogers was in his natural environment, punching and kicking his adversaries with a vicious flair. In St. Louis on Feb. 15, 1961, blood was shed during a TV taping, a particular rarity under the careful watch of Sam Muchnick.[55] Buddy's opponent was Navy veteran John Paul Henning of Florida, and there was no shortage of action. Outside the ring, blood was drawn from both wrestlers as Henning suffered a dislocated nose and cut above his eye. For his troubles, Buddy was slammed on onto a table, and received a slice along his right arm "from his wrist to his elbow."[56] The referee stopped the bout, declaring it a no-contest, and Rogers was stitched up by a physician.[57] St. Louis grappling aficionados packed the Kiel Auditorium for their grudge match on April 7, and a total of 12,482 people were in attendance. Rogers won another "wild" one, pinning Henning in 10:43.[58]

The income derived by Rogers was jaw-dropping and Capitol Wrestling wasn't the only entity looking at the numbers. The NWA was, as well, and its upper management was seriously considering the proposal discussed by Vince McMahon and Toots Mondt at the last convention. Money was the principal reason. Currently, the organization wasn't making enough in booking fees on the heavyweight champion to cover all the NWA's bills. In an attempt to make up for the deficiency, Muchnick imposed a $500 assessment on members, on top of the regular $100 a year for dues.[59] But it still wasn't enough. To pay Muchnick, his secretary, legal fees, and other expenses, the Alliance needed much more in its coffers than existed.[60] The enduring debate of whether to elevate a performer over a shooter had gone on for years, and the NWA always went with the latter over the former. Now, in a financial crisis, the answer was easy, and Buddy Rogers was the only real choice.

A more colorful champion was desirable to members. They wanted to utilize a wrestler they knew would boost their attendance, and in the case of Rogers, he was a guaranteed draw. Dick Hutton and Pat O'Connor were world-class wrestlers, but they were hit or miss in terms of excitement. In the right situation, a consequential money match-up was arranged, but with Rogers, his backers felt he was persistently a "must-see" attraction. Muchnick, perhaps the last holdout against a performer as titleholder, realized the benefits, and knew that a moneymaking champion would help the NWA survive. Approving Rogers wasn't a logical decision, it was an absolute necessity. On the other hand, the booking problems surrounding Buddy as U.S. champ were never really addressed. If Rogers was elevated to world champion, would he suddenly become more available to all Alliance members? At a time of desperation, that question was almost irrelevant.

Muchnick called for a special meeting of the NWA board of directors in early 1961. Beyond that, little is known about when it took place and who actually attended, but with the board made up of a majority of pro-Rogers promoters, the verdict was finalized.[61] The wheels were immediately in motion and Buddy couldn't have been more thrilled. After being ignored for so long, he was finally getting his due. As for O'Connor, he was well into his second year as Alliance king, and as an in-ring competitor, had met all expectations. His new responsibility, along with Rogers and the other parties involved, was to set the stage for the match that would see the title officially change hands. Chicago was selected as the host site, and Fred Kohler envisioned an outdoor summer spectacular at Comiskey Park.[62] Since Chicago was also O'Connor's adopted hometown, and he was the favorite headed into such a bout, his role in the build-up was very important.[63] But the real heavy lifting was the job of Rogers and Bobby Davis.

Their promotional effort started slowly in March 1961. By April, it was going full force and Bridgeport was ground zero for their TV campaign. The Bridgeport program aired in Chicago on Sunday mornings at 12:05 on the local NBC affiliate.[64] Fred Kohler did his own commercial advertising during the broadcast and hyped live events with exclusive interviews. The taped footage, which had Ray Morgan calling the shots, was packed with wall-to-wall action. O'Connor and Rogers each appeared four times on the show between March and June, and their matches highlighted their best attributes before the cameras.[65] Throughout this same period, Rogers and Davis, two of the best talkers around, were hammering O'Connor in interviews, and their attack was relentless. They demanded a world title shot and engaged in a level of verbal warfare never-before-heard in pro wrestling.[66] The way Davis talked trash was unparalleled. He made it personal, exaggerated with clever quips, and in the end, broke O'Connor down.[67]

That's how fans saw it play out. O'Connor was browbeaten into accepting a title match, and to protect his good name, he had to defend his NWA belt against Rogers. The final push toward their date at Comiskey Park occurred during the June 10 Bridgeport show, and if there ever was a reason to cheer for Buddy to get pummeled, this was it. He started by soundly trouncing Mr. Puerto Rico, only to have Sweet Daddy Siki enter the fray. Buddy then threw Siki from the ring, rendering him unable to continue, and irate fans were about to blow the top off the City Arena. O'Connor jumped into the ring to confront Rogers, and the U.S. champion sent him to the floor in a heap as well, but Pat immediately bounced back, battering Rogers and Davis, and chased the heels from the ring.[68] Back in Chicago, Kohler worked his magic, called in every favor, and had the sports media completely enraptured.

David Condon, the renowned columnist for the *Chicago Daily Tribune*, penned an article entitled, "He's the Greatest! (He Thinks)," about the "Nature Boy," and featured outrageously egotistical quotes by Rogers in his full heel mode. He put down O'Connor, talked himself up as the best wrestler in the business, and again gave people a thousand reasons to hate him.[69] The exposure was immeasurable for a wrestling show, and sales were going to surpass the Lou Thesz-Baron Michele Leone affair from 1952 for the largest gate in wrestling history.[70] In fact, Kohler anticipated a crowd of 52,000 and a gate of over $150,000.[71] The true numbers were closer to 38,000 and $125,000, and on Friday, June 30, 1961, history was made on the south side of Chicago.[72]

Appearing unfazed by the size and scope of the spectacle, Rogers was utterly confident as he strolled to the ring.[73] With Bobby Davis by his side and a stadium packed with enthusiastic followers of the sport he loved, Buddy was locked into the moment and prepared to have the best match of his career. The significance of the world heavyweight champion facing off against the United States champion wasn't lost on the audience, and the weeks of promotion had everyone on edge. All of Buddy's flamboyance and conceit was bounding through the heads of onlookers, and a decisive victory for O'Connor was all the latter's fans wanted. But for the percentage of the crowd supporting Rogers and his villainous style, they knew that he was surely headed for glory. And after 8:30 of the first fall, Buddy was on his way. He had pinned O'Connor following a high knee to the head and had taken a lead in the match.

It took six-minutes for O'Connor to even things up with a pinfall. But Rogers was cool entering the third, strutting around the ring, and pointing to his head to demonstrate his quick wit after slyly outsmarting his opponent. O'Connor took the advantage, though, and Buddy resorted to placing his foot along the bottom rope to stop a pin count, also begging off to display his weakness. All seemed to be over for the "Nature Boy" as they went into the final sequence. O'Connor attempted a dropkick and landed in the ropes, injuring his midsection. Rogers maneuvered toward him and applied a body press, securing a three-count and the victory. Buddy Rogers was the new National Wrestling Alliance world heavyweight champion. A moment later, he spoke into the microphone in the center of the ring, and declared: "To a nicer guy, it couldn't happen!"[74]

ENDNOTES - CHAPTER 14

[1] The Bridgeport show, promoted locally by Joe Smith, debut on Feb. 11, 1959 on WNEW-TV.

[2] McMahon's problems included a loss of key talent. Between December 1959 and March 1960, several of his key main event stars departed, like Ricki Starr, Amazing Zuma, and Johnny Valentine.

[3] The suit was filed by Alta Contos and Edward A. Contos Jr. *Washington, D.C. Evening Star*, Feb. 27, 1960, p. 10.

[4] Interview with Bobby Davis, Sept. 18, 2018. Also Interview with Bobby Davis, Buddy Rogers Tribute Tape.

[5] Interview with Bobby Davis, Sept. 21, 2018.

[6] Ibid.

[7] It was Buddy's first Washington, D.C. appearance since Aug. 30, 1956. A newspaper report incorrectly claimed that it was his "first appearance at the arena in several months." *Washington, D.C. Evening Star*, April 13, 1960, p. 62.

[8] Biographical information on Rosen appeared in *Pat Schnee's International Set*, Winter 57-58, p. 27.

[9] Interview with Bobby Davis, May 7, 2019. Davis also spoke about the Rogers-Rosen match during his interview on the Buddy Rogers Tribute Tape.

[10] In the non-televised main event, Sammartino beat Skull Murphy and Pat Kelly. Lou and Red Bastien defeated Swede Hanson and Zebra Kid in the tag bout. *Washington, D.C., Evening Star*, April 15, 1960, p. 14.

[11] *Bridgeport Post*, April 21, 1960, p. 34, *Bridgeport Telegram*, April 21, 1960, p. 47. Buddy's finisher was often called the "figure-eight" submission by the Bridgeport press.

[12] On July 27, 1942 in Atlantic City, Rogers (as Dutch Rohde) beat Vansky. The next day in Baltimore, he defeated Jim Austeri. According to existing records, Vansky also had the distinction of wrestling Bruno Sammartino in his professional debut in 1959.

[13] Rogers interview with Tom McDaid. *Wrestling Revue*, September 1983, p. 41.

[14] *Bridgeport Telegram*, May 5, 1960, p. 49.

[15] *Bridgeport Telegram*, June 16, 1960, p. 54.

[16] The gate was $89,675. Sportswriter Frank Mastro noted that fans were disappointed by the short match. The other part of the double feature was NWA World champion Pat O'Connor versus Yukon Eric. *Chicago Daily Tribune*, July 30, 1960, p. 40.

[17] Video tape of the Bridgeport show aired on Tuesday nights at 7:30 on channel 5 in Washington, D.C. *Baltimore Sun*, July 3, 1960, p. A8.

[18] Wright beat Rogers by disqualification. *Washington Evening Star*, July 19, 1960, p. 12.

[19] Londos defeated Dusek before the record audience. *Washington Evening Star*, Aug. 13, 1931, p. D1.

[20] Willie Gilzenberg letter to Jack Pfefer dated May 31, 1960, Jack Pfefer Collection, Joyce Sports Research Collection, Hesburgh Library, University of Notre Dame, Notre Dame, Indiana.

[21] Gilzenberg also complained about the lack of "discipline" in the territory. Letter from Willie Gilzenberg to Jack Pfefer dated May 9, 1960, Jack Pfefer Collection, Joyce Sports Research Collection, Hesburgh Library, University of Notre Dame, Notre Dame, Indiana.

[22] Letters from Willie Gilzenberg to Jack Pfefer from May and June 1960, Jack Pfefer Collection, Joyce Sports Research Collection, Hesburgh Library, University of Notre Dame, Notre Dame, Indiana.

[23] McMahon's workers appeared at the Garden on June 4, 1960, but were gone from the next event, on July 16, 1960. Rogers wrestled on the May 21 and June 4 Garden programs.

[24] Letter from Willie Gilzenberg to Jack Pfefer dated June 27, 1960, Jack Pfefer Collection, Joyce Sports Research Collection, Hesburgh Library, University of Notre Dame, Notre Dame, Indiana.

[25] According to Gilzenberg, McMahon had spent over $6,000 to assist Lake by 1960. Willie Gilzenberg letter to Jack Pfefer dated July 26, 1960. He was still helping Lake in 1965, having established the "Jimmy Lake Trust Fund." *Washington, D.C. Evening Star*, April 1, 1965, p. 22.

[25] *Bridgeport Telegram*, July 28, 1960, p. 50.

[27] 17,206 saw the show. *Chicago Daily Tribune*, Aug. 20, 1960, p. F2.

[28] McMahon was admitted into the NWA without having submitted an application and his initiation dues, which was customary.

[29] This incident occurred in 1953 when Verne Gagne was United States champion. Fred Kohler sanctioned that title, but the NWA refused to officially acknowledge it as an Alliance championship.

[30] NWA Bulletin #2, Dec. 1, 1960, p. 3.

[31] Balkin worked in the office of Houston promoter, Morris Sigel, who didn't make the trip to Mexico.

[32] The Rogers and Kohler photo appeared in *Wrestling Revue*, Spring 1961, p. 28. The Rogers and Muchnick picture appeared in a special Buddy Rogers Promotional Brochure, Circa. 1961.

[33] This U.S.-shaped belt was previously used to represent the West Virginia championship, the American Tag Team Title, and then the Eastern crown. Among the others to wear it, besides Rogers, were the Great Scott and Fritz Von Goering. Correspondence with Dan Westbrook, May 2020.

[34] The incident was shown on TV. Karol Krauser also got into the brawl on the side of Calhoun. *Bridgeport Post*, Aug. 18, 1960, p. 37.

[35] Davis was rushed to St. Vincent's Hospital. Ibid. He reportedly received 21 shots of morphine in 18 days.

[36] Calhoun had previously worked as "Country Boy Calhoun." He feuded with Rogers in 1958 in California, Ohio, and Arizona.

[37] *Chicago Daily Tribune*, Sept. 17, 1960, p. 36.

[38] Rogers and Valentine hadn't feuded since the summer of summer of 1956 in Texas. Their last known singles match occurred on Aug. 10, 1956 in Houston.

[39] Valentine accidentally hit referee Tommy Geldhauser in 20:30. *Paterson Morning Call*, Nov. 7, 1960, p. 20 and *Paterson Evening News*, Nov. 7, 1960, p. 56.

[40] *Paterson Evening News*, Nov. 17, 1960, p. 33.

[41] *Paterson Evening News*, Nov. 21, 1960, p. 38.

[42] Rogers and Valentine were advertised to wrestle at the Philadelphia Arena on Nov. 24, 1960, but no results were found in the *Philadelphia Inquirer* or the *Philadelphia Daily News*.

[43] *Paterson Evening News*, Nov. 28, 1960, p. 29.

[44] In Washington on December 1, Rogers beat Chief Big Heart in a preliminary bout. He continued to beat on his foe after the match, and Valentine came to Big Heart's rescue. Later, in the main event, Rogers and Valentine drew. *Washington Evening Star*, Dec. 2, 1960, p. B7. In a later interview, Rogers claimed that Valentine handed over his half of the title. "Valentine and myself would have been a perfect team," he said. *Wrestling Revue*, September 1983, p. 41.

[45] *Chicago Daily Tribune*, Dec. 10, 1960, p. F4.

46 NWA Bulletin #2, Dec. 1, 1960, p. 3.
47 Ibid.
48 McMahon initially planned a show for December 12, but it was snowed out. *New York Daily News*, Dec. 24, 1960, p. 26.
49 According to the latest version of the Buddy Rogers Record Book maintained by Haruo Yamaguchi, May 2020. Graham, for a time, was also managed by Bobby Davis. *Bridgeport Telegram*, July 14, 1960, p. 49.
50 *Tampa Tribune*, Oct. 12, 1960, p. 30.
51 Ibid.
52 It was a 60-minute draw, tied one-fall apiece. *Tampa Tribune*, Nov. 16, 1960, p. 3C.
53 *Capital Times*, July 18, 1961, p. 16.
54 Thomas talked about Rogers in *Wrestling Archive Project*, Volume II, p. 312-314.
55 The program was taped at the Chase Hotel in St. Louis.
56 *Flat River Daily Journal*, March 31, 1961, p. 6.
57 Rogers received "five stitches." *Wrestling*, St. Louis Wrestling Club Program, April 1, 1961, p. 1. The match aired on television on March 4, 1961. The day following the TV taping, Rogers wrestled and beat Count Corroni in Milwaukee. *Milwaukee Journal Sentinel*, Feb. 17, 1961, p. 38. Rogers had been booked to wrestle "Fred Von Hess," but that match was changed after a series of no shows on the card.
58 *St. Louis Globe-Democrat*, April 8, 1961, p. 9.
59 NWA Bulletin #2, Dec. 1, 1960, p. 1.
60 The ongoing legal battle between the NWA and Sonny Myers in Iowa was a major cause for concern, and was specifically cited by Muchnick in bulletins.
61 The board consisted of Fred Kohler, Toots Mondt, Morris Sigel, Jim Crockett, Sam Muchnick, and Frank Tunney. NWA Bulletin #3, Dec. 28, 1961 (sic).
62 Kohler rented Comiskey Park for $5,000. *Wrestling Revue*, Spring 1961, p. 29.
63 O'Connor resided in the Chicago suburb of Glenview.
64 "Heavyweight Wrestling" aired at 12:05 on channel 5, WNBQ.
65 O'Connor was slated for a fifth appearance, but no showed on March 4, 1961. *Bridgeport Post*, March 5, 1961, p. D2.
66 Rogers claimed he had "waited close to three years for a crack at O'Connor." *Boxing and Wrestling*, April 1962, p. 46.
67 Davis went into detail about his verbal onslaught on O'Connor during the Buddy Rogers Tribute Tape.
68 *Bridgeport Post*, June 11, 1961, p. D1.
69 The article claimed Rogers was 33 years old, but Buddy was really 40 at the time. *Chicago Daily Tribune*, June 25, 1961, p. B30.
70 On May 21, 1952, Thesz and Leone drew a $103,277 gate in Hollywood, California, setting an industry record.
71 Promoter Fred Kohler took credit for the success of Rogers-O'Connor, saying: "I realized the possibilities of a match between these two about six months ago. I worked up to this climax through repetitious exposure. I permitted O'Connor and Rogers to dispose of one less-skilled opponent after another." *Chicago Sun-Times*, June 28, 1961.
72 *Chicago Sun-Times*, July 1, 1961, p. 51. Enhancing the numbers for publicity purposes, Kohler's Chicago publication stated that attendance was 38,622 and the gate was $141,345. Wrestling Life, August 1961, p. 1. However, a 1972 letter from the Illinois State Athletic Board confirmed that the gross was actually $128,071.74. Brian Last/The Arcadian Vanguard Wrestling News Archive. This show held the national gate record until August 27, 1971 when Fred Blassie and John Tolos drew a gate of $142,158 in Los Angeles. It also held the national attendance record until WrestleMania III shattered it on March 29, 1987 with a purported crowd of 93,173.
73 Rogers told a reporter that he was "always nervous before each bout in my whole career." *Gong Magazine*, June 1979.
74 *Wrestling Classics* ESPN TV Series Footage of Match, *A Buddy Rogers Tribute* by J Michael Kenyon, *Buddy Rogers Record Book*, Circa 2005, p. 26-28.

Chapter 15
An Arduous Journey

The exhaustive publicity surrounding the grand title match in Chicago did a wonderful job of painting Buddy Rogers as the haughty and contemptuous wrestler he was. Of course, the "Nature Boy" played a significant role in advancing that side of his public persona, and the stunning draw at Comiskey Park was the result. The new NWA champion had long enjoyed a vacillating relationship with fans, and his contradictory ring style had a lot to do with it. "The champ is both hated by fans and opponents, and respected by the very same fans and opponents who fall into the aforementioned category," a Columbus, Ohio pundit noted eight years earlier.[1] When Buddy was performing at his highest level outside the ring, he was verbose, boastful, and irritating. Antagonizing crowds was his specialty, and few were better at getting underneath the skin of spectators.

"I know deep within they can't help but admire me," Rogers told Lou Sahadi in a kayfabe interview, "I know that. They love to hate me. They'll boo me and squeal at me, but down deep they love me. I crave the public booing me. That's what gives me my drive, my incentive. That's another reason I emphasize my cockiness. I give 'em my cocky strut and I love to hear them yell. They really holler. They light a fire under my feet. Sure, I'm cocky. I know it. When you're great, you can't help being cocky. You're good and you know it. I know I am the best. I mastered my business and it's evident at the box office. I am to wrestling what penicillin is to a sick man. I am [the] Mr. Box Office of wrestling."[2] There was no end to his pompousness, and it made for great content. For that reason, reporters couldn't get enough of him, and readers were thoroughly entertained.

At arenas, Buddy took a lot of verbal abuse for his outrageous behavior, and he knew it came with the territory. But sometimes things took a dangerous turn. In Washington, he was sliced "across his shoulder blades" by an attacker, receiving a wound that left a "nasty scar."[3] He was sucker-punched by a rabid ringsider at Madison Square Garden following a main event battle with Vittorio Apollo, and could have easily been seriously injured.[4] Another incident occurred at Kansas City years earlier, and he often mentioned it as being one of his most troublesome. "I beat Otto Kuss, a local hero," he explained in 1950. "As I was leaving the ring, I stepped on Kuss' face, accidentally-like. Then I had to start ducking chairs. They broke $500 worth of them and tore down the fire hose to play water on me. [It] took five police squads to get me out of the hall."[5] Near riots had been customary throughout his tenure in wrestling, and he relied heavily on police protection, both to the ring and back to the dressing room.

Financially speaking, the hazards of being wrestling's greatest heel were worth the risk. "Every time they boo me, I put another dollar in the bank," Rogers bragged to *Wrestling Revue* magazine. "In my opinion, the fans are a bunch of morons. They've shown their respect for me by stabbing me with knives, picks and hat pins. Look at these scars. I've never hurt anybody but a wrestler – I never laid my hands on a fan. All I do is give them the world's best wrestling, and send them home feeling five years younger. For this they hate me."[6]

Buddy's interview with *Wrestling Revue* after winning the world title was completely in character, and he talked his standard amount of trash. The interviewer asked him about being the "first villain" to hold the world championship, and Buddy replied, "I couldn't care less."[7] It should be pointed out that while the National Wrestling Alliance had never recognized a predominantly rule-breaking titleholder, the National Wrestling Association did in the 1940s with Bill Longson.

Rogers was much more subdued in a second interview, this one with a correspondent for his New York-based fan club.[8] Evelyn Lesh caught up with him backstage at Forbes Field in Pittsburgh and "found him to be very charming and quite easy to talk to." Without his usual sarcasm, he answered all of her questions, and seemed to perk up with a sense of pride when she asked him how he felt to win the NWA championship. "I've reached the peak," he said. "It's what I've been working for all my professional career. It's a wonderful feeling. Now the problem is to maintain my standing and hold on to the belt as long as I can."[9]

In addition to taking possession of the physical world title belt in the match with Pat O'Connor, Rogers collected the biggest single payday of his entire life, estimated by one publication to be upwards of $17,000.[10] The ramifications of becoming the heavyweight champion of the world were immediate, and the rush was on for promoters to lock in his first available dates.

The Capitol Wrestling circuit was advantageous for Rogers. He was able to spend more time in Camden with his mother, and the trip home to Columbus was less than a two-hour flight. Even though his previous recognition as United States champion had called for a wider disbursement of appearances for NWA members across the country, his schedule never really changed. Sam Muchnick, who coordinated Buddy's bookings with Vince McMahon, sent him to seven sanctioned territories during the first six months of 1961.[11] The other 11 were ignored. The powers-that-be were able to get away with the disproportionate arrangement to that juncture, but now that Rogers held the world heavyweight crown, the expansion of his schedule was mandatory. If Muchnick failed to book Rogers as he had previous champions, he risked a fracture and potential mutiny of Alliance members, and the organization he worked so hard to build would likely be headed for dissolution.

Visits by the NWA titleholder meant big money for promoters, and O'Connor, Dick Hutton, and Lou Thesz had been tireless workhorses for the organization. In theory, Rogers was supposed to emulate his predecessors in that regard, and in July 1961, his first month as champion, he reached six different territories. Lou Thesz had typically visited four or five regions a month when he was kingpin, and on paper, Rogers appeared to be right on track. But there was a certifiable disparity in the number of dates he worked per territory. Instead of Buddy wrestling three, maybe four matches per area, he worked 12 dates in the Northeast, four in Texas, two each in Charlotte and St. Louis, and one in Chicago and Pittsburgh.[12] It was very unusual for the champ to spend so much time in his base region, and it was simply a continuation of the booking patterns seen when he was the U.S. titleholder. The only difference was his six-day stint in Texas for Morris Sigel.[13]

The Houston office was considered priority. In fact, of the six territories Buddy visited, five of them were controlled by the same NWA board of directors that voted him to the title.[14] The sixth was the Northeast, of which Pittsburgh's Toots Mondt had an interest.[15] Rogers looked to be giving back to the men who pushed him to the belt, and that was wrestling politics at its finest. Being on the road was always a challenge, and Buddy managed to navigate things to the best of his ability. But his new schedule and the pressures of the world championship were intense, and Buddy had to adjust day-by-day. Exactly one week after he beat O'Connor, he was in Pittsburgh to face Capitol's favorite son, Antonino Rocca. Since feuding in Montreal in 1960, they had met a half dozen times in places like Baltimore and Paterson, New Jersey, and their May 1960 encounter at Madison Square Garden drew nearly 18,000 people.[16] Most of their bouts ended inconclusively, a purposeful tactic to prolong the lifespan of their rivalry.[17]

On June 24, 1961, Rogers and Rocca locked up in a high-profile contest at the Philadelphia Arena, and Buddy's "roughness" earned him a disqualification before 7,200 fans.[18] Expectations for their Forbes Field skirmish in Pittsburgh on July 7 were in the 20,000 range, but a mere 12,510 turned out to see the two competitors collide mid-ring in the third fall of an aggressive match.[19] Rogers revived first and won by countout.[20] A short time later, Buddy, Bobby Davis, and Reggie (Crusher) Lisowski created a raucous scene in Pittsburgh, resulting in all three being suspended by the Pennsylvania State Athletic Commission for "conduct detrimental to the best interest of the sport."[21] A hearing was held on July 22 at the State office building in Pittsburgh and the parties involved were issued a "substantial fine" for their actions.[22] The suspension was lifted, paving the way for Rogers and Lisowski to headline the Aug. 4 show at Forbes Field.[23] That particular program drew 14,415 and Rogers was victorious by DQ.[24]

Going back to April and May 1961, there was a concerted effort by Vince McMahon to elevate the tag team of Rogers and "Wildcat" Bob Orton, a 6-foot-2 ruffian from Kansas City.[25] The duo was featured in six television squash matches taped in Washington, D.C. and Bridgeport, building toward main event bouts at Madison Square Garden and Griffith Stadium. The latter, in addition to the aforementioned shows at Comiskey Park and Forbes Field, was part of a massive summer stadium series brokered by Capitol Wrestling, and Rogers was the star attraction at each of the eight events staged in Chicago, Pittsburgh, and Washington.[26] Collectively, the eight shows drew 129,205 people, and the total gate was slightly under $400,000.[27] At the Garden, the financial figures were equally impressive, as four programs headlined by the "Nature Boy" over the summer drew $184,840.[28] His primary adversaries were Antonino Rocca, Johnny Valentine, and the Fabulous Kangaroos.

Of the four Garden main events, Rogers teamed with Orton for three of them, and their natural chemistry as partners roused the ire of New York enthusiasts like few others in history. McMahon had a winning combination on his hands, and his longtime strategy to highlight tag team wrestling at the Garden continued to be successful. After all, local fans loved the nonstop chaos those type of matches brought. But not everyone was thrilled by the idea of promoting Rogers in tag team scraps instead of straight championship contests. Sam Muchnick abhorred it, and advised McMahon several times by letter to avoid the practice. Apparently, Buddy also disagreed with the concept, but there was little he could do about it.[29] The pressure had to come from the headquarters of the NWA. Muchnick tried his best to sway McMahon, but to no avail. "No champion before has been in tag matches and I most agree that this certainly does not dignify the title," Muchnick declared.[30]

Several things were at play here. For one, McMahon and his cohorts were demonstrating their rebelliousness against the rules of the NWA. It was almost as if there was one set of standards for Capitol Wrestling, and a completely different rulebook for the remainder of the Alliance. McMahon believed tag team action was the key to a high turnout at the Garden, and he wasn't going to be influenced otherwise. On top of that, there was an important money issue. If McMahon didn't book Buddy into a solo contest, he didn't have to pay him the required champion's percentage, which at the Garden would have been considerable. And not only would Rogers miss out on the added income, but the Alliance would, as well. The standard terms were 15 per cent of the net to the titleholder, with 11 per cent going to the champion and four to the NWA.[31] Muchnick and the Alliance relied on that percentage to pay his personal salary as executive secretary, the salary of his assistant, legal fees incurred by the organization, and a $150 monthly stipend to the destitute Ed (Strangler) Lewis.

Muchnick's gripes against tag team matches represented his larger frustrations on the NWA's inability to derive income from Garden shows. He knew that money would have been a big boost to the Alliance's treasury, and had been part of the allure of making Rogers champion in the first place. As far as Muchnick was concerned, there were two other problems with the way McMahon was managing Rogers and his end of the NWA world title deal. They were booking Buddy into small Northeastern towns for relatively no money and refusing to send fees due the Alliance in a timely manner.[32] They were only a couple months into Buddy's reign, but the problems were already adding up. Muchnick hoped to resolve the disagreements at the NWA's annual convention in Toronto, held from Aug. 24-27, 1961.[33] Over the course of meetings lasting 47 hours, a plethora of topics were debated, including the need to dwindle down the number of heavyweight title claimants to a single, undisputed champion.[34]

"Rogers is the real champion," Muchnick announced. "There can't be any doubt about that. He won the title fairly and squarely from Pat O'Connor in Chicago last June. All the others who claim the title have only token recognition within their own territories. However, in my opinion, the way to clear this whole thing up once and for all would be for Rogers to meet these so-called sectional champions to prove his superiority, which I have no doubt he will do."³⁵ Rogers, also in attendance at the conference, agreed to wrestle his rival claimants in a series of elimination matches. In an article for *Wrestling Revue*, Stanley Weston specifically mentioned Verne Gagne and Fred Blassie, the AWA and WWA champions, respectively, as potential opponents in that kind of endeavor. With regard to other business, Pat O'Connor was named the NWA United States titleholder and Fred Kohler replaced Frank Tunney as Alliance president.³⁶

Money was always a point of interest at the NWA convention, and members decided to amend how Rogers and the organization were paid per the champion's appearances. The promoter who used Rogers would continue to be responsible for setting aside 15 per cent of the net for each booking, but from that point forward, Buddy would receive 11.25 per cent, whereas 3.75 would go the NWA for administrative costs.³⁷ The adjustment was beneficial to Rogers, as he could use the additional quarter toward his booking fees due to Capitol Wrestling, while keeping most of his 11 per cent. Another aspect of being the NWA champion was something called an "appearance guarantee."³⁸ The appearance guarantee was a large sum of money that the champion was responsible for depositing into escrow to protect the Alliance from a possible double-cross. For instance, Pat O'Connor was asked to put up $10,000, and had he ever decided to go off script, or refused to drop the championship when the NWA ordered him to do so, he would have forfeited his money to the NWA.³⁹

Buddy Rogers was a unique case. His reputation was not as pure as the champions that had preceded him, and after he won the title, insiders speculated that he had been asked to put up four times the amount of money that O'Connor had.⁴⁰ A 1961 deposit of $10,000, in today's money was an astronomical $86,036, but $40,000 was over $340,000.⁴¹ Such a financial demand was unheard of in professional wrestling. Buddy's manager at the time, Bobby Davis, later revealed that he posted $20,000 of his own money to cover the mandatory performance bond when Rogers won the championship.⁴² Since the NWA never stipulated a larger escrow amount for Buddy, despite the rumors, $10,000 went to the St. Louis office of Muchnick, and the other half was kept by Capitol as an in-house performance guarantee.⁴³ It was unusual, but it seemed as if McMahon himself wanted another layer of protection in place to ensure Rogers did what he was told.⁴⁴

In the aftermath of the 1961 convention, there was a customary surge of unity and brotherhood amongst NWA members, but many of the core problems were unsettled. Checks from Capitol Wrestling to St. Louis continued to run late, Rogers remained a fixture in the occasional tag team match, and non-essential promoters were snubbed when they asked for dates on the world champion. Heartland promoter George Simpson told a journalist that, due to the "Nature Boy's" busy schedule, it was "extremely difficult" to bring him to Kansas City.⁴⁵ Dory Funk, co-owner of the West Texas territory, spoke about Rogers from a kayfabe wrestling point of view, saying: "I've wrestled him twice and have defeated him both times. It was before he held the title and he will try and avoid another match with me now that he holds the title."⁴⁶ Rogers last wrestled in Amarillo in 1958 and, the truth was, he had no desire to go back. In fact, he would never meet Funk in the ring again.

The optics of the situation was strange to say the least. Karl Sarpolis, Amarillo's promoter of record, was elected the 1st vice-president of the NWA at the Toronto conference, and it was assumed that he would have a measure of influence within the structure of the union. His position alone was consequential enough to maneuver obstacles in his favor, as other NWA officers had done in the past, but Sarpolis couldn't make it happen. Rogers simply evaded the Amarillo region completely. In September 1961, Buddy appeared in eight territories for the top tier of the organization, and did television in Pittsburgh, Bridgeport, Washington, St. Louis, Montreal, and Evansville. Strangely enough, Jim Barnett, the promoter in Evansville, wasn't even a member of the NWA, although he was in the midst of trying to obtain admittance to the Alliance. His application was tied up by politics, but with Muchnick nervous about possible government interference, he authorized bookings to Barnett to keep tensions low.[47]

But that didn't make sense in conventional terms. The 1st vice-president of the NWA couldn't get a booking on Rogers, but Jim Barnett, a non-member, could? Even George Simpson in Kansas City would get three dates on Buddy in late 1961 and early '62.[48] In addition, Rogers turned up in Memphis and Nashville for matchmaker Nick Gulas.[49] Looking at existing records, he wrestled at least 68 matches in 88 days between September and November, leaving less than three weeks for travel time, recuperation, and to see family.[50] He was regularly doing battle with the best in the business, and giving his all from bell-to-bell. He wrestled fan-favorites Johnny Valentine, Dory Dixon, Art Thomas, and Billy Watson, while also brawling with heels Fritz Von Erich, The Sheik, and Killer Kowalski. Cowboy Bob Ellis was a star hero in St. Louis, having won a series of TV bouts building towards a title match with Rogers. On Oct. 6, 1961, Buddy beat Ellis with his figure-four in front of 11,562 spectators at the Kiel Auditorium.[51]

An important fact should be observed at this point in the timeline. Coinciding with Vince McMahon's utilization of Rogers in tag team matches at Madison Square Garden was the New York Athletic Commission statute recognizing pro wrestling matches strictly as exhibitions. Championship contests were explicitly outlawed. Nevertheless, Buddy was frequently acknowledged as the titleholder by the New York press. Al Buck of the *New York Post* actually, and accurately, referred to him as the "National Wrestling Alliance" champion in a 1961 column, and noted that advertising for an upcoming match was for Buddy's "jewel belt," instead of being for any designated title.[52] The Garden was packed to the rafters for the huge Rogers-Antonino Rocca clash on November 13, and it was only Buddy's third singles bout at that venue all year. With 20,253 excitable patrons in the audience, Rogers beat the popular Argentinean in three falls, the third by DQ."[53]

Generally, Rogers was in good physical condition. When afforded the time, he enjoyed five-mile swims to improve his stamina, and like most other eminent wrestlers, he had his own personal philosophies on health and fitness. "I feel that every man's body is his empire," he told a reporter, "and he ought to take care of it. Too many men abuse their bodies. A wrestler becomes more mature between 30 and 40, providing he keeps in good condition, and should be good until he's 45."[54] Rogers claimed to be 36 years old, but he actually was approaching his 41st birthday, and he felt every bit of his age from the heavy workload. For weeks, he had worn a protective pad on his right elbow, and he dealt with regular soreness from an earlier injury.[55] As the year progressed, the pain in his left elbow became substantially worse, and it was believed to have been caused by bone chips. However, he gamely fought through the issue and continued to meet all of his responsibilities with the same gusto he had always shown.

His pain increased measurably by October, and frightening new symptoms exacerbated his private anguish. Not only did he have numbness in his left hand, but he was having a tough time completely opening his palm.[56] The onslaught of injuries had Rogers worried about his future. He knew he wouldn't be able to continue with things as they were, and he needed to give serious consideration to surgery. He also knew, however, that if that option failed, his time in wrestling was likely over. After consulting with Stanley L. Brown, a leading orthopedic surgeon in Camden, Buddy decided to go forward with a procedure, which called for the transplant of his ulnar nerve.[57] It was a delicate operation, and upon speaking with Sam Muchnick, the latter expressed a need for Rogers to give him a week's notice before taking a leave of absence. Rogers understood the strain it put on every promoter with whom he had upcoming dates, and rather than give the NWA just a one-week advance, he told Muchnick that he would work another month before going under the knife.[58]

Rogers went hard during those next few weeks, and in his last two matches before his surgery, he faced off with Johnny Valentine in St. Louis on November 24, and Bearcat Wright on November 27 in Washington. Interestingly, both of those matches would be used in wrestling storylines and cited as the cause of Buddy's arm injury and sudden convalescence.[59] By blaming Valentine and Wright, promoters had ready-made feuds when the champion returned.[60] On November 29 at West Jersey Hospital in Camden, Rogers underwent a successful surgery to repair his arm damage.[61] As amazing as it sounds, that was the first major operation of Buddy's 19-year career. He had endured smaller procedures, including work to fix his nose and teeth, and a tonsillectomy, but each time, he bounced back in relatively short order. His elbow surgery however, was a much-more serious operation, and it was critical that he give it the proper amount of rest, which doctors anticipated to be somewhere between three weeks and three months.[62]

It was reported that Rogers recuperated in Florida, and if true, that wouldn't have been a surprise.[63] Florida, particularly the southeast part of the state, had always been a refuge for the "Nature Boy," and the brilliant sunshine was good for his mental state. The entire ordeal had been exhausting and Buddy wanted to get back to doing what he did best, and that was making the box office cash register ring.[64] On Dec. 30, 1961, about four weeks into his recovery, Buddy made a non-scheduled appearance in Bridgeport and "flattened" Pete Sanchez in a TV match.[65] He slowly eased back into condition and participated in at least 14 bouts in January 1962. On January 22, he gained some revenge from both Johnny Valentine and Bearcat Wright in a tag team match with Bob Orton at Madison Square Garden. Fans bought every ticket in the house, and a record 20,777 saw the "Blond Bombshells" defeat Valentine and Wright in two of three falls. The gate was in excess of $63,000.[66]

The groundwork had been perfectly laid, and the sellout was a beautiful reward for the expert on-camera handling of Buddy's injury. Everyone performed flawlessly, and the carefully manipulated storytelling resulted in a historical achievement at the Garden. Rogers and Valentine were getting insane mileage out of their feud. A few days after their Garden battle, they met again in Chicago and drew 10,279 people to the Amphitheatre. Buddy won this time, as well, taking the first and third falls.[67] In Philadelphia, Rogers resumed his perpetual warfare with Antonino Rocca and captured a victory there by disqualification. A reported 6,800 fans braved a snowstorm to witness the must-see action, and Buddy gave them their money's worth. "We would have doubled the crowd if not for the elements," he told Stan Hochman of the *Philadelphia Daily News* after the match. "If you gave us newspaper space, we'd outdraw baseball in this town."[68] Buddy, in his classic form, strutted around the dressing room as he spoke.

The wrestling public in Pittsburgh was just as enthusiastic as the fans in Philadelphia as 7,139 die-hard aficionados ventured out in a blizzard to see Rogers and The Crusher batter each other at the Auditorium on March 5, 1962. The weather was absolutely brutal, and Buddy struggled to reach the venue himself, arriving well after the show had already begun.[69] In the ring, Buddy and his opponent stepped it up for the benefit of the animated crowd and wrestled to an exciting draw.[70] One specific hazard for promoters was the constant replication of certain match-ups, and with Rogers, his handlers had to be wary of overdoing his feuds with Rocca, Valentine, the Crusher, and Art Thomas. On the positive side, Rogers, while known for working within his standard routines, was smart enough to avoid repeating finishes against rivals in their second or third bouts in the same towns. He craftily changed things up to keep the intensity and attention of the fans, without squandering the heat they had worked so hard to build.[71]

That didn't mean Buddy wouldn't repeat a specially designed finish with the same opponent in different locations on the circuit because it happened all the time. For example, during matches with Art Thomas, they did a spot in which the popular "Sailor" would hoist Rogers up into a bearhug, and the latter would scream in agony. Then, thinking he had won, Thomas would prematurely release the champion and gesture toward the audience in a shared celebration. But the contest wasn't over. Rogers quickly maneuvered into a position of attack and caught Thomas unawares for a quick pinfall, as those in attendance stood in shock.[72] It was a variant of his old "pat on the back" trick, and it was an effective way to antagonize fans. And if promoters wanted to send the crowd home happy, they usually booked a match after Buddy's controversial affair, and gave the hero the final sendoff with a jubilant victory.

In terms of fresh rivalries, Rogers had a memorable clash with a talented 5-foot-9 strongman in Houston on Feb. 16, 1962. His foe was Dory Dixon of Jamaica, a former weightlifter turned grappler, who was the reigning Texas titleholder. Rogers and Dixon had wrestled before, but this was the match area fans were waiting for.[73] Using his high knee to the noggin, Buddy won the initial fall, but lost the second. In the third, Dixon's injured right leg buckled while attempting a body slam, and he was pinned.[74] Following the grueling contest, Rogers was nothing but complimentary toward Dixon, and called him a "great wrestler."[75] On the opposite end of the height scale, the 6-foot-10 Shohei Baba from Japan was the tallest competitor he had ever faced, and the two battled nearly a dozen times over the course of 1962.[76] Baba's extraordinary stature was a challenge to Rogers, but similar to his in-ring adjustments against the enormous Haystacks Calhoun, Buddy exploited the size differential and got the best from his opponent.

Vince McMahon's promotional machine went into high gear to advance a feud between Rogers and Cowboy Bob Ellis, and they fought a trio of big matches at Madison Square Garden. The hype was more than successful. All three bouts were sold out with a combined attendance of 56,477 and a total gate of $177,261. Buddy's figure-four leglock played a huge role in the series, and although Ellis was unable to break the famous hold, he did reverse it, shifting the pain back onto the "Nature Boy."[77] It occurred during their May 25, 1962, encounter, and the slick maneuver had spectators jumping for joy as it appeared that the champion was about to submit. Both wrestlers were ultimately counted out, though, and Rogers narrowly survived with his title intact.[78] Rogers won the other two matches, held on March 19 and June 22, capturing the finale when Ellis was unable to continue because of an injured knee.[79]

Capitol Wrestling also had top attractions Edouard Carpentier and Bobo Brazil in line for a number of important money matches beginning in May and June 1962. Carpentier, known as the "Flying Frenchman," was exceptionally popular for his lightning speed and acrobatic style.[80] Brazil had comparable support from audiences and was admired for his great strength. Originally from Arkansas, Bobo grew up in Western Michigan, and played baseball before making the transition to wrestling in 1949. In 1955-'56, Rogers and Brazil fought ten times in the Ohio territory, and Buddy realized the marketability of his ring adversary.[81] There was a special characteristic to their ring chemistry and they were predestined to make a lot of cash together. Flash forward to 1962, and the timing for a lengthy Rogers-Brazil feud was perfect. McMahon and his compatriots were chomping at the bit for explosive box office receipts from Washington, D.C. to Chicago.

The popularity of Brazil and other black stars, such as Art Thomas and Bearcat Wright, were instrumental to the turnout in many of Capitol's major cities. Officials shrewdly mapped out a booking strategy for each wrestler when it came time for a run against Rogers, and they knew they were setting the table for potentially massive returns. The promotion did it exactly right with Brazil and the payoff came on July 17 at D.C. Stadium in Washington.[82] Record attendance and gate figures — 20,959 fans and a gate of more than $45,000 — were established for the show headlined by Rogers and Brazil. The result of the main event wasn't overly satisfying as Rogers and Brazil battled to a draw, but McMahon wanted to milk more from their conflict over a longer period of time.[83] The match ended in a near riot and Rogers required police protection away from the ring.[84] For Bobo's followers, it was a close call, and they firmly believed he was going to be the next world champ.

"You know how many places Rogers and Bobo could draw big?" Willie Gilzenberg asked in a letter to Jack Pfefer. "In every city in the United States where there is a colored population. I would be willing to wager that Rogers and Bobo could draw at least $150,000 in Yankee Stadium or at the

Polo Grounds."85 On Aug. 18, Gilzenberg staged a rematch between Rogers and Brazil at the Newark Armory, and it was a complete sellout. Fans were on edge, expecting something big to happen, and behind the scenes, those involved agreed to run a unique finish to set up an even larger financial climax to their feud, perhaps outdoors in either New York or New Jersey. The angle they used was the accidental foul, and at the 18-minute mark, Rogers was on the mat, clutching his mid-section in pain. Referee Tom Geldhauser proceeded to count him out and declare Brazil the victor. Bobo, being the sportsman that he was, refused to accept the title since he didn't pin Rogers, but that wasn't the end of the story.86

The following day, the Newark paper announced that Brazil was the world heavyweight champion "whether he [wanted] to be or not."87 Seeds of confusion and doubt as to who the rightful titleholder was were sown, and fans wanted to believe Bobo was more than just the uncrowned wrestling king.88 News of his victory over Rogers was spread far and wide, giving additional credence to his status, and the anticipation of a final battle to settle the controversy was substantial in Northeastern cities. But before another record-setting house could be achieved, and the title situation cleared up, an unscripted event was going to take Buddy Rogers by surprise. And that one moment was going to change everything.

ENDNOTES - CHAPTER 15

[1] *Haft Nelson*, Oct. 22, 1953, p. 6.
[2] *Boxing and Wrestling*, April 1962, p. 46, 49.
[3] *Washington, D.C. Evening Star*, July 11, 1961, p. 16.
[4] Rogers went after his attacker and landed a punch in return. He had wrestled Apollo to a double countout on March 27, 1961. *Long Island Star Journal*, March 28, 1961, p. 14.
[5] *Akron Beacon Journal*, June 12, 1950, p. 17. This story, said to be Buddy's "most terrifying experience," was told in a slightly different manner in *TV Guide*, Nov. 13, 1953, p. 7. Notably, the only Rogers-Kuss match in Kansas City on record happened on Nov. 30, 1948. There was no mention of this incident in the *Kansas City Times*, Dec. 1, 1948, p. 21.
[6] *Wrestling Revue*, December 1961, p. 21.
[7] Rogers also said that he didn't consider himself a "villain." *Wrestling Revue*, December 1961, p. 18.
[8] Buddy's fan club was headed by Georgiann Mastis (Makropoulos) of Astoria, New York.
[9] *Nature Boy's News*, August 1962, p. 5.
[10] *Boxing and Wrestling*, April 1962, p. 46. Rogers was quoted as saying that he was going to receive "about 17 or 18 per cent of the gate." *Chicago Daily News*, June 30, 1961, p. 33.
[11] The territories included Florida, Charlotte, Toronto, St. Louis, Chicago, Pittsburgh, and the Northeast.
[12] Two of the St. Louis dates (July 12 and July 15) were television appearances and the dates may have been incorrect. Buddy Rogers Record Book by Haruo Yamaguchi, May 2020.
[13] He wrestled in Houston, Beaumont, Fort Worth, Dallas, and San Antonio. He hadn't wrestled in Dallas since March 1957 and Houston since March 1958.
[14] The only NWA Board member that didn't receive a visit in July 1961 was Frank Tunney in Toronto.
[15] Mondt had his own NWA membership headquartered in Pittsburgh.
[16] The show had a gate of $53,000. *New York Daily News*, May 22, 1960, p. 132.
[17] They wrestled to a no contest at the Garden, a draw in Paterson on June 25, 1960, and a no decision in Baltimore on Dec. 27, 1960.
[18] Rogers hit the referee, Tom Finley. *Philadelphia Evening Bulletin*, June 25, 1961, p. S4.

[19] *Pittsburgh Post-Gazette*, July 7, 1961, p. 21.
[20] The gate was $40,418. *Pittsburgh Post-Gazette*, July 8, 1961, p. 11.
[21] *Pittsburgh Post-Gazette*, July 18, 1961, p. 19. The incident reportedly occurred on Saturday, July 15, 1961. *Pittsburgh Post-Gazette*, July 22, 1961, p. 10. It's likely it happened at the WIIC Studios during the live telecast. The New York State Athletic Commission and the National Wrestling Association also suspended Rogers and Crusher. Although the New York Commission suspended Rogers in concordance with Pennsylvania, Buddy was allowed to wrestle in Commack on July 19.
[22] *Pittsburgh Post-Gazette*, July 23, 1961, p. 40.
[23] The suspension was lifted on July 27. New York State Athletic Commission Records, Aug. 18, 1961, p. 7.
[24] The Crusher, regularly a heel, was the crowd's favorite versus Rogers. *Pittsburgh Post-Gazette*, Aug. 5, 1961, p. 9.
[25] *Wrestling Revue* called them a "new and sensational tag team combination." *Wrestling Revue*, Summer 1961, p. 25.
[26] There were three shows in both Chicago and Washington, and two in Pittsburgh. There was another stadium effort in Charlotte on July 17, 1961, but the attendance for that program is not known.
[27] Included was a rematch between Rogers and O'Connor at Comiskey Park on Sept. 1, 1961, which drew 20,015 and a gate of $63,326. Rogers won again. *Chicago Tribune*, Sept. 2, 1961, p. F2.
[28] *Wrestling in the Garden: The Battle for New York* by Scott Teal and J Michael Kenyon (2017), p. 158.
[29] Letter from Sam Muchnick to Vince McMahon dated Sept. 28, 1961, Sam Muchnick Collection. In a magazine article, Rogers admitted to hating tag team matches, saying: "I was always against them. However, when they teamed me up with Bob Orton, my feelings changed. I feel very fortunate having Bob as my partner. He has so much to offer in the way of talent." *Boxing and Wrestling*, April 1962, p. 53. In later interviews, he spoke about tag team wrestling, including *Wrestling Revue*, September 1983, *Wrestling's Main Event*, September 1983, and *New Wave Wrestling*, April 1992.
[30] Ibid.
[31] Rogers liked to tell the press that he, as the champion, received 25 per cent, while his opponents got 17 ½. *Philadelphia Daily News*, Jan. 20, 1962, p. 35.
[32] Correspondence between Sam Muchnick and Vince McMahon, 1961-1962, Sam Muchnick Collection.
[33] The convention was held at the King Edward Sheraton Hotel.
[34] *Wrestling Revue*, December 1961, p. 56-59.
[35] Ibid.
[36] Rogers had relinquished the U.S. Title when he became World champion.
[37] Letter from Sam Muchnick to Mike London dated June 5, 1962, Sam Muchnick Collection.
[38] It was also called a "performance bond," "appearance forfeit," or "belt deposit."
[39] Certified Public Accountant for the NWA Statement of Operations, Aug. 31, 1960, Sam Muchnick Collection.
[40] Letter from Willie Gilzenberg to Jack Pfefer dated Sept. 18, 1961, Jack Pfefer Collection, Joyce Sports Research Collection, Hesburgh Library, University of Notre Dame, Notre Dame, Indiana.
[41] Inflation calculator, April 2020. www.data.bls.gov.
[42] Interview with Bobby Davis, Aug. 25, 2019.
[43] The NWA's $10,000 appearance guarantee for Rogers was confirmed in a letter between Sam Muchnick and Vince McMahon dated Dec. 28, 1962, Sam Muchnick Collection.
[44] Gilzenberg speculated that Rogers had put up money to "behave himself." Letter from Willie Gilzenberg to Jack Pfefer dated Sept. 18, 1961.
[45] *Kansas City Times*, Sept. 15, 1961, p. 41.
[46] *Canyon News*, Sept. 7, 1961, p. 2.

⁴⁷ The Department of Justice was being kept in the loop on the NWA membership requests of Jim Barnett and Johnny Doyle in 1961.

⁴⁸ He wrestled in Kansas City, KS on November 2 and Nov. 23, 1961, and again on Feb. 1, 1962.

⁴⁹ Rogers beat Doug Gilbert on November 20 in Memphis and Mike Paidousis on November 21 in Nashville.

⁵⁰ Not counting the end of November 1961, when he was out of commission.

⁵¹ Ellis won the first fall, but Rogers took the second with his figure-four. Ellis was unable to continue due to a leg injury. *St. Louis Globe-Democrat*, Oct. 7-8, 1961, p. 4E.

⁵² *New York Post*, July 24, 1961, p. 41.

⁵³ The gate was $61,995.50. *New York Daily News*, Nov. 14, 1961, p. 59. Years later, Rogers recalled a win over Rocca, and said: "'After I beat him, I thought to myself, 'You dumb s.o.b., you just beat a Latin wrestler, and now you've got to walk through 17,000 Latin fans to get to the locker room.' It took 30 cops but we made it." *Charlotte Observer*, Aug. 18, 1979, p. 7A, 9A. It's not known which match versus Rocca he was referring to, but the sentiment was the same with regard to this specific bout at the Garden.

⁵⁴ *Wrestling*, St. Louis Wrestling Club Program, Nov. 18, 1961, p. 3.

⁵⁵ Earlier in the year, he suffered a cut on his arm during about with John Paul Henning. He later claimed to have been stabbed by a fan in a contest versus Lorenzo Parente. He said he needed 19 stitches. *Boxing and Wrestling*, April 1962, p. 50. Rogers wore the elbow pad during his famous bout with O'Connor in June 1961. He was still wearing it in early 1962, and used it to his advantage during matches. *Boxing Illustrated, Wrestling News*, June 1962, p. 50-54.

⁵⁶ *Wrestling Life*, January 1963, p. 9-16.

⁵⁷ Rogers said that his elbow was broken in two places. *Camden Courier-Post*, July 30, 1963, p. 21. Brown, of Camden's West Jersey Hospital, had over 30 years experience.

⁵⁸ Letter from Sam Muchnick to Harry Light dated Oct. 30, 1961, Sam Muchnick Collection.

⁵⁹ Rogers "re-injured" his left elbow during his Nov. 24, 1961 bout with Johnny Valentine in St. Louis. *Wrestling*, St. Louis Wrestling Club Program, March 31, 1962, p. 3. Rogers beat Valentine by DQ. *St. Louis Globe-Democrat*, Nov. 25-26, 1961, p. 3C. Rogers claimed to have suffered a broken elbow versus Johnny Valentine in Washington, D.C. Rogers interview with Ray Tennenbaum, February 1985. His match with Wright was stopped because of his injured arm after three minutes. *Washington, D.C. Evening Star*, Nov. 28, 1961, p. A21.

⁶⁰ Willie Gilzenberg wrote that Wright got the "credit" for breaking Rogers' arm. Letter from Willie Gilzenberg to Jack Pfefer dated Dec. 4, 1961, Jack Pfefer Collection, Joyce Sports Research Collection, Hesburgh Library, University of Notre Dame, Notre Dame, Indiana.

⁶¹ Ibid. Also *Wrestling*, St. Louis Wrestling Club Program, March 31, 1962, p. 3.

⁶² Letter from Willie Gilzenberg to Jack Pfefer dated Nov. 20, 1961, Jack Pfefer Collection, Joyce Sports Research Collection, Hesburgh Library, University of Notre Dame, Notre Dame, Indiana.

⁶³ Rogers had his arm in a sling. *Wrestling Life*, January 1963, p. 9-16.

⁶⁴ A writer for *Wrestling Life* stated that the situation was "one of the darkest hours in Rogers' life to date." *Wrestling Life*, January 1963, p. 9-16.

⁶⁵ *Bridgeport Post*, Dec. 31, 1961, p. D1. Sanchez's original opponent was advertised to be Steve Stanlee.

⁶⁶ *New York Daily News*, Jan. 23, 1962, p. 42.

⁶⁷ *Chicago Daily Tribune*, Jan. 27, 1962, p. F3.

⁶⁸ *Philadelphia Daily News*, Jan. 20, 1962, p. 35.

⁶⁹ It was said that Rogers needed nine hours to travel 160 miles in the bad weather. A number of other wrestlers failed to appear. Letter from Willie Gilzenberg to Jack Pfefer dated March 10, 1962, Jack Pfefer Collection, Joyce Sports Research Collection, Hesburgh Library, University of Notre Dame, Notre Dame, Indiana. More than 10,000 fans were expected for this show. *Pittsburgh Post-Gazette*, March 5, 1962, p. 24.

⁷⁰ The gate was $22,335.30. *Pittsburgh Post-Gazette*, March 6, 1962, p. 20.

⁷¹ Rogers also refrained from using his better stunts and gimmicks on television, which would have reduced the effectiveness at live events.

[72] Two known examples of this occurred in Chicago on July 29, 1961 and in Albuquerque on June 11, 1962. *Chicago Daily Tribune*, July 30, 1961, p. B5 and *Albuquerque Journal*, June 12, 1962, p. 13.
[73] Rogers and Dixon had wrestled at least three times before beginning in July 1961.
[74] *Boxing Illustrated, Wrestling News*, June 1962, p. 50-54.
[75] *Kingston Daily Gleaner*, May 29, 1962, p. 12.
[76] Between March 1962 and November 1962, Rogers wrestled Baba at least nine times.
[77] The *New York Daily News* called the move, the "patented figure 14." *New York Daily News*, March 20, 1962, p. 50.
[78] Match description by wrestling historian Michael Tereshko, Facebook, Oct. 9, 2018.
[79] *New York Daily News*, June 23, 1962, p. 29.
[80] Rogers and Carpentier had several big matches in Montreal in 1962, and also headlined a Comiskey Park program in Chicago on July 27. Rogers won in three falls in front of 18,010. The gate was $55,719. *Chicago Daily Tribune*, July 28, 1962, p. F5.
[81] Rogers and Brazil also had one match in Los Angeles on June 29, 1955, which they drew.
[82] The show was originally scheduled for Monday, July 16, 1962, but was rained out. The postponement didn't damper the enthusiasm of fans.
[83] *Washington, D.C. Evening Star*, July 18, 1962, p. B9.
[84] *Wrestling World*, November 1962, p. 68.
[85] Letter from Willie Gilzenberg to Jack Pfefer dated July 21, 1962, *Buddie Rogers and The Art of "Sequencing"* by Max W. Jacobs, p. 17.
[86] The match lasted 18:20 and the attendance was 6,112. *Newark Sunday News*, Aug. 19, 1962, p. S2. In an interview, Brazil was quoted as saying: "If I didn't pin his shoulders, I don't want the title." *Bristol Courier and Levittown Times*, Sept. 13, 1962, p. 26.
[87] *Newark Sunday News*, Aug. 19, 1962, p. S2.
[88] One newspaper on Long Island, in promoting a show at the Long Island Arena, billed Brazil as the "newly crowned world's mat champion." Unsourced newspaper, Sept. 19, 1962.

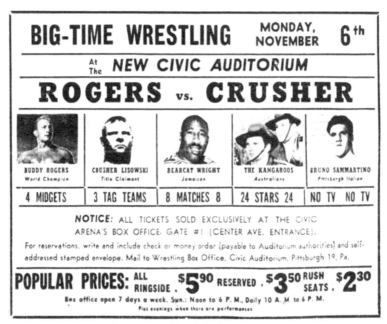

Pittsburgh, Pennsylvania: Monday, Nov. 6, 1961

Chapter 16
A Champion on the Ropes

The life of a traveling world heavyweight wrestling champion was a mixed bag. On the plus side of things, the perks were fantastic, the first of which was a drastic increase in personal revenue. Money flowed like a fine wine, and because of the great demand, the titleholder was never at a loss for his next booking. Everything was well-arranged with appearances set in stone going months into the future. It was an unusually consistent environment in terms of moneymaking in the paradoxical realm of professional wrestling. The champion was guaranteed to generate an ample income based on his expansive and essential travels. Wherever he went, he was highlighted at the top of the card and featured as the ultimate superstar of superstars, a distinction that all fans recognized regardless of his individual popularity. Buddy Rogers relished in his financial prosperity and thrived on performing before tens of thousands at the largest venues on the wrestling circuit.

Being champion was a way of life and Rogers embraced every aspect of it. The constant attention was consuming, and it didn't matter if he was walking into an arena or through an airport, all eyes turned his way. Buddy looked like a movie star – his blond ducktail hairstyle was perfectly combed, his suit impeccable, and when dealing with the public, he put his best foot forward. He signed autographs, shook hands, and happily took the time to speak with fans. The VIP treatment he received in towns both big and small was enthralling, and depending on his audience, Buddy navigated in and out of kayfabe. During interviews, he usually went full heel to promote upcoming shows, but when the cameras went off, people found him to be down to earth, friendly, and sociable. Carl Funk, a correspondent for *Boxing and Wrestling* magazine, saw the more affable side of Rogers six years earlier, and wrote that he was "amazed at the polite and poised gentleman ... with his gracious manner and soft voice."[1]

"Nature Boy Buddy Rogers, who generally portrays the villain in his pro mat bouts, is one of the friendliest guys you could meet outside the ropes," said George Kirchner of the *Lancaster New Era*.[2] By the early 1960s, many people were anxious to join a fan club dedicated to Rogers because they appreciated his athletic ability, even though they hated his methods. One enthusiast, upon meeting him, declared: "Outside of the ring, Buddy is the greatest. Once you meet him, you can't help liking him."[3] Who could believe that the same guy who ranted and raved so freely could also be so likeable? Of all the journalists Rogers dealt with during his active career, no one played to his "in character" strengths more than David Condon of the *Chicago Daily Tribune*, whose column, "In the Wake of the News," was instrumental in Buddy's upsurge at the box office in the "Windy City." But, at the same time,

Rogers enjoyed a personal camaraderie with Condon, and the latter was afforded a rare opportunity to see the man behind the gimmick.[4]

When it was time to promote an upcoming event at the Amphitheatre or Comiskey Park, Condon was relentless in his negative description of the "Nature Boy." He colorfully painted Rogers as a "sneaky creep," a "crybaby," and a "nasty spoilsport."[5] His "He's the Greatest! (He Thinks)" article in advance of the Rogers-Pat O'Connor NWA world title match in 1961 was legendary, and put Buddy over as perhaps the most egotistical heel in grappling history.[6] In his column, the ever-talented Condon had license to do a little storytelling with regard to wrestling, and was encouraged to do so by the Chicago office, as well as Rogers himself. After all, his column was selling a lot of tickets. On occasion, Condon stepped away from the mat madness to acknowledge Buddy's warmer side. In March 1962, he wrote that Rogers attended a Holy Name Society meeting where he was named Man of the Year. "If there is a more popular champion than Rogers in America, you will have to show me," Condon wrote.[7]

In addition, he noted that Rogers not only refused the $500 appearance fee, but donated $100 out of his own pocket to an organizational fund. Buddy was said to have been a guest at Condon's home and the godfather to one of his children, but both items were creatively scripted, as confirmed by his daughter, Barbara Condon Marrs, in 2019.[8] In total, the Rogers-Condon friendship was valuable on a personal and professional level, and promoter Fred Kohler loved the publicity.[9] The overall atmosphere in Chicago was electric and Rogers made the most of his time there. He visited ritzy restaurants along the Magnificent Mile, then danced the night away at a fashionable nightspot such as the Playboy Club on Walton Street. In April 1962, Herb Lyon, in his "Tower Ticker" column in the *Chicago Tribune*, reported that Rogers had partied at the Rumpus Room and called him, "A real champagne champ."[10] He epitomized the "work hard, play hard" mentality.

The sacrifice for making astronomical money as the champion was a fierce road schedule, and his itinerary was mind-numbing at times. In May 1962, Rogers wrestled approximately 24 matches in five territories, including a six-day run in Texas the first week of the month.[11] He made TV in Washington on May 10, returned to Houston the next day for a Friday offering for Morris Sigel, and then went back east to Bridgeport for a television program on Saturday, May 12.[12] The following weekend, he did two shots on Saturday – the first a matinee in Sunnyside, Queens, New York, and a night show in Philadelphia.[13] On May 26, the day after his punishing second contest with Bob Ellis at Madison Square Garden, he wrestled, and won, two bouts in Bridgeport, one on TV versus Paul Jones, and a dark match against Arnold Skaaland.[14] Altogether, Rogers worked predominantly in the Northeast, and aside from his trip to the Houston territory, he went to Chicago, St. Louis, and Montreal.

The month of June was one of the busiest of Buddy's career with at least 25 appearances in seven NWA regions. On June 10, he wrestled to a double-count-out with Bobo Brazil at the Akron Armory, and then boarded a plane headed to Albuquerque, New Mexico.[15] The jaunt was his first to the Southwestern United States as champion. At the Civic Auditorium on June 11, he beat "Sailor" Art Thomas in three falls before a "near capacity crowd."[16]

Quickly turning around, he ventured 2,000 miles in the other direction to Bridgeport for a match the next day. A week later, Buddy deviated from his normal schedule once again and trekked to the Pacific Northwest for matches in Seattle and Portland. Rogers had been wrestling for 20 years and had never toured that part of the country prior to June 18 and 19. That trip, combined with his recent excursion to Albuquerque, displayed his willingness to support the non-essential wing of the NWA, a collection of dues-paying members who had previously been ignored.

Bob Verlin of *Boxing Illustrated, Wrestling News* magazine, felt Buddy's travels were an effort to prove he was a "fighting champion."[17] But it was more about politics and settling the nerves of tense Alliance promoters. While in the Northwest, Rogers exemplified the real role of the traveling NWA kingpin, which was to bolster the local office by putting over their talent without actually conceding a match. In Seattle at the World's Fair Arena, he battled Luther Lindsay, an extraordinary talent from Virginia.[18] Lindsay was a three-time former Pacific Northwest champion and a top babyface for booking agent Don Owen. He was being groomed for a fourth title reign and won a 12-man tournament on May 22 to earn a shot at Rogers.[19] During their bout, the first two falls were split, and Buddy was selling everything Lindsay had to offer. When it appeared as if fans were about to see a new champion crowned, Lindsay missed a flying tackle and flew out of the ring. Rogers was barely conscious on the mat, seconds from defeat, and Lindsay was knocked out on the floor, where he was counted out.[20]

To the audience, Lindsay was a hero, despite his loss, and his near-win of the world championship boosted his reputation and credibility.[21] Rogers was seen as a sniveling coward, and as he hobbled from the ring area holding his prized NWA belt, fans let him know how much they hated him. In Portland, the premise and result was the same, but portrayed a little differently. Facing Billy White Wolf, Buddy scored the initial fall, but dropped the second by submission to White Wolf's Indian deathlock. He again seemed to be on the cusp of losing, and White Wolf went through the motions, rousing the crowd as he went for his final offensive push. Rogers caught him off guard and twice managed to send him from the ring. The second time, White Wolf didn't beat the referee's count, and the champion retained his title.[22] People may not have been satisfied by the result, but they were definitely enthusiastic about the efforts of their local stars.

In July and August 1962, Rogers had roughly 50 matches in 12 territories.[23] That included two trips to Texas, one to Florida, and an extraordinary stop in Vancouver on July 30 which drew 13,000 spectators to Empire Stadium.[24] The traveling was becoming harder and harder for Rogers, and his body was showing signs of breaking down. His physical well-being was a significant concern, but there were additional stress factors mounting, as well. The internal politics of the National Wrestling Alliance was changing, and a segment of the group was trying to mend fences and bring members back together. This pressure was directed at Capitol Wrestling and Fred Kohler, with Sam Muchnick in the middle being squeezed by both sides. Whereas money was prioritized the year before, members wanted to eliminate favoritism and streamline booking of the world heavyweight championship, placing all promoters on equal footing.

Obviously, the call to have Rogers appear for every member at an even greater frequency would have a negative financial impact on Vince McMahon. As it was, the head of Capitol Wrestling was already compromising a lot. By the NWA's convention on Aug. 25-26, he had only used Buddy in the Northeast six times that month, a drop from 11 the month prior. The truth was, his cities were more populated and presented a far better chance to make good money than a majority of the towns on the NWA circuit. Having Rogers in Des Moines, Dubuque, Corpus Christi and Lake Charles were necessary to keep the harmony, but wasteful of dates that could have been better served in the Northeast. Now, NWA members wanted to expand Buddy's scheduling to increase the number of secondary towns he worked. For the sake of the Alliance, it made sense, but for McMahon, and especially Rogers, it was a disastrous idea.

Buddy's road schedule was extremely tiresome. His personal life suffered as a result, and he later recalled an incident between himself and his wife, Terry. "I remember the day I came home after being on the road for almost a month," he said. "I grabbed her in my arms and kissed her. She was as cold as ice, but her eyes blazed and her voice filled with anger. 'So you finally decided to come home. Well, you didn't have to bother. I forgot what you looked like.' I tried to kiss her again, but she pulled away and stalked from the room. She went straight to our bedroom and locked the door. I had to sleep in the guest room."[25] With the Alliance pressing for Rogers to travel more than he already was, things were going to get progressively harder, and that had McMahon thinking about alternative plans.

McMahon's membership in the NWA was paper-thin. After a series of disagreements with Sam Muchnick in October 1961, he abruptly resigned from the Alliance.[26] He remained cordial with fellow promoters, and ultimately withdrew his resignation, but his actions symbolized his indifference toward the union. On one hand, membership had its privileges, and there were positives to Rogers wearing the "NWA" belt, but the benefits were in decline and McMahon had to weigh his options. He also needed to consider what things were going to look like in his region after the NWA forced Rogers to drop the championship. There was no way he would have the same kind of influence on the next titleholder as he had with Rogers, and he would be stuck waiting in line for an appearance like everyone else. That just wouldn't work. Nevertheless, McMahon continued to play ball with his promotional brethren, and at the 1962 convention, he was elected the 2nd vice-president of the NWA.[27]

Replacing Fred Kohler as NWA president was "Doc" Karl Sarpolis of West Texas, who was elevated from his 1st vice-president role over the previous term. Sarpolis, it could be remembered, hadn't received a single booking on Rogers since he won the world championship, and things were noticeably unchanged. In fact, he had billed Gene Kiniski as a claimant to the world title in the Amarillo territory going back to March 1962, demonstrating his independence in the face of perceived NWA mismanagement. Sarpolis planned to usher in a new administration with new goals, and from a unity standpoint, getting the belt off Rogers took priority over any other matter. Capitol's recent unilateral decision to give Bobo Brazil a victory over Rogers in Newark was another bone of contention as the NWA had not approved splitting the title as it had with Leo Nomellini in 1955 and Edouard Carpentier in 1957. It was a move pulled off without higher approval and was widely condemned.

For the 14 months Buddy wore the world heavyweight title belt, he brought a prestige to the championship measured by box office success, and not solely individual athletic skill. He was the performer the NWA board of directors had hoped he would be, but instead of drawing praise for his technical abilities, he was hissed at by audiences for using illegal tactics and receiving outside help. Earlier in Buddy's career, he was lauded by sportswriters and non-insiders for his prowess. *Sports Pictorial Review*, a New York-based publication, claimed in 1948 that he reminded "old-timers" of William Muldoon, the 19th century Greco-Roman great.[28] Two years later, an overzealous pundit wrote: "Buddy has a perfect physique and an ability to wrestle that is a combination of Frank Gotch, Earl Caddock, Ed 'Strangler' Lewis and Jim Londos all rolled into one."[29] The exaggeration was comical, and sounded like something Rogers might have said in his most grandiose of moments.

At other times, creative publicists tried to beef up his resume by giving him fake credentials. A Midwestern newspaper stated that Rogers was a former AAU amateur wrestling champion, while the *Montreal Daily Star* reported that he grappled at the University of Pennsylvania.[30] In 1961, shortly before Buddy's match with Pat O'Connor, an original detail was added to his life story, which up to that point had never been printed. David Condon, ironically or not, was the writer behind the revelation, and quoted Rogers as he talked about his time as a carnival wrestler, taking on all comers, when he was 15 years old. He provided unique insight into the trials of a "strong-boy" facing off with 300-pound miners, and the tricks they employed to swindle money.[31] The story was altogether fascinating, but peculiar when one studied the career of Rogers and examined previous interviews and biographical works. The legitimacy of being a carnival wrestler, versed in shooting and hooking opponents, would have been a pillar of his background going back to his pro debut. That is, if the claim was true.

A review of more than 15 biographical sketches on Rogers between 1942 and 1961, printed in various publications, found no mention of his experience as a carnival grappler.[32] The entire tale appeared to be fiction, and seemed to be a personal account more attributable to Buddy's trainer Fred Grobmier than an event from his own history. Historians have long searched for even an inkling of supporting evidence to back up Rogers' claims. In 2004, noted researcher J Michael Kenyon wrote that the then "19-million plus pages" of a particular online newspaper archive had zero mentions of the carnival Rogers said he worked for.[33] Sixteen years later, there are more than 600 million pages of archived newspapers online, and still, there is no substantiation of Buddy's statements. The one thing that seems to ring true is that Rogers, perhaps with NWA support, tried to strengthen his background and reputation prior to winning the world heavyweight title. He may have thought he needed stronger qualification if he was going to add his name to the likes of Lou Thesz, Dick Hutton, and Pat O'Connor.

From the stories they had read, fans might have believed Buddy was a skilled legitimate wrestler, but his contemporaries knew better. Over his two decades in the business, he had wrestled hundreds of rivals, and his peers, especially those with genuine mat knowledge, were wise to his limitations. They knew what he could do and what he couldn't, but at the same time, they gave him room to work his gimmick. That's what people wanted to see. Authentic wrestling didn't interest Rogers, and he avoided training sessions in the gym to focus on cardio exercise, specifically swimming. He would rather spend a day at the beach than grind out a workout on a gymnasium mat with a shooter, even if it would have proved beneficial.[34] That perspective bothered the segment of wrestlers who *did* put in the time to learn how to shoot and defend themselves. They judged him by his actual grappling knowledge, while promoters judged him by his box office success.

The two aspects were not equally valuable in professional wrestling. The latter was much more important. Spectators didn't pay to see wrestling's shooters in genuine matches. They yearned for excitement and entertaining personalities. Generally, fans in those days weren't interested in who was legitimately tough behind-the-scenes. It just didn't matter. But for certain wrestlers, it was always important. They were annoyed that Buddy's push didn't match his aptitude, and others were just plain jealous. But comparing *anyone* to Thesz, Hutton and O'Connor, the top one percent of the industry, was silly. Only a handful of wrestlers were even close to physically measuring up. Rogers had fashioned a successful career without having to follow their same path, and in that respect, he was a trailblazer. Talented performance-based wrestlers were world championship material, despite the alleged evil connotations, and his personal achievements were eye-opening.

Regarding his toughness, Buddy was a military veteran and a former policeman. He made it through boot camp and faced down violence on the streets of Camden.[35] In the worked environment of the squared circle, he participated in many brutally physical blood matches and his brawling ability was well above average. However, his heel character purposely made him look weak, as if he was running from the might of the hero, and always cheating to gain an advantage. That was the image he conveyed, and individuals not entirely smart to the business believed that was the true Buddy Rogers. But the act and the real man were completely different. That being said, he still wasn't a premier shooter, and there was room for concern if someone wanted to test him in the ring. Since he was the NWA champion, a lot was riding on the line, and both the Alliance and Capitol Wrestling wanted to avoid a double-cross at any cost.

In 1962, McMahon arranged for Rogers to have protection on the road by securing the services of 52-year-old Fred Atkins, one of the most hard-nosed, tough guys in the industry. Atkins, originally from New Zealand, began his wrestling career in 1934. He had recently mentored Sailor Art Thomas and Shohei (Giant) Baba on behalf of Capitol Wrestling, and as a "policeman" for Rogers, he watched his back and ensured that nothing irregular occurred. Atkins accompanied Rogers to his adopted hometown of Columbus several times in June and July 1962, in what should have been routine visits. But there was turmoil in Ohio, and Buddy's relationship with Al Haft was on the brink. Haft was nursing a private grievance toward Rogers for the way he abandoned his promotion in 1960, and by early 1962, his promotion was falling apart. He made a deal with McMahon for Capitol Wrestling to supply him with talent, which included appearances by Rogers and Antonino Rocca.[36]

After a few shows in Columbus, Cincinnati, and Dayton, the relationship quickly soured, and Haft continued to struggle.[37] He had lost a majority of his top wrestlers, and to his chagrin, a couple of them, Big Bill Miller and Karl Gotch, were now working for his rivals. The pair had joined the expanding operations of Jim Barnett and Johnny Doyle, a promotional troupe which steamrolled into Columbus in the summer of 1962 with programs at Jet Stadium.[38] Facing mounting pressure and unable to compete with superior star-caliber wrestlers, Haft was forced to mend fences with McMahon to import recognizable attractions. It all circled back to the drawing power of Buddy Rogers, who remained popular in Columbus, and Haft needed him to sell tickets.[39]

On Thursday, Aug. 30, Rogers wrestled Bruno Sammartino at Maple Leaf Gardens in Toronto and drew a house of nearly 14,000. The champion was victorious in 12:31 when his Italian foe was unable to continue following a missed dropkick. Rogers, Bobby Davis, and Fred Atkins traveled 427 miles from Toronto to Columbus for a card at the Fairgrounds Coliseum the next evening. Interestingly, Buddy was booked against Johnny Barend, his friend and tag team partner. In Washington, D.C. on July 5, Rogers and Barend won the United States tag championship from Johnny Valentine and Bob Ellis, and they were still champions at the time of the Columbus match-up.[40] Buddy was surrounded by his manager and his policeman, and had an ally as an opponent in a friendly town. Never in a million years did he expect anything to go wrong. But in the locker room that Aug. 31, as he prepared for his main event contest and discussed business with Al Haft, he was confronted by Bill Miller and Karl Gotch, the two wrestlers that had deserted Haft's group for the opposition.[41] Neither man had any involvement whatsoever with the show, and their presence at the Coliseum was startling.

Outside the dressing room, just moments before, Davis and Atkins had been escorted away by uniformed security officers in what appeared to be a planned and coordinated event.[42] "It's a mystery to me," Rogers later explained. "I was in my room when [Miller and Gotch] walked in, and said they had come to make a challenge. Before I could ask them what challenge, one grabbed me from behind, the other started hammering me in front. They dragged me over to the door of the room, jammed my left arm in, and then began smashing the door against it. Obviously, they were trying to break my arm, but before they could do that, I got free, but fell, and they gave me the boots. My arm was very badly bruised."[43] In an article in *Big Time Wrestling*, Buddy specifically identified Gotch as being the wrestler who "struck him" on his side, while Miller hit him from behind.[44] He was rushed to University Hospital and treated for a possible broken arm and a concussion.

The real-world assault on the heavyweight champion was scandalous. No NWA champion had ever been attacked in such a manner, and Rogers' bookings were cancelled for the foreseeable future. Of course, his bout with Johnny Barend was cancelled on the spot, and $2,500 was refunded to fans.[45] Buddy was released from the emergency ward, but then admitted for further treatment at Riverside Hospital the next day. He also spoke with a Franklin County prosecutor with the intent of filing assault and battery charges on Miller and Gotch.[46] On September 3, the two wrestlers appeared before a Municipal Court judge and were released on $25 bond each.[47] Rogers was angry, and wanted all of his injuries recorded for both criminal and civil prosecution. It was reported that he had initiated a $200,000 suit against the grapplers, but the chances of attaining even a quarter of that amount was small.[48] Al Haft was the only party involved with a bankroll, and Buddy seriously considered filing against him, as well.

At the heart of the entire incident was the question of why it happened in the first place. Was it promotional or personal? Was there one central reason or multiple? According to columnist Charley Bailey, Gotch owned up to the whole thing when he said he was motivated by "Rogers' refusal to give me a match. He kept telling me I didn't have a strong-enough reputation to meet him. Well, he knows I have now."[49] Rogers wrestled Gotch at least two times in 1960, but as Karl's standing in Ohio grew, calls for a return bout were ignored. The cover of Haft's publication *The Wrestler* on February 11, 1961, discussed "Rogers v. Gotch," but despite the interest, it never happened.[50] Rogers was known for wrestling people he trusted, and it's possible he believed Gotch was too much of a rogue to meet in the ring for the championship.

When he returned to Ohio in 1962, Gotch immediately joined Miller in what was dubbed the "American Wrestling Association," the outfit backed by Jim Barnett and Johnny Doyle.[51] Less than two weeks after the attack on Rogers, he was pushed to the AWA world title in what could be construed as an effort to capitalize on what had occurred. Since he was credited with having beaten up the NWA world champion, Gotch was the better wrestler, and, in turn, made the AWA crown more important. That is, if you thought like a promoter. But for most fans, this was a non-story about backstage drama, and it failed to intrigue the masses. There was no redeeming value anywhere in the information released to the public, and it didn't build towards a winner-take-all worked match between Rogers and Gotch. At best, Gotch's reputation as a tough guy was bolstered, and others might have decried Buddy's lack of courage. But honestly, Rogers had encountered two incredible shooters, and escaped relatively unharmed.[52]

His arm wasn't broken, nor was his neck severely injured. He wore a cast and sold his injuries for dramatic effect, including the claim that he had developed a speech impediment and lost 40 percent vision in his right eye.[53] Willie Gilzenberg, the Newark promoter for Capitol Wrestling, heard that Buddy took a "couple of hard falls while fainting" in the aftermath of the Gotch-Miller assault.[54] Whether that was true is unknown.

The 75-year-old Al Haft found himself in a precarious position following the Columbus episode. Rogers instantly divorced himself from the local office and anything to do with Haft, which meant all ties to Capitol talent were severed. The notion that Haft was behind the entire affair surfaced and was embraced by Rogers and his allies. The attack wasn't considered to be an ego-driven plot by Gotch, or a deliberate message from Gotch and Miller, or even a promotional weapon used by Barnett and Doyle. The blame was pinned directly on the shoulders of Al Haft.[55]

The reasoning was simple. Haft was paranoid that Capitol Wrestling was trying to take over his territory. He was the one who wanted to send a message, thinking there was enough confusion and potential villains to avoid having anyone point the finger at him. But the façade broke down and everyone involved picked a side. Rogers and McMahon withdrew completely from Columbus, leaving Haft to cancel a scheduled show on September 8.[56] Within a matter of days, Haft aligned with Barnett and Doyle, and booked a show at the Fairgrounds Coliseum headlined by Gotch and Don Leo Jonathan.[57] It was suspiciously timed, and perhaps that was his intention all along. As for the cause of his paranoia, the belief that Capitol was going to annex the territory, there was truth to that story. McMahon had discussed the idea with his lieutenants, but no official plan had been set in motion. When Haft seemingly got wind of their plot, he decided to strike first, and sent a dagger right into the heart of the NWA champion.

Although Rogers wasn't seriously injured, he did suffer physical and mental anguish. His cuts and bruises healed, but his love of Columbus diminished to the point that he was prepared to sell his home and move back to Camden.[58] In fact, on Nov. 1, 1962, he did just that. His property at 53 West Tulane Road, which he had owned since 1953, was sold to Frank and Esther Humphrey.[59] The bad press also proved embarrassing. In Akron, one headline read, "Nature Boy Not So Tough Out of Ring."[60] A Buffalo newspaper stated that the "AWA and Gotch" were the "big winners in the deal."[61] Even worse were the exaggerations and embellishment of the incident that circulated in locker rooms across the wrestling landscape. His enemies, jealous workers, and insiders with a flair for the dramatic took the opportunity to slay Rogers' reputation, criticizing him for running away from Gotch and Miller, and not standing up to face their challenge.

As mentioned earlier, there was a top tier of legitimate wrestling shooters, which included the likes of Lou Thesz, Dick Hutton, and Pat O'Connor. Gotch and Miller were in that same class. Gotch was a student of the legendary "Snakepit" gymnasium in Wigan, England, and was unquestionably one of the best real grapplers in the business. Miller was a former Big Ten wrestling champion at Ohio State University. In terms of size, Miller stood 6-foot-5 and weighed more 260 pounds, whereas Gotch was 6-foot-1, 240. Together, they were a dangerous pair, and any condemnation toward Rogers for not displaying "heart" in tackling both simultaneously was genuinely unfair. For argument's sake, individually, Thesz, Hutton and O'Connor would have been at a similar disadvantage against two world-class opponents in a straight fight. But Buddy's enemies got a good laugh out of the situation, and continued to disparage him decades later.[62] If the shoe was on the other foot, it's hard to imagine a grappler of any stature having success in that situation, especially if they cared about self-preservation.

Rogers would never live it down. In the end, he didn't file a lawsuit against Al Haft, and the case against Gotch and Miller was dropped.[63] He missed at least nine matches as a result of the assault, and promoters lost six-figures in total gates. Among the bouts he no-showed was an important contest versus Cowboy Bob Ellis in St. Louis, and Sam Muchnick was furious. He heard that Rogers was faking his condition, and questioned Vince McMahon as to the rumor. "I like to believe Buddy," Muchnick wrote. "I have always liked him. However, some people say he is a terrific actor and that he is not hurt at all, and that you know he isn't hurt."[64] The information McMahon had at the time, and his response to Muchnick is not known, but it's true that the loss of Rogers was also significant to Capitol Wrestling. He missed shows in

Washington, Baltimore, and at Madison Square Garden, but Muchnick wasn't buying it. He received confirmation that Buddy would be available on September 14, only to hear two days prior to the program that the champion would be unable to appear.[65]

"I'm still groggy," Muchnick said afterwards. He hated last-minute no-shows, but the Rogers-Ellis feud was given special publicity and promotion, making it even more important.[66] With little time to reshuffle his card, Muchnick brought in Lou Thesz as a substitute for Rogers, and the show lost its original luster. This was probably a turning point for Muchnick in his support of Rogers as champion. For months, he had dealt with complaints by members about Buddy's lopsided schedule and heeded comments regarding the NWA's lack of unity. He had struggled to get timely payments from Capitol Wrestling, and pleaded with McMahon to submit money owed to the Alliance office. He knew Rogers' days as champion were numbered, but there were a few bright spots left on the calendar. Sept. 14, 1962 in St. Louis, headlined by Rogers and Ellis, was one of them. After Buddy pulled out, Muchnick went to the 46-year-old Thesz, and was ready to admit that Thesz was the NWA's answer to a prayer.[67]

The Alliance needed a stabilizing champion and Thesz was "Old Reliable." He would do the necessary traveling to bring NWA promoters back together and encourage membership growth.[68] It was a shift in the right direction, and Muchnick understood the consequences, the good and the bad. In the meantime, he had to manipulate the chess board to get all players on the same page. As for Buddy Rogers, despite his rocky road, he didn't want to yield his championship. At least, that was his natural instinct. He had waited too long to reach the pinnacle of the sport and he wasn't ready to concede his spot. Soon, though, without any warning, Buddy would face another round of heavy adversity, and his personal convictions were going to be tested to the maximum degree. Not only was his reign as National Wrestling Alliance world heavyweight champion in doubt, but his future as a professional wrestler, as well. 1963 was going to be the most difficult year of his career.

ENDNOTES - CHAPTER 16

[1] *Boxing and Wrestling*, September 1956, p. 39, 76-77.
[2] *Lancaster New Era*, June 28, 1951, p. 36.
[3] *The Ringsider*, September 1964, p. 12.
[4] Rogers admitted that his act was "manufactured color." *Chicago Daily Tribune*, Sunday Magazine, June 25, 1961, p. 30-31.
[5] *Chicago Daily Tribune*, March 30, 1962, p. 51, *Chicago Daily Tribune*, Aug. 24, 1961, p. 79.
[6] *Chicago Daily Tribune*, Sunday Magazine, June 25, 1961, p. 30-31.
[7] *Chicago Daily Tribune*, March 9, 1962, p. 53.
[8] Ibid, *Chicago Daily Tribune*, Sept. 19, 1962, p. 51. Correspondence with Barbara Condon Marrs, May 27, 2019.
[9] Condon mentioned Rogers in his column at least 30 times between September 1960 and September 1962.
[10] *Chicago Daily Tribune*, April 16, 1962, p. 22.
[11] Rogers wrestled six matches in six nights in Texas between April 30 and May 5, 1962.
[12] He beat Pepper Gomez in Houston, and then defeated Carlo Milano in Bridgeport with his figure-four. The Bridgeport TV appearance on May 12 also set up future matches with Edouard Carpentier. *Bridgeport Post*, May 13, 1962, p. D1.

[13] The afternoon show at the Sunnyside Garden began at 2:00 p.m. *New York Daily News*, May 18, 1962, p. 77. Rogers defeated Pampero Firpo. The Philadelphia program started at 8:40. *Philadelphia Daily News*, May 19, 1962, p. 33. He beat Edouard Carpentier at the Arena.
[14] *Bridgeport Post*, May 27, 1962, p. D1.
[15] *Akron Beacon Journal*, June 11, 1962, p. 12.
[16] *Albuquerque Journal*, June 12, 1962, p. 13.
[17] *Boxing Illustrated, Wrestling News*, June 1962, p. 50-54.
[18] Lindsay got his start in wrestling in 1951, training at Al Haft's gymnasium in Columbus.
[19] *Seattle Daily Times*, May 23, 1962, p. 28.
[20] *Seattle Daily Times*, June 19, 1962, p. 29.
[21] On Aug. 24, 1962, Lindsay beat Fritz Von Goering for his 4th PNW Heavyweight Title. *Portland Oregonian*, Aug. 25, 1962, p. 21.
[22] *Portland Oregonian*, June 20, 1962, p. 26.
[23] Notably, when Rogers had to make a long jump, Muchnick often booked the appearances to begin on a Monday, so he could use Sunday as a travel day. It worked out this way for his trips to Seattle, Vancouver, and Des Moines between June and August 1962.
[24] Rogers defeated Gene Kiniski by virtue of a third fall disqualification. *Vancouver Sun*, July 31, 1962, p. 12.
[25] *Big Book of Wrestling*, September 1970, p. 56-57.
[26] Telegram from Vince McMahon to Sam Muchnick dated Oct. 24, 1961. Sam Muchnick Collection.
[27] *St. Louis Globe-Democrat*, Aug. 27, 1962, p. 28.
[28] *Sports Pictorial Review*, Jan. 26, 1948, p. 1.
[29] *Wrestling As You Like It*, April 14, 1949, p. 4.
[30] *St. Joseph Gazette*, Jan. 7, 1949, p. 10, *Montreal Daily Star*, May 19, 1951, p. 20. Also see *Television Guide*, Feb. 25, 1950, p. 22.
[31] *Chicago Daily Tribune*, Sunday Magazine, June 25, 1961, p. 30-31. The carnival story took on a life of its own and appeared in various other publications, including the *Chicago American*, Undated article from 1961, the *Detroit Free Press*, Feb. 2, 1962, p. 41, and the *Atlantic City Sunday Press*, March 7, 1982.
[32] Biographical information appeared in *Sports Pictorial Review*, the *Camden Courier-Post*, *NWA Official Wrestling*, *Wrestling World*, *Wrestling USA*, and *Boxing and Wrestling* magazines, and a handful of programs.
[33] *A Buddy Rogers Tribute* by J Michael Kenyon, *Buddy Rogers Record Book*, Circa 2005, p. 10.
[34] Lou Thesz told a second-hand story from Bill Miller, which claimed that Miller tried to work out with Rogers at the gym, and teach him some real wrestling. Rogers reportedly gave up after less than 30-minutes. *Whatever Happened To...?*, Issue #31, p. 8.
[35] For instance, in 1944, Rogers and another officer were confronted by three verbally abusive shipyard workers in Camden. The situation deteriorated into a bloody fistfight, and Rogers used a headlock and half-Nelson to subdue two of the aggressors. His fellow officer, Joe Reno, was a former boxer. *Camden Courier-Post*, Aug. 2, 1944, p. 11.
[36] "I told you that the boys made a deal with Al Haft and are booking five of his best towns." Letter from Willie Gilzenberg to Jack Pfefer dated Feb. 2, 1962, Jack Pfefer Collection, Joyce Sports Research Collection, Hesburgh Library, University of Notre Dame, Notre Dame, Indiana.
[37] On a rare occasion, Rogers and Rocca teamed up in Columbus to defeat Moose Cholak and Zebra Kid. *Columbus Dispatch*, April 1, 1962, p. 34B.
[38] Barnett ran Jet Stadium on Aug. 12, 1962 and drew 3,603. Gotch drew with Don Leo Jonathan and Miller partnered with Dick the Bruiser in a loss to the Nielsens. *Columbus Dispatch*, Aug. 13, 1962, p. 25.
[39] Rogers' popularity was demonstrated during his recent Columbus feud with "Giant" Baba. A local wrestling fan, Terry Scott said: "Here Buddy is a hero, not a villain. He wrestles a lot here and everybody loves him. When he steps into the ring, all you hear are cheers not boos. Buddy is the greatest." *The Strutter*, September 1962, p. 6.
[40] *Washington, D.C. Evening Star*, July 6, 1962, p. 29.

A Champion on the Ropes • 237

[41] *Columbus Dispatch*, Sept. 1, 1962, p. 11, *Big Time Wrestling*, December 1962.

[42] There were two differing reports as to where Haft was when the attack happened. Rogers stated that Haft was in the dressing room, and that he went "flying through the air" when the assault began. Columbus Dispatch, Sept. 1, 1962, p. 11. Another report claimed that Haft was outside the locker room. Letter from Willie Gilzenberg to Jack Pfefer dated Sept. 6, 1962, *Buddie Rogers and The Art of "Sequencing"* by Max W. Jacobs, p. 17.

[43] *Montreal Star*, Nov. 8, 1962, p. 66. Miller described the incident much differently. He said that he slapped Rogers and that he stood in the door while Gotch went after him. Then, Rogers made his escape and cut his elbow on a jagged nail. "We in no way harmed Rogers," he said. *Big Time Wrestling*, December 1962. Miller explained the matter again in an interview with Dr. Mike Lano in 1992. He said: "Rogers had been ducking us, badmouthing us behind our backs, and one day here in Al Haft's dressing room we began issuing challenges to him, calling him a false champion. We got him, Gotch and myself in a dressing room, and I stood in front of the [doorway]. Gotch slapped him, then I slapped him, and he ran right past me, pushing me out of the way to get out of there. We never slammed or crushed or broke his hand in the doorway. [Rogers] was a different guy back then, he was only looking out for himself. But he was a phenomenal worker, and could really work and take on people." Bill Miller interview with Dr. Mike Lano, Sept. 23, 1992, *Canvas Cavity* Transcript, *Wrestling Then & Now*, February 1993, p. 5.

[44] *Big Time Wrestling*, December 1962. Reports surfaced years later that Art Nielsen may have also been involved.

[45] *Columbus Dispatch*, Sept. 1, 1962, p. 11.

[46] Ibid.

[47] *Columbus Dispatch*, Sept. 4, 1962, p. 18A.

[48] *Buffalo Courier-Express*, Sept. 23, 1962, p. 2C.

[49] Ibid.

[50] *The Wrestler*, Feb. 11, 1961, p. 1.

[51] It was alleged that Rogers had gotten Gotch and Miller blacklisted, but since they had spots with Barnett and Doyle in the AWA, that claim was difficult to understand.

[52] Interestingly, in June 1961, Gotch and Miller were involved in another backstage incident. They teamed up against the Great Antonio, who wrestled a stiff match against Rikidozan in Japan. They proceeded to rough him up in the locker room and sent a strong message in the process.

[53] *Boxing Illustrated, Wrestling News*, January 1963.

[54] Letter from Willie Gilzenberg to Jack Pfefer dated Sept. 13, 1962, *Buddie Rogers and The Art of "Sequencing"* by Max W. Jacobs, p. 17.

[55] Billy Darnell was quoted as saying, "I believe Al Haft engineered that attack." Letter from Darnell to Bill McCormack, Undated. Bill Miller said, "Haft was a weasel who liked to stir up trouble among the wrestlers." Interview of Miller by Kit Bauman, Circa 1988.

[56] Haft was promoting a Shohei Baba vs. Johnny Barend main event. *Columbus Dispatch*, Sept. 2, 1962, p. 30B.

[57] Bill Miller also took part in this program. *Columbus Dispatch*, Sept. 29, 1962, p. 12.

[58] Rogers was quoted as saying: "I do know I've had all I want of Ohio for wrestling purposes. I sold my home there, and moved back to Camden, NJ." *Montreal Star*, Nov. 8, 1962, p. 66.

[59] Property Records, Franklin County Recorder's Office, Columbus, Ohio.

[60] *Akron Beacon Journal*, Sept. 5, 1962, p. 46.

[61] *Buffalo Courier-Express*, Sept. 23, 1962, p. 2C.

[62] For example, Fred Blassie wrote about it in his autobiography. *The Legends of Wrestling "Classy" Freddie Blassie: Listen, You Pencil Neck Geeks* by Fred Blassie and Keith Elliot Greenberg (2004) (117).

[63] Letter from Al Haft to Jack Pfefer dated Jan. 4, 1963, Jack Pfefer Collection, Joyce Sports Research Collection, Hesburgh Library, University of Notre Dame, Notre Dame, Indiana. An article claimed that Rogers "lost" his suit against Gotch and Miller. *Wrestling World*, October 1963, p. 64.

[64] Letter from Sam Muchnick to Vince McMahon dated Sept. 11, 1962, Sam Muchnick Collection.

[65] Rogers' doctor sent a certificate "attesting to his injuries," to Muchnick, and the information was forwarded to the Missouri State Athletic Commission. *Wrestling*, St. Louis Wrestling Club Program, Sept. 29, 1962, p. 4.

[66] Rogers and Ellis did a key TV angle in St. Louis, likely filmed on Aug. 20 and shown Aug. 25.

[67] Thesz reportedly came out of semi-retirement to wrestle Ellis and this would lead to his full-time return. *Wrestling at the Chase: The Inside Story of Sam Muchnick and the Legends of Professional Wrestling* by Larry Matysik (2005), p. 19. Ellis defeated Thesz by disqualification in the third fall. *St. Louis Post-Dispatch*, Sept. 15, 1962, p. 7.

[68] It is probable that Thesz was selected as Buddy's replacement as NWA Titleholder at the Aug. Alliance convention. In a letter from Albuquerque promoter Mike London to Sam Muchnick, London wrote: "I want Lou's [Thesz] phone number and address so I can get in touch and give him exposure before the day of reconing (sic)." Letter from London to Muchnick dated Aug. 28, 1962, Sam Muchnick Collection. This differs from the account that Thesz was chosen after Rogers no-showed the September 14 show in St. Louis.

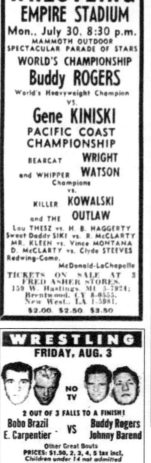

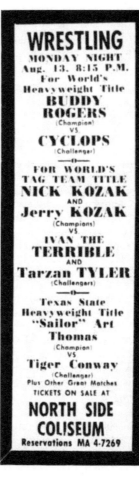

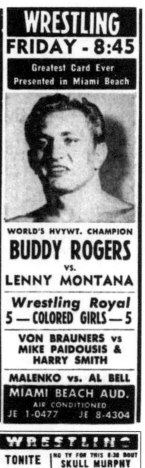

Chapter 17
Blind to the Consequences

Throughout his time in professional wrestling, newspaper and magazine writers lauded Buddy Rogers for his astute business acumen. His primary outside-the-ring avocation was real estate, and by age 29, he was reportedly the owner of nine homes in Camden, New Jersey.[1] Most of his properties were rented out, including his childhood home on Arlington Street, and his mother, Frieda, acted as his business manager while he was on the road. His brother John, a proficient plumber by trade, assisted in the family enterprise, and lived with Frieda at a residence near Camden High School.[2] In 1952, *NWA Official Wrestling* magazine referred to John as a "real estate agent" and claimed he kept "a sharp eye peeled for good investments."[3] A Lancaster newspaper that same year called Buddy's brother a "lawyer," but neither occupation was true.[4] He was a working-class laborer and joined his mother in handling the day-to-day operations of his brother's properties.[5]

The Arlington address had been in their family for over 30 years. By 1956, it was being rented to Frieda's nephew, Christian Stech, and his family.[6] Rogers bought a new home for his mother in the borough of Haddon Heights along Kings Highway, and invested in nearby land, as well.[7] Following the debacle in Columbus, Buddy pulled up stakes and moved back to New Jersey, purchasing a sizable house in an affluent area of Audubon in Camden County.[8] On the whole, it was a stressful time, and the turbulence of his professional life was disheartening. Now living a little more than a mile from his mother, near his old haunts, there was an upside to things and an opportunity to start fresh. Overall, he was pleased with his tenure as champion. His income was in the six-figures, and he had already made a strong case for being the most successful National Wrestling Alliance world heavyweight champion in history.[9]

From multiple sellouts at Madison Square Garden to drawing more than $1 million in Chicago, he had surpassed his predecessors and set a new standard for the NWA kingpin.[10] *The Ring* named him "Wrestler of the Year" for both 1961 and 1962, and he routinely received heavy coverage in newsstand periodicals.[11] Editors saw the marketability in Rogers, who was naturally photogenic, and several magazines stood out for their iconic covers featuring the "Nature Boy." One of the most popular was *TV Wrestling* magazine, a special photo album of superstars printed on glossy paper in 1962.[12] Buddy graced the cover wearing his black leather, gold-plated title belt, and to this day, it remains a highly coveted item among collectors. *Wrestling World* and *Wrestling Revue* also gave him cover editions, and *Boxing and Wrestling* featured an eight-page layout on Rogers in its April 1962 issue.[13] Rogers enjoyed the attention, regardless if the articles were positive or negative. "All I asked was that they spell my name right," he later said.[14]

The eminence of the NWA champion was recognized around the globe and added to Buddy's international celebrity. Organizations far and wide were eager to import him for big money appearances, and the Japan Pro Wrestling Association was at the top of the list. *Tokyo Sports* newspaper touted a possible contest between Rogers and the legendary Rikidôzan, to be held in Tokyo on November 18, 1962.[15] Rikidôzan, a former sumo wrestler, was a national hero in Japan, and four years earlier, beat Lou Thesz for the NWA International title.[16] Rikidôzan v. Rogers was a dream match in many respects, but the anticipated battle was not to be. Another promoter tried to land Rogers for a tour of Australia the summer before, but it was also nixed due to dates on the North American continent.[17] The only time Buddy made a departure from his regular circuit was in late April 1962 when he purportedly ventured to Puerto Rico for bouts in San Juan and Caguas.[18]

That same month, Rogers returned to Montreal after more than a year's absence and had significant backstage influence. He booked talent in coordination with Eddie Quinn and Lucien Gregoire and brought in the Great Scott, Bob Orton, Bobo Brazil, and a number of others.[19] On April 4 and April 26, he defeated high-flyers Edouard Carpentier and Antonino Rocca, respectively, and the latter event drew the largest house in Montreal in more than two years with 11,622 people in attendance.[20] Rogers and Carpentier fought again in a remarkably brutal and bloody contest on Aug. 9, 1962, before 10,000 spectators at the Forum. The result was a no-contest after the official stopped the bout, and both men needed stitches.[21] Toots Mondt and Vince McMahon attended the show, which commemorated Quinn's 23rd anniversary as a promoter in Montreal.

Veteran columnist Elmer Ferguson got in touch with Toots during his stay in Montreal and asked him who the best modern wrestler was. "Buddy Rogers is probably the greatest," Mondt replied. "He has the physique, and the grips. He's a cocky guy, readily admits he's good, is inclined to sneer at all his rivals, makes the most money of any wrestler, dresses like a rich college student, drives a high-priced pink car, [and] wears a diamond that would knock your eye out. He can wrestle, all right, and he has that leg-hold that can damage any wrestler he hooks. Rogers is the biggest card in the Garden, surpassing Antonino Rocca. He drew $26,000 recently in Vancouver, which is unheard of. He figured in a $50,000 gate in our last Garden show."[22]

Quinn's top heel was Killer Kowalski, a 6-foot-7, 270-pound behemoth from Windsor, Ontario. Kowalski was the reigning 12-time world heavyweight champion in Montreal and a natural terror of the ring. Rogers and Kowalski were no strangers to each other. They had wrestled upwards of 30 times in the past and had teamed together on about a dozen occasions. Personally, Kowalski respected Buddy, stemming from a contest they had in Kansas City early in his career.[23] "He led me throughout the match, helping me with this and helping me with that," Kowalski later explained. "Finally, when the match was over, the wrestling promoter said to me, 'Boy, you are good!' He thought I was really good. Meanwhile, it was Buddy Rogers that carried me to a good match and made me look good."[24] Kowalski never forgot Buddy's kindly deed, and their shared esteem translated to memorable matches in the squared circle. On Oct. 24, 1962, the "Nature Boy" successfully defended his NWA title against Kowalski in the main event at Madison Square Garden.

Despite Rogers being booed by the New York crowd, it was Kowalski who was disqualified for illegal tactics in 22:43.[25]

Two weeks later in Montreal, they switched things up by teaming up against Edouard Carpentier and Johnny Rougeau at the Forum. But Rogers wasn't in the mood for cooperation, and during the bout, he refused to be tagged into the affair. Even though Kowalski was forced to wrestle alone, he did pretty well for himself ... until Buddy attempted an ill-timed double-team and accidentally smashed the "Killer" squarely in the face. That opened the flood gates for an all-out war between the partners, and their opponents were a secondary concern. Kowalski chased Rogers from the ring area and tried to continue their brawl in the locker room.[26] After the match, Kowalski said: "It's no wonder other wrestlers beat him up in Columbus recently. He must have double-crossed them, just as he tried to double-cross me."[27] The comment blurred the line between kayfabe and the real world, and served to build the tension for their noteworthy battle on November 21 at the Montreal Forum.

Putting that crucial match on hold for a moment, it's important to examine what took place in the aftermath of the Columbus attack. Since returning to the ring, Rogers had been extremely careful with his bookings. Between September 25 and November 21, he had wrestled approximately four dozen matches in six NWA regions, including the Northeast, Chicago, Montreal, Pittsburgh, Toronto, and St. Louis.[28] Nearly 30 of the bouts were in Capitol territory and his opponents were handpicked from the organization's roster. He faced off with Antonino Rocca, Bobo Brazil, strongman Bruno Sammartino, and teamed with pal Johnny Barend. Rogers and his handlers were in protective-mode, leery of a mid-match betrayal or a similar backstage incident. The last thing they wanted was for Buddy to be put into another precarious situation, or have to deal with a second unforeseen injury that could cost Vince McMahon and his partners a fortune.

The Montreal contest with Kowalski was a safe bet. Kowalski was thoroughly trusted and promoter Eddie Quinn ran a tight ship. Fred Atkins and Buddy Austin were on the card with him, and Rogers was in good shape for a classic encounter.[29] But the deck was stacked against Rogers, and fate was going to impose another cruel tax on the NWA world champion. Within the first minute of his clash with Kowalski, Buddy suffered a devastating ankle fracture. It was the worst case scenario, and entirely accidental.

The match started with Kowalski rushing out of his corner at Rogers, a strategy Buddy himself had employed scores of times. However, Rogers avoided the blitz by jumping from the ring apron to the concrete floor. That was the mistake. Upon hitting the ground, Buddy landed wrong and broke his right ankle.[30] Buddy didn't realize the extent of his injury and got back into the ring, where he was body-slammed twice by Kowalski. At that point, he knew he was seriously hurt. "Pin me, my ankle is broken," Rogers told his opponent.[31] Kowalski followed through and scored the first and only fall of their championship match.[32]

Buddy was removed from the ring and rushed to Montreal General Hospital. He received X-rays and doctors placed his leg in a cast.[33] Acknowledging the gravity of the moment, a writer for the *Montreal Star* wondered if the injury was going to end "one of the most glamorous and stormy wrestling careers of modern times."[34] The thought of losing Rogers permanently was too farfetched for his closest supporters to imagine, but his immediate future was in doubt. News of his broken ankle went out across the Associated Press wire and the bureaucratic National Wrestling Association formally added Rogers to its suspension list on Nov. 23, 1962. The ailing champion went home to Camden and had his injury examined by Stanley Brown, the renowned orthopedic surgeon, who had helped him with his elbow issues in 1961.

While Buddy's recovery was being orchestrated, a sense of panic gripped the promoters who had scheduled bookings for the champion in late November and December. Altogether, the missed matches added up to a financial calamity, and gates were impaired in Chicago, Philadelphia, Pittsburgh, and Washington, D.C. Capitol Wrestling also lost a bundle on a scheduled Rogers-Dory Dixon match-up at Madison Square Garden on December 10, which was expected to sell out the venue. Rogers and Dixon had a hot feud going at the time, and their previous effort at the Garden on November 12 drew more than 15,000 spectators.[35] An early estimate for Buddy's recuperation was three months on the sidelines, and that information was distressing on every level.[36] A layoff of that kind would cripple the National Wrestling Alliance, and Sam Muchnick knew that better than anyone else. Since at least September, he had been working on a plan to supplant Rogers as champion, and this injury, in an instant, changed everything.

In fact, it happened only eight days before a consequential show in Toronto at Maple Leaf Gardens. It is believed that the November 29 card, headlined by champion Rogers and challenger Lou Thesz, would see the world title change hands. It was the match Muchnick and his colleagues had been waiting for, and the opportunity to take the belt off Rogers slipped through their collective fingers. On top of that, for the second time in two months, Muchnick was in damage control mode, laboring to adjust the calendar because Rogers was out of commission. Like the last time Rogers was on the sidelines, Muchnick fielded commentary from fellow promoters as to the legitimacy of Buddy's injury, and a rumor circulated that his reported fracture was invented to save him from having to lose the title to Thesz.[37] The allegation was unproven, and seemed to be perpetuated by the same cynics who took pleasure in hearing about the Columbus assault.

Kowalski was embraced as a title claimant following the Montreal bout and assumed Buddy's bookings in Chicago, Pittsburgh, and Ottawa.[38] On Dec. 14, 1962, at the Coliseum in Houston, he defended his championship against Thesz, and the two went to a competitive 90-minute draw.[39] In a unique twist, the promoter in Trenton, New Jersey, decided to credit "Killer" Buddy Austin with having put Rogers on the shelf, and Austin took over a handful of the latter's Northeastern appearances.[40] Where it was convenient, Austin was also billed as a title claimant, and his status further complicated the championship picture. As for Rogers and his injury, he received weeks of treatment and had his light cast removed on December 20.[41] Around that same time, it was said that he would miss two additional months of action.[42] Already, his cancellations had racked up an estimated loss of $70,000, and if there was truth to that recovery timeline, things were only going to get worse.[43]

Fortunately, Rogers' ankle healed a lot faster than anticipated, and he made a surprise return in Bridgeport on December 26 to do an angle with Austin.[44] Over the next three days, he participated in three successive six-man tag team matches, partnering with Johnny Barend and Magnificent Maurice (Gene Dubuque) in Washington, D.C., New Haven, and Philadelphia. Such bouts were perfect for Rogers as he eased back into competition. He could engage in slight physical combativeness, yet still hide his limitations. Essentially, his partners did the heavy-lifting, giving him more time to regain his full strength. During the first week of January 1963, Buddy appeared for TV in Bridgeport, Washington, D.C., and Cleveland, and promoters did everything in their power to reestablish the "Nature Boy" in advance of live arena shows. Capitol Wrestling needed its number-one star back in the saddle, drawing large crowds and generating massive gates. The company's future depended on it.

By early 1963, Vince McMahon was facing a financial meltdown. A downturn in business had put him in a terrific bind, and he needed an immediate cash influx. In recent weeks, he had invested considerably in a Cleveland outfit alongside Toots Mondt and local impresario Larry Atkins, and started up a live TV program on Saturday evenings on WJW.[45] Cleveland was known to be a profitable wrestling town under the right conditions, and it was strategically important for Capitol Wrestling as they continued to book talent to Akron and Chicago. The entire circuit hinged on having a healthy Buddy Rogers in the top spot, and his reemergence from injury couldn't have come at a better time.[46] But McMahon still needed money and was contemplating taking out a high-interest bank loan to cover his expenses.[47] The tenderhearted Sam Muchnick wanted to help, and even though he had some reservations, he agreed to transfer half of Buddy's performance bond back to Capitol, thus rescuing McMahon from economic ruination.[48]

Sending $5,000 to McMahon even before Rogers dropped the belt was a thoughtful gesture, but risky. He firmly expected Buddy to lose the strap to Lou Thesz on January 24 in Toronto or February 1 in Houston.[49] But, as shown in recent months, anything was possible, and another postponement of the inevitable title switch was going to erode Muchnick's kindly disposition. That wasn't going to be a problem, though. Rogers was tired of being on the road and was ready to pass the NWA title and all of its harsh responsibilities to someone else.[50] It made sense. The endless traveling and the constant battle to get to the next town – fighting weather and chasing airplanes – had worn him down. With the addition of the injuries and the stress of being away from his family for long periods of time, Rogers was burned out. In his darkest moments, he wondered if the "strain and tension" of holding the belt had been worth everything he had gone through to keep it around his waist.[51]

Since winning the Alliance championship in the summer of 1961, Rogers had received unparalleled attention from the media, and the press coverage was astronomical. He had drawn magnificent numbers and was acknowledged as wrestling's top superstar. Always looking fit and bronze, he was the picturesque professional wrestler, and on the outside, he appeared to be weathering the demands of the traveling champion well. But in private, things in his life were anything but ideal. For more than a year, Rogers had been secretly experiencing a range of abnormal health symptoms, which included shortness of breath and chest heaviness.⁵² At times, usually after a strenuous match, he was in more serious pain. In fact, his discomfort typically arose when he exerted himself, a symptom which corresponded with angina pectoris and was caused by the narrowing of the heart's arteries. His father had died from a type of coronary artery disease, and hereditary concerns were genuine. When the stress attributed to the world heavyweight championship was added, his risk for a heart attack was higher than it normally would be for an average 41-year-old athlete.

For the most part, his condition was manageable, and throughout the latter half of 1962, he tempered his in-ring style when necessary to alleviate his symptoms. Having not seen a doctor, he still wasn't convinced it was overly serious, and he coped with the pain privately. But it was becoming harder and harder to dismiss, and altogether, it was a tough pill to swallow. He was the champion of the world, and now, instead of dealing with an arm or ankle injury, he was being challenged by a strange internal health problem. Rogers had been known as "Mr. Perpetual Motion" and the "wildest chance-taker in the game," and his reputation extended across the wrestling universe.⁵³ That version of Buddy Rogers was no longer physically possible, and his pride was suffering along with his mind and body. With so much riding on his back, including Vince McMahon's new promotion in Cleveland, Rogers was in a position he didn't want to relinquish. But it was out of his hands, and he knew it.

"Fellas, I can't take it anymore," Rogers proclaimed in a meeting with his handlers. "My heart ... everything lays back with you, Vince, and I want to be with you, and I'm sorry this thing turned out the way it did, but, man, let's drop that NWA title back again. I wasn't about to double-cross Sam Muchnick."⁵⁴ Neither was McMahon. By sending back half of Buddy's belt deposit, Muchnick did Capitol Wrestling a huge favor, and they were ready to reciprocate. On Jan. 24, 1963, in Toronto, Buddy lost the NWA crown to Lou Thesz in 14:54 of a one-fall bout. Muchnick was on hand to present the belt to the new champion, and fans loudly applauded the decision.⁵⁵ However, the title switch, and the acceptance of a new NWA champion, wasn't going to impact what McMahon did in his territory, and a new course was established separate from the Alliance. McMahon didn't yet have all his ducks in a row, but the gist of things was clear: The Northeastern region was declaring its independence from the NWA.

This was McMahon's reaction to the NWA putting the belt back on Thesz. Thesz was a respected champion, but his value was far less than Rogers in New York City and Chicago, two of McMahon's most important cities. Capitol Wrestling could field a traveling champion in its territory full-time – a wrestler capable of working Chicago, Cleveland, Pittsburgh, and the entire Northeastern circuit. Such a champion could appear without NWA interference and without having to send booking fees to another office. That was McMahon's plan. He wanted Capitol to have its own designated heavyweight champion, and Rogers was the obvious choice. However, there was a key public relations issue. Rogers had already been defeated by Thesz, and his title claim lost. McMahon had an answer for that. He insisted that since the Toronto bout was only one fall, Buddy was still the rightful champion. In the kayfabe realm, it was sound, but after Thesz beat Rogers for a second time in three falls on February 7 in Toronto, that argument was futile.[56]

Nevertheless, Buddy continued to reign as champion in Capitol cities. His billing wasn't exactly uniform, but fans understood that he was the heavyweight titleholder. In places like Baltimore, Paterson, and Chicago, he was actually acknowledged as the "National Wrestling Alliance" kingpin, an erroneous claim that muddled the situation a great deal.[57] In St. Louis, Sam Muchnick wasn't playing that game. He advertized Rogers as a "former world champion" for his Feb. 1, 1963, show at Kiel Auditorium.[58] At the same time, he pushed back on any misleading publicity of an "NWA" champion other than Thesz, and reiterated his belief that a single heavyweight champ was best for the business. Nat Loubet of *Ring Wrestling* and Lou Sahadi of *Boxing and Wrestling* magazine complained about the state of affairs in the Northeast, and specifically about Rogers' claim to the title.[59] The latter explicitly pointed out Buddy's losses to Thesz, and stated that the increased number of champions was "damaging the sport."

Rogers was completely on board with Vince's strategy, particularly since it meant he would retain his championship status across the circuit he had worked so hard to strengthen. His calendar of routine TV appearances in Washington, D.C., Bridgeport, Pittsburgh, and Cleveland, plus an upcoming new program in Baltimore, allowed him to maintain his vise-grip on the wrestling populace.[60] In turn, arena shows remained a hot ticket and money flowed once again. But the reality of Buddy's health and the desperate need for him to play his standard headliner role were concurrent, and the pressure was becoming insurmountable. For Rogers, despite the warning signs, he was making the realizations a little at a time. Bobby Davis, his loyal friend, probably knew him better than anyone else. He was the first person close to Rogers to recognize the seriousness of his health problems, and he recommended that Buddy see a cardiac specialist for immediate diagnosis and treatment.

When Rogers resisted, Davis had no choice other than to give him an ultimatum, and it was very simple. If Buddy didn't agree to see a physician right away, Bobby was going to leave his side. The threat was powerful considering the level of devotion and admiration Bobby had for Rogers. The 25-year-old Davis grew up worshipping the "Nature Boy," and he was in his ideal role as Buddy's manager. But the last thing he wanted to see was Rogers overextend himself to the point of a catastrophic heart attack mid-match, and the possibility that Buddy was headed for an early grave. Rogers was blind to the consequences of his choices and felt he had more gas in the tank. He refused to slow down, and for that reason, Davis followed through with his promise. He walked away from his dream job and his best friend, hoping Rogers would find the inner fortitude to do what needed to be done.[61] It was out of his hands and there was nothing more he could do.

Rogers stubbornly pushed forward and fought to keep up appearances. He had the ability and intellect to hide his ailments, and went to great lengths to conceal his health problems. His matches were purposely shorter, and by design, typically in the eight to 14-minute range. In tag team bouts, it was easy to procrastinate and elude much of the action, but he was experienced enough to employ certain maneuvers in singles encounters to keep his pain in check. For instance, in a late 1961 bout with Crusher Lisowski in Pittsburgh, he was held in a headlock by his opponent "for almost 20 minutes."[62] Fans probably grew antsy and annoyed by the extended hold, but Rogers and Lisowski sold it effectively well, and in a long match, it aided both men in terms of conditioning. Rogers' health concern was justifiably worrying, and when it got to an advanced stage, Rogers took his rival aside prior to a scheduled contest and laid out an abbreviated match to limit his own exertion.

"A wrestler must have three things: Ability, showmanship and personality," Chicago promoter Fred Kohler told the Associated Press. "There are about 75 wrestlers in top demand today, but none has all three of those assets like Buddy Rogers."[63] The good publicity continued to stream in, and the accolades for Rogers were plentiful. Jim Wallington of the *Lansing State Journal* got Buddy talking in February 1963, and his comments were enlightening. "Wrestling, professional style, uses fanfare and antagonism to draw fans," Rogers said. "Boxing is a dead sport because it lacks these colorful gimmicks and colorful fighters, except for Cassius Clay." The 21-year-old Clay was a leading contender for the world heavyweight boxing championship held by Sonny Liston, and he had gained a tremendous reputation for his over-the-top verbal campaign against his foes. His exaggerated commentary was similar to a talkative wrestling heel, and Clay later divulged having received advice from the legendary Gorgeous George.[64]

Soon to be known as "Muhammad Ali," Clay also admittedly watched Rogers on TV in his youth in Louisville, and undoubtedly saw Buddy's classic mannerisms.[65] "Clay is attracting so much attention because he acts like a wrestler," Rogers explained. "He is good for the sport because he has a big mouth. Clay is the first fighter since Max Baer to capture fans with his colorful approach. Clay's best technique is naming the round he'll knock out his opponent. I bet he can't do that to me. As a matter of fact, I challenge him to try and put me down in a certain round. I'd bet him $20,000 he couldn't beat me. I'll wrestle and he'll box." The idea for a mixed match between Rogers and Clay gained traction, and Vince McMahon's Cleveland partner Larry Atkins wanted to make it a reality for a massive stadium show during the summer of 1963. He sent Clay a $100,000 offer for the bout, only to learn that the boxer wouldn't have accepted anything less than a quarter of a million to take such an extraordinary contest.[66]

Following his NWA title loss to Thesz, Rogers engaged in approximately 41 matches in February and March 1963, mostly in the Northeastern territory. He went to St. Louis once and back to Toronto to drop the three-falls rematch to Thesz, while venturing to Chicago, Pittsburgh, and Cleveland to satisfy the interests of Capitol Wrestling. Buddy didn't lose his in-ring stature by a long shot, and went over Killer Kowalski seven-times, Bobo Brazil four, and Edouard Carpentier on three occasions. On March 7 in Washington, D.C., Rogers and Johnny Barend lost their U.S. tag team belts to Buddy Austin and the Great Scott at the Capitol Arena.[67] Keeping things lively, Rogers and Barend soon entered into a feud, and headlined at Madison Square Garden on March 25.[68] Buddy defeated his former partner before 13,150 spectators.[69]

Aside from the loss to Thesz on February 7, Rogers only suffered one other defeat in a singles match during that stretch. It occurred in Cleveland on

March 28 and his opponent was the popular Dory Dixon. There was a greater significance to this particular bout as the winner received the newly created championship belt of the "World-Wide Wrestling Association." The WWWA was the recently established sanctioning body of Vince McMahon and his Cleveland cronies, an organization that would stand independent of the NWA.[70] By forming their own exclusive association, they now had structured backing for their world champion, just like Muchnick's NWA and the AWA in Minneapolis. It was almost out of necessity to provide their champion the credible sponsorship the media and fans were accustomed to, and which had been an element of wrestling's foundation going back decades. The WWWA would also aid their continued booking strategies in Chicago, Pittsburgh, and parts of Michigan.[71]

The Rogers-Dixon rivalry was successfully promoted in Cleveland, and was really pushed over the top by a remarkable studio bout earlier in March. At the outset, Dixon attacked Buddy and sent him to the mat with two flying dropkicks. He proceeded to dominate the champion in incredible fashion, and Buddy was at his best, selling everything to the best of his ability. According to the report in The Ring, "Dixon had Rogers pinned at least nine times during the match," and Buddy was saved by the bell when the 15-minute time-limit expired.[72] As a result of his otherworldly effort, Dixon was granted the title match with the "Nature Boy" on March 28. In the ring prior to their championship affair, Buddy was presented with the diamond-studded WWWA belt, but he didn't leave the Cleveland Arena with the strap in his possession.[73] Dixon was declared the victor when Rogers left the ring and refused to continue after being caught cheating to score a pin.[74] Dixon was the new WWWA world heavyweight champion.

Despite the solid action, the experiment in Cleveland was already on shaky ground, and money was the root issue. Vince McMahon's financial troubles were unceasing, and the WWWA investment was proving to be more of a burden than a profitable venture. It was crunch time, and McMahon needed a good run of houses to right the ship. A big rematch between Rogers and Dixon in Cleveland on April 18 was crucial, but the fate of the WWWA was pretty much decided. McMahon was preparing to abandon all of his interests outside the Northeast and Pittsburgh, and focus all of his energy on another new sanctioning organization, this one headquartered out of Newark, New Jersey. Like the WWWA, this promotion would rely heavily on the broad shoulders of the tanned grappler from Camden. But Buddy Rogers was in the worst physical shape of his life, and his health was a ticking time bomb. All things considered, and at the rate he was going, he would be lucky to survive the month of April.

ENDNOTES - CHAPTER 17

[1] *Windsor Star*, Nov. 17, 1950, p. 31.
[2] Interview with Jerry Hauske, June 21, 2018. The Rohdes lived at 1487 Greenwood Avenue, a property they purchased on Oct. 26, 1950. Camden County Property Records, Camden, NJ.
[3] *NWA Official Wrestling*, April 1952 p. 10-11.
[4] *Lancaster New Era*, Oct. 28, 1952, p. 16.
[5] One of his properties was near the corner of Locust and Saunders Avenues in Bellmawr, although the address is not known. It might have been 209 Saunders Avenue.

[6] Christian Stech was a brother of Frank Stech, who employed Rogers when he got out of the Navy. He was involved in the family's trucking business as a driver. The Stech Family lived at 2033 Arlington from at least 1956 to 1960. Christian passed away on July 22, 1963. *Camden Courier-Post*, July 23, 1963, p. 7. It appears that Buddy sold the property sometime in the 1960s. On March 15, 1990, Buddy's childhood home was destroyed in a fire that killed two men. *Camden Courier-Post*, March 16, 1990, p. B1. Arlington Street was completely razed in 2004 because of its close proximity to the former General Gas Mantle Factory, which contaminated a large area with radioactive waste. See Phil Cohen's excellent website for more information at www.dvrbs.com.

[7] The address was 1832 Kings Highway. Rogers bought land in the area of Kings Highway and St. Martins Avenue, not far from their home, for $2,600 in 1954. *Camden Courier-Post*, Dec. 7, 1954, p. 10. He was represented by lawyer Albert J. Scarduzio, who was a cousin of Samuel Scarduzio, a neighbor of the Rohde Family in the 1930s. Albert Scarduzio handled most of Buddy's non-wrestling business.

[8] The address was 215 E. Kings Highway, at the intersection of Kings Highway and Crystal Lake Avenue. They purchased the home on Nov. 8, 1962. Camden County Property Records, Camden, NJ. It was reported that this home cost $102,000. A description of the house appeared in *Wrestling Confidential*, May 1964 and July 1964.

[9] Articles routinely claimed that Rogers was making in excess of $100,000 a year. Rogers' actual earnings are unknown. A promoter wrote that he made $17,000 in February 1962. Letter from Willie Gilzenberg to Jack Pfefer dated March 13, 1962, Jack Pfefer Collection, Joyce Sports Research Collection, Hesburgh Library, University of Notre Dame, Notre Dame, Indiana. He reportedly made $146,000 in 1962. *The Wrestler*, February 1964, p. 16-17. Another article claimed he made $150,000 "last year." *Paterson News*, Feb. 15, 1963, p. 21. Ernie Ladd said that Rogers had made $75,000 in seven months. *Buffalo Courier-Express*, Dec. 24, 1964, p. 11.

[10] *Wrestling Life*, May 1963, p. 1.

[11] *Ring Wrestling*, September 1963, p. 56. The Chicago-based *Wrestling Life* magazine also acknowledged him as "Wrestler of the Year" for 1960. *Wrestling Life*, February 1961, p. 12.

[12] This magazine was put out by Stanley Weston's Champion Sports Publishing Corporation. It was not sold on newsstands, but offered for $1.00 through mail order. Advertisements were featured in *Wrestling Revue* and *Boxing Illustrated, Wrestling News* in 1962 and 1963.

[13] *Wrestling World*, November 1962, *Wrestling Revue*, Winter 1961, *Boxing and Wrestling*, April 1962, p. 46-53.

[14] Rogers believed magazines were a "great media device," and helped sell out arenas. "Magazines gave me as much public exposure as TV did," he said. *Wrestling's Main Event*, September 1983, p. 20-24.

[15] A second bout was mentioned as well, to be staged on November 22 in Osaka. *Tokyo Sports*, Oct. 31, 1962, p. S31.

[16] *Los Angeles Times*, Aug. 28, 1958, p. D4. Rikidozan had also helped train Rogers' ring rival, "Giant" Baba.

[17] Unsourced Sydney, Australia newspaper, July 19, 1962.

[18] Rogers was booked to wrestle Eugenio Marin on April 28 in San Juan at Sixto Escobar Stadium and Haystacks Calhoun on April 29 at Parque Sola Morales in Caguas. It's not known if Rogers made either date.

[19] Chris Colt discussed Rogers' booking of Montreal. *Wrestling Archive Project*, Volume II, p. 27.

[20] *Montreal Gazette*, April 5, 1962, p. 26, *Montreal Gazette*, April 27, 1962, p. 30.

[21] Rogers needed six stitches and Carpentier four. The bout was called the "most rugged battle fought here in years." *Montreal Star*, Aug. 10, 1962.

[22] *Montreal Star*, Aug. 9, 1962.

[23] Rogers and Kowalski had two bouts in Kansas City during the early stages of "Killer's" career. The dates are Dec. 30, 1948 and Jan. 13, 1949.

[24] 1wrestling.com Interview of Killer Kowalski, Undated.

[25] 12,238 paid $36,796.08. *New York Daily News*, Oct. 25, 1962, p. 83.

[26] Carpentier and Rougeau won the tag team match. *Montreal Star*, Nov. 8, 1962, p. 68.

[27] *Montreal Star*, Nov. 16, 1962, p. 43.

[28] It is unclear if Rogers wrestled on Sept. 22, 1962 in Philadelphia. He had two matches in Akron and two in Toledo, in what would've normally been the Ohio territory. However, these bouts were not for an NWA member in that region, and likely booked directly by McMahon.

[29] Atkins would accompany Rogers to the hospital.

[30] Rogers fractured the medial malleolus of his right tibia. Years later, Rogers told the story of his bout with Kowalski. He said that Kowalski attacked him from behind and kicked his leg, causing the broken ankle. He stated that the promoter had to refund 15,000 tickets. Buddy Rogers Interview by John Arezzi, *Pro Wrestling Spotlight*, Aug. 4, 1991.

[31] Kowalski suggested a disqualification, but Rogers was adamant about it being a pinfall finish. 1wrestling.com Interview of Killer Kowalski, Undated.

[32] The match lasted a total of three minutes. *Boxing Illustrated, Wrestling News*, March 1963, p. 55-58. Also see *Montreal Star*, Nov. 22, 1962, p. 58.

[33] A report describing his injury was sent to Sam Muchnick in St. Louis. The one-page document was also printed in *Boxing Illustrated, Wrestling News*, March 1963, p. 55-58.

[34] *Montreal Star*, Nov. 22, 1962, p. 58.

[35] *New York Daily News*, Nov. 13, 1962, p. 71.

[36] *Montreal Star*, Nov. 24, 1962, p. 18.

[37] Muchnick heard the claim that Rogers used an "old X-ray" to fabricate his current injury. Letter from Muchnick to Vince McMahon dated Dec. 17, 1962, Sam Muchnick Collection.

[38] In Ottawa, Kowalski was billed as the "North American Wrestling Association" champion. *Ottawa Citizen*, Dec. 7, 1962, p. 25. Kowalski talked about his reign as champion. 1wrestling.com Interview of Killer Kowalski, Undated.

[39] *Houston Post*, Dec. 15, 1962, p. D3. Historians have long wondered if the NWA had wanted Rogers to lose the championship to Thesz on December 14 in Houston, as opposed to the switch occurring in Toronto in late November.

[40] The promoter was Jean Pellettieri. Austin was said to have fractured Rogers' "leg" in Ottawa. *Trenton Evening Times*, Nov. 29, 1962, p. 39. Among the dates Austin assumed for Rogers was November 26 in Washington, D.C., against Antonino Rocca. *Washington Evening Star*, Nov. 26, 1962, p. 25.

[41] *Montreal Star*, Dec. 13, 1962, p. 73. In a later interview, Rogers claimed to have needed an operation on his "fractured tibia bone," performed by Dr. Stanley Brown. *Camden Courier-Post*, July 30, 1963, p. 21.

[42] *Montreal Star*, Dec. 13, 1962, p. 73.

[43] *Paterson News*, Feb. 15, 1963, p. 21. Rogers said that he personally lost "around $10,000 in purses," and expected to "lose three times that much before he got back into action." *Montreal Star*, Dec. 11, 1962, p. 56.

[44] *Bridgeport Post*, Dec. 27, 1962, p. 12. A Philadelphia newspaper stated that Rogers was "pronounced physically fit." *Philadelphia Daily News*, Dec. 21, 1962, p. 55.

[45] The Cleveland organization was incorporated as Buckeye Sports Enterprises, and the partnership was announced on Nov. 14, 1962. The first show was slated for Dec. 17, 1962 at the Public Hall. *Cleveland Plain Dealer*, Nov. 15, 1962, p. 10.

[46] McMahon was operating in Cleveland in opposition to an old adversary, Pedro Martinez, who had many big named wrestlers working for him. To successfully compete, he needed an equal number of superstars, and having Rogers was essential. Despite earlier success in Cleveland, Rogers hadn't appeared there since Oct. 18, 1957, when he wrestled Billy Darnell to a double DQ. *Cleveland Plain Dealer*, Oct. 19, 1957, p. 28. He made his return on Jan. 5, 1963.

[47] Letter from Sam Muchnick to Vince McMahon dated Dec. 17, 1962, Sam Muchnick Collection.

[48] Ibid.

[49] Muchnick initially thought January 31 was the date for Toronto. Ibid. After discussing things with Frank Tunney, they settled on January 24.

[50] *Wrestling at the Chase: The Inside Story of Sam Muchnick and the Legends of Professional Wrestling* by Larry Matysik (2005) (19). Thesz claimed that Rogers didn't want to lose the NWA championship. He also told the story that Muchnick threatened to donate the "$25,000" performance bond Rogers put up to charity if he didn't go through with a bout with Thesz. Thesz said, "That did the trick." *Hooker* by Lou Thesz with Kit Bauman (2011), p. 216.

51 In 1971, Rogers said he still wasn't sure. *The Wrestler*, October 1971.
52 His chest pain may have started as early as 1960 or 1961. According to one source, his chest pains began during his match with Lou Thesz. *Buddie Rogers and The Art of "Sequencing"* by Max W. Jacobs, p. 18.
53 *TV Digest*, Dec. 6, 1952, p. 21.
54 Buddy Rogers Interview by Tom Burke and Dan Reilly, *Wrestle Radio*, Nov. 9, 1991.
55 *Toronto Globe and Mail*, Jan. 25, 1963, p. 38. Also see *The Ring*, April 1963, p. 32. In Thesz's autobiography, he offered a much different view of what occurred in Toronto, including the claim that Muchnick had $25,000 in cash, which amounted to Buddy's belt deposit. *Hooker* by Lou Thesz with Kit Bauman (2011), p. 216-217. Additional details of their title switch have appeared in print, and most of them are erroneous. The legendary line, "We can do this the easy way or we can do this the hard way" has been attributed to Thesz with regard to this bout. However, it doesn't make sense. Rogers was in Toronto to lose his belt, and the result was prearranged with no hard feelings. It should be noted that Thesz didn't recite that comment in his book. The other claim, that Thesz snuck into the building and caught Rogers off-guard, in an attempt to win the NWA belt in a shoot, is also false. Muchnick sent McMahon a check for the remaining $5,000 for the belt deposit on Jan. 28, 1963. Letter from Sam Muchnick to Vince McMahon dated Jan. 28, 1963, Sam Muchnick Collection.
56 Wrestling historian Terry Dart, who attended this show, wrote: "Rogers looked very tired, however, still put on a good show." Email correspondence from Terry Dart dated Jan. 4, 2002. McMahon didn't want the news of Rogers losing to Thesz getting out, and asked Stanley Weston, a well-known magazine publisher, not to print news of the title switch in Toronto. *Is Wrestling Fixed: I Didn't Know it was Broken* by Bill Apter (2015). However, Weston covered the match in detail with eight pages of information and photos in *Wrestling Revue* magazine. *Wrestling Revue*, June 1963, p. 8-15.
57 *Baltimore Sun*, Feb. 6, 1963, p. 21, *Paterson News*, Feb. 15, 1963, p. 21, *Chicago Tribune*, Feb. 23, 1963, p. 44. In Fred Kohler's Chicago arena program, he listed Rogers as the "World Heavyweight champion," without the "NWA" designation. *Wrestling*, Feb. 8, 1963, p. 1, *Wrestling*, Feb. 22, 1963, p. 2. Kohler discontinued billing Rogers as champion in March 1963.
58 *St. Louis Post-Dispatch*, Feb. 1, 1963, p. 18.
59 *Ring Wrestling*, July 1963, *Boxing and Wrestling*, June 1963, p. 64.
60 The Baltimore studio show debut on Saturday, March 2, 1963 on channel 11, WBAL-TV, with Ray Morgan as commentator.
61 "The real reason for the split between Bobby Davis and his champion Buddy Rogers was the champ's refusal to follow the advice of his manager." *Wrestling World*, August 1963, p. 50. It is believed that Davis left Rogers around December 1962.
62 *Pittsburgh Post-Gazette*, Nov. 7, 1961, p. 21.
63 *Binghamton Press*, May 2, 1963, p. 26.
64 *Miami Herald*, Dec. 21, 1969, p. 9F.
65 *Muncie Star Press*, Jan. 19, 1975, p. 21.
66 *Cleveland Plain Dealer*, April 14, 1963, p. 9C and April 18, 1963, p. 53.
67 Scott's original partner was Pete Sanchez, who was knocked out of the match by Rogers. *Washington, D.C. Evening Star*, March 8, 1963, p. D3.
68 Promoter Walter Johnston described a near out-of-the-ring battle between Rogers and Barend in his office. *Brooklyn Daily Eagle*, March 20, 1963, p. 23. Johnston expected a crowd of 15,000 and Rogers was billed as an "ex-champion." *New York Post*, March 25, 1963, p. 80.
69 *Wrestling in the Garden: The Battle for New York* by Scott Teal and J Michael Kenyon (2017), p. 163. Attendance at the Garden was down from 18,777 a year earlier.
70 Notably, McMahon, Mondt, and Fred Kohler each resigned their membership in the NWA.
71 The original plan was for a Rogers versus Dixon championship match at Comiskey Park in Chicago during the summer of 1963. *Wrestling World*, August 1963, p. 50. It's probable that it would have been for the WWWA Title.
72 The bout was held at the WJW-TV studio. *The Ring*, July 1963, p. 43.
73 *Cleveland Record*, March 25, 1963, p. 7.
74 *Cleveland Record*, March 29, 1963, p. 6.

Chapter 18
A King Dethroned

Since joining Capitol Wrestling in 1960, Buddy Rogers had wrestled the cream of the crop on a consistent basis, and it often didn't matter if his opponent was a fan-favorite or heel. When he was pitted against an equally charismatic rival, audiences were electrified, and his matches against Antonino Rocca and Bobo Brazil were legendary. Beginning in late 1959, promoters in the Northeastern territory groomed a powerful ex-weightlifter from Pittsburgh named Bruno Sammartino, and he proved to be a naturally gifted performer. Originally from a small village in Abruzzi, Italy, he was dubbed the "Italian Superman," and Bruno, with his 58" chest and 22" neck, lived up to the hype.[1] His clean-cut image and magnetic personality inspired crowds all across the region. It was evident that Sammartino was headed for bigger and better things. In 1960, and again in 1961, the strongman ran into some problems with Vince McMahon and Capitol, but peace was made and he returned in the summer of 1961.[2]

In September of that year, Sammartino received his first shot at Buddy's NWA title and they went to a draw in Queens, New York.[3] Over the next 16 months, they wrestled 15 additional times and the "Nature Boy" won 12 of their contests. As the crooked villain, Rogers resorted to underhanded stunts and bent the rules far beyond the norms. During one Pittsburgh contest, he was locked in Sammartino's finisher, the crushing bearhug, in the third fall, and vocal enthusiasts expected a submission. Suddenly, Bruno released the hold, thinking he had won, and Rogers capitalized. He tossed Sammartino from the ring and the latter was counted out.[4] A few months before, also at the Arena in Pittsburgh, Bruno used his bearhug to win the initial fall over Rogers, but then dropped the second. In the third, Sammartino actually pinned the champion and apparently won the world title. It was an explosive moment for fans, but Bruno displayed his integrity by admitting he had fouled Rogers and refused the belt.[5]

The good-guy persona was important to Sammartino and his supporters loved his combination of brute strength and everlasting honor. Rogers, in the way he portrayed his in-ring character, was the antithesis of Bruno, and their rivalry was box-office gold. Their Aug. 2, 1962, encounter in Toronto drew more than 13,000 spectators, and incidentally, the wrestlers used the same "refused the victory" angle. Later that month, on Aug. 30, their rematch drew nearly 14,000 people, an astronomical number, to Maple Leaf Gardens. In that bout, Rogers was victorious after Sammartino missed a dropkick and was unable to continue. At that juncture, Bruno was unaffiliated with Capitol Wrestling, but in early 1963, he received several calls from Vince McMahon asking him to return to the promotion.[6] Their reasoning was multifaceted. In simplest terms, business was down and their main ethnic hero, Antonino

Rocca, had departed the territory under questionable circumstances in January.

Sammartino was initially hesitant to rejoin Capitol. His previous disagreements and the bad blood that surfaced between himself and McMahon was not yet resolved. Having found success wrestling out of the Toronto office, he felt the only thing that would make him change his mind was a run with the world heavyweight championship.[7] (I apologize for so many rewrites, i.e. the sentence above, but I'm trying to avoid the overuse of "and" in sentences.) With Toots Mondt in agreement, McMahon made the promise to Sammartino, but the promoter's game of three-dimensional chess was just getting started. He was in the midst of an unfortunate retrenchment plan and was withdrawing his talent from outlying cities. The Cleveland enterprise had been a bust, and even though they had a few shows scheduled in April and early May, the WWWA was heading out of business. By April 1, 1963, Buddy's recognition as the heavyweight champion remained inconsistent in the media. He lost title billing in Bridgeport, Chicago, and Ottawa, while being hailed as champ in Baltimore and Boston.[8]

In New York City, die-hard aficionados read the news of his loss to Lou Thesz in the April 1963 issue of *The Ring*, which hit the streets in early March.[9] In addition, columnist Al Buck reported Buddy's defeat in the March 17 edition of the *New York Post*.[10] But that proclamation didn't exactly jibe with the official dictum from the promotion of Vince McMahon. Despite the fact that Rogers had lost to both Thesz and Dory Dixon, he remained the top heavyweight in the Northeast. In Newark on March 30, he was casually announced as the reigning world champion before a tag team match with the Shadow (Clyde Steeves) against Bobo Brazil and Johnny Barend.[11] The promoter in Newark, notably, was Willie Gilzenberg, one of McMahon's most important allies. Gilzenberg was not only experienced, but wily, and his loyalty was unmatched by his peers. As a reward, Gilzenberg was elevated to an on-camera leadership role, and was pronounced the president of the newly established World-Wide Wrestling Federation, a role that McMahon seemingly wanted to personally avoid.[12]

The WWWF was created for the same reasons as the WWWA in Cleveland, but for McMahon, this promotional organization would be operated out of his own backyard, rather than a city several hundred miles away. Capitol Wrestling would continue to administer the business end of the territory, but the WWWF was now positioned to be its public face, and Gilzenberg would run its headquarters out of his Newark office. Buddy Rogers was a key figure during the infancy of McMahon's new federation. Since he was already acclaimed as the heavyweight champion, and his credentials verified time and again, he was proclaimed the initial WWWF titleholder. Fan recollections of the events surrounding Rogers becoming the WWWF champion differ slightly from person to person, and that makes sense 57 years after the fact. There are memories of him being affirmed as the champ and "returned" the title belt by Gilzenberg, who clearly said his loss in Canada [to Thesz] was non-title. Soon thereafter, he was formally declared the WWWF king.

However, some people recalled the dismissal of his NWA claim and the announcement of his WWWF championship standing as happening all on the same telecast.[13] To take it a step further, it was alleged that Rogers won a special tournament in Rio de Janeiro, Brazil, to attain WWWF recognition, a completely fictional assertion.[14] In April 1963, Buddy gave a "candid" interview to Robert D. Willis of *Wrestling World* magazine, and was acknowledged as the WWWF champion in a national publication.[15] "Rogers is professional wrestling," Willis wrote in his preamble. "His name is box office magic to promoters from coast to coast. He is, truly, money in the bank." Rogers talked up the WWWF, stating that it was "governed by a group of men around the country," and explained that Gilzenberg made sure he wrestled "none other than the best of talent."[16] When he was asked who was the strongest man he had ever met, Buddy answered definitively and demonstrated his willingness to push company workers. "Without a doubt, it would be Bruno Sammartino," he declared.[17]

The article offered a revelatory look at Rogers and was nice exposure for McMahon's new organization. His particular comments about Sammartino reflected his understanding of their feud's value and, with potential big money matches ahead, Rogers was willing to do even more to put Bruno over. As it was known, Buddy elevated an opponent like no other, probably better than anyone else in the business, and he had been doing it most of his career. Just recently on TV in Cleveland, he significantly boosted the esteem of Dory Dixon by selling nearly an entire match for his foe, and his actions were unselfish and business savvy. That single deed was going to transform into a pile of greenbacks, and he expected an even greater financial return from his series with Bruno. For weeks, Sammartino had eclipsed rivals in televised and arena contests, and the time had come for him to meet the champion in what would be a star-making performance.

On April 18, 1963, before the expansive Capitol Wrestling viewing audience, Rogers entered the ring in Washington, D.C. for a special non-title bout against the Italian powerhouse. As soon as the bell rang, Buddy pulled out one of his cunning tricks, attacking Bruno from behind and landing a couple swift blows. But Sammartino immediately turned things around, using his brute strength to dominate the WWWF titleholder and hoisting him into his backbreaker finisher. Rogers was done, unable to continue, and had the bell officially sounded and had his championship been on the line, he would have lost his belt fair and square.[18] The match was instead declared a no-contest. Witnesses to the affair were stunned. Buddy had never been so thoroughly trounced on the D.C. telecast. On occasion, he would struggle with a determined competitor, which was part of his gimmick, but by no means was he ever subdued in such a quick and embarrassing fashion. Fans were now sure Sammartino was the real deal, and Vince McMahon had his ace in the hole.

Rogers was situated for main event matches with Bobo Brazil, Johnny Barend, Edouard Carpentier, and Dory Dixon, but in the aftermath of the Washington broadcast, fans really wanted to see a title bout between the veteran champion and the muscle-bound hero. And Madison Square Garden seemed to be the perfect venue. McMahon still had some time to build things up as the Garden had been closed to the grappling industry since March, and wasn't set to reopen to the wrestling public until May 17.[19] For Rogers, he remained on the road, and refused to let up. The April 18 bout in Washington had actually been taped the week prior, and he was in the middle of a three-city jaunt to Ottawa, Pittsburgh, and Cleveland, when his life suddenly went off the rails. Following a defeat of Dick (Bulldog) Brower at the Coliseum in Ottawa on April 16, Rogers ventured to Pittsburgh for a six-man tag team bout, where he was slated to team with Buddy Austin and the Shadow against Sammartino, Brazil and Argentina Apollo.

Comparatively speaking, Buddy was dealing with a lighter schedule than when he was NWA champion. He had wrestled 10 matches in the past 16 days, and it should have been a relief, but Rogers was hurting more and more, and he could hide it no longer. Typically, wrestlers were given a brief medical screening before their matches, mandated and performed by the local state athletic commission. If an athlete neglected to disclose their medical maladies, but nothing turned up in a basic examination, they were approved for ring combat. The pre-match physical included a check of the vital signs, listening to the heart and lungs with a stethoscope, and an overall bodily inspection. To that point, Rogers had made no effort to inform a commission doctor of his chest pains for fear of losing his license. He knew if he was suspended for medical reasons in one state, it was acknowledged elsewhere, as per the working relationships between the various commissions.

That kind of domino effect could end his career. However, if he didn't start dealing with the realities of the moment, his untreated health problems could expose him to a possible tragedy. The truth of the matter was, Buddy wasn't improving on his own. Whatever personal changes he had made to his lifestyle weren't sufficient to mend his ailment, and by the time he arrived in Pittsburgh, he was at his breaking point. It's not entirely clear what transpired in the dressing room of the Civic Arena on April 17, but as a result of his examination, Rogers was blocked from participating in the evening's show by the on-duty physician. "Chest pains" were the stated reason.[20] During previous flare-ups, wrestling in a six-man tag team bout would have given him the necessary cover to hide his illness. He could rely on his partners to carry the match, while he remained mostly on the apron. This time around, though, even that was too much to ask.

The next morning, prior to heading to Cleveland for a title contest with Dory Dixon that night, Rogers went to Mercy Hospital in Pittsburgh for a more comprehensive exam.[21] He felt weakened and tired, and although the details of his hospital visit are unknown, he turned up at the Cleveland Arena in no better condition. Once again, he was prevented from wrestling by the in-house physician, disappointing his local supporters, but he managed to step out from the back area for a quick bow to the crowd.[22] The charade, however, was over. Buddy's back-to-back non-appearances sounded the alarm in the D.C. offices of Capitol Wrestling, and Vince McMahon direly wanted to know what was going on. Rogers was forced to reveal his condition, and McMahon wanted him back in Washington for immediate diagnosis and treatment at the famed Georgetown University Hospital.[23] Buddy agreed. A few days later, an Ottawa paper claimed Rogers had suffered a heart attack in Cleveland on April 21.[24]

Luckily, the report was false.[25] Based on all known information, including the recollections of Buddy's daughter, Lee Rogers, Buddy did not suffer a devastating heart attack in Cleveland.[26] Despite his rough shape, he returned eastward, and was admitted to Georgetown Hospital, where it was soon discovered that he had experienced "a series of small heart attacks and was [indeed] working himself up to a major one."[27] Essentially, one or more of his arteries were clogged, resulting in his bouts with angina, and between his stress and family history, he was an ideal candidate for a fatal myocardial infarction. A Georgetown doctor bluntly advised him not to return to the ring, making the entire situation difficult to process.[28] Rogers later admitted that when he got out of the intensive care unit, and realized he might never wrestle again, it was one of the toughest things he ever dealt with.[29] With regard to his career, Buddy obviously had a lot to think about going forward.

As the mainstream wrestling media was engrossed by Dick the Bruiser's feud with NFL star Alex Karras, the big story at the time, Rogers laid in a hospital bed, and his condition went unreported. No one knew what was happening outside a handful of trusted people, and that's exactly what the leaders of Capitol Wrestling wanted. Vince McMahon was laboring to save his company from an economic collapse, and any public news of his WWWF champion being hospitalized was potentially crippling. He needed his top star strong and fit, or at least give that impression until they could figure out an alternate plan. The best case scenario, which had Rogers returning at full strength, seemed to be impossible in light of what transpired. The next option was to get Rogers into the ring for a hastily booked title change and move the belt to an interim champion. But since Rogers had already been told not to wrestle again, there was definitely a big problem.

In the meantime, Rogers missed five additional bookings, two in New York State, and one each in New Jersey, Massachusetts, and Ontario.[30] The no-shows were risky, especially in states that had rigid athletic commission enforcement. If Rogers' career was effectively over, it didn't matter if he was suspended for medical reasons, but if there was the slightest chance he could go one last time to put someone over, McMahon had to protect his active status.

Mentally, Rogers was burned out. The cumulative effect of all of the trials and tribulations in his life since 1961 were beyond exhausting. His elbow and ankle injuries, the attack in Columbus, and the boundless pressure, were too much for even the most experienced wrestlers to endure. There were anxiety-filled moments when he wondered if he would bounce back from injury and regain his health. This time, though, his mortality was in question, and for a man with a young family, he couldn't risk it all, regardless of his love of wrestling.

Rogers was also a man of principle. He always had the utmost respect for McMahon and trusted him through and through. Contracts were never a necessity when working with Vince. "Anything Vince McMahon told you was his word," Rogers later explained, "and his word was as good as a contract."[31] Unwilling to leave McMahon out to dry, he agreed to go against his doctor's wishes and enter the ring for the specific reason of dropping the WWWF title. McMahon was appreciative, and because of the April 18 televised bout between Rogers and Bruno Sammartino, he already had Buddy's successor lined up. Unquestionably, Sammartino was McMahon's best option. The beating he gave Rogers in Washington, D.C. was a landmark occasion, and there was no better way to set up a main event at Madison Square Garden.

And fortunately, the angle was in motion before Buddy's life entered crisis mode.

But to further sell the heat between the two wrestlers, Rogers appeared on TV and talked trash, just like old times. He instigated Bruno and his fan base, focusing on Sammartino's Italian background, and poked and prodded until he got the reaction he wanted.[32] On camera, things initially started with Buddy flatly refusing to defend against Bruno, and fans saw right through that ruse. They knew Rogers was scared, and that Sammartino had his number. "I'll face him when I'm good and ready," the champion defiantly declared.[33] He threatened to ruin the Pittsburgh strongman "financially and physically," and refused to put his title on the line for anything less than $25,000.[34] With his chance at the belt hanging in the balance, Sammartino made a bold move. "Sammartino is taking 50 per cent of the gate, and [personally] paying Rogers $25,000," Garden promoter Walter Johnston announced. "We will have to sell out for Sammartino to make a couple of thousand dollars."[35]

It was all part of the storyline, but it sold perfectly. The highly anticipated Rogers versus Sammartino contest was scheduled for May 17, 1963, and was promoted in the newspaper as early as May 3.[36] That gave McMahon two weeks to build upon the excitement. A man of the people, Sammartino carried heavy emotional support, and the Italian populace in the New York metropolitan area rallied to his side in record numbers.[37] He was friendly, humble, and during interviews, he would often speak Italian, connecting him to the audience on a personal level. Rogers still had enthusiastic fans, but the up-swell in popularity for Sammartino couldn't be ignored. For that reason, Buddy wanted an agreement from McMahon for a high-profile rematch with Bruno during the summer, under the presumption that he would regain his health. The money to be made from their feud was substantial and he didn't want to miss out. With a lot of rest and prescribed treatment, Rogers hoped to be back in position to win a rematch from Bruno by Aug..

Promises were made and Rogers was comfortable with their long-term plan. He worked on a strategy for his bout with Sammartino and fulfilled several mandatory appearances in Newark and Washington. On May 4 at the Newark Armory, he briefly fought with Johnny Barend, and then put his foe in the figure-four. Barend was immobilized and injured by the hold, ending their bout before the initial bell even rang.[38] Buddy's physical effort was minimal, and it's assumed a similarly abbreviated bout occurred at the Washington Coliseum on May 13 between Rogers and Bobo Brazil. Rogers was disqualified for refusing to release a hold in that contest.[39] In *The Ring* magazine, Nat Loubet acknowledged these short matches, and noted that the "Nature Boy" had experienced a "physical disability since late April or early May." He pointed out that his recent bouts each had been "completed in less than seventy seconds."[40]

Vince McMahon was the master manipulator at the center of things. His dealings with Rogers, and then separately with Sammartino, were individually crafted to appease both men. It was a delicate operation, and Vince handled his star performers with care and immense skill. Years after the fact, Sammartino revealed his perspective of the May 1963 match with Rogers, and explained that he entered the ring to dethrone him, truly believing the latter wasn't in on the finish. He felt if Buddy knew he was going to lose the championship, he would fake an injury and not show up for the match.

However, Bobby Davis recalled it happening much differently. "In the week before the match," Davis explained, "Buddy and Vince and Bruno sat down and Vince said, 'Bruno, we're switching the title. We're giving it to you in the Garden. Buddy will tell you the finish.' No promoter in the business, at that time, would have sent the world champion into the ring with any opponent without laying out the finish first."[41]

Buddy's daughter, Lee, remembered something along those lines, but she actually recalled Sammartino visiting their home in Audubon, New Jersey, to "discuss the fight."[42] The later kayfabe versions of the important contest took root, and superseded logic in some instances. Overall, it was difficult to challenge the memories of a pro wrestling legend like Sammartino, whose integrity was well-established. He was a credit to the sport. But when it came to Rogers, he admittedly disliked him, and his stories reflected that natural aversion. McMahon, in the moment, had to balance the whims of Rogers and Sammartino, and told his grapplers what they wanted to hear. He was keeping Buddy's health a secret, as well, and no one outside the inner circle was wise to all facets happening behind-the-scenes. The New York State Athletic Commission was the last obstacle, and Capitol Wrestling had to ensure Rogers was approved to compete on May 17 without a hitch.

Since Buddy already had a state license to wrestle in New York, all he had to do was pass the pre-match examination on the night of the contest. Surprisingly, there had been no ramifications for his medical emergencies in Pittsburgh and Cleveland, or for his no-shows in at least seven towns. The normal consequences were overlooked, likely by design over ignorance, and the pathway to May 17 was clear. On the evening of the historic match, Rogers arrived at Madison Square Garden ready to do his job. He appeared his customary self to observers, smoking a cigar and not drawing any unusual attention.[43] When it was time for his pre-bout assessment, he went through the motions, and without any hesitation, was ultimately granted permission to perform.

The sanctioning of a wrestler with serious health issues was not extraordinary, despite the connotations. More than two years before, Charles (Chick) Garibaldi was given the green light to wrestle at Sunnyside Gardens. After his match, he collapsed in the dressing room and died. The 46-year-old Garibaldi passed away of a heart attack and his underlying health problems were undiagnosable with a simple exam.[44] In 1961, one of Buddy's old rivals, Oyama Kato, died in Vancouver, British Columbia, also following a contest.[45] An autopsy revealed hardening of his arteries had caused a heart attack, and there was significant pressure on the local commission to explain what happened. "We check all boxers and wrestlers before they perform in Vancouver," commission secretary Jack Henderson said. "This is done by Dr. W.J. MacKenzie. He puts a stethoscope on their hearts. He thumps their chests and checks their hands and eyes. The doctor is careful about their hearts, but how can he know about their arteries?"[46]

That was the same for Rogers in New York, and it was just impossible to identify that issue without more elaborate testing. And if Rogers had suffered a minor heart attack, a basic exam wouldn't have revealed it. Dr. Charles M.

Geller, Chief of Cardiac Surgery and Associate Chairman of the Department of Surgery for the Crozer Keystone Health System in Delaware County, Pennsylvania, said: "Given his impeccable external appearance, without Buddy volunteering the information or without them having access to his hospital or private physician records, the commission doctor would have had no way of knowing about [any possible previous] heart attack."[47] Even though the New York commission had a reputation for being medically tough, that didn't exactly make it so. In 1962, Lou Sahadi did an interview with Rogers backstage at Sunnyside in Queens, and in the middle of their conversation, Buddy had to be dismissed for his pre-match check-up. Sahadi explained that Rogers "wasn't gone two minutes when he returned," having completed whatever testing the commission required.[48]

In 1988, Rogers was asked why the New York commission allowed him to wrestle considering his grave condition. "That's a very touchy subject," Rogers answered. "I don't want to get people involved."[49] A short time later, during the same interview, he added: "They [the commission members] weren't that stringent."[50] While it's uncertain as to who performed Buddy's examination and how thorough it was on May 17 at the Garden, it is known that he was given consent to wrestle.[51] The match against Sammartino would take place as scheduled. In advance of the big event, there were three other details of importance. Rogers brought in his 26-year-old brother-in-law, Jackie Jackson, to work as his corner man, and physically, Jackie fit the bill. Having adopted the name "Diamond Jack" with a purported background from Calcutta, India, Jackson was actually a former Golden Gloves boxing champion from Ohio.[52] He was tall and thin, wore a turban or Derby and a tuxedo jacket, and wielded the trademark cane.

After losing the world championship to Lou Thesz in January, Buddy turned over the prized title belt owned by the NWA, as was custom. To accommodate his continuing claim to the title, he retrieved his old U.S.-shaped belt, which he held in 1960-'61, from mothballs, and began wearing it to the ring. That was the strap he had around his waist for his bout with Sammartino.[53] On the morning of the championship affair, the *New York Post* inaccurately touted the Buddy-Bruno main event as being two-out-of-three falls, instead of a one-fall contest, which it ended up being."[54] Rogers wasn't going longer than a minute or two, and according to the match layout he designed, it didn't need to for it to be effective.[55] On the way to the ring, he experienced a rush of adrenaline, and the exhilaration of the sold out Garden, with 19,648 people in attendance, caused his heart to beat harder and faster.[56] With that came his all-too-familiar chest pains.[57]

In his mind were the words of his doctors and the ominous warning that he was taking his life into his hands.[58] "No one knew when I climbed into that ring that I could have died right there," Rogers later admitted. "But I kept it to myself. That was just the way I was."[59] Sweating under the bright lights and from the mounting anguish, Rogers was said to have been suffering from a fever, and if true, it was another symptom purposely disregarded by the commission.[60]

The anticipation for the first lock-up was palpable, and the emotions were high throughout the arena. Referee Ed Gersh brought both Buddy and Bruno to the center of the ring for his pre-match instructions, and released the two competitors to their corners. The ever-sly Rogers wasn't about to adhere to the rules, and he apparently hadn't learned much from his April TV bout with the Strongman from Abruzzi. Buddy attacked Sammartino in a flash, striking him several times from behind, but instead of disqualifying the champion, Gersh called for the bell.

The match officially started, but in that same instant, Bruno seized control of the action. He landed forearms and dropkicks, and Rogers flailed backwards, disorientated and dazed. Sammartino wasted no time grabbing the WWWF champion into a bearhug and Buddy was squeezed by perhaps the most powerful man in professional wrestling. But Rogers didn't stay in that hold for long. He managed to break free, only to be subjected to a few additional dropkicks. The crowd, standing in unison, was screaming wildly at the sudden turn of events, and although fans who knew Buddy's resourcefulness waited for him to turn the tides, his typical in-ring recovery wasn't in the cards. It was all Bruno. The popular hero stunned the audience by lifting Buddy into his backbreaker and extracting a rapid submission.[61] The finish was clean and the WWWF championship changed hands in spectacular fashion.

Rogers succeeded in putting Sammartino over, incredibly, in just 48 seconds.[62] Fans were jubilant at the result and the lid was blown off the Garden as the crowd went crazy in celebration. The bout was a brilliant textbook example of how to elevate a wrestler to the top spot in the most dominant way possible, and Buddy's efforts displayed both his loyalty to Vince McMahon and a sincere demonstration of unselfishness. For people unaware of Buddy's health problems, the 48-second crushing triumph by Sammartino was likely a surprise, especially for naysayers with a longstanding anti-Rogers sentiment. Rogers essentially gave Bruno the entire match and bowed out as world champion by submitting away his title. It was as clear cut as could be, and Sammartino launched into his championship reign by finally silencing the "Nature Boy." The king was dethroned, once and for all.[63]

The manner in which Rogers lost was a gift to McMahon. In recent wrestling history, no claimant to the world heavyweight championship had succumbed in such a lopsided fashion. A title-change contest was usually three falls and full of back-and-forth combat, allowing the defending champion and the titleholder-to-be a credible performance worthy of the heavyweight crown. In this instance, it was a complete mismatch, and it went down the way Buddy planned. McMahon was the recipient of the hottest commodity in wrestling as a result of the contest, and the WWWF was off and running with a convincing young superstar at the helm.

In the weeks and months, even years, following the May 1963 match between Rogers and Sammartino, there was a constant stream of inconsistencies related to the bout. At the center of the varied reports was Bruno's unwavering insistence that Rogers was not ill that night, but Bruno also referenced the story that claimed Rogers left a hospital bed to go to the Garden and defend his title, which he said was patently false.[64]

Sammartino was correct. That didn't happen, but it also wasn't true that their match was a shoot.[65] Bruno was adamant that Rogers wasn't informed of the finish going into the bout, and that he was victorious in a contest

Buddy believed he was going to win.⁶⁶ With that rationale, basically, the affair was a double-cross, according to Sammartino's version of events.⁶⁷ But how could there be any double-cross if the champion not only agreed to lose the title, but scripted his defeat beforehand? But Bruno didn't see it that way. He recalled telling Rogers when they got into the ring, "I'm going over and that's it. I'm going over, Buddy."⁶⁸ If Rogers had disagreed with that finish, and was warned about a double-cross in this manner prior to a title defense, would he have run over and attacked his opponent before the bell? Would he have worked in cooperation with Bruno in any way? No! Given his experience, Buddy would have protected himself and his belt by getting out of the ring as quickly as possible. He knew what to do in that situation.

On the whole, it appears that Bruno's point of view was influenced by the theory that Rogers was trying to discredit him by claiming a heart attack. Simply put, Sammartino thought Buddy was damaging his reputation by claiming he was less than 100 percent. And the heart attack "two weeks" before their match and the "getting out of bed to wrestle" stories were hurtful exaggerations of the truth. In defense of his honor, Sammartino sounded off, and his voice was heard loud and clear. But it's also highly probable that Vince McMahon never told Sammartino about Buddy's condition, and as part of his manipulations, gave Bruno the task of beating Rogers by whatever means necessary. McMahon knew Rogers would go through the motions because of his health limitations, and Sammartino would end up riding a high of confidence based on a win he believed he really earned. This is possibly the only way to rationalize Sammartino's later comments.

From his own viewpoint, Bruno was actually right about what transpired. Rogers had his own version of events, as did McMahon. In a 1988 interview conducted by Blackjack Brown, Rogers said: "I feel that Bruno had no knowledge of what was wrong with me. I feel that Bruno didn't know what was going on, and I do feel that Bruno felt that he beat me in 48 seconds."⁶⁹

The downfall of Buddy Rogers caused an economic ripple across the wrestling landscape, and hastened the demise of business in Chicago and Cleveland. "Windy City" promoter Fred Kohler, the man who presided over the 1961 record-shattering gate at Comiskey Park, was nearing bankruptcy. His planned Rogers-Dory Dixon program at that same venue, slated for the summer of 1963, was off the table.⁷⁰ The WWWA in Cleveland was a distant memory, and the big-time mixed contest between Rogers and Muhammad Ali was never going to happen. The dominos were falling one at a time, and the reality was, the wrestling business would likely have to find a way to go forward without the services of the famed "Nature Boy."

ENDNOTES - CHAPTER 18

[1] Philadelphia Wrestling Program, Jan. 23, 1960, p. 4. Also see *Ring Wrestling*, September 1963, p. 7-8.

[2] Sammartino's first issue with McMahon occurred around July 1960 when he jumped to the booking office of Kola Kwariani. The second incident happened in March 1961 and resulted in his suspension following a missed booking. See *Bruno Sammartino: The Autobiography of Wrestling's Living Legend* by Bruno Sammartino with Sal Anthony Corrente (2019), p. 97-103.

[3] The bout took place in Sunnyside, Queens on Sept. 5, 1961.

[4] *Pittsburgh Post-Gazette*, Feb. 5, 1963, p. 19. Rogers did a similar finish with Dick "Bulldog" Brower in Ottawa on April 16, 1963. In this bout, Buddy tapped Brower on the shoulder and the latter thought he'd won. *Ottawa Journal*, April 17, 1963, p. 17.

[5] *Pittsburgh Post-Gazette*, Nov. 6, 1962, p. 21.
[6] Interview of Bruno Sammartino, *Wrestling Perspective*, Issue #71, p. 8.
[7] Sammartino said in his book that he only agreed to return to Capitol Wrestling "if [McMahon] put [him] in the ring with Buddy Rogers for the title." *Bruno Sammartino: The Autobiography of Wrestling's Living Legend* by Bruno Sammartino with Sal Anthony Corrente (2019), p. 109. Also Also Bill Apter interview of Bruno Sammartino, June 2017.
[8] *Bridgeport Post*, April 3, 1963, p. 54, *Chicago Tribune*, April 5, 1963, p. 65, *Ottawa Citizen*, April 17, 1963, p. 25, *Baltimore Evening Sun*, April 1, 1963, p. 26, *Boston Sunday Advertiser*, April 14, 1963, p. 33.
[9] *The Ring*, April 1963, p. 32. The issue was reportedly released around March 3, 1963.
[10] *New York Post*, March 17, 1963, p. 70. A week later, the same newspaper reiterated Buddy's status by labeling him the "ex-champion." *New York Post*, March 25, 1963, p. 80.
[11] Correspondence with Michael Omansky, March 2020. Rogers and the Shadow were defeated.
[12] Gilzenberg was acknowledged as the head of the WWWA "Rating Committee" in Cleveland. *Cleveland Plain Dealer*, April 15, 1963, p. 36.
[13] *Is Wrestling Fixed: I Didn't Know it was Broken* by Bill Apter (2015).
[14] It is unclear when the Rio de Janeiro tournament was first mentioned on WWWF TV, if at all. There is some belief that it was a more modern assertion, perhaps invented in the 1970s or '80s. An investigation of publications from 1963 turned up no mention of a Rio tournament. It was alleged that Rogers defeated Antonino Rocca in the finals. Rogers and Rocca was called "one of the classic duels of all time." *Ringside Magazine*, Spring 1983, p. 56-60.
[15] Willis worked as a publicity man at WIIC in Pittsburgh.
[16] *Wrestling World*, December 1963, p. 39-43.
[17] Ibid. Rogers was also asked, "Who's the toughest wrestler you've faced?" He answered: "I'd say this guy Bruno Sammartino is very outstanding."
[18] *Wrestling World*, February 1966, p. 57. Correspondence with Michael Omansky and William Morrisey, March 2020.
[19] *New York Post*, March 25, 1963, p. 80. In the interim, the Ringling Bros. and Barnum & Bailey Circus took center stage at Madison Square Garden. The original main event for May 17 at Madison Square Garden may have been Rogers vs. Edouard Carpentier, as mentioned in Donald R. Jordan's *The Wrestling Weekly*, Vol. 1, No. 3, April 29, 1963, p. 4.
[20] Rogers was replaced by the Great Mortier. The heels were defeated by Sammartino, Brazil and Apollo in three falls before 3,200 fans. *Pittsburgh Post-Gazette*, April 18, 1963, p. 31.
[21] Ibid. Another report stated that Rogers "underwent a four-hour physical check-up" at St. Margaret's Hospital in Pittsburgh. *Wrestling World*, December 1963, p. 39-43.
[22] Dixon wrestled and beat Adolph Von Hess in the main event. *Cleveland Plain Dealer*, April 19, 1963, p. 42. "Buddy Rogers failed a physical examination and was not allowed to appear." *Akron Beacon Journal*, April 19, 1963, p. 35.
[23] A friend of Rogers named Terry Milam claimed that McMahon "had known about [Buddy's] heart condition for years." Interview of Terry Milam by Steve Johnson, February 2006.
[24] *Ottawa Citizen*, April 23, 1963, p. 17.
[25] This Ottawa paper was the only known source for the heart attack in Cleveland story.
[26] Correspondence with Lee Rogers, April 18, 2020.
[27] It was said that Rogers was checked out at Johns Hopkins University Hospital in Baltimore. *Buddie Rogers and The Art of "Sequencing"* by Max W. Jacobs, p. 18. In two separate interviews, Buddy mentioned that he was treated at Georgetown University Hospital. *Jim Barniak's Sports Scrapbook*, PRISM Network, Dec. 2, 1981 and *Wrestling Hotline* with Blackjack Brown, March 1988. It's important to note that Buddy's daughter, Lee, didn't recall Rogers suffering a heart attack. He did have "chest pains" and was "taken to the hospital." Correspondence with Lee Rogers, April 18, 2020.
[28] Buddy Rogers Interview, *Wrestling Hotline* with Blackjack Brown, March 1988.
[29] *Jim Barniak's Sports Scrapbook*, PRISM Network, Dec. 2, 1981.

[30] The matches were scheduled for Kingston and West Hempstead, NY, Highland Park, NJ, Boston, MA, and Ottawa, Ontario.
[31] Buddy Rogers Interview, *New Wave Wrestling*, April 1992, p. 31-32. Rogers also made similar comments in his interviews with John Arezzi, *Pro Wrestling Spotlight*, Aug. 4, 1991 and with Dr. Mike Lano and Gary "Gerhardt" Kaiser, *Canvas Cavity*, Circa. 1991-1992.
[32] Interview with Fred Rubenstein, July 6, 2020.
[33] *Wrestling World*, February 1966, p. 57.
[34] *Jersey Journal*, May 18, 1963, p. 8.
[35] *New York Post*, May 15, 1963, p. 81.
[36] *New York Daily News*, May 3, 1963, p. 77, *Greenpoint Weekly Star*, May 3, 1963, p. 7.
[37] Joe "Joey G" Frustaci told a story about the importance of Sammartino in his Italian household, and how his support for Rogers created problems between himself and his grandfather. *Wrestling Chatterbox*, September 1995, p. 8.
[38] *Paterson News*, May 6, 1963, p. 25.
[39] *Washington Daily News*, May 14, 1963, p. 40. Buddy also beat Pete Sanchez "quickly" at the Capitol Arena on May 9. *Washington Daily News*, May 10, 1963, p. 57. He may have appeared for a Baltimore TV bout on April 27, and defeated Tony Manousos.
[40] *The Ring*, August 1963, p. 35.
[41] Interview with Bobby Davis, Aug. 25, 2019.
[42] Correspondence with Lee Rogers, April 18, 2020.
[43] Interview of Bruno Sammartino, Ringside Live with Mark Nulty, Jan. 8, 2005, wrestlingclassics.com.
[44] *New York Daily News*, Feb. 19, 1961, p. 4.
[45] Kato died on Jan. 9, 1961.
[46] *Vancouver Sun*, Jan. 13, 1961, p. 18.
[47] Correspondence with Dr. Charles Geller, Aug. 8, 2019.
[48] *Boxing and Wrestling*, April 1962, p. 49.
[49] For decades, rumors have circulated that pressure or some kind of inducement was made to the commission to get Rogers approved to wrestle that night.
[50] Buddy Rogers Interview, *Wrestling Hotline* with Blackjack Brown, March 1988.
[51] There were five main doctors for the New York State Athletic Commission in May 1963, handling wrestling and boxing events in the New York metropolitan area. They were Dr. Aaron Harry Kleiman, Dr. Alexander Schiff, Dr. Edwin Campbell, Dr. Samuel Swetnick, and Dr. Felice Viti.
[52] See *Gallipolis Daily Tribune* articles 1957-1959. Jackson's father, Malcolm Jackson was a boxing promoter, manager and trainer in Gallipolis, Ohio.
[53] In 2012, this belt was discovered in the attic of Johnny Barend. It was later sold to the WWE. See articles at slamwrestling.net and wwe.com.
[54] *New York Post*, May 17, 1963, p. 101.
[55] Rogers admired Joe Louis's "quick knockout." *Buddie Rogers and The Art of "Sequencing"* by Max W. Jacobs, p. 18.
[56] The attendance surpassed expectations. Promoter Walter Johnston stated he believed 18,000 would be at the Garden that night. *New York Post*, May 17, 1963, p. 101. Joe O'Day said that Rogers was "the big draw." The gate was $58,966.10. *New York Daily News*, May 18, 1963, p. 29.
[57] *Jim Barniak's Sports Scrapbook*, PRISM Network, Dec. 2, 1981.
[58] Buddy Rogers Interview, *Wrestling Hotline* with Blackjack Brown, March 1988.
[59] *Atlantic City Sunday Press*, March 7, 1982.
[60] Rogers was suffering from a fever as high as 103 degrees. Interview with Fred Rubenstein, July 6, 2020.
[61] *Wrestling World*, February 1966, p. 57. Also, Interview with Fred Rubenstein, July 6, 2020.
[62] *New York Daily News*, May 18, 1963, p. 29. A New Jersey paper stated that the bout lasted "28 seconds." *Jersey Journal*, May 18, 1963, p. 8.

[63] It was said that Rogers made $25,000 for his bout with Sammartino. *Jersey Journal*, May 18, 1963, p. 8. Sammartino said he received $6,500, which was the largest payoff of his career to date. *Hackensack Record*, March 9, 1964, p. 32.

[64] Interview of Bruno Sammartino, Ringside Live with Mark Nulty, Jan. 8, 2005, wrestlingclassics.com.

[65] Sammartino admitted that it wasn't a shoot. Interview of Bruno Sammartino, *Wrestling Perspective*, Volume IX, Issue #71, p. 5-8.

[66] *Bruno Sammartino: The Autobiography of Wrestling's Living Legend* by Bruno Sammartino with Sal Anthony Corrente (2019), p. 115.

[67] Sammartino said that Rogers complained about the double-cross during a meeting at McMahon's home in Delaware. Interview of Bruno Sammartino, *Wrestling Perspective*, Volume IX, Issue #72, p. 4-11.

[68] Interview of Bruno Sammartino, *Wrestling Perspective*, Volume IX, Issue #71, p. 5-8.

[69] Buddy Rogers Interview, *Wrestling Hotline* with Blackjack Brown, March 1988.

[70] *Wrestling World*, August 1963, p. 50.

Buddy and his brother-in-law, "Diamond Jack", who accompanied him to the ring the night Buddy lost the WWWF heavyweight title to Bruno Sammartino.

From the Dan Westbrook collection

Chapter 19
The Next Chapter

The dramatic match against Bruno Sammartino at Madison Square Garden was a turning point in the life of Buddy Rogers. Up to that juncture, he had been a fixture as world champion and acknowledged amongst the top heavyweights in the business for many years. His loss and his health concerns had forced upon him a new direction, and he needed to take specific measures to ensure his future. Rogers, though, was playing the long game, and through his conversations with Vince McMahon, had set up a preliminary timetable for his return during the summer. He wasn't entirely convinced his career was over and he was dedicated to a recovery plan that would lead him to his goal. A man of great pride, Rogers wanted to keep his heart problems secret, especially when it came to the general public. Surprisingly, the day after his loss to Sammartino, a sportswriter for the leading periodical in Calgary, Alberta, Canada, announced that Buddy had "suffered a recent heart attack."[1]

News of Buddy's condition was circulating inside the business, as well. In a letter from Sam Muchnick to Vince McMahon, the former wrote: "Hope Buddy recovers from his setback and is well again real soon."[2] The perils of active competition before he was physically capable were front and center in Rogers' mind, but to maintain his license, he was required to fulfill a handful of dates for Capitol Wrestling. That included a bout in Baltimore on May 18 against high-flyer Vittorio (Argentina) Apollo. In what was his standard fare, Rogers attacked his opponent prior to the bell, but was repelled by dropkicks. He quickly maneuvered away, causing Apollo to miss his target, and Rogers applied his figure-four. At the 22-second mark, Apollo gave up. "Many at the Civic Center had no idea of what happened as it occurred so fast," wrote Paul Dowling in *Ring Wrestling* magazine. "It was one of the most mismatched bouts I've ever seen."[3]

Rogers was in Chicago at the International Amphitheater, the site of many of his great triumphs, on May 24 for a contest with Bobo Brazil. The affair went a little longer than his last couple bouts, and lasted one minute, 4 seconds, ending with Buddy's disqualification when he refused to break his figure-four.[4]

In terms of booking, Buddy was the focal point of so many storylines, and Capitol had big matches lined up involving the "Nature Boy" in most of its towns. McMahon wanted a run of Rogers-Sammartino battles, with one scheduled for Westchester County Civic Center in White Plains on June 5, but it was called off.[5] There was also talk of the two getting together at Forbes Field in Pittsburgh sometime in July, but that idea was scrapped and the public was sold the notion that Rogers "refused to sign a contract."[6] In the 55 days following Buddy's loss of the WWWF championship, he competed in exactly five matches, and the two aforementioned singles bouts lasted a combined 86 seconds.

The other three engagements, with Rogers in a minor role, were tag team contests held in Washington, D.C., Newark, and at Madison Square Garden. He would normally participate for 30 seconds to a minute, and work other angles to attain heat and crowd reaction.[7] In the middle of this stretch of semi-activeness, Rogers was indefinitely suspended by the Pennsylvania State Athletic Commission for medical reasons.[8] Despite the attempts to keep his health quiet, officials on June 4 banned him pending a cardiological examination. The New York commission added him to its own suspended list based on that information, and since Capitol had a Garden program planned for July 12, Vince McMahon moved swiftly to get him reinstated. Buddy's cardiologist report was in the hands of Dr. Ira A. McCown, the medical director of the New York commission, within two weeks. Upon review, McCown recommended the wrestler be restored to good standing, and the members of the commission agreed.[9]

It really didn't matter if it was minimizing or whitewashing the truth. Rogers was positioned to resume his career, regardless of his physical state. The time off from competition was mentally agonizing, and Rogers later admitted how tough it was.[10] As he convalesced, pundits continued to discuss his sudden exit and the gossip surrounding his health. Nat Loubet, the publisher and editor of *Ring Wrestling*, stated: "Rumors that Buddy Rogers is ill and has retired are so much bunk. I have spent several hours with Buddy in recent weeks and he is not only well but is better than ever."[11] Robert D. Willis of *Wrestling World* magazine, agreed, and wrote that Buddy was "not seriously ill."[12] Georgiann Mastis, 22-year-old head of the "International Buddy Rogers Fan Club," declared that Rogers did not have a "heart condition" in her July 1963 newsletter to the club's membership. Georgiann actually said that Buddy had tax issues and owed the Government "$102,000 in back taxes."[13]

Spinning the story was relatively simple, and without dirt sheet writers or the internet to reveal the facts, fans were essentially in the dark. That made it easier for the confusion to perpetuate. Norman H. Kietzer authored a special "Salute to the Nature Boy" in the September 1963 edition of *Ring Wrestling*, and proclaimed: "He is one of the most colorful performers in wrestling. The originator of such important wrestling gimmicks as the Buddy Rogers strut, wearing expensive jackets into the ring, and bleaching of the hair."[14] The acknowledgment was deserved, and supporters undoubtedly enjoyed the article. But for Buddy, he was recoiling in the unknown, and his future on the mat was uncertain. If he was going to remain relevant, he had to be involved and lively, or else he was going to lose everything he had gained in the business. Getting back into the ring with Bruno Sammartino and regaining the championship was his central goal, and Vince McMahon gave him the time he needed to recuperate.

In his downtime, Buddy did some serious thinking. He considered life after active wrestling and decided to form a corporation to facilitate his business initiatives, which ranged from real estate to the promotion of athletic events. "Buddy Rogers Enterprises" was created with his brother John and mother Frieda as shareholders, and recorded in New Jersey on May 23, 1963.[15] The move coincided with his purchase of a 31-unit apartment building at 700 Station Avenue in Haddon Heights.[16] Transitioning to a promotional position had been on his mind for years, and he saw the opportunity to possibly run shows in Southern New Jersey.[17] In a July 1963 interview with Charlie Schuck of the *Camden Courier-Post*, Buddy mentioned wanting to "see what happens in this business from the front office viewpoint."[18] He negotiated with Philadelphia promoter Ray Fabiani to represent the latter's Keystone Athletic Club in the Camden area, and booked his first program for August 19 at the Convention Hall.[19]

Working with Fabiani and becoming an affiliate promoter for the WWWF in Camden was a major step in the right direction, but Rogers yearned for a full-time return to the ring.[20] On July 25, 1963, he reemerged on television for a match from the Capitol Arena, his first such appearance in more than two months. Buddy partnered with his more-recent adversary, Johnny Barend, and reformed their successful tag team. They squashed their opponents, Bob Boyer and Eugenio Marin, setting up a Madison Square Garden main event against Bruno Sammartino and Bobo Brazil eight days later. In that bout, the heels won two of three falls, and took the winner's purse. The contest was significant for several reasons, particularly the way Rogers was reestablished as the top villain and challenger to the world championship. During the initial fall, he pinned Bruno, the reigning champion, which affirmed to the 14,667 in attendance that he still had the skill and aptitude to prevail over the Italian strongman.

In the kayfabe environment, rebuilding Rogers into a credible force was incredibly important. He had lost the title in 48-seconds, turning Sammartino into a Superman-like hero, while diminishing his own reputation. For there to be any hope of capitalizing on the Rogers-Sammartino feud, the time was now for him to illustrate his vigor and refocus on taking back his throne. Not only did Rogers pin Sammartino, but he also won the match for his team by finishing off Bobo Brazil in the third fall.[21] It was a tremendous boost for Buddy and he appeared to be on his way. But was he physically ready? Had he recovered enough for another big-time run? In a 1988 radio conversation between Buddy and Bruno, Sammartino highlighted this bout, and mentioned that Rogers bodyslammed Brazil. In response, Buddy reiterated that it was a "tag match," and that he [still] "could not go over a minute."[22] It's not known how much of the nearly 18-minute match Rogers participated in physically, but from his later comments, it was clear that he was in no condition to resume wrestling on a regular scale.

So the answer was, "No," Rogers was not well. He was not any better, but to Vince McMahon and the public, Buddy acted like he was fine.[23] His scheduled bookings and an outdoor stadium bout with Sammartino, which McMahon envisioned would break the all-time attendance record, were going ahead as planned.[24] According to the angle playing out, Rogers earned a title shot as a result of the tag victory over Sammartino and Brazil at the Garden, stipulated by WWWF President Willie Gilzenberg.[25] A few weeks later, on Aug. 29 at the Capitol Arena, Buddy and Bruno did a special on-camera contract signing for an October 4 contest at Roosevelt Stadium in Jersey City. This was the match Rogers, Capitol Wrestling, and the fans were waiting for. "We expect to break all attendance and gate-receipt records with this match," Gilzenberg announced.²⁶ Between 30,000 and 40,000 people were anticipated, and Buddy knew the payoff was going massive, perhaps the greatest of his career.

Before the end of Aug., Rogers wrestled 10 additional matches, and eight of them were tag team encounters. Six were straight tag bouts alongside Barend, one was a six-man contest with Barend and Buddy Austin, and another was a TV scrap from Washington with the robust Gorilla Monsoon. Buddy engaged in only two singles bouts during that time-frame, a five-minute clash with the Black Shadow in Camden on August 19 and a 47-second collision with Hans Mortier at Madison Square Garden on Aug. 23.²⁷ Both matches ended in a Rogers victory. The Garden showing was remarkably brisk, and featured two dropkicks by Rogers and his figure-four leglock.²⁸ Demonstrating his continued enthusiasm for the business, he turned up at his old high school in Camden with upstart Ron Reed on Aug. 13, for an exhibition. Buddy displayed a handful of moves and offered his brand of philosophical advice to students, telling them: "It's important to get an education or some smart guy'll come along and take you over the hurdles."²⁹

Politically, the intrigue within the WWWF was escalating, and not everyone agreed on the next step. Vince McMahon was growing confident in Bruno Sammartino's ability to draw at the box office. Bruno worked for less money than Rogers and was less inclined to manipulate things backstage than the "Nature Boy." In some respects, the higher-ups at Capitol were thrilled to have replaced Buddy and rid themselves of the problems Rogers brought to the table. As for Bruno, he was happy in his championship slot and was thriving. The numbers were noteworthy, so he had every reason to think his reign was guaranteed to continue unabated.³⁰ From Buddy's vantage point, he believed he was smartly situated and would be getting the title back. Not only that, but Rogers considered his promotional spot in Camden secure. But the voices opposing his push back to the top were gaining steam, and McMahon went ahead and altered his strategy.³¹ Sammartino would continue to be the WWWF champion for the foreseeable future.

"Rogers the champion" and "Rogers the promoter" were problematic to McMahon's business. Based on previous experience, Buddy was known for building up a territory with use of his talented crew of workers, and then applying pressure on the territory promoter in an attempt to obtain more power. Even if that wasn't his objective, the speculation and concern for such a move had the hierarchy of Capitol Wrestling fearful. They couldn't control Rogers. For that reason, Buddy was squeezed out. His role as a promoter and WWWF agent were snatched away in an instant, and after a heated conversation with McMahon, his October 4 title shot was withdrawn as well.³² Although he tried to persuade McMahon to change his mind, Rogers failed, and he knew he was aced out. With regard to his physical activeness, it was probably for the best, but Rogers never wanted to leave money on the table, and losing the Jersey City bout was painful. It was a small fortune, and would have been his last real hurrah as a professional wrestler.

For months, Rogers had struggled with the mental realities of his situation. He had endured the pain, the risk assessments, and the concern of his family. The decision to leave the business he had devoted 21 years to didn't come easy, and he had wavered a lot since April. Rest and basic treatment were not a cure for his condition, and barring a surgical procedure, the problems were going to remain a fixture in his life. The faithful fans of the Northeast, who had awaited the second Rogers-Sammartino contest with bated breath, were stunned by the rapid developments. Things began to fall apart at the seams when Rogers no-showed a September 16 tag team affair at Madison Square Garden.[33] He was supposed to have teamed with Gorilla Monsoon against Sammartino and Bobo Brazil, but was replaced at the last minute by Hans Mortier.[34] Fred Cranwell in the *Jersey Journal* reported that Rogers "said he was sick," to justify his non-appearance. Sammartino called Buddy a "chicken," and said, "He's afraid of me."[35]

Monsoon took Buddy's spot in the Roosevelt Stadium contest against Bruno on October 4, but the show lost its luster after Rogers dropped out. Only 8,103 people paid $23,236 to witness the program, and Sammartino retained his WWWF title despite being disqualified.[36] As Rogers went out the door, McMahon decided to purge Capitol of Buddy's crew, and sent Johnny Barend, Great Scott, Ron Reed, and Buddy Austin packing.[37] Monsoon, interestingly, mentioned Buddy's "bad heart" in a kayfabe article, while the old-time sportswriter, Dan Parker, referred to an "injury, or whatever it was," as being what kept Rogers from his Garden date.[38] In Chicago, Rogers' friend David Condon of the *Tribune* boldly announced that the wrestler had been "sidelined by a heart condition," settling the confusion for local wrestling fans.[39] The New York athletic commission suspended Buddy indefinitely for medical reasons effective Sept. 16, 1963, and that was the final dagger silencing the career of the legendary "Nature Boy."[40]

Buddy Rogers always seemed indestructible. He possessed no fear in the ring, taking dives through the ropes and performing difficult stunts, and bounced back from injury with ease. "I am like a Cadillac," he told a reporter in 1962. "The Cadillacs keep rolling and the Fords fall apart."[41] That was the image Rogers wanted to convey to the world. He didn't want people to feel sorry for him.[42] Personally, he was satisfied by retiring as a headliner, and for years, had expressed his desire to leave wrestling on top. From his perspective, his health was a private matter, and it was downplayed in subsequent articles printed in *Wrestling Confidential* magazine. Terry Rogers was the author of a partially ghostwritten article in the July 1964 issue of that publication, which was entitled, "Mrs. Buddy Rogers Own Story: I Made My Husband Quit Wrestling." In the six-page exclusive spread, she stated that she wanted Buddy home more so he could spend time with family, and that's why he gave up the mat business.[43]

"Our daughter Lecha was five years old," Terry explained, "and her father was almost a stranger to her. She would ask almost every day, 'When is daddy coming home?'"[44] Buddy later said: "I had to choose between Terry and wrestling. It was a decision that had to be made very quickly, but there wasn't the slightest doubt which way it would be. I would start to live a normal life. I would be a good husband and father."[45]

Terry dismissed the notion that Buddy's health had anything to do with his retirement. "I read such ridiculous reasons as Buddy had to quit because of a bad heart, or that Buddy quit because he lost his zest for wrestling," she wrote. "How can a big hunk of man like Buddy have a bad heart?"[46] That was the official public statement from the Rogers family, and from their viewpoint, the case was now closed.[47]

Before the end of 1963, Rogers received at least two proposals to return to wrestling. The first was a nonstarter. Antonino Rocca had branched out and formed an independent promotion with regular shows at Sunnyside Gardens in Queens. Buddy's brother-in-law, Diamond Jack, and Johnny Barend jumped to the small-time organization, but the group was destined to fail. On December 9, Rogers was advertised to face Gregory Jarque at Sunnyside, but needless to say, he didn't appear.[48] In fact, Rogers said the promotion was "silly to even consider that [he] would wrestle for them for what they offered."[49] The other proposal was more enticing. English promoter Arthur Green visited him at his New Jersey home and offered just over $30,000 for a 16-week tour of Europe.[50] Rogers respected Green's enthusiasm and was apparently persuaded by the big money deal. He surprisingly agreed to sign a contract and launch a tour as early as January 1964.

Perhaps he was swayed by the money, and the opportunity to explore Europe with his family was too good to pass up. In typical "Nature Boy" fashion, he bombastically claimed he would beat any opponent on that continent inside of 15 minutes, and he was going to get into shape for a future bout down the line with NWA champion Lou Thesz.[51] However, with his health still questionable, Rogers venturing overseas to actually compete was exceptionally farfetched. But it didn't matter because fate was going to intercede. On December 2, Buddy was in Hollywood, Florida, at the Carlsbad Spa Hotel, reportedly working himself into condition for his trip abroad.[52] He sat down for a bite to eat when the chair underneath him collapsed. Rogers fell to the floor in agony, suffering from hip and back injuries, and was taken by ambulance to the hospital.[53] He was hurt worse than he originally believed, having ruptured a disc in his back, and immediately withdrew from his European commitment.[54]

Dealing with great pain, Buddy had a hard time walking, and he needed regular injections to relieve the relentless throbbing. Upon returning to New Jersey, he made an appointment to see his longtime orthopedic physician, Dr. Stanley Brown, who diagnosed his herniated disc at the base of the spine. Dr. Brown recommended surgery and informed Rogers that he would likely never wrestle again.[55] Buddy had received that same news months earlier, and to a certain extent, was probably used to the foreboding connotations, as depressing as that sounds. He knew the score. With increasing medical bills and a loss of income, Rogers brought a lawsuit against the spa and its parent company, and went to trial in Broward County, Florida, in September 1964. His lawyer, Maurice Fixel, charged the spa with negligence and said Rogers suffered "permanent injuries" as a result of his fall.[56] Appearing uncomfortable in what was, admittedly, his first time in a courtroom, Rogers was anxious, and he wanted the whole situation quickly resolved.

But the case didn't turn out the way Rogers hoped. His lawyer had asked for $209,881 in damages, not including pain and suffering, but the jury wasn't convinced.[57] Civil defense attorney Paul Meltzer aggressively went after Rogers during the three-day trial, questioning the legitimacy of his back injury and wondering why he didn't disclose his heart problems. The jury received the case on September 25, and after deliberating for two hours, awarded

Rogers $15,000, a fraction of his desired figure.[58] "What can I say," Rogers dejectedly asked after Judge Otis Farrington pounded the final gavel. "That's the jury system. You can't fight city hall. I don't know what I'll do. I can't wrestle no more."[59]

Meanwhile, a new opportunity sprang up that capitalized on his name value and love of sports. Buddy was appointed general manager of the Cherry Hill Arena, a venue only a couple miles north of his New Jersey home, and he planned to feature Roller Rama skating competition, boxing, and wrestling.[60]

Roller Rama, a type of Roller derby, provided fast-paced, exciting action, and drew thousands to the Cherry Hill Arena. The Jersey Jolters, the home club, were managed by Ronnie Robinson, son of the former boxing champion, Sugar Ray Robinson.[61] In promoting the sport, Rogers brought Sunnyside Garden TV wrestling announcer Erik Paige aboard to do commentary, broadcast on WRCV, and held evening events on Fridays, Saturdays, and Sundays.[62] Wrestling, of course, was his passion, and he wanted to bring big-time grappling to his arena. Ray Fabiani still maintained the franchise rights to Southern Jersey, and without the blessing of the powers-that-be, Rogers was blocked from getting a license to promote wrestling.[63] George Oetting of the *Queens Ledger* offered a deeper level of insight, claiming that the National Wrestling Alliance was "mad" at Rogers and that he was "'persona non grata' as far as the wrestling syndicate [was] concerned."[64]

The disappointments were adding up, but Rogers reveled being around his family and friends. Buddy spent time at home, enjoying his wife's cooking and listening to his daughter play the piano, and when he felt good enough, he went golfing.[65] But walking away from wrestling was immensely difficult for the 43-year-old Rogers, and as months went by, he struggled more and more. "I missed everything about it; the excitement, the recognition," he later said. "You hang in there for 25 years and the next day the curtain falls, you know there's got to be a transition.[66] I didn't get as great in wrestling as I did by not loving it. It was my whole life. I can't explain it. It really takes you down. It's something that you spent your whole life in this particular field [and] all of a sudden, it's no more. You don't get another penny out of that field. You don't have anything to do with that field. Imagine you doing something all them years and loving it, all of a sudden you never do it again."[67]

Through it all, there was constant speculation about his return and fans were clamoring for it. In a 1964 letter to the editor of *Big Time Wrestling*, an enthusiast from Florida wrote: "Wrestling hasn't been the same since Buddy Rogers retired. Wrestling needs him to make a comeback as he will bring back the color and excitement. Without him, wrestling cannot survive." In response to the comment, the editor stated that Rogers was "expected to hit the trail again soon."[68] Rogers was advertised to appear in Upstate New York for two matches in April 1964, but he no-showed the scheduled cards in Buffalo and Troy against Johnny Barend and Magnificent Maurice, respectively.[69] Buddy himself apparently told Georgiann Mastis that he was thinking about having a match at the Cherry Hill Arena in October of that same year, but it failed to materialize.[70] Promoters called him from time-to-time with inquiries, but Rogers would tell them he wasn't interested. If he changed his mind, he'd call them.[71]

Rogers frequented the gym in his free time, much more than when he was actively wrestling, and was devoted to keeping his trim physique. Taking into consideration his physical limitations, he devised a routine to strengthen his back, legs and upper body, and stretching was an essential element of his workout. He enjoyed a special diet and, once a year, he endured a personal detoxification program to cleanse his system.[72] Instead of gaining weight, which many wrestlers did during retirement, Buddy dropped about 10 pounds and held steady just shy of 230. He possessed a 50" chest and 18½" biceps, and felt his conditioning was first-rate. In December 1964, Buddy received some sad news as his old friend, ex-Montreal promoter Eddie Quinn, had passed away at the age of 58.[73] Quinn had always been one of his biggest boosters and helped him in the aftermath of his break from Jack Pfefer in 1951. In his place, star heavyweight Johnny Rougeau took over with Buddy's longtime pal, Bob Langevin, as the central promoter.[74]

Among the others affiliated with the group were Edouard Carpentier and Larry Moquin, two guys Rogers had wrestled many times in the past. For the sake of nostalgia and lending a hand to people he personally liked, Buddy agreed to wrestle in Montreal on Sept. 16, 1965, against his former protégé, Don Fargo, who was then using the alias, "Jack Dalton." In a subsequent interview, Rogers explained: "The desire to climb back into a ring, to hear the cheers of the people and have my hand raised at the end of a bout, never left me."[75] That yearning was satisfied as he beat Dalton in the main event of the card at the Paul Sauve Arena. The following year, in October 1966, Buddy returned to Quebec for at least three bouts beginning on October 17 in Montreal. An estimated 3,000 fans saw him lose the first fall to Tony Marino, but win the second with his figure-four. Nursing his wounds outside the ring, Marino refused to continue, and Rogers was awarded the match.[76] The next day, he wrestled Carpentier in Chicoutimi.[77]

Two months before, on Aug. 7, 1966, the legendary Ed (Strangler) Lewis died in Muskogee, Oklahoma. Rogers and Lewis had a strange relationship dating back several decades. Aside from the alleged match between them that never seemingly occurred, it was reported that the "Strangler" trained Rogers early in his career, and that Buddy socialized with his mentor in St. Louis in the late 1940s.[78] There is little evidence that Lewis offered any mat instruction to Rogers, and if they were friends, it certainly soured by 1959. In a St. Louis publication, the "Strangler" gave his opinion as to the "top ten" superstars of the day, and neglected to name Rogers anywhere on the list. He included a couple upstarts and a handful of perennial champions, but completely omitted the "Nature Boy."[79] Three years later, Rogers admitted that Lewis hated him "for some reason."[80] Did Buddy's purported private comment about Lewis to Lou Thesz make it back to the "Strangler?" It's unknown, but the rift didn't diminish Rogers' admiration for Lewis. He said Lewis was the best wrestler he ever saw.[81]

On Jan. 18, 1967, Buddy suffered more loss. His 82-year-old mother, Frieda, died at her Haddon Heights home.[82] "Mom Rohde," as she was known to family and friends, was the center of Buddy's world, and he worshipped the ground she walked on. For many years, she refused to watch him on TV for fear of seeing him injured. Frieda changed her tune after Buddy became a national sensation and never missed a match.[83] To help settle her nerves while he was on the road, he would call her after every bout to tell her he was okay.[84] A collector of beautifully designed German beer steins, Frieda was a "kitchen impresario of the old school," and Buddy loved her old country cooking.[85] "Mom is the world's greatest cook," he told a journalist in 1961, "[but it's] a drawback. If I ever let myself go, I'd blow up like a balloon."[86] In addition to buying her a house, Buddy showered her with gifts and ensured she was always taken care of. Her death had an immeasurable effect on Rogers, one that he would struggle with for years.

That same month, he received a call from Montreal, asking him to return for a series of matches. "I owed this promoter friend a lot, and he sounded so desperate in his last call that I decided to give it a try," Rogers said. "So, with Terry's blessing, off I went."[87] Feeling the best he'd felt in years, Buddy ventured back to Quebec and participated in around a dozen contests between March 13 and May 1, 1967. A few of the bouts were extraordinarily brief, lasting in the one-minute range, such as his encounter with Zelis Amara in Montreal on April 24. Amara, who would later gain fame as Abdullah the Butcher, was easily defeated by Rogers at the Paul Sauve Arena.[88] A week later, he wrestled 23 minutes with Johnny Rougeau in what was probably his longest match in four years. The bout ended in a no-contest after the referee was knocked from the ring.[89] Altogether, he went undefeated in singles competition, scoring wins from Manuel Cortez, Sweet Daddy Siki and Edouard Carpentier, the latter by disqualification.[90]

Bringing in Rogers was a highlight for wrestling during the Montreal Expo, and Buddy was a big hit.[91] Burt Ray, the influential writer behind the *Matmania* publication, heralded his comeback, noting that Buddy "still [had] all of the fire, the power and the ability as in his younger days." Ray added, "According to reports I have seen, Buddy looks better now than during his tour as champion," and recommended seeing him wrestle in person "even if you have to travel a hundred or more miles."[92] Caught up in the excitement, Ray teased his readers with some of the rumors going around, including talk of a match between Rogers and Verne Gagne in Chicago that summer. Then he brought up a Rogers-Bruno Sammartino contest, which he said "would out-draw any other match humanly possible." He concluded, "Yankee Stadium would not be big enuff."[93] But Rogers had other things in mind.[94] His new business responsibilities back in the Camden area and changes in his personal life were centrally important, and once again, he walked away from the mat business, leaving his fans wanting more.

ENDNOTES - CHAPTER 19

[1] Gorde Hunter, a veteran scribe, was the author, and it's unknown where he got his information. *Calgary Herald*, May 18, 1963, p. 6.

[2] Letter from Sam Muchnick to Vince McMahon dated May 24, 1963, Sam Muchnick Collection.

[3] *Ring Wrestling*, September 1963, p. 54. Rogers was billed as the "locally recognized world heavyweight champion." According to the local newspaper, the match went 48 seconds. *Baltimore Sun*, May 19, 1963, p. 8D.

[4] Attendance was 6,013. *Chicago Tribune*, May 25, 1963, p. B2.

[5] *Rockland County Journal-News*, May 23, 1963, p. 31. Rogers was replaced by Skull Murphy.

[6] *Pittsburgh Post-Gazette*, July 9, 1963, p. 19.

[7] The six-man tag bout in Newark was described in *Ring Wrestling*, December 1963, p. 60.

[8] New York State Athletic Commission Meeting Minutes, July 24, 1963, p. 2.

9 New York State Athletic Commission Meeting Minutes, Aug. 10, 1963, p. 3.
10 *Jim Barniak's Sports Scrapbook*, PRISM Network, Dec. 2, 1981.
11 *Ring Wrestling*, December 1963, p. 52.
12 *Wrestling World*, December 1963, p. 39-43.
13 *The Strutter*, July 1963, p. 9. This was reportedly the exact amount of Rogers' Audubon, NJ home.
14 *Ring Wrestling*, September 1963, p. 56.
15 The corporation was founded on May 21, 1963 and its principal office was 716 Market Street, Camden. Buddy Rogers Enterprises Certificate of Incorporation, New Jersey Division of Revenue, Trenton, NJ.
16 *Camden Courier-Post*, May 18, 1963, p. 10. John Rohde would later live in this building. Rogers seemingly bought additional property and had a total of 62 apartments. *Jim Barniak's Sports Scrapbook*, PRISM Network, Dec. 2, 1981.
17 Rogers expressed an interest in becoming a promoter upon retirement as early as 1952. *Columbus Star*, July 19, 1952, p. 2.
18 *Camden Courier-Post*, July 30, 1963, p. 21.
19 *Camden Courier-Post*, July 25, 1963, p. 36. Rogers also acted as an agent and booker for Fabiani in Philadelphia. Buddy Colt interview by Daniel Chernau, *Peach State Pandemonium*, Fall 2004, Bruno Sammartino interview by Greg Oliver, March 23, 2012.
20 Ibid.
21 Rogers pinned Sammartino in 9:04 for the first fall, then pinned Brazil in 4:02 of the third. Brazil beat Barend for the second fall in 4:49. From the files of Fred Hornby, unsourced newspaper, Aug. 3, 1963.
22 Buddy Rogers Interview, *Wrestling Hotline* with Blackjack Brown, March 1988.
23 It appears that Rogers did confide his condition with a few close friends, including Ron Reed, who he was mentoring. Buddy Colt interview by Daniel Chernau, *Peach State Pandemonium*, Fall 2004.
24 *Boxing Illustrated Wrestling News*, October 1963, p. 61.
25 *The Strutter*, July 1963, p. 9. Rogers initially said that he wasn't going to wrestle any matches until Sammartino gave him a rematch. He said Sammartino was ducking him. He later admitted to having changed his mind. *Long Branch Daily Record*, Aug. 14, 1963, p. 16.
26 *Jersey Journal*, Aug. 29, 1963, p. 32. Since the Washington show was taped, the contract signing probably occurred on Aug. 22.
27 Rogers won in 5:15 when the Shadow was unable to continue. 5,000 fans were in attendance. *Camden Courier-Post*, Aug. 20, 1963, p. 27. Shadow was Clyde Steeves. To maintain the illusion of separation between wrestler and promoter, Rogers was not listed as the man in charge behind-the-scenes for the August 19 show in Camden. Ray Fabiani was said to be the promoter. The newspaper said it was his first local appearance in "four years." *Camden Courier-Post*, Aug. 13, 1963, p. 20. It is believed that this bout was really was going to be his first local match in Camden in more than 10 years. The last was on April 27, 1953.
28 Photos and details were offered in *Boxing and Wrestling*, January 1964, p. 49-51, 66. A report in this same magazine stated that the contest lasted 43-seconds.
29 Red Berry was also on hand, acting as a referee. *Camden Courier-Post*, Aug. 17, 1963, p. 23.
30 In interviews, Sammartino complained about Rogers' role behind-the-scenes in the WWWF, and felt Buddy was purposely trying to hurt his reputation.
31 A rumor may have also influenced McMahon. Reportedly, Georgiann Mastis, the head of Buddy's fan club heard the latter's wife Terry say something about his future promotional plans – specifically a move to expand in the northeast. Georgiann told the story to Sammartino, who, in turn, informed McMahon. The only aspect of this story that remains questionable is Georgiann's relationship to Sammartino in 1963, the time in which this happened. Georgiann was much closer to Buddy at that point, and it doesn't seem likely that she would've said something with the potential of hurting Rogers. Georgiann was quoted: "If Buddy was out of town wrestling, his lovely wife, Terry, would always try to help us in answering our questions." *The Ringsider*, September 1964, p. 12.

32 From another angle, the match was cancelled because they couldn't agree on the finish. Sammartino wanted to pin Rogers to retain, while Rogers wanted to recapture the WWWF belt. Ron Reed (Buddy Colt) was present after a bad phone call between Rogers and McMahon. Rogers admitted that he was through with McMahon, saying, "I'll never work again." Buddy Colt interview by Daniel Chernau, *Peach State Pandemonium*, Fall 2004.

33 The tag bout went to a draw at the curfew. The Garden card drew 17,576 and a gate of over $50,000. *New York Daily News*, Sept. 17, 1963, p. 52.

34 Rogers was advertised for the show up until the day of the program. *New York Daily News*, Sept. 16, 1963, p. 50.

35 *Jersey Journal*, Sept. 17, 1963, p. 5.

36 *Jersey Journal*, Oct. 5, 1963, p. 1.

37 Diamond Jack, who was managing Gorilla Monsoon, was also "fired." Monsoon took Bobby Davis as his new manager. *Jersey Journal*, Sept. 25, 1963, p. 35.

38 Ibid. *Warren Times-Mirror*, Oct. 1, 1963, p. 12. Parker stated that Rogers was supposed to be out of action for "six months," and it's unclear if that was something Rogers or the WWWF put out to explain his inability to wrestle.

39 *Chicago Tribune*, Sept. 11, 1963, p. 65.

40 It is believed that his final match occurred on Sept. 12, 1963 at the Capitol Arena in Washington, D.C., where he wrestled to a draw with Hans Mortier. It's unlikely this was a "time-limit draw." No results were found in the *Washington Post* or the *Washington Evening Star*. Georgiann Mastis, the head of Buddy's fan club wrote that Rogers retired in "August 1963," and quoted him as saying, "I don't think I'll be back." *The Strutter*, December 1963, p. 13.

41 *Boxing and Wrestling*, April 1962, p. 51.

42 Interview with Debbie Rogers, July 15, 2020.

43 *Wrestling Confidential*, July 1964, p. 22-27. In 1959, Rogers said: "My wife hasn't seen me wrestle more than twice – and I like it that way. Her only concern is that when I retire I come out in one piece." *Montreal Gazette*, Sept. 26, 1959, p. 10.

44 *Wrestling Confidential*, July 1964, p. 22-27.

45 *Big Book of Wrestling*, September 1970, p. 57. Rogers told a reporter in 1967: "When I quit wrestling at my wife's request to live a normal life, I meant it." *Camden Courier-Post*, Nov. 25, 1967, p. 21.

46 *Wrestling Confidential*, July 1964, p. 22-27.

47 Years later, Buddy's daughter Lee confirmed that he reevaluated his life at that juncture, and that was a key aspect of his transition away from wrestling. Correspondence with Lee Rogers, April 18, 2020.

48 *Long Island Star-Journal*, Dec. 9, 1963, p. 14.

49 *Wrestling Confidential*, May 1964, p. 56.

50 *Wrestling Confidential*, April 1965, p. 56. Green was the secretary of Joint Promotions.

51 *The Wrestler*, February 1964, p. 16-17. Also see *Mat Wrestling Review*, Issue #311, January 1964, which included photos of Green at Rogers' home.

52 The hotel address was 3800 S. Ocean Drive in Hollywood, FL.

53 Former U.S. Representative James A. Roe of New York, another guest at the hotel, was the first to rush to his aid. *Wrestling Illustrated*, January 1965, p. 58-61.

54 Rogers wrote a letter to Green, explaining what happened, and added, "I promise you that as soon as I am ready, I will make the trip." *Mat Wrestling Review*, Issue #318, Feb. 20, 1964. Green later testified at Buddy's Fort Lauderdale trial.

55 *Wrestling Illustrated*, January 1965, p. 58-61. Rogers reaffirmed his intention to retire from wrestling in May 1964. *Camden Courier-Post*, May 28, 1964, p. 16.

56 Ibid. *Fort Lauderdale News*, Sept. 23, 1964, p. B1. Fixel's brother Irving, was also Buddy's physician in Hollywood, Florida.

57 The amount included $25,000 a year for approximately seven years of continued wrestling, plus his medical bills. *Wrestling Illustrated*, January 1965, p. 58-61.

[58] An in-person request for the case file was made, but no records were found. Archives Division, Broward County Central Courthouse, Fort Lauderdale, FL.
[59] *Fort Lauderdale News*, Sept. 26, 1964, p. 8.
[60] *Camden Courier-Post*, May 28, 1964, p. 16. It was also said he was planning to open a health facility in Cherry Hill. *The Wrestler*, February 1964, p. 16-17.
[61] *Camden Courier-Post*, Aug. 22, 1964, p. 34-35.
[62] Georgiann Mastis attended a game and wrote about it in *Wrestling Confidential*, January 1965.
[63] Rogers was quoted about this particular issue in the *Philadelphia Daily News*, June 20, 1967, p. 60. Rogers also tried to obtain a franchise in the Eastern Basketball League for the Cherry Hill Arena, but was denied. *Camden Courier-Post*, Aug. 4, 1964, p. 20.
[64] Oetting also named Antonino Rocca as being in the same boat. *Queens Ledger*, April 23, 1964, p. 3.
[65] In an exclusive look at Buddy's private life, a 4-page spread included 19 rare photos of Rogers and his family at their home. *Wrestling Confidential*, May 1964, p. 16-19.
[66] *Charlotte Observer*, Aug. 18, 1979, p. 7A, 9A.
[67] *Jim Barniak's Sports Scrapbook*, PRISM Network, Dec. 2, 1981.
[68] *Big Time Wrestling*, September 1964, p. 9.
[69] The Troy Armory show was promoted by Ted Bayly. Rogers and Maurice were to wrestle two-of-three-falls in the co-feature. *North Adams Transcript*, April 23, 1964, p. 20.
[70] *The Ringsider*, September 1964, p. 12.
[71] *Big Book of Wrestling*, September 1970, p. 56-57.
[72] A description of his workout routine and diet appeared in *Muscular Development*, November 1966, p. 32-33, 55-57. Beginning around 1966, he trained at Jim Corea's Gym and Athletic Club and at the Universal Health Spa, both in Cherry Hill. *Camden Courier-Post*, Nov. 25, 1967, p. 21.
[73] *Montreal Gazette*, Dec. 15, 1964, p. 25.
[74] The promotion was known as the International Wrestling Association.
[75] *Big Book of Wrestling*, September 1970, p. 56-57.
[76] A rival promotional outfit was staging a show at the Montreal Forum on October 18 featuring Killer Kowalski, Don Leo Jonathan, Dick the Bruiser, Bobby Managoff, Pat O'Connor and others. *Montreal Star*, Oct. 18, 1966, p. 56.
[77] The result is unknown. Chicoutimi was a borough of Saguenay, Quebec. Rogers had a tag team match in Montreal on Oct. 31, 1966, teaming with the Beast against Carpentier and Johnny Rougeau. This result is also unknown.
[78] *Chattanooga Times*, Dec. 22, 1946, p. 51, Rogers sat with Lewis to watch a bout featuring Gorgeous George at the Kiel Auditorium. *Buddie Rogers and The Art of "Sequencing"* by Max W. Jacobs, p. 11.
[79] St. Louis Wrestling Program, Jan. 3, 1959, p. 4.
[80] *Wrestling World*, November 1962, p. 40-41.
[81] *Buddie Rogers and The Art of "Sequencing"* by Max W. Jacobs, p. 20.
[82] *Camden Courier-Post*, Jan. 20, 1967, p. 9.
[83] *NWA Official Wrestling*, April 1952, p. 10-11. Frieda was given an "honorary" membership in the Buddy Rogers Fan Club. *Wrestling World*, July 1954.
[84] *Boxing and Wrestling*, September 1956, p. 76-77.
[85] Correspondence with Lee Rogers, Aug. 2018, *NWA Official Wrestling*, April 1952, p. 10-11.
[86] *Wrestling Revue*, December 1961, p. 19.
[87] *Camden Courier-Post*, Nov. 25, 1967, p. 21. Rogers, "for personal reasons," didn't want to say who the promoter was who called him. *Big Book of Wrestling*, September 1970, p. 56-57.
[88] *Montreal Star*, April 25, 1967, p. 40.
[89] *Montreal Star*, May 2, 1967, p. 19.

276 • **Master of the Ring**

[90] Rogers participated in two tag team matches with Johnny Valentine, and lost both by DQ. On September 9 and Sept. 13, 1967, Rogers had two additional matches in Quebec. Interestingly, Rogers was advertised for a match against Gwynn Davies at Queens Hall in Leeds, England on March 6, 1967. Buddy did not appear, and Davies instead wrestled and lost to Billy Robinson. *Yorkshire Evening Post*, March 7, 1967, p. 17.

[91] It was said that Rogers was offered $15,000 to wrestle during the Montreal Expo '67. *Philadelphia Daily News*, June 20, 1967, p. 60.

[92] *Matmania*, June 1967, p. 17-25, 27-35.

[93] *Matmania*, June 1967, p. 45.

[94] A writer asked Rogers if he was making his full-time return and looking for a title match with Bruno Sammartino. Buddy answered, "No, it's not that serious." *Camden Courier-Post*, Nov. 25, 1967, p. 21.

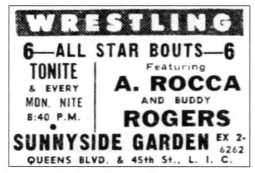

New York, New York: Monday, Dec. 9, 1963

Chapter 20
Passing the Torch

Stepping through the ropes for matches in Quebec was rewarding to Buddy Rogers, and he achieved the personal goals he set to attain. He had no illusions about a full-time return, nor did he envision becoming a world champion again. "I simply wanted to pump new life into fading memories and feel young again," he explained.[1] "The convincer was the look in Terry's eyes. She had been great about my trying a comeback. It was obvious she didn't want it to go on and on."[2] Rogers refocused on his family and the interests of Buddy Rogers Enterprises, which expanded with the purchase of a drive-in liquor store in Lindenwold, New Jersey, in June 1966.[3] "Buddy takes pride in announcing he wishes to extend you champion service by giving all his customers prompt, courteous, personal attention," an advertisement for his business read, and he welcomed fans to come in and meet him in person.[4] Four months later, he added to his concerns by opening up the "Buddy Rogers News and Gift Shop" next door, and offered free gifts to patrons during its commencement weekend.[5]

Rogers envisioned something better for his property, and by the following summer, he began construction on a lounge and supper club.[6] The "Buddy Rogers Covered Wagon Lounge" was erected as part of an adjoining building and officially opened on Nov. 1, 1967.[7] A semi-casual, family-friendly establishment, his lounge offered lunch and dinner seven days a week, and had an "all you can eat" special for $2.50.[8] For the adult crowd, Rogers had a fully-stocked bar and live music, and the big band sound kept people dancing well until the early morning hours.[9] His signature five-piece "Buddy Rogers All Star Band" supplied a diverse selection of musical favorites, and when they weren't tearing the house down, the talented Buddy LaPata was behind the piano, entertaining the crowd. The lively atmosphere made it a fashionable hangout, and Rogers was always the central attraction. Dressed impeccably in a suit, he worked the audience by shaking hands and ensuring everyone was having a good time.

There was no question about it, Buddy loved people, and this kind of environment played to his strengths. He was eternally charismatic, and wherever he went, he was surrounded by a gaggle of fans. Rogers embraced the attention, smiling all the time, and reveled in the success of his enterprise. But at the same time, he was remarkably down to earth. He would take the time to discuss matters one-on-one with a customer or employee, and routinely offered advice from the heart. Even when he was busy, he would pause to make certain his staff was in good spirits. George DiFlavis Jr. worked at the lounge while in high school and formed a friendship with Rogers. One day after turning up for his shift a little late, he explained that he had been at wrestling practice. Rogers asked what he had learned, and DiFlavis offered to show him. Buddy moved the nearby tables aside and got down on the floor, where DiFlavis placed a hold on him. Within seconds, Buddy turned the tides, and had the young man yelping in pain. "We all had a good laugh and a few people clapped with approval," DiFlavis later said.[10]

The patronage of his businesses and the coverage he received in both the *Camden Courier-Post* and the *Philadelphia Daily News* demonstrated the sustained interest in all-things "Nature Boy."[11] He made social appearances at functions in Camden County – events for the YMCA, Rotary Club, and the Square Circle Sportsmen Club among them, and attended local sports events to show his support.[12] On Jan. 5, 1968, he was lured to St. Louis by NWA boss Sam Muchnick to referee a championship match between world heavyweight titleholder Gene Kiniski and Edouard Carpentier. Kiniski, who had succeeded Lou Thesz as champion in 1966, was a highly rated heel wrestler of his own, although with a much different style than Rogers. The NWA champ won his match against Carpentier after the latter suffered a back injury and was unable to continue.[13] It was reported that Buddy looked "fashionable," but that he counted too fast against both wrestlers.[14]

When asked if he had plans to return to the ring, Rogers said he doubted it. "But if Sam talks me into a comeback, it will have to be with the understanding that if I prove myself, that I will get a title match with whoever is the champion," Buddy said.[15] He had known Muchnick for 20 years, and Rogers had been instrumental in pushing him over the top in the 1948-'49 St. Louis wrestling war. But, in private, Muchnick grumbled about Rogers' style of business, particularly the way he haggled over payoffs. As Larry Matysik, Muchnick's right-hand man remembered it, Rogers "really was arrogant, with a sharp, nasty tongue."[16] However, Muchnick respected his ring ability and called him "probably the greatest showman in the history of the game, considerably better than Gorgeous George."[17] Rogers was complimentary toward Muchnick as well. "Sam Muchnick was one of the greatest promoters who ever lived, along with Vince [McMahon] Sr. He was one of the most respected guys on the planet, and I love this guy."[18]

Professional wrestling was very difficult on the Rogers family, and his extended time on the road during his heyday on the mat was immensely burdensome. "By not having you around, it's a hard situation – that's why so many marriages don't make it," Buddy later told Ray Tennenbaum. "You know the old saying, 'Absence makes the heart grow fonder for somebody new.'"[19] Buddy and Terry's relationship survived his wrestling career, and he acknowledged in 1967 that he wanted to give her a "normal life" away from the chaos of grappling.[20] His businesses proved to be equally demanding, though, and his late-night hours at the lounge put a crimp in his marriage. By mid-1968, the family was living at 1921 Chapel Avenue in Cherry Hill, but it was soon thereafter that Buddy and Terry divorced.[21] Rogers was putting in long hours at his nightspot, and in the coordination of performers for his club, he met an exceptional musician recently back in New Jersey after a lengthy stay in Las Vegas.

Her name was Debbie Hayes, a talented entertainer, who for years lit up the stage in the Sinbad Lounge at the Dunes Hotel and Casino. Hayes was well-known for her incredibly versatile musical abilities and could play a variety of instruments, including her famous trumpet, as well as sing and dance.[22] Having toured internationally in addition to her years of success in Las Vegas, she recently appeared at the Showboat Hotel and Casino during the winter 1967 season.[23] By early March 1968, the blonde-haired Hayes was the featured act at Buddy's Covered Wagon Lounge, and was billed as the "Nature Girl," with the "body that turns you on."[24] Wearing leopard and zebra-skinned outfits, and surrounded by an adept group of musicians, she electrified the local audience with their Tijuana Brass style.[25] Rogers adored the music and promoted Hayes to no end. "Nature Boy discovers Nature Girl," he told a reporter with a smile.[26]

Called a "natural beauty" by Las Vegas photographer and columnist Jay Florian Mitchell, Hayes was a "fireball on stage," and her act was a boon to business at Buddy's club.[27] Debbie was originally from Gloucester County, New Jersey, about 14 miles south of Camden, and since her return from Nevada, was living in Turnersville with her mother and three-year-old son, David.[28] A relationship between Buddy and Debbie quickly blossomed, and by April 1969, the two were engaged to be married.[29] On Aug. 17, 1969, they were wed at the Grenloch Presbyterian Church in Washington Township, near Turnersville, and the location was symbolic to Debbie, as it was the church she had attended in her youth.[30] The newlyweds bought a scenic new home in Haddonfield at 600 Coles Mill Road, on top of a hill overlooking the Cooper River. The secluded house was a fixer-upper, but the couple was ready to spend the time needed to completely refurbish the property.[31]

That summer, Rogers purchased Charley Grip's Trailer Park on Black Horse Pike in Camden, and admittedly, it was one of the best investments he ever made.[32] Grip was an old-time local wrestling celebrity and a longtime friend of Buddy's dating back several decades. Following Grip's passing on June 1, 1969, at the age of 75, his trailer park complex at Black Horse Pike and Crescent Boulevard was sold to Rogers for an undisclosed price. The property was seven acres and held approximately 150 homes.[33] "It's the most economical way of living," Rogers said with regard to life in a mobile home community, "and it's becoming more and more attractive to more people."[34] With rarely a vacancy, the investment would be a constant moneymaker in Buddy's portfolio. Similarly, his Lindenwold lounge, liquor store and gift shop were financially stable endeavors, but were verifiably doomed.

The ill-fated luck was palpable on July 8, 1968, when a fire tore through the lounge's kitchen and bar areas. Fortunately, the fast actions of the Lindenwold Fire Department had the blaze under control within 20 minutes, but serious damage was done.[35] The establishment was closed until September 30 for repairs, and even then, Buddy was only able to open the lounge and bar. The kitchen needed four additional months of work. It was a destructive fire, but nothing compared to the utter ruination from a second inferno on Nov. 1, 1969. This time, Buddy's liquor store and gift shop were leveled by flames, costing upward of $500,000 in damages. A fire wall prevented further devastation, but the loss was immense.[36] On the bright side, no one was injured in either fire, and Rogers had the option to rebuild again. But the *Camden Courier-Post* revealed that Buddy had sold the complex "two weeks" prior to the second blaze.[37] The buyer, Ted DuBois, rechristened the club the "Gaslight Restaurant and Lounge," in early 1970.[38]

Rogers returned to pro wrestling in 1969, appearing for two different organizations in the Ohio and Michigan territories. The first was for a unique independent group headed by his former manager, Bobby Davis, and an advertising guy from Cincinnati named Ed Blatt. Davis and Blatt formed "Wrestling Show Classics" after the sponsor for a Dayton studio TV show demanded a revamp in talent in June 1969. Thus, the powers-that-be dropped Big Time Wrestling, the Detroit promotion led by The Sheik, and touted the return of Buddy Rogers on June 20.[39] In fact, Rogers was a lead fan-favorite, along with Mark Lewin and opposing heels Killer Karl Kox, Stan (Krusher) Kowalski, and Bob Orton. According to known records, Rogers wrestled seven matches for this organization, and five of them were against Kowalski. He made appearances in Dayton, Columbus, and Cincinnati, and with an eye on his heart condition, held back from doing anything overly strenuous.

Despite his concerns, Buddy was happy to be back in his old stomping grounds, and did as much as he could to help the promotion. It was a difficult situation, though, because of the promotional war being waged against The Sheik, and gains were minimal. By the first week of Aug., "Wrestling Show Classics" was on its last legs, and ultimately folded. The following month, Buddy turned up in Detroit for a campaign in that region, and a smart booking strategy was devised to build towards a match between Rogers and the Sheik. In a series of short contests, Buddy dominated opponents, typically winning with his figure-four leglock. During a TV interview in Detroit, he informed viewers that he was the inaugural holder of the United States title, and it was an honor he had never lost in the ring. He was forced to give up the belt after winning the world title in 1961. "Now, for me to see a creep like the Sheik and that thing with him, his Weasel [Abdullah Farouk], wear that belt, makes my stomach wretch," he said.[40]

"I am willing to go this far, to bring back some dignity and class to the U.S. heavyweight championship," Rogers continued. "I want the Sheik – I repeat – I want the Sheik. But I don't care where I get him. I just want him. I will give the Sheik $5,000 to wrestle me on TV and will give $5,000 to charity."[41] Notably, the Sheik's manager, Abdullah Farouk, was portrayed by Ernie Roth, someone Rogers knew well. In December 1952, Buddy appeared on Roth's radio show in Canton, Ohio, to promote an upcoming card.[42] Roth later became a wrestling announcer for a Rogers-affiliated studio telecast in Steubenville in 1959.[43] Working for the Detroit outfit, Buddy wrestled approximately 15 matches, and may have gone undefeated.[44] Over half of his bouts were against preliminary opponents, and likely ended in quick time. The anticipated contest against the Sheik never came to fruition, nor did the possibility of him regaining the prized United States championship. And just like that, Rogers retired again.[45]

As much as Buddy enjoyed the limelight and the applause of the crowd, he was content living the quiet life in picturesque Haddonfield with family. He worked long hours remodeling his residence from the ground up, and took great pride in creating a "spectacular" home.[46] It was a massive undertaking, but Rogers embraced the challenge. The landscaping and gardening was of the utmost importance, and Buddy became known for his green thumb. "I love working with the soil," he told a journalist in 1976.[47] And what he was able to achieve was noteworthy. The breathtaking scenery of the Rogers' property was listed amongst the exclusive houses on a special garden tour by the Haddon Fortnightly organization in 1977.[48] Buddy remained a folk hero in Southern New Jersey and around Philadelphia, and he frequently interacted with fans in his distinctive friendly style. He would venture out for dinner with Debbie, and over the house microphone, the restaurant host would announce, "Ladies and gentlemen, we have a celebrity in the house," and all eyes would focus on the tanned, muscular ex-wrestler.[49] Buddy loved it.

In the 1970s, Buddy lost a number of friends and former colleagues, which included Gene Dubuque, Al Haft, and Antonino Rocca.[50] His former manager, Jack Pfefer, passed away on Sept. 13, 1974, in Massachusetts at 79 years of age. More than any one person, Pfefer shaped and influenced Buddy's career when he needed it the most, and the development of the "Nature Boy" gimmick was a game changer. He helped Rogers become a household name, and after their emotional 1951 split, Pfefer used unmerciful tactics in attempts to hurt Buddy's career. He sent out damaging flyers, contacted reporters with insider information, and spread rumors. It's not surprising that after the attack on Rogers by Karl Gotch and Bill Miller, people actually suspected Pfefer as having paid a bounty for the assault.[51] The vitriol aside, Buddy learned a lot about booking and business affairs from Jack. He also developed a sense for cultivating talent, and how to manipulate within the framework of a territory for monetary gain.[52]

Rogers was in amazing shape for his age when he turned 55 years old in 1976. A photograph of him at the gym in Cherry Hill appeared in the *Camden Courier-Post* on April 19, and Roger Cohn observed Buddy lifting two 50-pound dumbbells and flashing his 18-inch biceps.[53] His blond hair was mixed with gray, but he was still tan and fit, and he looked to be in peak condition. By that time, Rogers had sold his trailer park and found a new livelihood, which was selling commercial real estate for Century 21. Once again utilizing his charming personality and keen business sensibilities, he was quickly successful, racking up millions of dollars in sales.[54] Other than the occasional article or casual mention in the newspaper, Rogers was out of the public eye, and people started to wonder about him. One curious fan inquired to the *Tampa Tribune*, asking sports editor Tom McEwen if there was any truth to the rumor that Buddy had died in a car accident. McEwen set the record straight, informing the reader that Rogers was alive and well.[55]

Another interested enthusiast was syndicated writer Bob Greene, the recent winner of the National Headliner Award for best columnist, who revealed his fondness for Buddy in an insightful 1978 article. Greene, as a young man watching wrestling in Ohio during the late 1950s, was enthralled by the antics of Rogers, and wanted to grow up to be like the "Nature Boy."[56] Years later, he reached out to Buddy, and the latter's first question, undoubtedly accompanied by his customary smirk, was, "How the hell did you find me?" Rogers was candid in his talk with Greene, divulging his favorite television shows, such as *60 Minutes* and *Kojak*, and that he liked to sit back and reminisce about the old days. "There was a time there," Buddy said, "I could do no wrong. I could take a gun and shoot you, and they'd clap. Those people screaming, that was my life. The roar of that crowd – that motivated my whole life."[57]

Ten years earlier, Buddy told a Philadelphia journalist that he wanted to help wrestling regain its glory. "I feel I could contribute toward bringing wrestling back to where it was once," he explained. "But a guy like me, he has no chance."[58] Disappointed by the evolution of the industry, Rogers only watched the sport on television occasionally and never attended shows live.[59] "Wrestling is a lost art," he said. "Today, it's a low form of mayhem. I can't knock a business that was once great to me and that I was great to, but I have to relate to a wrestler as a performer. If his performance leaves any doubt in the public's mind as to what he's doing, then he's a lousy performer."[60] In late 1978, Buddy was ready to commit himself to wrestling again, and he discussed an in-ring comeback with his old friend, Eddie Graham, head of the Florida territory.[61] Graham was for the idea, and Buddy's intentions were multifaceted. He wanted to perform and also have a say in the direction of the promotion.

Championship Wrestling from Florida was a lucrative operation with a strong circuit of weekly cities, plus secondary towns throughout the "Sunshine State." Graham was lauded for the way he ran the territory, and his strategies were emulated by promoters throughout the world. Creatively, he saw a role for Rogers, and gave him booking power to adjust matches and script angles.[62] Buddy took the opportunity very seriously. Florida was one of his favorite places, and the chance to wrestle in front of his son, David, who had never seen him in the ring, encouraged his decision.[63] The Rogers family found a luxurious vacation home near the edge of Old Tampa Bay and, by Jan. 1, 1979, Buddy was on the road with the CWF crew.[64] Rogers, Graham, the Fabulous Moolah, and others were in West Palm Beach for a program at the Auditorium. More than 2,100 fans witnessed Buddy's first match in nearly a decade as Rogers battled Jim Garvin to a draw.[65] Two nights later, Rogers appeared at a Tampa TV taping and beat Tenryu with his figure-four. He also issued a $10,000 challenge to reigning NWA champion Harley Race.[66]

Being around wrestling again stirred up many forgotten emotions for Rogers, and although he disappeared almost as quickly as he arrived, he returned to the territory in late March as a fan-favorite. In Miami Beach on March 28, he teamed with Killer Karl Kox to defeat Ox Baker and the Missouri Mauler, and Kox wrestled most of the match for his team. At the finish, Rogers scored a hot tag, landed three dropkicks, and pinned Baker.[67] Buddy was still conscious of his health limitations, and privately, Debbie worried about his heart.[68] There was only so much the 58-year-old could do in the ring, and his Miami bout was indicative of his typical in-ring contributions. When he felt better, and could do more, he would. Soon, Rogers assumed the management of Jimmy Garvin, holder of the Florida and Southern championships, and was said to be helping train him for an upcoming series of matches with Harley Race.

Rogers had a big night on April 28, 1979, in St. Petersburg. He ran to the aid of Mike Graham and Steve Keirn to fight off Don Muraco, Thor the Viking and Bugsy McGraw after their partner Dusty Rhodes was incapacitated by a pre-bout attack.[69] Then, after Harley Race beat Garvin to retain his NWA crown, Rogers placed the champ in his figure-four to the delight of the crowd.[70] Rogers spent most of his Florida campaign feuding with manager Sonny King and his stable of villains. On May 2, during a TV taping, King boasted that he could break Buddy's figure-four. At the last second, King substituted

Thor the Viking in his place, but proceeded to attack Rogers as Viking struggled to get free.[71] Rogers and King brawled again on May 9 at the Sportatorium, setting up a boxer versus wrestler match for May 15 in Tampa. That match was booked like something out of Buddy's past. King attacked Rogers prior to the bell, but the "Nature Boy" rebounded and pinned his rival in 40-seconds.[72]

As a booker, Rogers got a lot of heat from the locker room, and much of it had to do with the way he edged himself into high-profile scenarios that didn't really make a great deal of sense. It was perceived to be a grab for power and fan attention, and worked against the wrestlers and the overall promotion. For instance, in Miami Beach on May 16, 1979, Rhodes challenged Race for the NWA strap, and towards the end of the contest, the referee was knocked from the ring. Dusty's onslaught took Race down for the count, but with no official, there was no winning pin. Buddy, at that moment, jumped into the ring to provide a three-count, popping the house, but the referee regained his senses and disqualified Rhodes. The audience cheered Rogers and Rhodes, and the near victory for the hero, but Buddy's role was unusual. This kind of positioning – combined with his efforts late in tag team matches to ensure he was involved in the finish – rubbed CWF talent the wrong way.[73]

A worked injury caused by King Curtis and Jos LeDuc in May was Buddy's swan song in Florida. During the two previous months, Rogers wrestled just over 20 matches, and his popularity was unrelenting. But it was time to move on and devote his energy to a new wrestling endeavor in the Mid-Atlantic area. Not only was it a territorial jump, but it was to mark his return to the heel character he made famous. His friend, George Scott, was booking the region, and it was notable that four years earlier, Scott contacted him to ask a very important question. He wanted to know if Buddy would mind if the promotion attached his famous nickname, "Nature Boy," to an up-and-coming talent named Ric Flair. Rogers didn't hesitate in his answer. He gave his blessing to the idea, and the blond-haired Flair soared to new heights as an arrogant and swaggering superstar.[74] With Rogers headed into the territory in 1979, Scott had the rare opportunity of pitting the two "Nature Boys" against one another to determine the superior athlete.

The feud between Rogers and Flair began on June 17 in Greensboro when Buddy refereed a United States title match between champion Flair and Dusty Rhodes. They had friction from the start, usually with Rogers admonishing Flair for violating the rules. Late in the bout, Flair collided into Rogers, and a well-placed knee dropped the champion, leaving him vulnerable for a pin.[75] Rhodes got the three count and won the U.S. championship.[76] Buddy and Flair scuffled afterwards, with Rogers putting his younger rival in the figure four, a move that Flair had also adopted as his finisher. In a subsequent TV interview, Rogers called Flair, "Nature's Mistake," and announced that he would be the next United States champion.[77] But in Greensboro on July 8, Flair defeated by Rogers in a "lopsided" affair "as Flair reversed Rogers' figure-four and won by a quick submission."[78]

Rogers, in the days following, went full heel and took Jimmy (Superfly) Snuka as his protégé, promising to make him the "next Nature Boy."[79] "I think there's nothing greater than Buddy Rogers," Buddy told Mark Wolf of the *Charlotte Observer*. "When I look in the mirror, I see the greatest thing God ever created. If he ever did anything better, I missed it."[80] Puffed up beyond imagination, Rogers added John Studd and Ken Patera to his clique, and went to war in a series of tag team matches against newly-turned babyface Flair and his cronies. Buddy participated in tag bouts involving Andre the Giant, Ricky Steamboat, Blackjack Mulligan and Tim Woods, and claimed to have had an injured ear that, of course, became the center of his opponent's attacks against him. In a special 12-man tournament held in Charlotte on September 1, Buddy guided Snuka to victory in the finals over Steamboat for the vacant U.S. title.[81] By cheating and making perfectly timed sneak attacks, Rogers and his stable terrorized the Mid-Atlantic territory.

There were two additional singles matches between Rogers and Flair – the first occurred on July 21 in Spartanburg, which Flair won.[82] Their final bout happened on Thanksgiving, Nov. 22, 1979, in Norfolk before a packed house. It was a brawl from beginning to end, and both unloaded violent punches to the noggins of their adversary. Rogers bled first, and was seemingly in trouble after a suplex, but he resorted to one of his oldest tricks; patting Flair on the back during the pin attempt and giving Ric the impression that he had won. Needless to say, the contest continued, and after the referee was bumped from the ring, Buddy removed a foreign object from his trunks and pummeled Flair. Now busted open, Flair was knocked to the arena floor, where he was counted out.[83] Nevertheless, the fans were firmly behind Flair, and considering his other two victories, and the respect Buddy had for him, Flair had been passed the torch, and carried the distinction of the "Nature Boy" with honor.

Buddy entered the ring for nearly 40 matches between July and December 1979. His appearances exposed his gigantic personality and style to a whole new generation of fans. In the annual *TNT Times* awards, voted by the correspondents of the publication, Rogers was named "Comeback of the Year."[84] The family, however, became homesick for New Jersey, and Buddy hung up his boots.

Meanwhile, an extraordinary friendship developed between Rogers and comedian Andy Kaufman, whose "Latka Gravas" character was the breakout star of the show, *Taxi*. Known for his unpredictable and offbeat style, Kaufman had admired Rogers when he was growing up, and had recently initiated a wrestling gimmick in which he offered $500 to any woman who could pin him. His "inter-gender" bouts gained widespread attention and Rogers reportedly became his trainer.[85] On Dec. 22, 1979, Buddy accompanied Kaufman for a segment on an episode of *Saturday Night Live*. Off screen, Kaufman became close to the Rogers family, and spent time with them at their vacation property in Ocean City, New Jersey, during the summer. Buddy would later be saddened by the premature death of Kaufman in 1985 at 35 years of age from lung cancer.[86]

Possessing the spirit of a much-younger man, Rogers was always up for trying something new. He managed a health spa for a time and attended a casino gaming school prior to obtaining his license to work in Atlantic City.[87] He was hired to work as a casino host at the Playboy Hotel and Casino, and his charming nature made him an instant hit with the public and the Playboy Bunnies.[88] Dressed like a million bucks, with his elegant jewelry and cigars, he was the kind of guy everyone wanted to be around, from the high-rollers to the casual sightseers. "It's a dynamite job," he said. "I'm with a lot of super people that I work for. I enjoy being around the crowd again."[89] Often recognized, he enjoyed talking wrestling and giving autographs to fans.

On Dec. 2, 1981, Buddy gave a noteworthy interview during an appearance on Jim Barniak's Sports Scrapbook, broadcast on the PRISM cable network in Philadelphia. For the first time in a major forum, he spoke openly about his health problems in 1963, telling the host: "I waited a long time to bring this up. I'm going to let it out to the public. I never said this to anyone else." Rogers went on to divulge that he had suffered a heart attack "six weeks" before his match with Bruno Sammartino, finally revealing the secret he had been harboring for 18 years. Previously, anytime questions about his heart came up, Rogers denied any type of problem.[90] And because he was proud, he brushed the comments off as if they were unsubstantiated rumors. That night, though, he told Barniak and the viewing audience what really happened behind the scenes, and his struggle of having to walk away from the business he loved.[91]

For all the naysayers who criticized and critiqued Buddy's every motive and move, his disclosure was taken with a grain of salt. Their minds were already made up. To them, it was an alibi by a swerve artist. From the opposite perspective, there was no logic or reason for him to lie. Rogers had waited nearly two decades to share his side of the story. If protecting his ego and image was so fundamentally important to him, he could have utilized the so-called heart attack yarn right away. He could have hammered that story home in 1963 and in the years that followed. But he didn't. He didn't mention his illness as being the reason he lost to Sammartino, and as to what really occurred, his sudden exit from wrestling did nothing to help his finances in support of his family. He certainly didn't abandon his career in wrestling to prop up a fake heart attack story simply to discredit Sammartino, or to provide an excuse for an in-ring loss. He had lost scores of times. That was part of pro wrestling, and he knew that better than anyone. So where was the massive work his critics alleged?

In 1982, Buddy was approached for another wrestling comeback, but this time, it was the World Wrestling Federation calling. Rogers had great affection for Vince McMahon "Senior," despite what had gone down all those years before. Buddy and Debbie spent time socializing with Vince and his wife, Juanita, at their South Florida home, and there were no bad feelings about the past.[92] Realizing Buddy's modern-day value, McMahon advised his son, Vincent Kennedy McMahon — who was also known as Vince "Junior" and currently headed up operations for the WWF — to hire Rogers.[93] The younger McMahon respected the abilities of Rogers, as well, and he brought the "Nature Boy" aboard starting on Sept. 14, 1982. That evening, Buddy was not only introduced to the live audience at Allentown's Agricultural Hall, but he debuted his new "controversial segment," dubbed "Rogers' Corner," with Vince "Junior" as his initial guest.[94] Buddy promised to tell it like it was, regardless of the subject, and fans were completely enthused.

"Rogers' Corner" became a weekly feature on both the WWF's *Championship Wrestling* and *All Star Wrestling* television programs.[95] In addition to his own regular segment, Buddy was primed to manage again, and from day one, he demonstrated his support for his old charge, Jimmy Snuka. He believed Snuka was the best wrestler in the world, and after some verbal sparring with "Captain" Lou Albano, he attained the "Superfly's" contract.[96] Instead of a heel run, like they had in the Mid-Atlantic territory, they were fan-favorites, and Snuka's high flying thrilled spectators across the Northeast. There seemed to be no limits to their success, including a possible reign for Snuka as WWF world heavyweight champion. While Buddy's faith in Snuka, as a wrestler, remained firm, he had real cause for concern about the man's personal life, and things were going to take a dramatic turn. Unfortunately, it was also going to cost a young woman her life.

ENDNOTES - CHAPTER 20

[1] *Big Book of Wrestling*, September 1970, p. 56-57.

[2] *Camden Courier-Post*, Nov. 25, 1967, p. 21.

[3] The establishment was at 411-413 White Horse Pike in Lindenwold, NJ. Interestingly, the previous owners, Harry Haltzman and Edward and Helen Gartman, had been doing business as "Rogers Liquor Store" (Rogers Liquor Corporation), with no prior relation to Buddy, since at least 1958. The purchase was made on June 14, 1966. Camden County Property Records, Camden, NJ. Notably, the Rogers Family moved to 216 White Horse Pike in Haddon Heights around early 1965. Their Audubon home appeared on the market as early as July 1964. *Camden Courier-Post*, July 23, 1964, p. 38. They were living in Haddon Heights as of May 1965, when Rogers caught the license plate for an escaping criminal who had burglarized the building. *Camden Courier-Post*, April 22, 1966, p. 9.

[4] The advertisement ran in the sports section. *Camden Courier-Post*, June 15, 1966, p. 49.

[5] The shop offered newspapers, magazines, paperbacks, Hallmark cards, Hummel figures, tobacco and accessories, and other items. The grand opening was Oct. 21-23, 1966. *Camden Courier-Post*, Oct. 20, 1966, p. 45.

[6] Two years earlier, his friend, Dutch Schweigert, who wrestled as the "Great Scott," opened up a bar in West Collingswood, NJ. *Camden Courier-Post*, Feb. 4, 1965, p. 34.

[7] As part of the opening night ceremonies, all liquor and food was reportedly on the house.

[8] *Camden Courier-Post*, Dec. 13, 1967, p. 36.

[9] The bar closed at 3:00 a.m.

[10] Correspondence with George DiFlavis, Jr., Feb. 4, 2019.

[11] Rogers received lengthy write-ups in the *Camden Courier-Post*, Nov. 25, 1967, p. 21 and *Philadelphia Daily News*, June 20, 1967, p. 60.

[12] *Camden Courier-Post*, May 12, 1976, p. 50. *Camden Courier-Post*, Sept. 29, 1967, p. 9, *Camden Courier-Post*, Oct. 5, 1967, p. 44.

[13] The match lasted 7:05. *St. Louis Post-Dispatch*, Jan. 6, 1968, p. 5.

[14] *Wrestling*, St. Louis Wrestling Club Program, Jan. 13, 1968, p. 3-4.

[15] Ibid.

[16] Correspondence between Larry Matysik and Steve Yohe, Sept. 4, 2005. *Wrestling at the Chase: The Inside Story of Sam Muchnick and the Legends of Professional Wrestling* by Larry Matysik (2005), p. 18.

[17] *The Role of Promoter in Professional Wrestling* by Max Jacobs, p. 68.

[18] Buddy Rogers unsourced quotes, March 22, 1992.

[19] Buddy Rogers interview by Ray Tennenbaum, February 1985. www.ray-field.com.

[20] *Camden Courier-Post*, Nov. 25, 1967, p. 21.

[21] Camden County Property Records, Camden, NJ. The exact date of divorce is unknown, but it is believed to have occurred between September.1968 and April 1969. An attempt to locate a divorce record turned up empty. New Jersey Office of Vital Statistics, Trenton, NJ.

[22] *Camden Courier-Post*, May 10, 1968, p. 31.

[23] *Las Vegas Review-Journal*, Dec. 3, 1967, p. 5.
[24] *Camden Courier-Post*, March 27, 1968, p. 28.
[25] She was accompanied by The Equals, a three-member band. *Camden Courier-Post*, May 10, 1968, p. 31. Hayes later performed with the Manhattans and the Natures "4" Four featuring Fred Bender, Chip Brancato and Del Lucas.
[26] Ibid.
[27] *Las Vegas Review-Journal*, Nov. 22, 1957, p. 15. Hayes once dated Elvis Presley. *Arizona Daily Sun*, Oct. 20, 1998, p. 6.
[28] *Camden Courier-Post*, May 10, 1968, p. 31.
[29] Their engagement was revealed in a column by Charles Petzold. "She's sporting a four-carat pear-shaped diamond." *Philadelphia Daily News*, April 14, 1969, p. 33.
[30] New Jersey Marriage Index, ancestry.com. Buddy and Debbie originally planned to get married in Florida in January 1970, but changed their minds. As it was reported, they were going to spend their honeymoon in Mexico. *Philadelphia Daily News*, Aug. 15, 1969, p. 15.
[31] The home measuresd 128-foot by 40-feet and was valued at $200,000. *Camden Courier-Post*, April 19, 1976, p. 17. It was a historic location, as it was the site of Elizabeth Haddon's (founder of Haddonfield) original home in the 1770s. *Philadelphia Inquirer*, June 10, 1979, p. 18J-19J. Rogers later said he loved Haddonfield. *Jim Barniak's Sports Scrapbook*, PRISM Network, Dec. 2, 1981.
[32] The trailer park was at the intersection of Black Horse Pike and Crescent Boulevard. *Philadelphia Inquirer*, Aug. 16, 1970, p. 2.
[33] *Philadelphia Daily News*, June 10, 1969, p. 47. Buddy's brother John was the maintenance man at the park. Interview with Jerry Hauske, June 21, 2018.
[34] *Philadelphia Inquirer*, Aug. 16, 1970, p. 2.
[35] *Camden Courier-Post*, July 8, 1968, p. 9.
[36] *Camden Courier-Post*, Nov. 3, 1969, p. 10.
[37] Ibid.
[38] The Gaslight opened on Jan. 14, 1970. *Camden Courier-Post*, Jan. 9, 1970, p. 14. According to property records, Ted-Mil, Inc., owned by Edward "Ted" DuBois, officially bought the property on Feb. 16, 1970, and paid $250,000. Camden County Property Records, Camden, NJ.
[39] The sponsor for the Friday night Studio TV show in Dayton was Super Duper Stores. Davis was the announcer. *Dayton Daily News*, June 13, 1969, p. 67. The show was broadcast on channel 16 in Dayton, on channel 6 in Columbus, and on channel 12 in Cincinnati. Davis called Rogers to be involved. Interview with Bobby Davis, March 17, 2019.
[40] *Body Press*, Issue Unknown, 1969.
[41] Ibid.
[42] The show was on WCMW. *Canton Repository*, Dec. 12, 1952, p. 10.
[43] The program appeared on WSTV, channel 9. *Canton Repository*, Feb. 27, 1959, p. 34.
[44] Records are incomplete or unavailable.
[45] It was reported that Rogers was to wrestle in Montreal on Nov. 24, 1969 against Dewey Robertson, but it's not known if that match happened or not.
[46] He reportedly spent $200,000 refurbishing the house. *Philadelphia Inquirer*, June 10, 1979, p. 18J-19J.
[47] *Camden Courier-Post*, April 19, 1976, p. 17.
[48] *Philadelphia Inquirer*, May 4, 1977, p. B1.
[49] Interview with Jerry Hauske, June 21, 2018. In the Camden area, Buddy's photo hung on the walls of many different establishments, from bakeries to tailor shops. An endorsement by Rogers was a significant thing for local businesses.
[50] Dubuque (Magnificent Maurice) died in a plane crash in 1973, while Haft died in 1976, and Rocca in 1977.
[51] Pfefer was alleged to have paid $1,500 for the attack. Tony Santos interview by Max Jacobs, March 16, 1981, *Buddie Rogers and The Art of "Sequencing"* by Max W. Jacobs, p. 17, 23.

52 Rogers spoke about Pfefer during an interview with WrestleRadio. With regard to Pfefer renaming wrestlers after him in a mocking way, Buddy recalled telling Pfefer: "Jack, I don't care how many guys you call 'Bummy Rogers,' 'Ruddy Bogers,' whatever you want to call them, they're still not gonna be 'Nature Boy' Buddy Rogers. And by golly, I proved myself right." Buddy Rogers Interview by Tom Burke and Dan Reilly, *Wrestle Radio*, Nov. 9, 1991.
53 *Camden Courier-Post*, April 19, 1976, p. 17.
54 Rogers was employed by Century 21, Pavulak and Green, Inc. in Camden. *Camden Courier-Post*, Nov. 12, 1976, p. 21.
55 *Tampa Tribune*, June 24, 1979, p. 8D.
56 *San Francisco Examiner and Chronicle*, Sunday Punch, Feb. 12, 1978, p. 2.
57 *Boston Globe*, Feb. 6, 1978, p. 2.
58 *Philadelphia Daily News*, June 20, 1967, p. 60.
59 It was said that Rogers enjoyed "Superstar" Billy Graham. *Is Wrestling Fixed: I Didn't Know it was Broken* by Bill Apter (2015).
60 *Camden Courier-Post*, April 19, 1976, p. 17.
61 Reportedly, Buddy also worked as a special referee in Cincinnati on Oct. 13, 1978, for a bout between The Sheik and Stan Stasiak. *Global Newsletter*, #37, October 1978, p. 4.
62 *Jim Barniak's Sports Scrapbook*, PRISM Network, Dec. 2, 1981.
63 Ibid.
64 They lived on Bay Way Drive. Interview with Debbie Rogers, July 15, 2020. Their Tampa residence was also mentioned in the *Tampa Tribune-Times*, June 24, 1979, p. 8D and *Charlotte Observer*, Aug. 18, 1979, p. 7A, 9A.
65 *Palm Beach Post*, Jan. 2, 1979, p. 37. Garvin was originally billed to team with Killer Karl Kox against Sonny King and Thor the Viking. *Palm Beach Post*, Dec. 31, 1978, p. 53.
66 *Main Event Wrestling*, Jan. 12, 1979, p. 5. Rogers appeared for two different interview segments. The taping took place at the Tampa Sportatorium and was aired on Jan. 6, 1979.
67 *All-Star Grappler*, #18, p. 11.
68 Interview with Debbie Rogers, July 15, 2020.
69 *TNT Times*, #118, p. 31.
70 *TNT Times*, #117, p. 8, 19.
71 *TNT Times*, #118, p. 26.
72 *TNT Times*, #122, p. 4.
73 KC Guest Booker interview with Mike Graham, youtube.com, Chris Colt interview by Scott Teal, Wrestling Archive Project, Volume 1, p. 106.
74 Interview with Debbie Rogers, July 15, 2020. Buddy Rogers Interview by Dr. Mike Lano and Gary "Gerhardt" Kaiser, *Canvas Cavity*, Circa. 1991-1992.
75 It was either a knee or a punch that dropped Flair, setting up the final pinfall.
76 *Greensboro Daily News*, June 18, 1979, p. B7. The U.S. belt was later returned to Flair.
77 *Wrestling '79* by Joseph Shedlock, June-July 1979, p. 2-3.
78 Ibid.
79 *Charlotte Observer*, Aug. 18, 1979, p. 7A.
80 Ibid.
81 *TNT Times*, #150, p. 16.
82 Their match was billed as the "Battle of the Nature Boys."
83 Five minutes of footage from this match is available on the WWE Network, www.wwe.com.
84 *TNT Times*, #136, p. 5.
85 *Charlotte Observer*, Dec. 24, 1979, p. 16B. Rogers was still working with Kaufman in 1981. He was said to be his "mentor and consultant," and the "technical mastermind behind Kaufman's latest comedic persona." *Camden Courier-Post*, June 10, 1981, p. 13. In much his own way, but influenced by Rogers, Kaufman would work audiences with his often outrageous style of performance.
86 Interview with Debbie Rogers, July 15, 2020.

[87] *Buddie Rogers and The Art of "Sequencing"* by Max W. Jacobs, p. 24, *Camden Courier-Post*, March 27, 1986, p. 25.
[88] A photo of Rogers as a casino host appeared in *The Wrestler*, April 1982.
[89] *Jim Barniak's Sports Scrapbook*, PRISM Network, Dec. 2, 1981.
[90] For instance, in 1970, he said "there wasn't a shred of truth" to the rumors that he had a "bad heart." *Big Book of Wrestling*, September 1970, p. 56-57.
[91] *Jim Barniak's Sports Scrapbook*, PRISM Network, Dec. 2, 1981.
[92] Interview with Debbie Rogers, July 15, 2020.
[93] Correspondence with Jeff Walton, Jan. 9, 2019. At the time, McMahon "Junior" was making payments to the shareholders of Capitol Wrestling to purchase the WWF.
[94] The graphic on the telecast of *Championship Wrestling* misspelled Buddy's last name as "Rodgers."
[95] It was alleged that Rogers made $400 per taping.
[96] *Jim Barniak's Sports Scrapbook*, PRISM Network, Dec. 2, 1981.

Cincinnati, Ohio: Saturday, Oct. 4, 1969

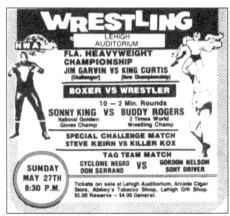

Fort Myers, Florida: Sunday, May 27, 1979

Charlotte, North Carolina: Sunday, Nov. 25, 1979

Chapter 21
The Legend Lives Forever

The return of Buddy Rogers to the World Wrestling Federation was heartily welcomed by old-school fans. His exploits on the mat were fondly remembered by a devoted segment of the wrestling community, and to see him back where he belonged was electrifying. For younger enthusiasts who were not aware of the "Nature Boy," commentators emphasized his iconic status, and put him over as the only man to have held both the NWA and WWF world titles. Once Rogers was joined by Jimmy Snuka, the popular star from the Fiji Islands, a defined feud against Lou Albano was established, and it was highlighted from late 1982 through most of 1983. On Nov. 22, 1982, Buddy made his first official wrestling-related appearance at Madison Square Garden in 19 years and sat in Snuka's corner as the "Superfly" trounced Albano. The beating Snuka gave his former manager was so thorough that the referee had to stop the match because of blood, and the crowd went wild.[1]

Three nights later at the Spectrum in Philadelphia, Buddy made his first in-ring start since late 1979, teaming with Snuka to beat Albano and Ray Stevens by count-out. Buddy was an active combatant for most of the nearly 10-minute battle, and demonstrated a fiery offense at times. He was also effectively double-teamed by Albano and Stevens, his one-time pupil. Snuka delivered his top rope splash on Albano before the "Captain" was pulled out of the ring by his partner at the conclusion.[2] Impressive in his appearance and ability, the 61-year-old Rogers was lauded by pundits. One publication stated that he displayed "signs of what had made him world champion nearly two decades ago."[3]

The "Rogers' Corner" segment continued to run weekly on WWF television, and he interviewed everyone from Andre the Giant to his old friend, the Grand Wizard (Ernie Roth).[4] It was a significant promotional outlet for ongoing feuds, and Buddy helped advance the storylines by asking the questions fans wanted to hear.

Buddy enjoyed doing "Rogers' Corner" and the fanfare was appreciated.[5] Being on the road, too, was pleasurable, and reminded him of his younger years. But despite his good intentions and the high hopes he had for Jimmy Snuka, things were quickly spinning out of control, and Rogers had no way to stop the momentum. The problems centered on Snuka's drug abuse, and it was enough of an issue to drive a serious wedge between the two men. Rogers was certainly no saint. He had partied with the best of them in his day, but cocaine was the drug of choice for Snuka in 1983, and it was not part of the healthy lifestyle Buddy prided himself on.[6] Their personalities clashed on that subject, and Rogers's interest in remaining with the WWF was fading fast.[7] On May 11, 1983, Snuka's girlfriend, Nancy Argentino, passed away from a traumatic head injury in Allentown, and the circumstances of her death were not altogether clear. Snuka said it was an accident caused by a fall, but there was reason to suspect otherwise.[8]

Even though Snuka wasn't charged at the time, he was surrounded by a cloud of suspicion, and the overall situation was unbearable.[9] In September 1983, Snuka and his wife Sharon bought a home on Coles Mill Road in Haddonfield and became neighbors to the Rogers family.[10] And as if things weren't bad enough, several weeks later, a domestic violence incident put Sharon in the hospital and Debbie Rogers took photos of her injuries to document the episode.[11] It was a depressing time, and the sudden death of the Grand Wizard on Oct. 12, 1983, at 57 years of age, only made matters worse. Buddy said the Wizard was the only manager to rank next to Bobby Davis "in greatness," and his loss was painful to the entire WWF family.[12] According to the booking plan, beginning late in the fall, Rogers was expected to team with Snuka for a series of bouts around the circuit against Albano and Don Muraco, and Vince McMahon wanted to capitalize on the popularity of their feud.

The campaign actually stated on Sept. 17, 1983, at the Civic Center in Baltimore, an important city in Buddy's history. Baltimore was the site of some of his earliest pro matches, and he always got a good reception in that Maryland city. Therefore, it was sort of fitting that he would end up participating in his final-ever contest in that metropolis. In the moment, the tag victory of Rogers and Snuka over Albano and Muraco was celebrated at the arena by fans who witnessed the affair, but no one knew it was the "Nature Boy's" last in-ring appearance. Buddy didn't know himself. After filming the conclusion of his weekly TV segments on October 25 and 26 in Allentown and Hamburg, respectively, he accompanied Snuka to New York City for a big match against Sgt. Slaughter on November 21.[13] Snuka and Slaughter fought evenly for 20 minutes, at which time their bout was declared a draw. Later that night, in the dressing room of Madison Square Garden, Rogers slipped and fell on the hard floor, and suffered serious injuries.[14]

Taken by ambulance to St. Vincent's Hospital, Rogers was examined for possible neck and pelvis injuries. Luckily, he didn't suffer any broken bones in the fall and was released the next day.[15] The WWF saw the incident as an opportunity to build upon Rogers' feud with Lou Albano, and published a two-page spread in its arena program, asking: "Who Did Hurt Buddy Rogers?" The article included a photograph of Rogers on a stretcher with a neck brace.[16] There was speculation that Buddy had a falling-out with Vince McMahon, was fired, and then filed a lawsuit.[17] Rogers convalesced from his injuries and disappeared from TV, adding apparent credence to his tiff with McMahon. Some months later, however, Rogers appeared on the Oct. 9, 1984, episode of *Tuesday Night Titans*, hosted by McMahon, and the WWF boss was exceedingly complimentary toward Buddy.[18] He praised his reign as world heavyweight champion and doubted that any wrestler could equal his accomplishments in wrestling. In turn, Rogers said he was "thrilled" to be on the program and stressed the importance of dedication in becoming a success on the mat.[19]

All in all, Buddy was shown great respect by the fans during his WWF run. Off-camera, it was more of the same, particularly when it came to the younger wrestlers looking for advice. Rogers was always responsive. "Buddy Rogers was the originator," Eddie Gilbert said in 1992. "His strut was adapted and taken by Jackie Fargo, [Jerry] Lawler, [Nick] Bockwinkel, [Ric] Flair, me and everyone. I really admire him because he always had time for me up there, always passed on what he could."[20] Two of Buddy's old friends, Dave Aquino and Don Robertson, met up with him at the Baltimore Civic Center, and brought a copy of his famous 1961 bout with Pat O'Connor. With a little help from the production crew, they played the match backstage, and Rogers watched the historic footage with several of the wrestlers. "They all treated Buddy like a celebrity," Aquino recalled.[21] On another occasion, at the Holy Child Forum in Staten Island on July 17, 1983, Rogers was honored by induction into the Staten Island Sports Hall of Fame.[22]

Following his departure from the WWF, Rogers reached out to 32-year-old Larry Sharpe, a fundamentally sound professional wrestler from Paulsboro, New Jersey.[23] Rogers was impressed by Sharpe and wanted to connect with a local athlete in hopes of starting a wrestling school.[24] Sharpe had idolized Buddy from a young age and credited him with sparking his interest in wrestling.[25] Of course, he agreed to work with his hero, and the "Buddy Rogers' Pro Wrestling School, Inc." was incorporated in the State of New Jersey on Nov. 2, 1984.[26] Their school was run out of a converted hanger at the Burlington County Airport, and Sharpe took the lead in teaching a class of upstarts everything they needed to know about the physical end of the business.[27] Rogers, now 63, taught ring psychology, and was happy to demonstrate the effectiveness of his famed figure-four on any daring student.

Dave Giegold, known in the ring as "Davey Gee," was part of that inaugural class, and agreed to experience Buddy's version of the figure-four. He said that Rogers was a "gentleman," but sunk the hold to let Davey know just who he was.[28] A sizable athlete, Giegold would later go on to work security on the controversial Morton Downey Jr. Show, but when he was at the wrestling camp, he spent a few months training alongside Buddy's son David.[29] In 1982, Rogers told a reporter that David was starting to work out, but was "afraid he [couldn't] beat what I did." He'd tell him, "Go out there and make your own mark."[30] Well, David was apparently inspired by his father's coaching, and by 1984, he had gained a ton of muscle mass.[31] He appeared with Buddy on *Tuesday Night Titans*, and the 19-year-old displayed his chiseled frame for a national viewing audience.[32] David was impressively built, and people wondered if he would follow his father's footsteps, but he decided against it, and took his life in an entirely different direction.[33]

By early 1985, Buddy withdrew his interest in the school, leaving it entirely to Sharpe, and the latter made the most of it. He rechristened the facility "The Champion's Choice Pro Wrestling School," and would later attain international fame as the "Monster Factory."[34] Among Sharpe's students would be Bam Bam Bigelow, Chris Candido, and Rocco Rock of Public Enemy fame. Rock, who's real name was Ted Petty, told the *Pro Wrestling Torch* in 1995: "Buddy Rogers helped me. He helped me a lot with psychology."[35] That same year, Buddy did some work for Verne Gagne's American Wrestling Association, but his time there was altogether brief. Although he was motivated to be around the business and willing to travel, Rogers was a "walking time bomb," according to his physician.[36] He desperately needed open heart surgery, and soon, he endured a quadruple bypass at the Lady of Lourdes Hospital in Camden. As a matter of pride, he asked Debbie not to tell anyone, and she sat in the waiting room by herself.[37]

Rogers made it through the operation and came out stronger than he had been in years. With healthy living and sensible training, he regained his strength and, in 1987, the Rogers family moved to South Florida.[38] They found a beautiful property within walking distance of the beach in Lauderdale-by-the-Sea, a suburb of Fort Lauderdale, and Buddy embraced a full retirement. "I love Florida," he said. "Oh, golly, I'm at home here."[39] When he wasn't swimming for exercise or at the beach worshipping the sun, he was working with his garden or socializing with friends. He possessed unlimited energy, even first thing in the morning, and would often surprise Debbie and David with his energetic personality. "Hey, everybody!" he'd shout upon opening the front door of his residence, and there wasn't a more personable individual in town.[40] He would greet friends and strangers with the same kind of enthusiasm, and if someone wanted to talk wrestling, he was more than happy to do so.

As could be expected, Buddy remained the center of attention wherever he went. He made friends easily and he frequently had people over to his house for parties or card games. A dog lover, Buddy had a black Labrador Retriever named "Blackjack," and before a hand of cards, Rogers and his pals would rub his dog for good luck.[41] Billy Darnell and George Scott were two of his closest friends from the wrestling industry, and both moved to Florida, although to different parts. Darnell initially moved to the Miami area, but relocated to Lauderdale-by-the-Sea and became Buddy's neighbor.[42] George Scott and his wife Jean settled in Indian Rocks Beach, on the west coast of the state, and got together with Buddy frequently.[43] The Gallagher Brothers, Mike and Doc, were also close to Buddy, and they worked out together a couple times a week.[44] Buddy spent a lot of time with Mike, who lived in nearby Pompano Beach, and was with him as he battled Lou Gehrig's disease. Mike died in 1990.[45]

In December 1988, Buddy was visited by one of his greatest fans, Bob Greene, for a special article to be featured in *Esquire* magazine. Once again, Greene got the best from the "Nature Boy," and the three-page piece was revealing from every angle. Buddy divulged that he had recently had an artificial hip put in, and was using a cane to walk, but he was every bit of his old self. "If I was in my prime right now," he said with authority, "there'd be no Hulk Hogan. I was born too soon. I'd inhale them guys today."[46] With that said, Rogers liked pretty much everything about the "Nature Boy" Ric Flair. "I love Ric," he told Georgiann Makropoulos. "He used everything I did — even my hold, figure-four grapevine."[47] In a separate interview, Rogers said: "[Flair has] done a superb job in the field of wrestling. And I do feel that, well, you know they say emulation is the greatest form of flattery. He copied my style of wrestling. And copied my name. All the way around, he did a superb job, and I will say this, I'm very happy for him."[48]

Rogers was 68 years old on July 24, 1989, when he was involved in a violent altercation at a sandwich shop near his home, and suffice to say, he more than held his own. The aggressor in the conflict was more than half Buddy's age, stood 6-foot-2, and weighed 200-pounds. Theodore Terhune, 30, entered LaSpades Original Hoagies in search of someone, and after learning that the individual was not there, he berated two women employees with foul language. Buddy was also in the establishment and verbally objected to Terhune's comments.[49] "If you want a piece of me, old man, let's go," the antagonist replied.[50] In the subsequent melee, Buddy landed several blows and had Terhune in a tight grip when the latter pleaded for him to halt his onslaught. Rogers suffered a cut lip in the exchange from a metal folding chair Terhune threw at him, and needed more than a dozen stitches.[51] The story made national news and Rogers was named "Citizen of the Year" by the City of Lauderdale-by-the Sea for his gallant efforts.[52]

In recent years, Rogers made a handful of public appearances. He joined a collection of local sports celebrities for a special meet and greet at Philadelphia Park horse racing track in early 1986.[53] Buddy was honored by the Cauliflower Alley Club at its annual banquet on March 12, 1988, in Studio City, California.[54] The next year, he went to New Orleans to attend a reunion of past NWA world heavyweight champions at a dinner arranged by World Championship Wrestling on the night before its Clash of the Champions show.[55] Rogers hobnobbed with Lou Thesz, Gene Kiniski, Pat O'Connor, Harley Race, and the Funk Brothers, as well as Sam Muchnick, and witnessed the epic Ric Flair-Ricky Steamboat two-of-three-falls encounter at the Superdome the next evening. Steamboat, the reigning NWA champion, retained his belt in a 55-minute match.[56] On March 23, 1990, he took a ten-minute drive from his home and turned up at a WWOW-TV taping at the War Memorial Auditorium in Fort Lauderdale.[57]

Buddy's love for wrestling never diminished. He trained a handful of up-and-comers in South Florida, and inspired Chris Chavis to pursue a career in wrestling.[58] Chavis would graduate from Larry Sharpe's Monster Factory and work as "Tatanka" in the WWF. Due to time constraints and a yearning to be around his family, he turned down a lot of prospective jobs.[59] In 1990, he received the "Stanley Weston Award" from *Pro Wrestling Illustrated*, an honor named after his longtime friend.[60] The following year, the wrestling community was energized by a massive convention promoted by John Arezzi in East Elmhurst, New York. Over two days, Aug. 24 and 25, 1991, fans interacted with the legends of pro wrestling, which included Lou Thesz, Bruno Sammartino, the Fabulous Moolah, and Ric Flair. Rogers enthusiastically agreed to attend, and appeared on Arezzi's radio show, *Pro Wrestling Spotlight*, to talk about the anticipated event.[61]

At the convention, Buddy reconnected with old acquaintances and made new friends.[62] He participated in a panel discussion and was candid with his opinions, as he typically was. He was gracious and easy to talk to, and everyone who saw him was stunned by his physical appearance. "I have never seen a man at age seventy look that good, and I have been interested in physical culture my whole life," said Bob Bryla, a well-known wrestling memorabilia collector.[63] "The man is in incredible shape," promoter Sheldon Goldberg wrote. "We should look that good at any age."[64] Overall, Buddy had a great time and hoped to do it again one day.[65] Rogers, interestingly, left the convention with a deal to return to the industry in an active role as part of the Tri-State Wrestling Alliance, a Philadelphia-based independent organization run by Joel Goodhart. Goodhart invited him to guest referee a match between Bam Bam Bigelow and Steve Williams on October 26 in Pine Hill, New Jersey, and Buddy "jumped at the opportunity."[66]

Being back in New Jersey was comforting to Rogers and he reminisced as he rode with referee Jim Molineaux for a radio appearance prior to the show. He stopped to have a meal at the Oregon Diner in South Philadelphia and was given the complete VIP treatment.[67] Nobody had forgotten the "Nature Boy." On the evening of October 26 for the card dubbed "Pine Hill Punishment," Rogers performed his duties admirably, but was forced to disqualify Bigelow after the wrestler ripped Buddy's shirt. Afterwards, he was confronted by "Nature Boy" Buddy Landel, the blond-haired TWA champion. Rogers and Landel brawled momentarily, and it seemed obvious that they were building toward a "Battle of the Nature Boys."[68] The promotion started the next day at Philadelphia's Original Sports Bar, with Rogers accepting the challenge to wrestle Landel on Jan. 25, 1992, at the Philadelphia Civic Center. Reportedly, there was a $16,000 advance for tickets, but Goodhart abruptly cancelled the show and folded the TWA.[69]

A facet of Rogers having a bout in the 1990s was to crown him with the badge of having a contest in seven different decades. It was a rare feat, but would have been technically impossible since Buddy didn't make his debut until 1942. However, it still was part of the Rogers "lore," and the claim that he began wrestling in 1939 was recited many times. Buddy believed he had one more "great match" in him and felt the Landel affair would have been it.[70] But the bout being called off ended any chance of him wrestling again. Back in 1983, Rogers was asked if he thought another grappler would ever hold both the NWA and WWF titles, as he had. "I doubt it very much," he replied.[71] After Ric Flair joined the WWF, Rogers reconciled the possibility that Flair might accomplish the goal, and he welcomed it. He even floated the idea of working with him. "Boy, can you imagine if I managed and handled Ric Flair?" he asked. "Against Hulk Hogan — there would not be a building big enough."[72] Flair, in fact, did accomplish the honor on Jan. 19, 1992, when he won the 30-man Royal Rumble and became WWF champion.[73]

On March 21, 1992, Buddy attended the 25th anniversary of the Cauliflower Alley Club in Los Angeles and enjoyed his time with the wrestling fraternity.[74] His best buddy, Bobby Davis, who had transitioned from the mat business to the ownership of a string of Wendy's franchises in the Bakersfield area, also attended the reunion, and the two spent a lot of time together. Rogers discussed the idea of forming a Florida chapter of the "CAC" with club officials, and was motivated to get the concept off the ground, possibly as early as March 1993. Receiving help from Billy Darnell and George Scott, Buddy planned for regular luncheons for the "boys" in the "Sunshine State," and really believed in the benefits of such a proposal.[75] The details were still being worked out and Rogers returned to Lauderdale-by-the-Sea. Three months later, Buddy was shopping in a local grocery store, mistakenly stepped on a discarded slab of cream cheese, and took an awkward tumble to the floor.[76]

Buddy suffered a broken arm in the mishap. In conversations with friends, he downplayed the seriousness of the incident and joked about why it happened.[77] The injury halted his normal routine, which included daily laps in the pool, and Rogers became a little depressed. He began to lose weight, and there were subtle indicators that something more significant was going on with his health. Soon thereafter, Buddy suffered a mild stroke and was hospitalized.[78] Debbie could see that he wasn't himself, and after a few days, Rogers was released despite her pleas to keep him admitted.[79] He spent Father's Day weekend at home, but Monday morning, June 22, he endured a second stroke while taking a shower, and this one was debilitating.[80] Rushed to Holy Cross Hospital, he was discovered to have suffered brain damage and paralysis, and was placed in intensive care. "He is such a fighter," Debbie told a reporter. "I talk to him. I was at his bed, and I said, 'Buddy, if you understand me, squeeze my fingers twice.' He was able to do that."[81]

The "Nature Boy," Buddy Rogers, passed away at approximately 11:00 p.m. on Friday, June 26, 1992.[82] He was 71. His death sent a ripple through the wrestling world.[83] For all the fans that had seen him at the New York convention, and thought he looked immortal, there was tremendous shock. "Nobody could ever believe his age," Debbie said. "They thought he was maybe 55."[84] Bobby Davis felt Buddy appeared even younger at the Cauliflower Alley Club in March. "Lord, he looked like he was about 30 years old, tan and muscled, and in fabulous condition," he explained. "[He] really wore us all out."[85] The news was sobering to Buddy's peers, and Bruno Sammartino paid tribute, saying: "I always respected his talents. I had some great matches with him. I don't know too many people who were as colorful as he was."[86] Lou Thesz added: "I'm going to miss him. We all are."[87] Upon hearing about Buddy's death, Dick Steinborn phoned Seymour Koenig and proclaimed, "The King is Dead! The King is Dead!"[88]

The funeral took place on June 30 and Rogers was entombed at Forest Lawn North Cemetery in Pompano Beach. Among those to attend his services were Bobby Davis, Larry Sharpe, Pedro Martinez, Brad McFarlin, and George Scott. Other friends like Johnny Valentine, who called Buddy two days before his death and told him he loved him, Billy Darnell, the Fabulous Moolah, the Poffos, and Georgiann Makropoulos, were unable to attend.[89] Buddy once acknowledged the fact that pro wrestling, in his experience, offered a wide range of acquaintances, but few friends. "You take it from Buddy, as long as you live, you'll be able to count on one hand your friends," he said. "And all the hair you have on your head, you'll get that many acquaintances, but on one hand, you can point out friends."[90] Without an overwhelming presence of wrestling insiders at his funeral, his comments rang true. But some of his closest friends, Vince McMahon "Senior," Eddie Graham, and Buddy Austin, had already passed.

Rogers was survived by two stepsiblings, John and Anna. Anna, incidentally, died five months later on Nov. 16, 1992, in Brooklawn, New Jersey, at 88 years of age.[91] As for John, he maintained a strong relationship with Buddy, and worked as a machinist, plumber, and a maintenance man for his brother's various properties. He retired to the Tampa area and died on June 25, 2005. Buddy's widow, Debbie, was known by friends and people inside the business as a "really sweet lady."[92] She attended the 1993 LIWA convention in Las Vegas as a guest of the Fabulous Moolah, and later became a member of the Cauliflower Alley Club.[93] In 1994, she posted a tribute to her late husband in a Camden newspaper, stating: "I can't believe two years have already passed, but never a day goes by that you are not in my thoughts. I love and miss you, along with your family, friends, and fans."[94] To this day, Debbie resides in Florida. David Rogers became a massage therapist, an occupation Buddy really appreciated, especially when he was the recipient of an expert rubdown.[95] Later, David went into business in Key West.

Buddy's daughter, Lee, followed in her father's footsteps by becoming a renowned performer in her own right. Beginning at age 15, she began touring the globe as a dancer, first in the successful Greek musical variety show, *Holiday in Greece*. She later studied the history of Mediterranean folk dancing, and, as one of the foremost experts, became a lecturer on the subject. "My father was an enormous presence, both on and off stage," Lee explained. "His influence on me was powerful. I learned a lot from him about showmanship, and about generating emotion from an audience. I inherited his standard of excellence, and his drive to be excellent at what I did. It seemed quite natural that I would become an entertainer. Pro wrestling and pro dancing have a number of aspects in common. Both require a unique set of skills, a high level of physical fitness, and a charismatic presence. Looking back on my father's career in wrestling, and my own career in dance, both roads had their challenges, but both roads beat working 9 to 5."[96]

If you ever had the privilege of speaking with the original "Nature Boy," you were quickly drawn in by his confident demeanor and style of speech. "He sounded like Robert Mitchum," Bob Greene wrote in 1998, "but [his] voice had even more authority, if you can imagine that."[97] Most of the time, he spoke slowly and deliberately, and his "jovial baritone" was a "stark contrast to his sneering public voice," as a writer in Charlotte noted.[98] Buddy had a way with words, and possessed an unlimited volume of unique sayings.[99] During interviews, he tended to show endearment to his interrogator by giving them a nickname, or simply adding a "y" or an "ie" to their first name. Buddy was famous for giving people in his inner circle a "handle." For instance, Billy Darnell was "The Will," Bobby Davis was "Bobaloo," and Fritz Von Goering was, "The Fritter." He also gave the wives of his friends nicknames, as Betty Darnell was, "The Betts." Amusingly, Debbie had one as well. She was, "The Hayes."

Typically, he'd call strangers "Pal" or "Pally," or sometimes "Coach."[100] Buddy didn't stop there. He had nicknames for inanimate objects, too. Cigars were "gars," and a pancake was a "panner."[101] Rogers was sarcastic, and his dry humor was apparent. If he was in character, it just was part of the show. In Philadelphia around 1961, he was informed that a spectator had died during a wrestling card, and Buddy replied, "Good, that's one less guy to throw things at me."[102] The duality of the Buddy Rogers persona was an incredible gift, and he worked fans, opponents, and promoters with a natural zest. Regardless of the city he was in or the size of the crowd, he always got a reaction from the audience, and it didn't matter if they loved him or hated him, the response was what he wanted. Usually patrons wanted to wring his neck, and some tried to get at him as he walked to or from the ring. With precise timing, Rogers ensnared the crowd and played them like a fiddle.[103]

Away from the ring, Buddy was just as flamboyant, wearing his bright-colored clothing, decked out in his gold rings, and casually strutting as he walked. He took pride in his appearance, and owned dozens of custom-made suits in his heyday.[104] After participating in a bloody match, he would put cocoa butter on his forehead to ensure he didn't scar. Gregarious through and through, he relished in the company of women, and it was never hard to find companionship on the road. Where some of his contemporaries complained about having women wrestlers on the bill, Rogers loved it. He knew they were a boost to the box office, and "what he couldn't draw, the girls would."[105] It was no secret that Buddy had relationships with women performers and the backstage drama incited turmoil of a different kind. More or less, the shenanigans were wrestling's version of a soap opera, and Rogers enjoyed the casual sexual atmosphere.[106] Feuds developed behind-the-scenes just as easy as in they did in the ring, many times for those reasons.

Extracurricular affairs with women fans were quite common in those days. They'd wait outside the dressing room and, in some cases, would throw themselves at him. "It was in front of you all the time," he explained. "It was expected of you."[107] In his 1989 article in *Esquire*, Buddy was forthcoming about his exploits. "I'd be lying to you if I said that the women didn't come around," Rogers said. "And the funny thing is, they seemed to be more attracted to me when I was a bad guy than when I was a good guy. I'd treat 'em like dirt sometimes. I'd treat 'em like they were wrestlers. I guess everyone else treated them sweet and nice and gentle. I know it's not a good thing to say, especially in this day and age, but it always seemed that the badder I'd treat them, they'd like it better."[108] Buddy developed a reputation as a womanizer and was judged by the clean-cut folk inhabiting the business. However, as anyone knew, hypocrisy was rampant in wrestling, and even the purported babyfaces weren't always shooting straight.

Rogers was a bit of a storyteller, and learned early on in his career how to manipulate the press to achieve his desired goals. "Let truth and falsehood grapple," he said in 1962, quoting John Milton, "and truth, like Buddy Rogers, will win every time."[109] His depiction of the truth, though, under the umbrella of kayfabe, was a mixture of exaggeration and cynicism. Buddy often claimed that he won the Texas championship in a 350-wrestler tournament, held the U.S. title for 11 years, and also beat Antonino Rocca for the initial WWWF belt. None were true, but they made for good copy. He was smart enough to know that if there was a work in progress, he wanted to be the one pulling the strings. He didn't want to be the victim. In the locker room, Buddy would never leave cash unattended, and placed it in his trunks if he had a match to wrestle.[110] Additionally, he'd wrap his valuables in a handkerchief, and his routines were central to protecting his own interests.[111]

The brotherhood of wrestlers that Buddy enjoyed in the 1980s and '90s was not the norm during his active career. Wrestling was cutthroat, promoters were scheming, and if a grappler wanted to be successful, they had to manipulate and maneuver. Working for Jack Pfefer taught him not to take guff from anyone, and he quickly earned a reputation as a troublemaker for questioning payoffs and demanding more from the till.[112] In other words, Buddy wanted to be paid fairly. And the more success he achieved and the more power he attained only served to turn the everyday journeymen against him. They weren't getting what he was, and they, in their jealousy, lashed out against Rogers.[113] These wrestlers spit venom, and their words were heard in subsequent books and shoot interviews, helping shape the modern reputation of Rogers. In essence, they claimed he was power hungry and selfish.

Buddy didn't care about their opinions.[114] Indeed, he was self-centered and eternally driven to make money. Whatever actions he took, even those that were misinterpreted, were for that end. From Buddy's generation on the mat, there was another premier superstar with an independent streak. He was Lou Thesz, and Buddy and Lou had a lot in common – much more than they would have admitted. At his peak, Thesz, too, was perceived as money-hungry, and guys believed that both Thesz and Rogers could have done more to help the industry instead of working to satisfy their personal egos. Thesz, honestly, disliked Buddy more than the other way around, and Rogers' comments about Ed (Strangler) Lewis were partially to blame. Buddy also supplanted Thesz as the top hero in St. Louis, and then jumped sides during Lou's wrestling war with Sam Muchnick, ultimately forcing him to compromise a multi-million-dollar enterprise. Thesz wanted to win that conflict, and Rogers stopped him cold.

Thesz never hid his animosity toward Buddy, although their relationship did seem to improve as they got older.[115] In various forums, Lou rejoiced in the "fact" that he didn't put Buddy over, and it was true, he blocked a possible NWA title switch to Rogers in 1957. But Buddy did beat Thesz once, on May 10, 1946, in Houston, capturing the Texas belt. It was a one-fall-in-90-minutes victory, but it was a victory nonetheless. Lou was also cooperative during their long history of warfare, giving Buddy quick falls to sell the intensity of their combat. In Louisville on Sept. 23, 1947, Rogers won the first fall in 18 seconds.[116] 11-years later, on Aug. 5, 1958, Buddy beat Thesz again in that same amount of time in Phoenix.[117] Aside from an NWA title change, Thesz and Rogers did what was best for business, and made a lot of good money together. They put their opinions on the shelf, and cashed in at the end of the night.

When Rogers was at his manipulative best, and his "Nature Boy" gimmick was firing on all cylinders, there was nothing he wouldn't do to garner attention. He was the "Frank Sinatra of wrestling" and had an image to uphold. It was all about the way he sold himself to the public, his arrogance in interviews, and the way he handled himself backstage.[118] Buddy wasn't above stealing another wrestler's heat, and in a match, there were times in which an opponent perceived him to be reckless or stiff, leaving them vulnerable to injury. Of all his moves, his piledriver, giant swing, and knee lift were his most dangerous in a legitimate sense, and accidents did happen.[119] On occasion, he was faced with an unruly opponent, someone yearning to test him or refusing to either sell or put him over, and without the surefire tools of a shooter, Rogers resorted to the only tricks he knew to send a message. He would adjust his timing and subtly put force behind his high knee, driving it right into the face of a rival.

Cooperation was necessary for the giant swing, but the "message" was all in at what point Buddy released his opponent – either high or low to the mat, which was considered much safer. If the release point was two or more feet off the ground, the chances for injury went up exponentially, and Rogers did toss a few foes from the ring over the course of his time on the mat.[120] His reasoning behind the perilous maneuvers was between himself and his opponent, and after such situations, they usually never wrestled again because of the bad blood.[121] While a high knee and giant swing weren't glorified like the dreaded submissions of Thesz or Karl Gotch, they were effective enough to get his point across. All told, Buddy got a lot of flack, and much of it was probably warranted. Some of it was based on resentment and envy, but many guys who cast aspersions were also quick to compliment Buddy's extraordinary showmanship and overall aura. At the top of that list was Lou Thesz.

As a blond heel, and specifically, a blond heel world champion, Rogers made a huge mark on the wrestling world, and his cool persona was remarkably influential. The in-ring character he created was studied and copied by a number of performers to include Roy Shire, Dr. Jerry Graham, and Jackie Fargo.[122] He didn't hesitate to label them imitators, and though he recognized it was flattering, he declared, "Nobody ever equaled Buddy."[123] Just like the situation amongst the fans, there was a love-hate element between Rogers and his peers. Guys might have disliked something he did, or a personality trait, but they still had to respect his game.[124] Many times, Rogers earned that admiration by putting over a competitor as a fierce threat, even if he didn't literally succumb at the finish. Buddy was inclined to help younger, promising athletes by giving them a star-making turn, typically on TV, and the showing was always a boost to their career. He did it for Donn Lewin, Dick Steinborn, Ray Stevens, Dory Dixon, Roger Kirby, Art Thomas, Bill Miller, Sweet Daddy Siki, Jay York, and Mark Lewin, as well as many others.

Who would have thought Jack Pfefer's madcap idea for a gimmick in 1948 would reshape the wrestling industry? After all, it was a clear takeoff on what Gorgeous George was doing, and the over-the-top histrionics was sure to burn itself out. But Buddy Rogers turned the "Nature Boy" character into a cultural phenomenon, and to this day, that nickname represents a certain image in professional wrestling – one that strikes deep into the heart of fans. The popularity and recognition of Rogers was far-reaching, and to the point that Nat King Cole would actually begin performing the hit song "Nature Boy" when he spotted Buddy in a nightclub.[125] The legacy of the heralded nickname was passed to Ric Flair, and he carried the "Nature Boy" tradition into the 21st century with his own original panache. Flair was not a carbon copy of Buddy in the ring. In fact, in terms of style, Nick Bockwinkel was closer to Rogers in the way he approached bouts in the squared circle.

The influence of Rogers was incalculable. He was an icon to fellow wrestlers and to a generation of fans. Everyone from Ray Stevens to Dick Steinborn to Les Thatcher idolized him, while others with similar ring characteristics were too proud to admit it. He trained dozens of future champions and helped shape the wrestling skills of ex-boxing kingpins, "Jersey" Joe Walcott and Joe Louis. Whether if it was the physical act of teaching a method or move, or sitting down to explain the psychological benefits of a specific angle, Rogers's advice was golden, and wrestlers listened to what he had to say. In many cases, promoters did, as well. Buddy lived for the business, listened to the audience, and he knew when to make the right play at the right time. Many of his protégés learned those same lessons and went on to have successful careers of their own. Notably, his 1961 match with Pat O'Connor was frequently shown to wrestling students as an example of athleticism and psychology.[126]

Rogers was once asked if he was in wrestling strictly for the money. "It's not far wrong," he answered. "The money helps soften the bumps."[127] Of all his qualities, Buddy was a pragmatist, and he knew that for a non-high-school graduate to become financially successful in the real world, it was going to take a lot of hard work. And he went all in, devoting his entire being to the wrestling craft. "I wish I had a dollar for every drop of blood I spilled in my career," he told a reporter in 1983. "I would need a truck to carry it to the bank."[128] Rogers saved his money, invested in annuities and real estate, and did everything he could to ensure he would leave wrestling with a small fortune. His biggest fear was leaving the industry broke, and he often proclaimed that he wanted enough money so "they won't have to throw any benefits for me."[129] His business transactions and financial decisions paid off, and Buddy never dealt with the financial hardships so many of his contemporaries struggled with.

Historically, Buddy's reign as world heavyweight champion from 1961 to '63 has brought much criticism for the way he was booked, and how preference was giving to certain cities over the entire NWA union. A handful of members in smaller territories were undeniably hurt by a lack of appearances by the champion. But, in accepting that truth, it has to be understood that Rogers's schedule was approved by the upper management of the organization, and Buddy's incredible box-office numbers literally saved the NWA from possible financial ruin. The organization was dealing with an ongoing legal action in Iowa brought by wrestler Sonny Myers, who charged the Alliance with an illegal monopoly.[130] The uncertainty of the lawsuit persuaded NWA leaders to push Rogers to the championship, and subsequently overlook complaints to keep money flowing in. In truth, Rogers did more to strengthen the Alliance than he did to erode the group. On the surface, though, it didn't appear that way.

In recognition of his illustrious career, Buddy was honored for induction into the WWF, *Wrestling Observer*, Professional Wrestling, and NWA Halls of Fame between 1994 and 2010.[131] Although he never lived to see his enshrinement, Buddy likely would have enjoyed the various honors celebrating his contributions to the sport. "Every fiber of his being was entwined with wrestling," Lee Rogers said. "The entirety of my father's identity was shaped by, and expressed through, wrestling."[132] Bobby Davis, after Rogers died in 1992, said that Buddy, "had more charisma, I think, than John Kennedy and Marilyn Monroe put together. The man had the ability to change your feelings, change your emotions."[133] Bob Greene declared unabashedly that Rogers was the "coolest person of the 20th century."[134] In 2015, WWE executive and Hall of Famer Triple H was asked if he had the ability to wrestle anyone from the past, who would he face, and he answered, without hesitation, "Buddy Rogers."[135]

Rogers once said that wrestling would "always be a part of me," and he strutted until he could strut no more.[136] In tribute, his lifelong buddy, Bobby

Davis said: "In addition to being a great man, and a great talent, he was a very loving husband, a devoted father, and a very, very dear and trusting friend. And I'm sure the likes of him I shall never see again."[137] The world of professional wrestling agreed wholeheartedly. But in the minds and hearts of all the fans who cherished the original "Nature Boy, they will never let their memories of him fade. To them, his trademark sneer, witty remarks, and larger-than-life personality will live forever.

ENDNOTES - CHAPTER 21

[1] *The Spinning Toe-Hold*, 1982, Issue #56, p. 11.

[2] Footage of this match was featured on the Buddy Rogers Tribute Tape.

[3] *Official Wrestling*, July 1983, p. 10-13.

[4] Rogers had a lot of respect for Andre the Giant and Andre visited Buddy at his Haddonfield home. Rogers said that he was the "greatest wrestler." Buddy Rogers interview with Rod Luck, WWDB Radio, April 1983.

[5] Interview with Debbie Rogers, July 15, 2020.

[6] Snuka talked at length about his cocaine use in his autobiography, Superfly: The Jimmy Snuka Story by Jimmy Snuka (2012).

[7] Snuka was not especially kind in his comments about Rogers. Ibid.

[8] Ibid. Jimmy Snuka Indictment Documents, *Commonwealth of Pennsylvania v. James Snuka*, Court of Common Pleas of Lehigh County, Trial Division, 2015.

[9] In 2015, Snuka was charged with third-degree murder and involuntary manslaughter for the death of Argentino. He was 72-years-old at the time. *New York Daily News*, Sept. 2, 2015, p. 5. He was later found not competent to stand trial. *Easton Express-Times*, June 1, 2016. Debbie Rogers was going to appear as a witness in the trial.

[10] Snuka and his family lived at 580 Coles Mill Road. Camden County Property Records, Camden, NJ.

[11] Jimmy Snuka Indictment Documents, *Commonwealth of Pennsylvania v. James Snuka*, Court of Common Pleas of Lehigh County, Trial Division, 2015.

[12] *Wrestling Revue*, September 1983, p. 42.

[13] These tapings were for shows airing between October 29 and November 12. Among his final guests were Tony Atlas and Rocky Johnson. Atlas told Rogers, "You're a champion to all the people and to us." Rogers' Corner from Nov. 12, 1983, youtube.com.

[14] The accident occurred at approximately 10:15 p.m. *Buddy Nature Boy Rogers v. Madison Square Garden Corporation, Madison Square Garden Boxing, Inc., Titan Sports, Inc., Capitol Wrestling Corporation*, Index No. 6005/87, Nov. 7, 1986, Supreme Court of the State of New York: County of New York. It was said that Rogers slipped on a bar of soap.

[15] *Global Newsletter*, Issue #98, November 1983, p. 3. Albano stated that Rogers suffered a broken leg in the fall. *Often Imitated, Never Duplicated: Captain Lou Albano* by Lou Albano and Philip Varriale (2008) p. 127.

[16] *World Wrestling Federation Program*, #108, January 1984, p. 14-15.

[17] *Wrestling King of Sports*, Vol. 8, Issue #18, Dec.-Jan. 1984, p. 2. Also see *Global Newsletter*, Issue #98, November 1983, p. 3. Rogers was replaced in upcoming tag matches by Arnold Skaaland. A search for any lawsuits filed by Rogers against the WWF in 1983-1984 turned up empty. A case was filed in 1986, though. In April 1987, the defendants asked for documents and to take depositions. *Buddy Nature Boy Rogers v. Madison Square Garden Corporation, Madison Square Garden Boxing, Inc., Titan Sports, Inc., Capitol Wrestling Corporation*, Index No. 6005/87, Nov. 7, 1986, Supreme Court of the State of New York: County of New York. According to court records, it doesn't appear that documents were submitted in a timely manner, and the case was likely dismissed. However, the case file might be incomplete.

[18] The show was taped in Baltimore. *Baltimore Sun*, Oct. 9, 1984, p. 8C.

[19] Buddy Rogers interview on *Tuesday Night Titans*, youtube.com. When asked about Vince McMahon "Junior" in a written interview by Georgiann Makropoulos in the early 1990s, Rogers wrote: "No comment." *Wrestling Chatterbox*, November 1991.

[20] *Fire...Away (In Memoriam) Sweet Prince* by Michael Lano, 1995. With regard to Buddy's strut, it has been said that Vincent K. McMahon's exaggerated swagger to the ring was adapted from Rogers' original version.

[21] Correspondence with Dave Aquino, Jan. 20, 2019.

[22] Buddy received a special trophy with his honor. *The Spinning Toe-Hold*, Issue #63, 1983.

[23] Sharpe (Larry Weil) was an amateur wrestler in high school and college. *Camden Courier-Post*, Nov. 22, 1984, p. 8D. Paulsboro was a 15-minute drive from Camden.

[24] Rogers said he had been asked by many people how to start a career in wrestling. Buddy Rogers interview on *Tuesday Night Titans*, youtube.com.

[25] Correspondence between Larry Sharpe and Bill McCormack, July 31, 2000.

[26] The board of directors included Buddy Rogers, David Rogers, and Larry Weil. Certificate of Incorporation, Filed on Nov. 2, 1984, Secretary of State, State of New Jersey, New Jersey Division of Revenue, Records Unit, Trenton, NJ.

[27] Outside the school, there was a sign that read: "We Guarantee the Future Stars of Wrestling" and was signed, "Buddy Rogers."

[28] Interview with Dave Giegold, Dec. 8, 2018.

[29] Ibid.

[30] *Atlantic City Sunday Press*, March 7, 1982.

[31] A magazine published photos of Buddy and David working out. *Wrestling's Main Event*, September 1983, p. 21-22.

[32] Buddy Rogers interview on *Tuesday Night Titans*, youtube.com.

[33] Interview of Larry Sharpe, *Whatever Happened To...?*, Issue #19. It is believed that David Rogers wrestled at least one professional match, competing on the Dec. 29, 1984 show at the Asbury Park Convention Hall. However, additional details are not known. Buddy Rogers refereed the main event on that card, headlined by Larry Sharpe versus Rocky Jones. *Asbury Park Press*, Dec. 20, 1984, p. 84.

[34] Certificate of Correction, Filed July 25, 1985, Secretary of State, State of New Jersey, New Jersey Division of Revenue, Records Unit, Trenton, NJ.

[35] *Pro Wrestling Torch*, March 11, 1995, p. 8.

[36] Interview with Debbie Rogers, July 15, 2020.

[37] Ibid.

[38] The Rogers Family relocated to Florida around June 1987.

[39] Buddy Rogers Interview by Dr. Mike Lano and Gary "Gerhardt" Kaiser, *Canvas Cavity*, Circa. 1991-1992.

[40] Interview with Debbie Rogers, July 15, 2020.

[41] Ibid.

[42] Correspondence with Linda Spiegleman, September 2018.

[43] Interview with Jean Scott, Sept. 10, 2018.

[44] Cauliflower Alley Club Program, March 12, 1988.

[45] *Sun-Sentinel*, Sept. 8, 1990, p. 19. Mike was married to women's wrestler, Juanita Coffman, who died in 1987.

[46] *Esquire*, April 1989, p. 59-60, 63.

[47] *Wrestling Chatterbox*, November 1991.

[48] Buddy Rogers Interview by John Arezzi, *Pro Wrestling Spotlight*, Aug. 4, 1991.

[49] *Sun-Sentinel*, July 28, 1989, p. 1.

[50] *New York Daily News*, Aug. 24, 1989, p. 43.

[51] *Sun-Sentinel*, July 28, 1989, p. 1.

[52] Interview with Debbie Rogers, July 15, 2020. Footage of the award ceremony was included on the Buddy Rogers Tribute Tape. Of note, there were two versions of the Buddy Rogers Tribute Tape. One was a six-hour video, put out by Dr. Mike Lano and Georgiann Makropoulos. It was entitled, "To A Nicer Guy," and proceeds went to Debbie Rogers. Then there was a four-hour tape offered by Makropoulos. These tapes were sold in the years following Buddy's death. Larry Sharpe released his own tribute video around 1995.
[53] This event happened on January 25 and 26 in Bensalem, PA. *Camden Courier-Post*, Jan. 22, 1986, p. 26.
[54] Among the others honored were the Fabulous Moolah, Mae Young, Roddy Piper, and Fred Blassie. Cauliflower Alley Club Program, June 1988.
[55] The show occurred on April 2, 1989. Brief footage of the dinner was shown at the beginning of the Clash on TBS. The event is available on the WWE Network. wwe.com.
[56] Rogers said that the Flair-Steamboat match in New Orleans "was the best match [he'd] seen in ten years." *New Wave Wrestling*, April 1992.
[57] Bruno Sammartino was also on hand to provide commentary. Backstage, Rogers and Sammartino briefly spoke and were photographed together by Bill Otten. *Swimming with Piranhas: Surviving the Politics of Professional Wrestling* by Howard T. Brody (2009), p.123. This was the first known Rogers-Sammartino photo together since 1963.
[58] *Carolina Indian Voice*, July 19, 1990, p. 1.
[59] Buddy Rogers Interview by John Arezzi, *Pro Wrestling Spotlight*, Aug. 4, 1991.
[60] *Pro Wrestling Illustrated*, March 1991 p. 56.
[61] Rogers appeared on the Aug. 4, 1991 show.
[62] Georgiann Makropoulos took a photograph of Buddy and Bruno Sammartino shaking hands at the convention.
[63] Correspondence with Bob Bryla, Aug. 14, 2018.
[64] *Mat Marketplace*, October 1991, p. 9.
[65] Buddy Rogers Interview by John Arezzi, *Pro Wrestling Spotlight*, Oct. 20, 1991.
[66] Ibid. Rogers had great respect for Steve Williams, calling him "the greatest wrestler in the world." *New Wave Wrestling*, April 1992.
[67] Rogers appeared for an interview on 610 WIP. Correspondence with Jim Molineaux, Dec. 16, 2018.
[68] *Wrestling Chatterbox*, October 1991, p. 12.
[69] Landel talked about the angle they were working. He said they were going to turn him into a fan favorite and Rogers was going to work as his manager. *Wrestling Flyer Interview Collection* #1, p. 36. Goodhart declared bankruptcy, as announced on Jan. 18, 1991. *Wrestling Chatterbox*, Janaury 1992, p. 5-6.
[70] Buddy Rogers Interview by Dr. Mike Lano and Gary "Gerhardt" Kaiser, *Canvas Cavity*, Circa. 1991-1992.
[71] Buddy Rogers interview with Rod Luck, WWDB Radio, April 1983.
[72] Buddy Rogers Interview by John Arezzi, *Pro Wrestling Spotlight*, Aug. 4, 1991.
[73] Following Rogers and Flair, A.J. Styles became the third man in history to hold both the NWA and WWE Titles on Sept. 11, 2016 when he defeated Dean Ambrose in Richmond, Virginia.
[74] Rogers was a presenter of a plaque for Maurice Vachon. Cauliflower Alley Club Program, April 1992.
[75] Interview with Karl Lauer, Sept. 12, 2018.
[76] *Wrestling Chatterbox*, August 1992, p. 2.
[77] Rogers didn't tell Georgiann Makropoulos about the injury during a call they had, and later said it was because he didn't want to worry her. Ibid.
[78] Ibid.
[79] Interview with Debbie Rogers, July 15, 2020.

80 It was reported in the newspaper that Rogers had suffered two strokes on Monday, June 22, one while taking a shower and the other after arriving at the hospital. *Sun-Sentinel*, June 26, 1992, p. B1.
81 Ibid.
82 *Sun-Sentinel*, June 28, 1992, p. 6B, *Wrestling Chatterbox*, June 1992, p. 1. Rogers was scheduled to have appeared at the LIWA event at the Dunes Hotel in Las Vegas on June 26. He was to have performed color commentary alongside Karl Lauer. David Rogers called Karl, informing him of Buddy's passing, and Lauer made the announcement from the ring. Many of the performers on hand for the show, including the Fabulous Moolah, were crying. Interview with Karl Lauer, Sept. 12, 2018, Steve Johnson interview of Terry Milam, February 2006.
83 Condolences were offered by Jim Ross during the July 4, 1992 episode of *WCW Saturday Night*. It is not believed that his passing was mentioned on WWF TV.
84 *Sun-Sentinel*, June 26, 1992, p. B1.
85 Bobby Davis Interview by John Arezzi, *Pro Wrestling Spotlight*, July 11, 1992.
86 *Pro Wrestling Torch*, Undated.
87 Ibid.
88 *Whatever Happened To...?*, Issue #52, p. 12.
89 *Wrestling Chatterbox*, August 1992, p. 2. Darnell missed the funeral because his wife was sick. Matt Langley attended on behalf of Makropoulos and *Wrestling Chatterbox*. Correspondence with Matt Langley, Feb. 22, 2019. Valentine said that Buddy was his "oldest and dearest friend." *Wrestling Then and Now*, Issue #55, August 1994, p. 8.
90 Buddy Rogers interview by Ray Tennenbaum, February 1985. www.ray-field.com.
91 Her full name was Anna S. Rohde Woerner. *Camden Courier-Post*, Nov. 18, 1992, p. 24. Buddy's other stepsister, Ida Rohde Hauske, died on May 10, 1989.
92 Interview with Karl Lauer, Sept. 12, 2018.
93 Interview with Debbie Rogers, July 15, 2020. Correspondence with Matt Langley, Feb. 22, 2019. Cauliflower Alley Club Program, April 1994, p. 12.
94 *Camden Courier-Post*, June 23, 1994, p. 17.
95 *Wrestling Chatterbox*, August 1992, p. 3.
96 Correspondence with Lee Rogers, Aug. 14, 2020.
97 *Chicago Tribune*, Sept. 6, 1998, p. 2.
98 *Charlotte Observer*, Aug. 18, 1979, p. 7A.
99 He'd often say that someone had or needed, "A little four letter word called, 'guts,'" and begin sentences with, "Let's take it this way."
100 Rogers reportedly called David Condon, "Coach." *Chicago Tribune*, May 18, 1962, p. 55.
101 Interviews with Bobby Davis, 2019.
102 *Philadelphia Daily News*, Jan. 20, 1962, p. 35.
103 Dick Hutton said: "It was like an orchestra. [Rogers would] pick 'em up a little bit, then settle 'em down, then he'd pick 'em up a little higher, then settle them back down." *Whatever Happened To...?*, Issue #44, p. 10.
104 Rogers got many of his suits from Walmart Tailors at 1209 Broadway in Camden. An advertisement mentioned him in the *Camden Courier-Post*, Jan. 27, 1949, p. 36. He also frequented Ace Tesone's shop in South Philadelphia. *Philadelphia Daily News*, July 19, 1971, p. 22.
105 Interview with Karl Lauer, Sept. 12, 2018.
106 The Fabulous Moolah recited an incident with Rogers on the road, in which Buddy allegedly demanded a sexual favor. She refused and got out of his car. *The Fabulous Moolah: First Goddess of the Squared Circle* by Lillian Ellison (2002), p. 63-65.
107 *Buddie Rogers and The Art of "Sequencing"* by Max W. Jacobs, p. 15-16.
108 *Esquire*, April 1989, p. 63.
109 *Chicago Daily Tribune*, April 13, 1962, p. D1.
110 *Miami News*, April 9, 1956, p. 13A.
111 *Fort Worth Star Telegram*, Aug. 16, 1962, p. 16.

[112] Kansas City promoter George Simpson said that Rogers was a "tough cookie" in negotiations. *American Sportscaster*, Nov. 2, 1953. Ed McLemore in Dallas said that Buddy was "always fussing" with the promoter. *Owensboro Messenger-Inquirer*, Oct. 2, 1950, p. 10.

[113] Some wrestlers would pick up and leave a territory if Rogers was coming in.

[114] Rogers said: "There's a tremendous amount of jealousy in our business. A lot of resentment. People undermine each other. Wish each other bad luck. What's that saying? 'The bottom's crowded. The top is lean.'" *Atlanta Journal-Constitution*, June 17, 1987, p. D1.

[115] After the Karl Gotch-Bill Miller attack on Rogers in 1962, Buddy called Thesz to vent his frustrations. *Whatever Happened To...?*, Issue #31, p. 8.

[116] *Louisville Courier-Journal*, Sept. 24, 1947, p. 4.

[117] *Arizona Republic*, Aug. 6, 1958, p. 30.

[118] During segments of Rogers' Corner, it was felt that Buddy took too much of the spotlight and didn't let his guests talk.

[119] A high knee by Rogers broke the jaw of Al Kashey in 1954. *Chicago Tribune*, Feb. 4, 1954, p. 56, *Paterson News*, March 4, 1954, p. 18. His piledriver reportedly injured the neck of his friend, Billy Darnell.

[120] It allegedly happened to Eric Pedersen, and Bruno Sammartino commonly referenced the incident during later interviews. Sammartino cited it as a major reason why he didn't trust Rogers in the ring. Other wrestlers, like Fred Blassie and Jackie Fargo, were in agreement. *The Legends of Wrestling "Classy" Freddie Blassie: Listen, You Pencil Neck Geeks* by Fred Blassie and Keith Elliot Greenberg (2004) (117-118), Interview with Jackie Fargo, *The Wrestling Archive Project*, Volume 2, by Scott Teal, p. 162.

[121] There were allegedly incidents involving Abe Jacobs and the Zebra Kid.

[122] Buddy had a real world feud with Shire, lasting many years.

[123] *Wrestling's Main Event*, September 1983, p. 20-24. Imitators were also called "vest-pocket Rogers."

[124] Among those to compliment Rogers were Thesz, Sammartino, Killer Kowalski, Bob Ellis, Dick Steinborn, Dory Dixon, Art Thomas, Johnny Valentine, Ron Reed, and Roger Kirby.

[125] Rogers mentioned this occurring at the Band Box in Los Angeles. Buddy Rogers Interview by Bill Apter, *Apter Chat*, Part One, 1979, youtube.com. The club was at 123 N. Fairfax and was operated by Billy Gray.

[126] It was a "great teaching match." Interview with Karl Lauer, Sept. 12, 2018.

[127] Buddy also said there were other factors. "I'd say that winning is the most important thing in the world to me. I'm a competitor and I hate to lose. *Wrestling Revue*, December 1961, p. 19.

[128] *Wrestling's Main Event*, September 1983, p. 20-24.

[129] *Philadelphia Daily News*, June 20, 1967, p. 60. Buddy claimed to have made $4.5 million in the ring. *Charlotte Observer*, Aug. 18, 1979, p. 7A, 9A. An article in 1964 had the headline: "Buddy Rogers – Millionaire Wrestler."*Mat Wrestling Review*, Issue #311, January 1964. Buddy Landel said that Rogers was "worth ten million dollars." *Wrestling Flyer Interview Collection* #1, p. 36.

[130] *Harold C. Myers v. P.L. George and National Wrestling Alliance*, Civil Action No. 3-630, District Court of the United States for the Southern District of Iowa.

[131] Rogers was inducted into the WWF Hall of Fame on June 9, 1994 in Baltimore, in its second HOF class. Bobby Davis gave his induction speech and presented the honor to David Rogers. Interview with Bobby Davis, March 24, 2019.

[132] Correspondence with Lee Rogers, Aug. 18, 2018.

[133] Interview with Bobby Davis, Buddy Rogers Tribute Tape.

[134] *Arizona Daily Sun*, Oct. 20, 1998, p. 6.

[135] Triple H interview by Steve Austin. *Stone Cold Podcast*, Feb. 2, 2015, WWE Network, wwe.com.

[136] *Charlotte Observer*, Aug. 18, 1979, p. 7A, 9A.

[137] Interview with Bobby Davis, Buddy Rogers Tribute Tape

INDEX

114th Infantry Armory (Camden NJ), 12
Adali, Ali, 38
Albano, Captain Lou, 258, 262-263
Albers, Karl Von, 130-131, 135-136, 139
Ali, Muhammad, 218, 232
All Star Wrestling (TV), 257
Allen, Charley, 40
Amara, Zelis, 244
American tag team title, 125-126, 165
American Wrestling Association (Columbus OH), 112-113
American Wrestling Association (Minneapolis), 205, 219
Amphitheatre (Chicago IL), 87, 90, 98, 178, 199, 236
Apollo, Argentina, 236
Aragon Club (Houston TX), 51
Arena (St. Louis MO), 100
Arena (Trenton NJ), 30
Arezzi, John, 266
Armory (Louisville KY), 68
Armory (Paterson NJ), 89
Arnold, Don, 112
Atkins, Fred, 203-204, 213
Austeri, Jim, 29, 34, 37, 40, 174
Austin, Buddy, 154, 164-165, 167, 213
Avey, Sam, 62-63
AWA world title (Columbus OH), 12, 112, 115-116
Axman, Dick, 64, 98
Baba, Shohei, 193
Baker, Frank, 115
Baker, Ox, 254
Balkin, Sid, 177
Baltimore Coliseum, 140
Banaski, Joe, 12
Barend, Johnny, 155, 167-168, 218, 228, 238
Barnett, Jim, 165-166, 204-206
Barniak, Jim, 67, 257
Baxter, Laverne, 42, 52
Beat the Champ title, 160-161
Becker, George, 72
Becker, Izzy, 85-86
Bell, Kay, 77
Big Heart, Chief, 174
Big Time Wrestling, 252
black Tuesday, 10
Blassie, Billy, 143
Blatt, Ed, 252
Boesch, Paul, 54
Bollas, George, 84-85
Boston Arena, 112

Bowser, Paul, 12, 101, 112, 141
Boxing and Wrestling (magazine), 211
Boxing Illustrated, Wrestling News (magazine), 200
Brazil, Bobo, 193-194, 201-202, 228, 238
Brazin, Moe, 28
Broadway Arena (New York NY), 35
Bromberg, Lester, 75, 89
Brown, Andy, 12
Brown, Blackjack, 232
Brown, Orville, 77-78, 80, 90
Bruiser, Dick the, 227
Bruns, Bobby, 78
Buddy Rogers Covered Wagon Lounge, 249-250
Buddy Rogers International Fan Club, 237
Buddy Rogers' Pro Wrestling School, 264
Buddy Rogers Trailer Park, 251
Burke, Frank J., 48
Burns, Farmer, 73
Butcher, Abdullah the, 244
Calhoun, Country Boy (Haystack), 160, 177-178
California state athletic commission, 128
Camden (NJ) YMCA, 13-14, 41, 111, 115, 118, 250
Camden Brewery, 8, 10
Camden High School, 14-16, 36
Campbell, Ian, 143
Capitol Wrestling Corporation, 166, 172-176, 180, 186, 188-189, 193, 200, 203, 205, 207, 215-216, 218, 223-225, 229, 236-237, 239
Carnera, Primo, 61, 67, 74, 87
Carpentier, Edouard, 143, 168, 193, 250
Casey, Jim, 52
Casey, Steve (Crusher), 60
Championship Wrestling (TV), 257
Championship Wrestling from Florida, 254
Chavis, Chris, 266
Cincinnati Gardens, 165
City Auditorium (St. Joseph MO), 78
Clash of the Champions, 266
Clay, Cassius, 218
Claybourne, Jack, 136
Cleveland (OH) Arena, 87-88
Cleveland (OH) boxing & wrestling commission, 116
Cleveland Arena, 127
Clinstock, Jim, 37
Coffield, Jimmy, 52
Coleman, Abe, 34
Coliseum (Baltimore MD), 29

Coliseum (Columbus OH), 104
Columbus (OH) boxing & wrestling commission, 111
Comiskey Park, 176, 178, 185, 199, 202, 232
Condon, David, 181, 199, 202, 240
Contos, Ed, 129
Convention Hall (Camden NJ), 29, 35, 98
Cotton Club (Houston TX), 51
Cox, Joe, 35, 41, 47-48
Craddock, Babe, 42
Crockett, Jim, 36, 140
Curtis, King, 255
Darnell, Betty, 269
Darnell, Billy, 11, 36, 41, 65-68, 76-77, 79, 84-85, 87, 90, 100, 117, 130, 143-144, 149-150, 265, 267, 269
Davis, Bobby, 6, 163-164, 166-167, 172-173, 175-176, 181, 229, 252, 268-269, 273
Davis, Sterling (Dizzy), 63
Davis, Sylvia, 6
DeCastro, Mike, 24
DeGlane, Henri, 12
Demon of Death Valley, 84-85
Dempsey, Jack, 11, 104, 127
DeVaiteau, Joe, 30
DiBiase, Mike, 105
DiPaolo, Ilio, 142
Dixon, Dory, 192-193, 214, 219, 224-226
Doganiero, Dominic, 24, 117, 130
Don George, Ed, 25
Doyle, Johnny, 72-73, 160, 165-166, 204-206
Drake, George, 105
DuBuque, Gene, 161-163
DuMont network, 86, 115, 129-130
Dundee, Chris, 141
Dusek, Emil, 35, 42-43, 51-52
Dusek, Ernie, 35, 47, 51-52
Dusek, Rudy, 12, 27-29, 35-38, 40, 47-48, 52, 55, 66, 98, 175
Eagle, Don, 79, 90, 101, 112
Eagle, Lone, 100
East Coast heavyweight title, 115
Eastern heavyweight title, 125-126, 130-131, 140, 165, 167
Eaton, Cal, 72-73, 160-161
Eiferman, George, 156
Ellis, Cowboy Bob, 190, 206
Emerson High School, 15
Estep, Elmer (Elmer the Great), 56
Etchison, Ronnie, 162
Evans, Don, 39, 42, 51
Fabiani, Ray, 90, 97, 130, 135-136, 166, 238, 242
Faieta, Eddie, 102
Fargo, Don, 165, 243
Fargo, Jackie, 165
Farnham Park Athletic Field, 14, 16
figure-four grapevine, 117
Flair, Ric, 255-256, 267, 272
Forbes Field (Pittsburgh), 186-187
Forum (Montreal QB), 101
Freeman, Herb, 37, 40

Funk Sr., Dory, 155-156, 189
Gagne, Verne, 105
Galento, Al, 41, 76
Galento, Two-Ton Tony, 61-62, 87, 137
Gallagher, Doc, 265
Gallagher, Mike, 265
Ganson, Jack, 87, 115, 128
Garden Pier (Atlantic City NJ), 28-29
Garibaldi, Chick, 229
Garibaldi, Gino, 12, 27, 35, 47, 55
Gehman, Doc, 89
Geigel, Bob, 105
Geohagen, Timothy, 140
George, Gorgeous, 7, 55, 72-75, 78, 88, 92, 101
George, Tom, 30, 36
Gersh, Ed, 230-2311
Giegold, Dave, 264
Gilbert, Eddie, 264
Gilzenberg, Willie, 62, 175-176, 193-194, 205, 224, 238-239
Givnin, Kathryn, 30, 39-40
Golden Angel (Jack Moore), 49, 64
Gomez, Pepper, 139
Goodhart, Joel, 267
Gossett, Eddie, 155
Gotch, Karl, 204-206, 253, 272
Graham brothers, 164
Graham, Eddie, 179, 254
Graham, Leon, 165
Grandovich, John, 12
Greene, Bob, 253, 273
Gregg, Christy, 76
Gregoire, Lucien, 212
Griffin, Wayne, 112
Griffith Stadium (Washington DC), 175
Grip, Charley, 11-12, 27
Grobmier, Fred, 26-28, 37, 47, 53, 117, 202
Gross, Milton, 137-138
Gulas, Nick, 190
Haft, Al, 67, 101, 103-105, 111-115, 117, 126, 128-130, 141, 149, 154, 163-166, 168, 203, 205-206, 253
Haft's Acre (Columbus OH), 111
Hanly, Frank, 12
Hanly, Ray, 12
Harben, George, 37
Hayes, Debbie (see Rogers, Debbie)
Helfand, Julius, 141
Henning, John Paul, 180
Hild, Helen, 76
Hill, Barto, 36
Hollywood Legion Stadium, 73, 75, 126, 128, 161
HOOKER, 55
Hornbaker, Tim, 6
Hornby, Fred, 6
Howlett, Dutch, 151
Hutton, Dick, 127, 156, 163, 176
Illinois state athletic commission, 90, 92
Indian Nature Boy, 100
Ivan the Terrible, 130

Jackson, Jackie (Diamond Jack), 230
Jackson, Terry, 124
Jacobs, Max, 62
Jamaica Arena (Queens NY), 60, 67
John W. Mickie School, 14
Johnson, Tor, 56, 67
Jonathan, Brother (Jack Moore), 50
Jonathan, Don Leo, 142-143
Jones, Marvin, 49
Jones, Paul, 49
Kangaroos, Fabulous, 178
Karlsson, Karl, 154
Karras, Alex, 227
Kato, Oyama, 126, 229
Kaufman, Andy, 256
Kelly, Gene, 139
Kenyon, J Michael, 6, 202
Kerr, Wilson, 13, 25
Kessler, Gene, 91
Kiel Auditorium (St. Louis), 65, 77, 79, 125, 180
Kietzer, Norman H., 237
King, Eddie, 37
King, Sonny, 255
Kiniski, Gene, 139, 250
Kohler, Fred, 64, 80, 86-87, 90-91, 97-98, 114-115, 140-141, 175, 177-178, 181, 189, 200-201, 218, 232
Koszewski, Irvin (Zabo), 156
Kowalski, Wladek (Tarzan), 113, 212-214
Kuss, Otto, 49
Kwariani, Kola, 176
LaChappelle, Maurice, 28, 36, 51
Landel, Buddy, 267
Lawrence, Sheik, 79
League, Jack, 63
LeDuc, Jos, 255
Lee, Cowboy Rocky (Don), 131, 137
Lee, Don, 52, 130
Lenihan, George, 49
Lenz, Henry, 156
Leone, Michele, 29-30, 36, 38, 42, 181
Lesnar, Brock, 153
Levin, Dave, 48-50, 55-56, 62, 65, 67
Levy, Martin (The Blimp), 48, 63
Lewis, Bill, 36, 129, 140
Lewis, Ed (Strangler), 13, 26, 38, 47, 55, 62, 113, 153, 188, 243, 271
Lex's Live Wrestling, 167
Lindsay, Luther, 200
Lisowski, Reggie (Crusher), 187, 192, 218
Londos, Jim, 12-13, 25-26, 38, 47, 62, 135, 175
Longson, Wild Bill, 50-54, 61, 65, 68, 91
Loubet, Nat, 237
Louis, Joe, 131, 136-138, 272
Ludlum, Joe, 41
Luttrall, Cowboy, 27, 142
Lutze, Nick, 72
Macricostas, George, 41
Madison Square Garden, 117, 130, 176, 179, 185, 188, 193, 211, 214, 218, 225, 227, 229, 236-238, 263

Mahoney, Tom, 68
Makropoulos, Georgiann, 237, 265, 268
Malcewicz, Joe, 161
Managoff, Bobby, 49-50
Manhattan Booking Agency, 87, 97
Mansfield boxing & wrestling commission, 151
Maple Leaf Gardens (Toronto), 204, 214
Marciano, Rocky, 127
Marcus, Henry, 36
Marigold Arena (Chicago IL), 97, 177
Markward, Bill, 30
Marlin, Farmer Don, 80
Marshall, Everette, 25, 62
Marshall, Floyd, 12
Martin, Joe, 28
Martinelli, Tony, 40
Martinez, Pedro, 172
Maryland state athletic commission, 126, 164
Masked Atom (Don Lee), 52
Mastis, Georgiann (see Makropoulos, Georgiann), 237
Mayer, Al, 35-36, 98, 102
Mayers, Lex, 164
McCarthy, Charley (Red), 62
McCune, Bob, 156
McEwen, Tom, 253
McFarlin, Brad, 268
McGuirk, LeRoy, 51, 63-64, 177
McMahon, Jess, 27
McMahon, Vincent James, 130, 140, 166, 168, 172, 175-177, 179-180, 188, 190, 193, 201, 203-204, 207, 212-213, 215-216, 219, 224-229, 231-232, 236-239, 257, 263, 268
McMillen, Jim, 25
McShain, Danny, 64, 67, 75, 127
Memorial Hall (Columbus OH), 110, 164
Midwest heavyweight title, 126
Miller, Big Bill, 105, 112, 125-126, 129, 204-206, 253
Miller, Ed, 139
Miller, Rudy, 87
Missouri sac, 141
Mitauer, Harry, 68
Mondt, Toots, 35-36, 38-39, 60-62, 65, 72, 80, 87-90, 97-98, 102, 129, 135, 140-141, 166, 168, 177, 180, 187, 212, 215, 224
Monsoon, Gorilla, 240
Monster Factory, 264, 266
Montana, Joe, 66
Moolah, Fabulous, 86
Moore, Tiger Jack, 48-49, 56, 64
Moore, Walter, 91-92
Morgan, Ray, 181
Moto, The Great, 116
Muchnick, Sam, 77, 79-81, 87, 100, 103, 125, 143, 152-153, 161, 176-180, 188-189, 200-201, 206-207, 214, 219, 250
Music Hall Arena (Cincinnati OH), 168
Myers, Sonny, 273
National Wrestling Alliance (NWA), 77, 80, 90, 97-98, 103, 112-114, 128-129, 135, 142-143, 149, 152-153, 155, 161, 163, 165, 169, 173,

310 • Master of the Ring

176-180, 185-188, 190, 200-201, 207, 211, 215-217, 224, 273
National Wrestling Association, 160, 214
Nature Boy (gimmick origin) 74-76
New York Athletic Club, 11
New York state athletic commission, 52, 67, 89, 99, 141-142, 190, 229
Newark (NJ) Armory, 194
Nichols, Hugh, 73
North American heavyweight title, 155-156
Numa, Leo, 54
NWA Official Wrestling (magazine), 113
NWA world heavyweight title, 68, 125, 173, 182, 185-189, 194, 200-205, 207, 211-217, 226, 230, 250, 254-255
O'Connor, Pat, 7, 127, 176-177, 180-182, 189, 202, 273
O'Hara, Pat, 137
Ohio tag team title, 165
Olsen, Cliff, 36
Olympic Auditorium (LA), 72-73, 156, 160-161
O'Mahoney, Danno, 47
Orton, Bob, 187, 191
O'Shocker, Pat, 12
O'Toole, Tommy, 27
packs t, 65
Packs, Tom, 53-54, 65, 77
Palese, Bill, 15-16
Parelli, Joe, 36
Parker, Dan, 66, 101
Parker, Zimba, 41
Patera, Ken, 256
Pedersen, Eric, 156
Pennsylvania state athletic commision, 40, 237
Pesek, John, 12
Petty, Ted, 264-265
Pfefer, Jack, 48, 49, 55-56, 60, 62, 64-68, 73-76, 78-80, 84-90, 92, 97-103, 125, 130, 143, 156, 165, 172, 176, 193, 243, 253, 270
Philadelphia Arena, 40, 187
Philadelphia Eagles, 11
Pinkerton, Lord, 156
Plummer, Lou, 51
Polish Angel, 84
PRISM cable network, 67, 257
Pro Wrestling Illustrated (magazine), 266
Pro Wrestling Spotlight (radio show), 266
Quinn, Eddie, 101-103, 129, 141, 168, 212-213, 243
Raap, Gus, 41
Race, Harley, 254-255
Rainbo Arena (Chicago IL), 64, 86, 90, 97, 103-104, 112
Ray, Burt, 244
Ress, Cyclone, 12
Rhodes, Dusty, 254-255
Ridgewood Grove (New York NY), 35, 80
Ring Wrestling (magazine), 237
Ring, The (magazine), 93, 224
Robert, Yvon, 47, 103, 115
Rocca, Antonino, 80, 87-90, 116-117, 140, 168, 187, 192, 241, 253

Rocky Mountain title, 62
Rogers' Corner, 257, 262
Rogers, Buddy (Charles), 128-129
Rogers, Bummy, 50, 102
Rogers, David, 264-265, 269
Rogers, Debbie, 6, 250-251, 253, 257, 263, 265, 268-269
Rogers, Frieda Alberta, 157
Rogers, Lee, 6, 226, 229, 269, 273
Rogers, Rip, 155
Rohde, Ellen, 79, 123
Rohde, Frieda, 157, 211, 237, 243-244
Rohde, Herman Gustav Max, 7-8, 10, 17, 21-22
Rohde, Herman Karl, 7-9
Rohde, John, 9-10, 17, 23, 41, 49, 211, 237
Rohde, Kathryn, 40
Rohde, Terry, 138, 156-157, 240-241, 249-250
Roosevelt Stadium, 240
Rosen, Buddy, 173
Roth, Ernie, 252
Rougeau, Johnny, 243-244
Sammartino, Bruno, 176, 204, 223-225, 227-232, 236, 238-240, 244, 257
Sarpolis, Karl, 190, 201
Savoldi, Angelo, 28, 34
Savoldi, Joe, 41-42, 52
Schmidt, Hans, 140
Schnabel, Hans, 49
Schneider, Gil, 126
Schwartz, Charles, 68
Schwartz, Leonard, 87, 97
Scott, George, 255
Scott, The Great, 115, 117, 125-127, 130, 265, 267-268
Sexton, Frank, 60-61, 90, 112
Sharkey, Babe, 38-39, 42, 50, 60
Sharkey, Jack, 127, 141
Sharpe, Larry, 264, 268
Sheik, The (Ed Farhat), 252
Sherry, Jack, 12
Shire, Professor Roy, 115
Sigel, Morris, 48-49, 51-52, 139, 187, 199
Siki, Sweet Daddy, 165, 176, 181
Silverstein, Ruffy, 104-105, 111-112, 127
Simon Gratz High School, 15
Simpson, George, 190
Sinatra, Tony, 84
Skaaland, Arnold, 173, 175
Slave Girl, 74-76, 86, 128, 155
Snuka, Jimmy, 256, 258, 262-263
Snuka, Sharon, 263
Snyder, Wilbur, 127-128
Spectrum (Philadelphia), 262
Sports Arena (Toledo OH), 100, 138
Sports Pictorial Review (magazine), 202
St. Louis wrestling, 53-54, 80-81, 100, 103, 125, 143, 250
St. Nick's Arena (New York NY), 35, 52, 67
Stadium (Chicago IL), 90
Stanlee, Gene, 64, 88-89, 103
Stanley Weston Award, 266

Index • 311

Staten Island Sports Hall of Fame, 264
Stech, Frieda, 8, 14, 22-24
Stecher, Joe, 25
Steeves, Clyde, 162
Steinborn, Dick, 268
Steinborn, Milo, 12, 29, 34-38, 87
Stevens, Don, 139
Stevens, Ray, 117, 139
Strongbow, Jules, 160
Studd, John, 256
Sucher Park (Dayton OH), 112
Super Swedish Angel, 56, 67
Superman Apollo, 156
suspensions, 52, 214
Swedish Angel, 48
Szabo, Sandor, 128, 157, 160
Talaber, Frankie, 116-117, 125
Teal, Scott, 6
team wrestling, 34
Terror, Golden, 136
Texas boxing & wrestling commission, 52
Texas heavyweight title, 54, 77, 139, 149
Texas tag team title, 49
Thesz, Lou, 47, 54-55, 65, 68, 79-80, 90-91, 98, 100, 103, 113, 125, 141-142, 144, 152-153, 161, 181, 186-187, 207, 214-216, 218, 224, 230, 241, 250, 271
Thomas, Sailor Art, 179-180, 192-193
Tokyo Sports (newspaper), 212
Torres, Enrique, 72
Torres, Ramon, 139
Townsend, Frank, 143
Triple H, 273-274
Tri-State heavyweight title, 112, 115
Tri-State Wrestling Alliance, 267
Tuesday Night Titans (TV), 263-264
Tulsa (OK) Coliseum, 67
Tunney, Frank, 189
Tunney, Gene, 11
Turk, Alex, 153-154
Turner's Arena (Washington DC), 39
TV Wrestling (magazine), 211
U.S. heavyweight title (Charlotte), 255
U.S. heavyweight title, 177, 189
U.S. tag team title, 218
U.S.S. Breckinridge, 23
Valentine, Johnny, 105-106, 116, 178, 191, 268
Vansky, Jack, 29, 41
Von Goering, Fritz, 151-152, 161-163, 269
Walcott, Jersey Joe, 138-139, 143, 168, 272
Wallace, Bobby, 154-155
Ward, Wally, 37
Watson, Whipper Billy, 65, 141-142
Weasel (Abdullah Farouk), 252
Weashing, Grover (Worm), 14
Weaver, Buck, 127
Weston, Stanley, 93, 189
White, Ed (Strangler), 36, 52
Wildwood Beach Patrol, 15-16, 28, 36
Windsor (Ontario) Arena, 85
Winter Garden (Bronx NY), 66
WLW television title, 104-105

WLW-TV tournament, 116
Wolfe, Billy, 79
Wolverton, Charles A., 23
Woodbury High School, 15
World Championship Wrestling (WCW), 266
world heavyweight title (CA version), 72, 77, 163
world heavyweight title (Montreal version), 168
world heavyweight title (Pfefer version), 79
World Wide Wrestling Federation (WWWF), 224-225, 238-239, 257-258
World Wrestling Entertainment (WWE), 273
World Wrestling Federation, 262-264
World-Wide Wrestling Association (WWWA), 219
Wrestling As You Like It (magazine), 64, 80, 88, 92, 98
Wrestling Confidential (magazine), 240
Wrestling Revue (magazine), 211
Wrestling Revue, 186, 211
Wrestling Show Classics (TV show), 252
Wrestling World (magazine), 211, 225
Wright, Bearcat, 175, 193
Wrigley Field (Chicago IL), 91, 150
WWF world heavyweight title, 225
WWWA, 224
WWWF heavyweight title, 225, 227, 230-231, 239, 262
Wyman, Ella, 51
Yellow Mask (Barto Hill), 36
Zaharias, Babe Didrikson, 141
Zaharias, Chris, 141
Zaharias, George, 141
Zarynoff, Count George, 12
Zbyszko, Stanislaus, 26
Zbyszko, Wladek, 26
Zebra Kid (George Bollas), 84-85
Zorro, Mighty, 151

Other books on wrestling by Tim Hornbaker available at www.crowbarpress.com

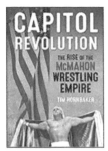

— Capitol Revolution —

The definitive take on the McMahon family's journey to wrestling domination.

For decades, the northeastern part of the United States was considered the heart of the professional wrestling world. Cities from Boston southward to Washington, D.C. enjoyed lucrative box-office receipts and New York's Madison Square Garden was center-stage. Three generations of McMahons have controlled wrestling in that storied building and have since created the most powerful wrestling company the world has ever known.

Capitol Revolution: The Rise of the McMahon Wrestling Empire documents the growth and evolution of pro wrestling under the leadership of the McMahons, highlighting the trials and tribulations beginning in the early 20th century: clashes with rival promoters, government inquests, and routine problems with the potent National Wrestling Alliance monopoly. In the ring, superstars such as Buddy Rogers and Bruno Sammartino entertained throngs of fans, and Capitol became internationally known for its stellar pool of vibrant performers.

Covering the transition from old-school wrestling under the WWWF banner to the pop-cultural juggernaut of the mid- to late-'80s WWF, this is the detailed history of how the McMahons fostered a billion-dollar empire.

— Death of the Territories —

By the early 1980s, Vincent K. McMahon believed cable was his opportunity to take his wrestling promotion national and was soon waged war on the territories, raiding the National Wrestling Alliance and the American Wrestling Association of their top talent. When he jumped into the pay-per-view field with *WrestleMania* and expanded nationwide, he changed pro wrestling forever. Including never-before-revealed information, this book is a must-read for fans to understand how McMahon outlasted his rivals and established the wrestling industry's first national promotion. At the same time, Hornbaker offers a comprehensive look at the promoters who opposed McMahon, focusing on their power plays and embarrassing mistakes.

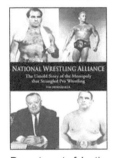

— National Wrestling Alliance —

In the 1950s in Las Vegas, a businessmen's conglomerate dominating a $25 million-a-year sports industry hid their illegal practices from the U.S. Department of Justice. The sport that privileged cold hard cash over honest competition was professional wrestling, and the conspirators were members of the famed National Wrestling Alliance. This book examines the NWA promoters' overwhelming success and the relationships to influential politicians and writers that protected their financial interests for over 50 years. It reveals how promoters twisted arms to edge out their opponents. Hornbaker documents the life of the NWA, from its humble beginnings in the Midwest to its worldwide expansion. He chronicles the legal investigation, providing readers with a never-before-told side of wrestling's legacy. Now, the conspiracies of a century-old brand of entertainment, that took place behind locked doors, will finally be revealed.

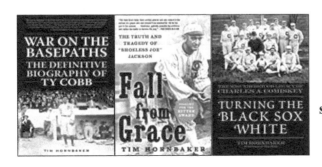

**OTHER BOOKS BY
TIM HORNBAKER
AVAILABLE AT
skyhorsepublishing.com**

Also available from www.crowbarpress.com

— RAISING CAIN: From Jimmy Ault to Kid McCoy —
by Frankie Cain & Scott Teal

"Antone Leone got John Swenski on the floor between the lockers and the bench and pounded on his head. Antone wasn't any kind of an outstanding wrestler, but he was on top, and Swenski couldn't move because he was wedged between the lockers and the bench. Of course, that's the way it always was. Anytime one of the wrestlers got into a scrap, it always wound up in a street-fight."

— Frankie Cain

If you ask any pro wrestler who plied their trade during the '50s and '60s who they consider to be the top minds in the wrestling business, invariably the name Frankie Cain will appear at the top of the list. Frankie has a keen recollection of things that took place in the wrestling business from the 1940s until wrestling evolved into what we know today as "sports entertainment."

But Frankie's story isn't only about his life as a wrestler. It's a fascinating journey that began when he was just plain Jimmy Ault, living on Depression-era streets of downtown Columbus, Ohio – learning hustles and cons from Gypsies, sleeping on rooftops, and selling anything he could – all simply to keep from starving. He came into his own and finally began to earn a decent living when prostitutes in Cherry Alley convinced him to work as their protector against the dangers they faced on the streets. Frankie, having fought on the streets almost every day of his young life, was born for the job.

Frankie tells about his discovery of pro wrestling and how he helped form the Toehold club, where young boys could mimic and learn the pro style. But it was his introduction to and training by tough shooter Frank Wolfe that set him on a path that would have him fighting in smoker clubs, athletic shows on carnivals, and eventually, pro wrestling. However, the majority of Frankie's early years were spent fighting on the road ... going into towns under assumed names and fighting ranked boxers. What his opponents didn't realize, though, was that he was there to "put them over," i.e. make them look good and give them a win to enhance their record. While they were trying to knock Frankie out, he was fighting back, but only enough to make it look like a real contest before he did what the promoters brought him there to do.

Frankie's story — presented in his voice just as he shared it with Scott Teal — will transport you back to a time of the true legends of both boxing and wrestling. Brutal, honest, and often hilarious, Raising Cain is an amazing look at the life and career of a self-made man who lived his life as none other.

— HOOKER —
by Lou Thesz, with Kit Bauman

Who was the greatest pro wrestler of the 20th century?

The debate is a real one among serious students of the sport. Like the arguments over any effort to crown "the greatest," "the best," or "the worst," that answer is unlikely to ever be resolved to everyone's satisfaction. One fact is indisputable, though. For those who watched wrestling before it became "sports entertainment," there is only one answer — Lou Thesz.

In the late 1940s and '50s, Lou Thesz was world heavyweight champion of the National Wrestling Alliance, and he carried those colors with dignity and class. "My gimmick was wrestling," he said, and it was evident to anyone who ever bought a ticket to see Lou Thesz that he was the real deal. Lou's book was one of the first published by a major wrestling star that discussed the business with candor from the inside.

This book contains pages and pages of new material — stories, anecdotes, and 215 classic photos — none of which has been published in any previous edition and all in the voice of one of the legendary figures of the game. Every sentence has been thoroughly combed over and vetted in order to answer any questions previously asked by readers, or to correct and/or re-order the "facts" as Lou recalled them, and each chapter now has detailed endnotes to supplement the text. Combined with all-new, spellbinding forewords by Charlie Thesz and Kit Bauman, an extensive 32-page "addendum" in Lou's own words, and a comprehensive name-and-subject index, and you have the definitive tome devoted to wrestling's golden era.

Also available from www.crowbarpress.com

This series, created by Scott Teal, features the most detailed books ever published on the history of specific wrestling cities and territories. Each volume contains a definite listing of every wrestling match we could find for each venue, illustrated with hundreds of images of program covers, advertisements, newspaper ads and headlines, and memorabilia. Also included, when available, are gate and attendance figures, match stipulations, and much more. These volumes represent an incredible amount of research that will be referred to over and over by both everyone.

v1 – Wrestling in the Garden, The Battle for New York
by Scott Teal & J Michael Kenyon

v2 – Nashville, Tennessee, volume 1: 1907-1960
by Scott Teal & Don Luce

v3 – Alabama: 1931-1935
by Jason Presley

v4 – Japan: The Rikidozan Years
by Haruo Yamaguchi, with Koji Miyamoto & Scott Teal

v5 – Knoxville, Tennessee, v1: 1905-1960
by Tim Dills & Scott Teal

6 – Amarillo, Texas, v1: 1911-1960
by Kriss Knights & Scott Teal

— Fall Guys: The Barnums of Bounce —
by Marcus Griffin, Annotated by Steve Yohe & Scott Teal

If you're like most people, who think professional wrestling was strictly "kayfabe" in the days before it morphed into "sports entertainment," then think again. In 1937, a book titled Falls Guys: The Barnums of Bounce was published. In the 215 pages written by sportwriter Marcus Griffin, the sport was exposed to the general public and the behind-the-scenes wheeling and dealing by promoters and wrestlers alike were brought to light. It was the first credible book ever published on the subject.

Fall Guys was, and still is, fascinating reading ... with one caveat. A great deal of the book was written by Griffin with an extreme bias for Toots Mondt ... his boss ... and against those whom Toots didn't like. It is filled with inconsistencies, contradiction, and ... yes, downright lies. Nevertheless, the book is the best resource of events that took place during that era, and wrestling scholars have used much of Griffin's writing as a launchpad for their own research.

That being the case, why would anyone want to read this book?

This is the annotated version, in which Yohe & Teal challenge Griffin's statements about events and correct errors that have been repeated through the years in other books and writings. They also add additional detail to the stories and the lives of the book's personalities.

Also available from www.crowbarpress.com

— Wrestling Archive Project —
by Scott Teal

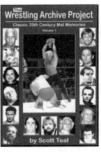

This series is chock full of interviews with the true legends of pro wrestling. Scott Teal, the force behind Crowbar Press, conducted most of these interviews in the days of "kayfabe," a time before anyone else was getting the inside scoop on the pro wrestling business, and most of the people he talked with have never been interviewed by or opened up to anyone else. Scott Teal has returned to doing what he does best — sitting down with the wrestling legends and asking them tough, probing questions that give us insight into what pro wrestling was all about in the days before "sports entertainment" became vogue. Go behind the scenes with the pro wrestling's legends

Volume 1: The main event is an interview with Buddy Colt, who opens the pages of his life and tells his story as he never has before. Also are Adrian Street, Benny McGuire, Dandy Jack Donovan, Dick Cardinal, Frank Martinez, Gene Dundee, Gene Lewis, Gorgeous George Grant, Ernie "Hangman" Moore, Joe Powell, Lord Littlebrook, Lou Thesz, Mac McMurray and Pepper Gomez. A massive 406 pages.

Volume 2: Killer Karl Kox, who steadfastly refused to grant an indepth interview to anyone other than Scott, headlines volume two. You'll feel like you're sitting across the kitchen table from Karl as he relates his life story. Also featured are Baron Von Raschke, Bob Orton Sr., Count Billy Varga, Bulldog Bob Brown, Gentleman Ed Sharpe, J Michael Kenyon, Jackie Fargo, Kody Kox, Larry Cheatham, Lou Thesz, Maniac Mike Davis, Nick Bockwinkel, Sailor Art Thomas, Karl Von Stroheim, Tom Jones & Violet Ray. 386 big pages.

A Complete History of Sam Muchnick's Missouri State Championship
by Roger Deem

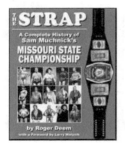

Roger Deem brings life to the story of the Missouri championship belt, the "crème de la crème" of pro wrestling's title belts, second only to the world heavyweight title. Deem covers everything about the title, from the creation of the belt in 1972 to its demise with the death of the St. Louis Wrestling Club in 1987. Also researched is the history of the St. Louis promotion during the time the title was in use; the genius of promoter Sam Muchnick; the behind-the-scenes manipulations that determined who would be given the opportunity to hold the title, or have it taken away; and the problems that beset the promotion both from within and without. Relive the memories of the days when St. Louis was the wrestling capital of the world and the Missouri heavyweight title was the goal of every wrestler.

Wrestling in the Canadian West
by Vance Nevada

Wrestling in the Canadian West accurately describes what it was like for those who traveled the roads on a daily basis in the unique and spectacular area of professional wrestling history. The author clearly illustrates how the business over the years has now come around full circle, as he is living it himself, and dealing with the same trials and tribulations wrestling's pioneers faced in the area more than a hundred years ago.
— Profiles on more than 100 promotions over the past century
— Championship histories and statistical rankings
— Road stories from the wrestlers themselves, including J.J. Dillon & Moose Morowski.
— A directory of the top drawing wrestling events of all time
— Statistics for more than 200 active Canadian wrestlers
— Much, much more!!

Also available from www.crowbarpress.com

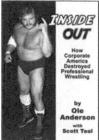

— Inside Out —
by Ole Anderson, with Scott Teal

The people who know Ole Anderson know that he is never hesitant to speak his mind — and this book is no exception. Ole tells of his feuds behind the scenes in the halls and offices of corporate giant, Superstation WTBS. In Ole's own words, *"The wrestling matches may have been staged and scripted, but there was nothing 'fake' about the corporate and legal battles."* This is a powerful story about a man who stood up to the establishment.

— "Wrestlers Are Like Seagulls" —
by James J. Dillon, with Scott Teal

For more than 40 years, James J. Dillon was involved in the world of professional wrestling. He speaks candidly on all aspects of both his career and his personal life, including his time in the WWF as Vince McMahon's right-hand man. Never before has someone from McMahon's inner circle written a book with an insider's perspective of the company. From the highs of making big money, winning championship titles, and rubbing elbows with top celebrities, to the lows of filing for bankruptcy, extramarital affairs, divorces, and drug use, no stone is left unturned.

— ASSASSIN: The Man Behind the Mask —
by Joe Hamilton, with Scott Teal

This autobiography of Joe "Jody" Hamilton takes the reader behind the scenes for a personal glimpse behind the mask of one of pro wrestling's hottest attraction — The Assassin! Joe takes readers on a journey as he tells about life both in and out of the wrestling ring—being attacked, stabbed, and shot at by angry wrestling fans; wrestling under a mask and trying to keep his identity a secret; legitimate fights and confrontations behind the scenes in the dressing rooms; and a war between two wrestling promotions in Atlanta.

— "Is That Wrestling Fake?" — The Bear Facts —
by Ivan Koloff, with Scott Teal

For decades, professional wrestling fans have asked the question – "Is that wrestling fake?" However, they wouldn't have dared ask that question directly to Ivan Koloff, whose work in the ring made believers out of the most cynical fans. In Madison Square Garden, he pinned Bruno Sammartino's shoulders to the mat and won the WWWF heavyweight title. Ivan tells the story of his life: the highs and the lows; admission of alcohol and drug abuse; reflections of a life spent on the road, and the toll it took on his body and soul; and the event that changed his life forever.

— BRUISER BRODY —
by Emerson Murray

Today, more than 18 years after his death, pro wrestling fans still talk about Bruiser Brody with reverence and awe in their voice. Hardcore fans consider him to be the greatest brawler in the history of the sport. He also was one of the most unpredictable men ever to step into the ring, marching to his own drummer and refusing to bow to anyone. Most promoters hated him, but they also loved him because fans turned out in droves to see him. This is the story of Bruiser Brody. No punches are pulled and the rulebook has been thrown out.

Also available from www.crowbarpress.com

— Wrestling with the Truth —
by Bruno Lauer, edited by Scott Teal

The story of Bruno Lauer, known professionally as Downtown Bruno and Harvey Wippleman, tells the fascinating, and often hilarious, story of his life. Direct and opinionated, he doesn't hold back anything. Even his close friends aren't safe from his scrutiny. Retracing every step of his career, this autobio is a fresh glimpse at life behind the curtain of professional sports entertainment — as much action, entertainment, heartbreak, and drama as anything inside a pro wrestling ring.

— The Solie Chronicles —
by Robert Allyn, with Pamela S. Allyn and Scott Teal

One of the most well-known pro-wrestling personalities wasn't a wrestler, but a commentator named Gordon Solie. Famous dead-pan style interviews and colorful play-by-play broadcasts of wrestling led to Gordon's induction into the WCW, NWA & WWE Halls of Fame. Background material was found in Gordon's personal files and taken from interviews with the people who knew him the best.

— Long Days and Short Pays —
by H.E. "Duke" West, edited by Scott Teal

By his own admission, H.E. West was never a well-known name in pro wrestling, but his story is a fascinating look at life on the road of a man whose only desire was to be a part of the world of pro wrestling, not matter how insignificant that part might be. Join him on his journey as he describes his time wrestling before small crowds in high-school gyms and armories, and his travels with his fellow wrestlers. West's narrative is peppered with honesty and humor, and told with humility by a man who never makes himself out to be more than he was — a wrestler whose sole purpose in the ring was to make other wrestlers look good.

— Drawing Heat —
by Jim Freedman

Freedman presents an insider's view of promoting a small, independent wrestling show ... putting the show together, setting up the ring, balancing the books, ring announcing, dealing with sports commissioners who are in the pocket of the big wrestling companies, and exactly what lures fans into arenas. Filled with wonderful characters, the focus is on Dave "The Wildman" McKigney and his wrestling bears, and his struggles and tragedies become the focus of the narrative. This is more than just a book about wrestling. It is a glimpse into a secret world unknown to most people.

— ATLAS: Too Much ... Too Soon —
by Tony Atlas, with Scott Teal

Tony Atlas was the first wrestler to be paid to learn his trade. By the late '70s, Tony was one of the biggest names in the sport and was wrestling in front of sellout crowds in the largest arenas in the country. Readers will live Tony's life through his eyes as he tells about his free-spirited and self-destructive journey through life. His out-of-the-ring stories are as compelling as those that took place inside the ring. This is the story of a man who had success handed to him—only to throw it all away—and the long, painful struggle he had to endure as he clawed his way back to the top.

Also available from www.crowbarpress.com

— The Last Laugh —
by Bill De Mott, with Scott Teal

The stories of Bill's life on the road are both hilarious and entertaining, and at other times, they are sad and insightful. His life has been filled with more backstage drama than is found in all the afternoon soap operas combined, and he doesn't pull any punches in the telling of his story. Considered by many to be a taskmaster with high expectations for his students, a softer side of Bill also reveals itself as his story unfolds. He speaks passionately about life on the road and how he missed seeing his children grow up. A fascinating memoir of one of wrestling's unique characters.

— When It Was Real —
by Nikita Breznikov

If you want to take a trip back to your childhood, your younger, less-stressful days, then journey with us back into the magical world of professional wrestling during the years 1970 to 1979 ... a time "when it was real" ... a time before Hulkamania took the world by storm. Author Nikita Breznikov tells the story from two perspectives — that of a starry-eyed fan, and as the manager and tag team partner of the legendary Nikolai Volkoff. Nikita details the matches and feuds that took place in the WWWF during the '70s and gives his insightful, often-hilarious perspective of the events that took place. Escape with Nikita as he transports you back to an era when wrestling was presented in an entertaining manner, but framed as legitimate competition.

— The Last Outlaw —
by Stan Hansen, with Scott Teal

Stan's writing is a guidebook of pro wrestling in Japan. He educates and entertains with stories about promoters and their promotions, how they operate business behind the scenes, touring the country, nightlife in the big cities, and how the sport in Japan differs from the U.S. And what would a "Stan Hansen book" be without personal stories about Bruiser Brody: how they first met, the story behind their becoming a team, spending time in the evenings on the streets and in the clubs of Japan, and his own, personal insight into the "real" Bruiser Brody.

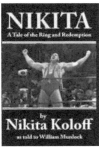

— NIKITA: A Tale of the Ring and Redemption —
by Nikita Koloff, as told to William Murdock

Nikita Koloff, better known as the "Russian Nightmare," stormed the wrestling world as few others have. Imposing, immovable, and unbeatable, Nikita left a trail of fallen opponents as he brought the Cold War that loomed over the globe into the ring. Nikita's name filled arenas and he captured five world titles in the process. And when he was at the top of his game, he walked away from the sport. This is not just the story of a wrestler. It is the story of a man ... a man who has touched hundreds of thousands of lives.

— BRISCO —
by Jack Brisco, as told to William Murdock

A former NCAA amateur wrestling champion, Jack had his first match in 1965 and soon became one of the top names in the wrestling business. He won both the Florida and Southern heavyweight titles and, just a few years later, took the NWA world heavyweight belt from Harley Race. Jack and his brother, Jerry, were responsible for convincing other Georgia Championship Wrestling shareholders to sell their shares to Vince McMahon, setting into motion Vince's dominance of the wrestling world.

Also available from www.crowbarpress.com

— "I Ain't No Pig Farmer!" —
by Dean Silverstone, edited by Scott Teal

In an era when few people were allowed into pro wrestling's inner circle, Dean pitched the idea of publishing an arena program to Seattle promoter Harry Elliott, and Dean's career as a wrestling publicist began ... when he was only 14 years old. Dean later formed Super Star Championship Wrestling, and in the process, faced anti-Semitism, unpredictable actions from his talent, crowd riots, warnings from the Hell's Angels, collapsing rings, the tragic death of one of his top wrestlers, and even a Molotov cocktail.

— The Hard Way —
by Don Fargo, with Scott Teal

As famous as he was for his ability to draw crowds to the arenas, Fargo probably was more famous for his hijinks behind the scenes. The stories about his pranks and wild lifestyle are talked about to this day by those who were witness to the events. This is the most detailed book ever written that ties together important events in wrestling history with hilarious shenanigans that went on behind the scenes. You've never read a more entertaining life story than this one.

— Whatever Happened to Gorgeous George? —
by Joe Jares

This is the story of the most outlandish personalities in sport—comic book figures with fanatical followings. Here you'll meet Gorgeous George, Bruno Sammartino, Haystack Calhoun, and a host of other arch-villains, prissy lords, masked marauders, and muscle-bound mamas. Loving and hating them along the way are the maniacal fans who follow them and turn the arenas into screaming, roving Theaters of the Absurd—Piccolo Pete, Hatpin Mary, and the septuagenarian sisters from Baltimore, to name a few. Then come backstage with the boys and see what the brutal world of wrestling's all about—cauliflower ears, fan-inflicted knife and gun wounds, matches fought in mud and ice cream, bloody grudge brawls, whacky practical jokes. This is a funny, irreverent look at the most colorful, theatrical sport.

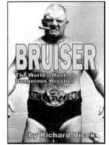

— BRUISER —
by Richard Vicek, edited by Scott Teal.03

There have been several "Bruisers" in wrestling history, but the name synonymous with pro wrestling for almost three decades was "Dick the Bruiser." A former Green Bay Packer lineman, Bruiser is a name people mention when talking about the golden age of the sport. Within a few months of his debut, Bruiser was cracking heads and pounding flesh from coast to coast across the United States. Words that desribe Bruiser's in-ring style are believability, belligerence, domination, unpredictability, explosiveness, intensity, and rampage. This book is his legacy.

— Pain Torture Agony —
by Ron Hutchison, with Scott Teal

Ron Hutchison, trainer of some of World Wrestling Entertainment's biggest superstars, is hailed as one of pro wrestling's unsung heroes. It is an account filled with history and insight into the fascinating world of pro wrestling, as well as tales of dreamers, muscleheads, a bomb threat, machine guns, Yakuza, midgets, and even a visit to the Playboy mansion in California. Fasten your seatbelt as Ron Hutchison, trainer of some of World Wrestling Entertainment's biggest superstars, takes you on an exciting four-decade journey into the wild, no-holds-barred, wacky & amazing world of professional wrestling.